WRITING THE PAST,

INSCRIBING THE FUTURE

WRITING THE PAST,

INSCRIBING THE FUTURE

History as Prophecy in

Colonial Java

Nancy Florida

Duke University Press

Durham & London

1995

© 1995 Duke University Press   All rights reserved
Printed in the United States of America on acid-free paper ∞
Typeset in Aldus by Keystone Typesetting, Inc.
Library of Congress Cataloging-in-Publication Data
appear on the last printed page of this book.
Portions of the Introduction were previously published
as "Reading the Unread in Traditional Javanese Literature,"
Indonesia 44 (October 1987).

for Joshua Nurhadi Suryolelono

CONTENTS

❋

LIST OF MAPS
AND FIGURES

❀

Maps

Figures

ACKNOWLEDGMENTS

※

This work has grown out of experiences and friendships that have spanned many years and many miles. For those experiences and for those friendships I am grateful to a number of individuals and institutions. When did this work begin? Was it some twenty-five years ago with my first experiences of Javanese culture through the study of *gamelan* music at Wesleyan University? Or was it in California and then in Java where I continued my study of the Javanese performing arts under the auspices of the American Society for Eastern Arts in the 1970s? It was during these early trips to Java, in 1971 and 1975–77, that I began my study of narrative traditions in Java, working under shadow puppet masters and beginning my studies in the manuscript archives of Surakarta, Central Java. I remember those many long nights, sitting motionless, enthralled by what seemed to me the near magical performances of the puppet masters as they spun their tales. To these Javanese storytellers, especially to Ki Anom Suroto and to the late Ki Suratno Gunowiharjo and the late Ki Sutrisno, I owe my fascination with Javanese narrative, with Javanese language and literature. My first encounters with Javanese manuscripts were in the library of the Mangkunagaran Palace and were encouraged by the late K.R.M.T.H. Sanjoto Sutopo Kusumohatmodjo, for whose many years of support and friendship I am deeply grateful. Others who influenced and shaped my early experiences in Java were K.R.T. Wasitodiningrat, the late R.L. Martopangrawit, the late Embah Jarwopangrawit, and the late Suranto Atmosaputro.

In 1978 I returned to America to begin graduate studies in Southeast Asian history at Cornell University. To my teachers at Cornell, especially to Oliver Wolters, David Wyatt, Benedict Anderson, and James Siegel, I owe a deep debt of gratitude. The opportunity to read with them both their own works and the works of others contributed to shaping my perspectives on writing and my approaches to reading. I am particularly indebted to Oliver Wolters; the inspiration that his work has provided me and the fellowship that his friendship has afforded me have been guiding forces in my scholarly life over the last seventeen years.

When I returned to Java in 1980 it was as field director of the Surakarta Manuscript Project, a project to microfilm manuscripts in the three royal manuscript repositories that are located in the ancient court city of Sura- karta. Through this project, which was generously funded by the National Endowment for the Humanities and the Cornell University Southeast Asia Program, I had the opportunity to go over almost three-quarter million pages of writing in Javanese script as I prepared the manuscripts for filming. My work on the manuscripts was made possible by the gracious permission of their Royal Highnesses I.S.K.S. Pakubuwana XII and the late K.G.P.A.A. Mangkunagara VIII, as well as by the support of the late K.R.M.T.H. Sanjoto Sutopo Kusumohatmodjo, the late K.G.P.H. Prabu- wijaya, K.R.T. Hardjonagoro, and the National Archives of the Republic of Indonesia. Others whose efforts were indispensable to this project were: David Wyatt, Haryati Soebadio, the late K.R.T. Mohammad Hoesodo Pringgokoesoemo, the late M.Ng. Kirnosayono, R. Pranadi Hartawiryana, Alan Feinstein, Mulyoto, M. Husni Djasara, and Bambang Hening Tjipto. Then in 1982, through a project that was funded by the Ford Foundation and was housed in the Sasana Pustaka Library of the Kraton Surakarta, this work was extended to preserve the original manuscripts as works of art on paper. I am very grateful to friends and colleagues who worked with me on that archival project at the Surakarta Palace, especially to G.P.H. Puger, G.R.A. Koes Moertiyah, Endang Tri Winarni, and Kasmir Efendi.

Meanwhile, in 1982, with the generous funding of the Social Science Research Council and a Fulbright-Hays fellowship and with the sponsor- ship of the Lembaga Ilmu Pengetahuan Indonesia in Jakarta, I began the field work on Javanese historiographical traditions that would eventually culminate in this book. A number of friends and colleagues influenced the course of that field work. At the Kraton Surakarta I am grateful to G.K. Ratu Alit, G.P.H. Poespohadikoesoemo, G.R.A. Koes Indriyah, the late K.R.T. Sastradiningrat, and Ibu R.T. Pamardi Srimpi for their assistance and advice. I am also deeply indebted to John Pemberton, B. J. Rianto, Thoriq Addibani, Tinuk Rosalia Yampolsky, and Halim H.D.; their insights, energies, and fellowship enriched my understanding and informed my perspectives during those years in Surakarta.

I began writing this book at Cornell in 1986 and wrote substantial portions of it there and at the University of Michigan over the next four years. During this period I learned from conversations with and comments and criticisms from Benedict Anderson, Judith Becker, Suzanne Brenner, Audrey Kahin, Victor Lieberman, John Pemberton, Takashi Shiraishi, Ann Stoler, Amrih Widodo, Thomas Williamson, Oliver Wolters, and David Wyatt.

In 1993–94, with generous support from the National Endowment for the Humanities and the Rackham Graduate School of the University of Michigan, I was provided the opportunity to reconceive and rework this project. A number of friends and colleagues commented on portions (and in some cases entire drafts) of the work as I was rethinking and rewriting it. Thanks here are due to Alton Becker, Katherine Bergeron, Joseph Errington, Valentine Daniel, Robert Hefner, Marilyn Ivy, Daniel Lev, Hendrik Maier, Adela Pinch, Vicente Rafael, Laurie Sears, Mary Steedly, and Amrih Widodo. I am also grateful for the editorial encouragement of Ken Wissoker of Duke University Press, and for assistance with maps and figures from Robert Cowherd, Ron Fraker, Annabel Gallop, and Adhi Moersid. The publication of this volume is supported with a grant from the Office of the Vice President for Research of the University of Michigan.

I am especially grateful to John Pemberton for his many and significant contributions to the writing of this book. Were it not for his insights and friendship I would, I am quite sure, have written a very different work. I have him to thank not only for encouraging my early interest in Java but also for, many years later, challenging me to take a critical stance on that same interest. Through his own writings as well as his criticisms of mine, he has enriched my understandings of Java in countless ways. And for his many and detailed comments on nearly every draft that this book has been through, I am truly grateful.

Finally a note of special thanks to my son, Joshua Nurhadi Suryolelono Florida, to whom I dedicate this book, with much love, in the hope that when, many years from now, he comes to read it, he will understand why I wrote it.

A NOTE ON MANUSCRIPTS,
SPELLING, PRONUNCIATION,
AND TRANSLATION

❇

Most of the original Javanese manuscripts referred to in this book are from three repositories in Surakarta, Central Java: the Sasana Pustaka in the Kraton Surakarta, the Reksa Pustaka in the Mangkunagaran Palace, and the Museum Radyapustaka. Citations of these manuscripts include two reference systems. The initial "MS." reference refers to the catalog entry of the local repository (with "SP" for the Sasana Pustaka, "RP" for the Reksa Pustaka, and "Rp" for the Radyapustaka). The "SMP" reference is based on the cataloging system of the Surakarta Manuscript Project. In this system, "KS" refers to the Kraton Surakarta, "MN" to the Mangku-nagaran, and "Rp" to the Radyapustaka. A complete bibliographic entry with author, title, place and date of composition and inscription, and double references appears as follows:

Ronggasasmita, Mas. *Suluk Acih*. Composed Aceh, 1815; inscribed Surakarta, 1867. MS. SP 15 Ca; SMP KS 502.

In many cases the provenance and dating of the manuscripts cannot be established. The abbreviation "s.a." (*sine anno*) indicates that the date is unknown; "s.l." (*sine loco*), that the place is unknown. Attributions are in brackets.

Microfilm copies of the Surakarta manuscripts are available for reading at the originating repositories and at the Indonesian National Archives in Jakarta as well as at Cornell University Library's Echols Collection and at the University of Michigan. The first of a four-volume annotated catalog for these manuscripts, my *Javanese Literature in Surakarta Manuscript*, vol. I: *Introduction and Manuscripts of the Karaton Surakarta*, was pub-lished by the Southeast Asia Program, Cornell University in 1993.

In addition to the Surakarta manuscripts, I also refer to several manuscripts from the Oriental Collection of the Leiden University Library and from the Oriental and India Office Collection of the British Library. The abbreviation "LOr" indicates Leiden Oriental manuscripts; "IOL" indicates India Office Library manuscripts.

My spelling of Javanese words follows, with some exceptions, the system standard in Indonesia today. The exceptions are as follows:

1. I distinguish the *taling* (*é* or *è*) from the *pepet* (*e*).

2. I spell and transliterate Javanese proper names as their owners do or did. I do not, for example, follow the standard academic Javanological spelling of "Ranggawarsita" for the poet Ronggawarsita.

The spelling of Javanese words, on the whole, reflects pronunciation. The following list gives the nearest English equivalents to the sounds represented by the letters:

Letter	Approximation in English	Example
/a/	in open syllables, similar to the *aw* in *law*	Jaka
	in closed syllables, as in *father*	babad
/c/	as in an unaspirated English *ch*	Centhini
/dh/	aveolar *d*, similar to the English *day*	Pandhanarang
/d/	dental *d*, produced with tip of tongue touching inside of upper teeth	Kudus
/e/	similar to the *u* in *cut*	semu
/é/	similar to the English *ay*	Déwaraja
/è/	similar to the *e* in *set*	Karèwèd
/i/	in open syllables, as the *ee* in the English *weep*	Jawi
	in most closed syllables, as in *bit*	Majapahit
	in some closed syllables, as in *sing*	Tingkir
/ng/	as in *sing*	ngéblat
/o/	in open syllables, similar to the *o* in *hope*	ngoko
	in closed syllables, similar to the *aw* in *law*	kraton
/r/	trilled or tapped *r* (no English equivalent)	rasa
/th/	aveolar *t*, similar to the English *later*	Centhini
/t/	dental *t* (see *d* above)	Tingkir
/u/	in open syllables, similar to the *oo* in *moon*	*suluk*
	in closed syllables, similar to the *u* in *put*	su*luk*

All translations are my own. A glossary of selected terms and titles follows the appendixes.

TITLES IN THE
KRATON SURAKARTA

❋

B.R.Aj.	Bendara Radèn Ajeng; granddaughter of a king
B.R.M.	Bendara Radèn Mas; grandson of a king
B.R.M.G.	Bendara Radèn Mas Gusti; junior prince (young son of a king)
B.R.T.	Bendara Radèn Tumenggung; a high courtier (*bupati*) of noble blood
G.K.	Gusti Kangjeng; usually, a queen
G.K.R.	Gusti Kangjeng Ratu; a queen
G.P.H.	Gusti Pangéran Harya; a senior prince (mature son of a king, twentieth century)
G.R.A.	See G.R.Aj. and G.R.Ay.
G.R.Aj.	Gusti Radèn Ajeng; a princess (in the twentieth century, an unmarried daughter of a king)
G.R.Ay.	Gusti Radèn Ayu; a princess (in the twentieth century, married daughter of a king)
G.R.M.	Gusti Radèn Mas; a junior prince (young son of a king)
H.	Harya; a prince
I.S.K.S.	Ingkang Sinuhun Kangjeng Susuhunan; ruler of the Kraton Surakarta
K.G.P.	Kangjeng Gusti Pangéran; a prince (son of a king)
K.G.P.A.A.	Kangjeng Gusti Pangéran Adipati Anom: the crown prince of the Kraton Surakarta
	(Kangjeng Gusti Pangéran Arya Adipati; the ruler of the Mangkunagaran Palace)
K.G.P.H.	Kangjeng Gusti Pangéran Harya; a high senior prince (mature son of a king)

K.P.H.	Kangjeng Pangéran Harya; a senior prince (mature son of a king; nineteenth century)
K.R.A.	Kangjeng Radèn Adipati; the vizier (*patih*)
K.R.M.T.H.	Kangjeng Radèn Mas Tumenggung Harya; a high courtier (*bupati*) of royal blood
K.R.T.	Kangjeng Radèn Tumenggung; a high courtier (*bupati*)
M.Ng.	Mas Ngabéhi; a middle-level courtier
P.H.	Pangéran Harya; a prince (usually the son of a king)
P.	Pangéran or Panji
R.	Radèn; a noble or prince
R.A.	Radèn Adipati; the vizier (*patih*)
	Radèn Ayu or Radèn Ajeng; a noble woman
R.L.	Radèn Lurah; a lower-level courtier
R.M.	Radèn Mas; a noble (fourth-grade royalty or lower)
R.M.H.	Radèn Mas Harya; the mature grandson of a king
R.M.Ng.	Radèn Mas Ngabéhi; a middle-level courtier of noble blood
R.M.T.	Radèn Mas Tumenggung; a high courtier (*bupati*) of noble blood
R.Ng.	Radèn Ngabéhi; a middle-level courtier of noble blood
R.P.	Radèn Panji; a noble (third-grade royalty or lower)
R.T.	Radèn Tumenggung; a high courtier (*bupati*)

ABBREVIATIONS

❋

ARA   Algemeen Rijksarchief (The Hague)
BJT   *Babad Jaka Tingkir*
BKI   *Bijdragen tot de Taal-, Land-, en Volkenkunde*
GR   J. F. C. Gericke and T. Roorda, *Javaansch-Nederlandsch Hand-woordenboek* (Amsterdam: Muller, 1901)
IOL   India Office Library manuscripts, British Library
KS   Kraton Surakarta
MN   Mangkunagaran
LOr   Leiden Oriental manuscripts, Leiden University Library
OJ   Old Javanese
RP   Reksa Pustaka manuscripts, Istana Mangkunagaran
Rp   Museum Radyapustaka manuscripts
SMP   Surakarta Manuscript Project
SP   Sasana Pustaka manuscripts, Kraton Surakarta
TBG   *Tijdschrift voor Taal-, Land-, en Volkenkunde*

INTRODUCTION:
ON THE POSSIBILITIES
OF READING IN JAVA

❀

> By day and night, read with care and diligence
> All the venerable laid-by works
> That they may be exemplars
> Of the language of the heart, be not deceived
>
> If you lack the time, read then every night
> If by night alone
> Study with utmost loving care
> Feel their meaning and their intent
>
> Bring out their sense, dare to try to comprehend
> If confused
> Or if they seem too simple
> —Mas Ronggasasmita, 1815[1]

Almost two centuries ago Ronggasasmita, a little-known writer from a well-known family of Javanese court poets, composed these lines calling his readers to active and careful readings of exemplary works no longer read.[2] He urges readers to approach the old texts with a kind of loving care, or quiet passion, that would provoke contemporary understandings

1. Mas Ronggasasmita, "Suluk Martabat Sanga," in *Suluk Acih* (compiled Aceh, 1815; inscribed Surakarta, 1867), MS. Sasana Pustaka Karaton Surakarta (henceforth SP), cat. no. 15 Ca; Cornell University Surakarta Manuscript Project (henceforth SMP), cat. no. KS 502, p. 55.

2. Mas Ronggasasmita was the son of R.T. Sastranagara (R.Ng. Yasadipura II, 1756–1844) and the grandson of R.Ng. Yasadipura I (1729–1803). Ronggasasmita's elder brother, R.Ng. Ronggawarsita II ("Sepuh"), who held the office of Mantri Lurah Carik Kadipatèn, was the father of the renowned court poet R.Ng. Ronggawarsita III (1802–1873). Implicated in revolutionary activities, the elder Ronggawarsita was exiled along with his younger brother "Mas Kaji" (Ronggasasmita?) in 1828 (*Babad Sengkala kang kaurut saking kagungan-dalem serat Babad* [composed and inscribed Surakarta, circa 1831, 1847], MS. SP 6 Ta; SMP KS 1C.7, II:127).

of their meaning and intent. The poet challenges readers to work toward comprehension, to learn that textual meaning is not a self-evident given served up for their passive consumption. And so he dares them to read in ways that will involve them in the active production of meaning—to enter into dialogue with the half-forgotten texts of the past.[3] "Try to comprehend," Ronggasasmita writes in words that also mean "take up and *extend* the language" of the texts, thereby subtly reminding readers to work toward meanings that will be partially of their own, that is, our own, making.[4]

These lines appear in Ronggasasmita's *Suluk Acih* (Songs of Aceh), a compilation of Islamic mystic songs, or *suluk*, written by the poet as he languished on foreign shores. Having made the holy pilgrimage to Mecca, Ronggasasmita was on his way home to the Central Javanese court-city of Surakarta where illustrious members of his family served the Pakubuwana ("Axis of the Universe") kings as professional literati. He was traveling with his uncle. When the two men reached the Sumatran port city of Aceh, the older man fell ill. It was then that Ronggasasmita took up his pen to reinscribe in Javanese verse the mystical teachings of his Sufi masters.[5] And in that text, written during a Sumatran interruption in his journey home to Java, the poet recalls prior texts expressly to call for their reactualization in present and future readings.

In the same poem Ronggasasmita goes on to remember one very spe-

3. The Javanese *lepiyan* ("venerable laid-by works") designates a written text which is no longer read, but has been laid aside (folded up) to be preserved—perhaps as a prototype for further copies. Old Javanese *lepih* means "to fold; double the sum, twice the amount" (P. J. Zoetmulder, *Old Javanese–English Dictionary*, 2 vols. [The Hague: Nijhoff, 1982] [henceforth *Zoetmulder*], 1:1014). Modern Javanese *lepih* means "to spit s.t. out" and by extension "to reject s.t. one had previously accepted or taken into consideration" (J. F. C. Gericke and T. Roorda, *Javaansch-Nederlandsch Handwoordenboek*, 2 vols. [Amsterdam: Muller, 1901] [henceforth GR], 2:134). For an imaginative reading, teasing from the word *lepiyan* the connotation of "an ornate protest," see J. Anthony Day, "Meanings of Change in the Poetry of Nineteenth-Century Java" (Ph.D. dissertation, Cornell University, 1981), pp. 275–76, 279, and 302.
4. The Javanese *nyambut-nyambut*, which I render as "try to comprehend," is the reduplicated form of the verb *sambut* ("to take up, to grasp; to borrow; to take up [s.o.'s] words, to reply, to continue [s.o.'s] language").
5. Ronggasasmita was a member of the Shattâriyyah tariq with an educational genealogy (*silsilah*) extending back to 'Abdallâlh ash-Shattâr (and ultimately to the Prophet Mohammad). That genealogy included Sèh Abdul Rauf of Singkel and Sèh Kaji Muhyi of Karang (Mas Ronggasasmita, *Suluk Acih*, pp. 52–55).

cial reader. The poet reports of his late grandfather, the renowned Kraton Surakarta (Surakarta Palace) writer Yasadipura I (1729–1803):

> And though already famed a master of knowledge
> Yet would he have with him
> The *wali*'s venerable laid-by works
> And those of the perfect masters
>
> I saw him on those nights
> When he had no guests
> Once resting from his writing
> Nothing else was seen by him
>
> Save *suluk* and Sufi texts.[6]

Recalling his famous grandfather surrounded at night by Sufi texts, Ronggasasmita is in effect admonishing his own readers to be mindful that successful writing is the fruit of thoughtful readings. For although the preeminent writer of his day, Yasadipura never ceased his readings of the "venerable laid-by works" that others had written. And what he read, according to Ronggasasmita, were the works of the Islamic saints credited with the conversion of Java—the *wali*—and "the perfect masters," their spiritual and intellectual heirs. "But nowadays," Ronggasasmita goes on to complain, there are many who neglect these texts and yet presume to teach, offering misleading thoughts on matters that they themselves little understand. Ronggasasmita's imagined punishment for these false and arrogant teachers: stuff their mouths with rocks, seven fistfuls each.[7]

This book responds to Ronggasasmita's call to return to works of the past by undertaking a close reading of one such work—*Babad Jaka Tingkir*, or "The History of Jaka Tingkir"—a singular and hitherto overlooked nineteenth-century Javanese writing of history that I came across in the library of the Surakarta Palace in early 1981 as I was cataloging all the manuscripts in that royal archive.[8] The text, written in the nineteenth

6. Ronggasasmita, *Suluk Acih*, p. 56. For biographical notes on Yasadipura I, see S. Soebardi, *The Book of Cabolèk* (The Hague: Nijhoff, 1975), and Sasrasumarta et al., *Tus Pajang* (Surakarta: Budi Utomo, 1939).
7. Ronggasasmita, *Suluk Acih*, p. 57.
8. *Babad Jaka Tingkir* (composed Surakarta, 1829) in *Kupiya Iber Warni-warni, Sampéyan-dalem kaping VI* (inscribed [Ambon], ca. 1849). MS. SP 214 Ca; SMP KS 78.2, pp.

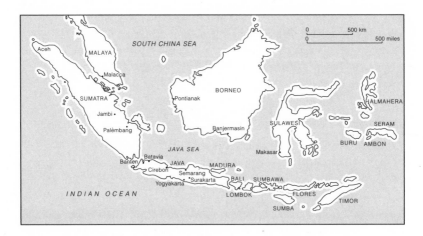

Map 1. The Indonesian Archipelago

century about a sixteenth-century past, was bound into a volume of diplomatic correspondence belonging to an exiled Surakarta king. This curiously positioned history veritably demanded my attention, while promising to compel my repeated returns to it. Even upon first encounter, *Babad
Jaka Tingkir*, which its writer "composed as a magic talisman,"[9] seemed to
anticipate and propel the future traces of its own potential readings. There
was no escaping it, and since that day I have returned many times to this
prophetic writing of Javanese history. My work here is an extended historical and literary exploration of this extraordinary text. I trust that my
efforts will not have earned me a mouthful of rocks.

My project involves situating, translating, and critically analyzing the
hauntingly prophetic *Babad Jaka Tingkir*. It is, in short, a close reading of a
particular text of Javanese historical writing which was itself produced
with an eye toward its own potential future readings. I begin with reflections on reading practices in Java, in the past and in the present. I then
consider historically the writing of *Babad Jaka Tingkir* by way of an introduction to the focus of my study: a translation of the manuscript in its

79b–152a. For an analytic inventory of the entire collection of some 1450 manuscript
titles, see my *Javanese Literature in Surakarta Manuscripts*, vol. 1, *Introduction and
Manuscripts of the Karaton Surakarta* (Ithaca: Cornell University Southeast Asia Program, 1993).

9. "Ginupita kang srat Babat Jaka Tingkir, malar dadya pusaka" (*Babad Jaka Tingkir* I:1).

entirety. This is followed by an analysis that moves in dialogue with the translated text to consider how this text makes sense in the contexts of its realities, textual and otherwise. My own reading of *Babad Jaka Tingkir* is very much engaged in this history's production of sense, for it is a reading that is self-consciously interested in the extension of this text's prophetic script for the future. In other words, my book is an attempt to perform just the kind of reading that Ronggasasmita seems to have had in mind.

Such a reading is itself a form of writing—a textual practice that involves the reader along with the text (and by implication that text's author) in a dialogic production which moves to realize the potential meanings that the text itself apparently intends. In a voice that perhaps would not have seemed alien to Ronggasasmita, Roland Barthes has noted that textual works are themselves "perpetual productions, enunciations through which the subject continues to struggle; this subject is no doubt that of the author, but also that of the reader."[10] The reader, partially undone by the text that she reads, struggles together with its author and through its perpetual productions to realize its work in her own reading of it. With the writing of this book as a practice of such reading, I thus attempt a dialogic encounter with a Javanese past, a text of that past, and the alternative futures that text suggests for the present. This encounter emerges, of course, from the interplay of various subjectivities across time, space, and languages—from the particularities of my own personal history and the realities inscribed in a specific work of Javanese historical writing to the potential readers that that work, and mine, would address.

The primary site of this interplay, this intensive reading, emerges from the work of translation. Hence, a translation of the entire text of *Babad Jaka Tingkir* is central to this book. For only by considering the composition of a particular Javanese writer in its entirety could I hope to discern the voices from the past that would make possible the dialogic encounter of which I speak. Indeed, it is only by allowing the text of this Javanese writer sufficient room to shape the contours of my own discourse, through

10. Roland Barthes, "Theory of the Text," in *Untying the Text*, ed. Robert Young (Boston: Routledge and Keagan Paul, 1981), p. 42. Reading, for Barthes, as a work of *signifiance* is a form of writing. He signals the eroticism of such reading/writing as a "work, not the work by which the subject (intact and external) might try to master the language . . . but a radical work (which leaves nothing intact) through which the subject explores how language works him and undoes him as soon as he stops observing and enters it" (p. 38).

translation, that I might resist both the pretense of "speaking for" Javanese subjects and the presumption of authority that would found a more
monological narrative of Javanese history. And, it is precisely by engaging
a particular text through translation that I am also brought into a more
expansive dialogue with a range of other texts and other Javanese pasts.
For the text that I read was itself composed against a background of
readings, of prior texts and contexts. Translating *Babad Jaka Tingkir* in full,
I am compelled to attend in a sustained manner both to its profound
intertextuality and to its historicity, to the stylistic, linguistic, and literary
modes through which its writer, in the particular reality of his or her
historical becoming, worked to generate its senses. Through the work of
translation I consider how the writer worked, prophetically, through other
texts—moving strategically among various literary, historical, and political contexts—to indicate what might lie beyond them. Translating this
historical prophecy thus has meant learning to hear and respond to its
writer's modes of signification and their historical determinations, in
order to produce—to recall Walter Benjamin's formulation—reverbera-
tions of these in my own writing *as* translation.[11]

The project of this book, then, is not simply to use indigenous texts to
reconstruct a history of Java; it is rather to engage a particular Javanese
text in an extended historical conversation in order to follow up on that
text's own prophetic tendencies and to imagine with it a historical space
for the future. The point is not to master the Javanese past or a text of that
past but to reinscribe, through dialogue, a particular text's apparent future intentions. In a text like *Babad Jaka Tingkir*, that is, a text that announces itself as prophecy, such future intentions are especially haunting.
My own reading and translation appear drawn up into this particular
text's afterlife, extending its future intentions into a world that was,
perhaps, not completely unforeseen by its prophetic Javanese author.[12]
The translation proceeds from this prophetic history to generate, with it,
a larger discursive space in which its future senses might move. For by

11. The task of the translator, according to Benjamin, is to produce an "echo," a rever-
beration of the original in the language of the translation (Walter Benjamin, "The Task
of the Translator," in *Illuminations* [New York: Schocken Books, 1969], p. 76). It is
worth noting here that Benjamin's *apologia* for translation was itself written as a
preface to his own translation of Baudelaire's *Tableaux Parisiens*.
12. On Benjamin's characterization of translation as a stage in the afterlife of a work,
see ibid., pp. 71–72.

opening this hitherto obscure "Third World" history to a whole range of readers who would otherwise have no access to it, the translation works quite concretely to push the limits *Babad Jaka Tingkir* now endures as a marginalized Javanese-language composition in a literary world that is dominated by Euro-American writings. Through translation, the remarkable Tingkir history enters into a wider comparative dialogue, where, read with interest not only by Javanese and Javanists, it can extend its prophetic potential into a more global register.

Imagining how *Babad Jaka Tingkir*, translated, might perform its work within the larger discursive spaces of a global comparative dialogue elicits further consideration of the political implications of this project. What might it mean to translate an "exotic" text under the postcolonial conditions of the late twentieth century? Whose interests does it serve to introduce an obscure text from a "Third World" literature into English? There are, of course, no unambiguous answers to these qustions.[13] I would hope, however, that by foregrounding the text of a marginalized Southeast Asian writer, I might just provoke a stutter in the universalizing projects of a dominant discourse that effaces marginal voices even as it would speak for exoticized others. *Babad Jaka Tingkir*, a text that *itself* both explicitly and implicitly questions the centrality of any center that would attempt to exclude margins, is perhaps uniquely suited to interrupt such projects. Through the translation of this particular Javanese text—a translation produced by writing across differences instead of against difference—I wish to introduce into the dominant discourse the potentially subversive agency of the authorial subject who composed it.

How, then, do I envision the practice of translation? If by translating the text of *Tingkir* in full I mean to work *with* it rather than *on* it in an imagined mastery of it, how do I account for the proverbial violence the act of translation may perpetrate upon an other's text? I certainly cannot fancy my translation an innocent reproduction of some original indige-

13. For extended and thought-provoking studies of the politics of translation, see Vicente L. Rafael, *Contracting Colonialism: Translation and Christian Conversion in Tagalog Society under Early Spanish Rule* (Durham: Duke University Press, 1993 [orig., 1988]), and Tejaswini Niranjana, *Siting Translation: History, Post-Structuralism, and the Colonial Context* (Berkeley: University of California Press, 1992). For a penetrating discussion of the (moral) position of the critic in postcolonial discourse on the "Third World," see Edward Said, "The World, the Text, and the Critic," in *The World, the Text, and the Critic* (Cambridge: Harvard University Press, 1983), pp. 31–53.

nous meaning. It goes without saying that my translation of this nine-teenth-century Javanese writing of history is itself an interested rewrit-ing of the "original" it translates. This translation, like any translation, is a rewriting, a writing-again which is at the same time an act of reading by a historically determined, desiring subject—a writing-again across lan-guages, literatures, cultures, and times that is itself located in the history of the conditions of its own production.[14]

Pure, unmediated translation is, of course, impossible. And it is this very impossibility that necessarily involves translation, intimately, with the worlds in and through which it moves. Reading not only across but also through differences, translation obviously can never hope fully to recover or to convey an originary meaning. Nor does it offer a locus of total expressive freedom. Rather, it is a practice which works through the senses of the imagined original in order to generate novel senses. Instead of a transparent reproduction and relay of an original truth, translation is a task, as Benjamin understood, that strives in dialogue with the original to realize and extend the *potential* truths the translated text apparently poses. Any translation is always both textual interpretation and textual supplement. And all translation is located in history. So I do not imagine my translation of this text—however invested I am in it—to be the last word on the text of *Tingkir.* Indeed, by offering it in translation I hope (if I may presume to ally myself with Ronggasasmita) to encourage others to read, that is, to "dare to try to comprehend" this and other of the "vener-able laid-by works" of Javanese writing.

Babad Jaka Tingkir

Babad Jaka Tingkir, the history of Jaka (or "the Youth from") Tingkir, is an epic history that concerns the emergence of Islamic power in Central Java. It is also a historical prophecy. Composed in indigenous sung meters and inscribed in Javanese script in the second quarter of the nineteenth cen-tury, *Tingkir* is an anonymous work. There is apparently only one manu-script witness of this singular history: I found that witness of the Javanese

14. Hendrik Maier, writing eloquently of the historical reception of Malay literary texts, reminds us that all readings, and rereadings, and readings of readings, are frag-mentary and selective; and that all readings bear with them traces of the centers of culture out of which they are produced (*In the Center of Authority* [Ithaca: Cornell University Southeast Asia Program, 1988], esp. pp. 1–12).

past tucked away in a volume of royal correspondence whose home is now the library of the Surakarta Palace. As shall become apparent, this anonymous manuscript was inscribed (if not composed) by the mysterious hand of one associated with that same palace—but not, as it turns out, the hand of one actually at court. For the hand that inscribed *Babad Jaka Tingkir* belonged to a marginalized subject who wrote the history as he or she languished, in political exile, on a distant island remote from his or her royal Javanese origins. It is in light of this discovery that this book begins to explore the relationship between the poem's prophetic foresight and the exile of indigenous power in colonial Java: that suggestive point where exile and prophecy, along with writing and history, converge in the textual work of a particular nineteenth-century Javanese subject.

With *Babad Jaka Tingkir*, a prophetic Javanese poet composed the history of a critical period in the Javanese past: the late fifteenth and early sixteenth centuries, a period that saw the transition from the ancient Hindu-Buddhist East Javanese regimes to the beginnings of Central Javanese Islamic hegemony. The poet wrote that history with distinctive style. For unlike texts of the more dominant tradition of Javanese history writing, this text does *not* chronicle a dynastic history preoccupied with the doings of kings and their armies in linear narrative fashion. Rather, this poem *interrupts* the dominant genealogical style of the dynastic chronicle to treat the past episodically, to generate a novel genealogy of the future. Rather than focus on the genetic antecedents of the ruling elite of his or her present-day Java, the poet writes, in a series of episodes, the stories of a handful of peculiar characters on the margins of the dominant literary, historical, and cultural traditions. These episodes, written from the vantage of exile, are deftly bound together to engender a new historical force which would emerge through contestation, rather than merely descend along royal bloodlines. Inscribing a new future out of a traditional past, the epic discloses a novel history whose effectiveness is self-consciously projected onto suggested tomorrows.

The *Babad Jaka Tingkir* motivating this book, this extended historical conversation, is certainly not the only history of Jaka Tingkir that was written in nineteenth-century Java. Nor is it the only historical prophecy. It is, however, perhaps the only history of Jaka Tingkir from which the famous "Youth from Tingkir" (legendary founder of the first of Central Java's inland Islamic kingdoms) is significantly absent. My reading of the text suggests that this absence discloses the revolutionary kind of future this historical prophecy writes for the Javanese past. Instead of writing a conventional foundational history of *the* "Youth from Tingkir," this history invokes the emergence of an alternative future: an alternative "Tingkir Youth" who might reign, not as yet another founding father, but as a sign of empowered margins, as a figure for new youthful forms of power. Rather than register a recuperation of past reality in the name of "objective truth" (as do many conventional master-narrative historical projects of the West), *or* a reinscription of the imagined pasts of dynastic presents with an eye to continuing traditional status quos (as do many of the more mainstream works of indigenous Javanese history), this text constructs an alternative past which, countering its oppressive colonial present, would move toward more autonomous, perhaps even liberating, futures. The text was written, I argue, to indicate to its readers a *context* out of which might emerge a profoundly changed future for Javanese history. And the implications of this contextualized text can be extended far beyond the world of nineteenth-century traditional Java to foreshadow possibilities, and to critique processes, still at work in contemporary Indonesia today.

Reading in Traditional Java

Before turning to *Babad Jaka Tingkir* in its contestatory particularity, I would first like to consider the nature of reading, and writing, in Javanese pasts and presents. In this discussion I will use the semifictional categories "traditional Java" and "the modern world," not as substantive entities but as fragile constructs that serve to delineate differences between conceptual orders that emerged in time through history. By "traditional Java," I mean the nonunitary discursive world in and through which a wide variety of Javanese subjects lived over a roughly 250-year period that closed (more or less conclusively) in 1942 with the Japanese invasion of Java and the consequent sudden end of Dutch colonial domination. A world that was generated and regenerated under the conditions of colonialism, traditional Java became recognized by emerging Javanese subjects as "Javanese" over the course of the nineteenth century.[15] This heterogeneous

15. For a wonderful tracing of the emergence of this world and its subjects, see John Pemberton, *On the Subject of "Java"* (Ithaca: Cornell University Press, 1994), chaps. 1–3.

and diverse world (or better, these worlds) became fixed as "traditional" *after* the fact, toward the beginning of what would later be considered its end; for "traditional Java" as such was born toward the end of the nineteenth century; and only in the face of its potential recession before its presumed opposite, "the modern world."

What do we know of literate audiences in the semifictional entity that I am calling "traditional Java"? How might we characterize the relationships among Javanese subjects and Javanese writings in these former times? Was literacy in traditional Java restricted to the insular members of a tiny elite class, an elite separated from and surrounded by a sea of illiterate peasants? Or was the traditional reading public a somewhat more popular and potentially populist entity?

Despite the abysmally low rates of literacy in Java preceding the 1945 Indonesian national revolution, the "literate" audience for written texts was not as small as might be imagined.[16] The great majority of texts written in the prerevolutionary era were composed in *macapat* meters which were (and are) meant for sung performative readings and hence for melodic aural consumption.[17] Indeed, even the solitary reading of these texts entails the intoning of the melody in the reader's mind. Sometimes the melodic phrasing of the poetry in performance actually determines the sense of a given passage.[18] Although solitary readings of these texts were clearly important to the professional literati (and others) who in-

16. Cf. Anthony Reid's discussion of the remarkably high level of literacy across Southeast Asia in the early premodern period (Reid, *Southeast Asia in the Age of Commerce, 1450–1680*, vol. 1, *The Land below the Winds* [New Haven: Yale University Press, 1988], pp. 215–25).

17. For technical discussions of Central Javanese *macapat* poetry, see Bernard Arps, *Tembang in Two Traditions: Performance and Interpretation of Javanese Literature* (London: School of Oriental and African Studies [henceforth SOAS], 1992); Maragaret Kartomi, *Matjapat Songs in Central and West Java* (Canberra: Australian National University Press, 1973); and Martin F. Hatch, "Lagu, Laras, Layang: Rethinking Melody in Javanese Music" (Ph.D. dissertation, Cornell University, 1980).

18. See Arps, *Tembang in Two Traditions*, esp. chap. 11. See also Timothy E. Behrend's description of Soeranto Atmosaputro's interpreting difficult passages of poetry ("The Serat Jatiswara: Structure and Change in a Javanese Poem, 1600–1930" [Ph.D. dissertation, Australian National University, 1987], p. 197). Compare this with Anthony Day's description of an old Kraton Surakarta scribe's reading to himself in "*Babad Kandha, Babad Kraton,* and Modern Javanese Literature," *Bijdragen tot de Taal-, Land-, en Volkenkunde* [henceforth BKI] 134, no. 4 (1978):442.

scribed them,[19] the majority of readings of *macapat* texts in the pre-revolutionary period were performed aurally by Javanese as they listened to public textual recitations, and it is precisely because of the usually public and oral performative nature of traditional Javanese textuality that the notion of *literacy*, at least as far as *macapat* texts are concerned, should be understood to have a different meaning in the context of prerevolutionary Java. The *literate* audience of Java's past included persons who were "illiterate" in the narrower sense of the word, and yet, through practiced and sensitive listening, had become highly conversant with literature.

Where, then, were some of these scenes of reading? And who were the audiences? Public recitations of texts were standard fare in the palaces of Central Java until relatively recent times. Notably, nightly *macapat* reading of texts entertained, up to the 1960s, large, fluid, and heterogeneous groups of court servants in the Kraton Surakarta. The texts were recited by the so-called "voice guards," male members of elite corps of military guards, who sang by turns throughout the night, every night except on Wednesday and Saturday nights when they were preempted by shadow-play performances.[20] Seated behind a low table at the edge of the palace's open Sasana Séwaka throne pavilion (figure 1), they read by flickering oil lantern, singing from a wide variety of texts that were selected from the same royal scriptorium that now houses what appears the sole manuscript witness of *Babad Jaka Tingkir*.[21]

19. Cf. Ronggasasmita's description of Yasadipura's solitary reading above. See also Behrend, "The Serat Jatiswara," pp. 358–72, for a strong argument on the visual aspects of scribal reproduction.
20. The "voice guards" (or *jagaswara*) were from the Tamtaman and Carangan corps; they read/sang the texts in a vocal style known as *lagu pringgitan*.
21. This description is rendered from several sources: (1) K.R.M.H.T. Daryonagoro, (then) Wakil Pangageng Paréntah Karaton, Karaton Surakarta, personal communication, 1984; (2) Padmosoesastra, *Serat Urapsari* (Batavia: Kolff, 1896), p. 238; (3) [R. Ng. Purbadipura], *Srikarongron*, 3 vols. [composed Surakarta, 1913], ed. Moelyono Sastronaryatmo and Sudibjo Z. Hadisutjipto (Jakarta: Departemen Pendidikan dan Kebudayaan, Proyek Penerbitan Buku Sastra Indonesia dan Daerah, 1981), 2:58–59; (4) *Serat Babad Langenharja*, vol. 2 (composed Surakarta, 1872; inscribed Surakarta, late 19th century). MS. SP 180 Na; SMP KS 100, p. 234 ff.

The *Babad Langenharja* passage is a contemporaneous account of a late-night reading at Langenharja that took place in 1872. What was read there were earlier "entries" in the same *Babad Langenharja*. This "frames within frames" depiction of reading is not unique (for example, see also Purbadipura, *Srikarongron*, 2:59). These scenes of reading suggest that the diarylike court *babad* functioned as aurally consumed local newspapers

Figure 1. The Sasana Séwaka throne pavilion of the Kraton Surakarta: a site of reading.

Although on occasion some of those listening at these palace readings were members of the royal family and their closest retainers, routinely most of the audience consisted of the less exalted workers at court who listened as they attended to their various duties—perhaps stopping their work at times to attend more closely. The consumption of "court litera-ture" was thus hardly the exclusive preserve of royalty and high cour-tiers. The audience for these texts, made up of the quite heterogeneous and socially stratified group of persons who were the actual participants in "traditional court culture" in Java, included the tailors, cooks, janitors, boatmen, nursemaids, washerwomen, and others employed by the palace. Indeed, the higher nobility were less likely to be present at these scenes of reading than their more humble subordinates, since the elite were seldom subject to the burden of night duty.[22] Many, if not most, of the audience

or news magazines for the court community. These "news magazines" were likely compiled largely from the official reports prepared in the Kraton's Secretariat (Sana-wilapa).

22. For a description of the higher nobility reading in the more relaxed environs of the king's Langenharja country manor, see Babad Langenharja, vol. 3 (composed Sura-karta, 1872/73; inscribed Surakarta, late 19th century). MS. SP 219 Ca; SMP KS 101, p. 120 ff. The royal reading of classical kekawins in this 1872 history features Western

were not resident at court; daily (or nightly) when their shift was done, they recrossed the palace walls to return home to their villages or urban neighborhoods, bearing with them what they had heard.[23]

Traditional Javanese writing, sometimes misnamed "court literature," has always had a life that extended well beyond the palace walls.[24] There is, for example, ample evidence that much of what is now called "court literature" grew out of and through textual traditions in the rural Islamic educational institutions, or *pesantrèn*, of Java. Indeed, it is a little discussed fact that *all* Java's most renowned "court poets" were products of (among other things) Islamic *pesantrèn* educations.[25] These court poets knew first-hand the classical literary prowess of the orthodox Islamic masters of the provinces.[26] They also knew by personal experience the popularity of *macapat* recitation in these provincial institutions of Islamic learning. It is not surprising, then, that we find among the texts of nineteenth-century court literature detailed descriptions of readings of Javanese poetic and

———
musical accompaniment, dancing Dutch *mevrouws*, and drunken toasts at the close of nearly every verse.

23. For a more detailed treatment of readings and readers in and around the traditional Javanese palaces, see my "Writing the Past, Inscribing the Future: Exile and Prophecy in an Historical Text of Nineteenth-Century Java" (Ph.D. dissertation, Cornell University, 1990), pp. 27–34.

24. Cf. Th. Pigeaud on the absence of a definitive line separating the performing arts of the Central Javanese palaces from those of the Javanese countryside (*Javaanse Volks-vertoningen: Bijdrage tot de Beschrijving van Land en Volk* [The Hague: Martinus Nijhoff, 1938], pp. 32–33).

25. The late-eighteenth-century poet laureate of the Kraton Surakarta, Yasadipura I, studied at a *pesantrèn* in Kedhu-Bagelèn. He later joined his king, Pakubuwana II, at the Tegalsari, Ponorogo *pesantrèn* of Kyai Agung Iman (Kasan) Besari (Sasrasumarta, *Tus Pajang*, pp. 10–15). Yasadipura II also studied at the famous Tegalsari *pesantrèn*; his fellow student was Kyai Kasan Besari II. The *pujongga* Ronggawarsita studied for approximately four years at the same *pesantrèn* under Kasan Besari II (his grandfather's classmate) (Komite Ronggawarsitan, *Babad Cariyos Lelampahanipun Suwargi Radèn Ngebéhi Ronggawarsita*, 3 vols. [Surakarta: Marsch, 1931–33], 1:5–110).

26. Yasadipura I brings this point home in his *Serat Cabolèk* when he has an orthodox religious scholar (*ulama*) from provincial Kudus worst all the Javanese aristocrats of the capital in reading skills. The (*ulama*) recites and provides exegesis on a few "difficult" verses from an Old Javanese classic, reads at length from and interprets the "neoclassical" *Déwaruci*, and finally recites in its entirety the text of the "mad" *Suluk Malang Sumirang* (Soebardi, *The Book of Cabolèk*, pp. 112–52). For more on the *Déwaruci*, see below, chap. 3; on the *Suluk Malang Sumirang*, see below, *Babad Jaka Tingkir* XXII:24–XXIV:22 and chap. 6.

other works at *pesantrèn*. Careful readings of these descriptions reveal the surprisingly diverse audience the traditional texts enjoyed in rural Java, an audience that included both men and women, and comprised teachers, pupils (or *santri*), and neighbors of the *pesantrèn* in which the reading was performed.[27]

Although the court and *pesantrèn* were crucial sites for the proliferation of traditional Javanese literature, persons associated directly with neither of these institutions were by no means excluded from the practice of reading (or of writing, for that matter). Among Javanese villagers, the recitation of *macapat* texts has been, and sometimes still is, a regular feature at certain ritual events, such as at the celebration of the birth of a child.[28] There is evidence which suggests that reading (or listening) was even more popular among the masses in the nineteenth century, though it is questionable (to some) how much they understood of what they read or heard. Take, for example, the evaluation of common literacy in C. F. Winter's elitist *Javaansche Zamenspraken* (Javanese Conversations), a textbook for Dutch students of Javanese language and literature which was compiled around 1840 at the Surakarta Institute of Javanese Language.[29] In Conversation 35, the Dutchman Tuwan Anu (Mister So and So) asks his prospective Javanese teacher, Gunawan, why "the Javanese"

27. See, for example, the descriptions of readings in the *Serat Centhini* (especially cantos 225–28) and *Serat Cabolang* (especially cantos 205–7) and my discussion of these passages in "Writing the Past, Inscribing the Future," pp. 35–36.

Undeniably important sites of production and dissemination of traditional Javanese writing, the *pesantrèn*, it must be noted, virtually monopolized indigenous paper production in Java up to the early nineteenth century. See C. Guillot, "Dluwang ou Papier Javanais," *Archipel* 26 (1984):105–15, and my "Writing the Past, Inscribing the Future," pp. 37–38, n. 77.

28. In contemporary Central Java, the text of choice for ritual events surrounding childbirth is the magical *Kidung Rumeksa ing Wengi* ("Song That Guards in the Night"), a text that affords supernatural protection to whoever recites, hears, or holds it.

29. C. F. Winter Sr., *Javaansche Zamenspraken*, vol. 1, 3d ed. (Amsterdam: Muller, 1882; orig. 1848). C. F. Winter Sr. (1799–1859) was a Java-born Eurasian philologist who himself authored a number of traditional Javanese literary works. He often worked in collaboration with the famed court poets of Surakarta (notably Ronggawarsita II, Ronggawarsita III, and Mangkunagara IV). The second director of the colonial government's Surakarta Institute (1834–43), he was enormously influential in the formation of academic Javanology. For a brief biographical sketch of Winter, see S. Kolff, "Een Baanbreker voor 't Javaansch," *Djåwå*, 2 (1922):75–82. See also below, p. 45.

Figure 2. A scene of reading, as depicted in an early-nineteenth-century manuscript. The woman in the audience appears to be massaging the reader's back. One of the men is smoking opium; the other is chewing betel. From *Serat Damar Wulan* IOL Jav. 89. Courtesy of the British Library.

like reading so much if they don't understand what they are reading. Gunawan answers:

> As for the *priyayi* [the bureaucratic elite], they are only interested in the story without troubling themselves with what the words mean. For most of the commoners, [reading] is just a prop to keep them awake so robbers won't come. As for the readers themselves, they usually don't know anything beyond the story-line; they don't understand a lot of the words. I'm not just talking about *Kawi* [Old Javanese or archaeized literary Javanese] texts either—given even ordinary Javanese texts, those who could really explain [what they're reading] are rare indeed. So all that singing ringing out in the night is nothing more than the night guard or maybe somebody showing off his voice to the neighbors—so that they'll be impressed that he can read and that he has a good voice.[30]

I wonder. That most readers-listeners were not attending to, nor perhaps understanding, the discursive meaning of every word of any text most certainly does not exclude the possibility of their having intelligently read that text. The active process of reading, that is *making sense*, of any text includes much more than being able to come up with appropri-

30. Winter, *Javaansche Zamenspraken*, 1:58.

ate glosses for unfamiliar words—perhaps especially in the case of traditional Javanese poetic forms in which textual sense is somewhat more sensuous and somewhat less literal. Reading-listening was undeniably a pleasurable activity to some nineteenth-century Javanese commoners (figure 2). And it was at least interesting and engaging enough to keep them awake, all night.

The popularity of reading among the common folk is attested to in *Zamenspraken*'s Conversation 69, in which Mister So and So is visited by the young poet Kawiswara ("Voice of Kawi"), who having heard the Dutchman is in the market for the classics, has come to sell him a Kawi manuscript. Kawiswara himself is not the owner, but is acting as middleman for a poor boarder he knows. The owner's asking price is a ream of good Dutch paper. Also working for Mister So and So and present at that time was the elder court poet Kawireja (roughly, "Rich with Kawi"). Kawireja considers the unusually well-preserved condition of the manuscript for sale:

> That's because he never read it and none of his neighbors ever borrowed it—none of them could have understood its words. *Usually Javanese books which are frequently read and frequently lent out* aren't that clean. They may have oil spilt on them and be all stained with betel chew or other filth. Using a cigarette butt to mark his place, when the reader gets sleepy, he uses the book for his pillow [emphasis added].[31]

Evidently the pleasures of going to bed with a good book were not unknown to Javanese in former times. Scenes of reading in nineteenth-century Java were many and varied.[32] What was read was also much more varied than is sometimes imagined today.

On Writing in Traditional Java

The body of writings produced by subjects who belonged to the world of traditional Java comprises the quite heterogeneous textual universe of works that is now known as "Traditional Javanese Literature." The texts

31. Ibid., p. 166.
32. For a description of a late-nineteenth-century reading "on the road," in which *macapat* reading apparently served as a traditional car radio, see my "Writing the Past, Inscribing the Future," pp. 41–43.

Figure 3. Reading by oil lamp in Java, as depicted in an early-nineteenth-century manuscript. From *Serat Damar Wulan* IOL Jav. 89. Courtesy of the British Library.

that make up this universe were, for the most part, inscribed in Javanese script and composed in Modern Javanese language, rather than Old Javanese or Kawi. Most of these texts were written in the 250-year period that ended with World War II and the Indonesian national revolution. These various textual works (and constellations of textual works) compose the discursive formations that delineate traditional Javanese writing, formations that apparently emerged among writers in eighteenth-century protocolonial Java and that retreated (almost finally) with early twentieth-century Java's turn toward modernity. It would be foolish to characterize "in general" what these writers wrote about, for their texts embrace a remarkable range of Javanese interests. Their writings—which include historical chronicles and documents, erotic lore, Sufi speculative lyrics, scripts for shadow-puppet plays, compendia of court lore, and manuals of magical practice—range, for example, from treatises on Islamic theology and law to manuals of horsemanship, from poetic histories of the Napoleonic Wars to catalogs of magic daggers, from moralistic platitudes on virtuous wifely behavior to inventories of royal liquor cabinets.[33]

33. For more on the diversity of the writings comprising this body, see vol. 1 of my *Javanese Literature in Surakarta Manuscripts*, pp. 15–21.

Almost all the texts that today's Javanese call *tradisional* would have been originally written, that is composed and inscribed, in Javanese script: the traditional literature of Java is, for the most part, a manuscript literature. As I mentioned above, a majority of these texts are composed in *macapat* verse forms written for sung performative readings. The language of many of these texts, though Modern Javanese, includes an admixture of archaic Kawi vocabulary. The texts tend to be written in a linguistic style which marks them as "literary" in distinction from the language of ordinary speech. Many, but by no means all, of the texts that make up this literature were written by persons in some way associated with the royal palaces of Central Java.

Despite the heterogeneous reality of these texts, there is, nevertheless, still a utility in pointing out certain characteristics that highlight the difference of *writing* traditionally in Javanese script from modern writing—both in the West and in Indonesia. How are we to understand this difference? What did it mean to *write*, to be a writer, in traditional Java? How is the notion of author related to the reality of text in this chirographic literature? At the outset, it is important to note that the words used in Java to designate "writer" do not share with English (and French) the cognate "authority" of the modern *author*. The Javanese words for "writer" connote a rather different status for "the textual worker" (*ingkang akarya sastra*) than does the modern Anglo-French *author*. The Javanese "writer" (*panulis, panyerat*) may be the person who physically writes or inscribes (*anulis, anyerat*) any text, the "scribe" by whose hand the written artifact is produced. Then again the writer may be the work's "composer" (*panganggit, pangiket*): she/he who "interlaces" (*nganggit*) and "binds together" (*ngiket*) words or texts in textually productive manners. Significantly, in traditional Java there is no clear distinction between these two categories of writing: that is, writing as physical replication of prior inscription and writing as original composition. On the one hand, the scribe enjoyed a modicum of poetic freedom in his or her "copying" (*nurun, nedhak*) of texts, which often engendered new variants and versions of old texts. On the other, the composer, working within conventions of Javanese textuality, would sometimes borrow (or "translate") from older works, interlacing (*nganggit*) and rebinding (*ngiket*) old textual fragments into new contexts to create his or her "original" work.

A dramatic illustration of this form of composition is a text which is today perhaps the best known of Javanese poems: the *Kalatidha* (Time of Darkness).[34] *Kalatidha* was written by R.Ng. Ronggawarsita (1802–1873), a nephew of the Mas Ronggasasmita who would have unread writings read. This most famous of poems, written by Java's most famous of poets, laments the oxymoronic impotence of perfect royal power in high colonial Java. Sometimes bruited as this "last of the court poet's" late-nineteenth-century expressive signature of the end of traditional Javanese power,[35] the poem is actually a rather more complicated reflection upon indigenous potencies. Composed of a cunning repetition of an early-nineteenth-century prophetic lament on future moral decline, which is interlaced with an inverted quotation about power's past excellence from that same earlier work, and then punctuated by the poet's own drolly provocative observations, *Kalatidha* is in effect a strategic *translation* of an old prophecy into a new prophetic context. The earlier work from which Ronggawarsita borrowed, or translated, is the *Cabolang-Centhini*, a work widely reputed to be "the first Javanese encyclopedia."[36] As it turns out, this "encyclopedia" itself is a profoundly intertextual work composed, in part, out of borrowings from and allusions to a host of still earlier works. My point here is not to expose the *Kalatidha* (or the *Cabolang-Centhini*) as derivative, but rather to point to the very intensely self-conscious intertextuality of Javanese writing. Indeed, none the less original an expression because of its intertextual reality, the meaning of the *Kalatidha* is doubly complicated as both a signature of the end of tradition and a critical commentary upon and reconfirmation of tradition's prophecy of its own end.

34. For text, English translation, and commentary on this famous poem, see J. Joseph Errington, "To Know Oneself the Trouble Times: Ronggawarsita's Serat Kala Tidha," in *Writing on the Tongue*, ed. A. L. Becker (Ann Arbor: University of Michigan Center for South and Southeast Asian Studies, 1989), pp. 95–138.

35. See, for example, Benedict Anderson's evocative treatment of this work in his *Language and Power: Exploring Political Cultures in Indonesia* (Ithaca: Cornell University Press, 1990), pp. 201–2 and 242–43.

36. Compare the text of the *Kalatidha* with *Serat Cabolang*, canto 248; verses 21–25 (in *Serat Centhini Latin*, vol. 3, ed. Kamajaya [Yogyakarta: Yayasan Centhini, 1986], p. 307), and canto 257, verses 34–43 (in *Serat Centhini Latin*, vol. 4, ed. Kamajaya [Yogyakarta: Yayasan Centhini, 1988], pp. 3–4). See also H. Karkono K. Partokusumo (= Kamajaya), *Zaman Edan: Pembahasan Serat Kalatidha Ranggawarsitan* (Yogyakarta: Proyek Javanologi, [1983]), pp. 20–29. For a provocative discussion of the *Centhini*, see Benedict Anderson's "Professional Dreams: Reflections on Two Javanese Classics," in *Language and Power*, pp. 271–89.

While not claiming the originary authority of authorship, writers in traditional Java were, however, often active participants in rather different forms of potency. Writing was a highly esteemed practice, and a practice that was self-consciously involved in its own worldliness, its being-in-the-world or circumstantial reality.[37] The best of the traditional writers—like Ronggawarsita, who is today revered as the *last* of the true court poets (or *pujongga*)—wrote with an acute awareness of the potential power of their words in the world. These writers wrote strategically to produce considered effects in the sociopolitical milieus in which they wrote. They meant to produce texts which were prophetic not just as records of already determined foreseen futures, but rather as kinds of writing whose very inscription itself could (or would) materially effect what was to come. Often writing about the very distant past, the sometimes anonymous *pujongga* wrote these texts of material prophecy self-consciously to affect the practical and political realities of both the historical presents in which they wrote and the imagined futures toward which they wrote. They wrote and rewrote history, not just after the fact, but also before and in suggestive anticipation of it.[38] Composing their works in the profoundly intertextual and reflexive world of writing in traditional Java, prophetic writers constructed their texts to contest and transform prior texts and contexts into something quite novel and often yet unknown. The orientation of such texts, original works composed out of, against, and as comments upon other texts, could be an as yet indeterminate future waiting beyond the horizon. *Babad Jaka Tingkir* is one such text.

37. On this notion of worldliness, see Said, "The World, the Text, and the Critic," esp. pp. 34–39.

38. Cf. C. C. Berg's discussion of "verbal magic" in the writing of Javanese dynastic histories from the eleventh through eighteenth centuries ("The Javanese Picture of the Past," in *An Introduction to Indonesian Historiography*, ed. Soedjatmoko et al. [Ithaca: Cornell University Press, 1965], pp. 87–117). Berg imaginatively argues that the professional poet-historians worked self-consciously—in the service of their (sometimes neo-) royal employers—both to impose and to effect (sometimes novel) dominant ideologies. He implies that when these poets wrote and rewrote history to effect their (sociopolitical) verbal magic they did so in a manner that intentionally distorted "the truth" (as an extralinguistic reality). My understanding of the work of the *pujongga*, though similar to that of Berg's, considers the work of these poets a less devious practice. It is my sense that the *pujongga* themselves realized in and through their work the discursive nature (the living historicity) of "reality" itself.

"Traditional Javanese Literature": A Colonial Heritage

The potentially radical genius of writing in traditional Java has not been realized in contemporary Indonesia. Conversely, this writing *as* "Traditional Javanese Literature" is apprehended instead as an inscribed monument to the refined quietism of an ever receding classical past. This *apprehension* has its own history—a history that I shall begin exploring in the Javanese present with the consideration of a peculiar kind of absence. A curious modern reality: although perhaps more highly esteemed than ever, the actual texts of "Traditional Javanese Literature" are today almost unread.[39] In this modern age of increasing literacy among Javanese subjects, and of increasing devotion to things "traditional" in New Order Indonesia, the sometimes extraordinary texts composed in traditional Java remain, for the most part, laid by on the shelf. Ronggasasmita's 1815 call to active reading with which I inaugurated this chapter has, it seems, been frustrated. Why, and how, has this come to be the case?

In late twentieth-century Indonesia, "Traditional Javanese Literature" is popularly understood as a particular genre of beautiful writing, a genre of elite (royal) writing characterized by difficult or esoteric texts of great refinement and philosophical depth: that is, *Literature* with a capital *L*. As a result of this generic misunderstanding, the diverse constellations of heterogeneous writings produced by a variety of writers in Java from the eighteenth through the early twentieth century have come to be reduced and confined (as Literature, or *Kesusastraan*) under the unitary, objectified category of "beautiful tradition" (*tradisi yang adiluhung*). Javanese writing of the past has thus been essentialized into an aestheticized object of tradition, a fantastic object whose contours are determined by (as they in turn help to determine) conventional wisdom on the nature of "Javaneseness." A construction of consciousnesses over time, the Literature, as object of tradition, is for most Javanese subjects today an imaginary ideal—or a spectral reminder of a vanishing past—rather than a diverse field of concrete inscription to be read.

The origins of the popular image of "Traditional Javanese Literature,"

---

39. This is not to deny that there are still avid readers of exemplars from this body of texts in contemporary Java; it is merely to note that their ranks are thinning. Bernard Arps treats several tiny enclaves of readers from among these diminishing ranks in his recent *Tembang in Two Traditions*.

which as we shall see is an image of rebirth and return as well as of refinement and exclusion, are to be found in nineteenth-century Dutch colonial philology. Dutch philology on Java was born in the second quarter of the nineteenth century along with Dutch consolidation of its first truly colonial authority over the island. These new colonial developments followed in the wake of two determinative moments in the colonial history of Java. The first of these moments was the temporary displacement of Dutch power on the island by the British from 1811 to 1816. As well as initiating institutional changes which transformed the political landscape of the colony, the British interregnum also saw the beginnings of scientific interest in native culture and literature.[40] Dutch administrators, upon their return to power in Java, were not blind to the usefulness of this new knowledge and in the coming decades strove to emulate British scholarship, citing in particular the proven political utility of British cultural policies in India.[41] Dutch authority now saw how "understanding the natives" could facilitate both the civil administration of—and the efficient extraction of profits from—what was, at long last, becoming a true colony.

The second critical moment in the colonial history of early-nineteenth-century Java was the final defeat of indigenous Javanese royal power that marked the end of the Dipanagara War in 1830. It had been a devastating war. Led by a Javanese prince and supported by a network of rural Islamic teachers, this last concerted Javanese rebellion against colonial authority (prior to the Indonesian national revolution) raged five years and claimed

40. Notably, Sir Thomas Stamford Raffles, *The History of Java*, 2 vols. (London: Black, Parbury, and Allen, 1817), and John Crawford, *History of the Indian Archipelago*, 3 vols. (Edinburgh: A. Constable and Co., 1820). It should be noted here, however, that Raffles in fact based much of his research on earlier published works of Dutch historiography (see Donald E. Weatherbee's "Raffles' Sources for Traditional Javanese Historiography and the Mackenzie Collections," *Indonesia* 26 [October 1978]:63–93). What was novel about Raffles' work was its scientific form and especially its publicity. With Raffles' *History*, "Java" became a proper subject for Anglo-European Orientalism.

41. See, for example, Dr. J. F. C. Gericke's lengthy memo to Governor General van den Bosch (T. C. L. Wijnmalen, "Nota van Dr. J. F. C. Gericke omtrent de Oprichting van een Instituut voor de Inlandsche Talen en Litteratuur," *BKI* 21 (1874):313–19. Written circa 1830, the memo calls, in the name of the colonial mission, for the systematic study of Javanese language and literature. Gericke, an important linguist and Bible translator, was to serve as the first director of the colonial government's Institute for the Javanese Language in Surakarta, which operated 1832–43.

the lives of over 200,000 Javanese—as well as the lives of some 15,000 colonials.[42] The experience of that war demonstrated both to the colonial authorities and to their subjects the fury that could be unleashed by "the natives" when mobilized by their elite under the banner of militant Islam. Having won the war, Dutch power would henceforth work to consolidate its authority in a way that would foreclose a recurrence of such fury. Already defeated militarily, after 1830 the final subjugation of the Javanese was to be sealed by a colonial strategy which would depend in part upon the cultural isolation and cooptation of the indigenous elite. As long as the indigenous elite could be held in colonial service, while at the same time held away, in a kind of cultural reserve, from both the masses and the sinister forces of "fanatical" Islam, Dutch authority, it was hoped, would reign supreme.

This strategy of control involved the implementation of a colonial cultural policy which worked to portray a sense of cultural remove on the part of the elite. Much of this policy, for instance the preservation and inflation of Javanese sumptuary practices to shore up sagging elite status and dignity, was quite studied and deliberate.[43] Other aspects of the policy were more implicit to the colonial project and less considered. The result of unconscious assumptions and wishful thinking, these other aspects assumed a certain logic of invisibility, what might be thought of as a structure of not seeing. This "not seeing," which was taking command of colonial perceptions in the 1830s just as the institution of forced cultivation was inaugurating the high colonial period of Dutch power on Java, worked to contain Javanese subjects within an ideological construct that would later become "traditional Javanese culture."[44] That construct was

---

42. The "colonials" who lost their lives included Javanese, as well as other indigenous soldiers who served in the Dutch colonial army. According to M. C. Ricklefs, of the 15,000 lives lost by government troops, 7,000 belonged to "Indonesian" soldiers and 8,000 to Europeans (*A History of Modern Indonesia* [London: Macmillan, 1981], p. 113).

43. See V. J. H. Houben, "Afstand van Gebied met Behoud van Aanzien: Een onderzoek naar de koloniale verhouding op midden Java in 1830" (M.A. thesis, Leiden University, 1976), and Heather Sutherland, *The Making of a Bureaucratic Elite* (Singapore: Heinemann Educational Books, 1979).

44. Cf. Nicholas Dirks on colonial investments in the cultural formations of colonized subjects in India. In the preface to the second edition of *The Hollow Crown: Ethnohistory of an Indian Kingdom* (Ann Arbor: University of Michigan Press, 1993), p. xxiv, Dirks writes of colonial involvement in the conceptual fixing of tradition: "It was not so much that traditions were invented as that the idea of tradition—as primordial and unchang-

articulated in part through a delineation and identification of high Javanese culture as an entity standing in opposition to Islam and as the exclusive and conservative preserve of a hyper-refined elite class. For among
the realities necessarily invisible in this field of colonial vision were the
Islamic and subaltern presences within even the most privileged sites for
the articulation of such a culture. And in post-1830 Indies' scholarship,
the Kraton of the Susuhunans (Kings) of Surakarta was positioned as the
most authoritative of these sites, as the truest, and therefore most *reserved*, exemplar of pure Javanese high culture.[45] Not seen, then, were the
Islamic *pesantrèn* educations of this palace's court poets, the Islamic content of its court literature, and the myriad commoners who populated its
court society.

Nineteenth-century colonial scholarship was dominated by the discipline of philology. Language and literature, philology's proper objects,
came to enjoy a favored position in the emerging image of Javanese high
culture. In 1832 a colonial Institute of Javanese Language and Literature
was established in Surakarta; it was there that the discipline of Javanology
first began to take shape. The moving forces behind the Institute were a
small group of Dutch—and especially Indo-European—philologists who
enjoyed strong ties both to the colonial government and to the Kraton
Surakarta. It was through the energies of these men that the canon of
what was to become "the literature of Java" began to emerge. At the same
time, and often through the hands of these same philologists, hundreds of
Javanese manuscripts were migrating westward to form the beginnings of
what would eventually grow into a massive colonial literary archive in

----

ing, as orderly and uplifting—was imagined, desired, and then deployed as the condition and mission of colonial rule. The more things changed the more they seemed to
remain the same."

45. The issue of the Surakarta Palace's position as the last and best preserve of Javanese
culture still rages. Witness the extensive national (and international) media coverage of
the "scandalous," and ultimately failed, project to build a five-star international hotel
within the Kraton walls. That project, which was to have been financed by one of
President Soeharto's sons, was widely condemned as a violation of the Surakarta Palace's sanctity as a "cultural reservation" (*cagar budaya*). See, for example, *Asia Week*
(23 October 1992); *Far Eastern Economic Review* (1 April 1993); *NRC Handelsblad* (24
October 1992 and 20 February 1993); *Kompas* (25–26 September 1992); *Editor* (12
September and 31 October 1992); and *Tempo* (17 October 1992). For an earlier valoriza-
tion of the Kraton Surakarta as a last holdout of high (Hinduized) Javanese culture, see
Clifford Geertz, *Religion of Java* (Chicago: University of Chicago Press, 1960), p. 237.

the Netherlands.[46] Because of the paired privileging of literature and of the Kraton Surakarta by the early colonial scholars, what these men *imagined* to be the literature of that court came to be a crucial factor in the framing of Javanese culture.[47] The implications of that frame are particularly evident in the history of Javanese literature produced by colonial, and also postcolonial, philology.[48]

As a classical discipline, colonial Javanological philology is preoccupied with the quest for golden ages, periods of alleged literary florescence succeeded by periods of decline or decadence. Such philology teaches that Javanese literature attained the zenith of its sophistication and aesthetic value in the distant pre-Islamic past with the classical Hindu-Buddhist Kawi literary culture. This classical culture is said to belong to the serial glorious courts of the Old Javanese heartland. Its products, the Old Javanese *kekawin* (poetic texts composed mostly in East Java from the ninth through the fifteenth century), are the closest things to genuine originals in Javanese literature; the real originals, however, are not to be found in Java at all but in the Indian subcontinent, which produced the Sanskrit prototypes on which the Old Javanese poems were based.[49] The classical discipline of philology teaches that the robust florescence of Old Java's literary culture was crushed by the coming of Islam in the late fifteenth century. Islam's coming meant the destruction of the old high culture and

46. For more on the Surakarta Institute, see C. Fasseur, "The French Scare: Taco Roorda and the Origins of Javanese Studies in the Netherlands," in *Looking in Odd Mirrors: The Java Sea*, ed. V J. H. Houben et al. (Leiden: Vakgroep Talen en Culturen van Zuidoost-Azie en Oceanie Rijksuniversiteit te Leiden, 1992); E. M. Uhlenbeck, *A Critical Survey of Studies on the Languages of Java and Madura* (The Hague: Nijhoff, 1964), pp. 44–47; and Kenji Tsuchiya, "Javanology and the Age of Ranggawarsita: An Introduction to Nineteenth-Century Javanese Culture," in *Reading Southeast Asia* (Ithaca: Cornell University Southeast Asia Program, 1990), pp. 79–82. See also vol. 1 of my *Javanese Literature in Surakarta Manuscripts*, pp. 13–14.

47. The Dutch colonial philological project belongs, of course, to the greater Western European tradition of Orientalism that was so brilliantly critiqued by Edward Said in his seminal *Orientalism* (New York: Vintage Books, 1979). My argument in the following pages has no doubt been inspired by his work.

48. For a fuller, and somewhat more complicated outline of the postcolonial Dutch philological history of Javanese literature, see Theodore G. Th. Pigeaud, *Literature of Java*, 4 vols. (The Hague: Nyhoff, 1967–80), 1:4–9.

49. See, for example, R.M.Ng. Poerbatjaraka's evaluation of Old Javanese literary practice in this Dutch-trained, ethnically Javanese philologist's introduction to Javanese literary history (*Kapustakan Djawi* [Jakarta: Djambatan, 1952], pp. vii–xii).

the pollution of its language and literature with the alien sounds and senses of Arabic. Philology calls what followed a long period of darkness, characterized by an Islamic literary culture coming out of the *pasisir* area (the northern littoral of Java).[50] It is said that the *pasisir* authors of the middle period produced derivative, and sometimes degenerate, texts on "foreign" Islamic topics.

For much of the seventeenth century and nearly the entire first half of the eighteenth century, the royal heartland of Central Java was torn apart by a series of dynastic, and other, wars. It is said that Javanese literary activity, presumably an activity proper to stable courts, ground to a near halt during this period of political chaos. Then in 1745, after the sack of the previous capital, the Dutch helped their ally, the reinstated king of Mataram, build a new court-city on the banks of the Solo river.[51] That new city was called Surakarta. Warfare continued unabated, however. Finally, in 1755, the Central Javanese situation, it is said, was normalized with the Dutch-overseen partition of Old Mataram into the twin realms of Yogyakarta and Surakarta. Peace and prosperity, we are told, at last came to Central Java.[52]

The philological canon teaches us that with this late eighteenth-century *pax Nederlandica*, Javanese literature came to experience a kind of rebirth at the new Surakarta palace, a rebirth that effected a partial recuperation of the lost greatness of old Java's literary culture. This renaissance is conventionally thought to have expressed itself most perfectly in the court poets' translations of the Old Javanese Kawi classics into Modern Javanese verse. Theodore Pigeaud, one of the greatest of the Dutch philologists, states succinctly the meaning of the rebirth as "the turning of the attention of Javanese scholars from Islamic texts to Old Javanese *kakawins*."[53] In effect: because the poets finally turned away from "foreign" Islam toward their

---

50. Interestingly, by the end of the colonial era the meaning of the word *pasisir* had expanded to designate all Javanese cultural areas outside the royal "heartland" (Poerwadarminta, *Baoesastra Djawa* [Groningen: Wolters, 1939], p. 475).

51. Canonical philology does not tell us that when the capital of Kartasura fell to the Chinese rebels in 1742, its king, Pakubuwana II, fled to East Java in the company of his court poet to be (Yasadipura I) to take refuge with the Islamic teacher (*kyai*) Imam Besari. See F. Fokkens, "De Priesterschool te Tegalsari," *Tijdschrift voor Taal-, Land-, en Volkenkunde* (hereafter *TBG*) 24 (1878) 318–19, and Sasrasumarta et al., *Tus Pajang*, pp. 14–15.

52. Actually, low-grade warfare continued well on into the nineteenth century.

53. Pigeaud, *Literature of Java*, 1:236.

native Javanese Hindu-Buddhist origins, Javanese poetry was reborn unto itself. It was to be, however, a short-lived rebirth (or, perhaps, but a stillbirth). For by the latter part of the nineteenth century, colonial philology had decided that the famed neoclassical productions of the Surakarta renaissance were "bad," as it were, translations. The renaissance would be declared dead, and with it newer classical literature as a serious art form.

In 1860 A. B. Cohen Stuart published the first systematically prepared philological edition and annotated Dutch translation of a Javanese literary work.[54] That work, the *Serat Bratayuda*, was a late-eighteenth-century Modern Javanese translation of a twelfth-century Old Javanese classic *kekawin*, which classic was itself a translation of the climax of the Sanskrit *Mahabharata* epic. The Modern Javanese version was composed by the man who is conventionally acclaimed the father of the Surakarta renaissance, the man who is thought to have fathered the rebirth of presumably dead Javanese letters from the grave in which the Moslem conquest had cast them. This man was Yasadipura I, Ronggasasmita's famous grandfather, the one who had been so fond of reading Sufi texts.

As it turns out, Cohen Stuart produced his philological work on Yasadipura's text with considerable embarrassment—and only because he was under orders from his civil service superiors at the Batavian Society of Arts and Sciences to do so. The philologist's prefatory remarks to his edition of this neoclassical Javanese text abound with apologies to his readers for subjecting them to such decadent, confused, and bastardized material. He would have much preferred, he explains, a commission to prepare an edition of the poem's much superior twelfth-century prototype. Disparaging Yasadipura's comprehension of Old Javanese as well as his literary skills in Modern Javanese, this father of Dutch colonial philology goes so far as to deplore the late king of Surakarta's choice of one so ignorant as Yasadipura to translate the fine *kekawin* classic into Modern Javanese verse. In the same vein, the philologist complains of the ignorance of his own "native informant," whose services, nevertheless, were doubtlessly indispensable for Cohen Stuart's Dutch translation of the poem. His disparaged "native informant" was none other than Yasadipura I's own great-grandson, Radèn Ngabéhi Ronggawarsita (1802–

---

54. A. B. Cohen Stuart, *Bråtå-Joedå, Indisch Javaansch Heldendicht*, Verhandelingen van het Bataviaasch Genootschap van Kunsten en Wetenschappen, vols. 27–28 (Batavia, 1860).

1873), who is regarded by Javanese today as having been the greatest of all Javanese literati.

After Cohen Stuart, Dutch philology turned its attention away from Modern Javanese to Old Javanese literature. Although nonacademic editions of Modern Javanese literary texts were still published (presumably as "appropriate" reading material for a small class of print-literate Javanese—and for Dutch colonial service trainees), these newer works were rarely considered worthy subjects for "serious" (read Dutch) scholarship.[55] Judged hopelessly involuted and derivative by the brokers of intellectual power, the new Javanese texts did not sell on the Dutch East Indies philological marketplace. Thus with the publication of the very first scholarly edition of a Modern Javanese literary text, the image of what was to become "Traditional Javanese Literature" was fixed in the halls of colonial scholarship as a monument to moribund involution.

And yet despite and alongside this disillusionment among scientific philologists of the later nineteenth and the twentieth century, the image of the neoclassical writing of the "Surakarta Renaissance" as the quintessential expression of high Javanese culture, quite remarkably, persisted—especially among romantic colonial officials "in the field." What the academic philologists meant to reveal as confused and garbled language, the romantics would see as expressions of the refined inscrutability of the elite native soul. For these romantics, the imagined neoclassical royal

55. According to Uhlenbeck's bibliography of Old Javanese and Javanese Literature, twenty-one text editions of Modern Javanese works and no editions of Old Javanese works were published by Dutch and Indo-European philologists in the seventeen-year period 1843–60. In the following seventy-nine years, the Dutch and Dutch-trained philologists published thirty-one editions of Modern Javanese works. Only a handful of these publications might be characterized as serious philological works. During the same seventy-nine-year period, the Dutch and Dutch-trained philologists published forty (serious) text editions of Old Javanese works, many of them Leiden University dissertations. See Uhlenbeck, *A Critical Survey of Studies on the Languages of Java and Madura*, pp. 145–73.

A notable exception to this scholarly disregard for Modern Javanese texts, however, was the continuing interest of Dutch scholars in the earliest Islamic texts in Java. See, for example, the Leiden doctoral dissertations of J. G. H. Gunning (1881), B. J. O. Schrieke (1916), and H. Kraemer (1921). Especially important in this regard have been the philological works of G. W. J. Drewes; see, for example, his *The Admonitions of Sèh Bari* (The Hague: Nijhoff, 1969) and *An Early Javanese Code of Muslim Ethics* (The Hague: Nijhoff, 1978).

writing of Surakarta, perhaps *because* it was seen as a dying and involuted form, best confirmed the "beautiful tradition" of Old Java, a tradition which colonial power would work to preserve and conserve.

This essentialized image of traditional Javanese writing as a desirably involuted neoclassicism came to take on a kind of truth. For although this narrow image does not in fact conform to the much more heterogeneous reality of written production in traditional Java, that image has, nonetheless, impressed itself into the reality of Javanese history. Such an image is, after all, a useful one. Generated in part by Dutch and Indo-European scholars whose interest was to understand the Javanese in order better to rule them, the neoclassical image of "Traditional Javanese Literature"—we should remember—first began to take shape in the aftermath of a devastating war waged against emerging colonial order by self-consciously Islamic opponents. The image was drawn, strategically, according to the philological romance of (pre-Islamic) golden ages and (non-Islamic) renaissances. It was and is an image which sees in the neoclassical writings of "Traditional Javanese Literature" a happy (if not totally successful) return, via texts, of the Javanese to their own native greatness, that is, to their timeless (docile) selves away from the interruption of Islam's sinister (political) messages. Internal to the logic of this image is the assurance that colonial order was ultimately responsible for the blessed return of Javanese writing to its "original truth."[56] The image, which had special appeal for the apologists of colonial authority, became in turn the intellectual property of emerging modern colonial subjects. In late-twentieth-century Indonesia it is still a variety of this image of "Traditional Javanese Literature" that reigns supreme.[57]

56. Benedict Anderson has suggested to me that among Netherlands East Indies intellectuals the philological ideal of the golden age was part of an ideological construct to justify the act of "colonization" or, better, the practice of empire. The imperial rationale of philology was as follows. "Our" colonized people at one time enjoyed a high civilization, which has since fallen into decay. In the case of Java, "Hindoo-Java's" decay was a direct result of Islamo-Arabic pollution and destruction. It was, then, both the right and the duty of the colonial power to bring that high culture/civilization back to its subject people; hence another buttress for the rectitude of the greater imperial "mission." Personal communication, Benedict Anderson, April 1987.

57. The canon of "Traditional Javanese Literature," as it is *popularly* construed and institutionally propagated in Indonesia today, features certain works composed by the "poets laureate" of the Surakarta Renaissance. The most often invoked canonical texts

On "Traditional Javanese Literature" in Modern Indonesia

The neoclassical image of "Traditional Javanese Literature" that prevails in the popular consciousness of late-twentieth-century Indonesia is articulated by Javanese subjects in two quite opposite (and interrelated) idioms. There is a tendency among today's Javanese to apprehend their traditional literature either as feudal fossil or as classic icon. The first image is one that emerges in the ostensibly modern or progressive consciousness, in the imaginations of those who view their traditional literature as an embarrassment, as the hopelessly conservative inscriptions of a self-indulgent and fatuous elite class. Calling the literature of the eighteenth and nineteenth century feudal or *féodal*, the progressive consciousness dismisses the writings of the Javanese past as summarily as had the colonial philologists who followed Cohen Stuart. The old writing inscribes the voice of decadence, a voice not worthy of being heard. Javanese writing thus apprehended means death, and underwrites the death of Java.

It is, however, the other contemporary image of "Traditional Javanese Literature," that of the classical icon, that is the dominant one in the discourse of late-twentieth-century Indonesia. Modern devotees of "traditional" texts, venerating these writings as classics, imagine them icons of high culture, mysteriously inscribed jewels from a rich cultural inheritance. And, as is probably true of acknowledged classics anywhere, such an exalted status is testimony to how little these texts are actually read. However, in modern Java the logic of the classic has achieved peculiar perfection in the contemporary image of traditional literature as ideally illegible writing, writing which is treasured precisely for (what is considered) its essential inaccessibility. Again, the association of the writing is with death: the classic standing as an indecipherable *monument* to a remote and essentially irrecuperable past.

---

of "Traditional Javanese Literature" in today's Indonesia are the Yasadipuran *Bratayuda, Rama,* and *Déwaruci* (Modern Javanese versions of the Old Javanese "classics"), Mangkunagara IV's *Wéddhatama* and Pakubuwana IV's *Wulang Rèh* (ultrarefined didactic works composed by the two Javanese rulers to teach proper behavior in the hierarchically stratified society of the nineteenth-century court), Ronggawarsita's *Kalatidha* (a didactic "prophecy"), and the "encyclopedic" *Centhini* (the overtly Islamic context of which tends to be ignored). For a contemporary survey of the "classics" as defined by the texts chosen for public readings in 1980s Yogyakarta, see Bernard Arps, *Tembang in Two Traditions*, pp. 121–23.

This classical image today belongs to a modern discursive formation I call "the cult of the *adiluhung.*" The word *adiluhung* translates as "the beautiful sublime." It has become in recent years the code word for what many modern Javanese appreciate as the super-refined (*halus*) sublime heights and profound depths of Javanese culture. The cult of the *adiluhung* idealizes a refined Javanese culture through the lenses of what is taken to be the culture of the traditional elite, that is, the *priyayi.*[58] The *priyayi,* and especially the neo-*priyayi,* in Java today are remarkable for their insistent preoccupation with the deep symbology they want to see underlying Javanese life. This preoccupation tends to linger on the alleged "high" arts, "traditional" rituals, linguistic etiquette, and the like. Modern devotees of the *adiluhung* are inclined to view "Java" as a traditional cultural unity whose true and essential center belongs to a more perfect past and behind ideally exclusive palace walls. Precisely because it is devoted to monumentalizing Central Javanese culture, the *adiluhung* view has little interest in analyzing the history and remarkable diversity of that culture.

The beginnings of this modern cult may be found in early-twentieth-century Indies theosophical circles, where conservative *priyayi* worked together with sympathetic Dutch Javanologists toward a spiritualized codification of elite culture.[59] A particularly well known product of this movement is the explication of the "true inner meaning" of the *wayang* (shadow puppet theater) published in Dutch by the Javanese prince Mang-kunagara VII in 1933.[60] It was this same Dutch-educated prince, inciden-

---

58. The word *priyayi,* originally from *para yayi* ("the younger siblings" [of the king]) came to mean the administrative and/or bureaucratic elite of the realm (kingdom and colonial state); in contemporary Indonesia, *priyayi* names the postcolonial Javanese elite. On the formations of *priyayi* culture, see Heather Sutherland, *The Making of a Bureaucratic Elite.*

59. This "movement" became active at precisely the same time (and in reaction to?) the immensely popular nationalist Sarekat Islam movement. Interestingly, the theosophical codification of elite culture tends to disregard or elide Islam from its considerations of essential "Java."

60. K.G.P.A.A. Mangkunagara VII, "Over de wajang-koelit (poerwa) in het algemeen en over de daarin voorkomende symbolische en mystieke elementen," *Djåwå* 13 (1933):79–97. The text of this influential article has been translated into English: *On the Wayang Kulit (Purwa) and Its Symbolic and Mystical Elements,* trans. C. Holt (Ithaca: Cornell University Southeast Asia Program, 1957).

tally, who as a matter of course translated into Javanese a portion of Cohen Stuart's dismissive introduction to the Modern Javanese *Bratayuda*.[61]

This early-twentieth-century move toward the construction of tradition has been repeated and intensified under the aegis of Soeharto's self-proclaimed New Order government. Perhaps reacting against a differently constructed relationship with the past enjoyed in the radically populist Revolutionary and Sukarno eras, New Order *adiluhung* rhetoric is eerily reminiscent of the late colonial voice. Highlighting what is imagined as the super-refined and spiritualized ways of traditional *priyayi* and then contrasting them with those of the so-called coarse and material West, the New Order Javanese elite have invented a vision of their very own *adiluhung* heritage as the somewhat endangered pinnacle of cultural development, the preservation (and reservation) of which they see as a "sacred duty."[62]

Within the cult of the *adiluhung*, the material texts of "Traditional Javanese Literature" in royal manuscript are perhaps the reigning icon of high culture.[63] Like the romantic colonial vision, the modern *adiluhung* view imagines that it was in the ultra-rarified world of nineteenth-century royal courts that Javanese writing attained the perfection of its literary expression—a perfection which can never again be achieved.[64] Among today's Javanese, it is widely believed that the language in which these royal manuscripts are inscribed is a kind of super-*krama* or super high-Javanese, Javanese language pushed to the limits of *halus*-ness. Indeed it is sometimes thought that the language of these texts has attained a degree of refinement which situates it beyond the limits of comprehension. A commonplace assertion among modern Javanese is that "the language of this literature is so sublime that we couldn't possibly understand it." And

---

61. Soeparta [= K.G.P.A.A. Mangkunagara VII], Surakarta, no year, 86 pp. See Uhlenbeck, *A Critical Survey of Studies on the Languages of Java and Madura*, pp. 139 and 149.
62. For a brilliant historical and ethnographic analysis of New Order cultural ideology and practice, see John Pemberton's recent book, *On the Subject of "Java."*
63. *Wayang kulit* is another popular icon. It is, however, *too* popular (still too accessible) to function perfectly as an icon in the sense of a fixed body.
64. For a perceptive analysis of the process of this golden-age construction at work in the present day (international) Indonesian literary establishment and the resultant dismissal of contemporary Javanese literature, see George Quinn, "The Case of the Invisible Literature: Power, Scholarship, and Contemporary Javanese Writing," *Indonesia* 35 (April 1983):1–36.

yet there remains a general consensus as to what that same unintelligible writing is about. The literature, it is said by the same people who are invested in its incomprehensibility, promises nothing less than the keys to life's deepest mysteries. However, since the literature is assumed unintelligible, those mysteries needs must remain forever shrouded. To support their assertions, many Javanese can sing from memory a line or two from one of the more famous nineteeth-century poems, the *Wéddhatama* ("The Noble Wisdom"). This poem, whose authorship is attributed to Mangkunagara IV (grandfather of the theosophical Mangkunagara VII),[65] is a highly alliterative, sometimes abstruse didactic and speculative poem. In many ways the *Wéddhatama* actually fulfills the dream of the *adiluhung*. The poem opens:

> Turning away from vain desire
> For the delight of teaching the young
> Rendered in song beautiful
> Embellished wrought elegantly
> That perfectly practiced be the knowledge sublime [*luhung*]
> Which in the land of Java is
> The religion of the rulers.[66]

65. There has been some dispute over the authorship of this poem, some claiming that the true author was rather a certain R.M.Ng. Wiryakusuma, one of Mangkunagara IV's courtiers. In a fascinating document from the Mangkunagaran Archives, Tarakusuma (a descendant of Wiryakusuma) reports to Mangkunagara VII concerning the disputed authorship. This report describes Mangkunagara IV's alleged method of poetic composition. The prince had installed about the palace a number of slates upon which he would write verses when so moved. The document notes that slates were positioned on the east and west verandahs of the royal residence as well as in the royal toilet. The prince would write as he walked back and forth along the verandahs and as he relieved himself. At the end of the day the slates were collected up and surrendered to the prince. The prince would then divide up the slates among his Javanese literature students (Mangkunagara IV with the assistance of R.Ng. Jayawiyata taught Javanese letters to a group of seven students). The prince then ordered the students to transcribe the contents of their assigned slates onto paper. Next he would order each student to compile his assigned writings into some order ("dhi dawoehi ngoeroetake panoelise"). It was to Wiryakusuma that Mangkunagara IV assigned the slates which were to become the *Wéddhatama* (Tarakusuma, *Serat Paturan ingkang sasambetan bab caranipun K.G.P.A.A. Mangkunagara IV nganggit serat* [Surakarta, 10 April 1941]. MS. Reksa Pustaka, Istana Mangkunagaran [henceforth RP], cat. no. Bundel 19; SMP MN 530A).

66. K.G.P.A.A. Mangkunagara IV, *Serat Wédhatama*, in *Serat-serat Anggitan-dalem*

My English rendering of these lines fails in a number of ways *as* translation, for it does not effectively re-register the modes of signification of the prince's text. Lost is the exuberant alliteration and assonance of the original poetry ("*Mingkar mingkur ing angkara . . .*"); lost too is the poem's treasured inaccessibility. My translation remains far too understandable to capture the tonality of the *adiluhung*. That tonality was much better rendered (without translation) into another universe of meaning by the late Indonesian pop singer Gombloh about ten years ago. What Gombloh did was to lift the first four lines of this stanza and then graft them onto an even less accessible Javano-Indic mantra. Sung soulfully to a rock melody, the mysterious words compose a sense of "tradition" which then opens out into a rock song.[67] Those who heard and repeated these lines of the *Wéddhatama* had no expectation of ever understanding what they meant, and instead appreciated them as a mantric emblem of "Javaneseness," which is precisely what they are—not just in Gombloh's song, but in everyday popular consciousness as well.

I suggested earlier that it is in manuscript form that the texts are most highly esteemed. There are at least three reasons for this phenomenon. First, the manuscripts are usually old and hence wear the patina of age that is among the marks of spiritually charged objects in Java. As material objects, the manuscripts are physical sites upon which the extraordinary powers of former writers and readers may have rubbed off. And so they offer the possibility of power by contagion. Second, the manuscripts are esteemed for their rarity. Access to manuscripts in Java is reserved, if not quite as reserved as many believe.[68] Third, the manuscripts are esteemed

---

K.G.P.A.A. *Mangkunagara IV*, 4 vols., ed. Th. Pigeaud (Jakarta: Noordhoff-Kolff, 1953), 3:108. There is a dearth of Western language translations of Javanese texts. The *Wéddhatama*, however, enjoys multiple English-language renderings. See, for example, Stuart Robson, *The Wedhatama: An English Translation* (Leiden: Koninklijk Instituut voor Taal-, Land-, en Volkenkunde [KITLV] Working Papers No. 4, 1990); Martin F. Hatch, "Lagu, Laras, Layang," pp. 258–355; and Suranto Atmosaputro and Martin Hatch, "Serat *Wédatama*: A Translation," *Indonesia* 14 (October 1972):157–82.

The final line, "agama ageming aji" may also read: "The religion [which] clothes/ ornaments the king(s)."

67. Gombloh, *Sekar Mayang* (Surabaya: Indra Records Golden Hand Series, 1980?).

68. Rumor among Javanese today holds that nearly all their manuscripts have been stolen by sinister outsiders, that these inscribed treasures were long ago carted off to distant caches in London and Leiden. And the small number of manuscripts believed still remaining in Java are often considered the sole preserve of the palaces—situated

for having been inscribed in Javanese script. The exaltation of this script has its own history. There are, for example, a number of nineteenth-century writings that specifically treat the hidden meaning, and power, of Javanese script in relation to Javanese bodies.[69] Much more recently, and in a rather different way, Indonesia's President Soeharto rearticulated the esoteric fascination of this script for New Order Javanese. It was at the 1991 National Congress on Javanese Language that the president presented his thesis: a consideration and affirmation of the relevance of the letters of the Javanese script, that is, the *alphabet*, for Indonesian political and economic development. Significantly, Soeharto's speech had nothing to do with actually reading Javanese writings. Instead, he focused exclusively on the mysteries of the script as such—apart from what the script might write. Among other things, he said of his native Javanese script: "And so, if we have difficulty nowadays comprehending Javanese script, at least we can pass on the philosophy contained in that script to the nation in order that our people may come to know their essential truth, their true identity (*jati diri*) as it has been ordained by God."[70] President Soeharto's acknowledgment of the simultaneous incomprehensibility and value of this divinely ordained script invites further comment.

In contemporary Java, the exalted and mysterious status of this form of

behind palace walls, which are ideally impenetrable. Although it is true that a large number of manuscripts have found their ways (by a variety of means) to European repositories, a vast number of manuscripts remain in Java—both inside and outside the royal repositories. And the royal repositories are not as closed as imagined: with the possible exception of the Pakualaman Palace, there is scholarly access to the manuscripts of all four courts of Central Java. Moreover, as a result of several microfilm projects over the last fourteen years, microfilm copies of manuscripts from the Kraton Surakarta, the Istana Mangukunagaran, and the Kraton Yogyakarta are now available at the National Archives in Jakarta, as well as in several research libraries in the United States and Australia. In addition to the palace collection, there are important collections of Javanese manuscripts in several public museums and libraries in Indonesia: for example, the Museum Radyapustaka in Surakarta, the Sono Budoyo Museum in Yogyakarta, the Perpustakaan Nasional in Jakarta, and the Fakultas Sastra Universitas Indonesia again in Jakarta. For further notes on the critical importance of these indigenously assembled collections of manuscripts, see my *Javanese Literature in Surakarta Manuscripts*, 1:11–36.

69. I have in mind especially the wonderfully complicated and recondite *Kridhaksara* texts which enjoyed some popularity in late-nineteenth- and early-twentieth-century Surakarta.

70. *Suara Merdeka*, 16 July 1991.

writing has been nurtured in the most common scene of confrontation between present-day Javanese and Javanese script: the public school room. As the president acknowledged, very few Javanese today are able to read this script despite the fact that most studied it briefly in the primary grades. It is precisely this brief study, so quickly stopped, as the curriculum dictates,[71] which endows many Javanese with a profound sense of failure (when, many years later, they remember what they have forgotten). That they tried and failed attests to what is already implied by the internal logic of the *adiluhung*'s modern ideal of inaccessibility. Knowledge of this divinely ordained script—because this script belongs to *adiluhung* literature and because it alone can really write that literature—apparently cannot be attained by study alone.

With this sense of the presumed inaccessibility of Javanese writing in mind, I turn now to the nineteenth-century Javanese writer who emerges as *the* cult figure around whom the fiction of the *adiluhung* has crystallized. By a curious quirk of history, this figure is none other than Cohen

71. The problem of the present generation's illiteracy in Javanese script, as a direct result of the national curriculum of 1975, was among the major issues discussed at the 1991 Javanese Language Congress. At the press conference that closed the Congress, a number of resolutions were announced; among them, resolutions (1) to return serious teaching of Javanese language and script to the public schools—from primary through tertiary educational institutions, (2) to prepare textbooks of Javanese script, language, and grammar, (3) to support research on Javanese language, literature, and especially on the philosophy of the Javanese alphabet. The resolutions were based on an affirmation of the relevance for the modern Indonesian nation of the noble values contained in the philosophical meanings of the letters of the Javanese alphabet [as proclaimed by President Soeharto at the opening of the Congress] (*Suara Merdeka*, 21 July 1991). In April 1994 the Yogyakarta Center of Research on Traditional History and Values, a division of the Indonesian Department of Education and Culture, hosted the National Seminar on the Meaning of the Letters of the Javanese Alphabet ("Seminar Nasional Pengkajian Makna Ha-na-ca-ra-ka"). The official invitation to the seminar explained its mission: "to unearth the noble cultural values of the Indonesian people and to realize (*merealisasi*) the speech that President Soeharto presented on 'The Hidden Meaning of the Letters of the Javanese Alphabet' at the opening of the Congress of Javanese Language on 15 July 1991."

Javanese script illiteracy is characteristically "modern Indonesian." Prior to World War II, among the numerically few literate (in the conventional sense) Javanese, reading and writing Javanese meant reading and writing Javanese script. Literate Javanese of the period were less likely to be literate in roman script. All this changed abruptly in 1942 with the coming of the Japanese and the banning of Javanese script in print and in schools.

Stuart's maligned "native informant," R.Ng. Ronggawarsita. Clearly a voracious reader and truly a prolific writer, Ronggawarsita is said to have written as many as fifty-nine books, several among them monumental tomes thousands of pages long.[72] In Java today, Ronggawarsita is accorded popular recognition as the greatest of all Javanese literati. And yet most of his writings are left unread. Even Ronggawarsita's most avowed admirers have rarely read anything beyond his celebrated *Kalatidha* and a smattering of his short prophetic poems. His longer works remain little read, perhaps assumed to be too refined for readability, too *adiluhung* for comprehension.

Although recognized as "the greatest Javanese poet," Ronggawarsita is remembered as the last, or better yet, as the seal, of the *pujongga*. Although *pujongga* may be glossed as "court poet,"[73] the English gloss misses *pujongga*'s implications in Javanese. To be a *pujongga* in Java means (or meant, as the case may be) to be a master of language with a prophetic pen. The writing of Ronggawarsita is revered not only for its reputed refinement, but even more so for its very material power to effect reality— that is, to make things happen. As a prophetic *pujongga*, Ronggawarsita quite literally *wrote* history, before and after the fact. If then one could really read his writing (which, of course, one cannot since it is situated at an ideal point beyond legibility), then one would really know the world in its past, present, and future.

Interior to the modern logic of the sublime *adiluhung* and its *pujongga*-ship, however, is the ultimate inaccessibility of both. It is out of the realm of conceivable possibility to learn how to become a *pujongga* or, for that

72. See Simuh, *Mistik Islam Kejawen Raden Ngabehi Ranggawarsita* (Jakarta: University of Indonesia Press, 1988), pp. 51–52.

73. Indeed, there was a spiritual-literary office of *pujongga* (or sometimes, *bhujangga*) at Javanese courts which dated from days of Majapahit and probably became reinstated with the "Surakarta Renaissance." For a retrospectively constructed listing of historical *pujongga* by the last Javanese to hold that office, see Ronggawarsita's *Serat Salasilah, Urutipun Panjenengan Nata ing Tanah Jawi, awit Panjenengan Ratu Prabu Déwata-cengkar, Medhangkamulan* (composed Surakarta [mid-19th century]; inscribed Surakarta, 1878). MS. B 84; SMP MN 245). The office has remained vacant since Ronggawarsita's death in 1873. It is widely accepted that there will never be another *pujongga*. Two rationales for this absence are offered: that the *pujongga*-ship is no longer relevant; and that no modern Javanese could ever fulfill the stringent intellectual, and especially supernatural, requirements for the position.

matter, to learn how to read the meanings of the *pujongga*'s words.[74] In a 1930s biography of Ronggawarsita, the "Ronggawarsita Committee" reports how, after a singularly unsuccessful course of study at the Tegalsari *pesantrèn* in Ponorogo, the uncanny linguistic mastery of *pujongga*-ship descended in a flash of divine light (*wahyu*) upon the young Ronggawarsita.[75] The youth, who had been up to that time a veritably intractable and delinquent pupil, at once knew and understood—without study!—Arabic, Javanese, and Dutch language and literature.[76] Presumably, it would take being hit by a similar flash of light for those who came after him to approach a real reading of Ronggawarsita's writing. Countless failed encounters with Javanese script in schoolrooms routinely bring this point home to the youths of modern Java.

And so traditional Javanese writing, when viewed under the modern aspect of the *adiluhung*, is caught in a multiple bind. In praise of its exalted status are offered a number of reasons not only why *not* to read it but why reading it is impossible. In the first place, the illegibility of script in which it is inscribed is intractable. It cannot be learned by study. Even should one by kind fate be graced with the gift of scriptural decipherment, then it is the language inscribed by that script that is too exalted to be understood. And were that language to become understandable (through an [en]lightening strike), the would-be reader knows that what that language writes is something so profound as to be beyond discursive comprehension. And

---

74. Traditionally, however, at least one text I have read writes how, step by step, one can through careful and diligent study learn to "be like a *pujongga* in excellence" (*ngèmpéri kaluwihaning pujongga*) by fulfilling eight heavy (*werit*) conditions of excellence (*Serat Wawaton Angger Tatakrama tuwin Adangiyah ingkang sampun kalampahaken wonten ing Karaton Tanah Jawi dalah Ada-ada Udanagara* [composed Surakarta, s.a.; inscribed Surakarta, {late 19th to early 20th century}]. MS. RP H3; SMP MN 542a, pp. 21–22). Ronggawarsita's *Wirid Hidayat Jati* provides an almost identical list as conditions for the teacher of *tassawuf*; see Simuh, p. 179.

75. A *wahyu* is a divine and manifest light which, when it falls upon the favored person, supernaturally invests that person with the power of, say, kingship or *pujongga*-ship. For notes (possibly composed by Ronggawarsita himself) on the triple *wahyu* of kingship, see *Serat Wawaton Tatakrama Kadhaton* (composed Surakarta, [mid-19th century]; inscribed Surakarta, [late 19th century]). MS. Museum Radyapustaka [henceforth Rp], cat. no. 74 carik; SMP Rp 76, p. 7.

76. Komite Ronggawarsitan, *Babad Cariyos Lelampahanipun Suwargi Radèn Ngabéhi Ronggawarsita*, 1:98–104.

so in contemporary Java the text of traditional literature remains on the shelf, an unread artifact of high culture, a dusty fetish.

Reading Traditional Javanese Writing Today: An Uncommon Moment

It was in this context of not-reading in contemporary Java that I decided to write a book which would suggest what actually reading the texts of traditional Javanese writing could still mean today. The real possibility of the regeneration of traditional meaning was suggested to me by an incident that occurred in 1984, when one of those books was pulled from the shelf, opened, and (quite traditionally) read aloud. Although reading texts of traditional Javanese writing was hardly popular among the avant garde youth of Solo in the early 1980s, it was then that a young art student and songwriter who went by the name BJ came up with the idea of putting the melodies of traditional verse to guitar music for performance at Solo's university. He remembered the basic melodies of most of the *macapat* meters as well as the words to one or two standard verses he had learned to sing as a child, but needed more lyrics to fill out the performance. Knowing that my work involved the texts of traditional literature, BJ came to me in search of material. What his generation had been taught to expect of traditional texts—and no doubt dreaded[77]—was something *adiluhung* like the *Wéddhatama*. What he read, that is, sang, was the following professional fantasy of an imaginary guru:

> A single line in Arabic is all I need to know
>
> Then that would I teach my pupils
> My students satisfied

77. In the case of BJ (that is B. J. Rianto, now a university lecturer and still a songwriter), the dread was clearly mixed with attraction. Indeed, the notion of putting *macapat* to guitar had been his idea after all. BJ spoke fondly and with awe of the haunting sensation the memory of his mother's voice reciting *macapat* at night still evoked for him. BJ's interest in the traditional texts was also sparked by memories of his late father, a well-known *dhukun* ("healer"; "practitioner of supernatural arts"), who some say was the son of the legendary Gusti Satriya, a magically marvelous son of Pakubuwana IX, who died (or perhaps vanished) in exile toward the close of the nineteenth century. Given his background, BJ's sense of the texts of tradition was not just the product of New Order schools.

Would think it knowledge brilliant new
In truth it would only show
How stupid are they who grovel
Hence I'd pursue it with zeal
Knowing nothing but *asyahdu'allah*[78]

With that would I hatch a scheme to get rich
A truly unscrupulous scheme
Really no more than a trick
In lieu of the goods to take offerings in cash
A full twenty-five in silver I'd take
Wrapped up in white linen napkins three
In different form, but still a bribe

. . .

And whenever I would be asked
To attend a reception
All reverence would be accorded me
Delicacies served up without cease
Rice tasties and puddings galore
My mouth would keep smacking away
Munching up all the treats

Then taking a little break, I would
Mutter and mumble so sweetly that
An incantation they'd take it for
Though in truth I haven't a clue
About incantations and such
But one thing rather worries me
Should a clever student come to me

Then would I be in fearful dread
That my secret be exposed
My face be stripped stark bare
With luck, only curses would fall
But were he to strike me 'longside my head

78. The name of the Moslem declaration of faith: "There is no god but God; and Mohammad is His Prophet."

'Til I reeled—still I'd count it fortune fair
That he hadn't brained me after all[79]

The reading almost broke down, not from the text's illegibility, but from BJ's howls of laughter. Where on earth had these outrageously funny, wholly irreverent, and clearly understandable lines come from? The verses are from *Serat Jayèngbaya* ("The Book of Him Who Conquers Danger"), an early poem composed by Ronggawarsita, that last of the *pujongga* himself. This is not what BJ had been taught in school to expect from the pen of Mr. Adiluhung. Understandable without being simple, it was parodic and biting with a slapstick sense of humor.

Serat Jayèngbaya is remembered fondly by the few contemporary readers of *macapat* texts I met who were familiar with it. I recall the glints of delight which shone in the eyes of those readers at the mere mention of the poem's title. One of them, a custodian at the Kraton Surakarta, could sing extended passages of the poem from memory. Most likely to be cataloged under the heading of "didactic literature," *Serat Jayèngbaya* is (among other things) a portrait of *pamrih* in nineteenth-century Java. *Pamrih* means desire, or rather the sinister under-belly of desire—the self-interested ulterior motive. The imaginary ego of the text, a certain Jayèngbaya, trying to decide just what to be in this life, moves through a series of fantasized career choices. In every imagined case, he falls from the enjoyment of pleasure's pinnacle to catastrophic ruin—often to disfigurement and death. For example, much in the idiom of a used-car dealer, Jayèngbaya imagines life as a horse trader. Reveling in the good life after making a killing off of an unsuspecting aristocratic customer, Jayèngbaya is then himself killed in a gory accident while taking one of his horses on a trial run. Again, our hero imagines a life of luxury as a Dutchman's houseboy. Enjoying the master's hand-me-down clothes, as well as the charms of the Indo-European missus, the houseboy's life is truly blissful until one day when the master returns home unexpectedly. "Caught in the act" with his master's missus, the houseboy's fate is not a pretty one. There is a rhythm to Jayèngbaya's fantasized career moves that invites further reading. To cite just a few of the sequences: from

79. R.Ng. Ronggawarsita [= Kiyahi Sarataka], *Serat Jayèngbaya* (composed Surakarta, ca. 1830) in [*Klempakan*] (inscribed Surakarta, 1920). MS. SP 135 Na; SMP KS 415.5, pt. 5, pp. 30–32 (verses 131–33; 136–38).

horse trader to performing artist to gambler to drug dealer (verses 2–41), from lawyer to thief to judge to Dutchman's houseboy (verses 56–74), from beggar to soldier to executioner to courtier (verses 176–214), and finally from dog to God Almighty to one struck dead by lightning (verses 241–49). A provocative opening into nineteenth-century Java both sociologically and literarily, the text energetically overturns the received images of Javanese literature and of palace literati.

And it was with this new perspective that BJ—and after him, his friends—went on to read other surprising texts of traditional Javanese writing. Attuned to the melodic curves of traditional verse, he created a range of sometimes bluesy, sometimes sweet guitar melodies for various poetic tonalities and maximum poetic effect—and perhaps, too, for cultural revenge. News spread, and one evening the host of Surabaya's TV talk show titled "Javanese Literature Appreciation" came to hear BJ sing these lines, again from *Serat Jayèngbaya*:

> But if I were a soldier to be
> Every day would be great fun
> And grief a thing long gone
> In time I'd rise to lieutenant in rank
> A station of some esteem
> I'd swagger and strut down the road
> With the air of a Major General
>
> Who could be the likes of me?
> All met would fall "plunk" to their knees
> As I'd be taken for high royalty
> Ah! My pleasure would know no bounds
> Like a dashing young *wayang* hero I'd be
> Except that I'm not good looking
> And I have no self-control[80]
>
> But I'd be trembling in my boots
> If ever there came the news
> That real battle were about to break
> Fine—if I could find a way

80. In the sense of the forbearance to perform ascetic practice (*tapa*).

To turn in my buckle and sword
But if sent to the front all 'a sudden
That would surely be the end of me[81]

Quite taken by what he heard, the TV host enthusiastically invited BJ to perform on his literature appreciation show, but only on the condition that something else be sung, something a bit more "traditional." Not that he didn't enjoy this "new" poetry, he explained, but it would never pass the state censorship board.[82] With a naughty gleam in his eye, BJ protested that this was real *adiluhung* stuff straight from the pen of the young Ronggawarsita. The talk-show host was silent. Youth singing tradition was fine—but the conventional image of tradition was shattered if old Ronggawarsita (tradition incarnate) was a youthful radical. The invitation was not repeated and the TV performance never materialized.

That Ronggawarsita would have entertained such a cynical view of the society around him is not really so surprising if one considers his personal history and the grievous conditions obtaining among Surakarta courtiers in the second quarter of the nineteenth century. *Serat Jayèngbaya* was probably written around 1830, toward the end of the Dipanagara War[83]— that is, just at the boundary which marks the disappearance from the Javanese courts of the last remnants of any real political power. After the war the courts of Central Java were impoverished, and the courtiers lived under straitened circumstances. Ronggawarsita's own poverty is legendary.[84] The last of the *pujongga* must also have borne more personal scars

81. Ronggawarsita, *Serat Jayèngbaya*, p. 40 (verses 178–80).
82. Perhaps the TV host heard in Ronggawarsita's poetry an allusion to the military operations that were under way in East Timor at the time.
83. A *sandi-asma* (a literary convention whereby the author and/or copyist inscribes a "hidden" signature into the poetry) in *Jayèngbaya*'s opening stanza reads "Kiyahi Sarataka." According to the Ronggawarsita Committee's biography, the poet—born Bagus Burham in 1802, to become Mas Rongga Pajanganom in 1819 upon his initial appointment as "Carik Kadipatèn Anom" at the Kraton Surakarta—was granted the name Mas Ngabéhi Sarataka by H.R.H. Pakubuwana V in Jimawal 1749 (1821–22) at the time of his promotion to the position of "Mantri Carik Kadipatèn Anom." In Jimawal 1757 (1829–30) his name was changed to R.Ng. Ronggawarsita when he was promoted (by Pakubuwana VII?) to the rank of "Panéwu Carik Kadipatèn Anom." See *Babad Cariyos Lelampahanipun Suwargi Radèn Ngabéhi Ronggawarsita*, 2:84–85 and 102–3. Since there are allusions in *Jayèngbaya* to events occurring in 1828 (see below), the poem must have been written sometime in the years 1828–30.
84. See especially Day, "Meanings of Change," pp. 185–86.

from that war. In 1830 he lost his king to exile and saw the kingdom he served reduced to near total colonial submission. Closer to home, in 1828 the poet's father, the elder Ronggawarsita (reputedly a brilliant literatus, whose works have been entirely suppressed), was arrested for his anti-Dutch intrigues and exiled to Batavia, where he died. The arrest was carried out personally by the Dutch Resident of Surakarta with the able help of his Indo-European translator, C. F. Winter Sr., author of the *Javaansche Zamenspraken* mentioned above.[85] The captured elder Ronggawarsita had been one of Winter's Javanese teachers.[86] This, of course, calls to mind the younger Ronggawarsita's position later as "native informant" (read teacher) to Cohen Stuart—to say nothing of the services the younger Ronggawarsita provided Winter himself for the three decades following Winter's betrayal of his father. The father's arrest and exile may very well be written into the *Jayèngbaya*, in the section on the teacher of invulnerability:

> But then some fateful day
> When gathered together in secrecy
> Discussing strange matters of mystery
> Without warning a thunder of feet
> And the blaze of the Resident's parasol[87]

85. For Resident Nahuys's proud account of the arrest of the elder Ronggawarsita, see Nahuys to the Kommissaris Generaal, Sourakarta den 19 April 1828, missive no. 41 geheim LᵃM, Ministerie van Kolonien (MvK) no. 4133 in the Algemeen Rijksarchief, The Hague. The account includes descriptions of Winter's role in the arrest and of the use of torture to extract the elder Ronggawarsita's confession. Likely arrested and exiled along with the elder Ronggawarsita was Mas Ronggasmita, whom I invoked at the beginning of this book (see note 2 above).

86. In the introduction to his 1846 translation of a Modern Javanese work into archaized Kawi, Winter gratefully acknowledges his teachers: Sastranagara [= Yasadipura II], the elder Ronggawarsita II [whom he had betrayed] and [the last of the *pujongga*] Ronggawarsita III; see Leiden Oriental (LOr), codex 2141. For more on Winter's literary activities in Surakarta, see above, note 29. V. J. H. Houben, in his "Kraton en Kumpeni: Surakarta en Yogyakarta, 1830–1870" (Ph.D. dissertation, Leiden University, 1987), writes of Winter's political role as official translator for the Surakarta residency.

87. That is, "The Full Moon," name of the pattern of ceremonial parasol (*songsong*) borne by the Surakarta Resident by regulations in force as of Dal 1735 (1808) (*Babad Sengkala: kawit Pulo Jawi dipunisèni tiyang nalika taun ongka 1 dumugi taun 1854*, MS. SP 220 Ca-A; SMP KS 1A, p. 71). Intricate regulations (*hormat* rulings) carefully

All my pupils put into chains
Arrested thrown into jail I'd be

Exiled to some foreign land
Tried and convicted a rebel
No teacher of invulnerability for me
Save secret my every move
The end is in some foreign land
Better to be just a medicine-man[88]

Thus wrote the palace *pujongga*, son of an exiled subversive, and sadly loyal, paid native informant to the local Dutch philologists.

Even a cursory reading of Ronggawarsita's *Serat Jayèngbaya* counters both modern images of "Traditional Javanese Literature." Literature imaged as merely *féodal*, as over-refined oozings from the reactionary courts of a decadent ruling class, has no room for a text so cynical, so biting in its satire. And the understandable, humorous language of the poem points to a literature quite different from that imagined as icon of the *adiluhung*. One of the features of this text which invites a vision of nineteenth-century Java not quite in accord with the received wisdom is the striking juxtaposition of images that do not seem to belong together, a literary device employed in this poem with parodic and comic effect. At one point in the poem, the pleasure at being touched by the flick of a prostitute's scarf is likened to the feelings enjoyed when promoted at court.[89] Yet another jarring image is of the moment of glory fantasized for the *kaum*, a professional chanter of Islamic prayers: when hired to pray at a *priyayi*'s funeral, he seizes the lucky opportunity to stuff some cups and saucers under his shirt.[90]

Always a vagrant of the imagination, the antihero Jayèngbaya (however high the fantasized position) seems incapable of conjuring an image of himself as anything other than marginal.

Could this be all there is to choose?
By luck it has not come to pass

---

governed the hierarchical distribution of the various patterns of the *songsong* as well as of many other ceremonial markers of respect and rank.

88. Ronggawarsita, *Serat Jayèngbaya*, p. 33 (verses 143–44).
89. Ibid., pp. 24–25 (verses 102–3).
90. Ibid., pp. 38–39 (verses 171–73).

For many my regrets may be
Save God I would become
With angels then as servants
All the world to dominate
Fulfilled would be my every wish

But still I'd be in fearful dread
'Tis said that the Lord Almighty
Is outside time and space
Is His then but a vagrancy?
And so I'd really rather not
Reign as God All-high
Better to be by lightning struck

'Twould be a sudden death
Without much suffering
For "zip" I'd be gone: "bang!"
Problem is I would not have told
My children and my grandchildren
That I was to be by lightning seized
To even the score with the Séla's Lord[91]

So there my corpse would lie
For days before discovered
Unknown, consumed by maggots
And so I'd really rather not
Be by lightning struck

91. Ki Ageng Séla was a sixteenth-century ancestor of the Mataram dynasty (grandfather of Ki Ageng Mataram). A farmer from the northern Central Javanese village of
Séla, he is noted for having captured a bolt of lightning. He transported that lightning
bolt, which had taken on the form of an old man, to the Kraton of Demak, where it/he
was imprisoned. The lightning bolt was eventually saved by an old woman (the lightning's wife). By Kraton Surakarta tradition, the tree to which the lightning bolt had
been chained was transplanted from palace to palace as the Kraton of Java moved (i.e.,
Demak to Karta to Plérèd to Kartasura to Surakarta) and now still grows in the Srimanganti Lor courtyard of the Surakarta Palace, just to the southeast of the northern
Mandhungan portal.

Benedict Anderson discusses folk traditions surrounding Séla's lightning in his "A
Time of Darkness and a Time of Light: Transposition in Early Indonesian Nationalist
Thought" (*Language and Power*, p. 259).

> Would it not be better then
> Though but tatters in the wind: to live[92]

Seemingly a perpetual loser, Jayèngbaya's name translates as "He-who-conquers-danger." And finally at poem's end, our antihero wins. In the wake of the naked exposure of the falseness of his Surakartan society, Jayèngbaya finally conquers danger by rejecting all the available options: first the God option when God turns out to be numbered among the homeless, and then the death option—thereby saving his neck. The momentary pleasure enjoyed at the fantasy of a quick and painless exit from the scene (by the good services of the lightning bolt) is quickly displaced by anxiety over the imagined silencing of his voice, and his consequent (future) absence from the memories of his children and grandchildren. That anxiety expresses itself in the ghastly image of maggots swarming over Jayèngbaya's unburied corpse. But our hero, having rejected his present in poetic joke, chooses, with similar irony, "to live"—a life that is nothing more than tatters in the wind. And so the poet concludes his 250-stanza work:

> Cast adrift by life's desires
> Jayèngbaya's writing
> Amidst works' foul madness
> Becomes but day-long darkness
> Blissfully doing what can(not) be done[93]
> Holy words evilly expressed
> Two hundred fifty verses are enough.[94]

It must be emphasized that Ronggawarsita's *Jayèngbaya* is not the only alternative textual opening into nineteenth-century Javanese literary and sociological worlds. Rather it is part of a larger body of contestatory writing that has been for the most part ignored. Another text which comes immediately to my mind is the early-nineteenth-century *Serat Mas Ngantèn*.[95] Composed by a high noble of the Surakarta court, this

92. Ronggawarsita, *Serat Jayèngbaya*, pp. 54–55 (verses 246–49).

93. The Javanese *sambawa* means both "that which is real or possible" *and* "the impossible."

94. Ronggawarsita, *Serat Jayèngbaya*, p. 55 (verse 250).

95. R.M.H. Jayadiningrat I, *Serat Mas Ngantèn* (composed Surakarta, 1819), in *Serat Wulang* (inscribed Surakarta, 1899). MS. Rp 104 carik; SMP RP 106B), pt. 1, pp. 1–48. See Suzanne Brenner's discussion of this spunky poem in her recent piece "Competing

poem is a comical satire on court etiquette in the hands of the nouveaux riches. Again, the cheeky humor of the later-nineteenth-century *Suluk Gatholoco* is a product of (among other things) angry plays on the formal constraints of traditional poetics and conventional morality.[96] Actually *Suluk Gatholoco* is but one of many spirited *suluk*, the so-called "Islamic mystical songs." Indeed, the *suluk* texts comprise a huge chunk of nineteenth-century writing characteristically overlooked by the devotees of the *adiluhung*.[97] It is of note here that, aside from historical texts (*babad* literature), the *suluk* comprise the single largest grouping of texts in the library of Surakarta Palace. In fact, that supposed bastion of conservatism and original Javanism has but a small smattering of the "belletristic Indic classics" and their translations.[98] Of the historical texts, the sometimes hilarious descriptions of royal dalliance in the often monotonous court chronicles of the late nineteenth and the early twentieth century are written with a kind of deadpan tonality that invites critical readings of what was, by that time, starting to become Tradition with a capital *T*.[99] And a whole range of historical poems written in the nine-

---

Hierarchies: Javanese Merchants and the *Priyayi* Elite in Solo, Central Java," *Indonesia* 52 (October 1991):55–83.

96. *Suluk Gatholoco* (composed East Java, ca. 1860–80; inscribed Kalinyamat, 1880). MS. RP A 34; SMP MN 357. See Benedict Anderson's delightful translation of the poem into English verse, "The *Suluk Gatoloco*, Parts One and Two," *Indonesia* 32–33 (October 1981 & April 1982):109–50; 31–88.

97. For a recent Indonesian turn to *suluk* literature, see the translations into Indonesian poetry of a selection of Javanese *suluk* texts produced by one who is certainly *not* an *adiluhung* devotee: the contemporary poet (playwright, essayist, and activist) Emha Ainun Nadjib (*Suluk Pesisiran* [Bandung: Mizan, 1989]).

98. By "belletristic Indic classics," I mean the renderings in Javanese poetry of the (originally) Sanskrit Ramayana and Mahabharata epics. Of the 1,450 titles in the Kraton's manuscript collection there are only seventeen of these renowned "Surakarta Renaissance" renderings of the Old Kawi classics into Modern Javanese verse. These texts comprise about 1 percent of the collection. In contrast to these sixteen, there are nearly five hundred titles belonging to varieties of Islamic literature (including a large number of *suluk* texts)—that is a solid third of the entire collection. For a descriptive listing of the Kraton Surakarta manuscripts, see vol. 1 of my *Javanese Literature in Surakarta Manuscripts*.

99. See especially *Babad Langenharja*, 30 vols. (composed and inscribed Surakarta, 1871–77). MSS. SP 187 Ra, 390 Ha . . . ; SMP KS 87–99; *Babad Langenharja*, 3 vols. (composed Surakarta, 1872–73; inscribed Surakarta, late 19th century). MSS. SP 180 Na & 219 Ca; SMP KS 100–101; *Babat Pémut ing Nagari Surakarta*, 14 vols. (composed

teenth century about much earlier times in Java—close readings of which could tell us much about Javanese imaginings not only of pasts, but of futures as well—wait on the shelf.

On Reading Babad Jaka Tingkir

The remainder of this book is an extended reading of one of those imaginative historical poems, *Babad Jaka Tingkir* (The History of Jaka Tingkir). In the course of this reading, it will become apparent that this history, a work composed to interrupt and contest the dominant dynastic historical tradition, was inscribed as a certain kind of prophecy. For the anonymous Javanese subject who wrote *Tingkir* inscribed with it a novel vision of Java's distant past in order to reflect, strategically, upon another yet-to-be-unfolded Javanese future.

The prophetic *Babad Jaka Tingkir*, not unlike the parodic *Jayèngbaya*, calls into question the center/periphery dichotomy that tends to structure conventional understandings of the Javanese past. *Jayèngbaya* effectively blurs the distinctions between the worlds of margin and center in a biting social critique of its contemporary Surakarta by moving back and forth from the worlds of entertainers, prostitutes, thieves, madmen, and beggars to those of courtiers, bureaucrats, businessmen, and educators. With a different, perhaps more guarded form of social critique, *Babad Jaka Tingkir* points toward the dissolution of the centrality of centers. Writing against the grain of hegemonic dynastic history, *Tingkir* inscribes moments of marginality, opposition, and exile from an imagined past into a stage upon which an alternative future just might be played out. If *Jayèngbaya* ("He Who Conquers Danger") is a parodic reading of a present, *Babad Jaka Tingkir* ("History of the Youth from Tingkir") is a prophetic rereading of a past.

This book, then, attempts to take seriously this prophetic rereading of the Javanese past and does so by reading it yet again. For with this book, I would write—in dialogue with this nineteenth-century Javanese writing of history—an alternative future for the Javanese past. I would thus suggest how actively reading the texts of tradition is one way to

---

and inscribed Surakarta, 1888–94). MSS. SP 5 Ca, 30 Ca . . . ; SMP KS 111–22; R.T. Arungbinang, *Serat Sri Pustaka Madyapada*, 29 vols. (composed and inscribed Surakarta, 1914–18). MSS. SP 249 Ca, 250 Ca . . . ; SMP KS 148–58.

refuse compliance with the authority of what has come in late-twentieth-century Indonesia to be accepted as the codified meanings of the past. Such reading has the potential to transform these curiously neglected texts—these laid-by works—into contexts for change. To read the texts means to "dare to try to comprehend" them, that is, actively to work through possibilities *with* them, possibilities that call into question an *adiluhung* aesthetics that suppresses historical sense. To do this is also to challenge the dominant assumptions of historiography. Reading the texts of tradition just might mean, then, looking forward to a kind of writing (somewhat akin to the writing of a Javanese *pujongga*) that could inscribe a very different future for Javanese history.

CHAPTER 1
THE WRITING OF
A HISTORY

❋

The writing of any history takes place in history and is itself, then, a kind of historical event. Traditional Javanese historical writing, I would argue, is a practice more self-consciously aware of this truism than is the practice of writing history in the post-Enlightenment West. The post-Enlightenment historical project is conventionally understood as the objective representation of past events as framed and explained by the historical contexts in which those events are construed to have "really" occurred. Such a historical project is premised on the assumed absolute alterity of a positively dead past, a past which is there to be known and faithfully reconstructed in writing by "objective scientists" who themselves exist (miraculously) in a place which itself seems outside history.[1] Traditional Javanese historical writing appears to have been a significantly different project with a significantly different relation to the past. Recognizing the presence of living pasts in the historically becoming presents in which they wrote, the writers of traditional histories in Java understood the inscription of these texts as historical *events*, and the texts themselves as potential *contexts*. Recognizing their own historical agency, these Javanese historians could, then, self-consciously employ traditional conventions of writing to effect a transformation of tradition itself. That is, such traditional Javanese historical writing, because it was self-consciously written in and of history, was capable, at times, of rewriting the conditions of its *own* production.

What, then, do we know of the history of the writing of *Babad Jaka Tingkir*? What kind of historical event does its inscription compose? How is the text of *Tingkir* situated as a writing of history? What manner of

1. See Michel de Certeau, *The Writing of History* (New York: Columbia University Press, 1988), pp. 1–6.

historical agent actually wrote this remarkably untypical traditional text? In this chapter, we will turn to the actual manuscript of *Babad Jaka Tingkir* to begin to address these questions.

In original manuscript there survives but a single witness of this unique telling of a Javanese past. This surviving manuscript witness is inscribed and bound into the end of a volume that is now stored in the library of the senior palace of Surakarta. That volume, titled *Kupiya Iber Warni-warni Sampéyan-dalem kaping VI* ("Copies of the Miscellaneous Correspondence of His Majesty the Sixth"; hereafter: *His Majesty the VI's Correspondence*),[2] appears a diplomatic archive associated with Pakubuwana VI, the Surakarta king who vanished into exile in 1830. How, then, does *Babad Jaka Tingkir*, this history of a legendary hero of the sixteenth century, belong to the correspondence of an exiled nineteenth-century king? To begin to answer this question I turn now to sketch a very brief history of that exiled king's life and times.

I.S.K.S. Pakubuwana VI

Born in 1807 to a secondary wife of Pakubuwana V, Pakubuwana VI was the ruler of the Kraton Surakarta from 1823 to 1830. He was not, apparently, a particularly popular monarch. Elevated to the throne when he was only sixteen years old, at least in part by the machinations of his foster

2. *Kupiya Iber Warni-warni Sampéyan-dalem kaping VI* (composed Surakarta and Ambon, 1812–48; inscribed [Ambon], ca. 1849). MS. SP 214 Ca; SMP KS 78. Microfilm copies of this manuscript, filmed under the auspices of Cornell University Southeast Asia Program's Surakarta Manuscript Project, are available for reading at the Kraton Surakarta, the National Archives of the Republic of Indonesia, and Cornell University Library (SMP cat. no. KS 78; reel nos. 224/1 and 104/1).

The library of the Sekolah Tinggi Seni Indonesia (S.T.S.I.) owns a photostatic copy of the portion of the original Kraton manuscript in which the *babad* is inscribed, a copy acquired by purchase from one Moelyono Sastronaryatmo, a Surakarta manuscript collector. Moelyono published a transliteration and Indonesian paraphrase of the *babad* under the auspices of the Indonesian Ministry of Education and Culture's Project for the Publication of Indonesian and Regional Literary Works (*Babad Jaka Tingkir: Babad Pajang*, ed. Moelyono Sastronaryatmo [Jakarta: Departemen Pendidikan dan Kebudayaan, Proyek Penerbitan Buku Sastra Indonesia dan Daerah, 1981]). Unfortunately, Moelyono's transliteration is less than flawless. For another transliteration of this MS, see my "Writing the Past, Inscribing the Future: Exile and Prophecy in an Historical Text of Nineteenth-Century Java," vol. 1.

father, the powerful Grand Vizier Sasradiningrat II (dates of office, 1812–46), the young king proved somewhat less tractable than his elders might have wished. A restless figure, the king (often appearing in Dutch dress, to the dismay of his colonial "guardians") was, it seemed to his detractors, all too often on the road.[3] Of the king's "dressing Dutch" and his incessant travel, Lieutenant Governor General H. M. de Kock complained: "[he] frequently goes off fishing and hunting, and often dresses up as a European, and has recently had the queen dress likewise; so that it can be said of him that he is doing whatever possible to make himself unpopular. A Mohammedan despot (*Mohamedaansch despoot*) must, if he is to inspire honor and respect, show himself little outside his Kraton."[4] Apparently the restless young king—who would not conform to the Dutch ideal of the "Mohammedan despot"—was an avid reader, especially of "traditional Javanese histories"; and it seems he was an accomplished writer as well. Of Pakubuwana VI's literary prowess, the hostile de Kock reported: "The Emperor has little natural intellect, and yet he has picked up an extensive knowledge of Javanese historical traditions (*gebruiken*); he writes fluently/smartly (*vlug*), and he has read extensively."[5] Pakubuwana VI was known to perform occasionally as *dhalang*, or shadow-puppet master,[6] and to waltz poorly.[7]

Pakubuwana VI ascended to the throne in September 1823, shortly after his father's untimely death and the notorious canceling of land rentals in the Principalities—and a scant year and a half before Prince Dipanagara, elder statesman of the Yogyakarta Palace (Central Java's other royal city), went into open rebellion against the encroachments of colonial domination. At the time of the outbreak of the Dipanagara War in

---

3. For a chronicle of Pakubuwana VI's movements, see especially *Babad Sengkala kang kaurut saking Kagungan-dalem serat Babad* (composed and inscribed Surakarta, [ca. 1831, 1847]) MS. SP 6 Ta; SMP KS 1C.7, part 2, pp. 129–61.

4. H. M. de Kock, "Beschrijving van het karakter en de hoedanigheden van den Keizer de Prinsen en de Rijksbestierder van Soerakarta," 1829. Solo Bundel 166, Arsip Nasional Republik Indonesia.

5. Ibid.

6. Algemeen Rijksarchief (The Hague) [ARA], Coll. H. M. de Kock no. 24, Resident Solo H. MacGillavry aan de Gouverneur-Generaal, 11 January 1826, and *Babad Sengkala kang kaurut saking kagungan-dalem serat Babad*, p. 89.

7. "Journal of an Excursion to the Native Provinces on Java in the year 1828, during the war with Dipo Negoro," *Journal of the Indian Archipelago and Eastern Asia* 7 (1853):17.

May 1825, Surakarta's king was barely eighteen years old. The popular Prince Dipanagara garnered a broad base of support for his rebellion: with the aid of a number of other aristocrats (including some from Surakarta) and with the extremely important backing of a powerful network of rural Islamic teachers, he earned the allegiance of a large number of ordinary villagers to his cause. The Dipanagara War, which was to rage for five long years, posed a serious threat to Dutch power in Java and marked the last stand of indigenous royal power against Dutch colonial hegemony. Where did the young Pakubuwana VI stand in this struggle? Although ostensibly supporting his Dutch overlords against the rebels, Surakarta's king was known to have sympathized with, and likely to have secretly assisted, the rebellious Dipanagara.[8]

The war ended in the spring of 1830, when the Dutch finally captured Dipanagara (in the course of ostensible negotiations) and straightway exiled him to Menado and then on to Makassar. After finishing with Dipanagara, the colonial authorities turned to settle with their putative ally, Pakubuwana VI. The victorious Dutch shocked their shifty comrade in arms by annexing all the outer districts (*mancanagara*) of *both* the Surakarta and Yogyakarta courts. This act provoked the young Pakubuwana to action; he protested the annexation by withdrawing secretly to the tombs of his ancestors and to the magical embrace of his spiritual consort. Almost certainly preparing for armed rebellion, the twenty-three-year-old Pakubuwana VI was arrested in June 1830 on Java's south-

8. Pakubuwana VI was long suspected of disloyalty to the Dutch colonial government. See, for example, Nahuys aan den Minister van Staat, Sourakarta den 28 November 1828, L.H.H. (Geheim); Missive van den Komissaris Generaal, den 17 Maart 1829 L[a]P (Geheim); Notes and report of Bousquet on the letter of 17 March 1829, Batavia den 28 Maart 1829, L[a]H (Geheim) and L[a]Q (Geheim); all in Solo Bundel 127, Arsip Nasional Republik Indonesia. See also Baron Nahuys van Burgst, *Herinneringen uit het Openbare en Bijzondere Leven* (Utrecht, 1852), p. 149 ff.; "Journal of an Excursion to the Native Provinces on Java in the year 1828, during the war with Dipo Negoro," *Journal of the Indian Archipelago and Eastern Asia* 8 (1854):87; and P. B. R. Carey, *Babad Dipanagara: An Account of the Outbreak of the Java War, 1825–1830* (Kuala Lumpur: Malaysian Branch of the Royal Asiatic Society, 1981), pp. 292–93. Recently published in Surakarta was a poorly documented volume inscribing Surakarta (court) oral traditions concerning the role of Pakubuwana VI as a partisan of Dipanagara in the war (Sunar Tri Suyanto, *Pahlawan Kemerdekaan Nasional RI: Sinuhun Banguntapa* [Surakarta: Tiga Serangkai, 1984]).

ern coast where he was communing with the spirit Queen of the South Sea.[9] The young king was deposed and exiled to the remote island of Ambon, located across a great expanse of ocean some 1,200 miles to the east of Central Java. Joining the young ex-king in exile were his favorite wife, Ratu Anom, one of his young daughters, and a tiny handful of faithful retainers.

With the exile of Pakubuwana VI and the ascension to the throne of his Dutch-favored uncle, Prince Purbaya, as Pakubuwana VII (r. 1830–58), whatever vestiges of political power the Surakarta rulers had managed to retain were finally lost. But at war's end, it was not just the ruling elite who suffered: five years' warfare had brought devastating losses to the people of Central Java. At a time when the population of the entire island of Java numbered but seven million souls, the war had claimed well over 200,000 Javanese lives; Yogyakarta's population was reduced by half.[10] After the war the Javanese peasantry, under the notorious *Cultuur Stelsel*, would be pressed into the forced cultivation of export crops, the profits of whose sale would go into the Dutch colonial treasury. The year 1830 is, then, a watershed year in Javanese history, marking the final end of indigenous royal political power, the defeat of the last serious military challenge to Dutch authority on the island (prior to the Indonesian national revolution), and the beginning of high colonialism in Java.[11]

Pakubuwana VI was never allowed to return to Surakarta; he died in exile in 1849 at the age of forty-two.[12] His remains were not returned to

9. The beach where the king was arrested is Parang Tritis, gateway to the watery abode of Kangjeng Ratu Kidul, spirit Queen of the South Sea and queen (serially) to all the rulers of Mataram. For more on Ratu Kidul, see my "The Badhaya Katawang: A Translation of the Song of Kangjeng Ratu Kidul," *Indonesia* 53 (April 1992):20–32. For an account of the arrest, see Nahuys van Burgst, *Herinneringen uit het Openbare en Bijzondere Leven*, pp. 173–85, and Nahuys aan den Gouverneur Generaal, Soerakarta den 10 June 1830 (Secreet H: 80) in Solo Bundel 153, Arsip Nasional Republik Indonesia.

10. Ricklefs, *A History of Modern Indonesia*, p. 113.

11. For a fine political history of the transitions in the *Vorstenlanden*, or Principalities, at the end of the Dipanagara War with the contracts of 1830, see the recent works of V. J. H. Houben: "Afstand van Gebied met Behoud van Aanzien" and "Kraton en Kumpeni."

12. There remain questions surrounding the circumstances of Pakubuwana VI's death. Based upon an examination of the late king's skull, G. P. H. Djatikusumo holds that Pakubuwana VI died from a gunshot wound to the head ("Sedjarah Politik ingkang

Java until 1957—after the Indonesian Republic had won its independence from the Dutch. In December 1830, six months after his arrest, a son was born to the exiled king by one of the queens he had left behind in Surakarta. That son, who was never to see his father, eventually succeeded to the throne of the Kraton as Pakubuwana IX (r. 1861–93).[13] Over a century after his death, Pakubuwana VI was proclaimed a "Hero of Indonesian National Independence" by presidential decree in 1964.

Babad Jaka Tingkir, item number sixty-three of the sixty-three items composing *His Majesty the VI's Correspondence*, somehow belongs to the documentary archive of this Hero of Indonesian National Independence. What manner of royal correspondence is compiled in this volume? In addition to the Tingkir history, the volume comprises a collection of letters and treaties (dated 1812–48) that appear to have been copied from documents in the Kraton Surakarta archives, the genealogy of a certain Sarifi Ibrahim Madyakusuma, two pages of captioned pen and ink drawings, and a single page noting that "this is a commemoration of His Majesty's dream . . ." This chapter explores historically the nature of this volume of "His Majesty the VI's Correspondence [or dream]."

The Manuscript

His Majesty the VI's Correspondence in manuscript measures 34.5 × 22 cm. and numbers some 304 pages (152 leaves, double-page numbered). A single hand, aside from a few duly noted exceptions, inscribes the entire manuscript. That hand writes in a cursive style that was prevalent in and around Surakarta around the middle of the nineteenth century. The hand appears to have been a fluent and practiced one (figure 4). The

---

Sinuhun Kangjeng Susuhunan Pakubuwana VI," 3 October 1971). According to a Kraton *babad*, the exiled king's death was the result of an illness brought on from a horse-cart accident in February 1849 (*Serat Babat Sampéyan-dalem ingkang Sinuhun Kangjeng Susuhunan Pakubuwana kaping VI: Sri Naluri* [composed Surakarta, 1906; inscribed Surakarta, ca. 1906]. MS. SP 177 Ca; SMP KS 80, pp. 220–21). Day cites a letter from Radèn Ayu Timur, the king's daughter who followed him in exile, to his brother K.P.H. Natadiningrat, attributing the death to a "lung infection" ("Meanings of Change," p. 156, note 101).

13. For more on Pakubuwana VI's exile, and on the accession to the throne of his son, see Day, "Meanings of Change," pp. 78–163.

Figure 4. Opening page of *Babad Jaka Tingkir*, in *Kupiya Iber Warni-warni Sampéyan-dalem kaping VI*, p. 79 verso. Courtesy of the Kraton Surakarta.

original text is preceded by a five-page table of contents inscribed in a different (likely later nineteenth-century) hand. The spelling and punctuation of the manuscript are consistent with nineteenth-century Surakarta conventions.[14] The manuscript is inscribed upon relatively lightweight European paper. There is no watermark. The leaves are brittle, and some are torn. Relatively mild ink bleed-through has perforated a number of the leaves.

The manuscript's binding is distinctive: the boards are covered with plain white cloth; the spine, with red velvet. The bound volume thus evokes the red and white *gula-kelapa* (sugar-coconut) motif of the royal flags of Java.[15] This use of the *gula-kelapa* motif in book binding is rare. In all the Surakarta repositories, I found only one other manuscript thus bound.[16] That other manuscript, also housed in the Kraton Surakarta library, resembles *His Majesty the VI's Correspondence* in other ways as well. The scripts and the papers of both manuscripts, though not identical, are remarkably similar. And, as it turns out, this other *gula-kelapa* manuscript is also associated with the exiled Pakubuwana VI. Inscribed on its cover is the title: *Serat Rama: Tilaran-dalem Sampéyan-dalem I.S.K.S. Pakubuwana kaping VI* ("The Book of Rama: Legacy of H.R.H. Pakubuwana VI"). The manuscript is a copy of Yasadipura's late-eighteenth-century *macapat Serat Rama*, which—though written in a Surakarta script, and stored in the library of the Surakarta Palace—was produced on the island of Ambon. The copy was commissioned by the exiled Pakubuwana VI in May 1846,[17] some three years prior to his June 1849 death.

14. See figures 4–5 for reproductions of MS. pp. 79verso and 152recto, the first and last pages respectively of *Babad Jaka Tingkir*.

15. According to Kraton Surakarta sources, the *gula-kelapa* flag motif dates from the kingdom of Majapahit and symbolizes the fertile union of male (white) and female (red) principles. In modern times, this motif has been taken over by the national flag of Indonesia: Sang Merah Putih.

16. R.Ng. Yasadipura I, *Serat Rama: Tilaran-dalem Sampéyan-dalem I.S.K.S. Pakubuwana kaping VI* (composed Surakarta, late 18th century; inscribed Ambon, 1846). MS. SP 106 Ca; SMP KS 428.

17. The manuscript opens in Dhangdhanggula: "Wedharing tyas, anénélad sungging / amituhu ing sabda naréndra / kang jumeneng prabu ping nèm / ngrat Jawi trah Mentarum / Sinuwun Jeng Suhunan Adi / Pakubuwana Sadrasa / ingkang angadhatun / ing Surakarta Diningrat / keng sudibya don akramanya menuhi / mring abdi kulawarga // Kang salagi karsa mangun tapi / wonten nagri Ngambon murwèng dhekah / kebon Batugajah ramé / purwanya duk tinurun / anuju ing ri Sukra Manis / tanggal ping

Were, then, both these *gula-kelapa* volumes produced in Ambon for the exiled Pakubuwana VI and then, following his death, brought home to Surakarta by one of the wives, children, or retainers who, having shared his exile, were repatriated to Java in June 1850?[18]

The Compilation

His Majesty the VI's Correspondence comprises some sixty-three textual items, the sixty-third and longest of which is *Babad Jaka Tingkir.*[19] Of the remaining sixty-two textual items, sixty-one comprise copies of Javanese language correspondence and archival documents, the overwhelming majority of which relate directly to the royal family and affairs of the Kraton Surakarta. Most of the documents (forty-five) originate from that court. The original documents date from 1812 to 1848, with a preponderance dating from 1823 to 1830, Pakubuwana VI's regnal years. The documents are not, however, copied into the volume in any strict chronological order. Seventeen of the volume's documents (fifteen of these at the close of the compilation) pertain directly to Pakubuwana VI's exile to Ambon. As I noted above, upon first reading, the copies appear to have been made from original documents that would have belonged to the Kraton Surakarta archives. A more careful examination of these documents, however, proves a very different source was consulted by the compiler of *His Majesty the VI's Correspondence.*

Royal correspondence constitutes the single largest category of documents copied. Included in this category is correspondence of Pakubuwana IV (r. 1788–1820), Pakubuwana V (r. 1820–23), Pakubuwana VI (r. 1823–30; d. Ambon, 1849), and Pakubuwana VII (r. 1830–58). The greater part of this correspondence comprises letters from these kings to colonial officials, Sultans of Yogyakarta, and members of the Surakarta nobility. The tone and content of the letters is formal and official, with the notable exception of the sometimes deeply personal Surakarta-Ambon correspondence of exile at the end of the collection. The final six of these personal

---

tigawelas / Madilawal tèngsu / warsa Jé kartining sabda / swara tunggal carita pruwa ginupit / Rama kawi jinarwan" (ibid., p. 1).

18. For a narrative description of that repatriation, see *Serat Babat Sampéyan-dalem Ingkang Sinuhun Kangjeng Susuhunan Pakubuwana kaping VI: Sri Naluri* (MS. SP 177 Ca; SMP KS 80), pp. 225–40.

19. For a detailed descriptive listing of all sixty-three items, see Appendix I.

royal letters are composed in *macapat* verse, three of them by Pakubuwana VI, one by the daughter who had followed him into exile (Gusti
Radèn Ayu Timur), one by his son (the future Pakubuwana IX), and one
by his brother.

In addition to the correspondence of these kings and their families, the
compilation contains several letters that concern land administration and
finance in the Surakarta region. Most of these letters were addressed to
colonial officials from various ranks of Surakarta royalty and court retainers. There is a single missive from a senior Surakarta prince to a
colonial official cum scholar of Javanese letters.

The volume opens with a complete copy of the famous and rather
lengthy treaty of 1812 between the ruler of the Kraton Surakarta and the
British colonial government. This treaty, which Sir Thomas Stamford
Raffles secured by threat of force, seriously compromised the royal power
of Surakarta kings—notably removing from them their military troops,
their control of tolls and markets, their rights to move their *kraton*, and a
goodly amount of land. When the Dutch regained control over Java in
1816, their first order of business in Surakarta was to ratify this important legal agreement.[20] For it was this British treaty of 1812 that was to
lay the foundations for the nineteenth-century colonial relationship the
Dutch overlords would enjoy with their royal Surakarta vassals. Also
copied into this volume are a report submitted by Prince Mangkunagara
to the colonial Resident of Surakarta on a (putative) death-bed wish of
Pakubuwana IV and copies of Pakubuwana V's accession treaties. Several
documents pertain to matters of concern to the Kraton Surakarta during
the Dipanagara War.

Another Compilation and Its Copy

In the course of my eight years' research in Java, I had occasion to examine a number of compilations of Javanese language correspondence and
archival materials. Most of the compilations I reviewed were in manuscript form. One, however, was a published text. That volume, which
I found at the Mangkunagaran Palace on the shelf of Surakarta's other

20. See *Pratélan Wontenipun Bongsa Éropah angambah Tanah Jawi, tuwin Pratélan Kawontenanipun Karaton Tanah Jawi, anggènipun lajeng Mamitran saha damel Prajang-
jiyan akaliyan Tiyang Bongsa Éropah* (compiled Surakarta, [late 19th century]; inscribed
Surakarta, 1922). MS. SP 179 Na; SMP KS 5, pp. 100–102.

royal library, was first published in the Netherlands in 1845. The book was T. Roorda's *Javaansche brieven, berigten, verslagen, verzoekschriften, proclamaties, publicaties, contracten, schuldbekentenissen, quitanties, processtukken, pachtbrieven en andere soortgelijke stukken; naar handschriften uitgegeven* ("Javanese letters, notices, reports, petitions, proclamations, publications, contracts, IOUs, receipts, legal documents, leases and other such documents; published from manuscripts"; later, and hereafter, known as the *Brievenboek*).[21] This publication, comprising a collection of 233 Javanese language documents dated from 1812 to 1843, was produced as a textbook for the Javanese language education of Dutch civil servants bound for the Indies. Roorda opens his preface to the compilation:

> It should be unnecessary to waste many words to point out the obvious utility and importance of this collection to any student of Javanese language, institutions, and customary practices—but most especially to him whose study of them is in preparation to become an official in the colonial possessions of the Government of the Netherlands East Indies.[22]

How did Roorda, who was himself never to set foot in Java, acquire the documents (most of which were from Surakarta) published in the *Brievenboek*? Comfortably positioned on his professor's chair in the Netherlands, Roorda relied on colonial officials "in the field" for his materials. In the same preface, he goes on to acknowledge the three individuals who provided the majority of the 233 indigenous documents he had compiled for publication. The generous individuals named by Roorda were Baron Nahuys van Burgst (Resident of Surakarta 1820–22 and 1827–30), J. F. C. Gericke (scholar of Javanese letters, Bible translator, and first director of the Surakarta Institute of Javanese Language), and C. F. Winter Sr. (literatus, scholar of Javanese letters, official translator for the Surakarta Residency, and second director of the above-mentioned Institute).

I first examined the *Brievenboek* some time after my first encounter with *His Majesty the VI's Correspondence* at the Kraton, and I found the Dutch publication's sometimes seemingly obscure contents uncannily familiar. After some reflection, I returned to the Kraton archive for an-

21. T. Roorda, *Javaansche brieven, berigten, verslagen, verzoekschriften, proclamaties, publicaties, contracten, schuldbekentenissen, quitanties, processtukken, pachtbrieven en andere soortgelijke stukken; naar handschriften uitgegeven* (Amsterdam: Muller, 1845).
22. Ibid., p. i.

other look at *His Majesty the VI's Correspondence*—this time with a copy of the *Brievenboek* in hand. A careful comparison of the two volumes demonstrated that the first forty-seven documents copied into the Kraton Surakarta manuscript are identical to documents dispersed through the 233-item published Dutch volume.[23] The first nine documents of *His Majesty the VI's Correspondence* both match and follow in sequence nine of the first eleven *Brievenboek* documents.

Which, then, of these two texts—one a product of a Dutch publishing house, the other a manuscript of the palace archive—is the more original; which, the more derivative? As it turns out, priority must be afforded the Dutch published textbook. The forty-seven matching documents in the Dutch publication could not have been copied from the Kraton manuscript: for, as I shall demonstrate below, *His Majesty the VI's Correspondence* was inscribed a good three or four years *after* the publication of the *Brievenboek*. Nor could both compilations have shared a third common Kraton archival source. We can know this with some certainty because there are among those forty-seven matching documents several which would *not*, it seems, have been housed in the Kraton archives. Take for example MS item no. 31 (*Brievenboek* 186), a letter from Prince Ngabéhi (a Surakarta prince who did *not* reside in the Kraton) to Mr. Gericke in 1834, answering the latter's inquiry on a point of court language use. Again there is MS item no. 35 (*Brievenboek* 219), in which two Surakarta nobles report to Mr. Winter in 1842 on the firing of a rural administrator. It is, then, almost without a doubt that it was from an exemplar of the published *Brievenboek*, which had made its way to the Indies, that the editor-scribe of *His Majesty the VI's Correspondence* selected out and copied the forty-seven matching documents.

On what grounds did the Javanese scribe make his or her selections? The *Brievenboek* comprises some 233 documents, of which only forty-seven correspond to documents in *His Majesty the VI's Correspondence*. Of the 186 published documents which do not appear in the Kraton manuscript, a great many treat the Chinese population and financial relationships between the Chinese and the indigenous nobility. Another large block of documents the *Brievenboek* does not share with *His Majesty the VI's Correspondence* concern rural provincial administration. The docu-

23. Appendix I provides correspondences for the contents of *His Majesty the VI's Correspondence* and the *Brievenboek*.

ments which do correspond (that is, which were selected for inclusion in the palace manuscript) are concerned primarily with the documentary history of the court, the realm, and the family of the Surakarta kings. It was these forty-seven documents that the compiler of the palace manuscript chose to adopt as the beginning of his or her documentary history of the exiled Pakubuwana VI—an edition of *His Majesty the VI's Correspondence* that would close with *Babad Jaka Tingkir.*

The Correspondence of Exile

Following these initial forty-seven items of *His Majesty the VI's Correspondence* are sixteen additional documents—none of which is to be found in the *Brievenboek,* and all save one of which are concerned with exile. These documents comprise fourteen royal letters that belong to the exile of Pakubuwana VI, the genealogy of an obscure Javano-Arabic character, and (finally and extensively) *Babad Jaka Tingkir.*

The fourteen letters are significantly different from the preceding correspondence copied from the *Brievenboek.* The focus of all fourteen is exile itself. The tonality of these letters tends to be less official than that of the preceding forty-seven documents. And these letters tend to convey more personal information than do the copied *Brievenboek* documents. Six of these letters date from the beginning of the deposed king's exile in 1830; their contents convey the poignancy and helplessness of the situation in which the incarcerated and newly deposed king found himself. On 11 June 1830, three days after Pakubuwana VI's arrest, the king's "old friend" Resident Nahuys writes that he "has no time" to visit the king in his prison (item 48). In a letter dated 1 July, one of Pakubuwana VI's uncles describes to the prisoner-king the 14 June coronation of his rival as Pakubuwana VII (item 53). In a farewell letter dated November 1830, the new Pakubuwana VII coldly informs Pakubuwana VI that his entreaty to serve his exile on Java instead of Ambon has been refused. The new Pakubuwana goes on to report that not one of the wives or retainers the prisoner had left behind in the Kraton will agree to join him in exile—and, the usurper adds, they do not even offer proper excuses. Pakubuwana VI's requests to his successor—that he be granted custody of his young daughters, that personal items of jewelry and clothing, as well as his diaries, be sent along to him—are all refused (items 49–50).

The remaining eight documents date from 1847 and 1848, a period shortly after the 1845 publication of the *Brievenboek* and just preceding the king's June 1849 death. As noted above, the tone of some of these later letters is deeply personal; six of the final eight are composed in *macapat* verse. In a tearful letter to the prisoner-king that is dated October 1847 (item 57), a brother of Pakubuwana VI writes to acknowledge receipt in Surakarta of the king's letter and gifts: among these gifts had been four of the exiled king's teeth. Answering that letter in June 1848 (item 58), Pakubuwana VI, referring to himself as "I.S.K.S. [H.R.H.] Sayiddi Mao-lana Mokahamat Salim," describes how very desperate his circumstances have become: writing in a rude hut in the middle of the dry fields that he keeps, the forty-one-year-old ex-king says that he feels very old, "like a sun about to set." In the same posting, Pakubuwana VI sends a tender love letter (item 59) to one of the queens he left behind in Surakarta, along with the gift of sarong that he has worn—that she may use it as her pillow. To another of his queens the ex-king writes on 27 July 1848 that "it is as though I am no longer of this world, that I am no longer at home in this world—my life hopeless, it were better that I die." He commends to her care their son (the future Pakubuwana IX) and advises her concerning her Islamic religious education. And in a postscript he records the loss of yet another tooth (item 60). The final letter (item 62) is from Pakubuwana VI's daughter Gusti Timur (the one who followed him into exile) to her younger half-brother, Prince Prabuwijaya (the future Pakubuwana IX). Writing, on 4 June 1848, with grace and some lyric beauty of her sacred duty to remain an exile with her father, the princess grants her little brother permission to precede her in marriage.

Interposed between the final two of these letters is a document that is apparently not concerned with exile: the *macapat* verse genealogy of a certain Sarifi [Sharif] Ibrahim Madyakusuma (item 61).[24] He is called, in Arabic, "al-fakuru illallahu / ghanniyul kammid" ("this poor man of Allah, rich with praise for Allah"), a title appropriate for one who has embarked upon the Sufi way. His name indicates his nobility (a Sharif is a descendant of the Prophet Mohammad) and points toward his mixed ethnicity: Ibrahim is Arabic and Madyakusuma is Javanese. The geneal-ogy records a distinguished lineage for Sarifi Ibrahim Madyakusuma, tracing his ancestry back through twenty-nine generations of Sharifs, then through the first seven of the twelve Shi'ite Imams, to the Prophet

24. For a transliteration of the complete poem, see Appendix II.

Muhammad, and then continuing on until finally reaching back to Adam himself(!).[25] Who was this man? Could he have been a teacher or a companion in exile of the unfortunate Pakubuwana VI?

On the Dating, Provenance, and Authorship
of Babad Jaka Tingkir

Let us now turn once again to the final document inscribed in this volume of *His Majesty the VI's Correspondence*: that is, *Babad Jaka Tingkir*. By far the longest of the manuscript's sixty-three documents, this anonymous history fills the final 143 of the manuscript's 304 pages. Markedly different from the rest of the royal correspondence, this extended piece of writing is a unique historical poem which offers glimpses of Java's past around the turn of the sixteenth century—the initial period of Java's conversion to Islam. The text of this history is, apparently, incomplete. An extended fragment, this *Babad Jaka Tingkir* ceases abruptly mid-line and mid-page on the final inscribed leaf of *His Majesty the VI's Correspondence* (figure 5).

When and where might this history have been written? And who, perchance, was its writer? Internally the poem dates its own writing with uncharacteristic hyperbole by no less than four time-reckoning systems: Javanese solar, Javanese lunar (A.J.), Hijrah (A.H.), and Gregorian (A.D.).

> It was Sunday when this writing of history began
> The twenty-second of Safar
> At the strike of eleven
> The reigning star was
> Jupiter at that time
> The year was Jimawal
> In Sancaya's eight-year turn
> In the third month of the solar year
> On the sixteenth—in chronogram: "The Excellent Sage
> Orders the Enormity of the World" [1757]

25. This pedigree would make Ibrahim Madyakusuma a distant relative of the Mataram kings. Royal Surakarta genealogies trace the right-hand descent of the dynasty from Adam through the Prophet Mohammad and then on through the first five of the twelve Shi'ite Imams ([Ki Padmasusastra] and R.Ng. Wirapratama, *Serat Sajarah Ageng ing Karaton Surakarta* [MS. RP B 77; SMP MN 690], pp. 1–18).

Figure 5. Final page of *Babad Jaka Tingkir*, in *Kupiya Iber Warni-warni Sampéyan-dalem kaping VI*, p. 152 recto. Courtesy of the Kraton Surakarta.

In the year of the Prophet's Hijrah
Chronogrammed: "The Sage Magical
Is Reverenced by all the World" [1237]
In the Dutch month of August
On the twenty-third rendered
In chronogram: "Ever Reverenced
Is the Person of the King" [1829]
(*Babad Jaka Tingkir* I:2–3).[26]

Each of the multiple dates, in accord with convention, is rendered not in numerals, but in *sangkala* (chronograms). *Sangkala* are aphoristic phrases, the words of which when read backwards signify—by a *logical* system of conventions—different numerical values.[27] To provide dates in *sangkala* indicates commemoration in time (in addition and contrast to mere temporal documentation). *Sangkala* work to make time into significant time. In the first place, calling attention to themselves as meaningful codes which have to be read (doubly for the discursive significance they might contain and for their numerical value), *sangkala* provide for the documented event a context in meaningful time. It is because *sangkala* name a certain kind of time that significant events are dated by them. To date any event by *sangkala* is to call it significant—both to inscribe it as worthy of remembrance and to commemorate it. This procedure for writing's self-inscription / self-commemoration in time is not at all uncommon for tradi-

26. The Javanese text, in Dhangdhanggula meter reads as follows: "Ing ri Akhad duk wiwit mèngeti / kaping kalihlikur sasi Safar / wanci pukul sawalasé / lintang ingkang lumaku / nuju sangat lintang Mustari / pareng warsa Jimawal / Sancayaning windu / lèk Jawi Mongsa Katiga / ping nembelas sangkala sang mahamuni [7] / anata [5] goraning [7] rat [1] // Héjrah Nabi tarèhnya marengi / sinengkalan pandhita [7] aguna [3] / sinembah [2] ing jagad [1] kabèh / lèk Walandi Agustus / kaping tigalikur winarni / sangkala trus [9] sinembah [2] / sariraning [8] ratu [1]."

27. For instance, words associated with eyes or arms (which are two) mean "two." *Sembah*, the gesture of reverence, indicates "two" because one offers it with his or her two hands. Words associated with fire mean "three" since *guna* ("fire" or "ability"), in Sanskrit, also means "three." Words associated with holes or openings indicate "nine" because of the nine openings of the (male) body. For a more comprehensive English language introduction to Javanese chronograms, see M. C. Ricklefs, *Modern Javanese Historical Tradition: A Study of an Original Kartasura Chronicle and Related Materials* (London: SOAS, University of London, 1978), p. 239 ff. The best explication of the *sangkala* dating system is still R. Bratakésawa's *Katrangan Tjandrasangkala* (Jakarta: Balai Pustaka, 1952).

tional Javanese poetic texts (including more typical historical texts, or *babad*). Nonetheless, by dating its writing four times over, *Babad Jaka Tingkir* overplays the conventional *sangkala* in a way that significantly intensifies its commemorative effect.

The redundant dating produces other effects as well: such a superfluity of systems all grinding together to commemorate a single moment (that is, 11:00 A.M., Sunday, 23 August 1829) lends an almost scientific sense of authority to the truth of this dating. However, this seeming precision—and, too, its truth—is contested by contradictions among the dates of these several systems. The Javanese lunar date of 22 Sapar Jimawal 1757 A.J. fell in the eight-year turn (*windu*) of Sangara, not Sancaya, and in the Hijrah year of 1245, not 1237. The date 22 Safar 1237 A.H. was 22 Sapar Jimawal 1749, *windu* Kunthara (and 18 November 1821 A.D.). The sixteenth day of the third Javanese solar month is 9/10 September, rather than 23 August. These several contradictions among the dates of these multiple time-reckoning systems, call into question, then, what had seemed the virtually mechanical certainty of the text's writing at a unique moment in August 1829.

But there is more. The hyperbolic dating of the text opens: "It *was* Sunday when this writing of history began" (Ing ri Akhad *duk* wiwit mèngeti). What would seem the immediate presence of the history's writing is already at the outset located in the past. With the little word *duk*, marking past time, the writer casts his or her writing out of the present, thereby distancing its inscription from the authority of authorial immediacy. I shall return to these special features which bear upon *Babad Jaka Tingkir*'s date of composition in a moment—after a brief detour to consider the history's provenance and authorship.

The linguistic and poetic idiom of this history situate it squarely in a tradition of writing associated with the court and city of Surakarta. The style is distinctly what is now considered "Surakarta renaissance"—that is, Surakarta writing of the late-eighteenth through the mid-nineteenth century. Even more definitively, the poem contains numerous citations, some of them lengthy, from texts that we know were written in, or around, the Surakarta court at that time. Notably, toward the end of this Tingkir history are extended passages, selectively quoted and strategically edited, from more mainstream texts of historical writing associated with the royal Surakarta palaces.

The text of *Babad Jaka Tingkir* contains a number of court scenes that are ostensibly set in the palaces of the ancient kingdoms of Majapahit and Demak. The palace described, however, is always the Kraton Surakarta. The poem incessantly maps the Surakarta palace, but it does so always elsewhere. On one occasion mapping the most interior geography of that palace, the poet provides intimate details about the Kraton's very private women's quarters (*keputrèn*), details that could not have been known to many. In the nineteenth-century Kraton Surakarta, only the king's women, their minor children, their female retainers, and the king himself had access to the *keputrèn*.

Babad Jaka Tingkir was, perhaps, composed in August 1829, apparently in Surakarta, and quite possibly at the Kraton Surakarta. We can say with some certainty that its writer knew the Kraton—including the zenana—intimately, that he or she was fully conversant with the Surakartan literary idiom, and that he or she had with him or her at least several other texts of that tradition from which he/she quoted. But could not this history have been written by someone *of* Surakarta who had been transported to somewhere else?

The Interpolations

Twenty-five pages into *Babad Jaka Tingkir* are six interpolated pages on three leaves of paper that materially rupture the text of the history.[28] Three surfaces of those leaves boast some remarkable inscription; the other three surfaces are blank. Drawn upon the first two of these leaves (back and front surfaces, respectively) are four pen and ink drawings: the portrait of a single figure on the first leaf (figure 6), and three smaller portraits on the second (figure 7). Such drawings were extremely uncommon in Javanese manuscripts. Aside from a book of portraits of Dutch governors general stored in the Mangkunagaran library,[29] this is the only example of such portraits among all the manuscripts of the three major Surakarta repositories. The third leaf is empty of writing save the following inscription: "This is a commemoration of His [or Her] Majesty's dream in the month of Mulud, in the year of Wawu, at the time of the west

28. MS. pp. 91verso–93recto; see figures 6–8.
29. *Serat Gambaripun para Gupernur Jendral ing tanah Jawa* (compiled and inscribed Surakarta, ca. 1926). MS. RP B116; SMP MN 270.

monsoon, in the year 1777 [February 1849]."[30] Following this "dream commemoration," it appears that a single leaf has been cut from the volume.

The interpolations bear no *obvious* relation to the text they interrupt; they are, however, shall we say, suggestive. The interpolated pages cut mid-line into a passage that relates the reading of a letter. The letter's reader and addressee is an exiled prince, who is himself a portrait painter. The letter the prince reads is from the jealous royal father who had banished him. The letter is interrupted by these interpolations as it writes of exile itself—more precisely at the very moment it writes of the utility of exile for the generation of future greatness.[31]

Bearing that text in mind, let us now examine these interpolations more carefully. The first ink drawing is a portrait, in frontal pose, of an unknown bearded man, wearing robes (*jubah*), turban, and a large medal in the form of an eight-pointed star (figure 6). The drawing is not captioned. The unknown character is definitely of an "Arabic-Islamic" cast. Could this be a portrait of the mysterious Sarifi Ibrahim Madyakusuma?—or is it perhaps an iconographic representation of one of the exiled heroes of the Dipanagara War: the charismatic Kyai Maja or even Prince Dipanagara himself?

The portraits on the facing page are captioned; the captioning hand, however, is not the hand that writes the rest of the manuscript. The portraits are of three figures (figure 7): a central, larger figure of a handsome man in frontal pose ("Sultan Malikil Salèh Banjarmas"), flanked by two smaller male figures in profile ("Pengéran Purbaya" and "Pengéran Harya Mentaram"). The central figure, which appears to be that of a Surakarta king, wears the regal *kanigara* fez, and *sikepan ageng* blouse and jacket. On his chest is a large multipointed, diamond-studded star strongly reminiscent of the Surakarta kings' medal of office, Kangjeng Kyai Suryawisésa. The portrait is captioned "Sultan Malikil Salèh Banjarmas." The name, or title, is Arabic and would translate, "Sultan Pious

30. "Punika pémut supenan-dalem, ing wulan Mulud taun Wawu, Mangsa Barat, angkaning warsa: 1777" (*His Majesty the VI's Correspondence*, p. 93recto). The lunar month of Mulud in the year of Wawu 1777 spanned a period from 25 January to 23 February 1849.
31. See below, *Babad Jaka Tingkir*, V:38.

Figure 6. Interpolation in *Babad Jaka Tingkir*: bearded figure with turban and medal, in *Kupiya Iber Warni-warni Sampéyan-dalem kaping VI*, p. 91 verso. Courtesy of the Kraton Surakarta.

Figure 7. Interpolation in *Babad Jaka Tingkir*: three royal Javanese figures, in *Kupiya Iber Warni-warni Sampéyan-dalem kaping VI*, p. 92 recto. Courtesy of the Kraton Surakarta.

Ruler [of] Banjarmas." To my knowledge there was never a Banjarmasin Sultan by that name. There were, however, two nineteenth-century Surakarta kings whose names, at different points in the courses of their very different lives, were similar to that of the mysterious Sultan Malikil Salèh Banjarmas. Pakubuwana VII was born B.R.M.G. Malikisalikin. As we mentioned above, shortly before his death, the exiled Pakubuwana VI called himself by the Arabic name: I.S.K.S. Sayiddi Maolana Mokhamat Salim.[32]

Behind and slightly above the central royal figure's right shoulder, the first of the two smaller flanking figures looks out in profile, away from the central figure into the spine of the book and hence toward the turbanned figure on the facing page. This smaller figure is a somewhat sinister looking man, with narrow eyes and a face blemished by spots. The man is wearing a military jacket with gold braid at his neck and a Javanese *dhesthar* (head-cloth). The figure is captioned "Pengéran Purbaya." Pangéran Purbaya was the uncle, enemy, and successor of Pakubuwana VI. Purbaya was enthroned by the Dutch as Pakubuwana VII in June 1830, as his nephew was en route to exile in Ambon. As I mentioned above, *His Majesty the VI's Correspondence* includes the "fairwell letters" that Pakubuwana VII sent Pakubuwana VI as the young ex-king sailed off into exile.

Partially behind the central figure's left shoulder, the second of the two smaller figures in profile gazes with determined eyes in the direction of that central figure. Unlike the other flanking figure, this figure seems to be on the same level as the larger central figure. The figure is a strongly handsome man wearing military uniform with epaulettes and a Javanese *dhesthar*; the portrait is captioned "Pengéran Harya Mentaram." The elder Harya Mataram (whose name was changed to Prince Mangkubumi in 1790)[33] was a younger brother of Pakubuwana IV; he was, therefore, an uncle of Pakubuwana VII and grand-uncle of Pakubuwana VI. Always a rebellious figure, Mangkubumi was exiled to Ambon in 1816 for his part

32. *His Majesty the VI's Correspondence* (item 58), p. 72.
33. Ann Kumar, "Javanese Court Society and Politics in the Late Eighteenth Century: The Record of a Lady Soldier. Part II: Political Developments: The Courts and the Company, 1784–1791," *Indonesia* 30 (October 1980):88 ff. Kumar describes how, in 1790, Pakubuwana IV's choice of the name Mangkubumi for this brother nearly provoked Yogyakarta to war.

in an anti-European conspiracy.[34] In late 1825 Mangkubumi was allowed to return to Surakarta, where he died in 1826. For that brief period of repatriation, the elderly Mangkubumi lived with his son, the younger Harya Mataram.[35] Following his father's death, that son was elevated to princely status with his late father's name. The younger Harya Mataram died K.P.H. Mangkubumi II in 1863. He was the brother-in-law and cousin of Pangéran Purbaya (Pakubuwana VII) and generational "uncle" of Pakubuwana VI. Unlike his rebellious father, this younger Harya Mataram was evidently loyal to the Dutch overlords.[36]

> This is a commemoration of His Majesty's dream in the month of Mulud, in the year of Wawu, at the time of the west monsoon, in the year 1777 [February 1849] (*His Majesty the VI's Correspondence*, p. 93recto).

The note recording that "this" is a commemoration of "His Majesty's Dream" is at the head of a page otherwise empty of inscription. Behind and below the inscription looms the ghostly impression of a Javanese king: in fact the shadow of the central royal figure on MS p. 92recto whose image appears to have migrated through the manuscript pages in order to witness this haunting commemoration (figures 8 and 9). The words that float above this royal ghost to commemorate "His Majesty's dream" are not inscribed in the captioning hand of the previous two pages, but rather in the same Surakarta cursive hand as the body of the manuscript. Which Majesty's dream, or what he dreamt, is not specified. However, the form of the dating of that unspecified dream provides a clue as to whose dream "this" commemorates, and where that dream was dreamt.

The dream is dated to the month of Mulud, in the year of Wawu 1777 (February 1849), "at the time of the west monsoon" (*mangsa barat*). Reckoning time in terms of the monsoons was not common practice in

34. See Peter Carey, "The Sepoy Conspiracy of 1815 in Java," *BKI* 133, nos. 2–3 (1977):294–322.
35. *Serat Babad Sengkala: Kawit Pulo Jawi dipunisèni tiyang nalika taun ongka 1 dumugi taun 1854* (composed Surakarta, s.a.; inscribed Surakarta, 1924). MS. SP 220 Ca-A; SMP KS 1A, pp. 132–36.
36. H. M. De Kock, "Beschrijving van het karakter en de hoedanigheden van den Keizer de Prinsen en de Rijksbestierder van Soerakarta," 1829. Solo Bundel 166, Arsip Nasional Republik Indonesia.

Figure 8. Interpolation in *Babad Jaka Tingkir*: "This is a commemoration of His Majesty's dream." Behind the inscription looms the ghostly figure of a Javanese king (the shadow of Pakubuwana VI?), in *Kupiya Iber Warni-warni Sampéyan-dalem kaping VI*, p. 93 recto. Courtesy of the Kraton Surakarta.

Figure 9. Interpolation in *Babad Jaka Tingkir*: migrating royal figures and the commemoration of His Majesty's dream in February 1849, in *Kupiya Iber Warni-warni Sampéyan-dalem kaping VI*, p. 92 verso–93 recto. Courtesy of the Kraton Surakarta.

nineteenth-century Central Java. Of the 233 documents that comprise the *Javaansch Brievenboek*, not one is so dated. However, a survey of the documents in this compilation of *His Majesty the VI's Correspondence* yields three such monsoon-dated letters: MS item nos. 58, 60, and 62, all of which are letters in *macapat* verse sent from Ambon to Surakarta. The letters date from the "east monsoon" (*mangsa timur*), in the lunar months of Rejep and Ruwah 1776 (June and July 1848). Two of the letters were written by Pakubuwana VI himself; the other, by his daughter R. Ayu Timur. Evidently the monsoons were of some import to these exiles on the tiny island of Ambon, who depended on the sea for whatever contact remained with Java and the rest of the outside world. Given the monsoon dating of this dream's recording, and the situation of the record in the context of this particular volume of royal correspondence, it may be assumed that Pakubuwana VI was the royal dreamer indicated here, and that the dream was dreamt on Ambon. May we then presume that his shade has moved onto the page in order to lay claim to that dream?

"This is a commemoration of His Majesty's dream" heads a blank page shadowed by a royal ghost, a page interposed in the middle of the text of *Babad Jaka Tingkir*. To what does that "this" refer? What was the nature of the dream the deposed king dreamt in February 1849, a mere four months prior to his death? And what form does its commemoration take? Allow me to suggest here that, for the Javanese writer who compiled this volume of *His Majesty the VI's Correspondence* (almost certainly in Ambon), the soon-to-be-departed exiled king's dream of the 1849 "west monsoon" was none other than *Babad Jaka Tingkir*. This book, then, is an exploration of the meaning of that dream.

Dating and Situating the Manuscript of the History

Because of the correspondence of exile preceding the text and the monsoon-dated dream which interrupts it, it is reasonable to conclude that this manuscript witness of *Babad Jaka Tingkir* was inscribed on the island of Ambon, sometime between August 1848 and June 1850. The inscription of the history could not have been begun prior to August 1848: in the manuscript the Tingkir text follows the copy of a letter written by Pakubuwana VI on 27 July 1848. Twenty-five pages into the text of the history, the poem is broken by the drawings and "dream-commemoration" discussed above. I have demonstrated that this "dream-commemoration," which is dated Mulud 1777 (February 1849), was almost surely inscribed on Ambon. Following Pakubuwana VI's death on 3 June 1849, the family and retainers who had shared his exile were repatriated to Java.[37] In June 1850, they returned to Surakarta, presumably with at least two of the late prisoner-king's manuscripts, *His Majesty the VI's Correspondence* and *His Majesty the VI's Book of Rama*, in hand.

How, then, was the manuscript produced? From his or her exile in Ambon, the Javanese writer (editor/scribe) worked from a variety of sources to compile *His Majesty the VI's Correspondence*. She or he had before her/himself an 1845 Dutch-published textbook compilation of Javanese letters (perhaps the gift of a thoughtful Dutch jailer), some original Surakarta-Ambon correspondence, a genealogy, and (perhaps) the text of a unique version of the *Babad Jaka Tingkir*. From these sources

37. There were, among these "returnees," some who were coming to Surakarta for the first time, i.e., wives Pakubuwana VI had married in Ambon and their children.

the writer constructed his or her *His Majesty the VI's Correspondence* as a kind of documentary history of an exiled king.

Let us now consider further the dating and provenance of this somewhat fanciful *babad* which concludes a history that was "introduced" with a selection of archival documents from a Dutch textbook. In the manuscript copy produced by this presumed editor on Ambon, the *babad* dates itself August 1829. However, as we have seen above, contradictions among dates from the several time-reckoning systems employed by the poet problematicize the veracity of this dating. One would assume that information indicating the day's correct Hijrah year and the correct *windu* would have been easily accessible to a poet/scribe beginning his/her writing in Surakarta on 23 August 1829. How then might we understand the discrepancies in the dating?

The confusion in the internal dating of *Babad Jaka Tingkir* invites several readings. The mistake could indicate nothing more than a carelessness in chronology on the part of the poet and/or the scribe. Or perhaps the opening section of the manuscript's Surakarta prototype, which had been carried or sent off to Ambon, was damaged. Indeed, the most likely pages to be damaged or missing in Javanese manuscripts are the opening ones. Perhaps the editor on Ambon erred in his or her attempt to provide readings for illegible portions of a damaged prototype. Access to accurate Javanese time-reckoning tables in late-1840s Ambon may well have been limited. Or perhaps the confusion in the dating points toward a willful antedating of the composition of the poem. We remember how the commemoration of the commencement of the text's writing begins in *past tense*. Perhaps rather than scribe of the poem, the writer of this late-1840s Ambonese compilation was instead its composer. This reading would suggest that for some reason the history's Ambonese-Javanese composer chose both to conceal his or her authorship and to push the date of the poem's composition back some twenty years to 1829—to a time preceding Pakubuwana VI's exile. There can be no definitive answer to this question of reading the *babad*'s dating. The implications of these various readings will be explored in the book's conclusion.

The single surviving manuscript witness of the *Babad Jaka Tingkir* presented here was inscribed in Ambon by an exile. It was written as the conclusion to a documentary history of Pakubuwana VI, large portions of which were in turn selected and copied from a Dutch-published textbook meant for the Javanese language education of colonial civil servants. We cannot be sure when or where the text was composed, or who its composer was. It could well have been composed in the 1840s on Ambon. Perhaps its writer was Pakubuwana VI's daughter, Radèn Ayu Timur. Or, its composer could very well have been Pakubuwana VI himself, admittedly a "fluent writer" with an "extensive knowledge of traditional history," who then wrote this history (for the future) by creatively piecing and binding together the materials available to a nineteenth-century royal exile. Perhaps.

In this chapter I have considered the historical production of the single extant manuscript of a unique *Babad Jaka Tingkir*; and in so doing I have suggested that this text in manuscript somehow commemorates the dream of a royal exile. I cast my narrative purposely in the mode of a mystery story, in which clues and teases are serially presented and then (tentatively) read. The mystery remains unsolved at chapter's end. I have ulterior motives. Among these: by playing on the mystery, I wish to replicate for my readers some of the haunting attraction this text has exercised upon me from the time of my first encounter with it—thereby to provoke in readers the desire to read, seriously and critically, the text of *Tingkir* themselves. I expect that such readings will generate understandings of the poem which will be other and likely counter to my own, and I welcome the projected extension of the dialogue. My analysis may be found in the chapters following the translation. But I strongly advise the reader to defer reading my critical analysis of the text until after completing his or her own thoughtful reading of this remarkable nineteenth-century Javanese (re)reading of a Javanese past.

CHAPTER 2
BABAD JAKA TINGKIR
IN TRANSLATION

❋

Babad Jaka Tingkir, inscribed by an exile on Ambon around the middle of the nineteenth century, presents a unique history of Java around the turn of the sixteenth century. As we shall see, this history was composed episodically, according to complex processes of enframement and reenframement against the background of a wider universe of traditional Javanese writing. Each of our individual readings of the translated text will move through these episodes and their frames, marking and remarking them, in our attempts to comprehend the text. But before turning to these readings, let us pause to consider very briefly some of the conventions that governed the composition of the text as Javanese poetry and some of the considerations that went into my English translation of it.

Prosodic-Melodic Semantics

Babad Jaka Tingkir, like most traditional Javanese writing, was composed in a metrical form (*tembang*) known as *macapat*.[1] *Macapat* texts, which are written for melodic recitation, are composed in fourteen or fifteen commonly recognized metrical sub-forms (again, *tembang*), each with its own melodic shape and its own name. For each of these meters there are specific formal requirements that govern (1) the number of lines per

---

1. For detailed discussions of *macapat* and *macapat* forms, see R. Hardjowirogo, *Pathokaning Njekaraken* (Jakarta: Balai Pustaka, 1952); in English, see Bernard Arps, *Tembang in Two Traditions*, esp. pp. 53–109; Martin F. Hatch, "Lagu, Laras, Layang"; and Margaret Kartomi, *Matjapat Songs in Central and West Java*. For a good concise English language introduction to Javanese prosody, see Pigeaud, *Literature of Java*, 1:18–24. See also Anthony Day, "The Meanings of Change," esp. pp. 14–45, and Timothy E. Behrend, "The Serat Jatiswara," esp. pp. 191–228.

Map 2. Java and Madura circa 1500

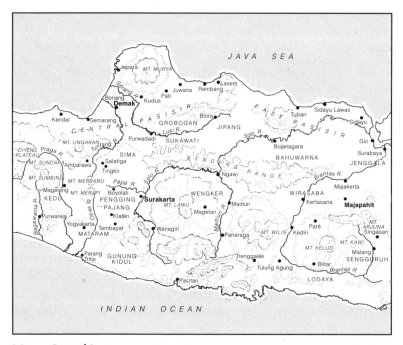

Map 3. Central Java

stanza (*guru gatra*), (2) the number of syllables per line (*guru wilangan*), and (3) the final vowel in each line (*guru lagu*). In addition to these formal rules, there are also structures of caesura (*pedhotan*) for divisions within and among lines. The caesura structures among lines in a verse work together with that verse's words to generate grammatically its *ukara*, that is, the verse's "sentences." It is through these "sentences," or syntactic units, that the words of the poem come to produce their potential meanings. The structures that formulate these "sentences" do not, however, comprise hard and fast rules that must be rigidly followed. For example, in seven-line *tembang* Asmarandana, the verse *tends* to be divided into two syntactic units, consisting of the first three and then the last four poetic lines. A verse of ten-line *tembang* Dhangdhanggula often comprises four "sentences," consisting of lines: 1–3, 4–5, 6–7, and 8–10. The caesura structures also relate to the oral melodic performance of the poetry. The caesura determine when the singer-reciter may breathe, thus shaping the melodic lines of the verses along with their potential meanings.

Each of the *tembang* has a variety of more or less elaborate standard melodies by which it may be intoned. Indeed, the word *nembang* (*tembang*'s verbal form) itself means "to sing." The various *tembang* songs have various melodic *watak* (roughly "character[s]"), which are evocative of various moods or tonalities. For example, *tembang* Asmarandana ("giving love") generates melodically a mood of longing or of passionate love; *tembang* Megatruh's ("to take someone's soul") song is evocative of sorrow or of deep regret. This melodic evocation of mood is indeed part of the process through which the poetry makes sense. For in *macapat* verse, language and the melodic texture of the song that intones that language work together—and sometimes in tension with one another—to generate textual meaning in any poetic work.[2]

Babad Jaka Tingkir consists of some 6,913 lines of *macapat* verse divided into thirty-two cantos in eleven different meters.[3] At the opening of each canto in the translation, I note the name of the meter and characterize its melodic mood. The reader of the translated text should try to bear these

2. See Appendix III for a listing of the eleven meters used in the present text, together with their respective rules of *guru gatra, guru wilangan,* and *guru lagu,* notes pertaining to *pedhotan* and *ukara,* and indications of poetic *watak.*
3. See Appendix IV for a listing of cantos, with the two opening lines of each canto in the original Javanese.

melodic moods in mind, remembering that the poet can and does some-times play the mood of the *tembang* against the words intoned in it.

Punctuation

The Javanese text uses punctuation only to mark (1) the division into metrical lines, and occasionally caesura within a line, (2) the division into verses, and (3) the division into cantos. For this punctuation, Javanese script of the nineteenth century knows only half stops, full stops, and something akin to markings that would indicate a change of movements in a musical score. The script knows no question marks, exclamation marks, or quotation marks—no colons, semicolons, dashes, parentheses, or brackets. This relative lack of punctuation often produces a significant semantic openness or ambiguity. Precisely because the syntactic units of the poetic lines are not impressed into determinate forms of singularly punctual coherences, the lines are sometimes opened to potentially multi-valent meanings or readings.

In the translation, I have moved to render the effects of the Javanese punctuation (and lack thereof) in and upon English. The poem is a narra-tive poem, and its English translation could—with "proper punctuation"—have been more consistently formed into grammatically contained En-glish sentences. I shunned this violence to the text. Instead, by purposely limiting the use of punctuation marks to the barest minimum, I have worked to translate into English the punctuational absences of the Java-nese original.[4] I have done so to avoid forcing the text's potentially multi-valent senses into the more determined closure of formal English sen-tences. I hope thereby to re-create in English some of the complexity and syntactical ambiguity of the original poetry.[5] Nevertheless, I have added an occasional question mark, colon, and comma in the service of textual intelligibility. And I have added quotation marks for direct speech.

In the translation the Javanese metrical forms are visualized through spatial punctuation and enumeration. Rendering the translation in the typographical conventions of European verse form, each poetic line is

4. See also G. W. J. Drewes's very cogent argument for a conservative policy of punc-tuation in the preparation of Javanese language text editions, in the introduction to his edition of *The Admonitions of Sèh Bari* (The Hague: Nijhoff, 1969), pp. 5–8.
5. See also my discussion of *plèsèdan* ("verbal play" or "slippage") in Javanese poetry, below in chapter 3.

accorded a line on the page. The first letter of the first word of each line is capitalized. Double-spacing separates verses. By numbering the verses and cantos, I have added to the translated text visual signposts not present in the Javanese.

Another Word on the Translation

This translation is the product of many years' struggle, the effect of my at times painful efforts to move across and between quite different universes of sense. Moving between the "senses" (discursive, emotive, and sensuous) of an obscure nineteenth-century Javanese poem and its late-twentieth-century English language rendition, I have engaged in an extended dialogue with a writing of the Javanese past. Through this intensive and sustained encounter, I have been involved with this Javanese text in the dialogic production of a new discursive space. That space itself, emerging through translation, comprises a shifting borderland between several worlds. These several worlds, brushing up against each other in this borderland, themselves exist in the particularities of their own historical becomings—while at the same time working changes each upon the other. Translation could be the name of this work of mutual transformation. The place of translation is neither to master the translated text nor merely to be mastered by it. With a humble nod to Benjamin, I would note that the task of the translator is not merely to convey "faithfully" the sense of the original into the text that she writes, but to work in dialogue with the imagined original in order to produce, with it, the novel senses to which that "original" itself already has potential claim.

   Babad Jaka Tingkir, presumably what Benjamin would have recognized as a translatable text (if he could have read Javanese),[6] was not an easy text to translate. Composed with an attractive linguistic and literary complexity, this prophetic history was purposively written to be a difficult, or challenging, text. The poet uses the rolling parataxis of Javanese *macapat* verse to maximum poetic effect—at times to create highly productive

6. Benjamin answers the question he himself poses as to a work's translatability: "Does its nature lend itself to translation, and therefore, in view of the significance of the mode, call for it?" (Walter Benjamin, "The Task of the Translator," p. 70). See Tejaswini Niranjana's analysis of this and other Benjaminian passages on translation and translatability; she argues that for Benjamin a text's translatability is the claim it has on coming generations (*Siting Translation*, pp. 113–19).

ambiguities. *Babad Jaka Tingkir* is marked as a highly textured literary composition by a number of features: its remarkably lush lexicon, its command of alliterative expression and of formal poetic conventions, its sophisticated plays on syntax, and its cunning intertextual allusions. The text is also marked by the deliberate archaisms that abound in it, providing it with a haunting sense of staged antiquity. At times obscure, and often allusive, the poem always demands of its readers active and creative readings.

Translating such a text has proven a daunting task. Working with this writing of the Javanese past, I have attempted to reproduce some of the complexities of its original Javanese in my English rendition. This attempt has meant, more than anything else, learning to attend carefully to the modes through which the Javanese writer of the text worked to produce its significance, and to try "lovingly and in detail" to "incorporate the original's mode of signification" into the text of my translation.[7] It has meant developing an ear for the poetic voices of the original in order that I might register those voices and then attempt to render them again, quite differently, in the new text that I was creating in dialogue with them.

The translation was premised, first of all, on a stubborn refusal to presume transparent glosses from Javanese to English meanings—a refusal born from an incessant questioning of any assumption of univocal meanings subsisting behind the language of the original for easy retrieval and removal to the translated text. This refusal has realized itself in a form of translation that bends toward what might be called "the literal." Pushing my English in the direction of nineteenth-century pseudo-archaic Javanese, I have worked to create a translation that would itself question the transcendental reality of the poet's meaning outside the language through which he or she composed his or her text. The text of the translation was generated, then, by a productive reading that moved from word to word, and from line to line, with passionate attention to linguistic and literary detail. Each line was translated in turn as its own contextualized unit of discourse. I would not allow myself the "freedom" of instead rendering the presumed semantic gist of a verse. In this way, moving in parallel line to the long-dead Javanese poet with whom I work, I have allowed his or her syntactical and semantic strategies to reconstitute my English.

7. Benjamin, "The Task of the Translator," p. 78.

Metrics were a constant concern, as were issues of assonance and alliteration. My translation makes gestures in these directions, but the constraints of trying to move between and among other of the poem's modes of signification sometimes foiled these more poetic intentions. Although my English text may at times reverberate with the *macapat* meters that it translates, it does not attempt to reproduce in English a form of *macapat*-like verse.[8] Instead—in dialogue with the Javanese original—I have nudged my English rendering toward something between rhythmic prose and poetry.

The translation was produced and reproduced (repeatedly) both visually and aurally. I would read and then often sing a verse of the Javanese text to myself in order to work through, with it, the poetry's potentially multiple "senses." Many times the discursive, emotive, and artistic senses of the text actually seemed to emerge from its melodic phrasing in song. Next, I would attempt an English rendering of the Javanese text, line by painstaking line. When the lines had become a verse, I would read the preliminary translation aloud and accept or reject it on the basis of its rhythms and tonalities—its poetic senses. The preliminary acceptance was usually reversed at a later date, upon another hearing. The translation, which I began some years ago in the shadow of the walls of the Kraton Surakarta, has been through many versions.

The translation that follows is provided with some editorial apparatus. (1) The translation is divided into sections, which are prefaced by editorial comments that are meant to direct the reader's attention to salient features of the poetic text that follows. Among other things, these divisions mark the episodes that compose the narrative. The comments are printed in italics. They are, of course, necessarily interpretive.[9] (2) In brackets at the head of every canto are notes pertaining to the melodic mood of the metrical form of the canto that follows. (3) The translation is provided with annotations that should facilitate the reader's participation in the world of the poem.

8. As did Benedict Anderson in his wonderful translation of *Suluk Gatholoco* ("The *Suluk Gatoloco*: Parts One & Two," *Indonesia* 32 (October 1981):109–50; 33 (April 1982):31–88).

9. I am very grateful to Oliver Wolters for having suggested the use and form of these commentaries to me: the style of the commentaries is borrowed from St. Teresa of Avila's introductions to the mansions of her "Interior Castle" (St. Teresa of Avila, *Interior Castle* [Garden City, N.Y.: Image Books, 1961]).

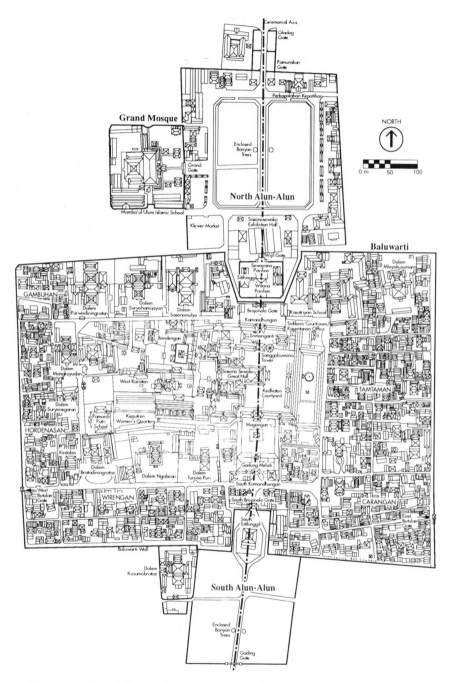

Figure 10. Plan of the Kraton Surakarta. Drawing by Robert Cowherd.

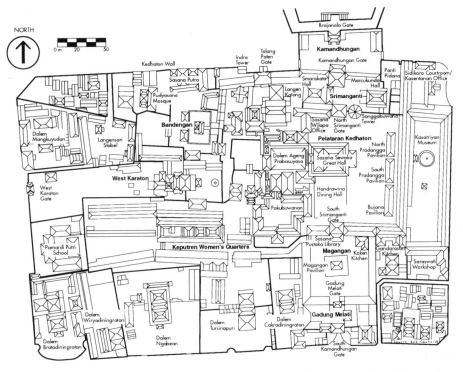

NORTH

0 m 20 50

Brajanala Gate

Kedhaton Wall

Kamandhungan

Indra Tower

Talang Paten Gate

Kamandhungan Gate

Sasana Putra

Panti Pidana

Sidikoro Courtroom/ Kasenanan Office

Pudyasana Mosque

Smarakata Hall

Marcukunda Hall

Langen Katong

Srimanganti

Dalem Mangkuyudan

Bandengan

Sasana Wilapa Office

North Srimanganti Gate

Sanggabuwana Tower

Langensari Stabel

Pelataran Kedhaton

Kasatriyan Museum

Dalem Ageng Prabasuyasa

Sasana Sewaka Great Hall

North Pradangga Pavilion

West Karaton

South Pradangga Pavilion

West Karaton Gate

Pakubuwanan

Handrawina Dining Hall

South Srimanganti Gate

Bujana Pavilion

Pamardi Putri School

Keputren Women's Quarters

Sasana Pustaka Library

Magangan

Koken Kitchen

Gandarasan Kitchen

Saraswati Workshop

Magangan Pavilion

Gadung Melati Gate

Dalem Wiryodiningratan

Dalem Tursinapuri

Dalem Cakradiningratan

Gadung Melati

Dalem Bratadiningratan

Dalem Ngabean

South Kamandhungan Gate

Figure 11. Plan of the Kedhaton: Kraton Surakarta. Drawing by Robert Cowherd.

Projecting its own significant future,
the poem dates the present of its
writing. An invocation to Allah and
His Prophet.

I. Dhangdhanggula/Sarkara
[Melodic mood is lithe, with didactic clarity and romantic allure]

1 Thus do I render the brilliant exemplar
In sweet meter to cheer
Troubled hearts with light
Ever commending the way to life felicitous
The vehicle of true being
The excellent virtuous man
The ground of becoming
Formed in subtle sign
This *Babad Jaka Tingkir* is composed
That it be a talisman[1]

2 It was Sunday when this writing of history began
The twenty-second of Safar
At the strike of eleven
The reigning star was
Jupiter at that time
The year was Jimawal
In Sancaya's eight-year turn
In the third month of the solar year
On the sixteenth, in chronogram:
"The Excellent sage
Orders the Enormity of the World"
[1757][2]

---

1. In line 2, "sweet meter" renders the Kawi *sarkara* "sugar." Insofar as Sarkara is another name for the ten-line Dhangdhanggula meter, the line also reads, "in Dhangdhanggula meter to cheer," and composes an internal melodic signal to the poem's reader. In line 5, the polysemic Kawi *wahana*, rendered as "vehicle," could also be read as "meaning" or as "screen." In line 7, the word *tumuwuh*, rendered as "becoming," could also be read as "development" or "creation."

In the final line of the stanza, I translate the word *pusaka* as "talisman." A *pusaka* is a thing or activity (or a class of things or activities) endowed with supernatural power(s). The *pusaka*'s powers may be available to the one who owns or

---

holds it. *Pusaka* are heritable property, often passed down as family heirlooms.
2. The Javanese text uses the Arabic name Mustari for the planet Jupiter. Safar is the second month of the Moslem/Javanese lunar calendar. Javanese time-reckoning marks four repeating eight-year cycles; these eight-year periods are called *windu*. Jimawal is the third of the eight years in any *windu*. The (Indic) solar year begins with the summer solstice. 22 Sapar Jimawal 1757 A.J. (23 August 1829) fell in the *windu* Sangara, not Sancaya.

The year date is in chronogram (or *sangkala*). An elaborate set of quite logical conventions indicates how to read the chronogram (back to front) as A.J. 1757: "sang mahamuni (7), anata (5), goraning (7), rat (1)." Mountains are associated with the number seven. Because sages (*mahamuni*) meditate on mountains, they too are "7s." *Gora* ("large" or "monstrous") is rare for "mountain" and hence a "7." *Tata* ("to order"), in Sanskrit, means "wind." In Javanese literary traditions, winds are sometimes named; those names are often prefaced with *panca*

3   In the year of the Prophet's Hijrah
Chronogrammed: "The Sage
   Magical
Is Reverenced by all the World"
   [1237]
In the Dutch month of August
On the twenty-third rendered
In chronogram: "Ever Reverenced
Is the Person of the King" [1829]
The object of worship
Is none but the Lord Creator
Ruler of the universe[3]

4   He who is generous in this world,
   compassionate in the next
Who created the seven levels of the
   earth
And the stars of the seven heavens
The contents of the entire world
Spread He forth over heaven and
   earth
Ordered by propriety
That there be order
To the ranks of creation
Created perfect was everything
In a space of six days

5   Then fashioning His throne
It was the Will of the Almighty
   and All-high
To teach His creatures
All the works
Of men minded by the principle
Let there be none of spirit savage
Nor of deed impetuous
May all observe the rule
Of order with wills open
To ever emergent time[4]

6   With the completion of my adora-
   tion
Of the Divine Lord Beloved of the
   World
Next comes worship of the Apostle
Of God Most-High
The revered Prophet Muhammad-
   dinil
Allah's chosen beloved
Chief of the apostles
Seal of the prophets
Master of the universe, torch of the
   world
Viceroy of God

7   Divine Light of the world, sign of
   the Almighty
For indeed creation's source
Is the Light of Muhammad in truth
O may
Always the Almighty's grace
The blessings of God
And His love

("5"). *Rat* ("world") is a totality and
hence a "1."

3. The chronogram for the Hijrah year of
1237 (= A.J. 1749 and A.D. 1821–22) is:
"pandhita (7) aguna (3) sinembah (2) ing
jagad (1)." The chronogram for the Gregorian year of 1829 is: "trus (9) sinembah
(2) sariraning (8) ratu (1)." 23 August
1829 (= 22 Sapar Jimawal 1757) fell in
A.H. 1245, not A.H. 1237. A.H. 1237 (= A.J.
1749) fell neither in *windu* Sancaya nor in
windu Sengara, but in yet another *windu*,
that is, Kunthara). And, according to the
calendrical system standardized in 1855,
the sixteenth of the third solar month
falls on 9/10 September.

4. The word rendered as "rule" in line 8 is
ukara, a word that also designates "order"
and rarely "greed." It is perhaps most
widely used as a linguistic or grammatical
term denoting "sense, sentence, syntax"
or, more generally, "correct grammar."

Be shed upon
The Prophet Muhammad, the
   chosen one
And on his lineage too[5]

8   And on his foremost associates
Sayid Abu Bakar
And Sayid 'Umar, and again
Sayid 'Usman
The fourth being Sayid 'Ali
All of these were caliphs
Viceroys of the Prophet
Who continued the works
Of the revered Prophet, spreading
   the faith
Bringing order to the world

9   And so having finished
Perfectly complete the invocation
Rendered in intricate substruction
In melodies entwined
Are interruptions in Java's story
The History of Java
The exploits
Of all the kings rendered in song
After the era of Sri Kalaraja-papati
Déwaraja then[6]

*Introduces Brawijaya V, the last king
Majapahit: his genealogy and his
vanishing into Perfection.*

10   He who closed that era
As His Royal Highness the King
Called the Little Prince as a boy
Reigned as His Majesty
Brawijaya the Fifth indeed
In the realm of Majapahit
Complete one hundred years
Was the age of that realm
Seven generations reigned as king
In the land of Majapahit[7]

———

Majapahit") and its relation to *Jangka
Jayabaya* prophecies, see chapter 3.
7. On Brawijaya V's names: the king's
name as a boy was Radèn Alit ("Prince
Little"); upon ascent to the throne, he
took the kingly name Prabu Brawijaya
("His Majesty Lord Victorious").

   Javanese proper names, royal or otherwise, are notably unstable. A person is
likely to assume a new name upon
achieving a new station in life: upon majority, marriage, career promotion, etc.
And, at any one time, a single person may
be known by a variety of proper names.
Proper names often semantically inscribe
a person's real or desired attributes.

   Royal names are prefixed by an array
of hierarchically graded royal titles. The
relatively common royal title *Radèn*
("Prince") could be used up to the fifth-
(or sometimes sixth-) generation descendant of a king. The title *Prabu* ("King" or
"His Majesty") was exclusive to mon-
archs.

   Majapahit ("bitter *maja* fruit") is the
name of a renowned East Javanese imperial kingdom which enjoyed hegemony
in the Indonesian archipelago in the fourteenth century.

5. *Nur Mukhammad* ("The Light of Muhammad") in line 3 is a key term in Islamic mysticism (see Annemarie Schimmel, *And Muhammad Is His Messenger*
[Chapel Hill: University of North Carolina Press, 1985], pp. 123–43). On the significance of Nur Mukhammad in Javano-
Islamic mysticism, especially as concerns
mystical cosmogony, see Dr. P. J. Zoetmulder, *Pantheisme en Monisme in de Javaansche Soeloek-Litteratuur* (Nijmegen:
J. J. Berkhout, 1935), pp. 181–83.
6. On the "proper name" Sri Kalaraja-
papati Déwaraja (meaning "kingship in

11   It began of old with King Suruh
      Who upon his death was succeeded
         by his son
      Lord Younger King, his name
      For those two
      Bore not the Brawijaya name
      Then with his son
      Began the name:
      Lord Brawijaya the First
      Whose son was named Brawijaya
         the Second
      Whose son again

12   Was named Brawijaya the Third
      Whose son was named Brawijaya
      The Fourth
      With the Little Prince
      As Brawijaya the Fifth
      The seven generations were com-
         plete
      Now to be related here
      Is an interrupted tale:
      With the Fall of Majapahit
      Was Brawijaya's vanishing

13   Vanished from the mortal realm
      Surging up in lightning body
      He rose to the realm of Release
      Not by way of death
      True return consummate
      To the realm divinely pure
      In absolute perfection
      His Majesty Brawijaya
      Perfectly realized *Jatimurti*
      Knowing the Whence and
         Whither[8]

8. In line 3, the "realm of Release" is
muksapada (the place of *muksa* and/or
moksa). oj *muksa* means "to vanish or

14   Not blind to the revelation of life
      Life which is eternal
      The magnitude of pleasure
      In the true *kraton*
      Truly is incalculable
      For 'tis countless times greater
      Than that enjoyed when still
      In the mortal realm
      It is said that the King's Release
      Was in company of his courtiers

15   The mighty Vizier Gajahmada
      With all the ministers and princes
      The courtiers both high and low
      All his subjects
      Those who were adept
      At realization of Release
      Not blind to knowledge
      Accepted into Emptiness
      Could follow their king in Release
      The ignorant could not

———

disappear"; whereas oj *moksa* (from the
Sanskrit) means "final liberation from the
bonds of the cycle of rebirth in the
world." In modern Javanese usage, the
verb *muksa* means to ascend to heaven
body and soul, often by vanishing in a
blaze of light.
   The compound *jatimurti* (line 9), "Reality Incarnate" or "Body of Reality,"
denotes a state of material-spiritual enlightenment. The phrase "Whence and
Whither" in the final line translates *sangkan paran*, a key term in Javanese mysticism. *Sangkan-paran* indicates the unity
of the ultimate source (*sangkan*,
"whence") and the ultimate destination
(*paran*, "whither") of life. In the present
context, that unity is *jatimurti*, the Reality Incarnate of man-in-God.

16 Be it in days bygone or be it now
    One who knows no discipline
    Is struck down by disaster
    Weeping in the end
    An ignorant fool, oblivious to the
        secret
    The secret of the sage
    The supreme knowledge
    The knowledge of Release
    Coming to the end, the ignoramus
        meets with doom
    Not so for the adepts

17 Following the king were about
    One-third Majapahit's court
    Just the aged ones
    The young were charged to stay
        behind
    To propagate their seed
    Charged were they to surrender
    To embrace divine Islam
    Except for those who had already
    Surrendered in their hearts, keep-
        ing holy Islam
    Were converts to the faith

18 But fortune was fair for those left
        behind
    Who could not follow in Release
    For they exchanged religions
    These infidels of Buda's way
    Taking on the Lord's religion
    Were converts to the faith
    Of Islam excellent
    The vanishing of Buda's way
    With the Fall of Majapahit
    Is rendered in chronogram thus:[9]

9. *Buda,* in Javanese, does not specifically
designate *the* Buddha. "Buda's way," my

19 "Gone, Vanished without a trace
        are the Works of the World"
        [1400][10]

*Treats the advent of a new era: the
ascendancy of Demak. New authority establishes new realms.*

    With that the era was changed
    To the "Age of Dark Oppression,"
        the world
    Of "Beautiful Hearts"
    In three lands were there realms
    In Bonang, Giri, and Demak
    The senior lord
    Was called the Pundit-king
    His Majesty Sovereign of the
        World
    Yea, Lord Sunan Bonang[11]

———

translation of "tata Buda," denotes the
multiplicity of pre- (and non-) Islamic
religious complexes in Java (Buddhism,
Hinduism, animism, and syncretic blends
of the three).
10. The chronogram reads: "sirna (o)
ilang (o) pakartining (4) bumi (1)" (Saka
1400 = A.D. 1478).
11. The proper names "Age of Dark Oppression" (Kalawisaya) and "Beautiful
Hearts" (Adiyati) in lines 2 and 3 are
drawn from the corpus of prophetic *Jangka Jayabaya* texts, where they refer to
the Demak period of Javanese dynastic
history. See discussion below, chapter 3,
pp. 272–75. Although the OJ *wisaya*
means "realm, dominion, kingdom; object of affection or of the senses; the visible world; passion" (Zoetmulder, 2:2296–
97), in nineteenth-century usage *wisaya*
was understood more darkly as "oppression; wrongdoing; evil; trickery" (C. F.
Winter Sr. [with R.Ng. Ronggawarsita]),

20 His title, Honored Body of Sub-
        limity
    Yea, Splendid Virgin Maharaja
    Celibate for all time
    Reigned as Axial Saint
    "He who Cleanses the Earth, Axis
        of Piety"
    His hermitage in Bonang
    Was silent and empty
    Built like a walled enclosure

Kawi-Javaansch Woordenboek [Batavia,
1880], p. 287).
    Bonang (rendered as Bénang in the
Javanese text), is the name of a town in
northern Central Java. But Bénang here
probably refers to Tuban, a coastal town
in northern East Java (see note to XVII:4).
Giri refers to the East Javanese town of
Gresik. Demak is the name of a town in
northern Central Java.
    I have translated the proper name/title
Prabu Anyakrakusumèng Bumi as "His
Majesty Sovereign of the Earth." The
name/title Anyakrakusuma, designating
(universal) overlordship, was also an ap-
pelation of the renowned Sultan Agung,
ruler of Mataram (1613–45).
    Sunan, and its variants *Susuhunan,
Susunan, Sinuhun* (from the root *suhun,*
"to honor and revere; to hold above one's
head") is a title which translates as "he
who is revered." Originally, the title of
Sunan was apparently restricted to the
hierarchy of Islamic saints (*wali*). Since
the eighteenth century, this title has been
used exclusively by the supreme rulers of
the Mataram dynasty. Since the partition
of Mataram into the realms of Surakarta
and Yogyakarta in 1755, the title has been
the exclusive right of the rulers of the
Kraton Surakarta. Official Dutch documents translate *Susuhunan* as *Keizer* (emperor).

A fortress: it was the beautiful fort
Truly the revered Capital of the
    World[12]

21 Now the second king
    Brother-in-law to Sunan Bonang
    Named His Majesty the Watchful
        One
    Reigned as "First among Kings"
    He was Lord Sunan Giri
    Mustafa Purbaningrat

12. "Honored Body of Sublimity" translates the title Sang Mahadimurti. "Splendid Virgin Maharaja" translates Sri
Mahanaréndra Wadat.
    "Axial Saint" translates the Sufi term
wali kutub. The wali kutub, "the saint
who is the hidden axis," is the greatest of
saints, on whom all existence metaphysi-
cally depends (see Marshall G. S.
Hodgson, *The Venture of Islam* [Chicago:
University of Chicago Press, 1974],
2:227–30). However, in the context of
this poem, an Axial Saint is a member of
the hierarchy of nine saints (*wali*) said to
have wielded spiritual and political authority over Java at that time. "He who
Cleanses the Earth, Axis of Piety" is a
translation of the Javanized Arabic *Ghosul
Alam Kutub Rabbani.* The office of Wali
Kutub Rabbani Ghosul Alam is the highest position in the hierarchy of saints
(*ridjal al-Ghayb*) both in Sufi cosmology
and in the spiritual-political structure
outlined in this poem. See also below, *BJT*
XIII:21 ff.
    "Capital of the World" conveys the
sense of *Hadiningrat* ("Finest in the
World"). Hadiningrat, the suffix attached
to the names of Central Javanese court
cities of the Pakubuwana (Axis of the
World) and the Hamengkubuwana (Sovereign of the World) kings, conveys the
universal pretensions of these polities.

Named Axial Saint
He was the "Pillar of Axial Saints"
Foremost in rule and authority was
he
In the world of Java's land[13]

22 He adorned the beautiful palace of
Giri
Yea, the Palace of Elephant Moun-
tain
Now the third king
Who was viceroy to
These two Revered Sunans
Made his seat in the land of Demak
Heir to the kingship
The son of Lord Brawijaya
Made successor to Java's *kraton*
Was the Prince-regent of Bintara[14]

23 They who installed him as king
Were the revered *wali* saints
With the weighty pundits
All the mighty Moslem faithful
Of Java bore witness
That the Prince of Bintara
Changing his title
From Lord of Palèmbang
Henceforth would be called: Pa-
nembahan Bintara
And further would be granted the
name[15]

24 Sénapati Jimbun, who, as
The Prophet's Caliph in Demak's
realm
Would rule over all Java
His ascent to kingship
Is chronogrammed: "The Fire
Went out
Showered by the King" [1403]
Falling silent now
On he who reigned in Demak

13. "His Majesty the Watchful One"
translates the name Prabu Satmata. For a
detailed discussion of this name, see
G. W. J. Drewes, *An Early Code of Muslim
Ethics* (The Hague: Nijhoff, 1978), pp. 71–
73. "First among Kings" translates the
office Ratu Tunggul. The name/title
Mustafa Purbaningrat, from the Arabic
mustafa and the Javanese *purbaningrat*,
could be translated: "Chosen Authority
of the World."

"Pillar" (line 8) is a translation of the
Sufi term *aotad* from the Arabic *awtad*
(pillars, stakes). In Sufi cosmology the
aotad indicate the four saints by whom
the four corners of the world are supported. In the hierarchy of the nine saints
as systematized in this poem, the office of
Wali Kutub Aotad is the second-ranking
position.

14. "Elephant mountain" is a translation
of Giri-Aliman. "Prince-regent" (in the
final line) is a translation of the title
Adipati. An Adipati was a semiautono-

mous ruler. Bintara is another name for
Demak.

15. The *wali* or *waliyullah* "friend(s) of
God, saint(s)" are the group of (usually
nine) lords to whom the Islamization of
Java is attributed. *Pundits* (line 3) translates the Sanskrit derived word *pandhita*
(sage, scholar, holy man), a term consistently used in this text to designate scholars or sages of Islam. "Moslem faithful"
(line 4) is a translation of *mukmin*, Arabic
for "the faithful."

The Javanese royal title Panembahan
means literally: the one to whom the
sembah (act of obeisance) is appropriate.
The title Panembahan is higher in the
hierarchy of court titles than is Adipati
("Prince-regent").

No more is said again turning the
    telling
To return to the tale[16]

A catalog of Brawijaya's progeny.
Particular note is paid to his son-in-
law, Handayaningrat, Central Java-
nese king of Pajang-Pengging and
ancestor to Jaka Tingkir. Traces of
the Princes and Princesses of Maja-
pahit mark the Javanese landscape,
forming a background against which
we expect Jaka Tingkir to emerge.

25   Recounted in narrative is the tale
    Of the last of the Brawijayas
    'Tis said that many were his chil-
      dren
    Born of his senior queen
    The King's first wife
    The Princess of Champa
    Whose beauty it is said
    Was unsurpassed on earth
    Her Majesty's name, Queen Dwa-
      rawati
    She of whom the tale is told

26   Possessed a mystic aura of beauty
    Every day transfigured seven times
      again
    Changing and rechanging ever was
      her form
    Three were her children

16. The title Sénapati designates "a military commander, a commanding general."
The word *jimbun* means "very old." The
chronogram in lines 6–7 reads: "dahana
(3) mati (0) siniram (4) ing naréndra (1)"
(Saka 1403 = A.D. 1481).

But the survivors are to be drawn
Drawn not are they who died
Now the eldest
The King's first-born
A daughter named Her Highness
    Ratu Pembayun
Was exceedingly beautiful[17]

27   Inheriting from her mother
    Tinges of beauty's mystic aura
    Her lustrous aura striking
    She married
    The King of Pajang-Pengging
    His Majesty King Handayaningrat
    With magic powers wonderful
    Heroic invincible
    A mighty warrior: many the for-
      eign kings who perished
    Downed on the field of battle[18]

28   In yesteryear when marching off
      to battle
    The King was still a youth
    It all began with Bali's king
    When he did rebel
    Spurning submission to Java
    King Kala Gerjita
    Bali's greatest king
    For three years then
    Had sent no tribute offerings
    To Majapahit

29   Making alliances with other realms
    Prepared an attack on Majapahit

17. The proper name Ratu Pembayun
means "First-born Queen."
18. The name Handayaningrat could be
translated as "He Who Wields Power
over the World."

Thirty thousand were his troops
Balambangan was beaten
Bali's troops carried the day
The Lords of the Eastern Provinces all
Were defeated in the field
For the Balinese at that time were
Graced with victory at war
The Javanese were shaken deep[19]

30 When westward marched the Bali-
      nese
    Then the troops of Majapahit
    Who came to meet their battle
    Were swept away in ruinous dis-
      array
    Not one of them could retaliate
    The great men's hearts were like
      unto
    Women, all of them
    None possessed of bravery

In terror they watched the cham-
  pions of Bali
Rouse rapturous love in battle[20]

II. Asmarandana
[Melodic mood is one of sorrow or
longing]

1 Thereat His Majesty the King
   Brawijaya of Majapahit
   Was anguished, his heart like
     blossom torn
   With ever swelling grief
   And Vizier Gajahmada too
   In ever deepening distress
   His heart in thrall was in turmoil
     rapt

2 Accordingly King Brawijaya
   Plighting his troth
   A contest did proclaim
   Whosoever could oblige
   To drive back the warriors
   Balinese effecting their surrender
   Would be taken as royal son-in-
     law

3 Becoming wedded husband to
   The first-born daughter of the King

19. Perhaps the Balinese king remembered here was Baturènggong of Gèlgèl,
whose sixteenth-century kingdom
stretched from Blambangan in the west
and Sumbawa in the east; see Adrian
Vickers, *Bali: A Paradise Created* (Berkeley: Periplus, 1989), pp. 41–49.
    "Eastern Provinces" is my translation
of *bang wétan*. Premodern Javanese
realms consisted of a core region (*negara
gung*) surrounded by outer provinces
(*mancanegara*). These outer provinces
were divided into eastern and western
sections, which were considered in balance (*timbang*) with each other. Hence
the terms *Bang Wétan* ("Eastern Balance"
or "Eastern Provinces") and *Bang Kulon*
("Western Balance" or "Western Provinces").

20. That the final line of this verse makes
minimal narrative sense is of little conse-
quence; its sense pertains rather to the
poem's melody and meter. *Asmara*, the
"rapturous love" roused in battle, points
to the verse form Asmarandana ("giving
love"). Hence, the line (in conjunction
with a dramatic visual sign punctuating
the end of one canto and beginning of another) alerts the reader/singer to change
her song to Asmarandana.

Many were the kings
Who came to aid in battle
Entering the contest
Wishing to be son-in-law
To the King of Majapahit

4 For the Princess was exceptional
Her beauty incomparable
Like the goddess Supraba lighted
    on the earth
Then came King Handayaningrat
Forward to the field
Triumphant he did the battle win
Defeated were the men of the float-
    ing isle[21]

5 The King of Bali surrendered
Then King Handayaningrat
Ranged far in pursuit of conquest
Setting his sails eastward
He made for the Isle of Sembawa
Beaten in battle, surrender did
The kings of all Sembawa

6 King Handayaningrat then
Made straight for the Isle of Pra-
    guwa
Worsted in battle, its king
Surrendered and offered tribute

Then His Illustrious Majesty
Set sail for the mighty island
Called the Celebes[22]

7 Making for Makasar of the Bugis
On the island called the Celebes
King Handayaningrat arriving did
    attack
Its kings in battle were worsted all
After they surrendered then
King Handayaningrat straightway
Setting out again, sailed on

8 His Highness of Pajang-Pengging
Making for Ternaté and Manila
Ranged far in pursuit of conquest
The kings of Ternaté and Manila
Did surrender all of them
Then His Majesty
Set sail for the ancient lands[23]

22. The island of Praguwa is unknown to
me. Celebes (*Selèbes*) was the colonial
toponym for the island now known as
Sulawesi.

23. Ternaté and Manila, of what are now
the Moluccas and the Philippines, are not
separated by a conjunction in the original
Javanese, perhaps suggesting the historical memory of a closer relationship in the
past between these polities that came
later to belong to separate colonies and
then to separate nation states.

"Ancient lands" at verse's close is *tanah
purwa* in the original Javanese. OJ *purwa*
means "east(ern)" as well as "ancient."
However, insofar as Kalimantan/Borneo
is west of Ternaté and southwest of Manila, the poet may understand *purwa* as
"west" (see II:10).

21. Supraba is the most beautiful of the
seven heavenly nymphs. These nymphs
sometimes appear in Javanese literary
texts (including the oral texts of the *wayang*, shadow-puppet theater) to tempt
meditating heroes. The "floating isle" (final line) is my translation of *nusa Kambangan*. There is off the southern coast
of West Java a small island called Nusa
Kambangan. Most likely meant here,
however, is the island of Bali.

9   Coming to the Isle of Borneo
    The realm of Banjarmas did fall
    Fallen its king surrendered
    Along with all his vassals
    All the kings of Borneo
    Surrendered themselves in bonds
    To King Handayaningrat

10 Thereafter His Majesty
    Knight Errant Handayaningrat
    Did set sail for west
    Coming to an island great and long
    Called the Isle of Sumatra
    He made for the mighty capital
       Palèmbang
    Whose king, worsted in battle[24]

11 Fell in the fighting's midst
    What troops survived surrendered
       all
    So having ranged then everywhere
    Penetrating each and every realm
    Beaten all, they did surrender
    Making offerings of tribute
    And so it was thereafter

12 The Luminous King of Pajang-
       Pengging
    Along with all his troops set sail
    Returning home to Java
    Made for Majapahit
    Now then not to be rendered
    In elaboration are the ceremonies
    Knight Errant Handayaningrat

24. In line 2, the title "Knight Errant"
translates the Javanese *kalana*. OJ *kalana*
is "an adventurer of noble birth wandering abroad."

   In line 3, geography demanded "west"
as a translation of *purwa* (normally "east"
or "ancient"); see note to II:8 above.

13 Was wed to the Princess
    Blissful was their marriage
    So very enamored were they
    Falling silent here: not to be ren-
       dered
    At length are their doings
    Lest too lengthy the telling
    That is hunted by the tale

14 Sketching one by one
    The royal children of Majapahit
    That they be accounted all
    The writer begs forgiveness
    For having forgotten the order
    Of younger and elder born
    Offers but the best her rapture
       births

15 The Princess's younger brother
    Was a handsome lad
    His name, Lembu Peteng
    Born too of the Cham Princess
    He was planted in Madura
    By his father granted the title
    Prince-regent of Madura[25]

25. The titles Lembu ("cow") and Kebo
("buffalo") were standard for high-born
male figures in Old and Middle Javanese
texts. The name Lembu Peteng means
"dark cow." Although this "dark cow" is
Brawijaya's legitimate child by a queen,
"lembu peteng" had, by the nineteenth
century, become a generic label for illegitimate and unacknowledged royal
children.

   The word "plant" is a literal translation
of the Javanese *tanem*, an agricultural
term that was used administratively to
designate the court's installation of officials (especially regent-princes, or *adipati*)
in the provinces.

16 Then came his younger sister
    Born too of the Cham Princess
    An exceptional beauty
    Named Ratu Mas Rara
    Devoted to her older sister, she was
    Adopted by the First-born Queen
    This sister was as though her
        child[26]

17 Following to Pajang-Pengging
    The maid, when she came of age
    Fell in love with her brother-in-law
    His Majesty the King, Handaya-
        ningrat
    Was incomparably handsome
    None would she regard
    Save her brother the King

18 Loath to be wed
    When pressed by her parents
    The lovely jewel was adamant
    Regarding but her brother
    Forgoing food and sleep
    In melancholy her body grew thin
    Fading in transport's ecstasy

19 Her elder sister, the Queen
    Of Pengging knew well
    Whither inclined the heart's desire
    Of Ratu Mas Rara
    Her heart sorely troubled
    Ever did she her little sister com-
        fort
    But 'twas all to no avail

20 Unwavering was her passion, of
        rapt intent

26. The proper name Ratu Mas Rara (line
4) means "Her Highness the Maiden
Queen."

But unrequited was this love
Thus the maiden's resolve
Bethinking not her parents
With no regard for kith and kin
Considering nothing save her
    shame
The lovely jewel took her life

21 The Princess died a suicide
    Wherefore to this very day
    The Princess's grave is known
    As "Grave of the Suicide Maid"
    Lying to the east of the palace
    Of Pengging at the edge of the
        spring
    Called the "Spring of the Suicide
        Maid"

22 Now the telling turns again:
    Brawijaya's son
    Named Prince Jaka Damar
    Whose mother was a demon maid
    Was planted in Palèmbang
    By his father granted the title
    High Prince Damar of Palèmbang[27]

23 Was sent forth with subjects, both
        male and female
    Numbering five-hundred house-
        holds
    And was granted authority

27. The name Jaka, which means "unmarried youth," is common as the first part of
a (young) man's name. The name Damar
means "torch" or "light."
    With "High Prince" (final line), I trans-
late the high royal honorific Harya. According to Kraton Surakarta rules of rank
and title, use of the title Harya is restricted to certain adult males in the first
two generations of descent from a king.

To sound the gong Lokananta
And authority to bear
The visible signs of kingship:
Only certain of them to be sure[28]

24 Presenting himself yearly
At the court of Majapahit
High Prince Damar, as the tale goes
Was he who spawned all the kings
And all the nobles
And all the mighty regents
Of Palèmbang and its vassals[29]

25 And further it is said
That Lord High Prince Damar
Was ancestor to
Sunan Candhibalang
Lord of Palèmbang
A king with magic powers wonder-
ful

Was His Majesty Sunan Candhibalang[30]

26 Now the telling is turned again
To a son of Brawijaya
Who, named Bathara Katong
Was planted in Panaraga
He it was who propagated
The nobles and the notables
Of Panaraga all

27 There were yet other children
Of His Highness Brawijaya
Two of them both daughters
Both born of a lower wife
Of one mother and one father
One of them was wed to
The Prince-regent of Lowanu[31]

28. Lokananta is the name of a sacred gong (and by synecdoche, the name of the *gamelan* ensemble of which that gong is a part) belonging to the Kraton Surakarta. The royal courts of colonial Java had highly developed and codified systems prescribing forms of deference (linguistic and behavioral) and paraphernalia of deference (i.e., ceremonial sunshades, royal regalia, etc.). Students of Indonesian society often call this system of deference the *hormat* system (see Heather Sutherland, *The Making of a Bureaucratic Elite* [Singapore: Heinemann, 1979]). Here the poet indicates that High Prince Damar was granted the extraordinary privilege of bearing designated items of royal *upacara* (ceremonial objects of state, e.g., golden spittoon, jeweled cock, etc.).
29. Prince Damar, as evidenced by his yearly trips to East Java, was in a tributary relationship to Majapahit's king. In turn, under-kings (in Sumatra?) paid tribute to him.

30. Sunan Candhibalang is Suhunan Abdurrahman, who ruled Palèmbang in the second half of the seventeenth century. He was the first ruler of Palèmbang to take the title "sultan" and the first to have an Arabic name. The construction of the Old Mosque of Palèmbang is attributed to him (H. J. de Graaf and Th. G. Th. Pigeaud, *De Eerste Moslimse Vorstendommen op Java* [The Hague: Nijhoff, 1974], p. 205, and M. O. Woelders, *Het Sutanaat Palembang, 1811–1825* [The Hague, 1975], pp. 118 and 487).
31. In line 4, I translate the Javanese *ampéyan* as "lower wife." Often mistranslated as "concubine"; there is, however, no English equivalent that might designate this connubial status. Modern Javanese kings can/could have as many as four primary wives (*pramèswari*) and countless *ampéyan* (or *prayantun-dalem*). Many of these women are legally wed by the king for shorter or longer periods of time in order to provide legitimacy to their children. Since by Islamic law any one man is permitted no more than four

28 The other one was married
    To the Prince-regent of Gawong
    There was yet another child
    Of His Highness Brawijaya
    Born again of a lower wife
    He was a handsome boy
    His mother hailed from Wan-
        dhan[32]

---

wives at a time, the women may be (and
often are) divorced again when the preg-
nancies of other of the king's *ampéyan*
call for legitimizing. An *ampéyan* who
bears a king several children may, then,
be repeatedly married and divorced by
him. These marriages are contracted in
the Kraton Surakarta, with what is (now)
known as "the traveling marriage license." Though legally married by Islamic law (*ningkah*), these minor wives
are not married to the king by Kraton
ceremony. The children of recognized
ampéyan are acknowledged as legitimate
princes and princesses, though lower
ranking than the children of a queen.

Lowanu (final line) was the name of a
region in western Central Java, comprising parts of Purwareja, Bagelèn, Banyumas, Pasisir Kilèn (B. Schrieke, *Indonesian Sociological Studies*, vol. 2 [The
Hague: W. van Hoeve, 1957], pp. 183–
85).

32. Gawong in line 2 must be Gowong, a
region in western Central Java: Gowong,
Bagelèn, Pasisir Kilèn (ibid., pp. 181, and
184–85).

The word *wandhan* designates "a wool-
ly haired negro, a Papuan" (GR 2:9). The
Mataram dynasty traces its descent to
this Wandhan woman. Because she is
their putative ancestress, Javanese royalty
have been invested in ongoing speculation concerning her ethnic identity. Some
of her royal descendants have hypothe-
sized that the Wandhan people composed
a mainland Southeast Asian "hill tribe."

29 Indeed the golden princess of
        Wandhan
    To narrate from the start
    The golden princess of Wandhan
    Was handmaiden to
    The Queen from Champa
    Her Highness Queen Dwarawati
    The golden one of Wandhan was a
        captive maid

30 A gift from her father the King
    Of Champa back when Wandhan's
        realm
    Fell in fighting to her father
    Surrender did its king
    Offering up his tribute
    And offering his daughter too
    To be carried off a captive

31 Then bestowed upon his daughter
    She was carried off to Majapahit
    After some time, it is related of
    His Majesty Brawijaya
    That his penis was afflicted
    Syphilitic was His Majesty
    He suffered so exceedingly

32 Incurable by medicine
    All the physicians did
    Exhaust their stores of remedies
    But none of them availed
    The King grew ever worse
    His heart was racked with grief
    Thousandfold was the Sovereign's
        woe[33]

33. An oblique cue at the close of the
verse, in conjunction with the punctuation mark for a new canto directly behind
it, signals the reader/singer to change to
the verse form of Sinom, which is also

III. Sinom, Srinata
[Melodic mood is "even"; appropriate for narrative]

1   One night the King lay down to
      sleep
    No sooner had he shut his eyes
      than
    He heard a voice so faint
    That voice's words rang clear
    "O King of Majapahit
    If you will recover
    Then lay you with
    The golden princess of Wandhan
    And after you have lain with her

2   "Your affliction shall be cured"
    The King awakened with a start
    In dazed silence he pondered hard
    Feeling his pain intense
    Not to be described here
    Is what His Majesty did
    For after having lain
    With the golden princess of Wan-
      dhan
    Cured was the Illustrious Lord's
      disease

3   That the princess of Wandhan then
    Was got with child was reported to
      the King
    When her time came she gave
      birth
    To a handsome boy
    But His Majesty the King
    Was more than mortified
    To acknowledge as his son

———

known as Srinata (Sri Nata = "The Sovereign").

The issue of the golden Wandhan
  maid
Was thus conferred upon the
  keeper of the fields

4   Stealing out a back gate
    Not a soul knew of it
    Commanded to avow the child
    His own was the keeper of the
      fields
    Not to be rendered here
    Are his exploits at length
    The Prince named
    Bondhan Kajawèn and called
    Prince Lembu Peteng resided in
      Tarub[34]

34. OJ *bondhan* designates a group of servants, or slaves, possibly of Papuan origin
(Zoetmulder 1:251). The name Bondhan
Kajawèn could be translated as "Javanized
[foreign] slave" (see also note to II:29
above). R. Bondhan Kajawèn (Lembu Peteng) is ancestor to the Mataram dynasty:
R. Bondhan Kajawèn → Ki Ageng Getas-
pandhawa → Ki Ageng Séla → Ki Ageng
Enis → Ki Ageng Pamanahan → Panembahan Sénapati. Tarub is a village in the
region of Grobogan, district of Séla, to
the northeast of Surakarta.
    In the "Major Babad" tradition, this
gift of an unwanted royal child to the
keeper of the rice fields is contingent
upon the keeper's promise to put that
child to death upon his eighth birthday. In
this tradition, it is not because of shame
that Brawijaya casts off his son, rather it
is to avert a prophesied danger to the
realm (*Babad Tanah Jawi*, 31 vols.
[Batavia: Bale Pustaka, 1939–41], 2:41–
46). The foster father does not in fact
murder the boy, who lives to pay an unin-
vited visit to the palace of his birth father.
The tale of that visit (ibid., 2:72–73) is

5 Let none misunderstand
All ye who would strive
To know well the tale
Two were the Lembu Petengs
The one born of the Queen
Who was planted in Madura
The other born of a lower wife
Who lived in Tarub to be sure
Again there was a son from a sanc-
    tioned union[35]

6 Born of the Chinese Princess
She was indeed a primary wife
Daughter of China's King
Queen of Majapahit
But junior queen was she
The Princess of Champa was senior
This Queen from China
It is told was conceived of child
When seven-months pregnant, the
    King

7 His heart filled with aversion
Did hate the very sight of her
And so the Princess of China
He gave in marriage to his son
High Prince Damar was charged
"Enjoy her not in bed
Before her time has come
And the babe is born
Once born, do with her as you
    will"

8 Carried off to Palèmbang
Was the Princess in her pregnancy
Coming to term, she gave birth
To a handsome son
Who was given the name
Prince Patah was the name
Indeed of the young
Panembahan Bintara
Again there was a son by a lower
    wife[36]

9 Jaran Panolih, by name
Was placed by his father the King
In the realm of Sumenep
Again three children more were
    there
Of a single father and mother
Born were they of a lower wife
The eldest was a son
Prince Gugur was he called
The second-born was a son again[37]

10 Prince Jaka Tèki was his name
Next born was a daughter
Ratu Tumus was her name
Though already come of age, the
    Princess
Would not marry
This beauty preferred maidenhood
Now let it be recited:

---

reminiscent of the Jaka Karèwèd story below (*BJT* X:30 ff.).
35. I have opted for "to know well" as a
translation of *mamerdawa* (line 3), which
could (and I think does) at the same time
mean "to take pleasure in." Concerning
the two Lembu Petengs (line 4), see note
to II:15.

36. According to Javanese historical traditions, Prince Patah (or Fatah) was to lead
the military assault that would result in
his father's death (or disappearance) and
the cataclysmic fall of Majapahit.
37. The name Jaran Panolih means
"Horse looking back." Sumenep is the
name of a polity in eastern Madura. The
name Gugur means "to fall" (before one's
time, as in battle).

In days of old, Prince Jaka Gugur
Was held by his father Brawijaya[38]

11 In the capital of Majapahit
For installed as commander of the
    troops
He answered for the safety of the
    realm
Along with his brother Prince Tèki
Now Prince Gugur, when of old
Majapahit did fall
So exceedingly deep was his shame
That he would follow his royal
    father
In Release ascending with the body
    of lightning

12 His father Brawijaya
Would not hear of it
Prince Gugur was charged to stay
    behind
Together with his siblings
And admonished were they all
To surrender to their brother
But Prince Gugur instead
Chose to slip into seclusion
Disguised as commoner his royalty
    forsook[39]

13 He plunged into the wilderness
Together with his siblings
Of one mother and one father
The progress of the three

38. The name Tèki means "ascetic practice." The name Tumus means "to pass
power on" (especially via blood to one's
descendants). Ratu is the title "Queen."
39. What is forsaken here are the visible
signs (clothing, regalia, etc.) and airs of
royalty.

Came to the foot of a mountain
Called Mount Lawu
To the southwest was this moun-
    tain
Far from Majapahit
From whence it was six days' jour-
    ney

14 There Prince Jaka Gugur
Stopped with his siblings
Pleased with the land
'Twas made a place of seclusion
For intent on ascetic practice
Prince Jaka Gugur
Built a hermitage
On that mountainside
Ardent was the practice of the asce-
    tic Prince Gugur

15 On that mountainside
And his place of dwelling
Was nigh upon the hermitage
The forest cleared
Established was a settlement
Not to be described at length
Many came to settle, raising
    houses
In long lines along the mountain
    ridge
Along its passes and its valleys

16 There were one thousand houses
And to this very day
This village named for its founder
Is called Gugur
Now again it is recited
In those bygone days Prince Gugur
For long was hunted
For long remained unfound
Found after three long years

17   Summoned was he to Demak
Having embraced holy Islam
Together with his siblings two
All converts to the faith were they
But Prince Gugur still
Preferred ascetic practice
In his hermitage
As for Prince Tèki
He was placed by his brother to the
    west[40]

18   There indeed at the river fork
And his settlement
Was called the village of Tersana
As for the younger sister
By then she had been married to
The Ki Ageng of Majasta[41]

40. Some Javanese believe that Prince
Gugur is *still* meditating on Mount Lawu,
having been metamorphosed into the
spirit king Sunan Lawu, as a result of his
many years of ascetic practice. Others believe that Brawijaya V himself was transformed into this spirit king after his disappearance from Majapahit. Still others
believe that Sunan Lawu is the invisible
twin brother of Pakubuwana IX (1830–
1893). In the spirit world, Sunan Lawu is
the counterpart of, and balance to, the
spirit Queen of the South Sea, Kangjeng
Ratu Kidul.
41. The title Ki (or Kyai) Ageng (*ngoko*,
Ki Gedhé) is an honorific title for (usually) rural leaders and/or teachers. The
honorific is often followed by a toponym,
the name of the village in which the
leader holds sway. *Kyai* is notably the preferred title for leaders of (often) rural
Moslem educational institutions, or *pesantrèn*.
   Majasta is a village in southern Central
Java in the District of Klathèn just to the

*Here begins the "first episode." The
poet introduces Jaka Prabangkara,
court painter and youth of kingly
potential. Revealed are the dangers
of representation.*

Now the telling turns
To Brawijaya's child
Born of a lower wife, this hand-
    some son

19   With brilliant radiance beaming
Like the moon at its fullness
Straight of body
With golden face alluring
Tall with silken skin
Enchanting of aura subtle
Named Jaka Prabangkara
He was adept at every work
As the tale goes, this Jaka Prabang-
    kara[42]

20   Was not owned as son by
His Majesty of Majapahit
It began when His Royal Highness
Was out on pleasure tour
Disguised as commoner, the King
With no escorting retinue
With but his betel bearers

———

west of Béji on the west bank of the Solo
River. A figure named Ki Ageng Majasta
was a student of the outlaw saint Sèh
Sitijenar (see below XVIII:21) and is well
known as an early associate of Jaka Tingkir.
42. "Of aura subtle" (line 6) translates
asemu from the root *semu*. OJ *prabangkara* means "painter" and "sun" (Zoetmulder 2:1377).

His little pages two
His Highness roamed outside the
walls[43]

21   Growing tired His Majesty
Heavy-eyed did long to sleep
Just as he drew nigh the house
Of the royal butchers' chief
And so His Highness stopped
There to rest the night
Now this chief of the palace
butchers
Had a daughter oh so fair
Once married now bereft of
spouse[44]

22   One child had she born
Her late lamented husband
But perish did the babe
So now a widow
At peak of beauty's bloom
She did serve His Majesty
His Highness mad with passion
Did not restrain his lust
She the Widow Woman did His
Highness bed[45]

43. The king's pages (line 8) were from
the Semut-gatel ("itchy ant") corps, a
corps of pages (punakawan) comprised of
little boys.
44. With "chief of the royal butchers," I
translate mantri lurah jagal. In the nineteenth-century court, a mantri was a
middle-ranking courtier. In Old Javanese
usage mantri designates "minister." This
usage continues in Modern Javanese texts
with the praméya mantri.
45. I translate the appellation "Ni Mbok
Rondha" as "She the Widow Woman."
Ni/Ni Mbok are honorifics for women.
Rondha means "widow."

23   Thereafter His Sovereign Majesty
Went home behind the palace walls
Not to be rendered at length
Of the Widow Woman is the story
now:
And so conceived of child
When her time came
She gave birth
To a handsome son
Indeed this very Jaka Prabangkara

24   Serving at His Majesty's court
Was installed chief of the palace
painters
A master at the art of drawing
Commanded was he by his father
the King
To portray all
Creatures who walked
Crawled or crept the forest
Both within and without the realm
And represented were all in perfect
likeness

25   The creatures of the sea he did por-
tray
The fishes great and small
Crawling and creeping creatures
All the oceans hold
In perfect likeness
Amazed His Royal Majesty
Showered down his love
On Prabangkara the Painter
Within his heart the King already
owned him son

26   But on the surface still he kept it
veiled
And so the King thereat
Commanded him to draw the
Queen

Her Majesty Dwarawati
Finished was the portrait
To the last hair perfectly
Like the Cham Princess
Boundless was the King's delight
In rapt daze he gazed upon the
    painted portrait

27   Seemed that it might speak
Finally as His Highness's
Gaze upon her secrets lit
The beauty-mark was spied
For marked by a drop of ink
Was the painting of Ki Jaka
The King tinged with anger
Asked how this had come to pass
The answer of Ki Jaka: "Verily
    marked

28   "By a drop of ink was my painting
That I failed to scrape it clean
Your servant begs the pardon
Of his master the Lord of Men"
His Majesty was speechless
His indignation shone
Brooding in his heart
The King considered to himself
"Could this our Prabangkara know

29   "The mark then of my Queen
Inside Her Majesty's *kèn*
The *as* there bears the mark
Her beauty-mark jet black
The placing is precise
Not a shade off the spot"
By *as* is meant "vagina"
While *kèn* is the word for "skirts"[46]

Swell did the Sovereign Master's
    rage

30   He mused within his heart
"So this our Painter has
It seems, lain with
My darling Dwarawati
For he knows her mark
The beauty-mark upon her cleft
This Painter is an evil man
That he dare adultery
With such my kindness does he re-
    pay"

31   Thus it was as time did pass
Swelling was His Highness's
Rancour at this Jaka
Whenever this Jaka was espied
Wakened was the royal rage
And so the Sovereign did decide
Young Jaka the Painter
Would be murdered in the night
The King called up his vizier with a
    summons sweet[47]

*In the following verses the Grand
Vizier counsels his king on kingly
virtue and the law.*

IV. Dhangdhanggula/Sarkara
[Melodic mood is lithe, with didactic clarity and romantic allure]

———

the "difficult" Kawi words in Brawijaya's
imagined thoughts.
47. The word "sweet" (*sarkara*) at verse's
end, in conjunction with the punctuation
mark for a new canto directly behind it,
signals the reader/singer to change to the
melody of Dhangdhanggula, or Sarkara.

46. In what seems a parody of reportage,
the poet-historian offers translations of

1 Grand Vizier Gajahmada coming
   Was told the Ruler's will
   That now indeed the Painter
   Was to be murdered
   Lest ever he aggrieve the royal
      heart
   And lest always he remain
   For His Majesty a speck
   Smarting and burning his eyes
   Most aggravated both day and
      night were denied
   A peaceful sleep

2 On hearing this, His Excellency
   Gajahmada called in earnest for re-
      straint
   Many, the words he pleaded:
   "There is a saying:
   However vicious the viper
   And however ferocious the tiger
   There is none so hardened as
   To devour his very own young
   Much less should a man thus en-
      dowed with spirit
   Be so callous to his own child

3 "Whose death in truth he could not
      bear
   There is another saying still:
   Though hardened to his suffering
   None is so hard as to bear his death
   And as for Jaka the Painter
   His sin is nothing damnable
   'Tis a misunderstanding mere
   Your Highness is he who mis-
      construes
   Lacking proof, precipitate Your
      Highness rages
   With no adjudication[48]

4 "Lacking patience, Your Royal
      Highness's heart
   Acts on rash impulse
   Unseemly is this lawless rage
   Why! Your Highness is a mighty
      king
   Revered by all the world
   Said to be amply qualified
   At government accomplished
   As well as wise
   Always vigilant even glimpsing the
      concealed
   Never wanting subtlety

5 "Always scrupulous in investiga-
      tion
   With no shortage of laws
   Always precise particular
   Weighing wisely all evidence
   Why! This Jaka the Painter
   Has yet to be investigated by care-
      ful
   Investigation of the accomplished
   There is no penetrating proof
   For a decision decisive that's defi-
      nite
   The ground of justice[49]

———

yumana") is conjectural. The meanings of
the word *yumana* (Kawi for "good-
natured, well-being, prosperity, enduring") make little sense in this context:
"His is not a good-natured / enduring
sin." Perhaps the poet means *yumani*
(Kawi for "hell") but writes *yumana*. Pro-
sodic rules (*guru lagu*) demand that the
line end with the vowel-sound "a."
49. The word *pamancas*, translated as "decisive" in line 9, could and does also mean
the cutting off of something (i.e., Prabangkara's head) at an angle.

48. The translation of line 6 ("dosané tan

6 "Should Your Highness's will be
        done
   Who then, Lord, shall be bereft?
   Doubtless bemoaning his days to
        come"
   Thus did the Excellent Vizier speak
   In tears imploring restraint
   Of the Illustrious Sovereign King:
   "Be not carried away
   Lest you regret your tomorrows
   Having followed rash desire
   For 'tis you who wields the law"

7 His Majesty's tears did flow
   Dazed, he was anguished in his
        heart
   Admonished by the words of
   The Grand Vizier was excellent in-
        deed
   Perceptive of his master's ways
   And so the Sovereign Lord
   Did rescind his plan
   His scheme to murder Ki Jaka
   Thereat His Majesty whispered
   To Vizier Gajahmada⁵⁰

8 Grasped well the subtle sign of his
        king
   That now it was the royal will
   For Young Jaka the Painter
   To be but banished
   From the realm of Majapahit
   Thus to escape the wrath
   Of his royal father the King
   But this would be a secret plan
   Concealed till brought to pass
   Forthwith the Vizier withdrew

50. Line 5, "Ing wawéka tanduking gusti,"
could as well be translated as "perceptive
of the ways of masters."

*A deception is perpetrated, and Jaka
Prabangkara sails off into exile carrying a sealed letter from his father.*

9 Meeting with Jaka the Painter
   He did convey the royal will
   In truth 'twas guised in delicate de-
        ceit:
   "Now by the will
   Of your father the Sovereign King
   You have been commissioned
   To portray all
   The contents of the skies
   To be imaged on your writing
        board
   Is all the heavens do contain

10 "The sun, the moon, the stars and
   Flashing lightning, rainbows, and
        radiances
   The starry Wind-trace Serpent
   Red fire balls of disaster, bluish ra-
        diance royal
   Lightning bolts and shooting stars
   Thunderbolts and lightning's crash
   Thunder's climax
   Thunderheads dark and billowing
        clouds
   Communing with golden clouds
        streaming
   At heaven's zenith⁵¹

51. In line 3, the Wind-trace Serpent is
the name of a constellation. Line 4 offers
a glimpse of Javanese cosmology, with its
highly developed typology of efficacious
radiances. For example, a bluish white radiance descending on a person from on
high (*andaru*) marks and makes that person a (future) king. Red fire balls rolling
along the horizon (*teluh bajra*) mean and
are disaster/disease.

11 "Cyclones, rain, great whirlwinds
All the contents of the skies
Commanded are you to portray
   them all
And too the birds
Those who live not on the earth
Those who soar the heavens
Are birds of many kinds
Like the bird of paradise
And others of the kind that are dif-
   ferent still of form
Still different is the eagle, mighty
   king of birds"

12 This Jaka offered his assent
Obedient to whatever was the
   royal will
Forthwith the Vizier returned
To the presence of the King
Bowing with a *sembah*, the Excel-
   lent Vizier
Reported how
He conveyed the King's command
And the answer of Prince Jaka
Prabangkara, that he obeyed the
   royal will
His Majesty was blithe of heart[52]

52. The *sembah* is a gesture of high es-
teem/deference in which one brings the
hands (palms together as though in
prayer) before the face with thumbs
touching the nose. In the nineteenth-
century Kraton Surakarta, there were
codified regulations governing to and by
whom, how many times, and in what
manner the *sembah* must be offered under varying circumstances. See *Serat
Wawaton Tatakrama Tembung Kadhaton*
(composed Surakarta, [mid to late 19th
century]; inscribed Surakarta, [late 19th
century]). MS. Rp 74 carik; SMP Rp 76,
esp. pp. 7–13.

13 Thus finished the Vizier withdrew
And so the King commanded built
A great and mighty kite
In breadth almost twelve meters
With a cagelike cabin for
Jaka Prabangkara
Along with all his fittings
His provisions all provided
Now after some time, finished was
A very handsome kite

14 Rigged with the semblance of a
   wind-swooping sail
Serpentine cords and sky-
   supporting sail
And streamers to catch the wind
In the center was the cabin
Like a house with all its trappings
Provided with provisions
Along with all his fittings
The appointments of a painter
Then the Sovereign summoned his
   Vizier
And all the courtiers too

15 Once assembled were the officials
   of the realm
The kite was tendered before the
   King
Complete with all its trappings
Its cord coiled in a mighty heap
Looked like unto a mountain
And was wound onto a spool
For reeling out the cord
Then Jaka Prabangkara
With a *sembah* to the King begged
   leave
His Highness held a letter

16 Folded and sealed close
Presented thereat to this Jaka

Thus spake His Majesty:
"Child, read now
The writing on the outside"
Prince Jaka made the *sembah*
Then forthwith did he read
The writing on the letter
Penetrating to his heart, the writ-
    ing sounded thus:
"A letter to our son

17 "Young Prabangkara the Painter
Receive this our letter
Our command to you
But we do forbid
You this our letter
To open
Before brought to completion
Is your portraiture
Of all the heavens do contain, by
    no means, lad
Dare you open it

18 "After you have finished, lad
Your painting of the skies
And all they do contain
At that time, child
Open this our letter"
Jaka having finished
His reading of
The writing on the letter sealed
Taken to his bosom, his answer was
    assent
With that he then mounted

19 The kite, inside the cabin to be sure
Then His Highness ordered it
    raised
The kite was set to soar
With brisk breezes blowing
The sails did catch the winds
Streaking up into the sky

Terrific was the howl
'Twas like a soaring eagle
The eagle, noble king of birds, on
    wing
Its image thus

20 The kite was nearly gone from
    sight
Then the King unsheathed his
    sword
Which was so very sharp
The sword shone flashing bright
His Majesty gazed on high
The kite in but a moment
Vanished out of sight
Having slipped into the skies
Thereat the King commanded its
    cord be held to fast
And bound onto a post

21 The post which was its spool
Then the King descended from his
    throne
Brandishing his sword
His Royal Highness spake:
"O Excellent Vizier and all ye
    princes-regent
Courtiers of Majapahit
Listen well all of you
Witness these our words
To our son Jaka the Painter
Who has ascended to the skies

22 "O my son, Young Painter, child
Dare you not descend
Ere you reach that place
In China's mighty realm
There may you descend, child
And once you have indeed
Come down in China yonder
There then shall be

One who takes you in and helps
    you, child
Be drawn to fortune fair

23   "A fortune fairer shall be yours,
    child
Casting your seed over China
Evenly over its lands
In the future your descendants
    shall
To Java by the many homeward
    wend
All sharing in authority granted
In days to come to feed upon
The fruits of Java's land
By whatever means their livings
    flowing in with ease
They shall be content, at home"

24   The Excellent Vizier and all the
    princes-regent
The nobles and high courtiers
All cried out in accord
Thundering in agreement all:
"Good fortune! May the handsome
    one
Be of good fortune upon his way
And may the future bring to pass
All these his royal father's words"
Instantly there was a sign with
    heaven's tumult
Thundering in the skies[53]

25   Answered by darkness and light-
    ning
Then the King did raise his sword
Forthwith the cord was cut
Cut in two was the cord
In a flash the higher cord flew loose
The metaphor for that cord:
Like a mighty savage serpent
Soaring into the skies
And like the whirling eye of a hur-
    ricane
Magnificent in the heavens

26   In no time vanished out of sight
The cord was carried by its kite
Fiercely the howling winds
Swirled as though by bellows
    fanned
So much for him which sailed on
    high
Now as for His Royal Highness
His sword again already
Sheathed, he thereat took his seat
Upon the throne still gazing at that
    cord
Streaking up into the skies

*Royal regrets and reflections on ex-
emplary kingship.*

27   His Majesty was stunned and
    speechless
His forsaken heart overwhelmed
By metaphor as one bereft
Now by the word *bereft*
Is meant: in one's hand is held a
    bird
A long-time pet
Beloved and devoted too
Slipped loose 'tis gone from hand

53. The response of nature to powerful
words is conventional in Javanese writing
and signifies that the speakers' words will
indeed be realized. Note here that it is not
the king's word which is answered by
heaven, but the echoing words of his
courtiers.

Vanished his piteous heart's *bereft*
The Illustrious One was stricken
    deep[54]

V. Mijil
[Melodic mood is one of longing:
erotic or mournful.]

1   Distraught and whelmed with woe
     Of troubled heart, aggrieved
     As if hopelessly anguish-stabbed
     Thousands, the torments pressing,
         whelmed
     By heartbreak unassuaged
     Bewondered sunk in doubt

2   In a swirling swoon as if quit of
     Strength was His Royal Majesty
     Wakened was awareness of love
     For his child as all living creatures
     Love their young
     For they are the becoming

3   Becoming man's vehicle to
     The excellence of continuity
     Continuity looking forward to that
         which is to come
     Hounded by his jealousy
     Naught was the King's design
     The carefully accounted plan

4   The assent of all the assenters
     The words consented to

54. The words *angeras driya* (translated
here as "stricken deep") at verse's end, in
conjunction with the punctuation mark
for a new canto directly behind them, signal the reader/singer to change to the
melody of Mijil (Rarasati).

Racing for division of fortune fair
Again and over again all but
    tempting death
A most imperfect death
Whose end is utter ruin

5   Were he to meet his death
     Forgetting the destination
     Of Perfection as the cure
     His wrath then brings destruction
     The undoing of creation
     Is to do then senseless acts

6   Senseless acts impetuously acted
     Impetuous without aim
     By a heart devoid of cause
     A rash, arrogant soul
     Filthy and dangerous
     A reverie of shamelessness

7   Shameless of deed, heedless of
         danger
     At the exalted core
     His virtue then is futile
     The way of the ancient kings
     Was to know the limits of
     Structured authority

8   A structure of rule/allusion that is
         hidden/expressed
     Has authority to see and be seen
     Such is the meaning of excellence
         true
     Which admonished the Celebrant
     Track down the tidings
     Prove the sublime word[55]

55. The opening line of the verse, "wangunaning naya kang winuni," is marked
by an exuberant polysemy. The Kawi

9   Of word sublime serene, swept not
        away
    Strive for certainty
    Of command, compassion is the
        ground
    The grounding of all kings
    Is mastery of investigation
    Always ever more and more

10 A foundation in ascetic practice
    Is the mark of royalty
    Tempered by trials, a mindful soul

———

naya ("prudence, wisdom; rule, politics")
can also be glossed as allusion (*pasemon*)
(Winter, *Kawi-Javaansch Woordenboek*,
p. 74). The Kawi *winuni* (*wuni* + *in* infix)
glosses as both "hidden" *and* "expressed"
(ibid., p. 272). Here, the word *winuni*
holds both meanings (retentive and expressive) at the same time in a productive
tension that is in play with the polysemic
naya that precedes it in the line. For further discussion of this verse, see below,
chapter 4, p. 292–93.
    "The Celebrant" in line 4 is a conjec-
tural translation of "Sang Miwahani."
The word *wiwaha*, Kawi for "wedding,"
by extension connotes "celebration" in
general. The word *miwahani* (*m* +
wiwaha + *i*) can mean "to perform a marriage" or "to celebrate" (i.e., as in a coronation celebration [*jumenengan*]). "Sang
Miwahani" could then be the one who
performs the celebration (the celebrant).
The sense of *celebrant* here is, then, that
of an elder statesman or kinsman, whose
officiating at a royal coronation includes
instructing the new, young king in matters of virtuous kingship. I am grateful to
Amrih Widodo for originally suggesting
the connection between *wiwaha* and
jumenengan. For similar usages of *wiwaha*
cognates, see below, XVII:7–8 and
XXIV:7.

Surveillant and perceptive
Observing the *darma* of kingship
He is revered, so excellent[56]

11 Too long were it expressed in
        words
    The heartfelt anguish of the King
    Oblivious his tears gushed forth
    And too the Excellent Vizier
    And all the princes-regent
    The foremost courtiers[57]

12 Stunned and speechless everyone
    Tears were shed by all
    Haunted by visions of his excel-
        lence
    Prince Jaka was brilliance consum-
        mate
    Able, his character refined
    Handsome, his appearance

*Treats the travels of Jaka Pra-
bangkara and his reading Brawijaya's letter.*

56. A *darma* is a code of conduct. Different codes are prescribed for different
stations of life.
    The Javanese text of the preceding ten
stanzas (V:1–10) is pleasurably obscure.
In these verses, which are marked by exuberant alliteration and assonance (*purwakanthi*), discursive sense seems less
important than other senses evoked by
plays of sound and association. The voice,
which is—almost directly—that of the
poet, is persuasive precisely because of its
beautiful sounds and its difficulty. The
voice is both didactic and obscure.
57. In line 2, the word *wulangun* ("heartfelt anguish") indicates that the source of
that anguish is either loss/longing or
confusion.

13 The King, resigned unto himself
Then retired to the inner palace
The Vizier did disperse the court
The princes-regent and high cour-
    tiers
Turned for home one by one
Now to be related:[58]

14 The hapless wind-borne one
Continued on apace
Rushing against the heavens'
    winds
Soaring as if to touch the skies
Vanish did the earth
He mingled with the clouds

15 Day and night whirling winds
Howling fiercely did assail
And so the kite's progress
Never failing soared ever higher
    still
Into the firmament
And so with time's passage

16 The kite then did arrive
In the realm of the king of birds
The eagle and the like
All those ordained to live on high
And too the bird of paradise
Portrayed was every one

17 Having finished with the birds
Then the noble youth
All the heavens did portray

58. The "inner palace," or *kadhaton* (line
2), designates the inner portion of a *kraton*. In the *kadhaton* are found the formal
audience hall, royal meditation chambers,
the apartments of the palace women and
of the magic regalia, etc.

Everything within the skies
There was nothing that escaped
His portraiture

18 With the completion of his work
Finished in perfection
For in the space of sixty days
His drawings were complete
Then the handsome one
Pondered in his heart

19 For now he longed to ascertain
His Majesty's command
Which fixed inside the writing was
Still sealed close as ordered
Ki Jaka longed to know
The nature of its secret

20 The letter then was opened
By the noble painter youth
Penetrating his heart, its words he
    read
"Note: this our letter, child
Which issuing from
The purest depths of our heart

21 "Together with our blessings
And with our prayers
Embellished with the fruits of our
    yoga
Is addressed to you, child
Prabangkara the Young Painter
Our very own son

22 "Who is accomplished in precise
    perfection
Even unto the play of subtle sign
Whose art shows in allusion
Receptive of mind, intelligent
Who is wholly able
At sublime noble works

23 "Who masters both gross and sub-
lime
Whose practices are practiced true
Who, loyal in service
Is fulfilling now
Our very own command
Following our orders

24 "We charged you to portray the
whole
Of the heavens yonder
Whatever seen there, all to be por-
trayed
And with our blessings, child
Together with our prayers
Having been granted you

25 "In opening, Jaka, Young Painter
Child, you who are our very own
son
This our royal letter
May it be a sign unto you, child
Our final instructions
Our royal word[59]

26 "Repudiated is our love
For you our very own son
From the moment of your leaving
hence
As you cast off for the skies
Soaring away with searching gaze
Sailing off on high

59. The missive's message begins with
this stanza, "in opening" (ing wiyosé). It
is conventional in formal Javanese letter
writing "to open" only after a lengthy
formulaic address, whose content is
largely standardized and depends upon
the relative social statuses of writer and
addressee.

27 "That, dear child, was your last
meeting
With this our royal person
Once to your destination come
You need not return home
To Majapahit
By no means, child

28 "And do not misconstrue, dear
child
Be not too distraught
With senseless needless dread
Should you fall to danger, child
Then take faith
In the Almighty Creator

29 "And thus it needs must be, dear
child
For even now
Our royal person is changed
The feelings of our heart are not
now as before
But are filled with ire implacable
Cast ever then at you

30 "Implacable, unappeasable
Our royal wrathful rage
Past hope of conciliation
Rather grows by bounds
Our fury ever mounting
Presses for the unthinkable

31 "Irrational of mind
Fury fused with confusion
We know only our hatred
Implacable for you
Perhaps it was destined thus
By the will of the almighty gods

32 "That you should be parted from
us

Not to be together
For thus, dear child, is our reality
By all means, child, abide by
This our directive
Take it not wrongly

33 "Your death is not our wish
It is but our will
To provide for you a way
The way to fortune fair
May you know exquisite tribula-
tion
In danger and discomfiture

34 "The difficult and uncanny
The distant and marvelous
May you know adversity on your
way
Afflicted by sickness, hunger,
heat, and piercing pain
Cast astray wandering
The skies ever straying

35 "O child, know well then
That words such as these
Mean we charge you to be clever
You shall grow to insight consum-
mate
Forging on with guide
Of exalted vision

36 "The companion on the way to
mastery
Of authority consummate
Is none but sorrowful trials at start
And steadfast heed of kingship's
code
In order that grace be granted
By the noble gods all-high

37 "Receiving the gift of divine grace

By the mercy of the All-Seeing
Released from sorrow and pain
Then is one called a noble master
and
Master of kingship's righteousness
And master of worldly goods as
well

38 "Master of wealth and master of
accomplishment
Master of prosperity perfect
Master of virtue and of conscious-
ness clear; the secret is
The harvest of the fruits provides
All of his descendants
With greatness in the time to
come[60]

39 "O child, hear now
My prayer
To the gods who master all
May you not descend, child
Before you have arrived
In China's mighty realm

40 "There may you descend, child
And let it not be rough
Gentle may your landing be
Then, there shall be one who helps
You, dear son
With true loving compassion

41 "And truly for that reason you
Shall reign as king
Beloved by your subjects all
More grand shall be your *kraton*

60. The Javanese text is broken in the
middle of this verse with the intrusion of
three interpolated MS leaves (figures 6–
8); see discussion above in chapter 1.

There in China, child
Fabulous your wealth

42 "And renowned in foreign lands
Your kingship shall be
Feared by all your enemies
A master of powers marvelous
You shall be victorious in battle
Valiant, invincible, unsurpassed

43 "And many shall be your children
Sons as well as daughters
Your descendants shall multiply
All fortunate and wealthy too
In the time to come
Many of them shall set forth

44 "Spreading sail for Java, child
Many of them shall come
To settle here in Java
Granted authority all to share
In feeding upon the fruits
Of Java in the time to come

45 "In all ways shall they be granted
ease
In their search for livelihood
Be vigilant in all things
O Prabangkara, our son
Heed and remember well
These our final words"

46 Finished was the writing's reading
By the young and noble hero
His tears flowed in gushing
streams
The handsome one's heart as
though pierced

Weeping with abandon
Engulfed by intimacy[61]

VI. Gambuh
[Melodic mood is vibrant and
rather brash]

1 Lapsing ever lower his heart dis-
tressed
Was assailed by anguish upon
anguish
As though plucked out and pierced,
his heart was rent
Torn out 'twas carried off
Lost, it pounded madly

2 His wildly pounding heart
Was nearly lifted to tumult's limit
As though clenched in reeling tur-
moil's grasp
Far gone, he fell into a faint
Swallowed in swoon of sorrow-
struck heart

3 Distrait and too distraught
Weary whelmed by anguished
agony
As though tired of agony's em-
brace
Ever more sorely his suffering
heart
Was ravished by miseries rapt

4 Dismayed in dreadful doubt
Suspended in speechless daze

61. The word *gambuh* (translated here as
"intimacy"), in conjunction with the
punctuation mark for a new canto directly following it, signals the reader/
singer to change to Gambuh meter.

His rapt longing sundered not
    from forlorn love
Moved, his longings passionate
Were then swept clean away

5   Cut off, in resignation
    Resigned heart swept off whirled
        away
    Waked from the longings of for-
        lorn love
    Bounded by a heart aware
    Vanish did his dread[62]

6   Having tucked away the letter
    Prince Jaka then cried out
    His prayer to the gods almighty
    Praying his journey be swift
    Was answered by the All-seeing

7   Merciful to His servants
    Affords help to His wretched slaves
    So at that very moment came a
        wind
    Exceedingly fierce from on high
    Descending it assailed

8   The kite with mighty force
    The ascending winds fell still
    And so the kite descended apace
    At incredible speed
    Carried off by the winds assailing

9   Like the mighty king of birds it
        shone
    Sailing down from out the skies

62. The Javanese text of the preceding five
stanzas (VI:1–5) is marked by exuberant
purwakanthi (alliteration and assonance),
the effect of which is to subordinate discursive sense to a sensual play of sound.

Flashing radiant; then came again
Southwest winds howling fierce
And lofty winds assailing

10   The kite relentlessly
    The kite followed those winds re-
        lentless
    Southwesterns lofty blowing fierce
    Ever northeastward whistling
    Swooping down and down

*Jaka Prabangkara in exile. Javanese
visions of others. Shown are the
benefits of industry and investment.*

11   After a lapse of time
    It was the Will of the Almighty
    Merciful to His miserable slaves
    To aid the wretched one
    Having to shelter come, the kite

12   Now blithely sailed along
    Over a mighty tract of land
    This mighty tract was in China's
        realm
    Far from the city, where villages
        lay
    At the edge of a desolate wood

13   There at the foot of the mountains
    Scrub growth did cover the hills
    Then the winds having died
    Just at the break of dawn
    Thereat the kite came down

14   Landing without a jolt
    Touching down gently, not hard
    At the edge of a wood it shone in-
        deed

A scrub wood nigh on a village
Isolated and oh so still

15   Far from the mighty Emperor
In Yut-wa-hi, as this village was
    called
A tiny village of the outer realm
There lived a wretched widow
The Widow Kim Liyong, her
    name[63]

16   A most impoverished wretch
Destitute, her hut was small
Bereft of husband long ago
Wretched, poor, so pitiful
Her state was near inhuman

17   'Tis said she had a child
Just one, a beautiful daughter
This maid, now newly come of age
Was in her youth's full bloom
Though as yet it hardly showed

18   For she was a maid of the village
Poor to be sure and hardship-
    bowed
And so her beauty yet shone not
    forth
Impoverished, most pitiful
Wretched without accoutrements

19   Kim Muwah was her name
Orphaned, bereft of father

With mother alone seeking food
Day in day out, the work
Of the Widow Kim Liyong

20   Wending to the wood nigh upon
    the village
The scrub wood at the mountain
    foot
The two of them: she and her child
Gathered dry leaves and twigs
Edible herbs and vegetables

21   Whatever they might find
Of herbs, vegetables, and twigs
Once gathered was sold forthwith
In the other villages
In the neighboring four and the
    five afar[64]

22   Whatever the take from these sales
Then was used to buy
Food for a single day, a single night
Thus it was day in day out
Then one day

23   The Widow did set forth
For the forest as on any day
The two of them: she with her
    child
Most pitiful wretches they
Trudged forth a twosome

63. The word translated as "outer realm" (line 3) is *mancanagara*, an administrative term that designates the outlying provinces (those under the king's "indirect rule" via the "outer regents") of the realm.

64. "The neighboring four" (*mancapat* or *merpat*) consists of the four nearest villages to, and lying to the cardinal points of, a central, reference village. "The five" (*mancalima*) would be the next nearest grouping of four. This four-five organizational grouping pertained (and pertains) especially to trade, with a system of rotating market days among the five villages.

24 Making for the mountain foot
    The sloping hills and valleys
    They dug for roots and gathered
        leaves
    Edible herbs and twigs
    And vegetables that sell

25 The time then was
    Still morning, barely eight o'clock
    When the Widow Woman startled
        was to see
    Before her something which
        appeared
    Like an enormous house

26 But this was no house
    Though like a house from the size
        of it
    All rigged out like a *kunthing* boat
    With sails to catch the wind
    Many were its readied sails[65]

27 Prince Jaka the Painter seeing
    Someone there forthwith came
        down
    From the cabin Prince Jaka gently
    Had descended to the ground
    Prince Jaka slowly did approach

28 This the Widow Woman
    The Widow showing fright stepped
        back
    And her child terror-struck
    Hung upon her mother
    All pale, her body trembled

65. *kunthing* (line 3) means "dwarf."
Zoetmulder speculates that the Old Javanese *kakunthingan* might refer to a short,
beamy boat (*Zoetmulder* 1:925).

29 The thoughts within the heart
    Of the Widow Woman: "Could it
        be
    A fairy who roams upon the earth?
    Or perhaps one of the spirits
    Who guards the forest yon?

30 "Or maybe a mountain spirit
    Or demon of the mighty wood?
    They who watch these mountains
        and woods
    Who all of them, such beings
    Are invisible and unseen?

31 "This one shows himself
    Having taken human form
    Looks to me like this fairy is male
    His clothes are oh so different
    His garments, wholly strange

32 "Not like the dress
    Worn by folks from here
    Why! This demon's a handsome
        one
    Cultured, serene, of aura subtle
    His radiance shines most brilliant

33 "It hurts your eyes to look at him
    Now if this *is* a real human being
    He's no son of a common man
    Only the son of a mighty king
    Could have a radiance like that"

34 Prince Jaka did observe with care
    The Widow Kim Liyong
    At once waked memories in Prince
        Jaka's heart
    Noting that her dress
    Her garments, and apparel

35 Were like the maid-servants
To the Queen of old
The Queen who'd come from
China
And the slant of her eyes
Her face was just the same

36 And too her skin
To be sure her skin was yellow
Prince Jaka did reflect, "Perchance
This woman is Chinese"
Now the Widow Kim Liyong

37 Then questioned him forthwith
Her question, in Chinese:
"Greetings, young man, who's
newly come
I ask in earnest now
That you tell me but the truth

38 "Are you then a spirit
A demon of wood or mountain
A fairy who roams the earth?
Or a spirit of the mighty forest
One of those who watch there

39 "Who's come to bring torment
To spread unnatural pestilence?
Or could you be a real human
being?
Speak the truth, O handsome one
Or are you the god Hong Tepè-
kong[66]

40 "Who has come to take
My life, to seize my soul?

If you are perchance a real human
being
What then is the name of
Your land: is it near or far?

41 "And what too is your name?"
Gentle, the reply of Prince Jaka
In perfect Chinese, his words were
sweet
Prince Jaka had been fluent long
Thus in speaking Chinese

42 And in its writing too
The handsome one was so adept
His teacher of old was nurse to
The Chinese princess who married
The Sovereign King of Majapahit

43 Many were her subjects
Mandarins of her entourage
These then were fellows at repartee
With Prince Jaka in days of old
Thus expert was the youth

44 Each and every question of
The Widow Kim Liyong
Prince Jaka Prabangkara fathomed
well
And so it is related
Softly did Prince Jaka sing the mel-
ody Pucung:[67]

VII. Pucung
[Melodic mood is lackadaisical]

66. Hong Tepèkong is identified in Javanese lexicons as the name of a Chinese
"heathen idol" (*brahala*).

67. Descriptive of the sound of Jaka Prabangkara's speech to follow, this line (in
conjunction with the punctuation mark
for a new canto directly behind it) also
signals the poem's reader/singer to
change to the melody of Pucung.

1 "Verily mother, I am not a specter
 Nor fairy to be sure
 Nor guardian spirit, nor demon
 Nor again Hong Tepèkong, not a
  god at all

2 "In truth, I am, dear mother
 Indeed a human being
 Hailing from the land of Java
 I'm servant to Majapahit's King

3 "I am His Highness's page, mother
 But one so very low
 Prabangkara is my name
 Rude and coarse, of wretched com-
  mon stock

4 "Ignorant to boot, I am an un-
  cultured brute
 Stupid, really useless
 Spoiled from childhood on
 A hopeless wicked wretch I am

5 "Verily mother, not nearly subtle
  enough
 To serve at royal court
 When charged by my Lord
 To study writing, I proved inept

6 "Befuddled always, most lacking:
  an ignoramus
 Many were my mates
 All of them, adept
 I alone, dear mother, was stupidest
  of all

7 "Knowing little, I could not tell
  north from south
 Thus did I catch the wrath

Of His Majesty the King
 And as for my arrival here

8 "I did not come to cause a stir
 It all began back when
 I was discharging
 The command of my Lord, Maja-
  pahit's King

9 "When charged to portray every-
  thing
 Within the heavens all
 The marvelous beheld
 Between the borders of the skies

10 "I was provided as means
 To climb into the skies
 A kite just like a *kunthing* boat
 Rigged like a ship with sails

11 "And provided was I all appurte-
  nances
 And ample provisions as well
 All held within the cabin
 No shortage of provisions, rather a
  surfeit

12 "Still manifold, why this excess
 Lies there inside my vehicle
 When my task
 Was finished, all my portraiture

13 "There came from on high a furi-
  ous wind
 Assailing then my kite
 The kite, refusing to turn back
 Sailed on day and night, ever down
  and down

14 "When nigh onto the mountains

It sheltered to the earth
As the winds then did die still
Last night just at the break of dawn

15 "So down onto the ground my
      vehicle did fall
    Right at this very spot
    Great was my wonder
    When you, mother, did thereupon
      appear"

16 Verily, the Widow, upon hearing
    Was dismayed, amazed
    Bewondered, deeply moved
    Wonder-struck was she, for it was
      so very far

17 And great then was her pity for the
      handsome one
    And so the Widow Woman
    Softly spoke again:
    "In that case, child, you are

18 "Cast astray ever straying lost
    Carried away by the kite
    Cut loose, swept off by the wind
    Tossed hither and thither, to light
      in a foreign land

19 "For your landing is exceedingly
      far
    From the land of Java
    From this realm of China here
    Java lies to the southwest

20 "But away an immense distance
    And the way is barred
    By oceans vast to be sure
    With passage by great islands
      manifold

21 "The mighty ocean, a three-
      months' sail
    That when the winds are fair
    Long ago, child, back when
    Your uncle, now long-dead, still
      lived[68]

22 "For he made the voyage way back
      then
    To the land of Java
    And went to Majapahit
    Back when the Emperor wed his
      daughter

23 "To the Illustrious Lord of Maja-
      pahit
    Back then your uncle did
    Escort Her Highness the Princess
    For it was his turn for king's corvee

24 "News is that that jewel among
      women
    Is now divorced
    From His Majesty the King
    The Queen, who is Princess of
      China

25 "Was seven months' pregnant
      when they did part
    Then by the royal will
    Of the King of Majapahit
    The Princess was bestowed upon
      his son

26 "Who, established in Palèmbang's
      mighty realm

68. By the familial "your uncle" (*paman
dika*), she means her late husband.

Goes by the name, High Prince
    Damar
Tell me, is it so?"
Jaka replied: "Indeed 'tis true

27 "And further, now she's given birth
    To a son
    An image of his royal father"
    Again spake the Widow Kim
      Liyong:

28 "O handsome one, what is it like
    Inside your vehicle?
    I truly long to see"
    Jaka replied: "As you please"

29 They then set off, Ki Jaka in the
      lead
    Next came the Widow Woman
    Behind was the daughter
    Coming to the kite, all of them sat
      down

30 Inside the cabin, the Widow
      charmed by what she saw
    And her daughter too
    Was charmed by the sight
    For it was like a well-appointed
      house

31 With the painter's appurtenances
      too
    Many were the paintings
    All of them exquisite
    Of heaven's sublime contents

32 The handsome one served refresh-
      ments
    Many kinds of breads

And Javanese dainties too
The kinds that last a long journey

33 And water with all kinds of fra-
      grant drinks
    For much did still remain
    All of which he did proffer
    To the Widow and her child

34 The three of them did eat of bread
    Spread with butter
    And many kinds of pastries
    Once they'd eaten their fill, Jaka
      then did speak:[69]

35 "And now, mother, if you will
    If you would so deign
    To adopt a hapless wretch
    Then, mother, shall I cleave to
      you[70]

36 "For I shall not return, mother
    To the land of Java
    As I am now far too ashamed"
    The Widow's heart was overjoyed

37 She said: "Why! How very fine

69. The bread, butter, and pastries that
Jaka Prabangkara served up comprise a
charming anachronism; these nineteenth-
century colonial dainties would hardly
have been common fare in fifteenth-
century Majapahit.

70. The word *ngèngèr*, translated in the
final line as "cleave to," denotes placing
oneself in unpaid menial servitude to another (surrendering oneself body and
soul). The term is often used for the relationship of subjects to a ruler (*pangéran*
= prince), students to a teacher, or
women (as mistresses or wives) to a man.

If you do then deign
To cleave unto a pauper
A lowly wretch without a thing"

38 The handsome one replied: "Indeed
     I will"
    Then this Jaka was
    Invited to their home
    Nothing loath, Jaka came bearing
     goods

39 The three did haul away the food
    And the trappings too
    The handsome one's appointments
    Back and forth they hauled the
     goods

40 And what provisions still remained
    For there was so very much
    And all the sails
    Of white cotton and the body of
     the kite

41 Great widths of finest cotton
    And all the cord
    And the frame they carried home
    In all it took four days to haul

42 Enough said, now after some time
    This the Widow Woman
    Kim Liyong grew to love dearly
    Ki Jaka, like her very own son

43 The handsome one had a ring
    Of ruby on his right hand's little
     finger
    And too his precious medal
    Crafted of burnished gold, embel-
     lished with enamel[71]

44 These gave he to the Widow
    Was ordered then to sell them
    As starting capital indeed
    For the Widow a living to make

45 Fabulous was the Widow's wealth
    For all of a sudden
    Her living came with ease
    Everywhere and always, the profits
     did flow in

46 Writing was the work of the hand-
     some one
    Pictures did he draw
    Of trees and of birds
    Once done, the Widow's charge to
     sell them

47 Famous were Ki Jaka's works
    Why! many of them sold
    Customers clamored to buy
    And his portraits of women and
     men

48 They struggled to outbid each
     other, regardless of the price
    Though wildly exorbitant
    Still many came to buy
    The bidding kept rising out of
     hand—they were both women
     and men

49 Heaped in piles was the Widow's
     wealth
    And so the Widow Woman
    Kim Liyong now was very rich

———

71. In line 3, I render *fartepènirèki* (from
the Dutch *waarde penning*?) "his precious
medal." *Fartepèn* could instead be a Java-
nization of the Dutch *vaarte pen* ("traveling pen") or *waarde pen* ("valuable pen").

From her foundling son's adherence[72]

VIII. Kinanthi
[Melodic mood is erotic and/or di-
dactic]

1   Thus was it bruited
All about the frontier
In the neighboring villages four
The neighboring five, six, seven
The neighboring eight, the nine
All rang in acclaim[73]

2   That the son of
The Widow of Yut-wa-hi
Her adoptive son, that is
Was exceedingly talented
Clever, accomplished at all things
For, to be sure, he was handsome

3   His face was like the moon
At its time of fullness
A master of language, of courtly
   mien
Charming, incomparably able
Polite, serene, unaffected
Fit to be the talk of the land[74]

4   And so his fame did come
To the provincial capital
Celebrated throughout the land
Many the provincial capitals
Who did acclaim Ki Jaka
Son of Yut-wa-hi's Widow

5   Exquisite were his looks
None was the like of him
All the youths of China
Were worsted in appearance
Unsurpassed in intelligence
He was praised by all the land

6   A master at drawing was he
Perfect likenesses were
His artful portraits
Seemed as if they'd speak them-
   selves
Of air his drawings seemed as not
Crafted of paper and ink

7   For as the truth were they
Of the subject crafted by art
In ceaseless stream did come
Emissaries of all the kings
And envoys of the nobles all
Of the courtiers and officials

8   All commissioning portraits
Artfully crafted and painted
Which seemed as if they'd move
   themselves
In perfect agreement with that
   desired

72. The word *kanthinya* (read here as "adherence"), in conjunction with the punctuation mark for a new canto directly behind it, signals the poem's reader/singer
to change to the melody of Kinanthi.
73. See above, note to VI:21. The "neighboring six" (*mancanem*) would be the
next nearest grouping of four to the
"neighboring five" (*mancalima*) and so
on.
74. The words *nor raga*, translated as
"of courtly mien" in line 3, mean to have
the quality of humbling oneself. Among
nineteenth-century Javanese, the art of

cultured self-abasement (that is, the
proper understanding of how, to whom,
and under what circumstances one must
humble oneself) would have been most
perfectly honed by servants of the court.

Rich were the returns
For Ki Jaka the Painter

9   Beautiful things and splendid trea-
       sures
     Money and elegant clothes

*Revelations and concealment: Jaka
Prabangkara vanishes into (China's)
court*

Then it came to the ears of
His Most Royal Highness Sov-
    ereign
Lord Emperor, greatest of all
Who reigned over all the kings

10 Of China's land entire
     It was he who had dominion
     Over all the land of China
     The tracts along the seashore
     As well as the oceans too
     Were under his authority

11 A mighty godlike king was he
     Famed in foreign lands
     And so His Majesty the King
     Captivated by the news
     Longed himself to see
     The person of Jaka the Painter

12 Thereat His Serene Majesty
     Sent a messenger to summon
     Jaka Prabangkara
     Before long did arrive
     Escorted by his master
     The provincial king

13 Came into the royal presence
     Bringing Jaka the Painter along
     The Emperor beckoned to Jaka

Commanding that he draw near
And Jaka did kowtow and *sembah*
His performance, charming to see

14 Crouching low, he did advance
     Like a peacock strutting
     Graceful, elegant, so agile
     Performed with decorum discrimi-
         nate
     Discriminate of the situation
     Exquisite was the swaying of his
         neck

15 Bowed low upon his elbows
     Expectant was his mien
     Seated humbly before the king
     Confirmed in perfect decorum
     His penetrating gaze did virtue
         shine
     Winsome, enticing, alluring was
         he[75]

16 Astounded were they who wit-
         nessed
     Stunned, struck speechless all
     And too His Highness the King
     And too His Highness the King
     Was amazed as he gazed
     Upon Jaka Prabangkara
     Gripped in the gaze, His Majesty

17 Did muse unto himself:

75. Prabangkara's performance is conventional for the approach of a beautiful
younger Javanese prince before a king in
audience, and it thereby comprises a form
of language through which the youth
presents himself as royal prince. The
meaning of the performance is not lost on
the (Javanese) perception of the Chinese
Emperor. Of course, Jaka Prabangkara
must deny his royalty.

"Most certainly this lad
Is not of humble stock
No child of a commoner
Clearly of noble blood is he
Of true patrician lineage

18 "Of honey-sweet aristocratic blood
A fragrant flower of royalty
A gentleman, I'd swear
'Tis manifest in his countenance
All his manners show him
Perfectly impressive

19 "There is no disguising the differ-
      ence
Between noble and commoner
But I surmise he'll not own up"
And so the King did speak:
"Greetings, child"
With a *sembah* Jaka the Painter
      replied:

20 "Deeply grateful am I, your slave
For Your Highness's royal greeting
Lifting it high above my head
May it be for me a magic charm
A talisman for my life
By Your Majesty's compassionate
      grace"[76]

21 Again spoke the Emperor
Inquiring of the handsome one
From whence his origins
With a *sembah*, Jaka the Painter
      replied:

"Hailing from Java, your servant
Is of mean and humble descent

22 "A page to His Royal Highness
Brawijaya of Majapahit
But all too stupid and simple
Your servant is exceedingly dense
Many are my fellows there
All of them intelligent

23 "I alone, Your Highness
Am stupidest of all
Of manner unfit to be
Courtier to a king
Short on intellect, fatuous
Ignorant of decorum

24 "I, a real ignoramus
A wretch spoiled from childhood
      on
'Needs must taste the flavors six'
A mere lad without discretion
A dunce unfit to know
The taste then of the six[77]

25 "*Amla, sarkara,* by which is meant
The 'sour' and the 'sweet'
Tikta and *kayasa*
Meaning the 'bitter' and the 'rich'
Lawana and *jatthuka*
Meaning the 'spicy' and the 'salty'

76. Jaka Prabangkara's hyperbolic acknowledgment of the Emperor's welcome
is purely conventional (even formulaic)
and is drawn from the language of the
opening audience scene in a *wayang* performance.

77. This reference to the "six flavors" (or
sadrasa) is an allusion to the Old Javanese
Nitisastra; see below, chapter 4, pp. 297–
98. See also the reference to *sadrasa*, as
part of the title of the exiled Pakubuwana
VI, in the opening stanza of *Serat Rama:
Tilaran-dalem I.S.K.S. Pakubuwana VI*
(MS. SP 106 Ca; SMP KS 428), quoted
above in chapter 1, note 17.

26 "Not nearly subtle enough
Knowing not the secret most
     essential
For service to a king
Thus did I ever incur the wrath"
And so this Jaka's telling told
From beginning unto end

27 How he had come to land
In the village of Yut-wa-hi
Upon hearing, the Emperor
Deeply moved, was most bewon-
     dered
His Highness's loving grace issued
To Jaka the Painter

28 His Majesty heedful of heart
Jaka was beckoned again
Charged to draw yet nearer still
With a *sembah* Jaka the Painter
Came close before the King
Beneath the golden throne

29 His Imperial Majesty bent down
Speaking in a whisper
He questioned then Jaka
Was charged to tell the truth
"Child, mince not your words
Just be frank with me

30 "Be not afraid
Whose son are you?"
With a *sembah*, Jaka replied:
"Alas, Your Majesty
Because of my great shame
Have I hidden behind a screen[78]

31 "Nonetheless, Your Highness
Since I, your slave, am now
Pressed by Your Majesty
Begging your royal pardon
Shameless do I now
Presume to tell the truth

32 "I, your slave, in fact
Am the son of His Majesty
Brawijaya of Majapahit
King of the Land of Java
But born of a lower wife
My mother an officer's daughter

33 "He the official with charge of
The butchers of Majapahit's realm
As for this my arrival here
'Twas by decree of my royal father
Set forth in an epistle
A letter from my father the King

34 "Which was his final directive
To me, Your Majesty"
Thus spoke this Prince Jaka
As he recited the letter's writing
From beginning unto end
Presented to His Majesty

35 When His Royal Highness the
     Emperor
Of China this did hear
His heart was torn by pity
Moved his tears did flow
In compassion for Prince Jaka
His Majesty seemed so sad[79]

---

78. The text of line 4, "kawula datan
wiwirang," actually reads "because I am
shameless." Since the context does not
support this reading, I am assuming a
scribal slip of *datan* ("without") for *dahat*
("very" or "great").

79. The word *kingkin* (sad, heart-sick), in
conjunction with the punctuation mark
for a new canto directly behind it, alerts

IX. Asmarandana
[Melodic mood is one of sorrow or longing]

1   His Royal Highness spoke:
    "In that case, child, you are
    Brother to our grandson
    And now it is our will
    That our address to thee
    Be that as to a grandchild"
    "By your grace," breathed Prince
        Jaka[80]

2   Again His Majesty did speak:
    "O Grandson Prabangkara
    You shall we conceal
    To your wish we do accede
    To bide in guise of commoner
    Behind a veil concealed, dear child
    By closely guarded secret

3   "But now by our royal will
    You we take to ourself
    We charge you to live here
    Together with your mother
    And with your sister too"
    Ki Jaka with a *sembah* said:
    "Be it as Your Highness wills"[81]

4   With gentle voice the King did tell

He who was Jaka's master
King Sitong Kisahé
That Jaka Prabangkara
He did take to reside there
Together with his mother
And with his sister too

5   Assenting with a *sembah*
    Submissive to the royal will
    Was King Sitong Kisahé
    With that the Divine Emperor
    His Royal Highness did retire
    The audience all dispersed
    And Jaka too withdrew[82]

6   Not to go on at length
    The tale told but in brief:
    Jaka with his mother
    And his sister too
    Were brought indeed to live there
    Given a house by the King
    Close by the royal palace

7   Nigh onto the *kraton* walls
    Cherished by His Majesty
    Many the gifts were granted him
    And the Crown Prince too
    Was most devoted to
    Jaka Prabangkara
    And all the royal family

8   The nobles and the courtiers
    All followed in devotion
    Many the gifts they offered
    Jaka Prabangkara
    Now with the passing of time

---

the reader/singer to change to the melody of Asmarandana.
80. The Emperor's grandson would be Prince Patah (= Panembahan Bintara), Brawijaya's son by the Chinese princess who had been removed to Palèmbang. See above III:6–8 and VII:22–27.
81. The word translated as "take" in line 2 is *pundhut,* a word which has the connotation of adopting someone as one's own child or property.

82. In line 3 of the Javanese text, the name of the provincial master reads "Sitong Sisahé"; see, however, above VIII:4.

Rumor billowed ever higher
It could not be concealed

9   That Jaka the Painter was
A noble flower of honey-sweet
    blood
Exposed, his guise of commoner
By the will of His Majesty
Made one with the royal children
Soon to be taken as son-in-law
Grandson-in-law to His Highness
    the King

10   Married to a child of the Crown
    Prince
The first-born of his daughters
Siti Umiyan, her name
But by His Royal Highness's will
Jaka Prabangkara
His grandson was charged to
    marry too
The daughter of the Widow

11   So Kim Muwah, the lovely jewel
Was married at the same level
They were devoted to each other
In connubial bliss both pairs
Now with the passing of time
High Prince Prabangkara
Was acclaimed throughout the
    land[83]

12   Unsurpassed in valor
Excellent of intellect
Heroic and heedful
He was adept at every work
With the sweet nature of an *ulama*
His character, burning incense
Striking his every word[84]

13   Wise, he was fearless
Virtuous and valiant
For, to be sure, he was handsome
His face was like the moon
At its time of fullness
Many were the fragrant ones
Enamored of his looks[85]

14   Now of him the prosperous one
High Prince Prabangkara
Nothing more is to be said
Breaking off this tale
Of adventures in China
Lest the story take too long
And so the telling turns

Here begins the "second episode."
The fathering and (especially) the
mothering of Jaka Karèwèd. Re-
sistance of the "little man."

84. The use of Arabic-Islamic *ulama* in
line 5 is notable. An *ulama* is one learned
in the field of Islamic religious and legal
studies, a religious scholar (pl. of the Arabic *'alim*). This remarkable image, describing this apparently pre-Islamic portrait painter, presages the Islamic figures
to follow in the poem. The word rendered
as "striking" in the final line is *kacap*, literally "struck, stamped, engraved."
85. By "the fragrant ones" (*para arum*) in
line 6 is meant "noble women."

83. That Kim Muwah was married "at the
same level" (*jinajar pakramanira*) means
that she was taken as a true co-wife (not
merely as lower wife or concubine) with a
status equal to that of the Emperor's
granddaughter. I presume the "they" (in
line 3) who were devoted to each other to
be the two co-wives.

15 Returning to the tale of old
In the realm of Majapahit
Child of His Royal Majesty
Brawijaya, his youngest
A son named
Jaka Karèwèd was
Born of a lower wife[86]

16 It began when His Majesty
Took to himself as handmaiden
A girl-child of the butcher folk
But not the daughter of
The butchers' chief officer
This daughter of a fourth-rank
   butcher-man
After some time had passed[87]

17 Was bedded by the King
The Maiden then was pregnant
Barely in her second month
Just showing listless pale

An aversion had the Maiden
She despised the sight of men
Now His Highness Brawijaya[88]

18 Decided then to summon
The Maiden of the butcher folk
As he was bent on bedding her
The Maiden, most averse
Would not yield to pressure
Ever adamant, the Maiden
Wept in dire distress

19 The King's desire frustrated
He was consumed with wrath
And so he turned his heart from
   her
His rage was gone too far
And so he did command
The leading lady-in-waiting
The Maiden to expel[89]

20 From the royal harem
Ordered was she to return home
To her father and her mother
His Highness thus would not abide
The sight then of the Maiden

86. The word *krèwèdan* means "a little profit" or "a little left over" (Poerwadarminta, *Baoesastra Djawa*, p. 250).
87. The word *parara-rara* (more commonly *palara-lara*), rendered in line 2 as "handmaiden," designates a little girl who, chosen by the king for her beauty or talent, is brought to the *kraton* (for education and "safe-keeping") at a very young age—to be taken as royal concubine when she comes of age (at her first menstruation). By noting that she is *not* the daughter of the chief officer, the poet takes care to distinguish this girl from Jaka Prabangkara's mother. This girl's father held the rank of *jagal panatus*. In the nineteenth-century Kraton Surakarta, a *panatus* was a fourth-rank palace official, after *bupati*, *kliwon*, and *panéwu*. See above, note to III:21.

88. "The Maiden" is my translation of the Javanese "Sang Rara."
89. The "leading lady-in-waiting" (*pawongan pinisepuh*) would be the mistress of the zenana who, in the nineteenth-century Kraton Surakarta, bore the title Radèn Ayu Adipati Sedhahmirah. Senior of the Sunan's minor wives, this powerful woman had charge of and dominion over the royal household (the *kenyapuri*). The *kenyapuri*, or harem, is the most inner/private part of the palace, wherein the female members of the royal house and their young children live.

His heart was turned from her
Now then in due course

21 With the coming of her time
The child of the Maiden's womb
Was born a son
She would inform the King
Too great though was her fear
For still His Royal Majesty's
Wrath was not appeased

22 So all of them remained in fear
That if they did indeed report
The unthinkable might befall
Thus it was as time did pass

Jaka Karèwèd is introduced: an exceptional village boy who is also a (very marginal) prince.

By the Will of the Absolute
That newborn baby did
Grow at a most amazing pace

23 And so with the passing of time
Now he was fourteen years old
His name was Jaka Karèwèd
In all his deeds shone clear
His difference from the other boys
With the air of his face profound
Truly none could be the like

24 It is said that the delight of
Jaka was tending buffalo
Beginning as a little boy
Daily making for the forest
As he tended his buffalo
And his goats and cows as well
To the middle of the woods

25 Many were his fellows

All of them butcher boys
Whose task it was to tend
Buffalo, cows, and goats
But this one Jaka
Often struck off alone
Preferring silent solitude

26 He would not join in play
Childish games and songs
Boisterous camaraderie
Assuredly in ancient times
Of those herd boys
Many were they who sang loud
   songs
Some sang in rustic melodious
   verse

27 Some told riddles and
Others tales of the masque
Some played with pokes and kicks
Others with ditties and verse
Rock skipping with piggy-back
Jaka ever was cajoled
By his friends the other boys

28 But still he would not play

Jaka Karèwèd discovers a charm of invisibility.

And so one day when Jaka
Had withdrawn apart
As he tended his buffalo
Wandering ever farther away
Deep in the mighty wood
There was a small clearing

29 There it was he rested
Jaka was very tired
The time approaching dusk
Jaka sitting on the ground

Before him saw there was
A tiny banyan tree sprouting
From the earth, a single finger high

30   Its trunk, the breadth of a palm-
          leaf rib
      A hardy sprout, its branches four
      Tiny were its leaves
      Of aspect supple, curling
      So very lush it shone
      Like a golden hair ornament
      Jaka delighted at the sight[90]

31   Thus he pondered in his heart:
      "It'd make a fine ear ornament
      I'll take it home with me
      Even when it's dried up
      Its form will still be nice
      With all its curls and knots"
      With that he plucked it from the
          earth

32   Pulled up too its roots
      Were clean with not a speck of dirt
      And lo! By the Will of the All-
          seeing
      Those roots twisted in magic knots
      Descending and ascending lush
      Placed at once behind his ear
      It was a charming ornament[91]

33   Becoming both from front and
          back
      With that Jaka Karèwèd
      Did vanish out of sight
      Invisible not just to man
      Why neither demon, ogre
      Fairy, spirit, nor sprite
      Could see Jaka Karèwèd

34   Jaka, bent for home then
      Set to herding his cows
      His buffalo and goats
      But loath were they to move
      All of them he coaxed and called
      But not a one did heed
      Unmoved were they by his com-
          mands

35   Even when he whipped them
      They still refused to budge
      Jaka in exasperation
      Mulled then to himself
      "Could this my ornament be
      The cause of all this bother?
      What if it takes my life?"[92]

───

90. The "golden hair ornament" of line
six is a translation of *cundhuk mentul,* a
springy bobbing ornament worn in the
hair coils of brides and female dancers.
91. In line 4, "twisted in magic knots" is a
translation of *sindhetan mimang.* The
word *mimang,* modifying the word for
root, designates a rare pattern of growth
for the aerial root of the banyan tree in
which the root sprouts again, reascending
from below. The word *sindhetan* means

"knotted" or "with a knot," and must describe the appearance of the root at the
node where it turns upward. Because such
roots are endowed with supernatural
powers, a person who steps over one of
them will become confused and lose her
way, perhaps repeatedly finding herself
back at the site of the root again. These
roots may be worn as a girdle or buried in
front of one's house to ward off evil influence and magic danger. See GR 2:519.
92. The words *anatas nyawa* ("to take
[my] life"), in conjunction with the punctuation mark for a new canto directly behind them, alert the reader/singer to
change to the melody of Megatruh ("to
take someone's life/soul").

X. Megatruh
[Melodic mood is one of sorrow or
deep regret]

1   Jaka then his ornament did
    Pluck and lay upon the earth
    Ki Jaka tried forthwith
    To herd his buffalo, cows, and goats
    Lo! Meekly they did follow

2   Stopping then, Ki Jaka pondered in
        his heart:
    "Perhaps this ornament indeed
    Makes one vanish out of sight"
    And so to try it once again
    The banyan tree he snatched forth-
        with

3   Thereat Ki Jaka's person
    Vanished again from sight
    And so the buffalo and cows
    Strayed and scattered yet again
    Commanded, still they would not
        budge

4   Beaten, they scattered to the winds
    To the north, the west
    The east, and south they fled
    Ki Jaka stopping then
    Did gently lay that banyan down

5   Jaka's person flashed to sight
    At once he tried again
    The goats, buffalo, and the cows
    He rounded up and
    Drove into a herd

6   He called and they did follow
    Meek, they strayed not from the
        way
    Jaka marveled for a moment

Pondering deep within his heart:
"So now 'tis surely true!

7   "Beyond a doubt 'tis the banyan
    That brings invisibility
    Making one vanish out of sight"
    Ki Jaka thereupon
    Caught one of his goats

8   Begirding it with ropes he tautly
        tied
    The banyan tree he stowed
    In a bamboo tube he tied
    To the back then of that goat
    Upright it stood, a single bamboo
        joint

9   Setting off for home, Jaka tended
        his herds
    His journey not recounted
    Now when he did arrive
    At home he was so late
    The cows he penned in haste

10 The goats and buffalo too, soon
        were in their pens
    Then Ki Jaka took
    The bamboo tube that held
    The banyan sprouting from the
        earth
    Jaka thereat was gone from sight

11 Invisible thus he entered the house
    His mother did not see
    Jaka so very hungry
    Forgetting the tube he held
    Came in with tube in hand

12 His mother was mulling to herself:
    "That boy is taking a mighty long
        time

Penning up the cows
Why! he's still not back!
Whatever is he up to there?"

13 As Jaka was exceedingly hungry,
      and
Yet his mother did not speak
Ki Jaka did cry out:
"Mama! Mama! I'm so hungry!
Give this empty belly rice!"

14 His mother, jumping with a start,
      replied:
"Where are you, Jaka?
Where are you calling from?
I've been waiting ages
You're nowhere to be seen

15 "But I hear your voice before me"
Ki Jaka did reply:
"Here I am, Mama
And I'm awfully hungry"
Tearfully then his mother spoke:

16 "You know I love you, child
Why then can't I see you?"
Of a sudden Jaka remembered
That he held in hand the banyan
Which was inside the bamboo tube

17 And so he put that tube forthwith
Just above the door
Jaka thereat was visible
His mother rushed to him
"O Karèwèd, my son

18 "O darling of my heart"
Wept she for her Jaka
And too his mother asked
"Now what is happening here
That you were just invisible?"

19 Ki Jaka then related how it had
      begun
When he found that banyan tree
Which sprouted from the earth
From beginning unto end
Ki Jaka did report

20 Upon hearing, his mother most
      amazed
Spoke thus unto her son:
"In that case, child
Perhaps 'tis by the grace of God
That you, my own dear son

21 "Are granted means to vanish out
      of sight
This is a precious magic charm
Wrap it up with care
Place it in a tube of ivory-bamboo
And store it in that chest"[93]

22 The son did as his mother told
Storing away the banyan tree
Thereupon Ki Jaka was
Served rice, and he did eat
Once he'd eaten his fill, the youth

23 Then slept, so very tired was he

93. In line 2, "precious magic charm" is
my translation of *paripih*. According to
Gericke and Roorda's nineteenth-century
lexicon, the word *paripih* or *jimat paripih*
designates the pad used by a girl at her
first menstruation, which pad is saved to
be worn later as a protective charm by
that girl's son (GR 2:306). In 1939, however, Poerwadarminta defined *paripih* as a
magic amulet upon which is inscribed the
Javanese character: aksara swara *u* diwulu
(*Baoesastra Djawa*, p. 472).

*Jaka Karèwèd embarks upon a new
career as subversive.
Invisibility and illicit penetration of
walls/orders.*

Speaking not now of the night
Let it be told that on the morn
Jaka did beg his mother leave
That he not go out to herd

24 Another instead was charged to
        herd
    With that Ki Jaka did set off
    Intent to try it out
    Holding the magic banyan tree
    Jaka was gone from sight

25 Coming to the market, not a soul
        did see
    Though penetrating every corner
    Still not a single soul did see
    At that Ki Jaka did turn back
    And arriving home, removed

26 From his head-wrap, the banyan he
        stored
    Thus it was as time went on
    Every morning Ki Jaka
    Ranged about the realm
    To the north, east, south, and west

27 For Jaka wished to see within
    The houses of the lords
    The great and mighty nobles
    And all the chief officials
    The courtiers of the King

28 He ranged inside their houses all
    The courtiers, nobles, and chiefs
    Even unto the home of

The Lord Grand Vizier
Gajahmada he did penetrate

29 Not a single soul there was who
        saw
    So through their inner gardens too
    He ranged through all of them
    And now Ki Jaka wished to see
    The sights within the *kraton* walls

30 Ki Jaka, making straight for it
    Through the Gate of Watchful
        Waiting came
    Not a soul accosting him
    Heading straight for the king's
        zenana
    The Inner Sanctum did he pene-
        trate[94]

94. The "Gate of Watchful Waiting" (or
Sri Manganti) is the name of a gate in the
Kraton Surakarta. This gate, which is enclosed in a building and heavily guarded,
is the third northern portal (after Kori
Brajanala and Kori Kamandhungan) into
the Kraton proper, the *kedhaton*. There
guests of, or emissaries to, the Susuhunan or members of his immediate family
wait (*manganti*)—under guard—to be received.
    The "Inner Sanctum" (or Dalem Ageng
Praba[su]yasa), located directly behind
(to the west) and adjoining the major audience pavilion Sasana Séwaka, was [is?]
the sacral center of the Kraton Surakarta
(figure 16). The most sacred (that is potent) regalia of the realm were and are
housed in this chamber. On royal ceremonial occasions, the queens, princesses,
concubines, and female courtiers were
and are seated in this Inner Sanctum.
Since the early twentieth century, no
men aside from the Susuhunan and a

31 From the Hall of Fragrant Flowers,
        to the Queen's boudoir, her bath
   In and about ranging everywhere
   All over the royal harem
   He did not miss a thing
   And after everything was eyed[95]

32 Ki Jaka then withdrew most tired
   And he was very hungry too
   Exhausted and famished indeed
   So then he paid a call at
   The Chief of the Exchequer's
        house[96]

33 As he came in, the lord of the
        house

        ——

   very few senior princes have been admit-
   ted entrance to this chamber. In nineteenth-century Kraton diaries, however,
   it is not uncommon to read of the Susuhunan escorting high-ranking European
   officials on tours through the Prabayasa.
   See, for example, [Krep, Josep = Joseph
   Kreeft], *Serat Baleniklan: Awit ongka 1771
   dumugi ongka 1773* (compiled and inscribed Surakarta, 1843–53). MS. SP uncataloged; SMP KS 81a, *passim*.
   95. Purwakanthi ("the Hall of Fragrant
   Flowers") and Purwalulut ("the Queen's
   boudoir") are names of pavilions in the
   zenana of the Kraton Surakarta. Flower
   offerings were (and are) prepared in the
   Purwakanthi pavilion. Purwalulut was
   formerly associated with the boudoir (and
   bath) of the queen (Personal Communication, Nyai Tumenggung Pamardi Srimpi,
   1984).
   96. The English "chief of the Exchequer"
   is a translation of *mantri gedhong*. The
   Gedhong (Exchequer) of the Kraton was
   in charge of the palace stores and the
   household expenses of the king and royal
   family.

He did descry about to eat
Ki Jaka was greatly relieved
Forthwith the feast began
With relish Ki Jaka joined in

34 That he was befriended at board,
        the Exchequer Chief knew not
   For Ki Jaka could not be seen
   That illustrious officer thought it
        was
   From the deliciousness of the feast
   That so prodigious a platter of rice
        was short

35 Taken aback were the servants all
   For as long as they remembered
   Never had he eaten like that
   "Perhaps he was helped by a
        demon
   Or maybe a ghoul has gobbled it
        up"

36 Once the feast was done, Jaka made
        for home
   And so then every day
   It was Ki Jaka's pleasure
   To eat with the royal officers all
   The courtiers, both old and
        young[97]

XI. Sinom
[Melodic mood is "even"]

1 The princes-regent and the nobles
        all

        97. The word *nom* ("young"), in conjunc-
        tion with the punctuation mark for a new
        canto directly following it, signals the
        reader to change to the melody of Si*nom*.

Were joined at their tables
By the very same Ki Jaka
And the Excellent Vizier
Gajahmada was not left out
Even His Majesty the King
Was joined at dinner too
Thus as time went on
All the realm did reckon alike

2 Everywhere seethed the news
That there was a secret outlaw
Marvelous and invisible
Who often stole in to eat along
And often ranged the *kraton* -
Striking His Majesty's gong
Majapahit's holy regalia
As well as the ancient war gong
Sir Thunderhead, the holy heir-
    loom of Jenggala[98]

3 And often drank up the liquor
His Majesty's private reserve
Whatever drinks there were
Every day he did drink up
And so His Royal Highness

98. The word *maling,* rendered in line 2 as
"outlaw," designates a thief (or lover)
who steals in somewhere under cover of
darkness.
    The "holy regalia" in line 7 and the
"holy heirloom" in the final line are both
for the Javanese *pusaka.* Sir Thunderhead
(Kyai Grah papat, literally "Sir Thunder
of the Fourth Month") is a *bendhé* gong,
an archaic flat gong without nobbed boss.
By Javanese historical traditions, Jenggala
was a thirteenth-century kingdom located near present-day Surabaya. The
most renowned ruler of this legendary
kingdom was King Suryawisésa (=
Panji).

Was deeply grieved of heart
And the Excellent Vizier
Plunged in anguish dire
Felt challenged as guardian of the
    realm

4 His Majesty's miseries
All the troubles of the realm
In truth it was the Vizier
Whose challenge it was to meet
    them
"Should it go on like this
Then turmoil shall come to reign
In the realm of Majapahit
This very well might be
A plot to fell the King"

The authorities strike back: Jaka Ka-
rèwèd, the invisible subversive, is
forced to light before his final van-
ishing.

5 Truly the world was in uproar
And so the Excellent Vizier
Consulted with the King
Proposing a perfect way
To still this bothersome care
To outvie in trickery
A means then if it worked
To make the outlaw come to sight
Endorsed was Gajahmada's plan

6 Speaking then not of the night
It is related that on the morn
His Majesty Brawijaya
Determined to hold a feast
For all the servants of the realm
By royal command, the Vizier
Did summon all the courtiers
The nobles and high officials

Princes-regent from afar and all
    the generals[99]

7   When everyone was assembled
    The King began to feast
    In banquet he did drink
    With his courtiers great and low
    The drinks were manifold:
    Fermented rice whisky, rice wine,
      grape wine
    Palm whisky, palm beer, ambrosia
    Fresh rice whisky and fragrant rice
      gin
    Dry wine, sweet wine, liqueur of
      anise

8   Their shouts did shake the walls
    And so again 'tis related
    Of Ki Jaka the butcher boy
    After watching for some time
    Did long to join the feast
    The banquet of His Majesty
    So then Jaka joined in
    Seated close to the Vizier
    Ki Jaka was caught in the readied
      trap

9   Of empty chairs there was but one
    And there set out already were
    Many kinds of drinks
    Before that empty chair
    All of them were doctored
    With heady potions and drugs
    That he to a drunken stupor would
      fall
    And in such stupor would come to
      sight

99. With "generals," I translate *huluba-
lang.*

Not one of the toasts did Ki Jaka
    miss

10 Now so very reeling drunk were
    The Divine King of Majapahit
    And all his courtiers
    The nobles and princes-regent
    The officials both great and low
    Their shouts did shake the heavens
    Along with the song of the game-
      lan
    So delicately alluring
    Like a flood of golden honey it
      charmed[100]

11 All them feeling their drink
    Looked pink like basil blooms
    Let it be recited now: Ki Jaka

100. This image of the shouting, drinking
king and courtiers would not have been
an exotic one at the nineteenth-century
Kraton Surakarta. Indeed, the description
calls to mind numerous accounts of toast-
ing Javanese kings and courtiers (usually
in the company of Dutch colonial officials) recorded in the palace archives and
elsewhere. For instance, an English visitor
to the residence of the Surakarta prime
minister in 1828 reported: "as usual we
had a number of toasts to honor, standing
up and cheering to each; our worthy host
pledged them all so faithfully, that he evidently felt the influence of the jolly god
before we rose from table and the last
toast he gave was quite unintelligible to
all present; it received however as much
attention and applause as the others"
("Journal of an Excursion to the Native
Provinces on Java in the Year 1828, during the War with Dipo Negoro," *Journal
of the Indian Archipelago and Eastern Asia*
8 [1854]:93).

Had fallen in the trap
Like a hibiscus bloom
A vivid violet hibiscus
His face, a flush of red
Bleary was his vision
Reeling, he had lost himself

12   Wobbling in his seat
Groping were his hands
Back and forth his head did reel
Tremble did his body
And sweat pouring forth
Drenched was he to the skin
Suffocating, his body burned
On the sudden vomiting blood
Down from his chair did Ki Jaka
        fall

13   Oblivious, he was as dead
It must have been the Will of God
That Jaka meet his ruin
Overwhelmed by the mighty King
Who was his father after all
Now then with the fall of
Jaka from his seat
His head-wrap did fly loose
Landing far from his head

14   The magic charm within the cloth
The banyan sprouting from the
        earth
Whose roots twisted in magic
        knots
Was borne along with the head-
        wrap
Jaka then was quit of
The state of invisibility
And Jaka's person flashed to sight
A lifeless heap sprawled on the
        floor

Now the soldiers who'd been given
        to know

15   The "Death Lovers," the "Hidden
        Ones"
And the "Lions of the Realm"
Who all along had lain in wait
In formation to either side
Vigilant to the danger
All together then did pounce
Together with a shout
Thundering, so horrible
Crying: "Outlaw! Here's the magic
        outlaw!"[101]

16   All present raised exultant cheers
Joining in they cried: "The outlaw!
The disappearing outlaw
The invisible unseen one
The sneaky little bully
Wonderful, magic, so devious
Presumptuous, so cocksure
As if there were no others of magic
        powers wonderful
Aside from this wretched outlaw of
        wondrous powers supreme!

101. The names of these various corps of
premodern undercover agents refer to actual troop divisions in the nineteenth-
century Kraton Surakarta. The Marta-
lulut ("Death" [or conversely, "Life"]
"Lovers") were a corps of executioners
who would execute secretly the punishment decreed/desired by the Susuhunan
(J. W. Winter, "Beknopte Beschrijving
van Het Hof Soerakarta in 1824," BKI 54
[1902]:71). The Kajineman ("Hidden
Ones") were a troop of secret police. The
Singanagara ("Lions of the Realm") were
a corps of public executioners.

17 "As if there were no other men
    Aside from this wretched outlaw!
    No others magically marvelous
    Aside from this wretched outlaw!
    No others with mystic powers
    Aside from this wretched outlaw!
    No others possessed of daring
    Aside from this wretched outlaw!
    Now try your wits on that, you
        wretched magic outlaw!"

18 Ki Jaka they did bind
    Tied hand and foot was he
    But Ki Jaka then
    Away in sleep's oblivion
    Was not the least aware
    So deep his stupor
    So strong the drinks
    So potent the potions
    And drugs, that he was half-dead

19 Once bound, Ki Jaka was
    Delivered up before the King
    By command of Brawijaya
    The head-cloth then was burned
    Jaka was provided another
    Head-cloth from the King
    Ki Jaka at that time
    Laughter's butt to right, left
    And behind, was oblivious still

20 Grand Vizier Gajahmada then
    Administered forthwith
    The antidote: young lime juice
    With *orang-aring* leaves
    And juice of the *nasandir*
    And mashed *kati gubug*
    Were given at his nose to snift
    And sprinkled on his lips

Camphor was sprayed into his
    eyes[102]

21 In a flash Ki Jaka started wide
        awake
    All too stark aware was he
    With pounding heart distrait
    He found himself tied up
    Bound and the butt of laughter
        cruel
    In the presence of the King
    Surrounded by the courtiers
    Jaka unable to move was
    Resigned in his heart and bowed
        his head in shame

22 Questioned was he by His Majesty
    "Who are you, churl?
    Why! You're but a boy
    And fine to look at too
    With power to vanish out of sight
    Who then sent you here
    In a devious cunning plot
    To topple thus our realm
    To subvert by a *darma* of de-
        ceit?"[103]

102. The Latin name of the *orang-aring*
plant is Eclipta alba. I have yet to identify
the *nasandir* or *kati gubug*.
103. Line 2, "èh sira bocah ing ngendi,"
could be translated more literally: "where
do you come from?" However, the question asks "who are you?" or "what kind of
person are you?" or "where do you stand
in the social hierarchy?"
    A *darma* is a code of behavior or an
ethics. A *darma* of deceit (or tricks) would
be a style of political/military strategy in
conflict with the recognized and accepted
(heroic) *darma* of the *satriya* (noble or
warrior) and the judicious "*darma* of
kingship" (see above, V:10).

23 Jaka Karèwèd's answer:
"O Majesty, my Illustrious Lord
I, your humble servant, do forgive-
   ness beg
From beneath the dust of your
   royal feet
That I do not a *sembah* make
Troubled thus by these bonds"
On hearing this, His Majesty
Did command him loosed
The officers then set to, loosening
   his bonds[104]

24 Still left, but as a formal sign
A cord draped over his shoulders
Ki Jaka then his *sembah* made
"O Majesty, my Illustrious Lord
I, your humble servant, am neither
   spy
Nor devious subversive foe
Nor emissary of a king
Prince or prince-regent
General, courtier, or high officer[105]

25 "I'm nothing but a reckless lad
Spoiled since I was small
I hail from the Butcher's Quarter
Where I live fatherless
The son of a poor widow
Low-born of common stock
Karèwèd is my name
My grandpa is a commoner
Named Kartimaya, a butcher of
   fourth-rank[106]

26 "As for what I've done
All that, Your Majesty
Was by my own design
No one told me what to do
It was because I wished
To prove, Your Royal Highness
The book I chanced upon
In the middle of the mighty wood
Its form a banyan tree sprouting
   from the earth[107]

27 "Straightway I pulled it up
Its roots came right along
Those roots were twisted in magic
   knots"
Young Jaka did continue
From beginning unto end
As His Majesty listened

104. The tonality of Jaka's reply is not
sarcastic. It is simply impossible for a
subject to speak to his king without the
gesture of obeisance.
105. The cord draped over Jaka Karèwèd's
shoulder marks him as prisoner. That
cord is analogous to the *samir* (a red-
bordered yellow sash worn to this day
over the shoulders of courtiers at the
Kraton Surakarta). I have heard from different servants of the court various interpretations of the *samir*'s significance and
utility. Some say that the *samir* protects
its wearer against the possibly pernicious
effects of the Kraton *pusaka* and/or of
Kangjeng Ratu Kidul (spirit Queen of the
South Sea and wife to all kings of the
Mataram dynasty). Others say the wear-

ing of the *samir* indicates the servant's
willingness to be throttled at any moment by his/her king.
106. The name Kartimaya indicates deception or illusion. The word *karti* means
"agent" or "maker"; *maya* means "illusion, fraud, deceit, sorcery."
107. In line 7, Jaka Karèwèd claims—by a
"slip of the pen"—to have found a book
(*pustaka*) instead of the expected "magic
talisman" (*pusaka*).

He pondered in his heart
Amazed the Illustrious Lord
Reflected on the words that from
the water rose[108]

XII. Mas Kumambang

[Melodic mood is one of deep sorrow or mourning]

1   His Majesty the King seemed sunk
in deep regret
For too rash of spirit
Had he ordered the head-wrap
burned
Prodded by passion impetuous

2   Had he been less rash, it could have
been of use
And so His Majesty
Thereat did summon forth
The chief of the royal butchers

3   Was ordered to bring forward his
fourth-rank butcher named
Kyai Kartimaya
Arriving in no time at all

Was commanded to advance into
the presence of the King

4   Kyai Kartimaya, on seeing
That his grandson was
Surrounded there before the King
Forgot the royal presence, and

5   Weeping loudly, wailed, more or
less:
"Alas! And now it's come to this
Because you dared
To enter here, O treasure of my
soul"

6   Many were the plaints of Kyai
Kartimaya
Then His Royal Highness
Did question the headman
Yea, the chief of the royal butchers

7   "Now, whose child is this boy in
truth?"
The butcher chief replied:
"Surrendering my life into your
hands
Your slave dare not, not to reply

8   "In truth, Highness, this Jaka is
Indeed the one that carried off
From the *kraton* still in his moth-
er's womb
Was born as this Ki Jaka[109]

9   "Back when the Maiden did the
kraton leave

108. The sense of the final line, "nga-
ngen-ngangen kang tutur timbuling
toya," though hardly discursive, is three-
fold: (1) the emotive sense, in which the
words by association are evocative of the
king's affective state (*ngangen* [reflected
on] with *kangen* [pangs of loss] and *toya*
[water] with recession/loss); (2) the sense
of sound—from the alliteration and assonance of the repeated *ng-*, *-ang*, and then *t*
sounds; (3) the sense as a sign (in conjunction with the visual sign marking the
change of cantos) signaling the reader/
singer to change to the Mas Kumambang
("Floating gold") meter.

109. An alternative reading for the initial
line "Yektosipun, pun Jaka punika Gusti,"
is "In truth, this Jaka is a prince."

Indeed 'twas none but I
Your Majesty, who knew of it
And who watched over her

10 "And to this very day, she does re-
fuse to wed
Content to watch her son
A child of the *kraton*
Hence exceedingly spoiled"

11 On hearing this, the King knew
then in his heart
Truly this boy was his son
But still he hid it in his heart
Breaking off a moment on the King

12 To tell of the one left behind:
She the Widow Woman
Of the butcher-folk, all the night
long
Was assailed by heart's foreboding

13 Unable to sleep all the night long
Ever pounding her heart
And still upon the morn
Her heart was ill at ease

14 The morning long Ki Jaka was
cajoled
By this his mother
"Do not go out, dear child
For my heart bodes ill"

15 But Jaka was not persuaded
And so then when
The Widow Woman heard
Clearly from the roaring mob

16 That the King had caught the
magic outlaw
Able to vanish out of sight

And that the outlaw was but a boy
The Widow hoisted up her skirts

17 Along with her mother; off rushed
the two
Eyes brimming with tears
The two of them scurried on apace
Straightway to the King's audience

18 Arriving in the presence, the
Widow let out a shriek
Rushing to her child
She wept most piteously
As she embraced her son

19 "Alas! For nought I bore this son!
Alas! There is none so
Ill-starred as I
Perhaps such is my fortune

20 "My words went all unheeded
I told you not
To go abroad this day
Headstrong, you went anyway

21 "Foreboding was my anxious heart
Now, treasure of my soul, you
Do suffer these bonds
In the clutches of the Realm

22 "Oh wretched disaster! My darling
son, O Lord!
Now is sunk to shame
Alas! Now where am I to turn?
How I prayed for a son

23 "And now he does but break my
heart
My heart is splitting
Ruined, ruptured, ripped to shreds
Alas! 'Tis not as it should be

24 "For you have yet to know of life's
      delights
    For orphaned from birth
    Living fatherless
    You've grown reckless and unruly

25 "O my darling, how could you dare
    To penetrate the *kraton*?
    Where many are the courtiers, the
      chiefs
    Many, the notables of the realm

26 "You have yet to know the ven-
      geance of the realm
    For you are but a commoner
    A lowly wretched wretch
    A villager who has no rule[110]

27 "And yet you dared, my darling
      child
    Draw nigh unto the presence of
    His Majesty the Imperial Lord
    And he a mighty king divine

28 "Beloved of the foremost gods
    Lord of all the world
    There is none who equals him
    You, my darling, are but a child

29 "A child of the village blind to
      ruled propriety
    Acting blind of the proper way
    You are ruined, my child
    Fallen now to torment"

30 The hapless widow wept in an-
      guished abandon

110. The word *ukara*, translated as "rule"
in the final line, reads most often as a
grammatical term for "sense," "sentence,"
or "syntax."

And too the plaintive cries
Of Grandma Kartimaya keen
Ki Jaka too began to cry

31 All those who heard were deeply
      moved
    And with abandon they
    Did give way to tears
    And knew that this was the son of
      their king

32 His Majesty the King was touched
      by wonder deep
    His heart pierced by care
    Tears welling in his eyes
    Bethought himself, his heart aware

33 Decreed the King to his Vizier
    "This our Jaka here
    Is verily my son
    Take him home with you"

34 The Vizier his assent did say
    Then His Royal Highness
    Retired to the zenana
    The Vizier the assemblage did dis-
      perse

35 Jaka was escorted out by the Vizier
    Behind them came his mother
    Along with her mother
    And Grandpa Kartimaya too

36 And the chief of the royal butchers
      was not left behind
    And the high courtiers
    All paid their respects
    Escorting Prince Jaka

37 Coming to the Vizier's stead,
      changed were the clothes

Of this Prince Jaka
Describing not that night
It is told that on the morn

38   There came His Highness's mes-
         sengers
     Bearing many trays
     Laden with fine garments
     Gifts from his father the King

39   Every day came trains of guests
     All the princes of the blood
     Princes-regent and high courtiers
     All presented him fine garments

40   Riches and rainments manifold
     And so Prince Jaka then
     Was of eminence wonderful
     And too so very rich

A return to the tale of Pajang-
Pengging. Introduces the princes of
Pengging: Kebo Kanigara and Kebo
Kenonga (Jaka Tingkir's uncle and
father respectively).

41   Falling silent on Prince Jaka who
         had come into his own
     Let now be told in turn
     The tale interrupted by poetry
     Of Pajang-Pengging sweet[111]

111. The word *kawi* rendered in line 3 as
"poetry" could as well be read as "the
Poet."
   The word *sarkara* (rendered here as
"sweet"), in conjunction with the punctuation mark for a new canto directly behind it, signals the poem's reader/singer
to change to the melody of Dhangdhanggula, or Sarkara.

XIII. Dhangdhanggula/Sarkara
[Melodic mood is lithe, with didactic clarity and romantic allure]

1   To tell of Pajang-Pengging's King
    The mighty Handayaningrat
    Did not enjoy a lengthy life
    With death His Majesty
    Left behind two children
    Both of them were sons
    The elder one was named
    Prince Kebo Kanigara
    The younger, Prince Kebo Kenonga
        indeed
    Both were handsome lads[112]

2   Succeeded they their father
    These princes of Pengging two
    By their grandfather's will
    Were not enthroned as kings
    For Pengging's realm was halved
    Into two mere regencies
    Of junior and senior Pengging
    Still living then their mother
    Indeed the Queen of Pengging,
        Handayaningrat
    Did nurture her children two[113]

3   Before long their mother perished
    Thus orphaned were the princes
        two
    While still of very young age

112. The word *kebo* ("water buffalo") was
a standard prefix to noble names in "medieval" Java. The words *kanigara* and *ke-*
nanga (or *kenonga*) designate a flowering
tree and flowering plant respectively.
113. The word I translate as "regencies"
in line 6 is *kabupatèn*.

Most piteous was their state
Bereft of kingly father
And queenly mother too
And so it is related:
By the will of their grandfather
His Highness Brawijaya King of
    Majapahit
Both of these his grandsons

4   Were brought then to Majapahit
By their grandfather adopted sons
Both of them indulged
For as his firstborn grandchildren
They took for him the place of his
    child
Overflowing was the love of the
    King
And too Her Majesty the Queen
Andarawati, surpassing
Was her love for these her grand-
    sons two
For neither mother nor father had
    they

5   And their realm of Pajang-
    Pengging
Was tended by the nobles all
All the gentry of Pengging
The great and mighty officers
Unchanged, it was the same as
    when
King Handayaningrat still reigned
Now not to be related here
Are their doings or time's passing

Returning to Brawijaya's vanishing,
the poet genealogically centers the
heirs to the kingdom of Pajang-
Pengging in relation to the saints

credited with bringing Islam (and a
new era) to Java.

That to be rendered: with the Fall
    of Majapahit
Was Brawijaya's vanishing

6   The Cham princess, Queen Dwara-
    wati
Followed not her husband in Re-
    lease
For in her heart she was Moslem
Embracing the religion
Of her son from Ngampèldenta
And with the death of that her son
She followed then her grandson
That is, Lord Sunan Bonang
Honoring the *shari'a*, ordained by
    the Prophet
Muhammad, Master of the Uni-
    verse[114]

114. Queen Dwarawati's "son" (actually
her nephew) was Sunan Ngampèldenta.
Following Dwarawati's marriage to Brawijaya, her younger sister was married to
the Arab "missionary" of Islam, Ibrahim
Makdum Asmara, who is credited with
the conversion of Champa. This sister
bore Ibrahim Makdum Asmara two sons:
Prince Rahmat (later Sunan Ngampèldenta) and Prince Santri (later Sunan
Ngali Murtala). Upon maturity these two
sons together with their mother's brother's son, Prince 'Alim Abu Hurérah (later
Sunan Majagung) traveled to Java in
search of their aunt, Majapahit's queen.
By permission of his uncle Brawijaya,
Prince Rahmat (who is often acknowledged as the originary bringer of Islam to
Java) settled and taught religion in Ampèldenta (Surabaya).
   Sunan Bonang was the son of Sunan

7 And the husband's charge of old
   To his queen the Cham Princess
   Ordered was she to stay behind
   To nurture all the children
   The grandchildren all who'd been
      left behind
   To honor the faith
   The Prophet's *shari'a*
   His Majesty Brawijaya
   Though but a heathen *Buda* still
      was brilliant bright
   Aware of the Whence and
      Whither[115]

8 Though Queen Andarawati was
   Borne away by her grandson
   His Majesty Sovereign of the
      World
   The Lord Sunan Bonang
   Did his grandmother deeply revere
   Many were the grandchildren
   Who did come along
   With their grandmother to Bonang
   Both the princes of Pengging two
   Came along to Bonang[116]

9 For indeed the Lord Sunan Bonang
   Was related as second cousin
   To these princes two
   The elder in relation
   Were the princes of Pajang-
      Pengging
   The Lord Sunan Bonang
   Stood younger in relation
   Deep, the reciprocal love of
   The elder brothers two and their
      younger brother
   The Lord Sunan Bonang[117]

10 Of good comfort were these lords
      of Pengging
   In Bonang they did study
   The faith, the *shari'a*
   Also there was the Lord
   Of Madura, Prince-regent
   Lembu Peteng of Madura
   At that time did sojourn
   At the ashram of Bonang
   Lord Sunan Bonang cherished so
   With love this father his[118]

11 For indeed as elder uncle to
   His Majesty Sovereign of the
      World
   Stood the King of Madura

Ngampèldenta by a daughter of High
Prince Téja, a Majapahit noble and ruler
of Tuban.
    Sometimes called the "Sacred Law" or
"Canon Law" of Islam, the *shari'a* is the
name of the collected body of more or less
codified laws that govern every aspect of
life for a pious Moslem.
115. A follower of *Buda*, as I noted above
(note to I:18) is not a Buddhist, but an ad-
herent to the pre-Islamic "Buda order."
On the "Whence and Whither," see
above, note to I:13.
116. The word *binoyongan*, rendered in
line 2 as "borne away," is the term used to
describe the carrying off of brides, captive
women, and the spoils of war.

117. The Pengging princes are genealogically senior in this relationship because
their grandmother, Queen Dwarawati,
was the elder sister of Sunan Bonang's
grandmother.
118. Lembu Peteng of Madura was the
uterine brother of Queen Handayaningrat, both of them children of
Sunan Bonang's elder great aunt (and
therefore generational "grandmother"),
Queen Dwarawati. Lembu Peteng, as
Sunan Bonang's genealogical elder-uncle,
was his generational "father."

This Lembu Peteng was indeed
Son-in-law to High Prince Baribin
Who ruled Madura's realm
And so it is told
Lord Lembu Peteng of Madura
Deeply did love these his nephews
Prince Kebo Kanigara[119]

12   And Prince Kebo Kenonga too
With the death of their mother and
    father
Of both he took the place
Showering down his love
As though to his own sons
Not like nephews mere
And even 'twere the case
Their mother and father still lived
Still special would be his love
For these his nephew-sons

13   And the Lord Sunan Giri too
Deeply loved his elder brothers
These lords of Pengging two
And as for the Lord Sunan
Darajat, it was the same again
And too their elder-uncle
Lord Sunan Majagung
Great was his love and respect
For these princes of Pengging two
Were like his own sons to him[120]

119. The kinship relations between Sunan
Bonang and Prince-regent Lembu Peteng
of Madura were further complicated: the
sister of Lembu Peteng's wife (High
Prince Baribin's daughter) was one Ni
Ageng Manyura. She was married to Kalipah Kusèn, former husband of Sunan
Bonang's niece (daughter of Bonang's
elder half-sister, who, like her daughter,
was also called Ni Ageng Manyura).
120. Sunan Giri was a distant cousin of
the Pengging princes. His grandfather

14   And Lord Sunan Muryapada
Now he was related as son
To these princes two
With Susunan Kudus
Related too as son
Both of them did deeply love
These honored royal children
And too the Lord Sunan
Kalijaga stood a younger brother in
    relation
To these royal princes[121]

——

was the Arab emigrant Maulana Abu
Ahmad Iskak (a brother of the Pengging
princes' great-uncle by marriage, Ibrahim
Makdum Asmara). Furthermore, Sunan
Giri's wife was also the princes' second
cousin (she was a daughter of Sunan
Ngampèldenta and a half-sister of Sunan
Bonang).
    A son of Sunan Ngampèldenta, Sunan
Darajat was the uterine brother of Sunan
Bonang.
    Sunan Majagung, known by the name
Prince 'Alim Abu Hurérah as a boy, was a
son of Sultan Sarip Judin of Champa. He
was the brother of Majapahit's Queen
Dwarawati and therefore the Pengging
princes' great-uncle.
121. Sunan Muryapada was a son of the
Princes of Pengging's "cousin," Sunan
Kalijaga, and hence their generational
"son."
    Sunan Kudus, a son of the younger Ni
Ageng Manyura (grand-daughter of Sunan Ngampèldenta) by Kalipah Kusèn,
was therefore a generational son of the
princes of Pengging; see also note to XIII:
11 above.
    Sunan Kalijaga, though (to my knowl-
edge) no blood relation to the princes of
Pengging, still stood in genealogical relation of younger brother (cousin) to them.
Kalijaga was a son of Tumenggung
Wilatikta of Tuban, whose sister (Ni
Ageng Manila) was married to Sunan

15 And Lord Sunan Gunungjati
     Deep too was his love and respect
     And their uncles all
     And all their aunts
     All the royal children of Majapahit
     Fondly did cherish
     These honored royal sons
     And all of the nobility
     Did always bear in mind the charge
     Of His Highness Brawijaya

16 All were commanded of old to care
       for them
     With none to be of heart aloof
     To these royal princes two
     Charged in solemn earnest
     With interdictions was this trust
     Of His Majesty Brawijaya
     To those whom he left behind
     And so with the passing of time
     It is told that Queen Dwarawati
     Had grown so very old

17 And after some time, Queen
      Dwarawati
     Fell ill unto her death
     Not to be rendered elaborately
     Her body was laid to rest
     There at Karang Kamuning
     Her children and grandchildren
     All they who were bereft
     Did solemnize her death reciting
     The Qur'ân and chanting the *tas-*
       bèh and *tahmid*
     Tahlil and *istigfar*[122]

Ampèldenta, cousin of the Pengging princes' mother.
122. Karang Kamuning is the name of a village near Bonang, in northern Central

Some notes pertaining to the establishment of Islam over newly converted Java. This includes a catalog of the religious authorities and an implicit mapping of the extent of Demak's political sway.

18 Thus with the passing of time
     It is said that the realm of Demak
     Did flourish most lush
     All Java did submit
     All the kings and princes-regent
     All those of the distant
     Mighty outer realms
     All of them submitted
     To the Lord Panembahan of Bin-
       tara
     The Caliph of Allah's Prophet[123]

Java. *Tasbèh* is an Arabic prayer consisting of a repetition of the phrase meaning: "I proclaim the glory of God." The Moslem rosary is also called a *tasbèh*. *Tahmid* is an Arabic prayer that praises God with the words "Praise is due to God alone." *Tahlil* is an Arabic prayer that consists of the repetition of the formula: "there is no god but God." *Istigfar* is an Arabic prayer that consists of the words: "I ask forgiveness of God." The chanting of these Islamic prayers at the Queen's funeral comprised a form of *zikir* (Ar. *dhikr*). The practice of *zikir*, in which such prayer formulas are meditatively and repetitively recited (often by groups of worshipers), is an important technique of Islamic mystics on their way to ecstasy. On Sufi *dhikr* practices, see J. Spencer Trimingham, *The Sufi Orders in Islam* (London: Oxford University Press, 1971), p. 201 ff.
123. "The Caliph of Allah's Prophet" of the final line is a translation of "Khalifah Rasullolah."

19 As deputy of divine dominion
        indeed
    With authority to adjudicate on
        discourses
    On the holy *sharî'a* of
    The Prophet who was Apostle
    Now at that time in Java's land
    All had become Moslem
    There was none who did resist
    All the mountain hermits
    The ascetics and acolytes, the de-
        votees and disciples
    Many converted to the Faith[124]

20 And the royal Buddhist and Saivite
        monks, the Hindu priests
    Were exchanged for *fuqaha* law-
        yers

124. The translation of line 2, "myang
wilayah kurus [i.e., kusus] ing rilasah
[i.e., risalah]," is problematic. The line
might as well read: "With special authority of apostleship." My translation of this
and the first line are influenced by the
new light on the institution of the Caliphate in the Arabic Islamic world provided by Patricia Crone and Martin
Hinds's *God's Caliph: Religious Authority
in the First Centuries of Islam* (Cambridge:
Cambridge University Press, 1986).
    In this and the next verse, the poet
translates from pre-Islamic Hindu-
Buddhist to Islamic "clerical" categories.
In this verse, the terms belong to rank-
ings among rural/mountain pre-Islamic
holy orders. The term "hermit" is my
translation of *ajar*. "Ascetic" is my translation of *wasi*. For *guguntung* I chose the
English "acolyte." By "devotee," I render
manguyu (a category of male religious
persons). "Disciple" is my translation for
cantrik.

Great and mighty pundits
Excellent learned *ulama*
Mystic *zahid* and *mungahid*
Mufti and *sulakha*
Great and mighty *khukama*
Why! Even of the foreign kings
Who were to Java vassal
Many had become Moslem[125]

21 Thus it was with time's passage
    To tell of Bintara-Demak
    It was on a Monday when

125. In line 1, the *sogata séwa* and *resi-resi*
("royal Buddhist and Saivite monks, the
Hindu priests") were classes of religious
persons often associated with the palaces
as spiritual officials of the realm. The
term *sogata* names the Buddhist monk-
hood. The word *séwa* refers to the Shai-
vite "priesthood." The word *resi* ("bhik-
shu") designates a kind of ascetic priest.
    Fuqaha (pl. of the Ar. *faqîh*) are experts
in Islamic law (*fiqh*).
    Pundits is my "translation" of *pandhita*,
Sanskrit for "scholar, sage, teacher, holy
man." Here and elsewhere the poet in-
stills this well-known Hindu term with
Islamic meaning.
    Ulama (pl. of Ar. *'âlim*) are religious
scholars.
    Zahid is Arabic for "an ascetic."
    Mungahid (variant of the Ar. *mujâhid*)
are those who fight in the way of God or
in the cause of religion. In Sufi terms the
mungahid is the one who strives along the
mystical way.
    Mufti are canon lawyers authorized to
promulgate *fatwâ*, or formal legal opin-
ions.
    Sulakha (pl. of the Arabic *sâlik*) are
travelers along the mystic way.
    Khukama (pl. of the Arabic *hakîm*) are
judges of Islamic law.

All the *wali* did assemble
With the pundits, *ulama, mufti*
The *khukama* and *fuqaha*
The great and mighty *sulakha*
Foremost of the *waliyullah*
Was the Lord Sunan Bonang, "The
    Axis of Piety
He Who Cleanses the Earth"[126]

22   Next came Lord Sunan Giri
"The Pious Pillar of Axial Saints"
Coming next again in rank
The one from Cirebon
Lord Sunan Gunungjati was
"The Alternate Axial Saint"
Next came Lord Sunan
Majagung, "Chief Among Axial
    Saints"
Then came Lord Sunan Darajat
"The Preeminent Axial Saint"[127]

23   Coming next again in rank
Was none but Lord Sunan Kalijaga
Known by the name Sèh Malaya
He was "The Substitute Axial
    Saint"
Coming next again in rank
Was none but the Lord Susunan
Of Muryapada, he was
"The Dutiful Pious Axial Saint"
Next, to be sure, came Lord Sunan
    Kudus
Succeeding his father[128]

24   Lord Susunan Ngudung of late
Who died upon the field
At the time of the great battle
Against Prince-regent Terung
Commander of Majapahit's troops
Now this Lord Sunan
Of Kudus was indeed
"The Chosen Pious Axial Saint"
Complete were the eight ranks of
    wali
Still there was another[129]

---

126. "The Axis of Piety, He Who
Cleanses the Earth" (Kutubur Rabbani,
Ghosul Ngalam) is the office of the supreme Wali Kutub, or Axial Saint. In this
poem, it is the office of the first-ranking
of the nine Javanese saints. See also
above, note to I:20.

127. "The Pious Pillar of Axial Saints"
(Wali Kutub Rabbani Aotad) is second-
ranking of the nine saints.

Wali Kutub Ngukba, third-ranking in
the hierarchy of saints, I render provi-
sionally as "The Alternate Axial Saint."
This translation presumes that *ngukba*
is a derivation from the Arabic root *'aqb*. I
am grateful to Mr. Usep Fathudin for this
suggestion.

"Chief among Axial Saints" (Wali Kutub Nukba) is fourth-ranking in the hierarchy of nine saints. The word *nukba*
is from the Arabic *nuqabâ* (pl. of *naqîb*).

"The Preeminent Axial Saint" (Kutub
Rabbani Nujba) is fifth-ranking of the

nine saints. The word *nujba* is from the
Arabic *nujabâ* (pl. of *najîb*).

See also above, notes to I:20–21, on the
ranks of axial saints.

128. "The Substitute Axial Saint" (Kutub
Abdal) is sixth-ranking of the nine saints.

"The Dutiful Pious Axial Saint" (Kutubur Rabbani Abwar), is seventh-ranking
of the nine saints. The word *abwar* is
from the Arabic *abrâr* (pl. of *bârr*). See
Trimingham, p. 300.

129. Prince-regent Terung was the son of
the Majapahit's ex-queen, the Chinese
princess, by her step-son, High Prince
Damar. He was, therefore, both half-
brother and nephew to Prince Patah (Panembahan Bintara).

"The Chosen Pious Axial Saint" (Ku-

25 The "Princely Saint" who came
after
To complete the enumeration
The nine ranks of *wali*
Included in the grouping
Of the *wali* eight
Was yea the Lord Panembahan
Sénapati Jimbun
Ruler of Palèmbang
At that time assembled were they
all
Along with all the princes-
regent[130]

26 All the notables from afar
The Prince-regent of Blambangan
Lumajang's Prince-regent
And the Prince-regent of Terung
Panataran's too and the Princes-
regent of
Basuki and Tunggarana
Japan and Surabaya
The Princes-regent of Madura
Lembu Peteng and High Prince
Baribin
And Sumenep's Prince-regent

27 That is Lord Jaran Panolih
And Bathara Katong of Panaraga
And Daha's Prince-regent
The Prince-regent of Madiun
Of Jagaraga, of Sukawati
Of Rawa, of Blitar

The one from Tambakbaya
Prince-regent Taruwongsa
The Princes-regent of Lowanu and
Gowong
Of Binarong, of Banyumas

28 The Prince-regent of Banten with
Prince-regent of Pajajaran
Of Ciyancang and Sokapura
The Lords of Sumedhang
Of Brebes and Wiratha
The Prince-regent of Pekalongan
He who was Lord of Tegal
With Prince-regent Pandhanarang
High Prince Damar of Palèmbang
having arrived
The assemblage replete accorded
love[131]

The poet tells how the wali *decide to*
build the Grand Mosque of Demak
to serve for all time as sacred talis-
man for kingship in Java (the Ca-
liphate).

XIV. Asmarandana
[Melodic mood is one of sorrow or
longing]

1 Then did all the *wali*
Discuss their plan to build
As magic talisman a mighty
mosque
To be the congregation site
For their communal *salât*

---

tub Rabaniyah Akyar) is the eighth-
ranking of the nine saints.
130. The ninth-ranking saint, who is invested by the others to complete the hierarchy of nine, is the Caliph or the
"Princely Saint" (Wali Ngumran). *Ngum-*
ran is apparently derived from the Arabic
umarâ (pl. of *amîr*).

131. The compounded word *danasmara*
(rendered here as "accorded love"), in
conjunction with the punctuation mark
for a new canto directly behind it, signals
the reader/singer to change to the melody of Asmarandana.

Whenever gather did
All the *wali* nine[132]

2 With all the princes-regent
Of Java and of foreign lands
Whenever they all might come
Wishing none be disappointed
And considering well
The means that it be meet
To be talisman for a king

3 The desire of all the *wali*
The eight who made the relic
A little something rather grand
Was to create a new mosque
A sacred site of power for the king-
    dom of Demak
A talisman for all the kings
Of all the Land of Java

4 As for the former Grand Mosque
Of old it was created by
The Lord Sunan Ngampèl
At the time of Majapahit's flower
Fit just for settlers new
It was created for
The Lord of Bintara

5 When he opened the land
Starting up a new settlement
A splintering off from Ngampèl
By the charge of his guru

The Lord Sunan Ngampèldenta
Prince Patah made that settlement
Clearing the forest of Demak

6 That land of fragrant sugarcane
In time became a court city
Many were the *santri* there
Honoring the Faith of Islam
All devout at their devotions
Thus it was that in those days
The Lord Sunan Ngampèldenta[133]

7 Came to build a mosque
For their communal *salât*
One but middling large
Let there be none who mistakes
All ye who read this tale
The Mosques of Demak
Are two, the stories say

8 One is the old mosque
The other the new
Let there be no mistaking
Take care and heed ye here
The sign is in the chronograms
Note ye the counting of the year
Thus to know the sequence clear

9 The chronogram of the older
    mosque:
"Excellence Straightway Knows
    the World" [1393][134]

132. The Javanese word that I render here
"magic talisman" is *pusaka*. The Arabic
salât in line 5 is the word for Islamic ritual prayer or devotional *performance*. For
an incisive description of the performance
of *salât* in an Acehnese context, see James
T. Siegel, *The Rope of God* (Berkeley: University of California Press, 1969), esp. pp.
109–15.

133. The Demak area is also known by
the name "Glagah-wangi" (fragrant sugarcane).
    Santri here denotes (often itinerant)
students of Islamic religion and theology,
rather than the more modern meaning of
"devout orthodox Moslem(s)."
134. The chronogram reads: "guna (3)
trus (9) uninèng (3) jagad (1)" (Saka
1393 = A.D. 1471).

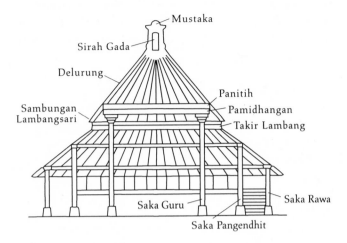

Figure 12. Tajug Lambangsari Pendhapa: The Demak Mosque. Drawing by
Ron Fraker.

The architectural plans for the
Grand Mosque of Demak are laid
(figure 12). Its architectonics, as de-
picted by the poet, mirror and map
structures of political power in the
realm.

Now let the telling proceed again
Those who did deliberate
The plan to make the talisman
The magnificent place of *salât*
To a consensus came

10   A division of duties they reckoned
The tasks to be assigned
Each independently worked
The measurements were deter-
    mined
The great and the small
The low and the high
The long and the short of its com-
    ponent parts

11   For all the mosque's component
    parts
Were drawn up plans with mea-
    surements
And plighted was the date
For the assembly of the parts
Of what would be its frame
The fitting of the fixtures of
The beams of the uppermost
    peak[135]

12   Now all the revered *wali*
Eight took for their task
Completed by the ninth *wali*:
Panembahan Bintara
The central master pillars four
These were assigned to
All the *wali* nine[136]

135. The technical term for the uppermost peak of a *tajug* house structure is
panuhun sirah gada (see figure 12).
136. The *saka guru* are the four central

13 As for the auxiliary pillars
    That is, the medial ones
    Which numbering twelve
    Are outside the master pillars
    And inside the peripheral ones
    Those were the task of
    All the lesser *wali*:[137]

14 His Highness Prince Atas-angin
    And His Highness Prince Siti Jenar
    And His Highness the Prince of
      Geragé
    Along with the Pundit-king
    Ruler of Gresik
    His Highness Prince Bawéyan
    And Sunan Candhana[138]

——

master pillars of a structure (see figure
12).
137. The auxilliary pillars, the *saka pangendhit* (or *saka pananggap*), are the
twelve medial pillars surrounding the
master pillars of a structure. The peripheral pillars, the *saka rawa* (or *saka goco*),
are the twenty outermost pillars of a *tajug*
structure (see figure 12).
138. According to this text, Prince (Pangéran) Atas-angin was an Indian (Bengali) prince and grandfather of Prince-
regent (*Adipati*) Pandhanarang (Sunan
Bayat). See below XVI:3 f. The compound
name Atas-angin designates "above the
wind," that is, "The West," including India and Turkey.
    Prince (or Sèh = Sheikh) Siti Jenar is
the most renowned (outlaw) saint of Java.
See below XVII:14 ff. The name "Siti
Jenar" means "yellow earth."
    Geragé is an alternative name for the
realm of Cirebon (located in western Pasisir).
    "Pundit-king" is my translation of
raja-pandhita.
    This Prince Bawéyan must be either a
son of Sunan Ngali Murtala (the original

15 And Sunan Geseng to be sure
    And His Highness Prince Cahyana
    Who buried on Mount Lawèt was
    The Prince of Jambukarang
    And His Highness Prince Kura-
      wang
    And Sèh Wali Lanang
    With Sèh Waliyu'lislam[139]

——

Pundit-king of Gresik) or Sunan Ngali
Murtala himself (a.k.a. Pangéran Burèrah
or Burèrèh or Hurérah).
    The title "His Highness [the] Prince"
(*Pangéran*) afforded these auxiliary *wali*
indicates that they were considered on a
level with high royalty. By nineteenth-
and twentieth-century Kraton Surakarta
rules of rank and title, the title *Pangéran*
is restricted to senior first-generation
(and select second-generation) princes,
both by the Susuhunan's favor. *Pangéran*
is derived from *ngèngèr* ("to submit oneself to, to go into the service of [while re-
lying upon]"); hence, the one to whom
ngèngèr is performed.
    Sunan Candhana probably refers to the
Sunan *of* C[e]ndhana, a central *pasisir* district in the Japara-Kudus area.
139. Sunan Geseng ("The Singed
Sunan") was a student of Kalijaga. Also
known as Ki Cakrajaya, Sunan Geseng is
best known for allowing himself to be
burnt, singed (*geseng*), rather than dis-
obey his teacher's order to keep watch
over his cane (Bambang Suwondo, *Ceritera Rakyat Daerah Istimewa Yogyakarta*
[Jakarta, 1982], pp. 77–82).
    Prince Cahyana was an Islamic saint
from the Cahyana district of Banyumas,
Central Java (Ann Kumar, *The Diary of a
Javanese Muslim: Religion, Politics, and the
Pesantrèn, 1883–1886* [Canberra: Australian National University, 1985], pp. 42–
43).
    Kurawang probably refers to Krawang,
West Java.
    Sèh Wali Lanang was the father of

16 And too the Sèh of Mahribi
    With Sèh Suta Maharaja
    Sèh Parak and Sèh Banthong
    The Pundit-king of Galuh
    Together with the Pundit-king
    Of the Pamalang hermitage
    And the Pundit of Karangbaya[140]

Sunan Giri and one of the many sons of
the prolific Arab emigrant Maulana Abu
Ahmad Iskak.

According to the *Serat Walisana*, Sèh
Waliyu'lislam was another son of Sèh
Maulana Abu Ahmad Iskak. Sèh Waliyu'lislam is said to have emigrated to Java
before his father's immigration, and to
have become the regent of Pandhanarang
(R. Tanojo, ed., *Walisana* [Surakarta:
Sadubudi, 1955], pp. 24–25). This, however, conflicts with the genealogy for Adipati Pandhanarang provided below (XVI:
3 f.).

140. According to the *Serat Walisana*, Sèh
Mahribi was yet another son of Sèh Maulana Abu Ahmad Iskak (*Walisana*, p. 30).
Traces of Sèh Mahribi, renowned for his
missionary zeal and magical prowess,
mark the contemporary Javanese landscape. On the plethora of grave sites associated with this saint, see Pemberton, *On
the Subject of "Java,"* pp. 286–87.

Sèh Suta Maharaja (whose name
means "son of the maharaja") was yet another son of Sèh Maulana Abu Ahmad
Iskak; he was also an adoptive son of
Brawijaya V. By some accounts, he was
the father of Sunan Gunungjati (*Walisana*, pp. 20–21, 31).

I have been unable to identify a character by the name of Sèh Parak. In the *Serat
Kandha*, a Chinese Kyai Banthong is the
father of Brawijaya V's Chinese bride; see
Pigeaud, *Literature of Java*, 2:362.

Galuh is a district in West Java.

Pamalang is a town of the western
Central Pasisir.

There are two Central Pasisir villages

17 And the Lord Susunan Katib
    And the Sunan of Pantaran
    Along with Sunan Tembalo
    The Pundit Ngusman-nuraga
    And the Pundit Ngusman-aji
    For them the task at hand
    Was the medial pillars all[141]

18 Now the peripheral pillars indeed
    Were twenty in number
    Their making was assigned to
    All those *wali* and pundits
    Who were the *pradikan*
    The great and mighty *ulama*
    The *mufti* and *khukama*[142]

---

by the name of Karangbaya: (1) in Mantup, Juwana, Jepara and (2) Singèn Lor,
Semarang.

141. According to the *Serat Walisana*,
Sunan Katib is another name for Sunan
Ngampèldenta (*Walisana*, p. 20). Of
course, it could not be Sunan Ngampèldenta who is indicated here.

There is a village named Pantaran in
Boyolali, Pajang Surakarta.

I have been unable to identify the
name (toponym) Tembalo. Perhaps what
is meant is Tambalang; see below XVII:
21.

Probably meant here (lines 4–5) are
Pangéran Kalipah Nuraga and his elder
brother, Pangéran Kalipah Kaji Ngusman.
Both were sons of Raja-pandhita Ngali
Murtala of Gresik and were married to
daughters of Sunan Ngampèldenta. Pa-
ngéran Kalipah Nuraga resided in Tandes;
Pangéran Kalipah Kaji Ngusman, in Ma-
lacca ([Ki Padmasusastra] and R.Ng.
Wirapratama, *Serat Sajarah Ageng ing
Karaton Surakarta* [composed Surakarta,
ca. 1900 and 1940; typed s.l., s.a.]. MS. RP
B 77; SMP MN 690, p. 26).

142. The *pradikan* (those of independent
status) were men of religion to whom the

19 The mystic *zahid* and devout
       ngabid
    The mystic *mungahid* and faithful
       ahlul-iman
    The elect *mukmin khas* and the
       pious *salèh*
    'Twas the peripheral pillars for
       them
    As for the master tie-beams
    The peak's base and the hip-rafters
    With the primary support beams[143]

20 The plate beams to be sure
    Those whose assigned task it was
    Were all the princes-regent
    As for the secondary support
       beams
    And all the slatted sheathing
    The border and the great roof
       boards
    All of it, both above and below[144]

———

king would grant tax-free lands (also
called *pradikan*). The *pradikan* were exempt from regular royal service but were
expected to watch over sacred sites (often
graves) and/or provide religious education. Many *pesantrèn* were located on *pradikan* lands.
143. The *ngabid* (Ar. *'âbid*) are "devout
worshipers." The Arabic *ahlul-iman* are
"men of faith." The Arabic *salèh* are "the
devout" or "the righteous." The Arabic
mukmin khas are "the elect of the faithful."
   The "master tie-beams" (*sunduk-kili*)
are the four beams attached to, and sta-
bilizing, the four master pillars. The
"peak's base" and the "hip-rafters" are
the *pamidhangan* and *delurung* respectively. The "primary support beams" are the
panitih and the *takir lambang* (see figure
12).
144. The "plate beams" are the *blandar*

21 These were the tasks assigned
    All the princes of the blood
    The royal family, both the high
       and low
    As for all the rafters
    And the fencing materials too
    Those whose assigned task it was
    Were the foremost generals[145]

22 The courtiers and high ministers
    Now as for all the shingles
    The roofing materials all
    Everyone would just chip in
    With that they did disperse
    Having set the date for
    Assembling the component parts

23 Each went off on his own
    To make his component part
    Now not to be described here is
    How long they went about their
       work
    Nor the fixing of the frame
    Of the structure's upper portion
    The fitting done was a success

24 The fittings so fetchingly fit
    And its interior portion too
    All its many pillars
    The tie beams and plate beams
    Were fitted together all

———

pangeret. The "secondary support beams"
are the *takir pananggap*. "Slatted sheathing" is my understanding of *dudur*. The
"border" and the "great roof boards" are
the *plisir* and the *wuwung* respectively.
145. In line 3, I translate *sentana* as "the
royal family." In the court of Surakarta,
the *sentana* includes first- through
seventh-grade royalty.

Sunan Kalijaga is shown to be a maverick wali, who absolves his "fault" by performing the miracle of the wood-chip pillar.

Remaining were but the master
    pillars
Four, when time it was to start

25 To set to the fitting of
The master pillars were still short
    one
Only three in number were they
And so the Lord Sunan Bonang
Inquired after Sèh Malaya
For nowhere to be seen
His task remained undone[146]

26 That single master pillar was
The task of Sèh Malaya
Of which there was no trace
Ever away, apart in contemplation
    rapt
He was coolly nonchalant
Though now the time did press
For the master pillars' fitting

27 'Twas pressing for upon
The morn they were to raise
The Grand Mosque sacred talisman
The Lord Sunan Kalijaga
Alarmed, drew nigh to the pres-
    ence

To be rebuked by Lord Sunan
Bonang, Master of the World

28 A *sembah* Sèh Malaya made
Bowing low he caught the wrath
From the presence he withdrew
Making for the work site
Then did Sèh Malaya
Collect the scattered wood chips
By the armsful many

29 These wood chips he did bind with
    cord
Did order and arrange with care
As though he were making a torch
The cylinder round and long
Bound up tall and slender
Was mighty long and round
Sèh Malaya felt familiar ease of
    heart[147]

XV. Gambuh
[Melodic mood is vibrant and
rather brash]

1 Turning his face to Mecca
Sèh Malaya focused in *semadi*
His expanding heart penetrating to
    consciousness pure
Dissolved, annihilated was he in
    vision unitary
His every thought granted real-
    ity[148]

146. Sèh Malaya is an alias of Sunan Kalijaga. See, for instance, the saint's history
in *Suluk Sèh Malaya*, a text which is none
other than an Arabicized version of the
Suluk Déwaruci (Faqier 'Abd'l Haqq, ed.,
Suluk Sèh Malaya [Yogyakarta: Kulawarga Bratakesawa, 1959]).

147. The word *gambuh* (rendered here as
"felt familiar ease"), in conjunction with
the punctuation mark for a new canto following it, signals the reader/singer to
change to the melody of Gambuh.
148. The word that denotes Sèh Malaya's
meditation in line 2 is *semadi manekung*.
Semadi, from the Sanskrit, is a yogic term

2   Thought whole the wood-chip pil-
lar was
Transformed, its "chipness" van-
ished
In length and breadth it was as
measured
Against the master pillars three
That were already fitted

3   Releasing his meditation
Sèh Malaya's miracle was done
Astounded were all who saw
Dazed in bewildered bewonder-
ment
They were in speechless awe

4   This wood-chip pillar once pre-
sented
To the Virgin King forthwith
Was measured and fitted too
And with that done
All that remained was the rais-
ing[149]

*Described in the following verses is
the raising of the Grand Mosque of
Demak. Particular note is paid to
difficulties encountered in the right
alignment of the finished Demak
Mosque to the Mosque of Mecca.*

5   Night having fallen
Together they did their *salât*

The sunset *salât* followed by that
of the eve
Then at the strike of three
everyone did wake[150]

6   Then they did the dawn *salât*
With the *salât* done, all forthwith
Did ready the parts for the
mosque's raising
All the great and mighty *wali*
Set to work in cheerful earnest

7   The great and mighty faithful
Along with the princes-regent
The princes of the blood and the
high courtiers
The generals and admirals
All stood in readiness[151]

8   Then straightway the work began
That morning the master pillars
Those four were raised at once
It was the *wali* eight
Who set to work all hoisting

9   And Sénapati Jimbun too
Joined in hoisting these pillars four
Once raised, the uppermost peak
was next
Finished was the upper portion
Next came the lower veranda[152]

150. It is obligatory for Moslems to perform the *salât* five times a day, at five
clearly prescribed times: *subuh* (dawn),
luhur (noon), *asar* (late afternoon), *mahrib* (sunset), and *isa* (evening/night).
151. The word translated as "admirals" in
line 4 is *lalang-laut*.
152. By "lower veranda" is rendered *pananggap panosor*.

for the final stage meditative practice.
That which I render as "consciousness
pure" in line 3 is *cipta ening*, the (non)site
whereat thought, volition, and emotion
disappear, merging into their seat.
149. The "Virgin King" (Sang Ratu
Wadat), was, of course, Sunan Bonang.

10 The medial pillars
    Twelve presently were raised
    The lesser *wali* set to work
    Hoisting these pillars with zeal
    Raising them all at once

11 Fitted were the support beams
    The sheathing, plate beams, and
        rafters
    The middle veranda thus finished
    Next the peripheral pillars
    Were raised without delay

12 Those twenty pillars
    Whose making was the task of
    All the *wali* who were *pradikans*
    The great and mighty pundits
    The foremost of the *ulama*

13 The great and mighty *khukama*
    All the *mufti* and the mystic
        mungahid
    All the *sulakha*, ascetics, and de-
        vout *ngabid*
    The elect *mukmin khas* and the
        learned ones
    In cheerful earnest they worked[153]

14 With the raising of
    The peripheral pillars, next the
        sheathing came
    With the peripheral support beams
        and the plate beams too

All the rafters raised on high
Finished was the lower veranda

15 Next came the shingling
    Now completely finished
    Then the *wali* eight forthwith
    Attended to the mosque's *kéblat*
    Lest it miss its mark[154]

16 That true its orientation be
    To the Ka'bah of Mecca
    Were the mosque's *kéblat* not true
    Invalid and in vain the *salât* then
    Of all who made their *salât* there[155]

17 Now it came to be that all
    The reverend *wali* nine
    In vision of the *kéblat* clashed
    One of them would claim
    That straight it faced to west

18 Another would call that wrong:
    Its facing more northerly should
        incline
    Then prodded to the north was the
        mosque's facing

153. Rendered as "ascetics" in line 3 is *tapa*, a Javano-Sanskrit word designating "asceticism," or "ascetic practice"; *tapa* here designates Moslem ascetics. The words translated as "the learned ones" in line 4 are *ahli ngilmu*.

154. The *kéblat* (Ar. *qiblah*) is the direction to which a Moslem must face when praying, that is, pointing in the most direct line to the Ka'bah of Mecca. The Javanese verbal form *ngéblat* means "to face Mecca" or "to obey."
155. The word *adhep*, rendered as "orientation" in line 1, means "belief" or "obedience" as well as "facing" and "direction facing."
   The Ka'bah is the sacred cubelike building located in the center of Mecca's holy mosque, Masjidu'l-Haram. Pilgrims to Mecca ritually circumambulate the Ka'bah as part of their *hajj*.

Considered once again: 'twas now
   too far
Far too northward its incline

19   Then prodded to the south
     Now the *kéblat* of the mosque too
     Southerly was shoved northward
        once again
     And still was wanting its incline
     Nudged then to the north it was

20   Considered wrong again
     'Twas now too northerly
     So back to the south it was pushed
        again
     'Twas not quite strictly straight
     But rather west to northwest

21   And thus on and on there was
     Incessant dispute on its strict
        straightness
     There was as yet no view precise
     The mosque, as though rocked to
        and fro
     Swayed back and forth from north
        to south

22   And then as dusk approached
     Still there was no certainty
     And so the Lord Sunan Bonang
     In consultation with Sunan
     Giri came to an agreement

23   Stopping for the meantime
     That night 'twas agreed that they
        meditate
     For enlightenment from All-holy
        God
     So that in true correctness
     The *kéblat* be not wrong

24   Now with the fall of night
     'Tis recited that all the grand *wali*
     Did meditate in utmost ardent zeal
     Their *semadi* most intense
     They prayed to God All-wise[156]

25   All the *wali* eight
     Plunging the depths of vision
        penetrant
     Saw in brilliant clarity all the phe-
        nomenal world
     There were no veils between
     From the east straight to the west

26   With Mecca coming into sight
     Allah's Ka'bah clearly shone
        thrusting upon high
     The Masjidu'l-Haram was mani-
        fest
     Then all the honored *wali* eight
     Gathered together as one[157]

27   And Sénapati Jimbun too
     Did join with all the *wali* eight
     And then considered was the *kéblat*
        of the mosque
     That its orientation be straightened
        strict
     To Allah's Ka'bah which was mani-
        fest

156. The word rendered as "meditate" in
line 3 is the Javano-Arabic *tafakur*, "contemplation" or "thought." The Arabic
tafakur is modified by the Javanese *aneru
dhiri*, which means to push one's person
to (and beyond) its limit.
157. The Masjidu'l-Haram is the sacred
mosque of Mecca. See above, note to XV:
16.

28 But all the *wali* eight
    Of vision still did clash
    The mosque nudged to right and
    left
    Swinging to and fro from north to
    south
    Still never came to rest

*Related here is the miracle by which
Sunan Kalijaga successfully brings
the Demak and Meccan Mosques
into correct alignment.*

29 Then did the Lord Sunan
    Bonang and the First Among Kings
    Drawing in their breaths will the
    world condensed
    In a flash accomplished was
    The sovereign *wali*'s miracle[158]

30 Condensed the world was tiny
    And Mecca shone close by
    Allah's Ka'bah was nigh, manifest
    before them
    To estimate its distance
    But three miles off it loomed

31 The Celibate Lord did beckon
    Sèh Malaya, ware to the subtle
    sign
    Lord Sunan Kali rose to his feet
    From north he did face south
    One leg he did extend to side

32 Both legs did stretch forth
    Long and tall, their stance astride

158. The "First Among Kings" (Ratu
Tunggul) was Sunan Giri.

His right foot reaching Mecca came
Just outside the fence
Of Allah's Ka'bah there

33 His left foot did remain behind
    Planted to the northwest of the
    mosque
    Allah's Ka'bah did his right hand
    grasp
    His left hand having taken hold
    Of the uppermost peak of the
    mosque

34 Both of them he pulled
    Stretched out and brought to meet
    The Ka'bah's roof and the peak of
    the mosque
    Realized as one being were
    Perfectly straight strictly on mark

35 All the great and mighty *wali*
    Watched in exultant joy
    Lord Sunan Bonang softly said:
    "Little brother Sèh Malaya, now
    'Tis right beyond a doubt"

36 Sèh Malaya did a *sembah* make
    Then his hands released
    Allah's Ka'bah and the mosque re-
    turned, each to its own place
    Then Sèh Malaya sitting down
    Before his elder brother made a
    sembah[159]

159. Sunan Kalijaga and Sunan Bonang
are not, of course, genealogical brothers.
Their brotherhood is of the Axial Saints,
of whom Sunan Bonang is the eldest
(most senior). The word *wotsinom*, a
synonym for *sembah*, in conjunction with

XVI. Sinom
[Melodic mood is "even"; appropriate for narrative]

1   Not to go on at length about their
      work
    At that time finished was
    The Grand Mosque of Demak
    The completion of the work
    Is remembered in the *babad* thus:
    "Remaining Two are the Works
    Of Man" [1420] in chronogram
    And so when reckoned both
    The interval between the old
      mosque and the new[160]

2   Is a span of twenty-seven years
    Now then the old mosque
    Was moved to Suranatan
    To serve as inside-mosque indeed
    For the *salât* of the king
    For his communal devotions
    Thus it was as time did pass[161]

———

the punctuation mark for a new canto directly behind it, signals the reader/singer to change to the melody of Sinom.

160. The chronogram reads: "kari (0) roro (2) kartinipun (4) ing jalma (1)" (Saka 1420 = A.D. 1498). On the old mosque's date, see above, XIV:9.

161. Suranatan is the name of the mosque of the Juru Suranata ("Corps of the Royal Valor"), a corps of religious officials in the Central Javanese *kraton*. The Juru Suranata are responsible for the preparation of offerings and the reciting of incantations (both Javanese and Arabic-Islamic) for the metaphysical well-being of the king, royal family, and realm. For more on the Suranata, see R.M.T. Bratadiningrat et al., *Karaton-dalem Surakarta Adiningrat Sasana Pustaka: Mèngeti kuwajiban Abdi-dalem Juru Suranata, Maésa Lawung,*

———

Rendered here is the tale of Sunan Bayat: the transformation of an embittered provincial lord into a candidate spiritual (over)lord.

Turning the tale that is told:
There was a scion of Our Lord,
    Master of the World[162]

3   From Atas-angin, Above-the-
      Winds
    He made his way to Java
    In olden days back in the time
    Of Lord Sunan Ngampèldenta
    He was appointed *mufti*
    In the town of Kaliwungu
    Known was he by the name
    His Highness Prince Atas-angin
    One race was he with the king of
      Delhi in Bengali land[163]

4   In Delhi of Bengali land
    Lord Sultan Sharif Asnawi
    Was chief of all the kings
    Of all Bengali

———

Donga-donga, Nglabuh, Pados Sekar Jay-akusuma, saha Mriksa Kasagedan Juru Suranata (compiled and inscribed Surakarta, 1941 and 1945), SP 547 Ka; SMP KS 189. In the Kraton Surakarta, the Suranatan Mosque is located in the outermost part of the inner palace, that is, between the Brajanala and Mandhungan gates.

162. By "Master of the World" is meant the Prophet Muhammad.

163. "Above the Winds" (Atas-angin) indicates the world north of the equator and often refers to "the West" in general. See above, XIV:14. Kaliwungu is a town in Central Pasisir, just to the west of Semarang.

His Highness Prince Atas-angin
Was taken then as son-in-law
By the Lord Sharif Sultan
Two were the Prince's sons
One of them in Bengali lived[164]

5   The other was in Java
In the town of Kaliwungu
Brother-in-law to the regent
He had fathered children
Four were they in number
Three of them were sons
The daughter was then married to
Him who succeeded as Prince-
    regent
Of Kaliwungu; whereas the sons
    all three

6   Did move to Pandhanarang
Which is in "Semawis"
That's "Semarang" in language
    short
The eldest became Prince-regent
Yea, of Pandhanarang
Fabulous was his wealth
And wise, his character
In every way he prospered well
His younger brother, preferring a
    life of trade

7   Made his home on Mount Pragota
And was devoutly religious
The youngest of the brothers
Devoted to ascetic practice
Was an excellent pundit
Accomplished at the subtle arts
He lived in Pandhanarang
Now it is related:
After the raising of the Grand
    Mosque in Demak[165]

8   Prince-regent Pandhanarang
Defiant, refused to show himself
At the Capital Demak
It all began when the princes-
    regent
Suffered humiliation deep
At the time the Mosque was built
All the *waliyullah*
With the pundits, the *mufti*
The *ulama*, the *khukama*, the
    fuqaha[166]

9   The pious *salèh* and ascetics
The elect *mukmin khas* and the
    mungahid
All these were seated above
On one level with the king
Whereas all the princes-regent
The great and mighty courtiers
And all the princes of the blood
The regents, the high ministers
Were seated, all of them, below

10   Prince-regent Pandhanarang

164. I have been unable to uncover any further information on Lord Sultan Sharif Asnawi, Prince Atas-angin's Bengali father-in-law. There was, however, a historical figure named Sultan Sharaf (the Amir of Bayana) who was forcibly expelled from his amirate by Sikandar Shah (the Lodi ruler of the Delhi Sultanate) in 1491 (R. C. Majumdar, ed., *The History and Culture of the Indian People*, vol. 6, *The Delhi Sultanate* [Bombay: Bharatiya Vidya Bhavan, 1960], p. 145).

165. Mt. Pragota is in Semarang. Rendered as "the subtle arts" in line 6 are the words *pasang semu*.
166. Refusal to show oneself at court is a clear sign of intention to rebel. See below XXVI:8–9.

Humiliated was sick at heart
And so he did hold out
In the city of Semarang
Attending not the opening
Of the Grand Mosque in Demak
And when he was summoned
    thence
Always made excuses
Then Lord Sunan Kalijaga

11   Did come to the town of Pan-
        dhanarang
To reason with his younger
        brother
So this his little brother-in-law
He questioned melodiously
His Highness Prince Pandhanarang
Disclosed how this had come to be,
        from start
Unto its end
And so Lord Sunan Kali
Looked with pity on the Prince of
        Pandhanarang[167]

12   Was instructed then in all
The sacred knowledge of *wali*-ship
The absolute of holiness
The perfectly consummate life
Life absolutely real
Called *Jatimurti*
"Whence and Whither" recuperate
Enlightened *lahir* straight through
    batin
Within his innerness, a potential
    waliyullah he[168]

13   The brother of the Prince-regent
The youngest wholly accomplished
    one
Who was an ascetic
Aware of mind did follow
Surrendering body and soul
Kissing the dust beneath the feet
Of the Lord Sèh Malaya
He too was taught the knowledge
    of
The *wali*-ship like his brother the
    regent

14   His Highness Prince Pandhanarang
Along with his youngest brother
For both of them high hopes there
    were
They made such excellent candi-
    dates
Now with that then
Abandoned were life's luxuries by
Prince-regent Pandhanarang
Along with his youngest brother
Never looking back at family or
    worldly wealth

15   With but their wives alone
As married couples two
The sons of the Prince-regent

---

167. The affinal relation between Kalijaga
and Pandhanarang remains a mystery to
me. Pandhanarang is alternately titled
Pangéran (High Prince) and Adipati
(Prince-regent).

168. In line 2, I render the Javanese *ngèl-*

mu as "sacred knowledge." *Ngèlmu*, from
the Arabic *'ilm* (knowledge; to know, especially as pertains to religious knowledge), often connotes mystical or magical
knowledge. On the concepts of *Jatimurti*
and the "Whence and Whither," see
above, note to I:13. The opposition between and the ultimate identity of *lahir*
("the outer") and the *batin* ("the inner")
aspects of man are key topics in this poem
and in the broader discourse of Javanese
Sufism.

Were charged to study the Qur'ân
In earnest to seek sacred knowl-
edge
From the Lord Sunan Majagung
Related as grandsons were they
To Sunan Majagung indeed
And so the Prince-regent of Pan-
dhanarang[169]

16 Relinquishing his realm, made off
In the dead of the night
Not a single soul did see
With only his younger brother
Now 'tis not to be described
In elaboration or at length
Or the events along the way
Resulting from the fulfillment of
Sunan Kalijaga's charge

17 Proceeding to the south and east
He came to Mount Tembayat
Settling there in Tembayat
His ascetic practice was intense
Now his younger brother
Ordered to live apart
Did settle in Kajoran
His ascetic practice was intense
Both of them became *waliyullah*
then[170]

18 His Highness Prince Pandhanarang
Had changed his name by then
To Lord Sunan Tembayat
His brother did change names

169. Presumably, this genealogical tie is
through the boys' mother.
170. Mt. Tembayat, in southern Central
Java (Klatèn, Pajang, Surakarta), is located some ten km. to the southeast of the
town of Klatèn. Kajoran is located near
Tembayat.

The Lord Panembahan indeed
Of Kajoran was his name
Breaking off here on these so
exalted
To have attained the rank of *wali*

*An abbreviated note on royal births,
deaths, and successions in the Kingdom of Demak.*

Let it be told: then in the realm of
Demak

19 The Panembahan of Bintara
After a considerable time
Having then fallen ill
Before long did perish
The ceremonies made brief
All the funerary rites
The body then
Was laid to rest to the north of the
Mosque
The Panembahan's death is chro-
nogrammed thus:

20 "Vanish did Excellence from the
Works of the World" [1430]
Lord Panembahan Bintara
Had lived to see ten years
From the building of the Mosque
Now it is related:
The children of His Majesty
Were four all told
The eldest of them was
A handsome son, High Prince
Sabrang Lèr, his name[171]

171. The chronogram reads: "sirna (0)
guna (3) kartining (4) rat (1)" (Saka
1430 = A.D. 1508). The name Sabrang Lèr
means "across/abroad to the north."

21 His second born, a daughter
   Was given in marriage indeed
   To His Highness Prince Widagda
   In the realm of Cirebon
   The next born was again
   A son, to be sure, whose name
   Was Prince Trenggana
   After him was then
   The last born, a son who was
      named

22 High Prince Sabrang Kidulan
   But since olden days known
   As the Prince of the River
   For he perished in the river
   Now again to be related:
   The one succeeding to the throne
   Was the son who was named
   High Prince Sabrang Lèr indeed
   They who installed him as sove-
      reign were[172]

23 The Lord Sunan Bonang
   And Lord Sunan Giri
   Endorsed by all the *wali*
   All Java did bear witness
   Now his title was
   The Lord Sultan of Demak
   But not for very long
   'Twas ordained by the Will of God:

172. The name Sabrang Kidulan means "across/abroad to the south." The repercussions from Sabrang Kidulan's death in the river continued on into the next generation. His son, Harya Panangsang (Harya Jipang), contending that his father had been murdered by Prince (later Sultan) Trenggana, feuded with (and was ultimately killed by) Trenggana's son-in-law and heir, Sultan Pajang (that is, Jaka Tingkir).

Soon to die was this Sultan of
   Demak

24 His reign as king
   Lasted but two years
   This Lord Sultan of Demak
   His body was then laid to rest
   To the north of the Mosque
   At the feet of his father
   His son did not succeed him
   To reign as sovereign king
   The brother of the king was in-
      stalled sweetly[173]

XVII. Dhangdhanggula/Sarkara
[Melodic mood is lithe, with didactic clarity and romantic allure]

1 Prince Trenggana then reigned as
      king
   Succeeding to his brother's *kraton*
   Sultan Demak was his title
   His *Pangulu* was Sunan Kudus
   The Grand Vizier changed as well
   The Excellent Wanasalam
   Was his name indeed[174]

*A note on deaths and orderly succes-
sions in the* wali *hierarchy.*

Now changing what is told:

173. The word *sarkara* ("sweetly") here, in conjunction with the punctuation mark for a new canto directly following it, signals the reader/singer to change to the melody of Dhangdhanggula (also known as Sarkara).
174. The *pengulu* (line 4) was an Islamic religious official, or *imam*. Here, specifically the highest religious official at court.

Lord Sunan Giri Kadhaton
Fell ill unto his death

2   In brief, with all the proper rites
His body was then laid to rest
In the palace of Giri
The chronogram is reckoned thus:
"Smoldering wicks of Excellence
    are the Works of the World"
    [1433]
Succeeding him was his son
Named the Lord Sunan
Giri Parapèn
"First Among Kings, Pious Axial
    Saint"
"The Pillar" was his rank[175]

3   For like his late father was he
In wisdom and awareness clear
And ascetic practice
Now changing what is told:
His Majesty Sovereign of the
    World
The Lord Sunan Bonang
Arriving at his destined end
Passed then from this world
Returning home to the everlasting
    kraton
The ceremonies not to be described

4   His body then was laid to rest
In the Ashram Sunya of Bonang
Related now in chronogram
Is the death of the Lord Sunan:
"Secret teachings Pure are the Fin-
    est in the World" [1445]

175. The chronogram reads: "siking (3)
guna (3) karyaning (4) bumi (1)" (Saka
1433 = A.D. 1511). On the ranks of Axial
Saints, see above, I:21 and XIII:21.

The one succeeding then
To his position was
The Lord Sunan Darajat
Presided like his late brother
As "He Who Cleanses the Earth,
    Axis of Mercy"[176]

5   It is related: with the death of
The Virgin Master of the World
It was not long at all
In barely half a year
Madura's Prince-regent perished
Lembu Peteng's body
Then was laid to rest
There in Karang Kajenar
At the feet of his mother, the
    Queen
His son succeeded him

6   Lembu Wara was his name
Yea, Prince-regent of Madura, he

*Returning again to the antecedents
of Jaka Tingkir, the poem tells of the
disappointment experienced by the
provincial rulers of Pajang-Pengging
and of their resolve to resist the authority of Demak.*

Now that of which is spoken here:
Indeed the royal princes of

176. The Ashram Sunya is the "Silent
Hall" or the "Hall of Absolute Void." Bonang's tomb is in Tuban, East Java.
    The chronogram reads: "wisik (5) suci
(4) adining (4) bumi (1)" (Saka 1445 =
A.D. 1523).
    Sunan Darajat's title is "Wali Ghos Ku-
tub Rahman." Note that *Rahman* here replaces *Rabbani* (see the title of the Supreme Axial Saint in I:20 and XIII:21).

Pajang-Pengging, the mighty
    nobles two
Prince Kebo Kanigara
And Kebo Kenonga too
With the death of the Virgin Lord
And the death of their regent uncle
    too
Lembu Peteng of Madura

7   The mighty nobles two, troubled in
    their hearts
Refused to show themselves at the
    capital Demak
So deeply shamed were they
Within their hearts these nobles
Did harbor deep resolve
No summons would they answer
Tormented by the fond hopes of
    old
That with tender words their
    grandfather had raised
Thus 'twas better they refuse
To witness the celebration[177]

8   Celebrating in their hearts, the
    mighty nobles two
In Pengging their own realm, apart
Considered then what they would
    do
At that these mighty nobles
Two did clash and disagree

177. Presumably the "fond hopes" (*ku-dangan*) expressed by Brawijaya were
that his grandsons would reign as sovereigns, succeeding to the independent
throne of their father—if not to that of
their grandfather.

    The *pamiwaha* ("celebration") probably
refers to the coronation ceremony of
Prince Trenggana as the new sultan of
Demak. See above, note to V:8.

Of will they were not one
Intense ascetic practice
Was the elder brother's will
Becoming an ascetic at Mount
    Merapi's foot
He cast off his royalty

9   Like a mountain hermit, his prac-
    tice was austere
In zealous passion, his body he
    denied
Disguised as commoner in truth
Hidden behind a veil, his way
Lest it be manifest
His wife as a disciple maid
And all of his children
Were disciples of various ranks
And so the ascetic at fiery Merapi's
    foot
Like a Sunyata hermit[178]

10 Forgot his royalty
Considered not his regency

*Describes the populist spirit of the
community of Pajang-Pengging and*

178. The word I render as "mountain hermit" is *ajar*. With "disciple maid," I render the pre-Islamic term *éndhang*, a
female ascetic or, more often, a female
attendant to a male ascetic. "Disciples of
various ranks" renders the words *manguyu jajanggan*. A *jejanggan* is a category
of male disciples to a holy master in a
pre-Islamic rural religious community or
hermitage. For *manguyu*, see above, note
to XIII:19.

    The word "Sunyata" names the Abso-
lute Void, or the mystic state of emptiness. Presumably here it names a category, or school, of ascetic practice or of
hermits.

the piety of its Moslem brotherhood.
Ki Ageng Pengging is described as
the "Kyai" of a rural pesantrèn.

Now to tell of the younger brother:
Kebo Kenonga, left behind
In the city of Pajang-Pengging
Had no desire to be paid court
In the manner of nobility
All the officials, the gentry
The royal ones, should they wish
    to pay him court
Did so in the manner of mere
    santri[179]

11 Gone was all *priyayi* glitter
In form, devices, and ways
Their ways were the ways of a
    pesantrèn
A place for seekers of knowledge
In truth living for Allah alone
Prince Kebo Kenonga
An earnest man of knowledge
Faithfully did the communal *salât*
Together with his disciples all
His subjects and royal brethren[180]

12 Both great and low, Pajang-
    Pengging's subjects
Both within and without the capi-
    tal
Approximating their number
They were three thousand men
All faithful at their *salât*
The inner disciples numbered
Only seven hundred
Prince Kebo Kenonga
Had not a single word to spare
For his Regentship

13 Changing his name to "Kyai
    Ageng Pengging"
The title "Prince" he did cast off
Merely "Kyai" then did he use
Detached was he of character
As though living but for God alone
Now after his worship of God
Farming was his work
Tending *gaga* rice and potatoes
In the fields, stopping at the wor-
    ship times
Thus it was day in day out[181]

179. Rendered as "manner" in lines 7 and
10 is the word *cara*, connoting styles of
behavior, language, and especially dress
or costume. Historical poems treating the
Surakarta period compulsively chronicle
the *cara* (costume and hence behavior
style—be it "European" or "Javanese") of
the king and royal family at various ritual
and other functions. For a good treatment
of this phenomenon and its significance,
see Pemberton, *On the Subject of "Java,"*
chaps. 1–3.
   By *santri* here is meant students of Islamic religion and theology.
180. The *priyayi* (from *para yayi*, all the
younger siblings [of the king]) are "the

courtly elite." A *pesantrèn* is a place of the
santri, an Islamic religious community
and educational institution where *santri*
live and study under a master/teacher,
called a *kyai*. The word rendered as
"knowledge" in lines 4 and 7 in *ngèlmu*.
181. The title Kyai (alternately "Ki") is
the usual one for the master of a *pesan-*
trèn. Kyai Ageng could be rendered as
"Great Master."
   Gaga is rice produced in dry fields that
are cultivated at higher elevations than
the more extensive irrigated rice fields
(*sawah*) of the lowlands.
   By the "worship times" are meant the
five obligatory times at which *salât* must

Introduces Ki Ageng Pengging's guru, the renowned "heretic" saint, Sèh Siti Jenar, as a master of the ngèlmu (Knowledge) of rasa ("Feeling" that is "Meaning" and "Mystery"). Here too is mapped the sway of Siti Jenar's influence across an expanse of rural Java.

14 Now to Kyai Ageng Pengging
Came a marvelous *waliyullah*
Of wondrous power renowned of
  knowledge
A wandering adept of practices
  austere
A nimble wit, there was no catch-
  ing him
Proud and never cringing
The consummation of knowledge
Knowledge of *rahsa-surasa*
Like sugar's *rasa*: form and sweet-
  ness
Indivisible[182]

15 Already encompassing all the
  world
The heart of this pundit did give
  forth
The fragrance of pure musk
The unity of Being-One
Creature-Creator inseparable
Truly of origin one
Not benighted of vision
Seeing ultimate Being-Non-Being
The Holy One was realized beyond
  all veils
Aware of the Whence and
  Whither[183]

16 The perfection of body manifest
A manifestation that never dies
Vanishing in the end
For ever ineffable is
Its telling voiced in speech
There are no magic formulae
Everything encompassed
The consummation of Release
Encompasses the entire universe
Truly absorbing-while-absorbed[184]

17 Bejewelling-while-bejewelled,
  begemming-while-begemmed

---

be performed by devout Moslems. See above, note to XV:5.

182. In line 4, it is the word *laku* that I render as "practices austere."

Line 5, "kesit datan kena pinethik," means "literally": [his words] could not be quoted/picked."

There is no translating the polysemic *rasa*, a word whose excess of sense escapes definition. *Rasa* evokes (often at the same time) a range of senses: "essence, meaning, feeling, taste, sense, secret, speech." The word *rahsa* means "mystery; secret; esoteric meaning; essence; ultimate essence." The compound *rahsa-surasa* ("the secret *rasa* of *rasa*") indicates both "the mystery of meaning" and the "meaning of mystery." See also, below, XIX:21–23.

183. The word rendered as "vision" in line 7 is *kawruh* (more commonly, "knowledge"), from the root *weruh* ("to see" or "to know").

184. Line 5, "kawuwusanira winuni," at the same time reads paradoxically as: "Hidden is its telling."

The verbal forms at the end of this verse and at the beginning of the next indicate reciprocity of action, presumably within One Actor who is (not) two. "For always ineffable [is] . . ."

Having come to the exalted place
Most exalted his exaltation
The Holy One was called
Ki Sèh Wali Lanang Sajati
And Lord Jati Minulya
As for his name, it was
His Highness Prince Siti Jenar
Known as Sèh Sunyata Jatimurti
Was the Susunan of Lemahbang[185]

18 The pundit stayed long in Peng-
      ging
Kyai Ageng received with rever-
      ence
Devotion and honor his guest
At that time, it is said
Kyai Ageng became a disciple
Of His Highness Prince Siti Jenar
He studied the sacred knowledge

The perfection of person
The meaning of discourses myste-
      rious and strange
The way to *rahsa*'s binding

19 Poured out to him, the teachings
The knowledge of Release in its
      every twist
All that he did receive
Now after a goodly time
The Holy One went home
To the village of Siti Jenar
Kyai Ageng did accompany
His master to Siti Jenar
'Tis said of this Kyai Ageng Peng-
      ging
Others were there with him

20 Fellow students of sacred knowl-
      edge
Under High Prince Siti Jenar
Forty were they in number:
Ki Ageng Banyubiru
And Ki Ageng Getasaji
The Kyai Ageng of Balak
The Ki Ageng of Butuh
And Ki Ageng of Ngerang
And Ki Ageng of Jati, Ki Ageng
      Tingkir
Ki Ageng Watalunan[186]

185. The name Ki Sèh Wali Lanang Sajati
reads discursively as "Sir Sainted Sèh the
Perfect Man." The name, emphasizing the
(sexualized) maleness of the Perfect Man
translates the Sufi concept of the *insan
kamil*, the Beginning and End of Creation,
the realization of Himself to which the
mystic aspires. The name Lord Jati Minulya reads discursively as "Lord Reality
Exalted." The name Sèh Sunyata Jatimurti, though semantically determined,
defies translation. Roughly, it "means"
the Sèh Who Has Attained the Absolute
Void as Reality Incarnate. See above, note
to I:13. The word/name *Sunyata* recalls
the ascetic practice of Kebo Kanigara (see
above, XVII:9). The words *lemahbang* and
sitijenar (alternatively *sitiabrit*) are syno-
nyms, meaning red or golden earth. Lemahbang names a number of villages
across Java, including one to the north of
Ambarawa in the district of Salatiga,
Central Java.

186. Although forty disciples (including
Ki Ageng Pengging) are claimed for Siti
Jenar, I count forty-three to forty-six.
The leeway of three depends upon how
one determines designation in counter-
distinction to alias.
   There are two villages by the name of
Banyubiru in Central Java: one, on the
western side of Rawa Pening, Salatiga
district; the other near Cawas in the Kla-

21 And Ki Ageng Pringapus with
    Kyai Ageng Nganggas [and]
       Wanalapa
    Paladadi's Ki Ageng

---

ten district. Ki Gedé Banyubiru is well
known as an early associate (teacher) of
Jaka Tingkir. Ki Gedhé Banyubiru and
Ki Gedhé Getasaji may well be one and
the same person. According to the Balé
Pustaka edition of the *Babad Tanah Jawi*,
Getasaji, a village southeast of Pengging,
was the residence of Ki Gedhé Banyubiru (*Babad Tanah Jawi* [Batavia, 1939],
3:61).

There is a sacred grave called Balakan
(burial site of Ki Ageng Balak) near the
town of Kartasura, just to the west of
Surakarta. Balakan is a popular pilgrimage site for thieves and other criminals, as
well as for any persons involved in litiga-
tion. There is also a village of Balak situated on the western slope of Mount Merbabu.

Butuh is located just to the west of the
Lawiyan district of Surakarta in an area
now known as Makam Aji ("King's
Grave," as the site of Sultan Pajang's
[Jaka Tingkir] grave). Ki Gedhé Butuh is
well known as an early associate of Jaka
Tingkir.

Ngerang is the name of a village in
Mantup, Juwana, Japara. Ki Gedhé Nge-
rang was married to a daughter of Bon-
dhan Kejawèn (Ki Ageng Tarub). Nge-
rang's daughter married her cousin, Ki
Ageng Séla—a son of Ngerang's wife's
brother, Ki Ageng Getas Pendhawa ([Ki
Padmasusastra] and R.Ng. Wirapratama,
Sejarah Ageng ing Karaton Surakarta [RP
B 77; SMP MN 690], pp. 66–67). Ki
Ageng Ngerang is well known as an early
associate of Jaka Tingkir.

The Jati of Ki Ageng Jati is probably
the village of Jati situated just south of
the town of Kudus. There is also a hamlet
called Jati near Karanganyar to the east of

Ngambat Karangwaru's
Babadan's and Wanantara's
Kyai Ageng of Majasta
The one of Tambakbaya
Of Baki and Tembalang
Karanggayam Ngargaloka, Kayu-
    puring
Pandhawa, Sélandaka[187]

Surakarta. A Ki Ageng Jati was married
to a daughter of Ki Ageng Séla (*Sejarah
Ageng ing Karaton Surakarta*, p. 67).

Tingkir is now the name of a village 4
km. to the southeast of the town of Salatiga; it formerly named that entire district. The wife of Ki Gedhé Tingkir became the adoptive mother of Jaka Tingkir.

I have not been able to identify the
name/toponym Watalunan.

187. Pringapus is the name of a village in
the district of Salatiga.

According to the Bale Pustaka edition
of the *Babad Tanah Jawi*, Ki Gedhé Wanalapa was an emigrant from Atas-angin
(above the equator) who helped Prince-
regent Bintara establish the settlement of
Demak. When the Prince-regent was invested with kingship, Wanalapa became
his vizier, Mangkurat (*Babad Tanah Jawi*
[Batavia, 1939], 3:14). Perhaps the Ki
Ageng mentioned here is that Vizier
Mangkurat's son or successor. There is a
village by the name of Wanalapa in East
Java (southeast of Malang).

I have yet to identify the names/topo-
nyms Nganggas, Paladadi, and Ngambat.

There are two villages in the Central
Pasisir named Karangwaru: one in Grobogan, the other in Jepara.

There is a village of Babadan in Ungaran, Salatiga. There are also a number of
villages named Babadan in southern Central Java. Wanatara is the name of a village in West Java near Indramayu.

Majasta is a village in southern Central
Java, in the district of Klatèn just to the

22 The Kyai Ageng of Purwasada
Kebo Kangan, Ki Ageng Kebonalas
Ki Ageng Waturanté
Kyai Ageng Tarumtum
Pataruman, Banyuwangi
Of Purna, Wanasaba
Of Karé, Gugulu
Of Candhi, Mount Pragota

———

west of Béji on the west bank of Benga-
wan Solo. *Babad Jaka Tingkir* (III:10–18)
agrees with the Balé Pustaka *babad* that
Ki Gedhé Majasta was married to Brawijaya V's daughter Ratu Tumus (*Babad
Tanah Jawi* [Batavia, 1939], 3:18). Ki
Ageng Majasta is well known as an early
associate of Jaka Tingkir.

There are several villages of Tambakbaya, including one in Sukaharja district
(see Pemberton, *On the Subject of "Java,"*
p. 272, note 6) and one in Grobogan, Semarang.

Baki is a village 6 km. southwest of the
city of Surakarta. The village of Baki has
traditionally provided porters to the
Kraton Surakarta. There is a villge of
Tembalang in Srondol, South Semarang.

There are a number of places called Karanggayam, including villages in (1) Cen-
dana, Kudus, (2) Semanten, Pacitan, and
(3) Kotagedhe, Yogyakarta. Ngargaloka is
the name of an area on the eastern slopes
of Mount Merbabu, situated to the southwest of Salatiga. There is a village called
Kayupuring in Ngasinan, Magelang,
Kedu. Mount Pendhawa is located on the
Diyèng Plateau. In some Javanese histories, Ki Ageng Sélandaka is identified as
the hunter who discovered the foundling
new-born baby Jaka Tarub (illegitimate
son of Seh Maulana Mahribi and Rasa-
wulan [Kalijaga's sister]; future father-in-
law of Bondhan Kejawèn) abandoned in
the Kepanasan forest (see, for example,
Babad Tanah Jawi [Batavia, 1939], 2:53–
54).

Ngadibaya, Karungrungan, Jati-
ngalih
Wanadadi [and] Tambangan[188]

188. I have yet to identify the names
Kebo Kangan, Kebonalas, Waturanté, and
Tarumtum. The name Kebo Kangan,
however, is likely to be the proper name
of a Kyai rather than a place name.

There is a place named Pataruman in
West Java in the district of Kuningan.
Banyuwangi is the name of a town on the
very eastern tip of Java.

Mt. Purna is located in Lorok, Pacitan.
A daughter of Ki Ageng Getas Pendhawa
was married to a Ki Ageng Purna (*Sejarah
Ageng ing Karaton Surakarta*, p. 66).
Wanasaba is a town in Ledok, Bagelen, on
the southern side of the Diéng Plateau. Ki
Ageng Wanasaba was the eldest son of
Bondhan Kejawèn. Wanasaba's daughter
was married to his brother Getas Pan-
dhawa's son, Ki Ageng Séla (*Sejarah
Ageng*, pp. 66–67).

According to the "major" *Babad Tanah
Jawi*, Nyi Ageng Karé was a daughter of
Ki Getas Pendhawa (*Babad Tanah Jawi*
[Batavia, 1939] 3:35). There is a village of
Karé in East Java, situated to the south-
east of Madiun. Gugulu is the name of a
village on the Progo River to the south-
west of Yogyakarta.

Candhi, Mt. Pragota is in Semarang
(see above, XVI:7).

Ngadibaya is the name of a village in
Sumawana, Temanggung, Kedu. Ni
Ageng Ngadibaya was a daughter of Ki
Ageng Getas Pendhawa (*Sejarah Ageng
ing Karaton Surakarta*, p. 67). There is a
Mt. Karungruman in the Priangan dis-
trict, West Java. Jatingalèh is a mountain
village just south of Semarang.

There are two villages by the name of
Wanadadi in the Semarang area: (1) in
Truko, Kendal, Semarang and (2) Grogol,
Semarang. Tambangan is the name of a
stream near Jepara, Central Java.

23   Kyai Ageng of Ngampuhan with
     Kyai Ageng Bangsri Panengah
     Now all these were fellows
     For all took as their guru
     His Highness Prince Siti Jenar
     All joined in brotherhood
     Brothers under one master
     Deeply loving one another
     As though real brothers, they were
     In harmonious accord all[189]

24   To tell of Lord Ki Ageng Pengging:
     Long was his stay in Siti Jenar
     When assembled all complete were
     The brethren under one master
     In Siti Jenar all of them
     Did discourse upon *rasa*
     Deliberating on the knowledge
     Of the Sufi way whose knowledge
       is *rahsa*
     Precisely was their discourse on
       the Perfect Man
     The binding of Release[190]

25   And after that they all took leave
     Of their master, High Prince Siti
       Jenar
     Granted leave, they all dispersed

189. I have yet to identify the name
Ngampuhan. There are two places in
Central Java called Bangsri: one to the
northeast of Jepara, the other to the
southeast of Surakarta. Ni Ageng Bangsri
was a daughter of Ki Ageng Séla (grand-
daughter of Getas Pandhawa and Wanasaba) (*Sejarah Ageng*, p. 67).
190. By "the Sufi way" in line 8, I render
tasawuf, the Javanese transcription of the
Arabic *tasawwuf*. In line 9, it is *insan khamil* (Javanese transcription of the Arabic)
that I render as "the Perfect Man." See
above, note to XVII:17.

     Each of them returning home
     To his respective dwelling place
     Now then it is told:
     This Ki Ageng Pengging
     His journey was in company
     Of seventeen whose progress was
       southward
     Ki Ageng Tingkir the eldest was
       with

26   Ki Ageng Pengging, Ki Ageng
       Banyubiru
     Ki Ageng Getasaji, Ki Ageng Balak
     Ki Ageng Majasta and
     The Ki Ageng Tambakbaya
     Of Tembalang, Ki Ageng Baki
     The Ki Ageng of Babadan
     The one of Wanantara
     Ki Ageng of Karanggayam
     Ngargaloka, of Pringapus, Kayu-
       puring
     Of Nganggas and Wanalapa

27   The seventeen to Tingkir came
     The home of Ki Ageng Ngadi-
       purwa
     Charged to spend the night there
     Two nights' long they stayed
     Favored with feasts replete
     Lavish was the reception of
     Ki Ageng Tingkir
     For these his sixteen guests
     After that, making their farewells
     They set off in a group[191]

28   Upon the road four did part ways
     To the southwest was the progress
       of

191. Ki Ageng Ngadipurwa is another
name of Ki Ageng Tingkir.

Kyai Ageng Ngargaloka
Kyai Ageng Pringapus
With Ki Ageng Kayupuring
And Ki Ageng Purwasada
Now then it is told:
Twelve they were who went south-
    east
Ki Ageng Pengging and his fellows
Describing not their journey

29 The progress of Ki Ageng Peng-
       ging
    Did come unto his palace
    With his eleven fellows
    All stayed over there
    Ki Ageng Pengging lavishly re-
       ceived
    These his eleven guests
    Resting there two nights
    Were favored with feasts replete
    Then making their farewells
    They did set off, each on his own
       way[192]

Tells of Demak's reaction to the in-
novations in Pajang-Pengging. Ki
Ageng Pengging is summoned to
Demak.

XVIII. Pangkur
[Melodic mood is intense, impassioned and/or weighty]

192. The compound *ungkur-ungkuran*
("each his own way") means literally
"with their backs to one another." Here as
sound signal, in conjunction with the
punctuation mark for a new canto directly behind it, the compound alerts the
poem's reader/singer to change to the
melody of Pang*kur*.

1   No more said on the travelers
       home
    Let the tale be turned again:
    In Bintara His Majesty
    Who newly come onto the throne
    Was beloved of all the great *wali*
    Loyal, all the princes
    The nobles, the high courtiers

2   All held him in respectful awe
    Not one had misgivings
    By then His Royal Majesty
    Had already heard the news
    That his elder brothers of Pengging
       two
    Changing the tune of their ways
    Their manners were strangely new

3   Casting off their royalty
    They dressed as *santri* in the man-
       ner of *fakir*
    And too they did refuse
    To come to the capital Demak
    For as long as His Highness had
       reigned
    Yet to present themselves to the
       court of Demak
    These nobles two remained aloof[193]

4   Away in their own realm apart
    His Majesty was troubled deep
    Most anxious was his heart
    The Honored Sultan of Demak
    Feared that these his elder brothers
    Might bring grief unto his reign
    Over the Kraton of all Java

193. The word rendered as "dressed" in
line 2 is *cara*. See above, note to XVII:10.
A *fakir* (Ar. *faqîr*) is a poor wandering
Sufi or a dervish.

5   The Lord Sultan Demak at that
Dispatched as envoys officers four
Were charged forthwith to sum-
mon
These his elder brothers two
The Princes of Pengging; thereat
the messengers
Sped off—their journey not de-
scribed
The messengers, come to Pengging

6   Did meet His Highness the Prince
Was charged by command of the
King
That the royal princes
Two were summoned
By the Lord Sultan Demak to come
straightway
With the messengers' return
Now then Ki Ageng Pengging

7   Did answer thus the messengers:
"Tell the Lord our King
That at present my elder brother
Kebo Kanigara
Has taken off to who knows where
Following but his heart's desire
With nary a subject attending

8   "With but his wife and children
Long have I searched to no avail
Now as pertains to me myself
Being summoned by the King
I needs must beg forgiveness of His
Majesty
Till my elder brother should return
Whenever his coming might be

9   "Then shall I present myself
To the Lord Sultan Demak

Both of us, with my brother too
Enough messenger. Be off with
you"
The officers four, faithful to his
every word
Taking leave from his presence
Departed the realm of Pengging

10   The progress of the envoys four
Relating not their adventures
along the way
Coming to Demak did proceed
straightway
Into the presence of the King
Offering a *sembah*, on their mis-
sion they did report
Beginning, middle, unto the end
Was reported to the King

11   On hearing this the Lord Sultan
Wondered in his heart, but with a
direful dread
From His Majesty's suspicions
Surmised he that perhaps this did
Spell trouble for his Kraton
But at least His Majesty
Still remembered in his heart

12   That these his elder brethren were
Both these nobles of Pajang-
Pengging
Cousins of His Majesty
Born of his elder-aunt
How could they harbor ill intent?
For still related closely were
These nobles and the King

13   And so it was as time went by
For the Sultan of Demak; turning
what is told:

The Lord Susunan Majagung
Had grown so very old
Falling ill, to death he did succumb
His body then was buried
Within his meditation cell

14 The son who did succeed him
Was called the Panembahan of
   Majagung
Many were his brethren
Went off their separate ways
Each and every one of them was
   titled a "High Prince"
Some settled in the capital Demak
Others lived at Ngampèldenta

15 Still others settled in Drajat
And Bonang while others lived in
   Giri
Others still there were who stayed
   in Majagung

Tells of the annual Garebeg Mulud festivities at the capital of Demak.

Now that to be recited:
In the capital Demak with the
   coming
Of the month Rabingu'awal
Assemble did the *wali* all[194]

194. Rabingu'awal, or Mulud, is the third month of the Islamic lunar calendar. On the twelfth of this month is the celebration of the Prophet Mohammad's birthday, Maulud Nabi.

16 And the *mufti* and *sulakha*
The *ulama, kukamah* and *ngabid*
The great and mighty pundits
With all the ascetics too
Assembled in Demak, together one
   and all
And all the princes-regent
The nobles and high courtiers

17 The princes-regent of the outer
   realms
All assembled in Demak
As was customary
Every Rabingu'awal
They came; thus it came to pass
On the twelfth of the month
They recited *The Prophet's
   Nativity*[195]

195. In the premodern Moslem Javanese polity, the three Garebegan ("tumultuous gatherings together") that celebrated the holidays commemorating the Prophet Mohammad's birth (Garebegan Mulud in the third month), the end of the fasting month (Garebeg Siyam on the first of the tenth month), and the sacrifice of Ishmael by Ibrahim (Garebegan Besar in the twelfth month) were the most important public state ceremonies. The most impressive of these occasions was the Garebeg Mulud, at which time "the entire realm" (i.e., all the provincial vassals of the ruler alongside his administrative elite) were *required* to gather at the capital to pay homage and taxes. The ruler would offer mountains of rice and food (*gunungan*), which would be conveyed in royal procession from the inner *kraton* to the courtyard of the Grand Mosque. The mountains were "divided up" among (actually torn to shreds by) the faithful and the people in the mosque courtyard.
   By *The Prophet's Nativity*, I render

18   In the Grand Mosque of Demak
     In spirited song they sang in verse
     The ancient tales in voices redolent
     The Lord Sultan of Demak
     Sang in refrain with the mighty
        wali
     When their *tahlilan* was done
     They sat to feasts replete[196]

19   On the morn then the procession
     Garebegan proceeded in parade
     Teeming the subjects great and low
     Were arrayed: a crowded sea
     Filling the Alun-alun brim full
     Over they spilled to the by-ways
     Thronging in unbroken streams[197]

20   Like a leafy young forest lush
     The grand parade of subjects from
        all of Java's land

Maulud Nabi, which indicates either the title of a text, or the name of a genre of (usually) poetic texts, treating the birth of the Prophet Mohammad.

196. The verse referred to in line 2 is *singir,* from the Arabic *syâ'ir,* for "verse" (especially religious verse).

Tahlilan (the act of saying "there is no god but God" in Arabic) denotes sessions of collective Islamic prayer, or more precisely, chanting (*zikir*).

197. On the Garebegan, see above, note to XVIII:17. The term *Garebegan* is from the word *grebeg* (tumultuous of sound). The *alun-alun* are the twin large plazas opening out both in front of and behind (to the north and south of) Javanese palaces. Here, the reference is to the Alun-alun Lor (the Northern Alun-alun) through which the courtiers proceed with the ritual rice mountains (*gunungan*) on their way to the Grand Mosque.

Loomed like a long lolling darkening cloud
Pressed in crowded crush
In swarming teeming mass
Like a thunderhead on high
With darkness, covering all the sky

Especially noted is the seating protocol for the culmination of the Garebegan festivities.

21   The Lord Sultan, holding audience
     In the Canopied Pavilion on the
        Elevated Earth, sat
     Upon his sapphire throne
     With the foremost of the *wali*
     Seated on thrones one and all
     On one level with His Majesty
     To the right and left of the king[198]

22   To the north they did face all
     As for the minor *wali*
     They were inside the Mosque
     And all the pundits
     The *ulama* and mighty *khukama*
     The *ngabid, sulakha,* and *fuqaha*
     Filling the Mosque's veranda[199]

198. The audience is depicted as if it takes place in the nineteenth-century Kraton Surakarta. The Sultan is seated in the Bangsal Witana ("Canopied Pavilion"), a small caged-in cubicle for the Susuhunan's throne. The Bangsal Witana is indeed located on the northern Siti Inggil ("Elevated Earth"), a man-made "plateau" about six feet tall.

199. The Surambi was the name of the veranda of the Mosque; it was also site of the religious court of justice.

23 Spilled over to the courtyard
   Now arrayed before the king
   Were the mighty princes of the
       blood
   The regents and royal family
   Ranged in rows sat before His
       Majesty
   Under the Awning below the
       King's Canopy
   All the senior princes[200]

24 Who were uncles to the Sultan
   Did sit on chairs to either side
   Before His Royal Majesty
   Grand Vizier Wanasalam
   Was in the Assembly Hall with the
       leading courtiers
   The princes-regent of the outer
       realms
   And the highest ministers[201]

25 Once the Rice Mountains had
       come forth

200. By "the Awning," I render Tratag, a
spacious veranda in front (to the north of)
and under a single roof with the Witana.
201. By "Assembly Hall" I render Pagelaran, a large roofed open pavilion situated to the north of, and below, the Siti
Inggil. It was in this pavilion that the
grand vizier would preside over his subordinates and the realm's military troops on
audience days. In the course of any audience, the vizier would be summoned from
the Pagelaran to the inner palace (Sasana
Séwaka) to report to the Susuhunan on
the state of the realm.
   By "highest ministers" in the final line,
I render nayaka praméya mantri. In the
administrative bureaucracy of the palace,
the nayaka were high court officials
ranked just above the bupati ("regents").

To the Mosque the royal offering
Then was blessed forthwith
And divided evenly
With that the Lord Sultan retired
Unto the inner palace
To feast with all the *wali*

26 When the feast was finished
   The *wali* then went forth
   Unto their own encampments
   The audience dispersed
   As did the troops' array

Tells of the design of the wali *synod*
to enforce strict adherence to Islamic
law. The indictment of Siti Jenar.

Now with the elapse
Of three days and three nights

27 Allah's *wali* all
   In the palace did collect
   With the mighty pundits all
   The *mufti* and the *khukama*
   None but the elder ones
   They'd come there to discuss
   Their will that the Faith be firmed

28 The strengthening of the *sharî'a*
   Heeding the Holy Prophet's word
   Lord Muhammad the Chosen One:
   Hold fast to the *sharî'a*
   The pillar of the foremost Faith
   Whosoever that impugns
   Verily impugns he God[202]

202. The word for "God" in the final line
is the Hindu appellation "Hyang Wid-
[dh]i."

29 Whosoever does God impugn
    Shall face the holy tribunal
    For trial and punishment
    There's no avoiding it
    Lord Susunan Kudus sweetly then
        did speak
    To the Lord Sunan Darajad
    Reporting the behavior of

30 His Highness Sèh Siti Jenar:
    "Who so blatantly dares in dis-
        closure rash
    The secret to unveil
    The End of Ends
    That on which all knowledge
        hangs, Being Absolute
    All too impudent of manner
    Eccentric are his ways

31 "He dares transgress the bans
    Of the Prophet's holy *sharî'a*
    Oft scorning its commands
    He impugns the rule of *sharî'a*
    No leading him is there to the way
        of righteousness
    He scorns the sacred pillars
    Forsakes *salât* in the mosque[203]

32 "He scorns the Friday worship
    He scorns prayer and *zikir* too
    Plunged headlong to damnation's
        way

He's arrogant, incorrigible
When reproached he does reproach
    in turn
Vanished all his dread
Nothing holds he secret[204]

33 "If cornered, the tribunal he'd dare
    With nary a care for his death
    Unappeasable, he's adamant
    Exposing the secret with nary a
        veil
    Making light of the Prophet's holy
        sharî'a
    Oft revealing the concealed
    Defiant, he'll not retreat"[205]

XIX. Durma
[Melodic mood is very impassioned, angry, or violent. Appropriate for battle scenes.]

1   Now spoke the Lord Sunan Drajad
    "In that case, son
    This does agree
    With what I have heard tell
    And witnessed too myself
    Why, it differs not
    From everything you've said

2   "If 'tis true the ways of Ki Sèh Siti
        Jenar

203. The "Sacred Pillars," or the *rukuning
Islam*, are the five ritual activities obligatory upon any Moslem. These five pillars
are: (1) *shahâdah* (Confession of Faith),
(2) *salât*, (3) fasting in the ninth lunar
month [Ramadan], (4) performing the
pilgrimage to Mecca (*hajj*) once in one's
life—if possible, and (5) annual payment
of the *zakât*, or religious tax.

204. *Zikir* (Ar. *dhikr*) is an Islamic ritual
activity characterized by chanting. See
notes to XIII:17 and XVIII:18.
205. The word *ngunduri* ("retreat"), in
conjunction with the punctuation mark
for a new canto directly following it, signals the reader/singer to change to the
melody of Durma. This cue works from
the conventionalized sound association of
durma with words formed from the root
un*dur*.

Do indeed break rank
And trouble do our course
There'll be no shielding him
He's truly subject to the justice
    then
Laid down by Allah's law
Unless he should reform"

3   Lord Sunan Drajad then canvassed
    All the senior *wali*
    And too the *khukama*
    The *fuqaha*, the pundits
    Along with all the *mufti*
    Came to the decision
    That His Highness the Prince of
        Siti Jenar

4   Was subject to be punished by the
        tribunal
    Unless he did reform
    He would be put to death
    Lest he go too far
    Stirring up the realm
    Ruining the *sharî'a*
    Straightaway summoned they

5   His Highness Prince Siti Jenar
        from his encampment
    Conducted by the messenger
        arrived
    Inside the palace he
    Was seated properly
    Together with the *wali* there
    Then it was the Sunan
    Of Kudus who declared:

6   "Receive you now the sentence
    Of His Holy Reverence
    If you do refuse
    To redeem your ways
    Which so strangely new

Do ruin the *sharî'a*
Blatantly with nary a screen

7   "Verily are you subject to the jus-
        tice which
    Comes straight from the Qur'ân
        and Hadîth
    The *ijma'* and *qiyâs*
    There's no escaping it
    Allah's punishment shall fall
    On you
    But if you should reform[206]

8   "Verily shall you be absolved
    And furthermore rewarded
    With all beneficence"

Siti Jenar's defense. A lyric expres-
sion of rasa *ecstasy.*

Then laughing in delight
Sèh Sunyata Jatimurti
Did slap his thighs
With beaming countenance[207]

206. The Hadîth, or "The Traditions," are
the collected body of tales detailing practices of the Prophet Mohammad and his
early associates. The Arabic word *ijma'*
(consensus) is an Islamic legal term for
the agreement of the community of Moslem (legal) scholars as a basis for juridical
decision. *Qiyâs* (rational argumentation)
is an Islamic legal term indicating a process of coming to legal decisions for novel
cases by way of analogy to "traditional"
cases (from the Hadîth and Qur'ân). Enu-
merated thus are the four bases of traditional Islamic legal decisions.
207. The name in line 5, Sèh Sunyata
Jatimurti, is an alias of Siti Jenar. See
notes to I:13 and XVII:17.

9 Speaking sweetly and precisely, his
       words were impudent
   "So! I've reached the heights
   Now of fortune fair if
   I am to be rewarded with
   A world more beautiful
   The source of all beauty
   In this world and the next[208]

10 "As for the pronouncement of the
       Lord Susunan
   Drajad, His Reverence
   With all that deep concern
   For my person's body
   Such sensitivity for life
   It is received with thanks
   For His Reverence's loving kind-
       ness[209]

11 "But I for one have not the least
       desire
   Now to betray my words
   Heretofore expressed
   For ever is it thus

This my-creature's being
Is merely then to move
As authored by the Lord[210]

12 "All my-creature's movements are
       without intent
   Seeing, hearing
   Gesture, voice
   Ways beyond compare
   Speech beyond limit
   Who holds authority?
   Why! The Being of the Lord

13 "Pervades my-creature's being
   As one, drawing-while-drawn
   Determining-while-determined
   Enamoring-while-enamored
   Being, exchanging-while-
       exchanged
   Moving-while-being moved
   There the lovers do unite[211]

208. The terms for "this world and the
next" are Arabic/Islamic existential ones
(sâghir, "empty" and qabîr, "experi-
enced/phenomenal"). Here they name
the Javanese spatial/temporal categories,
realms eternal and transient, that I render
"this world and the next." It is intriguing
that in the poem there is no conjunction
separating sahir from kabir. Rather than
regard it a mere result of metric constric-
tions, I read this absence of conjunction as
a device to reject this spatial/temporal
duality—qua simple duality. Unfortunately, the ambiguity does not translate
into English.
209. The Javanese badan manira ("my
body") in line 4, also (and at the same
time) reads "my person" or "my personal
being."

210. The word kawula, rendered as "my-
creature" in line 5, can and does refer to
Siti Jenar's personal self (functions as a
first-person pronoun)—while at the same
time denoting his personal "creatureness"
as well as "creatureness" in general.
   With this verse begins a poetic exposition of the well-known Javanese kawula/
gusti doctrine, which espouses the unity
of creature and Creator; servant and Master. For a sketch of the centrality of this
doctrine in Javanese thought, see Soemarsaid Moertono, State and Statecraft in Old
Java, pp. 14–26.
211. The repetitive verbal form (reduplica-
cated verb with the passive in infix for the
second of the pair) in lines 1–6 indicates
reciprocity of action. In this case the reciprocity is presumably within One Actor
who is (not) two. See also above, XVII:
16–17.
   In the final line, the Kawi pulangsih re-

14 "Uniting as lovers in the Being
Encompassed by the Lord
Vanish does the creature
Dissolved, extinguished and de-
stroyed
Replaced by the Being of the Lord
His life is
Then the Life of the Lord

15 "*Lahir* and *batin*, his then is the
Absolute's Being
The one worshipped is the Lord
The Lord it is Who worships
Self worshipping-while-
worshipped
Self adoring-while-adored
In reciprocity
And so, in this life²¹²

16 "Be ye aware of life in perfection
Life restored to Reality
The Reality of Life

---

fers more specifically to "sexual intercourse."

212. The words *lahir* and *batin* (line 1) are
Arabic loan words which denote the dual-
istic opposition of exteriority vs. interi-
ority; revealed vs. concealed; expressed
(born) vs. reserved (hidden); material vs.
immaterial. It is precisely this opposition
which is collapsed by Siti Jenar's discourse. See also note to XVI:12.

In the same line, "the Absolute" renders the OJ *Suksma*, the nonmanifest essence of God.

In lines 4 and 5, the words (*dhéwé* and
pribadi) are rendered as "self"; however,
these words mean, at the same time,
"alone" or "by oneself," and hence denote
here the autonomy of divine Agency.
There is no single English word which
can hold the tension of these two meanings.

Subject not to death
The very tremble of a hair
Though but a single strand
Is then indeed adoring prayer

17 "For then adoring prayer is per-
petual
When 'tis such indeed
The being of man is
Blithe though he be naked
Untroubled though hungry
Should he be insulted
His joy then knows no bounds

18 "When met with danger dread
Or tried by disaster dire
He merely laughs
For his heart is without care
And he knows no fear
His is but strength serene
From *lahir* straight through to
batin

19 "He knows no joy when graced
With pleasure consummate
Or praise
Desiring no reward
Disaster, disease, and fortune fair
To him are all the same
Not his to pick and choose

20 "For all of these are too rewards
Gifts divine; for the receiver
There is but acceptance
Eternal evermore
Beyond the limits of life
His life is beyond
The compass of the mind²¹³

---

213. It is the word *panarima* that I render
as "acceptance" in line 3. *Panarima* also

21 "For he who has grasped the ulti-
mate of *rasa*
Rasa that is Reality
The reality of *rasa*
Is surely not *rerasan* voiced in
speech
Nor the six *rasa* flavors
Nor again the *rasa*
Which is *rasa*-ed by the lips[214]

22 "Nor the *rasa* which is *rasa*-ed by
the heart
Nor *rasa* fabricated
Nor again the *rasa*
Which is *rasa*-ed by the body
Nor *rasa* which is *rasan*-ed by the
voice
Nor again the *rasa*
Of pleasure and afflicting pain[215]

23 "The Reality of *Rasa* which au-
thors *rasa*
Rasa Real mastering
Rahsa-surasa
Rasa which is *rasa*'s navel
The king of *rahsa* all
Rasa exalted
Is *Jatimurti* recuperate"[216]

*Found guilty of heresy, Siti Jenar is
sentenced to death. Reports Siti
Jenar's response to the sentence.*

24 The Lord Sunan Kudus did angrily
retort:
"Aha! In which case 'tis so
You stand exposed
As one who claims Godhood
Though hiding behind a veil, still
manifest

---

means "reception," as in "gratitude" and
in "resignation." The supposed Javanese
character trait of *panarima* or *nrimo* (as
quiet resignation) has become a clichéd
emblem of "Javanese fatalism." The *panarima* of which the feisty Siti Jenar speaks,
however, is certainly not fatalistic.

214. A wonderfully polysemic word, *rasa*
(and its cognates) indicates "feeling, taste,
emotion, voice, speech, gossip, sense,
meaning, mystery, essence." In this and
the following stanzas, the poet plays on
this polysemy. In order to retain the play,
I have left the *rasa* words in the original
Javanese, sometimes with the addition of
English *-ed* verbal endings. See also note
to XVII:14.

The word *rerasan* (line 4) means "discourse," often in the sense of gossip about
a third party. For more on the "six *rasa*
flavors" (line 5), see above, VIII:24–25.

215. The passive of *rasan* (line 5) could be
rendered "voiced" or "spoken."

216. The word *rahsa* (in lines 3 and 5)
denotes "Mystery." The word *surasa* denotes "meaning," and sometimes "pleasure." *Rahsa-surasa* (line 3), then, signifies "the mystery of meaning" and "the
meaning of mystery," as well as the reciprocal relationship between these two
significations *and* the pleasure that reciprocity affords. See also note to XVII:14.

In line 5, "rahsaning sakalir" is "the
mystery of everything" and/or "all mystery."

By placing the verb *to be* at the head of
the final line, my translation reads the
line "is *Jatimurti* (Reality Incarnate) recuperate" as predicating both the clauses
that immediately precede it *and* the extensively modified "he who's grasped the
ultimate of *rasa*" which opens verse 21. I
am grateful to I. Kuntara Wiryamartana
for his suggestions pertaining to the verbal structure of this complicated "sentence."

As fallen to Jabariyah
Baring blatant these pretentious
    claims[217]

25 "Lost are you and wayward
Fallen to the devil's way
Without a doubt you shall
Meet disaster in this world
Felled by the wrath of the realm
Transgressing thus the bans
You bring trouble on the realm

26 "Making light of the Holy
    Prophet's *shari'a*
Yea is punishable by death

On the coming Friday
There is no escaping it
After we've done our *salât*
You shall be executed
By a sword of potent might"

27 His Highness Sèh Siti Jenar ever
    more defiant
Was not the least afraid
Dauntless and unflinching
His face shone brighter still
With refulgent radiance keen
And with sweet allure
Smiling he answered triumphant:

28 "Hark ye well, my fellows all
All ye *wali*
And ye pundits too
Are acting childishly
Twice over do ye do the deed
Why! You do explode
With empty threats in this attempt

29 "In a waste of windy surfeit words
You think to threaten
A suckling babe
Who might fall in a fit
To be rubbed with salves, as he
    trembles and cries
With rolling eyes
And horrible plaintive wails[218]

30 " 'Twould be a shame were I afraid

217. Siti Jenar stands "exposed" (*kakan-dhangan*) in the sense of "coralled" or "exposed to public ridicule in a stockade."
    Jabariyah names, for those who oppose it, a variant of Islamic thought characterized by radical determinism. To be called "Jabariyah" is to be charged with heterodoxy, if not heresy. Jabariyah is mentioned with concern in other nineteenth-century Surakarta texts: for example, in his *Wulang Putra*, Pakubuwana IX cautions his children to observe strictly the *shari'a* lest they fall prey to Jabariyah (Pakubuwana IX, *Serat Wira Iswara* [Jakarta: Departemen Pendidikan dan Kebudayaan, Proyek Penerbitan Buku Sastra Indonesia dan Daerah, 1979], p. 102). A modern Indonesian dictionary of Islamic terminology notes that Jabariyah teaches that all existential phenomena (including human behavior) are determined by the Will of God (*kudrat* and *iradat*), thus relieving man of all responsibility for his actions (Shodiq H. Shalahuddin Chaery, *Kamus Istilah Agama* [Jakarta: C. V. Sienttarama, 1983], p. 155). See also P. J. Zoetmulder, *Pantheisme en Monisme in de Javaansche Soeloek-Litteratuer* (Nijmegen: J. J. Berkhout, 1935), pp. 146–49.

218. The fit is *sawan*, a disease of infants characterized by convulsive seizures. The seizures are caused by the pernicious influence of spirits. A remedy or prophylactic for *sawan* is to rub the infant's brow with certain medicinal preparations, especially turmeric and lime.

Either now or on the morn
Never then shall flee
This the man Siti Jenar
'Twould be a shame that I
Did take the name
'Sunyata Jatimurti'[219]

31 "If lost I am and wayward
Fallen to the devil's way
Better had I died
When still a suckling babe
What sense is there to live
Submitted to the devil
Borne away to error?

32 "And now liable to justice
I stand by all my speech
Never to forswear
Though finished on the scaffold

219. This is an especially problematic stanza to translate. The sense of the lines diverges significantly depending on how the reader understands their syntactic divisions. The Javanese text: "Éman-éman babo manira wediya / ing mangké nadyan bénjing / monsa ta uncata / lamun wong Sitijenar / éman-émané wak mami / asi-lih aran / Sunyata Jatimurti." Another plausible reading of these lines is: "A pity it'd be were I afraid / Either now or on the morn / Never shall I turn heel / Should the man Siti Jenar / Pity this my person [body] / Then I take the name / Sunyati Jatimurti."

The Javanese original manages to hold *both* these meanings in tension with each other. The alternative and alternating readings turn on the parsing of the fourth line, *lamun wong Siti Jenar*. This clause can be (and is!) subject to both the preceding (*mangsa ta uncata*) and the succeeding (*éman-émané wak mami*) predicates.

Were I to flee my speech
Could never then be true
True *lahir* straight through *batin*

33 "And true it is: true in the morn-
ing, in the evening true
True by day and night
Beyond confines of season
'Tis true, indeed the Truth
In past, present, and future too
For it is the Truth
Call it what you will"

34 Now the Lord Sunan Darajad
Astounded was to hear
So staunch was the resolve of
His Highness Prince Siti Jenar
And all of them who heard
All those assembled there
Were amazed indeed aghast

35 The Lord Susunan Darajad did
order then
That they be adjourned
Till the coming Friday
And so they did adjourn
Each to his encampment

The execution of Siti Jenar.

Now then in due course
Came the appointed time

36 'Twas on Friday they were assem-
bled all
All the *wali*
With His Majesty the King
And all the pundits
The *ulama* both great and low
The princes of the blood
The princes-regent and courtiers

37 Inside the Mosque when the hour
        had come
    They did their Friday *salât* all
    And after they were done
    With the Friday *salât*
    Then they went outside
    Sunan Darajad
    And His Majesty the King

38 Sat in a pavilion which was newly
        built
    To the east of the Mosque's main
        gate
    The outer gate that is
    To the east of the courtyard
    Encircling them were the *wali*
    The pundits
    And the faithful *mukmin* all[220]

39 Joined by the princes-regent and
        the nobility
    Arrayed were the high courtiers
    In a crowded crush
    The Alun-alun was brimming
    Sèh Sunyata Jatimurti
    Was clearly manifest
    Seated rather to the fore

40 Sunan Kudus read the sentence
    Of His Holy Reverence
    Unto Sèh Siti Jenar
    That executed then would be
    The punishment of Allah which
        was death
    Dauntless did retort
    His Highness Prince Siti Jenar

41 With a smile, his radiance beam-
        ing:
    "Indeed, would you please
    Just get on with it
    Without further ado"
    And so Sunan Kudus forthwith
    Did bare his sword
    So very sharp

42 Sunan Siti Jenar then was put to
        the sword
    His neck, severed
    Down his head did fall
    Onto a readied carpet
    Spread with white *genis*
    Writhing on the ground
    His blood did gush forth hard[221]

Described is the death of Siti Jenar.
The testimony of the blood.

XX. Mijil
[Melodic mood is one of longing:
erotic or mournful]

1   Red blood appeared glowing bright
    And all they who did see
    Spoke with words like these:
    "That's not a pretty sight to see
    I thought him powerful
    Potent, yea invulnerable

2   "Why! a weakling he—laid low by
        a single blow

220. In other words, the execution was
carried out on the Alun-alun Lor (as were
public executions in nineteenth-century
Surakarta).

221. By *genis* perhaps is meant *gendhis*, or
"sugar."
    The word *mijil* ("to go [gush] forth") at
verse's end, in conjunction with the punctuation mark for a new canto directly following it, signals the reader/singer to
change to the melody of Mijil.

It didn't take a second strike
So, that is all there was to him
Crowing loud he claimed to truth
At the top of his voice
Pretending to sublimity

3   "And there, his blood is red
Just common human blood
I'd thought somehow that it'd look
    strange"
At that His Highness Prince Siti
    Jenar
From his body spewed
Blood as black as pitch

4   Brilliant black like jet-black ink
And all they who did see
Said: "Why! That's nothing special
Everybody's got black blood"
With that flowed yellow
The blood from the body

5   'Twas like fluid yellow powder
    flowing
And all they who did see
Said: "Still that's nothing special
For each and everybody's got
Blood of yellow hue"
With that the august body

6   Then issued blood bright white
A whiteness radiant with light
And sweet of fragrance redolent
And they who saw spoke yet again
"This too is nothing special
For each and everybody has

7   "Got blood of colors four
For God Almighty's creatures

Are primally from these colors
    four
Red, black, yellow, and white
Indeed the origin of yore
Is these fundamental four"

8   Now the blood of colors four
Able to hold forth
Did extol in joyous thanksgiving:
"However many the joys of life
By avail of death
Those joys are had

9   "In death, a death perfected
It's more than marvelous
The True Man truly
Of sacred knowledge consummate
Never then does die
But lives forevermore

10 "To call it death is false
For by the grave untouched
He merely moves on to another
    place
Bearing his *kraton* along with him
The delights of death
Are beyond number"

11 Now then all they who witnessed
Momentarily stunned
Bewondered at the blood's dis-
    course
And then they all did speak again:
"This must be some sorcery
That is, an act of conjuring

12 "Who's ever heard of talking blood
Holding discourse thus?
Was perhaps his knowledge but
    spiritism mere

Was that the best then he could do
This our 'Most Revered'
But fraternize with fiends?[222]

13 "Damnably lost fallen deeper still
      to error
    Anxious dread results
    Making difficult his death
    Just like the knowledge of the
      coarse and low"[223]

*Herein depicted is the apotheosis
and ascension of Siti Jenar.*

With that the Honored Dead
His head, that is

14 Roared with laughter, while speak-
      ing oh so sweet:
    "Blood of my body all
    Return ye now in haste
    Lest ye be left behind
    And enter not into
    There your paradise"

222. The art of the spirit medium is considered particularly apt for "empty" persons, especially hysteric women. For
more on spirit mediums and their maligned status in Javanese society, see
Ward Keeler, *Javanese Shadow Plays, Javanese Selves* (Princeton: Princeton University Press, 1987), pp. 119–24.
223. It is widely held in Java that one possessed of an excess of *magic* powers and
especially of power objects, may experience great difficulty and pain in his or
her death throes. Such a person may attain release in death only after ridding
himself or herself of these powers. This is
not an easy matter, since these powers, or
charms, are usually firmly "stuck" to
their owner.

15 The blood then did return
    All of it, as if inhaled
    Vanished without a trace
    Then the head did circle
    Around its body
    Three times round

16 Speaking all the while: "My fel-
      lows all
    None of you believed in me
    Your skepticism most extreme
    You took it as ridiculous
    Union with the Lord
    Fused in Being One"

17 Thereat the head fixed on again
    Perfectly in place
    Healed was the wound leaving
      nary a trace
    His radiance brilliant beaming
      bright
    Gently hailed he them, "Peace!"
    In dulcet voice so sweet[224]

18 Answered was his greeting
    By all assembled there
    Thunderous did their voices sound
    Marvel did all who witnessed
    Dazed they were struck dumb
    In bewondered awe

19 Deathly still as if bewitched
    With speechless mouths agape
    They hadn't thought 'twould come
      to this
    'Twas true that subject not to death

224. Hailing "Peace!" Siti Jenar voiced
the standard Islamic greeting: "assalam
'alaikum," which is answered "alaikum
salam."

Death was his in life
Life was his in death[225]

20 Life forever without death
    Returned unto the end
    Spirit body eternal evermore
    Then His Highness Prince Siti
       Jenar
    Drew nigh unto the presence of
    The Most-High Lord Bhikku[226]

21 Exchanging *salâm* with His Rever-
       ence
    And with His Majesty
    And all the other *wali* too
    Every single person there
    Salâm did exchange
    With He-Who-Is-Exalted[227]

22 After the exchange of *salâm*
    With each and everyone
    He-Who-Is-Exalted softly did be-
       speak
    His Reverence the Lord Sunan

225. The final two lines, "mati j[r]oning
urip / urip jroning lampus," repeat a
"metaphysical cliché" that describes the
stage of mystic perfection in which the
mystic attains a durable state of subsistence under the aspect of the Absolute.
226. "Spirit body" in line 3 is my rendering of *badan suksma*, words that signify a
materialized spirituality like that of *jatimurti* (see note to I:13).
    In the final line, "The Most-High Lord
Bhikku" (Sang aMaha Wiku), literally,
Highest Buddhist monk, refers to Sunan
Drajad as "patriarch" of the "synod."
227. *Salâm* are greetings of "peace" (see
above, note to XX:17).
    "He-Who-Is-Exalted" is my rendering
of the appellation Sang Wus Linuhung
(Siti Jenar in the state of apotheosis).

"And now given that
My punishment's been paid

23 "I beg your leave for I would move
       on
    To the realm of sublimity
    So fare thee well in days to come
    And thou, my Lord and King
    Fare thee well
    In future days to come

24 "And ye my fellow *wali* all
    And ye excellent pundits too
    Ye *ulama* and ye *mukmin* all
    Fare thee well in your tomorrows
    As well as all of ye
    Nobles great and mighty

25 "Ye ministers, regents, and officers
    Courtiers to His Majesty
    Begging leave from all of you
    I bid ye all the best
    Fortune fair be with you
    In all your tomorrows"

26 Thundering they did answer "Yes!
    In the end may all
    Meet with fortune fair
    Both he who's moving on and
       those now left behind"
    Now he who was set to vanish
    Brought forth his radiance

27 Radiant refulgent flaming flashing
    A lustrous lambent light
    Blazing brilliant striking
    Verily dimming the daystar's rays
    Blinded by the dazzle were
    All those who did see

28 Sèh Sunyata Jatimurti

Softly then did say
"I now have work to do"
Then that radiance bright did as-
    cend on high
In no time vanished into Mystery
Was He-Who-Is-Exalted[228]

29 Leaving in his wake a fragrance
        redolent
    Perfectly pervasive
    An eddied swirl of balmy musk
    Wide-eyed was the wonder of all
        those who did watch
    Each and every one of them
    Was plunged in awed regret

30 Among them there were those who
        cried: "Oh! Oh!
    Oh! Alas! Alas!
    I never thought that thus 'twould
        be!
    Verily, he was in truth a truly ex-
        cellent man
    His excellence exceeding
    All the rest"

31 No more said of him who was now
        Mystery

*Gravestones are erected to mark Siti
Jenar's tracks across the landscape.
His students mourn the loss of their
master.*

228. The "Mystery" into which Siti Jenar
vanished is *ghaib*, a technical term in Sufi
literature. In this state of perfection, the
seeker's soul, having attained *fanâ*, ex-
tinction which is absorption into the Divine, has its (non)existence in the *'Alam
al-Ghaib*, the uncreated world of God's
Mystery.

Now it is related:
Lord Sunan Drajat did command
On all the sites used of old
By Sèh Jatimurti
Whereat he'd meditated

32 And all the sites whereon he'd
        taught
    It was charged on all
    To mark them with tombstones
    Like graves the monuments
    Lest these sites bring curses on
    Foolish unripe men[229]

33 Now all the *wali* did adjourn
    Unto their encampments
    His Majesty the King retired to the
        palace
    The assembly thus dispersed
    Coming each unto his place, they
        were
    Ever whelmed by transports of
        deep passion[230]

229. Depending upon the "parsing" of the
lines, the *aja* of the *aja milalati* (line 5) can
be read either "Don't!" or "Lest . . ."
Hence, alternatively, this line could refer
to the actual engraving on the tomb-
stones and would translate: "[Engraved:]
'Don't bring curses on . . .' "
    The word *milalati* is a verbal derivative
of the noun *walat*, which denotes the dangerous aspect of the supernatural powers
belonging to exceptional persons or objects. It may mean disaster or even death
for ordinary persons to come into contact
with such powers, especially should such
persons in some way (even inadvertently)
offend the source of the *walat*. The word
milalati here means to exude *walat*.
230. A number of words in the stanza's
final emotive line, in conjunction with
the dramatic visual sign indicating a new

XXI. Asmarandana
[Melodic mood is one of sorrow or longing]

1 And so the Excellent Vizier
   Wanasalam thereat sent forth
   Officers four whose charge it was
   To erect markers on the sites
   Whereat His Highness the Prince
   Siti Jenar had meditated
   His retreats and hermitages

2 And the sites whereat he'd taught
   Richly endowed with funds
   The work did not take long
   Soon they all were done
   Now turning what is told:
   All the disciples of the Lord
   His Highness Prince Siti Jenar

3 Were sorely struck with grief
   Brooding in their hearts
   Their sorrow ever swelled
   Bereft of their master
   Their hearts were torn with pain
   Like children bereft of mother and
      father
   Pondered they his love for these
      his disciples

4 Hence broken were their yearning
      hearts
   No more said on the mourners
      here
   Turning what is told:
   All the *wali* of Allah
   Who were present in Demak

   ——

   canto that follows, alert the reader to
   change to Asmarandana ("giving love")
   meter.

Then did wend their homeward
   ways
Each to his separate seat

5 And the faithful *mukmin* all
   And all the princes-regent
   From the outer realms
   Wended homeward all

*A return to the tale of Jaka Tingkir's
father. The Sultan of Demak sends a
second summons to Ki Ageng Pengging, reminding him by letter of his
obligation to show himself at court.*

Now that which is related:
His Majesty Sultan Demak
Recalled, brooding in his heart

6 His senior kinsman, Ki Ageng
      Pengging
   Whose promise made of old had
      been
   To await his brother's coming
   Prince Kebo Kanigara
   Who'd left for parts unknown
   Along with his wife and children
   Such had he professed

7 As soon as he were met
   Together to Demak they'd go
   But now indeed 'twas overlong
   Already a full year had passed
   And he'd yet to keep his promise
   Brooding further, His Majesty
   Sensed there something sinister

8 And so the King did dispatch
   Officers eight entrusted with
   His Majesty's letter
   Departed from Demak

Telling nothing of their journey
The progress of these envoys eight
Had come to Pengging's realm

9   Meeting with Ki Ageng Pengging
The messengers eight forthwith
Did execute the charge
Of Demak's Royal Lord
Delivering the letter
It was then received
By Ki Ageng Kenonga

10 Opened, 'twas received deep within
        his heart
The letter's words were these:
"Note: A letter from the King
Which issues most sincerely
From the pure depths of his heart
From your little brother, Sovereign
Of Demak who is Viceroy

11 To the Holy Prophet
Muhammad, Master of the World
Who has been granted authority
To rule over all Java
And all her tributaries
All those foreign kings
Who are to Java subject

12 "Addressed here now to you
O brother Kebo Kenonga
Prince-regent of Pengging
Who are now in mourning
Bereft of your elder brother
Vanished to oblivion is
Brother Kebo Kanigara

13 "Firstly, my greetings
I convey to you
Greetings done, to open now:
O Brother, Kebo Kenonga

I have watched so for your coming
It has been a full year now
Since I did dispatch

14 "My men, those officers four
With a summons hence for you
You asked them for a stay of time
Till the coming of your brother
Our brother Kanigara
And surely were he not met with
While reporting thus to me

15 "You were to have come to meet
        with me
How I have watched for your
        coming
And now 'tis far too long
I've had no word of news
Even though I myself
Most assuredly do share
This loss just as do you

16 "How distant are we indeed?
Why, related as first cousins
Is not away at all, 'tis said
And now this my request:
May you, my elder brother
Honor in your heart
This summons to Demak

17 "Await no longer
Your elder brother's coming
Finding him shall be simple
Once you have met with
Me myself in person
Truly I shall join forces
Sharing in the search

18 "But, O Brother, now
You needs must meet with me
For there are matters of import

I wish to weigh
With you, Brother
Whose counsel may I seek
If not my senior kinsman's?

19 "On all matters of the State
'Tis best I seek the counsel of
The eldest of my kinsmen
Majapahit's royal grandsons
Are all but callow youths
Save you who are mature
Eldest grandson of the King

20 "And son of a mighty king
Pengging's Handayaningrat
On both sides of royal descent
Verily duty-bound
Am I to seek your counsel
In all consultations
On matters of the State

21 "Brother, be now escorted
On the way by these my envoys
It is the true intent
Of my heart, O Brother
That is held in this letter"
Finished was the letter's reading
Its every word taken to heart

22 Kyai Ageng spoke softly:
"Tell me, Envoy, is there perchance
A message from the Lord and King
In addition to this letter?"
The messenger's humble reply:
"Indeed there is, Your Majesty
A message from Your Highness's
   brother

23 "If Your Majesty does indeed
Decide to go hence to Demak

I, with these my friends, am
   charged
To escort Your Royal Highness
Be it now or on the morrow
I await Your Majesty
Whatever your pleasure, Sire"

24 Kyai Ageng spoke softly:
"O Messengers, wait ye
Here for two days' time"
The envoys assenting
Were provided lodgings then
Outside the palace walls
Entertained both night and day

25 Feasted with feasts replete were
   they
And presented raiments fine
Into which they were charged to
   change
All the envoys eight
Reckoned it success
Kyai Ageng Pengging
Thought they, was coming to
   Demak

*On Ki Ageng Pengging's answer to
the second summons to Demak.*

26 And so with two nights' passing
Ki Ageng had finished
Composing his reply
In letter to the Sultan of Demak
On the morn Ki Ageng seated
In the Pringgitan
Summoned the messengers from
   Demak[231]

231. In a "traditional" upper-class Javanese house (*joglo*), the *pringgitan* is the

27 Having arrived, the officers eight
   Seated themselves in the presence of
   Ki Ageng did gently say:
   "This, messengers, is my word
   My letter of reply
   Which I offer to His Majesty"
   The chief envoy a *sembah* made

28 As he took the letter
   Ki Ageng did speak again:
   "And tell His Royal Highness
   Indeed should it come to pass
   That I am permitted by God
   Verily then shall I
   Present myself before the King

29 "And tell His Majesty
   That I remain in mourning
   With grief that's deepened further still
   By the loss of my guru"
   Making the *sembah* the messengers all
   Withdrew from the presence
   Of Ki Ageng Kenonga

30 In hasty retreat, once they'd come outside
   The messengers made off straight-away
   Proceeding thence from Pengging
   Not to be rendered then
   Is their tour along the way

The progress of the envoys eight
Had come to the realm of Demak

31 Then entering in the palace
   Into the presence of the King
   They were questioned by His Majesty
   How then their mission fared
   With a *sembah* the messengers spoke
   Reporting how the mission fared
   As they offered up the letter

32 The reply sent from Pengging
   Was taken by the Sultan
   And the message was delivered
   Thereat the letter was opened
   By His Majesty the King
   Taken deep within the royal breast
   Its words enthralled his heart[232]

XXII. Mijil
[Melodic mood is one of longing:
erotic or mournful]

1 "This letter issuing in sincerity
   From the certainty of
   A heart instilled with purity
   Adorned with prayer
   And with deep respect
   That knows no bounds

2 "From your elder brother, Ki
   Ageng Pengging

veranda which separates, and conjoins,
the open front pavilion (*pendhapa*) from/
with the enclosed back-inner portion of
the house (*dalem*). Guests of some stature and familiarity would be received in
the *pringgitan*.

232. The words *angraras driya* (translated
here as "enthralled his heart") in conjunction with the punctuation mark for a
new canto that follows, signal the reader
to change to the melody of Mijil (also
known as "Rarasati").

Who is most ignorant
Who is base, a thousandfold base
A wretched begging *santri*, poor
    and low
Abject, devoid of intellect
Of culture unpossessed

3   "And who is now accorded
A heart in sorrow's thrall
By grief blinded to the jasmine
    bloom
Is addressed to His Royal Majesty
Who does adorn
The mighty realm Demak[233]

4   "Who is Viceroy to the Prophet
Apostle of All-knowing God
Who rules o'er all Java
With authority o'er all her subjects
Who is graced with the love
Of the Lord God Almighty

5   "Who masters the realm of Java's
    kingship
To whom all kings do bow
Who is wise and accomplished at
    rule
Skilled at the magic arts of war
Brilliant of intellect
Forgiving, patient, understanding

6   "With that affirmed, O King
Now I shall begin:

233. I am unfamiliar with the allusion in line 3, "duka-cipta tan wrin wratma-kané." Perhaps with it Ki Ageng Pengging means to say that he is so heartsick that he is unable even to appreciate the simple beauties of life.

That which you sent I have re-
    ceived
The letter which does summon
Me your brother of Pengging
Charging me to come

7   "To Demak into your Royal Pres-
    ence
The reason for this being
The need for consultation on mat-
    ters of state
Regarding this, Your Majesty
God willing
Should it come to pass

8   "That I am granted by Almighty
    God
Relief from grief's thralldom
Should this heart that feels so
    wondrous strange
Be graced release from this plague
    of woe
Then indeed shall I
Come before Your Highness

9   "But as for now I do remain
Distraught with faltering heart
In lovelorn passion's close embrace
So now, O King, do I
But abiding your wrath
Beseech your understanding

10   "May you be forgiving
Your Highness tolerant
Let not the fancies of your heart
    lead you into error
For a king is one possessed
Of compassion for the little man
Of patience and forbearance"

11 The reading of the writing done
Then His Majesty
Asked his envoy if there were a
  message
From brother Ki Ageng Pengging
The envoy with a *sembah* said:
"This, Your Royal Highness

12 "Was your royal brother's mes-
  sage:
'Tell His Majesty that
I remain in deep mourning
One loss still unconsoled, then an-
  other followed on
As though compassed by grief I am
Bereft of my guru'

13 "Just that, My Lord, was his message"

*An intelligence report on the state of
affairs in Pengging delivered to the
Sultan of Demak by his envoys. On
categories of* sepi *("absence") and*
ramé *("presence").*

The king then spoke again:
"What is the manner of things
  there
At the seat of my brethren in
  Pengging
Is it *ramé* or *sepi*?"
The envoy with a *sembah* said: [234]

234. The words *ramé* and *sepi* elude translation into English. Each of the two words
composes a semantic constellation that is
(normally) defined in binary opposition
to the other. The word *ramé* connotes

14 "The manner of your brother in
  Pengging
A secret does conceal
His manner's both *ramé* and *sepi*
'Tis *sepi*, as he fancies not
The ways of a provincial lord
Or the ways of nobility

15 "His are but the simple ways of a
  poor *santri*
With all his people
All the nobles of Pajang-Pengging
Both great and low, their tune's the
  same
With no *priyayi* ways
They play a village tune

16 "Casting off his royalty
He has no use of display
Forsaking awesome luxury
He fancies not the practices of
  prestige
Refusing to hold audience
In the way of a nobleman [235]

———
presence: noise, bustle, crowds, activity.
Sepi, conversely, connotes *absence*: silence, solitude, emptiness, loneliness.
235. The word rendered as "way(s)" in
these stanzas is *cara*; see above, note to
XVII:10.
  "The practices of prestige" (rèh kang
mawi singgih) means social and linguistic
practices that recognize and conform to
conventional structures of hierarchy—in
effect, those practices that constitute almost all traditional Javanese social intercourse. To reject such practices is, then, to
reject "traditional Java" as such—in order
thereby to move into another more egalitarian Javanese world. This egalitarian re-

17 "Ki Ageng delights in contempla-
    tion
    Worship without cease
    But wishing not his practice be re-
    vealed
    Like a pundit he prefers the her-
    mit's life
    Oft retiring in seclusion
    To places that are obscure

18 " 'Tis *ramé*, with his delight in the
    Holy Faith
    The excellent *sharî'a*
    All his subjects earnest at *salât*
    Their communal prayer resounds
    by day and night
    All the royal family
    Are ardent in their zeal

19 "Their Grand Mosque is indeed ex-
    ceedingly lovely
    Seen towering on high
    For it was but lately built
    Still new, 'tis not yet old
    Kyai Ageng Pengging is
    A steadfast master of sacred
    knowledge

20 "And after his worship is done
    He makes straightway for the rice
    fields
    In the fields he enjoys farming
    Were it not there remains the hint
    Of a sign
    He would be like a real peasant

21 "The sign is that he still resides

    ———

    jectionism, a radical subversive gesture, is
    presumably the result of taking seriously
    the precepts of Islam.

In the palace of Pengging
Of old his father's talisman
Built as the palace of Pengging"
Now upon hearing this
Astounded was the King

22 His heart growing ever more anx-
    ious
    He worried to himself
    That trouble loomed ahead
    Manifest this reply
    Rang of hollow diplomacy
    Within lurked other signs[236]

23 But at least the words in the letter
    Were words humble and meek
    Redolent sweet in embellishment
    Alluring, they touched the heart
    And so His Majesty's
    Heart was captivated

24 The messengers withdrew from
    the palace
    No more here on His Majesty

*Introduces the impassioned/mad
"heretic" saint, Sèh Malang Sumirang. Tells of his flagrant disregard
of Islamic law.*

Turning the telling of what is told:
In the remote village of Ngudung
There was an exceptional man
Austere, his asceticism[237]

236. The word rendered as "signs" in the
final line is *semu*.
237. Ngudhung is said to have been located in Jipang Panolan, north of Blora
in the Central Pasisir (Solichim Salam,
Ja'Far Shadiq [Kudus: Menara Kudus,
1986], p. 12).

25 Graced with Divine Light, he was
    joined of one Will
With God All-knowing
Ki Sèh Malang Sumirang, his
    name
He was a cousin to
The late departed
Lord Susunan Ngudung[238]

26 Ki Sèh Malang Sumirang, 'tis said
Was then still rather young
But thirty years of age
In the flower of his youth
Brave he was and able
With magic powers wonderful

27 Surpassing all the rest
He stood out from the crowd
There was no catching his nimble
    wit
Impudent, there was nothing he
    revered
Dauntless, he spilled his heart
Which heart did soar on high

28 Imbued with knowledge sacred
    since childhood
Taking as his guru
Sunan Giri Parapèn
When he was instructed in the
    True Knowledge
His age was but
Seventeen years

29 Having mastered the *rahsa* of
    Knowledge
To practice he did turn
Mortifying self, his practice was
    austere
Dauntless making into spectral
    woods
Deep ravines
Deadly gorges

30 Into deep caverns he plunged
Hills and valleys traversed
To the peaks of mountains climb-
    ing
In austere contemplation he
    roamed the mountain tops
The edges of the ocean
Its bays and capes

31 For ten full years he wandered thus
Then he changed to the way
Called *Tarîq Majnûn Rabbânî*
Which means "the way of mad-
    ness" indeed
Madness whose mad passion is
For the lover's Lord[239]

32 Lost in visions of rapt fancy
He sat with absent gaze
In thrall of excess ecstasy
Heeding neither body nor soul

238. The word rendered as "Divine Light"
in line 1 is *wahyu,* a divine radiance that
descends on certain persons (prophets,
kings, poets), instilling them with supernatural powers and authority.
    The name Malang Sumirang means
"indecent" or "unseemly."

239. A *tarîq* is a Sufi order. The Arabic
word *majnûn* translates as "lunatic," or
"one possessed." Ar. *rabbânî* means "of
God." I have been unable to locate any or-
ganized order with the name Majnûn
Rabbânî. It makes perfect sense that there
would be no such order, since the definition of the lunatic is precisely one who is
outside of order and rule.

Idling at home he sat
In empty vacant musing

33 Having forsaken all activity
Nothing did he do
And turning from the Faith
The rule of *sharî'a,* law of the
   Prophet
Apostle of Almighty God
He regarded not

34 Forsaking the *salât,* Ki Sèh would
   have none of
Bowing before All-knowing God
Resisting the commands of Qur'ân
   and Hadîth
Heeding none of that
Transgressing the law
He broke the *kukunthung*[240]

35 As pet he kept a little dog
Trained to faithfulness
Humanlike, a docile dog
For understanding human speech
Well he apprehended
Whatever the command[241]

36 Just like a faithful servant boy
That dog did his bidding
And whenever this Kyai Sèh
Went forth, wherever he would go

240. I have yet to determine the meaning
of the word *kukunthung.* Perhaps, from
kukuncung (child's topknot), "he'd left off
childish ways." See below, XXIV:11.
241. Dogs, for orthodox Moslems, are
filthy animals. Contact with dog saliva
renders one so ritually impure that one
must bathe seven times before one may
again perform *salât.*

His dog followed behind
The Youth was in the fore[242]

XXIII. Sinom
[Melodic mood is "even"; appropriate for narrative.]

1 And so Malang Sumirang
Went forth encompassing
The compass of many lands
He traversed the outer realms
Having nothing in mind
But to keep on the way
The way which is auspicious
The way of the exceptional man
Whose doing done becomes
   "Screen of the Universe"[243]

2 He oft watched those who gathered
   for

242. "The Youth" in the final line renders
"Sang Anom," which, in conjunction
with the dramatic scriptural punctuation
following it, signals the reader to change
to the melody of Sinom ("youth").
243. The word rendered as "way" in line
8 is the OJ *sasana* ("way" in the sense of
discipline, especially codified rules for the
behavior of those in religious orders).
Rendered as "way" in line 7 is the word
laku (ascetic practice).
   In the final line, "Screen of the Universe" renders the Javanese "keliring
buwana." A screen is that which both
conjoins and separates front from back,
inner from outer. The word here for
screen (*kelir*) is specific for the *wayang*
screen. In symbolic discourse, the *wayang*
screen is said "to stand for" the world
upon which God (the *dhalang*) plays out
the actions of the puppets (mankind). The
screen, then, is a kind of background
upon which something might happen.

Communal worship in the mosque
But he would not join in prayer
His dog came with him to the
    mosque
And thus provoked a stir
Charged to do *salât*, he would not
Pressed and too coerced
Ki Sèh remained silent
Rebuked, he merely chuckled in
    delight

3   And so it was the news was rife
Throughout these many lands
That Sèh Malang Sumirang
In manner most blatant aggrieved
The practice of the Faith
Transgressing the Prophet's *sharî'a*
Even for the capital Demak
Ki Sèh knew no respect
When threatened, more fearless
    still he'd forward press

4   Without the least anxiety
All fear was gone from him
For three years long had he
Persisted in these grievous ways
Thus Ki Sèh did enter
Into his thirtieth year

The wali *synod sentences Malang
Sumirang to death by fire for multiple transgressions of Islamic law.*

Then in the capital of Demak
Assemble did the *wali* all
The *mufti, sulakha,* and the pundits

5   Discoursing on the Law of God
They came to a consensus all
That Sèh Malang Sumirang

Was subject to state discipline
Sentenced to death by the Faith
Punished for daring to cross
The prohibitions of the *sharî'a*
He claimed to spirit-body
And further did he claim to Divine
    Existence[244]

6   And so there was no escaping
The penalty of death
Since he could not then
Be saved or edified
Cured or pacified
By his nephew
Sunan Kudus was
Related as his nephew
So loving his uncle, oft entreated
    him in tears

7   And yet Sèh Malang Sumirang
Stubbornly to sight laid bare
Without a veil his way
Openly he made his claims
With the decision thus decided
Then it was decreed
To Malang Sumirang that
He would be put to death
Yea, be burned alive on
    Demak's Alun-alun

8   Hearing this Malang Sumirang
Was filled with fond delight
Eager, without a trace of fright

244. The "spirit-body" of line 8 is a rendering of *badan rokhani,* an existential
state in which the body is spirit and the
spirit, body, in a nonduality hearkening
back to the *jatimurti* of Siti Jenar (and
Brawijaya). "Divine Existence" in the
final line is *kahananing Hyang.*

And so the Mighty Vizier
Wanasalam did erect
The pyre whereupon
He would be burned
And thus it was finished
Complete with all appointments of
    a pyre

Seating protocol for Malang Sumi-
rang's execution.

9   On Monday's coming
All the *wali* did assemble
With all the pundits too
And His Royal Majesty
Came forth from his palace
To audience on the Alun-alun
Just south of the Twin Banyans
Under a temporary pavilion
His Royal Highness sat upon the
    throne[245]

10 Beside him sat the Lord Sunan
Darajad Most Revered
And all the leading *wali*
Sat alongside the King
The lesser *wali*
Faced in from right and left
In ranks then were the pundits
The *khukama*, *ulama* and *mufti*
The assembled throng gathered
    into groups

11 Grand Vizier Wanasalam
With all the princes-regent

245. The "Twin Banyans" (*wringin kem-*
bar) are the sacred Fenced Twin Banyans
on the Northern Alun-alun. These trees
comprise important regalia of the realm.

The courtiers and princes of the
    blood
Were arrayed before the king
The foremost ministers
Amassed sat motionless
The Alun-alun brimmed over
Malang Sumirang having arrived
Took his seat with the lesser *wali*

12 The little dog he'd brought along
Sat there in front of him

The execution of Malang Sumirang.
The condemned man prepares to
write his testament.

Malang Sumirang's radiance
Shone forth calm indeed
His manner did not seem
Like one close on punishment
Of manner his was much the same
    as
Prince Siti Jenar of late
As he awaited death by sword

13 Unflinching, he remained most
    calm
Yea, boundless his delight
And so the Lord Sunan
Drajat straightway gave the com-
    mand
To Sunan Kudus then
Was charged to order forthwith
The execution of justice
The Law of God beyond a doubt
Spelled death for Malang Sumi-
    rang

14 There could be no escaping
And Sunan Kudus forthwith did

Decree unto his uncle:
"Uncle, receive now
The verdict of the Most Revered
In compact with the King
And all the *waliyullah*
All Java's *khukama*
Princes-regent, courtiers, and
    nobles all

15 "You are subject to justice
By the Law of God indeed
According to the rule of *sharî'a*
Directly from the Qur'ân and
    Hadîth
Ijma' and *qiyâs* most certainly
Which cannot be altered even a
    hair
All this is but born of
What you yourself have done"
Ki Malang Sumirang at that did
    voice assent

16 And this is what he said:
"O my son of Kudus, now
Be quick and light the pyre
And when the flames are ready
Then shall I enter in
Plunging down onto the pyre
And further do I
Request some paper and some ink
I shall compose in writing my final
    testament

17 "Should I meet my end"
Lord Sunan Kudus then straight-
    way
Gave him ink and paper
About two signatures
While commanding Grand Vizier
Wanasalam he bid at once

To light the pyre
The Vizier did assent
Forthwith the pyre was lit; its
    flames blazed up on high

18 Engulfed were the oil and kindling
In a ghastly blaze
The flames soared heavenward
The inferno's voice bellowed
Those who watched were terrified
Sèh Malang Sumirang thereat
Taking leave with kind *salâm*
Forthwith did ascend
To the pyre just north of the Twin
    Banyans

19 Not leaving without his dog
Followed along behind
Coming to the top of the pyre
Then plunged down into the fire
And came to the heart of the blaze
Ki Sèh sat there cross-legged
Before him sat the dog
Untouched by the flames
Then Ki Sèh did command his dog

20 Bidding him return and fetch
The paper, pen, and ink
Which, left behind there at his seat
Ki Sèh would use to write
The dog scampering back
Came to the designated spot
Then fetching the paper
Left behind with the pen and ink
That dog then did return again to
    the blazing pyre

21 Plunging in, bearing the paper
Together with the pen and ink
Were presented to his master

Then Malang Sumirang at once
Did set about his writing
In the midst of the blazing fire

*The poet describes Ki Sèh Malang
Sumirang, allowing the saint narrative space in which to compose his
testament. The description comprises
a treatise on the conditions for
Knowledge (ngèlmu).*

Ki Sèh Malang Sumirang
Was True *lahir-batin*
Truly glorious, a *wali* most sublime

22 Sublime authority incarnate
    Granted the right to trade himself
    With the Lord God Almighty
    A master of miracles
    Boundless was his mind
    Whatever he wished became
    The consummation of Reality
    The *rahsa* of Knowledge Ultimate
    In Release, knowing the end of
        Being-Nonbeing[246]

23 Not blind to the Whence and
        Whither
    His it was to die in life
    And to live in death
    He was immortality manifest
    How few who understand
    This utterance:
    "Were there being, then there is
        not"
    Difficult is the way of him who
        seeks knowledge
    So hard, so complex, so very dan-
        gerous

24 Most horrible the danger
    A single slip spells ruin
    How different for him who knows
    Lahir straight through *batin*
    The true forbidden secret
    He who does know that
    Perfect both here and there
    Can be in this world and the other
        too
    Having already ascended to salva-
        tion's eternal realm[247]

25 For his Knowledge is Truth
    That then is supplemented
    With ascetic practice ripe
    Such a one indeed is beyond com-
        pare
    Truly it is forbidden
    To tread upon his shadow

246. Line 2, "winenang aliru dhiri," could
as well be rendered: "Granted the right to
trade personal existence[s]."
    Line 6, "whatever he wishes becomes"
(dadi barang karsanipun) is meant literally, and designates the material creative
power of the saint's mind, and especially
of his language. Should he, for example,
see a dead branch and say/think "flower!", flowers immediately would grow
from the branch. Or should (as often hap-
pens in *wayang* plays) he witness the
boorish behavior of another and say/
think, "You're a pig," a real pig indeed
that other would become.

247. In the final line, it is *jaman kasala-
metan* that I render as "salvation's eternal
realm." The spatio-temporal word *jaman*
here designates a time and place which is
outside, and beyond, the categories of either time or space.

Far from all danger
Provided with life's necessities
Gone is all worldly ill and disaster

26 Knowledge without ascetic practice
Is flat as liquor short on yeast
Wherefore in this life it is
Everyone's duty a guru to take
Always to the utmost striving
To embrace the guru's teaching
So that he will impart
His Knowledge which is Truth
The *rahsa* locked in the inner
vault[248]

27 The jewel set in jewels
The diamond set in diamonds
Which absolutely perfect
Which precisely to the mark
Quibbles not in redundancy
The consummation of life consum-
mate
So in deadly earnest press
To the utmost your guru
Otherwise never shall you gain

28 Your guru's teachings of
The Knowledge which is Truth
Unless you beg and cry enough
The best you shall be granted is
Knowledge of gross numeration
Yea, but ordinary knowledge

For an ordinary life
Not the knowledge that is sublime
The ignoramus takes as Knowledge
True

29 For indeed the saying goes:
Once came a fool from the moun-
tains
To the house of a goldsmith
Keen to buy pure gold
By the goldsmith was he given
Sparkling yellow metal fake
And yet delighted was
The fool on receiving
Fool's gold he fancied gold most
pure[249]

*A comparison is drawn between
Malang Sumirang and the Prophet
Ibrâhîm.*

30 And so Sèh Malang Sumirang
Who was within the fire
Blithely did write on
Attended by his little dog
Furious did the fire
Flame up, blazing on and on
And yet he remained cool
As though sheltering beside a crys-
tal pool
Those who watched were like unto
the prey of swooping carrion
crows[250]

248. The image in line 2 is shared with
(derived from?) R.Ng. Yasadipura I's
Suluk Déwaruci (*Déwaruci* canto V, vs.
53–54) in *Serat Suluk: Jaman Karaton-
dalem ing Surakarta* (composed Surakarta,
1794 & early 19th century; inscribed
Surakarta, 1870). MS. SP 244 Na; SMP
KS 481.18, p. 239.

249. The image of the fool and the goldsmith is shared with (derived from?)
R.Ng. Yasadipura I's *Suluk Déwaruci*
(*Déwaruci* canto IV, vs. 28–29), in ibid.,
p. 223.
250. The word *dhandhang* ("carrion
crow"), with the conventional punctua-

XXIV. Dhangdhanggula
[Melodic mood is lithe, with didactic clarity and romantic allure]

1   Malang Sumirang's image was:
As long ago in ancient times
The story set in the great country
Of Babel that mighty realm
When burned was the Holy
    Prophet
Ibrâhîm, Beloved of God
By His Majesty
Namrûd the Mighty Tyrant
The burning was done in a tall furnace
The flames pumped by bellows[251]

2   When ready was the blazing fire
Then the Holy Prophet was hoisted
    up forthwith
Thereat they plunged him down
Into the great furnace
Protected was the Prophet by Almighty God
His body was unscathed
By the blazing fire
That furnace had become

———

tion for a new canto immediately following it, signals the reader by sound association to change to the melody of *Dhangdhanggula*.

251. The tale of the Prophet Ibrâhîm's burning by the tyrannical heathen king Namrûd (in the Judaic tradition, Nimrod) belongs to the sacred history of Islam. For précis of several versions of the story, see H. A. R. Gibb and J. H. Kramers, eds., *Shorter Encyclopedia of Islam* (Leiden: Brill, 1953), pp. 437–38.

A charming pavilion richly
    adorned
Encircled by a garden

3   The flowers were many and beautiful
And provided with a throne of
    pearl
On which to sit was the Holy
    Prophet
And granted was he from above
A garment from heaven
Redolent its fragrance
Breathed sweet ambrosia
In all the world there is no
Fragrance like unto the garment of
    Lord Ibrâhîm
Which descended from heaven

Malang Sumirang emerges from the fire unscathed. A reading of his testament, the Suluk Malang Sumirang.

4   Now again the telling turns:
By then Sèh Malang Sumirang
Had finished his writing
His composing a *suluk*
Tinged with the Knowledge that is
    Truth
A framework for the self
Its allusions striking
Its allure imbued with Life
Its precision precisely transporting
Its transport in *dhangdhanggula*[252]

252. *Suluk*, from the Arabic *sulûk* (traversing [the Sufi way]), names an important and extensive genre of Javanese liter-

5 With that Ki Sèh then did emerge
 From the flames in ecstasy
 Accompanied by his dog
 Carrying the writing
 As well as the pen and ink
 Ki Sèh Malang Sumirang
 Returned unto his place
 His seat in the assembly
 By him sat the dog bearing as
  regalia
 The writing, the pen, and the ink[253]

6 As for all the *wali*
 And the Sultan of Bintara
 And all the *mufti*
 The great and mighty pundits
 The princes and princes-regent
 The officers and courtiers
 Everyone of them
 Was astounded
 Bewondered in amaze of speechless
  daze
 They shook their heads

7 Their voices breathing praise
 Did extol Malang Sumirang

The people who did witness all
Pressed in a crowded crush
Buzzed with wonder: "Lo!
Lo and behold, 'tis true!
True! Really true!
'Tis truth manifest
Truly he dared to celebrate
The vehicle of Truth"[254]

8 Then Ki Sèh straightway did ex-
  change *salâm*
 With Lord Sunan Drajat
 And all the principal *wali*
 As well as with the King
 All the *wali*, pundits, and *mufti*
 Did greet him too
 Crowding in from behind
 Was everybody there
 All eager for the blessings of the
  Honorable Marvelous
 Ki Sèh Malang Sumirang[255]

9 Then Ki Sèh presented the writing
 That he'd written in the fire
 That framework for the self
 Was received by His Majesty
 To be a relic in future times
 A sign that was wakened
 In song to be *suluk*
 Yea, *Suluk Malang Sumirang*

---

ature comprising Islamic mystical songs,
mostly composed in *macapat* verse.
 The translation of "panggalanging sarira" (line 6) is wonderfully problematic.
I translate the polysemic *panggalang* as
"framework," in the sense of a scaffolding
or foundation upon which a structure is
constructed. The word *sarira* ("self") also
means "body" or "person."
 Dhangdhanggula is, of course, the name
of the verse form in which the *suluk* is
composed.
253. Rendered "bearing as regalia" is the
verb *ngampil-ampil*. On *ampil-ampil* (syn.
upacara), see above note to II:23.

254. The word rendered as "celebrate" in
line 9 is *amiwahani*; see above, note to
V:8.
 In the final line, *sunyata* is the word
rendered as "Truth." *Sunyata* also, and at
the same time, reads as "Absolute Void."
255. The "blessings" that they crowd each
other for are the saint's *safangat*, real material powers which others may contract
by physical touch.

Was it called, a stepping-stone to
the Knowledge of
The *rasa* that authors *rasa*

10 Then commanded to read the writ-
ing was
The soldier whose office it was to
read
Was charged to make his reading
loud
So that it could be heard
By everyone at audience
In the middle of the assemblage
Then read it was
Honey's elixir its words
Thus the writing sounded
Beginning from the start:[256]

11 "Malang Sumirang breaks the
rules
Blind to danger, he sings his song
A mere youth blind to his error
Sounds forth a false discourse
Most lacking, he's blind to the dan-
gers
Speaking blind to ordered rule
He breaks the *kukunthung*

His language is a joke
Though an empty fool, he claims
excellence
He's not to be restrained[257]

12 "Heedless, he holds forth overlong
Excessive, outrageous are his ways
Brazenly plunging on headstrong
Anyung short on practice
Lost in error is his discourse
Confused and gone astray
Implacable is he
Overbearing in his ways
Disrespectful, his arrogance brazen
From nothing does he shrink[258]

13 "As far as far can be, I set my heart
To come near, then, is to be neared
In life manifold are
Matters not to be mistook
The nearness which is neared
Is the binding of *rahsa*
The *rahsa* of Knowledge

256. On professional readers at court, the
"wadya kang juru pamaca" or *jaga swara*,
see above, Introduction, p. 12.
    The following three verses, XXIV:11–
13, compose a very abbreviated version of
the well-known *Suluk Malang Sumirang*.
For a fuller version of the *suluk*, see
G. W. J. Drewes, "Het Document uit den
Brandstapel," *Djåwå* 7 (1927): 97–109.
Yasadipura's *Serat Cabolèk*, edited and
translated by Soebardi in his *The Book of
Cabolèk*, pp. 147–52, *Wali Sana*, ed.
R. Tanojo [Surakarta: Sadubudi, 1955],
pp. 181–85, and *Kitab Suluk 41* LOr. [Lei-
den Oriental Collection] 7375.

257. Line 7 reads "amegat kukunthung,"
a reading that corresponds to several
other *Malang Sumirang* versions I have
consulted (for example, in the *Wali Sana*
edition and *Kitab Suluk 41*). I have yet to
determine the meaning of *kunthung*. In
both the Drewes and Soebardi editions,
however, the line reads instead "amegat
kekuncung." The word *kuncung* designates the topknot traditionally worn by
small Javanese children. Drewes translates the line: "hij acht zich de kinder-
schoenen ontwassen" ("Het Document
uit den Brandstapel," pp. 104, 107). Soebardi's translation reads: "he regards
himself as fully adult" (*The Book of Cabolèk*, p. 147). See also above, XXII:34.
258. I have yet to determine the meaning
of *anyung* in line 4. A nasalization of *sung*
("to give") seems unlikely in this context.

Knowledge of the vanishing realm
The satisfaction of sweet wealth's
    works
Swept off in death"²⁵⁹

*The reading of the Suluk is cut short
by the poet. Malang Sumirang's
sainthood is recognized, with a reminder of the need for adherence to
the Law.*

14   Thus, the revealing of the secret
Words writing the concealed
The warning of the Watchful One
To reason I will not refer
This lesson of total knowledge
I'll cut it off, I'll not unfold
The unfolding of the sweet fra-
    grance
For I but follow the tale
Done was the reading of the writ-
    ing that is
*Suluk Malang Sumirang*²⁶⁰

259. Line 4, "ing rèh tan kena korup,"
could instead be rendered: "matters beyond compare."
    The "vanishing realm" in line 8 is con-
jectural for *alam panikar* (from the Ar.
fânî ["the disappeared"]?).
260. "The Watchful One" of line 3 glosses
"Sang Manginté." The Kawi *inté* means
"to peer, to peek, to watch carefully." In
the same line, the word *pamènget*, rendered as "the warning," could also be read
as "being ware" or "being aware."
    Line 5, "nalirahing ngèlmu sakalir"
could be rendered instead as "a total theory of Knowledge" or again as "an exposition of all [this] Knowledge."
    Line 8, "mung ingsun amburu kon-
dha," literally "I am just hunting down
the story, or discourse" (cf. above, II:13).

15   Amazed were all those who did
    hear
Their voices thundered praise
Lovely was what they said
To tell would take too long
With that the Most Reverend
Lord Sunan Drajat
Did give a sign
To Sunan Kudus forthwith
Sunan Kudus at once pronounced
    the ruling
To Sèh Malang Sumirang:

16   "O! Honored Uncle, do receive
The command of our Lord Panem-
    bahan
As regards you Uncle, now
'Tis proven truly true
Truly without bounds, you are
Peerless in this world
In all of creation
You exist a perfect soul
Body-soul through and through
    penetrant
Consummate in the Truth of Truth

17   "But Uncle, you must now
Protect the prestige of the Faith
Abide by its confines
Leaving off error
To keep as best you can the *sharî'a*
Of the Prophet, Master of the
    World
That in this world may come
Adherence to the holy *sharî'a*
Keeping the full meaning of the
    Qur'ân and Hadîth
Ijma' and *qiyâs*

18   "In rulings which rule the realm
The precepts of Islam

Reign with the *sharî'a*
Yea with the law
Whose wisdom is manifold
Every last deed that might be done
The good and bad
The right and wrong
Evil and virtue are laid out in the
    Qur'ân and Hadîth
Ijma' and *qiyâs*

Malang Sumirang vanishes into in-
ternal exile.

19 "Hence, O honored Uncle, now
    Ponder in the clear light of your
        heart
    And take this not wrongly
    Uncle, be resigned
    That better you go off far away
    Lest you bring about
    Confusion by subversion
    Loosening the knot
    Pulling down the palisades, break-
        ing through the ranks
    Bringing low the flag

20 "Where, O Uncle, would you pre-
        fer
    Your hermitage, that altogether fit
    Yea more, a sacred site of power'd
        be
    By duty it is the realm
    That must furnish as is fit
    The furnishings of your hermitage
    With all its appointments
    Which as talisman of the realm
    Will refresh all the land
    Touching all with its power"

21 Sèh Malang Sumirang answered
    "My child, I do consent

With great pleasure in my heart
There is in the great thorn forest
Of Kalampisan a spectral place
Quiet, far from men
There shall be my stead
A small hut will suffice
I wouldn't fancy something fine
Just whatever you can do"[261]

22 Lord Sunan Drajat, hearing this
    Was overjoyed, as was the King
    With all of the *wali*
    Their voices all sang praise
    With that they all dispersed
    Wending homeward
    Each to his own place
    Not to be rendered at length
    Sèh Malang Sumirang had gone
        off by himself
    To the forest of Kalampisan

Ki Ageng Pengging meditates. His
prayers answered, he is promised a
son of prowess who shall be king.

23 Enough for now on the capital
        Demak
    Turning the telling again:
    At that time Ki Ageng Pengging
    Was there inside his palace
    But being most griefstruck
    Ate and slept but little
    In the nighttime
    Taking no shelter
    He lay in the open, in focused
        semadi

261. The forest of Kalampisan is the place
of the *kalampis* trees, a wild acacia (*tor-*
mentosa) whose branches are covered
with long sharp thorns.

Clearing his mind, delving the Will
of God[262]

24 The source of his heart's sorrow
was
That never had he a child
To survive infancy
Four had been his children
Sons and daughters both
But all of them had perished
When they were still babes
Thus Kyai Ageng did truly
Wish to have a child
A son, who'd be long-lived

25 Who'd be handsome and intelli-
gent
And fit to be the staff
Of all the lineage
Who'd be meet in future days
To finish out the tale
Thus his practice was intense
And then upon
The night of a Friday eve
'Twas three in the morning and Ki
Ageng
Was exceedingly sleepy[263]

26 Nodding off, he closed his eyes
There in the yard of his retreat

Before long at all
There did call out
From Mystery a voice so clear:
"O! Kebo Kenonga
Answered shall be
Your prayers unto the Supreme
Soul
You shall be spared a child
A son who'll be long-lived[264]

27 "And he shall be most handsome
His radiance shining brilliant as
the sun
At the height of the dry season
And endowed with powers mar-
velous
He shall be wholly able, most intel-
ligent
Strong he'll be from childhood on
Heroic, invincible
Renowned for his might
Capable of anything, a master of
the arts of war
His bravery, beyond compare

28 "Challenging danger, he shall be
victorious
'Tis he in the future whom God
has ordained

262. In the final line, I render "aneges karsa" as "delving the Will of God." The quest is to grasp (to know—and to influence) what is to come, the future.
263. Friday eve (Thursday night), as the eve of the Islamic day of communal prayer, is the preferred night of the week to perform meditative practice in Java, and the one most likely to yield results. The best time for practice is between midnight and 3:00 A.M.

264. Ki Ageng's "retreat" (line 2) is called a *pamelengen* (meditation chamber). Javanese palaces are provided with special meditation chambers whose use is restricted to the ruler. It is the *duty* of the ruler periodically to go there in retreat and practice meditation (and/or commune with members of the spirit world) in order to ensure the prosperity of the realm.
  "Mystery" in line 5 is *aib*. "Supreme Soul" (line 8) is *Suksma*.

To be the staff of the multitude
That means to be the king
Who masters all Java
For indeed your son
Will reign a mighty king
With his palace in Pajang
But 'tis not your court of Pajang-
    Pengging
That shall your son's court be

29 "He shall clear the forest to the
        east
    Just west of the village of Lawiyan
    For there shall his *kraton* be
    His reign shall be inviolate
    But you will not live to see
    Your son's coming of age
    For it has been ordained
    That you will go home to Release
    By your own desire
    To turn your eyes from this
        world[265]

30 "Defiled by the sight of unclean
        filth
    Pressing for return to the *kraton*
        eternal
    Delight will be yours when the
        way appears
    For your return home
    To Release in the realm of Purity
    O! Kebo Kenonga
    These words shall not be betrayed

265. The Kingdom of Pajang was indeed
located near the ancient district of Lawiyan. Now a division of the city of Surakarta, located in the city's southeast
corner, Lawiyan has historically been a
center of the Javanese textile industry and
of Islamic orthodoxy.

For thus has God ordained"
Ki Ageng, startled by what he
    heard so clear
Wakened to give love[266]

XXV. Asmarandana
[Melodic mood is one of sorrow or
longing]

1   And so Ki Ageng Pengging
    Pondered in his heart
    Recalling what the voice had said
    His heart in awed amaze
    He sat in contemplation
    Silent his mind filled with
    Thanksgiving unto God

2   At the break of dawn
    Ki Ageng did the *salât*
    Of dawn complete
    Then Ki Ageng did take a seat
    In the cloister of his retreat
    Ever pondered in his heart
    Was what the voice had said

3   And so with time's passing
    The wife of Ki Ageng
    'Tis said was great with child
    Enough for now on Pengging

The Sultan of Demak's concerns re-
garding Ki Ageng Pengging's con-
tinued reluctance to submit to his

266. The word *andanasmara* ("to give
love"), with the conventional scriptural
punctuation for a new canto immediately
following it, signals the reader by sound
association to change to the melody of
Asmarandana.

authority. *A third summons is sent
to Pengging commanding his presence at court. Ki Ageng Pengging
grows ever more defiant.*

Changing the tale to be told:
The country of Bintara
Was then truly flourishing

4 To review the tale again
   Back when the Sultan of Demak
   Had summoned the Ki Ageng
   Of Pengging who then plotted in
      his heart
   To make a rupture in the realm
   Hence the King so dearly
   Wished that he come to Demak

5 At his coronation as King
   The Sultan of Demak did first
   Wish him to come to court
   Ki Ageng was defiant
   Refusing to come to court
   Even unto death he would
   Hold fast to his resolve

6 His Majesty the King
   Prospered; revered was his *kraton*
   Nothing was amiss
   Content were the common folk
   All the crops flourished
   Now it is told, His Majesty
   Was holding audience

7 Enthroned in the Pengrawit Hall
   He summoned his Grand Vizier
   Along with all the sages:
   Ki Ageng Wanapala
   Was seated before the king

Along with His Highness Prince
   Kudus
And Ki Ageng Sidik-iman[267]

8 His Majesty the King did speak
   To the Vizier Kartanagara
   "O Vizier, what news is there
   These days of Pengging's Master?"

267. The Pengrawit Hall, "Hall of Intricate Beauty," is a small, elevated screened
cubical for the Susuhunan's throne which
is located in the Pagelaran Assembly Hall.
The king held audience in the Bangsal
Pengrawit (i.e., Miyos Siniwi) only when
he installed or removed his grand vizier
or when he decided and pronounced legal
judgments (*Serat Wawaton Tatakrama
Tembung Kadhaton*, MS. Rp 74; SMP Rp
76, pp. 20–21).
   Although the manuscript reads "Wanalapa" for the sage's name in line 4, I
render it the more usual "Wanapala" (as
it indeed appears both elsewhere in this
poem [XXV:11] and in the more dominant *babad* tradition [i.e., the Galuh variant; see below, note to XXVI:1]). Ki
Ageng Wanapala is sometimes mentioned
as the father of Demak's vizier (*Serat
Babad Tanah Jawi: Sri Majapahit pungkasan dumungi Demak pungkasan* [com-
posed s.l., s.a.; inscribed Surakarta, 1871],
MS. RP B15a; SMP MN 196, p. 167).
Elsewhere in our *babad*, a certain Ki
Ageng Wanalapa is numbered among the
"opposition" to Demak as one of Sèh Siti
Jenar's forty disciples (see above, XVII:
21).
   Hitherto with the spiritual title "Lord
Sunan," the saint of Kudus appears now
with the more worldly, court title of "His
Highness Prince" (Pangéran).
   The name Sidik-iman means "true
faith."

With a *sembah* answered the
    Vizier:
"The news is everywhere
Ki Ageng a signal *santri* is[268]

9   "I have heard, Your Serene High-
        ness
    Of Your Lordship's brother
    That Ki Ageng Pengging
    Will not present himself to Your
        Royal Majesty
    In my estimation, Sire
    The allotted time is up
    Though summoned he is yet to
        come"

10 His Highness Prince Kudus with a
        sembah said:
    "As for me, Your Majesty
    It would be advisable
    That Your Highness send an envoy
    To your brother in Pengging
    Then manifest will be his fault or
        innocence
    Such is my advice"

11 Ki Wanapala sweetly spoke:
    "Well spoken are the words of
    Your Highness's son, the Prince of
        Kudus
    'Twould be best to send an envoy
    To summon this brother of yours"

268. Elsewhere in the poem, Wanasalam
is named as Sultan Trenggana's vizier; see
above, XXI:1, XXIII:11, and below, XXXII:
5.
    Rendered as "Master" in line 4 is the
title *Ki Bahyi/Bayi*. The title probably de-
rives from the Old Javanese *baye/bayai* (a
particular functionary in the temple service; Zoetmulder 1:230).

Then spoke His Majesty:
"Vizier! Send as envoys

12 "Two officers of quality
    Who, wise and heedful
    Know allusions' mysteries
    Who can conceal their true intent"
    The Vizier bowed: "As My Lord
        wills"
    Thereat His Majesty retired
    The Vizier arranging the mission

13 Forthwith appointed the officers
        two
    Who, wise and heedful
    Brilliant of intellect
    Knowing the text of Truth
    Were truly eminent
    The King's envoys departed
    The two of them made haste

14 Their journey not to be described
    Having made their way to Peng-
        ging
    The envoys then gave notice to
    The Chief Lady-in-Waiting:
    "May you report now
    To Ki Ageng Pengging post haste
    I am the envoy of the King"[269]

15 The Lady then did sweetly speak
    To Ki Ageng reporting:
    "My dear Young Royal Lord
    Your Highness has some guests

269. Rendered as "Chief Lady-in-Waiting," in line 4 is "pawong lurah parekan."
Historically, Javanese rulers/palaces have
been guarded by highly influential corps
of female retainers. It is these female retainers who convey messages and guests
between inner and outer palace environs.

Envoys from Demak are they"
Spoke Ki Ageng in dulcet tones:
"Escort my guests in"[270]

16 The Lady did withdraw at once
To meet with those envoys:
"Sires, ye are invited now
Into the Central Chamber"
Thereat the envoys did proceed
Meeting Ki Ageng there
In the Central Chamber[271]

17 The envoys straightway did pro-
claim
To Ki Ageng the King's command:
"Your Highness is commanded
now
By your brother to come to Demak
To repair hence now with me"
Ki Ageng spoke softly:
"As you will. Be seated, mes-
sengers."

18 At once the envoys two sat down
After all had shaken hands
They were served up betel chew
And the usual feast
Whereupon they ate
And when the feast was done
Ki Ageng did softly speak:[272]

19 "I, having been summoned
By His Majesty the King
Needs must beg pardon
For I shall not go"
Softly did the envoy speak:
"Pray what reason for this?"
Ki Ageng did softly speak:

20 "I have no more reasons
Just tell His Majesty
That such is my reply"
Softly did the envoy speak:
"Your Highness, Ki Ageng
Are you certain, My Lord
That such is your desire?"

21 Softly Ki Ageng answered:
"Like a mere child, O messenger
Are you blind to my allusion?"
Softly did the envoy speak:
"I wished it not to come to this
But to your wish accede
If thus you are determined"

22 The envoys then took leave
To return to Demak
Ki Ageng spoke softly:
"Mind that you do tell
His Royal Majesty
That such is my reply"
From his presence the envoys
withdrew

23 Their journey not to be described
—

270. Since Ki Ageng Pengging is no
longer a particularly young man, it must
be assumed that this senior lady at court
is of a very advanced age, or rank. She
speaks to him as though he were her son,
perhaps her "milk-son."
271. Rendered as "the Central Chamber"
in lines 4 and 7 is the word *madyasana*.
272. The "handshake" (anjawab tangan)
in line 2, would be the mutual touching of
hands after which each party would draw

his own hand to his heart. This gesture
signifies the equality of both parties in
the Islamic brotherhood (*ummah*) and is
in contradistinction to the *sembah* which
defines the relative hierarchical statuses
of the giver and receiver of that gesture of
homage and subservience.

The envoy's progress having come
To Demak, relayed was the reply of
Ki Ageng Kebo Kenonga
Most astounded was the King
Pondering deep within his heart
He felt unripe of intellect[273]

XXVI. Sinom
[Melodic mood is "even"; appropriate for narrative]

1   The envoys of Demak withdrew
From the presence of their King

*The counsel of Ki Ageng Tingkir to
Ki Ageng Pengging regarding the
latter's defiance of the State.*

And now to be related:
Indeed Ki Ageng Tingkir
Had then heard the news
That his little brother of Pengging
Had been summoned to Demak
Ki Ageng Tingkir coming to Pengging
Met with Ki Ageng Kenonga[274]

2   Once both men were seated

273. The word *nom-noman* (rendered here, "unripe"), with the conventional scriptural punctuation for a new canto immediately following it, signals the reader by sound association to change to the melody of Sinom.
274. On the fraternal relationship of the two Ki Agengs: this younger/elder distinction marks the brothers' relative position of seniority in the spiritual brotherhood rather than difference in chronological age.

Spoke Ki Ageng Tingkir:
"O Brother, you are summoned
By the Sultan of Demak
What is the secret, Brother?
Why will you not go?"
The younger brother did reply:
"What could be the use of it
That a villager be summoned by
the King?"

3   "Come now, Brother, how is it
That summoned, you will not go
To the capital Demak?
What will come of it, Brother?
Are you not, Brother
Subject to the King?
The earth on which you move
Yea, everything in Java
Is all the property of him who
reigns as king"

4   Softly spoke the younger brother:
"It is Allah who owns the earth
What then does he really want
With summoning villagers?"
Ki Ageng Tingkir spoke:
"O Brother, be not stubborn
Take this not simply
Regard it not lightly
Consider the dangers, o my
brother

5   "For Brother, one like you is called:
'A water jug that once held fish'
The smell is there to stay
You are the grandson of a king
The King of Majapahit
In you his trace is not faded
Moreover your father was
A hero of marvelous might

Wherefore he was taken as Brawijaya's son-in-law[275]

6 "Brother, can it be that you
   Take leave of your senses?
   You've been summoned by the
     King
   Have you then forgotten that
   He is your own uncle
   Your mother's little brother?
   Perhaps he's moved by pity
   Now that he is become king
   To have family away in a village so
     remote

7 "You really should now go
   I will follow along behind
   How could he suffer you harm?
   And I will guard should trouble
     come"
   The younger brother softly spoke:
   "Now I think it is not so
   Brother, that is most absurd
   Wherefore should becoming king
   Move him to bethink his distant
     relatives?"

8 Then Ki Ageng Tingkir's query:
   "What then, Brother, is your will?"
   Ki Ageng Pengging's answer:
   "Indeed, what is there to do?
   Should he summon me yet again
   Still I will not go"

The elder brother harshly spoke:
"O my little brother, a man
Who refuses the summons of his
  king

9 "Indeed does stand in rebellion
   So then raise an army now
   Do not stop half-way
   You must not vacillate
   Where there is jealousy
   Comes ignominy in the end:
   The jealous one does but despoil
   So if you can, devise a plan
   By which to win the loyalty of sub-
     jects"

10 The younger brother chuckled in
     delight:
   "Brother, you labor the obvious
   Carrying timber to a wood
   Of misfortune, sickness, and death
   Who is the Master?
   That Master is Almighty God
   Before this body did exist
   Its destiny was created first
   The good and the bad, inscribed in
     the Lauhu 'l-Mahfûz"[276]

11 The elder brother gently said:
   "Yea, Brother, what more then?
   If so determined is your will
   You have your brother's blessings"
   The day long he counsel gave

275. The saying "a water jug that once
held fish" describes a person upon whom
the traces (however faint) of past behavior, station, or ancestry remain evident. See C. F. Winter Sr., *Javaansche
Zamenspraken* (Amsterdam: Muller,
1858), 2:107.

276. According to Hadîth traditions, the
Lauhu 'l-Mahfûz (Jav. *lukil makful*) is
"the preserved tablet" upon which the decrees of God for mankind are inscribed
from eternity (Thomas P. Hughs, *A Dictionary of Islam* [Clifton, N.J.: Reference
Book Publishers, 1965], p. 285).

And with the fall of night
They did their *salât* in the little
  mosque
Then after their *salât* was done
The elder brother was received
  with great esteem[277]

*Tells of the portentous birth of Mas
Karèbèt (the future Jaka Tingkir).*

12 That night there was a *wayang*
The Ki Ageng of Pengging did
Present his elder brother
An all-night *wayang bèbèr* show
And then it was that
His wife thus great with child
Did give birth
In the month of Jumadilakir
On the eighth day; it was the year
  of Dal[278]

13 In the fifth of the solar months

On the day of Sweet Wednesday
At the break of dawn
Born was a handsome baby boy
It was Ki Ageng Tingkir
Who brought forth the afterbirth
Ki Ageng Kebo Kenonga
Rejoiced in his heart
In an uproar was the *wayang* audi-
  ence[279]

14 Great rainbows did appear
Three of them sipping the river
Together with a fine rainfall
Ki Ageng Tingkir spoke:
"Brother, this your son
I give the name
Mas Karèbèt
For at the time
Of his birth I held a *wayang bè-
  bèr*[280]

15 The younger brother said softly:
"Thank you; 'tis most fitting
By Your Lordship's blessings
May he be spared all illness
I am but the means

277. The "little mosque" in which they did their *salât* was the *langgar*, a small room or pavilion for performance of Islamic ritual obligations or for religious education.

278. The *wayang bèbèr* is a form of puppet performance in which the puppeteer unrolls long painted scrolls upon which scenes from the tale he recites are depicted. Nowadays this form of *wayang* is almost never performed. For an interesting discussion of this fading art form, see Benedict Anderson, "The Last Picture Show," *Proceedings from the Conference on Modern Indonesian Literature* (Madison, Wis., 1974), pp. 33–81.

Jumadilakir is the sixth month of the Islamic lunar calendar. Dal is the fifth year in the eight-year *windu* cycle of the Javanese calendrical system. No year date is provided for this birth.

279. On Ki Ageng Tingkir's part in the birth: it is almost surely *not* the case that this man assisted in the actual delivery of the afterbirth. What is probably meant here is the bringing of the afterbirth (by Javanese belief: the baby's younger brother) out of the birth chamber to be buried or (more likely) cast into water. While the afterbirths of commoners' children are usually buried near their front doors, it is the practice of high royalty to have their children's afterbirths cast into running water.

280. Mas K[a]rèbèt was the birth name of Jaka Tingkir. *Wayang krèbèt* is another name for *wayang bèbèr*.

'Tis you who are his father
May long life be granted
To this newborn babe
May the grace of God be ever shed
    on him"

16 'Tis said, for three days long
    Ki Ageng Tingkir stayed there in
        Pengging

*Related here are the Sultan of De-
mak's continuing concerns regarding
Ki Ageng Pengging's defiance of the
court. The King dispatches Ki Ageng
Wanapala to deliver his* bantah *(debate, riddled questions): Pengging is
to be forced to make a choice. Ki
Ageng Pengging holds fast to a position beyond choice.*

Turning now the telling:
In Demak, His Majesty the King
Then did summon
The great and mighty *ulama*
Along with his vizier
And all of his *wajir*
With His Highness Prince Kudus
    sitting to the fore[281]

17 And Ki Ageng Wanapala
    Forthwith summoned
    Was there before the King
    Then said His Royal Majesty:
    "O! All ye *wajir*
    And ye mighty *ulama*
    Know ye that
    My brother in Pengging now
    Would surely play my *kraton* false

281. *Wajir* in line 8 is Arabic for "ministers."

18 "O! Dear brother Wanapala
    'Tis you whom I do charge
    My argued *bantah* to convey
    You shall be my deputy
    To our brother in Pengging
    My *bantah* concerns two things:
    'O Brother, you must designate
    Which of them choose you?
    'Tis one or the other: the outside or
        inside?"[282]

19 Ki Wanapala did reply:
    "As Your Royal Highness wills
    'Tis mine but to obey
    Bearing high the royal charge"
    Then said His Majesty:
    "Now be off at once"
    Ki Wanapala withdrawing
    From the presence of the King
    Set off at once, traveling in *santri*
        attire

20 Not telling of his journey
    In three days he'd come to Peng-
        ging
    Thereat word was given
    That a guest had come
    For Ki Ageng Pengging

282. Roughly, "argumentation" or "debate," *bantah* (especially *bantah kawruh*)
is a specific kind of argumentation in
which two or more sages debate matters
of esoteric truth. The "argumentation"
almost always involves exchanges of riddles, sometimes with interpretive discussions of those riddles' solutions. The
"truth" is revealed (or more often,
glimpsed) in the course of the argumentation. *Bantah kawruh* exchanges are
often found in "heavy" *wayang* plays and
in *suluk* literature.

The envoy of His Majesty
The Sultan of Bintara
Ki Ageng replied sweetly:
"See him to the meditation cham-
ber"

XXVII. Asmarandana Canto[283]
[Melodic mood is one of sorrow or
longing]

1   Whereupon escorted was
Ki Ageng Wanapala
Proceeded to the little mosque
Meeting there with Ki Ageng
Then said he his *salâm*
To receive *salâm* in turn
Seated were they both

2   Then the Ki Ageng two
Took each other's hands
Said Ki Ageng Pengging:
"Your coming, My Lord
Is dearly welcomed"
The other Ki Ageng answered:
"Thank you
My Lord, for your gracious hospi-
tality"[284]

283. The caption "Asmarandana Canto" is
inscribed at the head of the canto with no
verbal cue indicating the change of verse
form.
284. A note on language use here: the
contest has already begun. The two Ki
Ageng attempt to outvie each other in
their use of the elaborate and elegant linguistic combination of *krama andap/kra-
ma inggil.* In this tricky combination of
speech levels, when spoken mutually by
equals of high status, the speaker *seems* to
humble himself while exalting his interlocutor. In this kind of language use, the
stress (and the pleasure) is with sound

3   Ki Ageng Pengging sweetly said:
"Wherefore, Little Brother, were
   you sent
My Lord, by His Majesty the
   King?"
Ki Wanapala did reply:
"Charged am I to convey
His Majesty's *bantah*
Answer this clearly:

4   "Yea, which do you choose:
Being of exceeding being
Or absence of exceeding absence?
Or again, to sleep but once
To wake forevermore?
Or every night to sleep
And every day to wake?

5   "To eat but once to fullness
For as long as you shall live
Or every evening to eat
To be hungry every day?
Now you needs must choose
By command of His Majesty
Should you choose being

6   "And eating every day
Then swallow the realm of Demak
While His Majesty still reigns"
Said Ki Ageng Pengging:
"Has then His Royal Highness
Come thus to be mistaken?
What then can this be?

7   "Most taken aback am I
His Majesty's command
———
and formal style rather than with discursive "meaning." The one who controls the
combination with the most grace and the
most flower "wins" the contest. This kind
of contest remains popular in Java today.

Does breed anxiety
Kyai, I had thought him
A king who, as Allah's Caliph
Truly most exalted of character was
Virtue's ultimate

8   "I will not choose
For all of it do I desire
Were I to choose
But one, 'twould be wrong
Brother, may this my answer
Be conveyed to His Majesty
No desire have I"

9   Ki Wanapala replied:
"That answer of yours, Lord
Has no end to it
Intrigue is your answer
To the Lord our King
Futile was my coming here
By order of Demak's King

10   "Your Lordship does not choose
As regards the King's *bantah*
Oh! What shall come of this?
Fare thee well, my elder brother"
Then the two exchanged *salâm*
Ki Ageng Pengging sweetly said:
"Little brother, this my message

11   "Convey to His Royal Highness:
No desire have I
Be it as His Majesty wills
All of it I do desire
'Twould be wrong for me to choose
There is no end to it
When one does pick and choose"[285]

285. Line 6, "tanpa wekasing tumuwuh,"
at the same time means "There is no Ultimate Being." One who has attained the

XXVIII. Pangkur
[Melodic mood is intense: impassioned and/or weighty]

1   Relating not his journey
Ki Ageng Wanapala arrived
In the land of Demak

*Hearing of Pengging's decision not
to choose, the Sultan sends Sunan
Kudus to Pengging to effect a final
solution to the problem.*

And so it is told:
At that time in the Demak court,
    the King was holding audience
Assembled were his courtiers
Along with all the *wali*

2   His Highness was seated on the
        throne
Spread with flower-strewn velvet
    drapings
Behind him were his golden goose
And his golden serpent
Golden cone with golden cock to
    the rear
The pundits were to his right
The *wali* were before him[286]

state of Absolute Perfection is beyond
"picking and choosing." See above, the
discourse of Siti Jenar (XIX:19 ff).
    In the final line, the word *ngungkurna*
("repudiate," translated in this context as
"choose"), with the conventional punctuation for a new canto immediately following it, signals the reader by sound
association to change to the melody of
Pang*kur*.
    286. Described here are the royal regalia
(*upacara* or *ampil-ampil*) of kingship, all

3   Sitting to the very front was
    His Highness Prince Kudus by
        name
    His Majesty spoke sweetly:
    "O! My brethren
    How fares the mission of my
        envoy
    The Ki Ageng of Wanapala
    Whom I sent to Pengging?"

4   His Highness Prince Kudus with a
        sembah said:
    "I do surmise our brother did suc-
        ceed"
    Before long came there
    Ki Ageng Wanapala
    All a sudden before His Majesty
    Forthwith he made a *sembah* to
    His Royal Highness the King

5   The King did softly say:
    "Elder Brother, I welcome thee"
    Said the Ki Ageng: "Highness
    My mission as envoy
    To convey Your Majesty's com-
        mand
    To brother Kebo Kenonga
    In Pengging was a failure

6   "None of it would he choose
    For all of it did he desire
    Wanting nothing at all
    His heart's intent is
    But to live the village life

    ———
    crafted in pure gold and borne by the
    king's female guard upon ceremonial oc-
    casions. See above, note to II:23.
        The scene here is a formal *wayang*
    scene (*jejeran*)—in its staging, language,
    and dramatic structure.

I render up to you, Highness
The answer of Kyai Pengging

7   "Begging a thousand pardons
    He refuses Your Royal summons
    Though hidden on the surface
    Within he harbors *rasa*
    Deep and involved are his designs
    I reckon I'm not wrong
    The decision is Your Majesty's"[287]

8   The King did softly speak
    To the Prince of Kudus he charged:
    "Little Brother, go at once
    To Pengging as elder to preside
    If in your consideration, he has in-
        deed designs
    Then I grant you leave
    To administer justice by the
        Qur'ân and Hadîth"

9   The Prince of Kudus assenting
    With a *sembah*, withdrew from the
        royal presence
    The King retired to the inner
        palace
    All the *wali* and the pundits
    And the foremost courtiers dis-
        persed one and all
    Each unto his home

*The Prince of Kudus travels to Peng-
ging. In the course of his journey he
marks the countryside.*

And now turning what is told:

287. Line 6, "kawula dugi tan cidra,"
could instead be read: "I reckon [him] not
disloyal."

10 He who preparations made
    The Prince of Kudus had readied
    Seven of his disciples
    All of them in simple dress
    In *santri* garb the Prince was
        dressed
    Borne along was his talisman
    A small gong named Sir Tiger[288]

11 The legacy of his wife
    From Terung's Prince-regent
    Was borne by his disciples
    Then he did set forth
    To the southwest escorted by the
        seven
    Not telling of the journey
    Thereat they had arrived[289]

12 In the land of Pengging
    At the edge of a remote village
    There was a great banyan tree
    In the middle of the fields
    The Prince of Kudus did stop there
        to rest
    Before, were his disciples
    Seven sitting in array

13 Before long there did come
    A village headman, Sir Monday
        was his name
    Kneeling off to the side

He addressed the noble prince:
"Welcome, brother!
And where do you hail from?
What do you call yourself?"[290]

14 His Highness Prince Kudus re-
        plied:
    "A *santri* from Kudus, my name,
        Kyai
    Is "Ahmad Who'd-ever-guess?"
    As for my intentions
    I'm off to Pengging to find my
        elder brother
    And you, Uncle, what is your
        name?"
    Sir Monday answered sweetly:[291]

15 "My name is Mister Monday
    May I invite you, son
    To stop by at my house
    I would serve refreshments
    Just humble village fare
    Water and coconut juice
    If Your Lordship deigns

16 "To mix with simple villagers
    Ill-bred, awkward, and wretchedly
        poor
    There's nothing pretty here to see"

288. The word rendered as "talisman" in
line 6 is the Arabic *wasiyat*. Sir Tiger's
proper name is Ki Macan.
289. Among Sunan Kudus's three wives
was a daughter of Adipati (Prince-regent)
Terung. Adipati Terung (the son of Harya
Damar and the Chinese princess) was the
half-brother, as well as uncle, of Radèn
Patah (= Panembahan Bintara).

290. The headman, Sir Monday, was a
bekel. In the nineteenth century, the *bekel*
was often the administrative representative of an absentee landlord (apanage-
holder) from the court. Sir Monday is a
translation of the proper name Ki Soma;
as well as "Monday," *soma* also means
"moon."
291. The proper name translated as "Ahmad Who'd-ever-guess?" is Ahmad Sapa-
nyana.

The noble prince spoke sweetly:
"Thank you, Uncle, for your gener-
osity
But I instead request merely
That you give these friends of
mine

17 "All of them most thirsty
Some coconut juice without delay"
Sir Monday was off at once
To the village to find
A servant to climb for young coco-
nuts
Once they were cut open
He rushed back to the fields

18 Presented were they to the prince
Said: "Thank you very much"
The coconut juice drunk
By the prince so refreshing
Was given to his disciples
All of them did drink
The noble Prince Kudus said
sweetly:

19 "I ask you now, Uncle
Which is the way to Pengging?"
Sir Monday answered softly:
"There to the south and west"
Before long came all the villagers
Young and old, male and female
To see those seated there[292]

20 Crowding to the right and left

In front and behind, they stood,
sat, and squatted
One then asked his fellow:
"Hey boy, what is that
That carried under cover there
looks so big and scary?"
His friend did answer gruffly:
"I'd venture it a platter[293]

21 "With chili plates, and saucers"
Another guessed a tambourine
His friend's retort: "Not that!"
Raucously they argued
All the herdsboys standing there,
crowding for a look
Mister Monday, furious
Would pummel then these boys[294]

22 Lord Sunan Kudus said:
"Patience, Uncle. They are but chil-
dren
Let them do as they will
They surely mean no ill
Uncle, this village I grant the name
Indeed of "All-were-seen"
For I do see many[295]

292. The word rendered as "to see" in the
final line is *anonton* (to see in the sense of
"to watch a spectacle"). The image is that
of a mass of villagers crowding around
with mouths agape to get a look at the
strange and marvelous outsiders.

293. Like most power objects, or *pusaka*,
the gong is covered with tailored-to-fit
cloth wrappings (*singep* or *ules*). These
wrappings, which are considered among
the *pusaka*'s "dress," act both to conserve
the object's energy and to protect its
bearer from the ill effects (*walat*) that
same energy may engender.
294. A tambourinelike instrument, used
to accompany singing, the *terbang* (line 2)
is associated with Islamic-Arabic forms of
entertainment.
295. The proper name of the village is
Samakatingal. I have yet to identify a village by this name.

23 "People here, both men and
women
Along with little children, coming
for a look"
The noble prince then set forth
Sir Monday followed behind
Attending Prince Kudus on his
way
After they'd gone a ways
Mister Monday was sent home[296]

24 The noble prince continued on his
way
To the southwest, his seven disci-
ples attending
Taking turns at carrying
The gong called Sir Tiger
The Prince's progress overtaken by
nightfall
He stopped then to sit down
In a field at the edge of the River

25 Cemara, beneath a tree
Called a *kapundhung*; his disciples
before him
Opened the gong's wrappings
Sewn of scarlet fabric
And hung it in the *kapundhung*
tree
It being sunset then
They all went down to the river[297]

26 Once done were the prince's ablu-
tions
The seven disciples followed be-
hind
When done, they all returned
To where they had been sitting
Prince Kudus to the fore led the
prayers
From sunset on to evening
Earnestly they prayed[298]

27 When they had finished their
prayers
The time was nine at night
And the moon shone full
The noble prince did bid
Them sound the gong, Sir Tiger
Then as it was struck
Its voice rose to the heavens

28 For like a tiger's roar it was
Terrified were all the surrounding
villages
The neighboring four and five
Were all in a tumult
Taken was it for a real tiger
Sounding the alarm they gathered
To hunt down the roaring tiger[299]

---

set" is *mahrib*, designating the time for
the dusk *salât*.

298. The ablutions (line 1) are the *wulu*
(Ar. *wuzū*), the specified ablutions which
must be made by a Moslem prior to *salât*.
In line 5, Prince Kudus was, literally, acting as *imâm* (*angimani*). The prince and
his disciples prayed from *mahrib* (sunset)
to *ngisa* (evening); see above, note to XV:
5.

299. On "the neighboring four and five"
in line 3, see above, note to VI:21.

In a Javanese tiger hunt, the hunters

296. Mister Monday accompanied the
prince for one *unjutan*, the distance one
can carry a heavy object before needing to
sit down for a rest.

297. The *kapundhung* tree (Pierardia race-
mosa Bl., genus Euphorbiaceae) is a tree
with fine wood and a sweet-sour fruit
(GR 1:510).

In line 6, the word rendered as "sun-

29 Foraying out to the waste lands
With torches they searched the
     brush at the edge of the ravine
But nowhere seen was the tiger
With the roaring voice
The multitude confounded; every-
     one wondered
Before long their progress
Came down to the river's edge

30 All of them wailing and screaming
Coming up the ravine then saw
Beneath the *kapundhung* tree
There were people seated
The eight forthwith they did ap-
     proach
Questioned by the multitude
His Highness Prince Kudus an-
     swered:

31 "A *santri* from Kudus am I
My plan was to make for Pengging
But overtaken by night on the way
I could not continue on
In turn I ask, what is it that you
     want?
So many of you coming at once
All flustered you appear to me"

32 They all cried out together:
"We came to catch the tiger
With the roaring voice
But now he is not here"
The Prince of Kudus sweetly said:
"In that case, I grant the name
Of "Tiger" to this place[300]
———
would form a human fence which would
encircle the tiger. Each of the hunters
being armed with a spear, the tiger would
impale himself trying to escape the circle.
300. The proper name of the village is

33 "For when I passed through here
A tiger's roar was heard"
All of them gave thanks
And to this very day
Those hamlets are known as the
     village of Tiger
By then the time was
Nigh upon the break of dawn

34 The prince performed the dawn
     salât
The seven disciples followed him in
     salât
Then after the hour of dawn
At seven o'clock they did set forth
With halting steps, their progress
     veiled in mystery[301]

*Related is the meeting and debate of
Ki Ageng Pengging and Sunan
Kudus.*

Now turning what is told:
In Pengging's heart there were
     signs of approaching doom[302]

———
Sima ("tiger"). The village of Sima is located on the Cemara River to the northeast of Boyalali, along one of the roads
leading to the Kudus-Demak area.
301. In line 2, what the disciples do is the
salât makmuman, that is, *salât* performed
behind and after the lead of an *imâm*.
302. The word *srengkara* in the final line
designates signs (such as eclipses, earth-
quakes, volcanic eruptions, etc.) that
foretell the impending fall of a realm. Followed here by the conventional punctuation for a change of cantos, *srengkara* signals the reader by sound association to
change to the melody of Sarkara (=
Dhangdhanggula).

XXIX. Dhangdhanggula (Sarkara)

[Melodic mood is lithe, with didactic clarity and romantic allure]

1   Kyai Ageng was rapt of heart
His consciousness fixed on Release
He neither ate nor slept
In the *kobongan* he sat in meditation
Absorbed in deep *semadi*'s light
He delved the Will of God
Mastering vision
Oneness of vision consummate
Beyond desire, vanished was the universe
Extinguished was all danger[303]

2   His consciousness shone clear
Revealed by grace was the Mystery
Benighted not to Oneness
Now turning what is told:
The progress of Prince Kudus came
To Pengging's outer walls
The time then was high noon
The noble prince did stop
After his *salât*, he made for an abode
To the east of the palace walls[304]

3   The dwelling of the Widow named Wujil
Once seated, the Widow Woman asked:
"Accept my welcome, son
From where do you hail, My Lord?
And what is it that you want?
I think I know you not"
The noble prince said softly:
"A *santri* from Kudus am I
Ahmad Who'd-ever-guess?, my name, ma'am
I wish to present myself[305]

4   "To Kyai Ageng Pengging now
Tell me, would he be at home?"
The Widow answered softly:
"Indeed he is, My Lord

303. The *kobongan* or *krobongan* is a ceremonial chamber located in the center of the inner room (*dalem*) of a traditional upper-class Javanese house. This chamber within a chamber is often glassed in and hung with curtains. Inside this hallowed space is a ceremonial bed which is invariably stacked high with bolsters. This sacred couch is widely held to be a shrine to the goddess of rice/fertility, Dewi Sri. This bed would never be slept upon. However, it is said that in the Kraton Surakarta, the Susuhunan would consummate his marriage to a queen in the *kobongan* (in the Dalem Ageng Prabasuyasa; see figure 16. *Pusaka* may be stored in the *kobongan*, or in the two small rooms located behind and to either side of it.

In line nine, rendered as "the universe" is *alam kabir*, that is, "the phenomenal universe." The line, "tanpa karkat lumuyut ing alam kabir," could also be read: "Beyond desire, vanishing into the universe."

304. Rendered as "high noon" in line 7 is *luhur*, the time for the noon *salât*.
305. The word *wujil* means "dwarf." Is this widow woman the wife of the famous Wujil after whom the *Suluk Wujil* was named? That Wujil, a one-time servant to Majapahit's Brawijaya, converted to Islam and became a disciple of Sunan Bonang. See Poerbatjaraka, "De Geheime Leer van Soenan Bonang (Soeloek Woedjil)," *Djâwâ* 18 (1938):145–81.

But melancholy is his heart
Neither eating nor sleeping
He meditates in the *kobongan*
The talk of the crowd is that such it
    has been
Since the King's envoy did leave
Up to this very day

5   "Ceaseless is his practice of *semadi*
None of his brethren will he re-
    ceive
Everyone is sunk in gloom"
The noble prince spoke sweetly
To his seven disciples:
"Stay here, all of you
I shall enter alone
But heed ye well my words:
Should you hear loud wailing from
    within the palace
Then be on alert!"

6   The disciples seven with a *sembah*
    did assent
The Prince of Kudus spoke again
This time to the Widow:
"To your care I do entrust
These my seven disciples
I am going in"
The Widow did agree
Whereupon went he to the palace
Coming to the gate, he asked
    sweetly
To the keeper of the gate:

7   "Tell me, Brother, does Ki Ageng
    Pengging
Find himself at home?"
Soft was the questioned one's
    reply:
"Indeed he is, My Lord
But he is not well

For days without food or sleep
He meditates in the *kobongan*
Refusing to receive anyone"
Then spoke the Prince of Kudus
    again:
"See that you tell him

8   "That come is the envoy of God
Jabara'il to dispatch His Word
Go now quickly and report"
He to whom these words were said
At that rushed in the palace
The message relayed to the Ladies
    of Court
Then was delivered
Ki Ageng Pengging did muse:
"In that case do invite at once
He who claims to be the messenger
    of God[306]

9   "Command him forthwith to pro-
    ceed into the palace"
The ladies two set off in haste
Coming to the gate
Met His Highness Prince Kudus
Was invited straightway into the
    palace
Escorted on the way
He entered the Inner Sanctum
The noble prince called out
    "Peace!"
Ki Ageng answered: "And with you
    too, peace!"
As he parted the curtain[307]

306. In Islamic traditions, the archangel
Jabara'il (Gabriel) is God's foremost an-
gelic messenger; among his duties are to
convey God's commands to the prophets
and to reveal to them His mysteries.
307. Rendered as "Inner Sanctum" in line

10 His Highness Prince Kudus
        climbed up onto the couch
    Exchanging *salâm*, they took their
        seats
    The curtain was closed again
    Ki Ageng spoke softly:
    "O My Young Lord, receive
    My welcome on your coming here
    To Pengging, Little Brother"
    The noble prince said sweetly:
    "By God's Will, Brother, are we
        well"
    Ki Ageng spoke again

11 To Rubiyah, his wife, charged then
        to serve
    Refreshments to the guest who'd
        come
    At once withdrew to the kitchen
    Of Ki Ageng is the telling:
    Seated together were the nobles
        two
    His Highness Prince Kudus did
        say:
    "O Elder Brother, the command
    Of your little brother, the Sultan of
        Demak
    Your Highness now is summoned
    To come along with me"[308]

12 Kyai Ageng Pengging replied:

----

7 are the words *Dalem Ageng*. See above,
note to X:30.
    In lines 8 and 9, the two men exchange
the standard Moslem salutation: "Assalam 'alaikum . . . Wa'alaikum salam."
308. The word *rubiyah* ("wife") from the
oɪ *rabi* ("wife") + the Arabic nominal
feminine ending—*yah*. See GR 1:376. In
this text, "Rubiyah" is the proper name
of Ki Ageng Pengging's wife.

"What could I be summoned for?
Here is a villager
Summoned by a king
From yesteryear unto this day
I do not serve as subject
Am subject to no king
Lord and subject are all the same
The being of the subject has its
    source in the lord
That of the lord in the subject"

13 The Prince of Kudus answered
        severely:
    "Why Brother, you are cornered
    Save firm you hold to what you
        think"
    Ki Ageng answered gently:
    "You waste your words, Master
    Once tasted by my smacking lips
    'Tis sure to be swallowed
    To spit it out would be a waste
    Old and worn out, 'twould be
        knowledge off the mark
    If you are benighted"[309]

309. Lines 2–3, "pan ki raka sira kekan-
dhangan / yèn tan mantep panggiluté,"
also may be read, variously, as (1) "Why
Brother, you stand exposed / As but half-
hearted at your practice (or contemplation)"; (2) "Why Brother, you stand exposed / As one who won't stick to what he
chews"; and (3) "Why Brother, you'll
stand exposed / If you don't stick to what
you chew." Part of the difficulty in deter-
mining the translation of these lines is in
the polysemic character of the word *pang-
gilut*, which glosses as "consideration,"
contemplation; striving (for knowledge);
and chewing."
    The word *dikecapena*, rendered as
"tasted by my smacking lips" in line 6, is
from the verb *kecap*, which means *both*

14 The Prince of Kudus spoke again:
    "O Ki Ageng, choose now:
    The outside or the inside
    The below or the above
    The right or the left
    The back or the front
    Being or non-being
    The *sepi* most *ramé* or
    The *ramé*, Brother, most *sepi*"
    Ki Ageng spoke softly:[310]

15 "Were I to choose the inside I'd err
    To choose the outside I'm lost
    Wavering then in faith
    Were I to choose the above
    'Twould be searching for an echo
    Were I to choose the front
    Truly I'd be most damnably lost
    Lost by seven schools of thought
    Below, above, left, and right are
        mine
    Nothing is mine"[311]

The death of Ki Ageng Pengging.

16 The Prince of Kudus's words were
        sweet:
    "Brother Ki Pengging, Your High-
        ness
    Can die within life
    That I would like to see"
    And soft was Ki Ageng's reply:
    "Indeed I can
    With or without you
    Make not light of faith
    If you wish to see the Beautiful
        Bird
    You must know the Whence and
        Whither"[312]

17 The Prince of Kudus answered
        severely:
    "Where then is your life and
        death?"

"to smack" and "to utter." Thus the line,
"lamun dikecapena," also reads "Once
uttered by my lips." K. A. Penging's response, then, replies to the polysemic
play of the *panggiluté* above in Sunan
Kudus's belligerent challenge.
    Rendered as "Master" in line 5 is the
title Ki Bayi; see note to XXV:8.
310. An alternative translation of lines 7–
9, "ana ora iku / kang sepi luwih ramé-
nya / ingkang ramé ki raka aluwih sepi,"
would be: "That which is, is not / The *sepi*
is most *ramé* / The *ramé*, O Brother, is
most *sepi*." On the terms *sepi* and *ramé*,
see above, note to XXII:13.
311. Rendered as "schools of thought" in
line 8 is the word *medahab* (Ar. *madhâhib*). Almost surely, this should have read
"four" (Jav. *patang*) rather than "seven"
(Jav. *pitung*), thus referring to the four
recognized *madhâhib* (pl. of *madhhab*) of

Sunnî Islam. Each *madhhab* comprises a
"school" or system of *fiqh*. Cf witnesses
of the Galuh variant.
312. The "Beautiful Bird" (*peksi kang adi*)
of line 9 is a trope for the way to Enlightenment. A meditation on "the Beautiful
Bird" concludes a version of *Suluk Malang Sumirang* found in the *Serat Walisana*. There, "the beautiful bird," encompassing heaven and earth, is *suksma*
(roughly [!], "soul, spirit"), the mount of
"the aware" to heaven (*Wali Sana*, ed.
R. Tanojo, pp. 184–85). See also *Kidung
Rumeksa ing Wengi* in *Sèh Amongraga*,
ed. Moelyono Sastronaryatmo (Jakarta:
Departemen Pendidikan dan Kebudayaan,
Proyek Penerbitan Buku Sastra Indonesia
dan Daerah, 1981), pp. 16–17. This publication is an unacknowledged transliteration of [*Suluk Warni-warni*] (composed
s.l., s.a.; inscribed Surakarta, 1820–21).
MS. SP 109 Na; SMP KS 480.

Softly said the Ki Ageng:
"Make a cut in my elbow
With that little knife of yours"
The cut made thereupon
He fell and died
And then he called out, "Peace!"
Prince Kudus answered softly:
"And with you too, peace!"[313]

18 Ki Ageng Pengging was dead
His wife, oblivious
Still readied refreshments

*Tells of Sunan Kudus's flight from
Pengging and how he eluded those
who pursued him.*

His Highness Prince Kudus
Did leave the *kobongan* and then
Make for the place where
His disciples had been
Coming to the Widow's house
The disciples seven he met ready
    for danger
Not about to retreat from battle[314]

XXX. Durma
[Melodic mood is very passionate,
angry, or violent; evocative of bat-
tle]

1 The noble Prince of Kudus said
    softly

313. Prince Kudus's "little knife" (*sase-
king*; Ar. *sikkin*) is a circumcision knife.
Again, in lines 8 and 10 are, in Arabic, the
standard Moslem salutation.
314. The word *mundur* ("retreat") in the
final line, with the punctuation for a new
canto following it, signals the reader by
sound association to change to the melody of *Dur*-ma.

To his seven disciples:
"Let us now be off
But heed these words of mine
Should we be pursued
By the relatives
Of Ki Ageng Pengging

2 "Let none among you join in battle
    against them
Ignore them, be unmoved
Proceeding on your way
The disciples voiced assent
And thereupon they did depart
Turning the telling:
The one left in Pengging

3 Ki Ageng's Rubiyah did ready re-
    freshments
Now everything was done
With all her cooking
Wanting to tell
Her husband, she entered the
    palace
With her coming
To the edge of the *kobongan* then

4 She waited expectantly for her
    husband's word
Time passed in total silence
Drawn shut were the curtains
Rubiyah pondered in her heart
And then did she the curtains open
The guest was gone
Her husband lay fallen

5 Thereat Rubiyah took her husband
    in her arms
He was already dead
Shrieking she beat her breast
Wailing in distress

In tumult were Pengging's
  brethren
Both women and men
Cried out, "Treachery!"

6   When assembled were the family
      all
    They divided up the tasks
    Laying out the deceased
    Once the body they had bathed
    And wrapped, it was then laid to
      rest
    At the head of the house
    In the Estate of Pengging

7   Telling not of the rites for him who
      had gained Release
    Turning again that told:
    All of the family
    Were busy preparing for war
    Weapons heaped in piles clattered
    With battle streamers
    Beautiful pennants and flags

8   Those who led the family were
    The elders of Pengging
    The high nobility
    Their names: Sir Wild Buffalo,
    And Sir Buffalo Horns, thirdly
    Sir Lightning
    Fourthly Sir Thunder[315]

9   They made off in hot pursuit of the
      treacherous one

315. All these nobles are titled "Lembu"
("Sir," literally "cow"); see above, note to
II:15. The proper names of these four
Lembu are: Lembu Handaka (Sir Wild
Buffalo), Lembu Singat (Sir Buffalo
Horns), Lembu Makilat (Sir Lightning),
and Lembu Thathit (Sir Thunder).

To the northeast proceeding
All of them weeping
Crying out for vengeance
For their murdered lord
Before long at all
The progress was sighted

10 Hazy and distant of the eight who
      went with halting steps
    Then were hailed forthwith
    "You there! Wait!
    O treacherous *santri*
    Try your hand on me
    Both of us valiant
    Let us meet in combat!

11 "Give battle now to Sir Wild Buf-
      falo
    And to Sir Buffalo Horns
    And to Sir Lightning
    And fourthly to Sir Thunder
    Champions of the people of
      Pajang-Pengging
    Stop there!"
    The Prince of Kudus listened

12 Hurled challenges, he was sur-
      rounded by the troops
    To right and left and behind
    Assailed by the screaming multi-
      tude
    Deluged by the weapons' fire
    The prince proceeded on non-
      chalant
    Eyes lifted to the skies
    He stretched out open hands

13 With that his prayers were an-
      swered
    By Almighty God All Pure
    His disciples wailed

Pressing to give battle
The noble Prince of Kudus did
refuse:
"Be still, all of you
Surrender to Almighty God

14   "There is no telling fortune fair,
disease, and death"
The noble prince thereat took up
His cane
And waved it to the right
The people of Pengging followed
Seeming to them that
Thousands of foe had appeared

15   All the troops of Pengging rushed
in frenzied rampage
None among them wished to live
Rapt with love
For their murdered lord
They danced forward in hot pur-
suit
Of nothing at all
The prince was moved by the sight

16   The troops of Pengging in confu-
sion did charge off
To the southwest weeping
His Highness Prince Kudus thereat
Did wave his walking stick
To the north; it was followed
Then the noble prince
Set off on an eastward course[316]

17   Mistaken were the Pengging folk
in their pursuit
Those they took as enemy

Before long did vanish
Those whom they did follow
And so they all turned back
Most disappointed
'Twas beyond comprehension

18   But there was among them one old
man
Who did advise his companions
That they had been tricked
That army of Pengging
Then decided to fall back
Paying the matter no further heed
All of them went home

*Tells how the Prince of Kudus's prog-
ress proceeds punctuated by* salât.

19   Now turning again what is told:
The Prince of Kudus proceeding
With his disciples
Seven stopped along the way
At the sunset time
Then doing his *salât*
The disciples followed his lead

20   After sunset they prayed on to the
night prayer time
Then after their prayers
They did the night *salât*
The *salât sunat* and then
The obligatory night *salât*
After the *salât*
They did not sleep all night[317]

316. The "walking stick" of line 4 is the
prince's *ecis*, a long walking stick characteristically borne by *ulama* (GR 1:275).

317. Rendered as "night *salât*" in line 3 is
"ebam ngisa." The word *ebam* can mean
"ordained in stone" (GR 2:748). The *salât
sunat* are nonobligatory prayers uttered
by a mosque official prior to communal
salât.

21 Reciting prayers, they prayed for
        fortune fair upon the way
    His Highness Prince Kudus was
        then
    Truly eminent
    Mastering both gross and sublime
    Earnest, mindful of sacred knowl-
        edge
    Accomplished and aware
    Enamored were all who saw[318]

XXXI. Asmarandana
[Melodic mood is one of sorrow or
longing]

1   After dawn *salât* they went on
    The noble prince with his disciples
    To the northeast proceeding

    *Returning to the tale of Jaka Ting-
    kir's antecedents, Pengging mourns
    the loss of its Ki Ageng.*

    And so to turn the tale that's told:
    The troops of Pengging then
    Upon their return from the chase
    Of the treacherous guest

2   A failure had their mission been
    Worsted were they in eminence
    Sunk in gloom were all
    The nobles of Pengging
    Both men and women wept
    Ni Rubiyah's heart was broken
    Absorbed in thoughts of him who
        was gone

318. The word *kasmaran* ("enamored"),
followed by the conventional punctuation
for a change of cantos, signals the reader
to change to the melody of Asmarandana.

3   Leaving behind an infant son
    Who most piteous
    Was called Mas Karèbèt
    At that time gather did
    All of the family
    For the seventh-day death rite
    The trays of food then coming
        forth[319]

4   Were divided up evenly
    Among family and friends
    Ketib, modin and *marbot*
    No one was left out
    Many were the trays
    The *salawat* just kept pouring
    The common *santri* were over-
        joyed[320]

319. Rendered as "the seventh-day death
rite" is "ngaos pitung dintenipun" (more
precisely, "the Quranic recitations performed on the seventh day [after
death]"). The Javanese funerary rite is an
extended affair: after the initial burial
rites, solemnized as soon as possible after
the person's death, there are a series of
further rites to mourn the deceased.
These rites are performed seven, forty,
one hundred, and one thousand days after
the person's death. They consist of (usually small) communal feasts (*slametan*),
which near neighbors and relatives are
obliged to attend, and the chanting of Islamic prayers in Arabic (*ngaji/ngaos*) by
hired professional *santri* chanters.
320. In line three are the names of (usually rural) mosque officials. The *ketib* is in
charge of the sermon (*khutbah*) at Friday
salât. The *modin* announces the *salât*
times to the faithful. The *marbot* acts as a
guard or custodian of the mosque.
    The *salawat* in line 6 (from the Arabic
salawât [pl. of *salât*]) is the money paid
out to the professional *santri* for their

5   Gathered together they did eat
Next they divided up the treats
Not to tell of the rites[321]

*Tells of a meeting of the Ni Agengs
of Pengging and of Tingkir.*

And so it is told:
Then in mourning was
Ni Ageng Tingkir, since
The death of her husband

6.   The Ki Ageng; then before long
Struck down again was she by the
    news
Of the death of Brother Pengging
And his wife's ensuing illness
Ni Ageng Tingkir forthwith
Made for Pengging in haste
Not telling of her journey

7   Arriving in Pengging
She went straight into the palace
Meeting, the two Ni Ageng

———

chanting of the prayers. The jarring image of the happy *santri* divvying up the
take at their master's funeral plays on a
nineteenth-century stereotype of lower-
class professional *santri*. See, for example,
the description of petty greed among the
vulgar *santri* for the *salawat* at a high-
class funeral in R.Ng. Ronggawarsita's
Serat Jayèngbaya (SMP KS 415.5), pp.
38–39.
321. Rendered as "treats" is *barekat*, the
parcels of leftover food that the participants in the rite take home to their families. From the Arabic *baraka*, this word
more usually denotes the beneficent spiritual power possessed by holy persons
and God, which may be granted to others
as a "blessing."

Embraced one another sobbing
Pondering in their hearts:
"O! Alas, my sister
Woe is hers who is bereft!"

8   And they took their seats
Both upon the couch
Ni Ageng Pengging spoke:
"Elder Sister, welcome
Upon your arrival here"
Said Ni Ageng Tingkir sweetly:
"Thank you, Little Sister[322]

9   "For your gracious hospitality
Now I have come, Little Sister
To pay a call on you
Upon the death of your husband
And more, you too have fallen ill
It breaks my heart to see"
Nyai Ageng spoke softly:

10   "O Elder Sister, since the death
Of your little brother till now
Neither have I eaten nor slept
Bethinking always your child
This our Karèbèt
For the boy though still a babe
Is now bereft of father

11   "To whom then can I turn?
I cannot bear, Sister, being left be-
    hind
'Twould be better were I to die"
Said Nyai Ageng Tingkir:
"Little Sister, speak not thus
Accept what has come to be
Inscribed in the Lauhu'l-Mahfûz
    are

322. The couch (*kathil*) in line 2 must be
the couch in the *kobongan*. Cf. XXIX:10.

12 "Fortune fair, disease, and death
Are destiny; never could there be
Fated an untimely death"
The younger sister nodded humbly
Ni Ageng did speak again:
"Sister, if you would permit
I would take your son with me"[323]

13 Said Ni Ageng Pengging softly:
"Aye Sister, whatever you will
However, it is my request—
Begging a thousand pardons—
That when I have recovered
Then will you get your son, Krè-
bèt"
Ni Ageng Tingkir answered:

14 "I honor your wishes, Sister
Mind you heed these words of
mine:
Accept your lot with strength
Beware of temptation
To unwholesome deeds
Not fit for emulation
Truly hold to this[324]

15 "Fare thee well now, Sister
I take my leave to go
To Tingkir; after I am gone
May you nurture well your son
And your family too

All rests on you now, Sister
Since your husband's death"

16 Ni Ageng Pengging, bowing down
Was cradled by her elder sister
Tears welled in their eyes
And when they had left off
Ni Ageng went home in haste
The one left behind, sunk in
reverie
Pondered her elder sister's words

17 And ever more grave her illness
grew

*Tells how the Prince of Kudus con-
tinues slowly on the way to Demak.
His progress is punctuated by* salât.

Now turning the tale that is told:
The progress of High Prince Kudus
Had yet to make Demak
Ever stopping and turning with
halting steps
He did try himself
Absorbed in thoughts of him who
died[325]

18 The Prince was aware of Mystery
Not blind to the Whence and
Whither
But 'twas hidden by his eyes
The seven disciples guessed it not:

323. The "humble nod" of line 4 was the
saying "Nuwun," the sense of which ap-
proximates a noncommittal nod in an English language world.
324. Line 3 reads "dèn-agedhé panri-
mané. On *panrima*, see note to XIX:20.
    The final line, "èsthinen ingkang san-
yata," also reads: "Hold fast unto the
truth."

325. By "trying himself" (amesu sarirani-
pun), in line 6, is meant that he was pushing himself (body and soul) in ascetic
practice. This was not just a journey back
to Demak, but a disciplined wandering
(*lelana brata*) performed in quest of en-
hanced spiritual (and material) powers.

"So long on the road are we
I surmise that our master has
Decided upon wandering[326]

19 "For ten nights have passed and yet
We've still not made Demak
This progress is so very slow"
And then when the time
Of the noon *salât* came
They stopped at the edge of a pool
Then all did their *salât*

20 *Pépé* leaves they made into
Carpets for their *salât*
After the *salât*, they chanted
    prayers
The disciples crying: "Amen!"
After finishing his *salât*
The noble prince asked sweetly:
"What, pray, is this river's
    name?"[327]

21 A disciple answered bowing:
"Highness, I do not know
The name of this river"
The noble prince said softly:
"I grant the name
Of Pépé to this river
For when I did sit here

22 " 'Twas on a carpet of *pépé* leaves"
The disciples all approved his will
Unto this very day the name
Of this river is the Pépé

326. In line 3, more usual than *nétra*
("eye"), would have been *nétya* ("facial
expression").
327. The *pépé* (line 1) is a plant from
whose leaves is made a tonic for newborn
infant boys (GR 2:180).

They then continued on their way
Not to be related at length:
They had come to the land of
    Demak[328]

23 The time was the afternoon *salât*
    time
After his *salât* was done
He then repaired for home
To rest himself
Exhausted from the road
On the morn would he go to court
To show himself before the King[329]

*Tells how the Prince of Kudus comes
before the court of Demak to report
on his mission to Pengging.*

XXXII. Sinom
[Melodic mood is "even," appropriate for narrative]

1 Awaiting the coming Monday
To show himself at court
When assembled replete would be
    the pundits
And all the highest courtiers
Senior princes and nobility
He would come to display his work
Like the Honored Kramadaya
Sent by his king, Sri Rama

328. The Pépé River runs just to the
north of Pengging; they had indeed not
traveled far at all.
329. The words *Sri Naranata* (rendered
"the King") in the final line, with the
punctuation for a new canto following
them, signal the reader to change to the
melody of Sinom (also known as "Srinata").

To Alengka to spy on Dyah Sinta,
   the Queen[330]

2   When he came to the audience hall
Assembled were the monkeys
   great and small
Truly an excellent envoy
Able, brave, and powerful
Accomplished was his mission
This noble prince's intention was
That he be emulated
By all royal envoys
That their works match his in vir-
   tue

3   His Highness Prince Kudus truly
Able and handsome to see
Dispatched his work most thor-
   oughly
Of sacred knowledge consummate
   and cunning too was he
For clear and precise was his speech
Strict, his observance of the Faith
Brilliant, his discourse
For sharp was he of intellect
At the break of dawn the prince set
   off for court[331]

330. In nineteenth-century Surakarta,
Monday and Thursday were the routine
days for audience at court.
   Kramadaya (roughly: "Way of Power")
must be an alias for Hanoman, the famous white-monkey emissary of the
Rama[yana] tales whom King Rama sent
to Alengka to deliver his ring to the kid-
napped Queen Sinta. However, I have yet
to track down a textual reference to
Hanuman that uses this name.
   Rendered as "to spy" in the last line is
the word *anukma*.
331. Rendered as "observance of the
Faith," in line 6, is *ngibadah*.

4   'Twas on a Monday morning
The King came forth in audience
There in the Assembly Hall
The attending subjects thronged
The regalia amassed
The *wali*, to His Majesty's right
With all the learned *ulama*
The *fuqaha* and devout *ngabid*
The pundits all arrayed before him

5   Grand Vizier Wanasalam
Had come before His Majesty
Arrayed were ministers and re-
   gents
All the courtiers, both high and
   low
Amassed was the palace guard
Forthwith arriving
The Prince of Kudus straightway
Took his place at audience seated
   on a chair
While making a *sembah*; said His
   Majesty sweetly:[332]

6   "Little brother, welcome
On your return from my errand
And did you meet success?"
The noble prince with a *sembah*
   said:

332. The text, lines 3–4, lists all the officials of court, in order of descending rank:
the *nayaka* (ministers), *bupati* (regents),
and then the *kliwon, panéwu,* and the
mantri.
   In the intricate grammar of seating
regulations in the nineteenth-century
court, Prince Kudus's place on a chair indicates his extremely high standing. Only
the most senior of princes (and European
officials) were allowed to be seated upon
chairs in the presence of the king.

"With the blessings of Your
  Majesty
Prosper did my mission
To convey the royal word
I did pronounce forthwith
To our brother Ki Ageng Kebo
  Kenonga

7   "But most averse was he
To come before Your Majesty
Not feeling himself subject
By pretext he pressed his claims

Refusing to pick and choose
For all of it did he compass
. . . ."333

333. Rendered as "by pretext" is *akiyas*
(Ar. *qiyâs*), the principle of drawing novel
juridical decisions (*fatwa*) by way of analogy with decisions in the Hadîth and the
Qur'ân (see above, note to XIX: 7). Prince
Kudus apparently means *kiyas* in its de-
rogatory sense of "to quibble with base-
less argumentation."
    The text breaks off abruptly in the
middle of this verse (see figure 5).

CHAPTER 3
INVOKING THE FUTURE IN
WRITING A PAST

❋

The hand that wrote the manuscript of *Babad Jaka Tingkir* laid down its pen, quite abruptly, at this textual moment:

> "Not feeling himself subject
> By pretext he pressed his claims
> Refusing to pick and choose
> For all of it did he compass"
> (*Babad Jaka Tingkir* [henceforth
> *BJT*] XXXII:7).

Sunan Kudus, describing the character of the man he had killed, has just begun to report on his final meeting with Ki Ageng Pengging when the manuscript so suddenly breaks off. The executed man of whom the Lord of Kudus was speaking, the recalcitrant *santri* who did not feel himself subject to royal authority and who refused to pick and choose, was the father of the Jaka Tingkir for whom the *babad* is named. Breaking off at this point, the narrative leaves that Jaka Tingkir (that is, Mas Krèbèt) a pitiful orphaned infant, whose birth, however, had occasioned auspicious portents of future greatness. Hence, although the poem's namesake "shows promise," he has yet to emerge as an effective actor on the narrative stage of history when the poem suddenly falls silent. The *babad* has, then, the curious identity of a "history of Jaka Tingkir" without—or, better, before—Jaka Tingkir. Before considering why this should be so, and hence the potential significance of the protagonist's absence from the text, we first need to know precisely who Jaka Tingkir was and how he is remembered in the more dominant Javanese historical traditions.

Jaka Tingkir is an important figure in Javanese history. Tales of his life and exploits are well documented in the literary archives of Java; his story also enjoys a prominent place in the oral traditions that have informed Javanese historical consciousness for centuries. He would certainly have been well known to, and borne in mind by, the nineteenth-century audience of this Tingkir history from which he is so conspicuously absent. When one thinks of the Jaka Tingkir of the more dominant historical traditions, several features come immediately to mind: asceticism, exile, marauding crocodiles, mad bulls, lethal betel leaves (or hair pins), and, of course, the Central Javanese kingdom of Pajang that he founded. Pajang, the ruins of whose *kraton* are located several kilometers west of present-day Surakarta, was the first inland Islamic kingdom in Java. The kingdom of Pajang was established and enjoyed a brief period of ascendancy in the second half of the sixteenth century. Pajang's hegemony passed to its successor Central Javanese kingdom of Mataram upon the death of Jaka Tingkir, who had ruled the realm he founded as prince-regent or, anachronistically, Sultan of Pajang.

Another "Babad Jaka Tingkir"

How, then, did the pitiful son of the martyred Ki Ageng Pengging come into his kingship? Our *babad* does not say, but according to more mainstream historical traditions, the boy's ascent to power was neither a regular nor an easy one. Let us now review that rise to power as it is related in another "Babad Jaka Tingkir," one that tells the story of Tingkir's career that our *babad* omits. This other telling comes from the so-called *Major Surakarta Babad*.[1]

With the deaths of both his parents, Mas Krèbèt was raised by the widow Ni Ageng Tingkir in the small mountain village of Tingkir near present-day Salatiga; hence the name Jaka Tingkir ("Youth of Tingkir"). As a boy he tended his adoptive mother's fields and displayed a remarkable predilection for ascetic practice. Upon his mother's advice that he study with a Moslem teacher, Jaka Tingkir presented himself as a disciple to the Ki Ageng of Séla, master of a small village to the southeast of Demak. And it is surely not coincidental that this *kyai*, a renowned puppeteer as well as Moslem religious teacher, is a direct genealogical ancestor of the Mataram dynasty. An excellent student, Jaka Tingkir became

---

1. *Babad Tanah Jawi*, 31 vols. (Batavia: Balai Pustaka, 1939–41), vols. 3–5. On the "Major Surakarta Babad," see my discussion below, in this chapter.

a noted puppeteer; the *Major Babad* says little of his Islamic education. Having recognized signs of future kingship in the boy, Ki Ageng Séla advised Tingkir to go into royal service at the court of Demak.

Before making for Demak, Jaka Tingkir returned home to bid his adoptive mother farewell and to help weed the fields. It was as he was weeding that a stranger (Sunan Kalijaga) appeared and prophetically advised him to abandon this lowly work, so unfitting for a king-to-be. Tingkir then departed for Demak, where he was received into royal service through his adoptive mother's family connections. His performance at court flawless, he rose quickly through the ranks. Before long, this youth of extraordinary prowess had attained the very high rank of commander of Sultan Trenggana's elite guard. When the Sultan decided to increase troop strength, Tingkir was the one designated to test applicants to the guard. All went well until a certain Dhadhungawuk, a hideously ugly but powerful champion from a mountain village, came forward to be tested. Tingkir, revolted by the applicant's appearance, stabbed him with a *sadak* (a hair-pin, or—in modern usage—a rolled betel leaf). Dhadhungawuk fell to his death. On Tingkir's orders, Dhadhungawuk's body was then hacked to pieces by the guard. The Sultan was horrified when news of this atrocity reached him. Tingkir was stripped of his command and exiled from the kingdom.

Following a period of hardship and intense ascetic practice, Tingkir allied himself with a network of rural southern Central Javanese *kyai* who had been associates of his late father. Upon their advice, he decided to return to Demak and win back the Sultan's favor. Making his way north on a river raft, he did battle with and defeated the king of the crocodiles and his crocodile troops near present-day Surakarta. Now in his service, the subjected crocodiles navigated the raft upstream to a spot near the Sultan's summer palace east of Demak. According to the texts of the dominant tradition, Tingkir employed a ruse in order to regain his position at court. With a magic charm from one of the *kyai*, Tingkir maddened a wild bull which he then set against the summer palace. The Sultan's troops were powerless against the bull's attacks. Jaka Tingkir alone (by secretly removing the charm from the beast's mouth) was able to save his king from the bull's ravages. In gratitude, the Sultan went further than reinstating him: he gave Tingkir his daughter in marriage and installed him as the provincial Lord of Pajang.

Only after Sultan Trenggana's death did his son-in-law, the prince-regent of Pajang, assume hegemony over "all Java." When his newly attained authority was challenged by a scion of the Demak house, Pajang's cause was championed and then won by the efforts of a clique of loyal courtiers. Among those courtiers were notably Ki Ageng Pamanahan (the grandson of Ki Ageng Séla) and his son, Lor ing Pasar. The former Jaka Tingkir rewarded Pamanahan with the wild forest tract of Mataram. Clearing the land with his family, Pamanahan ruled there as Ki Ageng Mataram. Mataram's son, Lor ing Pasar, was recognized as foster son by ex-Jaka Tingkir (now Sultan Pajang). This son of dual fathers was known in his maturity as Panembahan Sénapati. It was he who, by means of his marriage to Kangjeng Ratu Kidul (spirit Queen of the South Sea), eventually established the kingdom of Mataram and put an end to Pajang's hegemony. Jaka Tingkir, the prince-regent of Pajang died a broken man. His "real" son eventually succeeded as Pajang's lord, but this son's status was that of vassal to Mataram. A final note: the Jaka Tingkir of the dominant tradition is said to have had a fatal weakness for pretty women.

A "Babad Jaka Tingkir" before and in Anticipation of Jaka Tingkir

It is important to remember that it would have been renditions of some or all of these tales that nineteenth-century readers of a text titled "Babad Jaka Tingkir" would have expected to read or hear. But the peculiar *Babad Jaka Tingkir* translated here, with its very different sequence of tales, repeatedly defers fulfillment of these expectations. Indeed, among the ways it achieves its distinctive effects is precisely by the subversion of accepted audience expectations. Instead of offering a rendition of Jaka Tingkir's well-known story, what this text depicts in a singularly pointed manner is a history of Jaka Tingkir's biological and ideological antecedents. The text composes its "History of Jaka Tingkir," a fragmentary account of a past that would *precede* Jaka Tingkir, in order, it seems, to construct a stage upon which the character of Jaka Tingkir should emerge. The text is, then, a pretext or, better, a context for a different kind of text, one that is yet to be written. But what kind of text, that is, what kind of "Jaka Tingkir," might emerge from such a context? And when does the poem anticipate that emergence might occur? This book will address these questions through a detailed reading of the text itself, a reading which will disclose that Jaka Tingkir's absence from the page prophetically signals his presence elsewhere, in the emerging text of the future.

The skeptic might point out that fragmentation, elision, and truncation are commonplace in Javanese manuscripts. Indeed, a manuscript rendition of a complete text as an integral whole (that is, with a clearly distinguished beginning, middle, and end) remains exceptional, especially among texts of history.[2] Nonetheless, I shall propose that the manner in which this text breaks off distinguishes it as something other than ordinary manuscript fragmentation. For in the case of this history in manuscript, deliberate truncation is an essential component of the text's production of meaning. I shall argue that in order to make sense this Tingkir history necessarily omits the well-remembered history of Tingkir's career. The focus of this Tingkir history must instead be upon those who would immediately precede him.

The skeptic might then point out that there is nothing extraordinary about histories of Jaka Tingkir's antecedents. Indeed, such histories are integral to the dominant *babad* tradition. And it has long been recognized that there is considerable variation among these "legendary" histories which precede the relatively standardized narrative sequence of Tingkir's exploits sketched above. Indeed, as early as 1913 it was in large part upon differences among variant pre-Tingkir Pajang-Pengging histories that the remarkable Indonesian historiographer Hoesein Djajadiningrat based his philological division of the dominant Central Javanese historical tradition into two major redactions. Djajadiningrat's bifurcation distinguishes the more extended versions, in which Jaka Tingkir actually descends from a crocodile, from the more condensed treatments in which our hero is provided a fine Majapahit pedigree.[3] More extensive intertextual comparisons among *babad* which treat this period prove, however, that the picture of Jaka Tingkir's past, and hence of Javanese historical traditions, is rather more complicated. The *babad* translated here, for example, clearly draws upon both variant textual traditions, without being subsumed under either of them. This circumstance, however, does not impugn the astuteness of Djajadiningrat's observations. For it was certainly not by

2. This material truth alone should caution us against imposing the Western criteria of textual unity for a literary valuation of Javanese texts.

3. Hoesein Djajadiningrat, *Tinjauan Kritis Tentang Sajarah Banten* (Jakarta: Djambatan, 1983), pp. 249 ff. and 298 ff.

chance that this seminal historiographer recognized the importance of the variant historical constructions of this particular period of the past for an understanding of Central Javanese historical thought. In remembering the half-forgotten antecedents of Jaka Tingkir, the writers of these *babad* remembered what was antecedent to the establishment of a new political authority in the Central Java that they called home. How they remembered his antecedents could tell us how they would remember him—or one like him.

The Invocation: A Web of Meanings

Let us now turn to a critical reading of the poem itself, a reading that will suggest how the text works to create the startling effects alluded to above. Consider the poem's opening stanza:

> Thus do I render the brilliant exemplar
> In sweet meter to cheer
> Troubled hearts with light
> Ever commending the way to life felicitous
> The vehicle of true being
> The excellent virtuous man
> The ground of becoming
> Formed in subtle sign
> This *Babad Jaka Tingkir* is composed
> That it be a talisman [*pusaka*]⁴

This single, seemingly abstruse stanza is highly significant. Indeed, the reader who attends carefully to this poetic preface will be provided clues that can inform the reception and understanding of all that is to follow.

The language of this stanza is absurdly difficult. This would not discourage its nineteenth-century Javanese audience, however.⁵ A display

4. [Dhangdhanggula] Nihan déning ngulun manulad sri / ring sarkara mamrih mamardawa / tyas wigena panjutané / juwet silarjèng tuwuh / wahananing kahanan jati / sujana paramarta / witaning tumuwuh / winangun ingkang sasmita / ginupita kang srat Babat Jaka Tingkir / malar dadya pusaka (*BJT* I:1).
5. By "audience" in the nineteenth-century context of Central Java, I mean both the reader/reciter of the script and those who would listen to that melodically intoned performance. In order to remind my reader of the performative, aural nature of the Javanese manuscript tradition, I sometimes use the words "reader" and "audience" interchangeably, and sometimes compound them as "reader/audience."

of linguistic obscurity and ambiguity is conventional for the opening stanzas (or *manggala*) of Javanese poetic texts. The audience would not expect a determinative discursive understanding of the stanza. Instead, they would know to expect a rather different kind of sense from such poetic prefaces. The prefaces were composed to set the mood of the poem and to initiate textual clues that would direct the readers' reception of the text that would follow.[6] In short, the *manggala* provides the audience a sense of what to expect from the text they are about to hear. And, to a literate nineteenth-century audience/reader,[7] this single stanza invites a remarkable array of expectations.

Let us begin with an analysis of the language of the *manggala,* language that I have characterized as absurdly difficult. Not merely a function of the abundance of archaic Kawi words, the difficulty of this language is more a product of its linguistic ambiguity, a deliberate ambiguity that would actively and purposively resist ordinary discursive sense. How, then, does the poet generate this artful ambiguity of language?

The stanza is composed largely of a series of paratactic nominal clauses. In ordinary spoken and written Javanese discourse, two successive paratactic nominal clauses tend to be apprehended (heard/read/parsed) as a "sentence," in which the second clause is apparently predicative of the first. Indeed, it is that apprehension of predication itself that produces the semantic closure following the second nominal clause (the "predicate"), thereby constructing the "sentence." For example, an ordinary reading of lines five and six of the *manggala* would seem to be: "The vehicle (or meaning) of true being [is] the excellent virtuous man" (*Wahananing kahanan jati / sujana paramarta*). If we stop here, we have what appears a "normal sentence." However, when we proceed to line seven, "The ground of becoming," the apparent closure of the presumed preceding sentence is reopened. With the apprehension of this succeeding clause, we then re-apprehend the clause that preceded it, and it seems that: "The excellent virtuous man [is] the ground of becoming" (*Sujana paramarta / witaning tumuwuh*). And again with lines eight and nine: "The ground of becoming

6. Many nineteenth-century *manggala* contain the acrostic signatures of their writers; some contain apologies from their writers as well. Dating in chronogram was another prominent feature in these prefatory lines.
7. As I discussed above in the Introduction, in the context of nineteenth-century literary practice, the *literate* audience might include "illiterate" but practiced and attentive listeners to recitations of the texts.

[is] formed in subtle sign . . . [and so is] *Babad Jaka Tingkir"* (*Witaning tumuwuh / winangun ingkang sasmita / ginupita kang srat Babat Jaka Tingkir*).

The absence of the copula in Javanese language lends itself to such slippage of predication.[8] In works of *macapat* poetry, this linguistic feature of Javanese is generative of a form of syntactic play or conceit that is difficult to render in English. I have borrowed the term *plèsèdan* to name this device. The word *plèsèdan* (from *plèsèd*, "to slip") translates both as "playful or musical slippage" and as "wordplay." In *plèsèdan* a single clause (or sometimes a single word) shifts its reference in a slip that causes it to be read (or heard) in two directions at once.[9] Through this slippage the more ordinary discursive structure of the closed sentence, in which one set of linguistic units seems clearly to predicate or complement another, is undone. Accomplished writers in traditional Java employed this device to maximum poetic effect, repeatedly tripping up expectations of semantic closure, thereby intensifying the potentially multivalent senses of the language that they wrote.[10]

8. The Malay languages share this characteristic with Arabic. For an interesting discussion of the difficulties and confusions this linguistic feature posed to the Islamic-Malay metaphysical discourse on the abstract concept of Being, see Syed Muhammad Naguib al-Attas, *The Mysticism of Hamzah Fansuri* (Kuala Lumpur: University of Malaya Press, 1970), pp. 147–75.

Interestingly, the word *wujûd*, which was adapted to mean the abstract concept of Being in Arabic and which was then adopted by Malay writers and translators of philosophical works to mean the same thing in the Malay language[s], has come to mean something quite different in modern Indonesian and Javanese usage. The third edition of Echols and Shadily, *An Indonesian-English Dictionary* (Ithaca, N.Y.: Cornell University Press, 1989), defines *wujud*: "shape into which s.t. has been formed" and *berwujud*: "(1) have the shape of . . . (2) concrete, tangible."

9. This poetic device, sometimes reminiscent of the *kakekotoba* of classical Japanese poetry, frequently involves the use of a single set of "pivot words" to mean two things at once or to parse in two different ways at once. In this usage, the "object" of one clause forms (or may form) the "subject" of the next, whose "object" may in turn be "subject" to what follows. An example of the device thus worked would be: "saksana dèn-timbali // Jeng Pangéran Siti Jenar nèng kuwunya / kèrit ing duta prapti / salebeting pura / sampun lenggah satata . . ." [Straightaway summoned they // His Highness Prince Siti Jenar from his encampment / Conducted by the messenger arrived / Inside the palace he / Was seated properly . . .] (*BJT* XIX:4–5).

10. Alton Becker has drawn my attention to similar conceits of shifting reference in Shakespeare's sonnets. For an intricate discussion of the poetic working of such conceits, see Stephen Booth's preface to his edition of *Shakespeare's Sonnets* (New Haven:

The effect of this device upon readers is vertiginous, producing in them an almost visceral sense of slippage. With their expectations repeatedly tripped up, readers experience the far from unpleasant sensation of being swept along on a current of language. To make ordinary discursive sense requires settled determination of predication. Since at these poetic moments of shifting reference that determination is undecidable, the issue of fixed discursive meaning waxes irrelevant and sense grows more sensuous. The audience loosens the desire for ordinary discursive sense, and this effort allows the generation of other senses, other significant pleasures. Enjoying the indetermination of predication, readers may be drawn into a more associative flow of language that can carry them away from the constricting moorings of ordinary discourse, toward the generation of new meanings.[11] I do not mean thus to suggest that such passages are nonsense: sense remains, but is transformed to become more sensuous, more associative.

What then is the sense—or what might be the senses—of this opening stanza of *Babad Jaka Tingkir*? On first reading, the verse seems a rather straightforward declaration of authorial intention: "Thus do I render the brilliant exemplar / In sweet meter to cheer . . ." The poet writes to cheer troubled hearts. What she or he writes is a history of Jaka Tingkir. And that history is written that it might become a magic talisman. We have a rationale for the work's composition, its title, and its intended efficacy.

First the title. The poet is forthright: *Babad Jaka Tingkir* is the title of the composition. The effect of this unequivocal pronouncement upon the audience is to evoke in readers' minds the well-known Tingkir tales sketched above. Consequently, the audience is prompted to receive (read and therefore interpret) what follows in light of a determined reference to those tales. Reception is conditioned by an expectation: "Ah yes, this is the history of Jaka Tingkir." Only much later will the audience realize that this expectation has been disappointed—in order that it might be deferred.

Yale University Press, 1977), pp. x–xvii. Consider also these lines from Sonnet 82: "And do so, love; yet when they have devised / What strainèd touches rhetoric can lend, / Thou truly fair wert truly sympathized / In true plain words by thy true-telling friend" (ibid., p. 72).

11. This feature of poetic language is perhaps most pronounced in the mystical texts of *suluk* literature, where it moves to realize in language the nonduality of Being—to say that which cannot be said.

The history opens: "Thus do I render the brilliant exemplar" (*Nihan déning ngulun manulad sri*). The poet's writing is a rendering—a transcription or re-presentation—of an exemplar, of something other than itself. That something other is called *sri*, "beauty, radiance, brilliance" or perhaps "the king." In the very opening line of the composition, the anonymous poet already disclaims full ownership of that which he or she writes; the poet's writing follows after a prior text that he or she calls *sri*. This work of poetic re-presentation is not, however, an act of simple mimesis.[12] The poet's rendering transforms *sri* "in sweet [that is, Dhang-dhanggula] meter to cheer / troubled heart[s] with light" (*ring sarkara mamrih mamardawa / tyas wigena panjutané*). The creative act, the poetic composition, is a transcription of a prior text into other words and another tune. And this act of translation across poetic texts is prompted by the desire to cheer troubled heart[s]. Insofar as this rationale for poetic composition is a commonplace in Javanese letters, its expression is conventional and is not meant as a revelation of a fancied "authentic authorial intention."[13] Rather, the convention signs the text as poetic—and in this case, specifically as poetry in the Dhangdhanggula meter. The literate nineteenth-century audience would have recognized the convention and have registered it as such. This is not to say that this stanza is without intentionality; but the inscribed intent, I would argue, goes far beyond the will to drive dull care away. The poet continues with the series of paratactic nominal clauses discussed above. Those clauses are laden with traces that suggest associations with texts of didactic and ontological literature: "the way to life felicitous, the excellent virtuous man, true being, the ground of becoming." What kind of history book have we here?

"This *Babad Jaka Tingkir* is composed / That it be a talisman [*pusaka*]" (*ginupita kang srat Babat Jaka Tingkir / malar dadya pusaka*). The verse closes providing the writing with a title and a genre (that is, of *babad*, or history) and projecting for it the hopeful status of *pusaka*.[14] A *pusaka* is a manifest thing endowed with supernatural powers, which powers may

---

12. For more on the aesthetics of Javanese "representation," see below, chapter 4.

13. Other conventional rationales for poetic composition were: in order to praise God/ the Prophet/the King, upon orders of the King. Many, if not most, poems open with no rationale.

14. I say "hopeful status" because of the subjunctive mode of the line: *malar* (in order that) *dadya* (the arealis form of *dadi*, "to become") *pusaka*. The text is proclaimed a potential *pusaka*. It can, perhaps, be finally realized as *pusaka* only by being read.

become available to persons, especially its owners or custodians, who come in contact with it.[15] Aside from a few naturally occurring *pusaka*, like the Kraton Surakarta's meteorite Kyai Pamor, *pusaka* attain their power by contagion. They were either created by persons of power or held by persons of power or held in contiguity with other objects of power. Persons of power, in turn, may become persons of even greater power by means of contact with *pusaka*, especially by prolonged or repeated contact. Weak persons, however, must be protected from contact with *pusaka* since the *pusaka*'s excess of power can harm or destroy the unworthy bearer. There must be a balance between the *pusaka* and its holder. *Pusaka* are hereditary property which may be passed down along family (or sometimes master-disciple) lineages as heirlooms. *Pusaka* both embody and promise the fulfillment of parental wishfulness for the success of their children and grandchildren.

Although many books (notably palace manuscripts) are considered *pusaka*, rarely does a poem declare its own promised *pusaka* status.[16] And even among those texts that do allude to their own supernatural efficacy,

15. Although usually it is a material object, such as a *keris* (Javanese dagger), musical instrument, cannon, or a *book*, a poetic text (such as the *Bedhaya Ketawang* song) or an activity (again, the *Bedhaya Ketawang* dance) may also be or become *pusaka*. The power that lives in *pusaka* is similar to the Sanskrit *sakti*. A number of Javanese terms denote such power in its various nuances; among these words are *sawab*, *angsar*, *kasektèn*, *sekti*, *mandi*. An object or person endowed with power is said to have *isi* (contents). Benedict Anderson eloquently describes and analyzes this power, for which he coins the usage *Power* with a capital "P," in his seminal article "The Idea of Power in Javanese Culture," in Claire Holt, ed., *Culture and Politics in Indonesia* (Ithaca: Cornell University Press, 1972), pp. 1–69.

16. Another history book which calls itself a *pusaka* (*pusaka pinustaka*) is the *Babad Tanah Jawi* redaction commissioned by Pakubuwana IV in 1788. See *Babad Tanah Jawi* (composed Surakarta, 1788; inscribed Surakarta, 1830, 1836, & 1869). MS. RP B 25c, B 25d & B 25b; SMP MN 189, 191, & 192. J. J. Ras quotes and translates the relevant stanzas from this *babad* in his "The Babad Tanah Jawi and Its Reliability: Questions of Content, Structure, and Function," in *Cultural Contact and Textual Interpretation*, ed., C. D. Grijns and S. O. Robson (Dordrecht, The Netherlands: Foris Publications, 1986), pp. 255 and 271–272. Another open declaration of textual potency is found in the patently magical *Kidung Rumeksa ing Wengi*, in which the poem incorporates a catalog of those whom it may benefit: "singa maca myang ngrungu / kang anurat tuwin nimpèni [whoever reads or hears / whoever writes or keeps]," as well as old-maids, madmen, crooks, and debtors (*Kidung Rumeksa ing Wengi* [composed s.l., s.a.] in *Serat Suluk: Jaman Karaton-dalem ing Surakarta* [inscribed Surakarta, 1870]. MS. SP 244 Na; SMP KS 481.1, p. 19).

the projection of power inscribed in *Babad Jaka Tingkir* is notable for its simple and forthright candor. The frank wishfulness written into the closing line of the poem's opening verse would have given the nineteenth-century audience pause to take special note. By declaring this *babad* a candidate *pusaka*, the poet projects the text's efficacy into the future. It is the poet's expressed intent and desire that *Babad Jaka Tingkir* become an enduring source of power for its future readers. And, as shall become apparent, that wishfulness also includes a vision of the kind of future that the poet would imagine for those anticipated readers of this prophetic history.

For the literate nineteenth-century reader/audience, the opening stanza of *Babad Jaka Tingkir* would have generated yet other deeply textured meanings. The production of those meanings in reading would have required of the audience considerable familiarity with the literary traditions and texts of the day. To be understood, the verse must be read intertextually. For the *manggala* of the Tingkir history is, in fact, a quotation: the slightly edited citation of another text's *manggala*. Compare the following stanza, the opening verse of a mid-nineteenth-century version of the late-eighteenth-century *Suluk Déwaruci*, with the *Babad Jaka Tingkir* stanza discussed above:

> Thus do I render the brilliant exemplar
> In sweet meter to cheer
> Troubled hearts with light
> Ever commending the way to life felicitous
> The vehicle of true being
> The excellent virtuous man
> The ground of creation
> Formed in subtle sign
> The Kawi-composed tale of Bimasuci
> Is given in translation[17]

Suluk Déwaruci, a Modern Javanese *macapat* version of the older Mid-

---

17. [Dhangdhanggula] Nihan doning ngulun manulat sri / ring sarkara mamrih mamardawa / tyas wigena panjutané / juwet silarjèng tuwuh / wahananing kahanan jati / sujana paramarta / witaning tumuwuh / winangun ingkang sasmita / ginupita ing kawi rèh Bimasuci / winangun lawan jarwa (R.Ng. Yasadipura I, *Suluk Déwaruci* [composed Surakarta, 1794 and early 19th century], in *Serat Suluk: Jaman Karaton-dalem ing Surakarta* [inscribed Surakarta, 1870]. MS. SP 244 Na; SMP KS 481.18, p. 198).

dle Javanese *Nawaruci,* was composed in the late eighteenth century by R.Ng. Yasadipura I (1729–1803). The oldest version of this *macapat* rendition that I have seen is dated 1794.[18] This older version, however, does not include the prefatory stanza cited above, the stanza which was later to be borrowed by the author of *Babad Jaka Tingkir.* That is because in 1794 the preface had yet to be written.

In 1803, Yasadipura I's son, Yasadipura II (later known as R.T. Sastranagara [1756–1844]), translated his newly deceased father's *Suluk Déwaruci.* The younger Yasadipura rendered that translation, which he titled *Serat Bima Suci,* in a peculiar Modern Javanese verse form known as *kawi miring,* or "crooked Kawi." Crooked Kawi verse is composed in Old Javanese *kakawin* meters; the language, however, is Modern Javanese, though with an abundant sprinkling of archaic Kawi words. The form is self-consciously "pseudoancient" or "pseudoclassic." The opening stanza of the younger Yasadipura's 1803 crooked Kawi *Bimasuci* is composed to introduce his work as an interpretation, seemingly but not actually, of another (even more) ancient Old Javanese original:

> Thus the reason that I adorn the spirit of the divine word
> In Great Meter is to cheer troubled hearts and too in everything
> Ever to commend the way to life felicitous the vehicle of true being
>   the excellent man
> Most virtuous in the world the ground of creation revealed in subtle sign to be interpreted[19]

Over the course of the following decades, this younger "ancient" *Bimasuci* gained legitimacy as a genuine text of antiquity, and the older "new" *Déwaruci* became derivative. By a curious twist, then, Yasadipura I's *maca-*

---

18. R.Ng. Yasadipura I, *Serat Déwaruci* (composed Surakarta, 1794), in [*Serat Déwaruci tuwin Raja Kapala*] (inscribed Surakarta, ca. early 19th century). MS. SP 271 Ra; SMP Ks 485.1, pp. 1–67.

19. Nihan karananira ndoning ulun rumancanèng sotanira kata diwya / ri lagu mageng mamrih mamardawa pragnya rikang manah lalu saniskara / juwet silarjèng tuwuh wahanané ring kaanan jati sujana nindita / paramartèng rat witaning tumuwuh winahya tékang sasmita winardia (R.Ng. Yasadipura II, *Bimasuci Sekar Ageng,* in Prijohoetomo, *Nawaruci: Inleiding Middel-Javaansche Prozatekst, Vertaling Vergeleken met de Bimasoetji in Oud-Javaansch Metrum* [Groningen: Wolters, 1934], p. 148). The translation is mine. See also R.M.Ng. Poerbatjaraka, *Kapustakan Djawi* (Jakarta: Djambatan, 1952), pp. 145–48.

pat Déwaruci came to be considered a translation of his own son's "ancient" *Bimasuci*. Hence many later versions and editions of Yasadipura I's *Déwaruci* (qua translation) are prefaced by a retranslation "back" into *macapat* of Yasadipura II's preface to his pseudoclassic crooked Kawi *Bimasuci* (translation). It is this retranslation which was then borrowed, with a few vital changes, by the author of *Babad Jaka Tingkir* to serve as the opening (or *manggala*) to his or her own original composition.

Having reflected upon the somewhat convoluted genealogy of the stanza, let us now consider what this particular act of citation might signify for the *babad* under investigation. In the first place, I should note again that intertextual citation, borrowing, and allusion are integral features of traditional Javanese poetic composition.[20] For the traditional poets, unconcerned with absolute authorial mastery over and hence ownership of their writing, the question of plagiarism was not an issue. To create good poetry involved, among other things, skillful borrowings from and intertextual weaving of a number of sources. The act of citation itself could be used as a literary device which would allude to "familial" relationships, and hence shared meaning, between the "parent" and the "derivative" texts. The literate audience, recognizing, even if only subliminally, at least some of these borrowings, would then read-in or hear-in the textual meaning alluded to by the citation.

What sense, then, might the literate nineteenth-century audience make of the opening of *Babad Jaka Tingkir* as a citation from the *Suluk Déwaruci*? To begin to address this issue, we must first consider the status of *suluk* as a category of writing in Java and then the perhaps surprising status of the classic Yasadipuran *Déwaruci* as a *suluk*. *Suluk*, or Islamic mystical songs, form a very important genre of writing in traditional Java. They are among the oldest extant texts of Modern Javanese poetry and, judging from the large number of manuscript witnesses, the popularity of these Islamic mystic songs survived well into the nineteenth century. The *suluk* (from the Arabic *sulûk*, "traversing the Sufi way")[21] are complex texts that write allusively and often symbolically of matters that concern

20. See my discussion of Javanese writing in the Introduction.
21. Dutch philologists have quite remarkably wished to deny or underplay the Arabic/Islamic etymology of the term *suluk*, while retaining its usage as a generic marker of "Javanese mystic songs." See, for example, Pigeaud, *Literature of Java*, 1:85, and G. W. J. Drewes, "Wat valt er te verstaan onder het Javaanse Woord *Suluk*?" *BKI* 148, no. 1 (1992):22–30.

Islamic mystical practice and belief. Among other things, *suluk* texts write of the nature of man (body and soul), often exploring the potential of human perfection in and through God. They frequently pose questions that concern the relationship between, and the paradoxical organic unity of, apparent binary opposites. Among the relationships treated in *suluk* are those between: inside and outside, body and soul, asceticism and activism, ritual practice and enlightenment, death and life, and ultimately the defining relationship between God and man.

Suluk Déwaruci, nowadays not usually considered a *suluk*, is among the most famous of Javanese writings, both among contemporary Javanese and scholars overseas. Indeed, the Déwaruci tale has been a favorite of the international Javanological community from at least the early twentieth century. It is a rare treatise on the refined heights and profound depths of Javanese culture, and especially of Javanese *wayang*, which does not mention this renowned tale of the Pandhawa Prince Bima's enlightenment. The international Javanological community has, however, resisted recognizing the Yasadipuran *Déwaruci* for what nineteenth-century Javanese literati took it as—that is, a *suluk*. Of the seven manuscript witnesses of this text in the Kraton Surakarta library, five are inscribed in *suluk* collections. The other two are paired with other self-consciously Islamic texts. That nineteenth-century inscriptions of this poem are so often inscribed *as* "Suluk," and appear so frequently in compilations of other *suluk*, clearly indicates that Yasadipura's *Déwaruci*, despite its lack of obvious Islamic content, was understood to be an Islamic mystical song by the palace scribes who compiled these volumes.[22] The resistance among Javanologists to register the *macapat Déwaruci* as *suluk*, in the face of this manuscript evidence, is of course due in part to the text's pre-Islamic genealogy, to its lack of obviously Islamic content, and to the absence of Arabic/Islamic terminology in its language.[23] Precisely because of these deviations from

---

22. See also Yasadipura's *Serat Cabolèk*, in which a Moslem scholar reads the *Déwaruci* as a work of *tasawwuf* after asserting that the Rama and Arjuna Wiwaha tales also merit such readings (Soebardi, *The Book of Cabolèk*, pp. 114–33).

23. Another determinative factor would have been the aversion to Islam and "things Islamic" which has characterized the tradition of Javanology from its nineteenth-century European beginnings. This aversion grows out of a tradition of anti-Islamic sentiment in Western Europe which dates from the crusades. For an outstanding treatment of the history of European apprehensions of Islam, see Edward Said's incisive *Orientalism* (London: Vintage, 1978). For a history of Dutch colonial apprehensions of

the "norm" of Islamic mystical textuality, however, it is even more notable that in the nineteenth-century palace scriptorium the classic *Déwaruci* nevertheless "belonged" to the community of *suluk*.

The effect, then, of opening the Tingkir history with this *Déwaruci* citation is deftly to situate *Babad Jaka Tingkir* within, or at least in relation to, the textual world of *suluk*. But what of the choice of this particular *suluk*? I would argue that the poet, artfully working through processes of intertextual allusion and association, chose the well-known *Déwaruci* text for quotation in order to indicate, subtly, the form of future empowerment that this Tingkir history would compose.

How might one characterize *Suluk Déwaruci*?[24] Yasadipura's poem on the enlightenment of the *wayang* hero Bima is composed as a treatise on gnosis and return; it is at the same time a meditation on knowledge and power. The hero of the *suluk*, the Pandhawa Prince Bima, braves and survives a series of horrible dangers finally to achieve union with God. That union is attained through knowledge gained by means of self-transcendence in the form of the hero's divine fusion with a tiny miniature of himself. Representing the hero's own "inner self," the miniature's name is Déwaruci.

Although the hero at first would prefer to remain suspended at the eternal moment of union, he learns that he must return to the phenomenal world in order to fulfill his duties as a warrior. Indeed, it is the apprehension of this lesson-of-return which comprises the gnosis itself. For in true gnosis, the distinction between inside and outside is collapsed in a gnostic transformation of all categories. The return, then, is to a point from which the hero has yet to depart—and to nowhere. A changed man, he remains "himself"; his "return" is to a changed world—and to one he never left. The change is in his knowledge; and that changed knowledge means, among other things, power to effect changes upon the temporal

---

Indonesian Islam, see Karel Steenbrink, *Dutch Colonialism and Indonesian Islam: Contacts and Conflicts, 1596–1950* (Amsterdam: Rodopi, 1993).

Interestingly, the text of this *macapat Déwaruci* was, however, later reinscribed as *Suluk Sèh Malaya*, with very few alterations besides a change of dramatis personae to a cast of Islamic saints, and a translation of its Javano-Indic religious and psychological terms into the standard Arabic terminology of Islamic mysticism. See *Suluk Sèh Malaya*, ed. Faqier 'Abd'l Haqq (Yogyakarta, Kulawarga Bratakesawa, 1959).

24. For an English synopsis and brief discussion of the *Suluk Déwaruci*, see Soebardi, *The Book of Cabolèk*, pp. 45–53.

realities of phenomenal existence. Through gnosis, the Pandhawa prince has attained the supernatural power which will sustain him in the real-world tasks that await him—notably his destiny as his brothers' champion in the coming apocalyptic fratricidal Bratayuda war. Within the logic of this numinous knowledge (this gnostic epistemology), there is nothing jarring about what might appear an unseemly mixture of material interest with spiritual enlightenment. For it is a logic that recognizes no absolutely "other-worldly" gnosis: in true gnosis the categories of "spiritual" and "material" collapse.

Indeed, an understanding of this logic lends intelligibility to the patent materiality of most traditional Javanese spiritual practices, practices which continue on into present-day Javano-Indonesian life. The dominant currents of spiritual practice in Java have (always?) been materially interested. By "material interest" I do not mean to imply the sinister self-interest or ulterior motive often conjured up by the Javanese word *pamrih*.[25] Rather, I mean to emphasize that, historically, spirituality in Java has not necessarily, or even ideally, meant a quietistic turning away from the world. Ideally, Javanese spiritual practices instead imply an activism, an interest—in a nonderogatory sense—in the transformation of the world. The quest for gnosis is a strategy for that knowledge (*ngèlmu*) whose transformation of all categories means (and hence is) power. *Suluk*, and perhaps especially *Suluk Déwaruci*, traverse in song the ways to that knowledge which is power. By means of literary quotation, *Babad Jaka Tingkir* would, it seems, partake of this power.

From a close reading of *Babad Jaka Tingkir's manggala* has come an awareness of several important features of the text. First, we know unequivocally that the text we read is a history—and a history of Jaka Tingkir, the first postclassical, Islamic king of interior Central Java. Secondly, we know that the poet who composed this history did so with the desire that it become *pusaka*. The text was written with the hope that its efficacy would be projected onto the future. Thirdly, we know that the poet, by means of intertextual allusion, has situated the text in the context of the *suluk* world of mystical Islam, thereby implying that its writing will

25. Nonetheless, many nights have been spent in meditation, fasting, and chanting, and many pilgrimages and graveside vigils have been performed *for*, say, a throne, an heir, a mate, a weapon, money, a winning lottery number, or even a passing exam score.

concern both spiritual enlightenment and worldly transformation. Finally, by tracing the textual genealogy of this opening stanza, this reading has demonstrated how this ostensible expression of authentic authorial intention, *as* a textualized product of citation and re-translation, itself decenters the original authority of authorship *without* thereby sacrificing its intentionality.

Postponing for the moment further consideration of the poem's internal dating (*BJT* I:2–3), which, as I suggested in chapter 1, gives rise to another interesting set of problems, let us continue this close reading of the poem's opening stanzas. The invocation, to Allah, the Prophet Muhammad, and the Prophet's associates (*BJT* I:3–8) is reminiscent of similar invocations introducing other Javanese Islamic texts that would have been familiar to a literate nineteenth-century audience—notably redactions of *Nawawi*, *Tajusalatin*, and *Ambiya* texts.[26] These other texts, which may be classed as didactic Islamic histories, treat the exploits and fortunes of Near Eastern Islamic saints and kings. The *Nawawi* and *Tajusalatin* texts are concerned with the ethics of statecraft, and especially of kingship.[27] That this *Babad Jaka Tingkir* redaction opens with an invocation that shares a common language with these well-known texts has the effect of further situating the poem within the textual world of self-conscious Islam while at the same time suggesting its quality as a textbook of political rule.[28]

26. See, for example, the invocations of: *Serat Nawawi* (composed Surakarta, 1789; inscribe Surakarta, ca. 1832/41). MS. SP 129 Na-A; SMP KS 527; *Serat Nawawi* (composed [Surakarta, 1817/18]; inscribed Surakarta, 1817/18). MS. SP 218 Na; SMP KS 525; *Serat Tajusalatin* (composed [Kartasura, 1726]; inscribed Surakarta, 1826). MS. SP 140 Ca; SMP KS 340; *Serat Tajusalatin* (composed [Kartasura, 1726]; inscribed [Surakarta, s.a.]). MS. SP uncataloged; SMP KS 341; *Serat Ambiya* (composed s.l., s.a.; inscribed Surakarta, 1862); MS. RP 1D; SMP MN 280.
27. The current ruler of the Kraton Surakarta, I.S.K.S. Pakubuwana XII, still holds that the *Tajusalatin* is the sole book that every Javanese ruler *must* read. Personal communication, G.P.H. Poespohadikoesomo (Putra-dalem I.S.K.S. Pakubuwana XII).
28. And yet although clearly related organically to the invocations prefacing these other self-consciously Islamic poems, the *babad* invocation distinguishes itself from them by its intensive focus upon images of order and propriety in Allah's creation. The terms for *order* are "tidy" (*urut, tata krama*) or "chilling" (*tartib*). Why this is the case is not entirely clear since, as we shall see, this *babad* seems to champion anti-order over order.

At the close of the invocation, in another semantically rich stanza, the poet provides the audience with further signs that, when read with care, draw the reader toward a better understanding of the poet's project, that is, to an apprehension of the form of history that he or she would compose:

> And so having finished
> Perfectly complete the invocation
> Rendered in intricate substruction
> In melodies entwined
> [Are] interruptions in [or "fragmentings/fragments of"] Java's story
> The History of Java
> The exploits
> Of all the kings rendered in song
> After the era Sri Kala Rajapepati
> Déwaraja then[29]

The stanza opens with a Malayo-Arabic formulaic marker for textual progression (*ammabakdu anapon*) that I translate as "And so." This phrase, a combination of the Malay/Arabic *ammaba'du* ("after that") and the Kawi *anapun* ("as regards"), is characteristic of traditional Islamic literature in the Malay world. It is especially characteristic of *suluk* literature.[30] Beginning with a signature formula of Malayo-Islamic literature, the stanza

29. [Dhangdhanggula] Ammabakdu anapon sawus ning / sampat paripurnaning pa-mudya / kang winarnèng panggalangé / lalagon kang ginelung / pamunggeling carita Jawi / babading tanah Jawa / lelampahanipun / para nata kang ginita / wusing jaman Sri Kala Rajapepati / Déwaraja semona (*BJT* I:9).

30. Javanese today mark such diction as Pasisir ("North Coast," that is, "coarse, non-Kraton, *santri*"). One Javanese scholar to whom I showed this verse claimed that the very presence of this phrase proved that this *BJT* text could not have been written in the Kraton. However interesting an observation, such language use is certainly not unknown to Kraton manuscripts. For example, such diction in relatively common in the Kraton Surakarta's substantial collection of *suluk* manuscripts, some of which were productions of the court—others, reproductions. What this observation does indicate is that, in the conventional image of what constitutes Kraton literature, there is no space for an Islamic/rural presence. As I discussed above in the Introduction, many late-twentieth-century Javanese have come to imagine "Court Poetry" or "traditional Java-nese literature" as consisting largely, if not exclusively, of the "Hindu-Buddhist Clas-sics."

then continues with a series of other clues that suggest to the reader other significant characteristics of this history that is beginning to unfold in entwined melodic tresses.

These textual clues are provided to be read, and their reading is not a simple matter: the language of the stanza is again a study in ambiguity. On the one hand: "Rendered in intricate substruction, in melodies entwined, [are] interruptions in Java's story." On the other: "Interruptions in Java's story, [are] *The History of Java*." First the poem itself comprises interruptions in, or fragments of (*pamunggeling*), "Java's story, *the* History of Java (*Babading Tanah Jawa*)." Next a *History of Java* is comprised of those interruptions or fragments. The reading depends upon the reader's parsing and can, I hold, be read both ways at once. As I noted above, at such textual moments, categorical choice of predication fades into insignificance.[31] Hence, over and above the frank admission of something interrupted or fragmented, the very ambiguity written into these lines resists the authority of a singular History of Java.

By the early nineteenth century there was, in the context of Surakartan court culture, a relatively circumscribed body[32] of texts called *Babad Tanah Jawa/Jawi* (*The History of Java*). This body of texts composed a constellation of versions of the dynastic history of the then-reigning house of Mataram and its antecedents, or putative antecedents. Although there is considerable variation among these versions, especially in their treatments of the histories of Mataram's antecedents, the texts share certain salient features which would have made them recognizable to nineteenth-century Javanese as constituting a relatively specified genre of texts about the past. It is to this body of texts I refer when I speak, for convenience's sake, of the "dominant" or "major" *babad* tradition.[33] I would like to

31. Preoccupation with determination of predication would be even less a concern for the audience at a recitation, where the text is received in a unidirectional aural flow.

32. By *body* I mean a constellation of texts (inscribed discourse) which were, or are, recognized as sharing common (or related) titles and common (or related) narrative contents. I thus distinguish *body* from *corpus*, as defined philologically by Timothy Behrend in his recent doctoral dissertation. Behrend establishes *corpus* as "the sum of all works derived directly or indirectly from the same original work" (Timothy Behrend, "The Serat Jatiswara," p. 6). By *body* here I mean a constellation of corpora.

33. Among the texts that comprise this "dominant tradition," I would include the thirty-one volume Balai Pustaka *Babad Tanah Jawi* edition (Batavia, 1939–41), the so-called "Meinsma edition" (The Hague: Nijhoff, 1941), as well as a number of manuscripts I have examined in Surakarta repositories, including: from the Kraton Sura-

emphasize, however, that it is only for convenience that I refer to this constellation of texts as "*the* dominant historical tradition"; for within this constellation, the textual variants are many and significant.[34]

If it may be granted that the early-nineteenth-century Surakartans had some sense of a major *babad* tradition, that sense was developed from shared exposure to and experience of the constellation of *Babad Tanah Jawi* texts then in public circulation. Over the course of the later nineteenth and the twentieth centuries, Dutch and Indies scholarship—to say nothing of the effects of the introduction of print technology—further codified and circumscribed the meaning of the modifier "major tradition" when applied to the term "Javanese historical literature." By the middle of the twentieth century it had become commonplace to talk of "*The Major Babad Tanah Jawi*" in contradistinction to the "minor *babads*" when referring to variant texts in the *Babad Tanah Jawi* corpora. What came to be known as *The Major Babad* developed from a variant apparently codified at the Kraton Surakarta in the years between 1788 and 1836. Yasadipura I is credited with the codification (that is, this particular literary form) of the poem. The manuscript which has come to be considered the definitive version of this *Major Babad* is an 1836 recension/copy which was made in or about the Surakarta Palace for export to the Netherlands under the supervision of the influential Indo-European scholar-translator C. F. Winter Sr.[35] In 1939, a little over a century after its production for export, the text of that manuscript was returned to Java in published form by the Nether-

---

karta: SMP Nos. KS 21 (SP 190 Na), KS 22 (SP 200 Na-A), KS 24 (SP 182 Ca), KS 24A (SP uncataloged), KS 25 (SP 200 Na-B), KS 29B (SP uncataloged); from the Mangkunagaran: SMP Nos. MN 169–71 (RP B 97a, B 99, & B 97b), MN 184 (RP B 100), MN 187 (RP B 4b), MN 189 (RP B 25c), MN 191 (RP B 25d), MN 192 (RP B 25b), MN 193 (RP B 31), MN 268 (RP B 24b); and from the Museum Radyapustaka, SMP Nos. Rp 13 (carik 140) and Rp 20A (uncataloged: D 82).

34. Although a detailed study of how (and what) the variations *within* the dominant tradition do/did signify has yet to be performed, an interesting short article by Anthony Day is a fine beginning to such an investigation (Day, "*Babad Kandha, Babad Kraton*, and Variation in Modern Javanese Literature," pp. 433–50). A complete study of variation within that tradition—on the lines, for example, of Timothy Behrend's recent work on the much more limited *Jatiswara* corpus—would comprise an investigation of truly massive proportions.

35. This eighteen-volume manuscript now comprises Cod. LOr 1786 in the Leiden University library. For a description of the artifact, see Theodore G. Th. Pigeaud, *Literature of Java*, 2:25.

lands Indies publishing house, Balai Pustaka, in thirty-one small volumes for the edification of the Javanese reading public.[36] In his inaugural address as professor of Javanese at the University of Leiden in 1985, J. J. Ras discussed at some length the genealogy of this text, which he calls "the official chronicle of the kingdom of Mataram."[37] For a version to be "official" implies the authorization of an "officiating" agent. The final agent, in this case, is not the Javanese king or kingdom, but Dutch-Indies Javanology culminating in Professor Ras.

The constellation of texts which I characterize as "the dominant Javanese historical tradition," although something less than an official chronicle of the kingdom, is nonetheless bound genealogically to the house of Mataram. Written as narrative histories that extend through linear time and across universal space, these *babad* organize their tellings of the distant, and not so distant, past into teleological (and even prophetic) trajectories that project purposefully forward along blood lines which are to culminate in the persons of the Mataram dynasts. The tellings differ, the trajectories enjoy variant curves, but all move in linear narrative toward the generation of this particular family. The histories that these texts of the dominant tradition construct of the more distant past tend to cast their genealogical nets as widely as possible, bringing all significant remembrances of the past into affinal relation to the rulers of Mataram. A number of these *babad* open with genealogical listings tracing the Mataram kings' lineage back to the Prophet Muhammad by the right branch and to the Hindu god Bathara Guru (Shiva) by the left branch—both branches proceeding ultimately from Adam, and hence Allah. Genealogical bonds linking Mataram's patrilineage to the Majapahit royal family are carefully drawn in these histories. Tales of the Demak dynasts and the house of Pajang are juxtaposed and related to tales of the rustic antecedents of the Mataram rulers. The saints (*wali*) who conveyed Islam to Java are brought into direct relation to the Mataram lineage, notably in the special relationship obtaining between Sunan Kalijaga and the scions of Mataram.

Stylistically, the texts of the dominant tradition are recognizable in kind.[38] Their style is marked by a mode of narrative in which everything

36. *Babad Tanah Jawi*, 31 vols. (Batavia, 1939–41).
37. J. J. Ras, "The Genesis of the Babad Tanah Jawi," *BKI* 143, nos. 2–3 (1987):343–56.
38. In terms of their language, the *Babad Tanah Jawi* texts tend to be relatively simple and straightforward. Indeed, in the *Javaansche Zamenspraken* compiled by the re-

and everyone is presented in turn along (sometimes parallel) lines of even linear progression. The narratives move, albeit poetically and variously, in the register of the chronicle. Within that linear narrative framework, the presentation of persons and events occurs under the aspect of their relations to the house of Mataram. Though the nature of the relationships may differ from variant to variant (telling to telling), Mataram blood genealogy remains the organizing principle for all the tellings. It is that organizing principle which, in the earlier sections of the dominant tradition, sews a pastiche of tales of the Javanese past together into the linear narrative of a dynastic chronicle.

An Alternative Structure: Fragments, Frames, and Episodes

Babad Jaka Tingkir is composed of "interruptions in (or fragments of) Java's story" (*pamunggeling carita Jawi*). How then might we characterize the relation of this unique Tingkir history to the more dominant tradition? Stylistically and organizationally (that is, structurally), *Babad Jaka Tingkir* distinguishes itself from (or, perhaps, in opposition to) the major tradition as I have described it here. Instead of recounting the past in the linear narrative form that characterizes the dynastic chronicle tradition, this *babad* interrupts that tradition to compose, instead, a structure of episodic fragments. These episodes tell the stories of six curious characters on the margins of the past: the exiled Jaka Prabangkara, the invisible Jaka Karèwèd, the recalcitrant Demak mosque, the would-be martyrs Sèh Siti Jenar and Sèh Malang Sumirang, and finally the murdered Ki Ageng Pengging—father of the *babad*'s invisible namesake and hero. The lines that bind these separate episodes together into a text are more thematic than blood ones.[39] The text, at times almost novelistic in tone, grows out

---

nowned nineteenth-century Indo-European Javanologist C. F. Winter, *Serat Babad Tanah Jawi* is recommended as the most appropriate text for one just beginning to learn to read Javanese (*Javaansche Zamenspraken* [Amsterdam: Muller, 1882], 1:59). It should be noted that *Zamenspraken*, vol. 1, was published first in 1848, a good quarter of a century prior to the first publication of the simplified Meinsma prose *Babad Tanah Jawi* in 1874.

This relative linguistic simplicity alone distinguishes the texts of the dominant *babad* tradition from the relatively difficult text of the *Babad Jaka Tingkir* presented here.

39. See for instance *BJT* II:14, where the poet (*kang amarna*) uncharacteristically speaks

of a thematics of marginality and undecidability. And yet, like the "dominant *babad* tradition," this *Babad Jaka Tingkir* recension is also genealogical—without reading the past in the narrow terms of the biological generation of the Mataram dynasty. For it is indeed, as implied by its title, a genealogy of "Jaka Tingkir."

Although it is these episodic fragments that compose the heart of the text, they are framed by narrative snatches which do relate directly to the blood antecedents of the ever invisible Jaka Tingkir. The heroic exploits of the protagonist's grandfather (Handayaningrat) and the mythic beauty of his grandmother form the first narrative account in the *babad* (*BJT* I:25–II:21). Then comes the lengthy "digression" that composes the poem's first two episodes: the Jaka Prabangkara and Jaka Karèwèd stories (*BJT* III:18–XII:41). That "digression" closes calling attention both to itself *as a* fragment and to the "story at hand":

> Let now be told in turn
> The tale interrupted by poetry [the poet]
> Of Pajang-Pengging sweet[40]

Following this reminder of what the *babad* is about comes a terse account that discloses the central position held by Jaka Tingkir's father (Kebo Kenonga) in genealogical relationship to the foremost *wali* and to the Demak dynasts (*BJT* XIII:1–25). Next comes the third episode: the lengthy exposition of the construction of the sacred mosque of Demak and the activities of the *wali* (*BJT* XIII:25–XVII:6). Separating this episode from the Siti Jenar tale that follows it as the fourth episode (*BJT* XVIII: 15–XXI:5) is a return to, and progression in, the story of Jaka Tingkir's father—now named Ki Ageng Pengging. Again it is the Ki Ageng Pengging narrative (*BJT* XXI:5–XXII:24) which marks the boundary between the Siti Jenar (fourth) and Malang Sumirang (fifth) episodes. With the disappearance of Malang Sumirang (*BJT* XXIV:22), the Ki Ageng Peng-

---

in direct authorial voice to ask forgiveness (*minta aksama*) for having forgotten the precise birth order of Brawijaya's progeny. The sense is that *babad* should get that kind of genealogical data right. The apology here, however, is a tongue-in-cheek one. For this poet is not really interested in the "right order" which comprises proper narrative sequence in "ordinary" *babad*. Written by an enraptured heart (*brongta*), this poem rather signals a different "order" of historical imagination.

40. [Mas Kumambang] gantya kawuwusa / ingkang pinunggel ing kawi / ing Pajang Pengging sarkara (*BJT* XII:41).

ging narrative is resumed, to continue on until the *babad*'s abrupt end. These narrative snatches, as frames, act both to distinguish and to highlight the episodes: they form the seams that bind the episodes into a coherent structure at the same time that they separate them one from the other.

It is these frames that repeatedly remind the audience to read as genealogy the fragments that compose the *babad*, to read these fragments in light of the coming emergence of Jaka Tingkir. The narrative frames act to highlight and organize; and yet it is the episodic fragments that prevail in the text. Together, the frames and fragments generate the distinctive construction of the past through which *Babad Jaka Tingkir* bequeaths to Javanese historiography a novel, alternative form of genealogy. And both histories (the dominant and this alternative) are genealogies of power.

The dominant *babad* tradition acts to inscribe the genealogy of the political power of a particular biological family. Although other powers, such as the power of Islam, are recognized by this tradition, those powers tend to be treated, or made sense of, in terms of that family. Power, in the dominant tradition, progresses down *the* royal family, through time, in more or (oftentimes) less orderly dynastic succession. The narratives that belong to this dynastic tradition focus on the wars, intrigues, and romances that contribute to the propagation of that family's power. This *Babad Jaka Tingkir* redaction is a significantly different form of narrative.[41] Written sometime between 1829 and 1849, that is, around the time that any truly significant political power passed from the grasp of the Mataram house, this *babad* dwells episodically on other powers which arise—repeatedly—at the edges or margins of society. The characters who embody these marginalized powers tend not to succeed to a more mainstream power. Rather, they vanish—serially and variously over the course of the structured series of episodic fragments that compose the *babad*. *Babad Jaka Tingkir* is a tissue of fragments bound together by a thematics of marginality and exclusion.

This presentation of the past in the form of discrete fragments valorizing marginality counters—and perhaps even subverts—the dominant tradition. Resuming our close reading of the opening stanzas of the *babad*, consider for example the lines: "Now to be related here / Is an interrupted

41. When the author of the Tingkir history does touch briefly on the story of the Mataram ancestor, Prince Bondhan Kejawèn, it is stated explictly that his exploits are *not* to be rendered at length (*BJT* III:4).

tale" (*kuneng kang winuwus / ing carita kang cinegat* [*BJT* I:12]). These lines act to cut off the introduction of Brawijaya V and the catalog of his ancestry. On the immediate level of the line, then, the "interrupted tale" refers to the Brawijaya story. On the deeper, structural level of the text, however, the "interrupted tale" signifies the dominant narrative tradition of Javanese historiography itself. And the agent of interruption is none other than the alternative telling of the past in fragments that composes *Babad Jaka Tingkir*. Consider the word *cinegat* (*cegat* + *in* infix) which I render "interrupted." The primary meaning of the verb *cegat* is "to ambush" or "to obstruct." In terms of dialogic discourse, *cegat* means "to interrupt" in a very special way, that is, to take up from someone else's words and continue them—often in a different direction. In narrative terms, an already existent other telling is taken up and transformed— perhaps subverted—into some other telling. *Cegat* is also a carpentry term, meaning to finish off a half-drilled hole in a board by boring in from the other side. If this meaning is associated with *cegat's* place in the realm of discourse, then to interrupt a tale could mean to finish off a telling (half-told) by telling "the other side of the story." Granted, these connotative musings are speculative, but the speculation is informed by the thematics of marginality and the stylistics of interruption that structure the particular telling of the past inscribed in this *Babad Jaka Tingkir*.

The Construction of Futures: Stage-settings and Prophecy

Returning to the stanza cited in full above (*BJT* I:9), let us now turn to the pivotal line: "Rendered in intricate substruction" (*kang winarnèng panggalangé*). Owing to the slip of *plèsèdan*, this line may be predicative either of the invocation before it or of the "interruptions" after it—or, perhaps, of both. And the reading of the line is further complicated by the semantic multivalence of the word *panggalang*.[42] With my translation of *pang-*

---

42. In modern Javanese, *galang* denotes a kind of scaffolding, or infrastructure, upon which something else is constructed (Poerwadarminta, *Baoesastra Djawa*, p. 128). In nineteenth-century Surakarta, *galang*, as a "Kawi" word, enjoyed a range of other meanings. The *Kawi-Javaansch Woordenboek*, compiled by C. F. Winter Sr. in consultation with R.Ng. Ronggawarsita, lists the following definitions for the root *galang*: *panggunggung* ("praise"), *palang* ("obstacle"), *pagol* ("hindrance"), *ceplok* ("circle-shaped mark"), *sarasah* ("veneer, plating"), *cethak* ("palate"), *papan* ("board"), *cithak*

galang as "intricate substruction," only two of its possible meanings are rendered—with semantic primacy according the meaning approximated by the curious English word *substruction*. By *substruction* is meant a framework or scaffolding upon which some structure, either concrete or abstract, is built. This translation choice was influenced by a consideration of the semantics of *panggalang* elsewhere in the poem. The word appears only three times in the *babad*. In the other two cases the word also refers to writing: the *suluk* which Malang Sumirang composed on the funeral pyre is twice called a *panggalang*—of self, or person (*BJT* XXIV:4 & 9).

"Rendered in intricate substruction [*panggalangé*] / In melodies entwined / Are interruptions in Java's story." The dominant reference of the word *panggalang* in this stanza is, I think, those interruptions that follow, the interruptions or fragments that compose the text of *Babad Jaka Tingkir*. These lines, thus read, underwrite the sense that this fragmented *babad* is a framework upon which, or out of which, a text of the future is to be written. The *babad*, in its capacity as a candidate *pusaka*, looks forward to something other than itself, something which is yet to be constructed upon a scaffolding, a kind of context, that the text itself is working to generate.

In this verse that concludes the poem's invocation is still another nod to the future. And this gesture is written in the register of prophecy. The stanza ends: "After the era of Sri Kala Rajapepati / Déwaraja then" (*wusing jaman Sri Kala Rajapepati / Déwaraja semona*). On first reading, it appears that "Sri Kala Rajapepati Déwaraja" is the proper name of a king. Kings' names are frequently prefaced by the honorific *Sri* ("The Illustrious"). The name could be translated as "The Illustrious Mighty-dangerous Lord of Kings, God-king." Who, then, was this Sri Kala Rajapepati, this mighty god-king? There is no king so named in Western reconstructions of the Javanese past. Nor does a survey of dynastic lists compiled from the dominant traditions of Javanese historical writing yield any king by that name. This is because the name Sri Kala Rajapepati Déwaraja refers to a dynastic period rather than to a person. For within the framework of a very specific Javanese textual tradition, "Sri Kala Rajapati Déwaraja" (the *pe* of

---

("die, mold"), *pathok* ("wooden stake; immobile; rule, law"), *watang* ("pole"), *anggung-gung* ("to praise"), and *renggan* ("elaboration, decoration"); *Kawi-Javaansch Woordenboek*, p. 524. The prefix (*pang-*) with the suffix *-é* work to transform the root substantive *galang* into a more complicated linguistic item, denoting the process of production of the *galang*.

pepati is an optional syllabic reduplication) designates "the illustrious era" (*sri kala*) of kingship that characterized the hegemony of Majapahit.

The textual tradition in which this proper name is found is the well-known genre of *Jangka Jayabaya* texts. Texts of this genre turn on historical periodization, political symbology, and, especially, prophecy. The schema for the periodization of Javanese history presented by these texts divides historical time into three major eras (*kala*), each consisting of 700 years. Thus these texts set the duration of Javanese historical time at 2,100 years, beginning with the (second) peopling of Java from the Sultanate of Rum (Turkey) in the "Saka" year one and ending with the Day of Judgment in Saka 2100. The *Jayabaya* texts relate the political history of Java—both for the past and the future—in the form of a cryptic symbology (*pralambang*) that invites active interpretation. These historical prophecies have been in popular circulation from at least the early nineteenth century, when one version of the *Jangka Jayabaya* was incorporated into the encyclopaedic 1815 redaction of the *Serat Centhini*.[43] Among the most widely circulating *Jayabaya* texts is the mid-nineteenth-century version that Ronggawarsita wove into his massive prose history of Java, *Pusta-karaja Purwa-Madya-Wasana*.[44]

How, then, does the name "Sri Kala Rajapati Déwaraja" work to designate Majapahit kingship in these *Jayabaya* texts? In Ronggawarsita's mid-nineteenth-century redaction of the prophecy, the ancient Hindu King Jayabaya reveals the future of Java as it had been previously taught him by Maulana Ali Samsujèn, a wandering Moslem saint from Turkey. Jayabaya reveals this prophecy to his bewildered son as he justifies to him the

43. *Cabolang-Centhini* (cantos 256–57) in *Serat Centhini Latin*, ed. Kamajaya (Yogya-karta: Yayasan Centhini Yogyakarta, 1986–88), 3:342–46 and 4:1–4; see also Suma-hatmaka, *Ringkasan Centini* (*Suluk Tambanglaras*) (Jakarta: Balai Pustaka, 1981), pp. 34–35 and 177–78.

44. R.Ng. Ronggawarsita, *Serat Pustakaraja Madya: Jayabaya* (composed Surakarta, mid-19th century; inscribed Surakarta, mid to late 19th century). MS. RP D-128; SMP MN 15, pp. 456 verso–476 verso. See also *Serat Pranitiwakya tuwin Jangkanipun Prabu Jayabaya* (composed Surakarta, mid-19th century; inscribed by R.M.Ng. Sumahat-maka in Surakarta, 1925). MS. RP A-101; SMP MN 409, 1:1–42; *Serat Pranitiwakya tuwin Jangkanipun Prabu Jayabaya* (composed Surakarta, mid to late 19th century; inscribed Mangkunagaran, Surakarta, s.a.). MS. RP B 177; SMP MN 409B, pp. 1–40; and Andjar Any, *Rahasia Ramalan: Jayabaya Ranggawarsita dan Sabdapalon* (Sema-rang: Aneka, 1979). Note that in the Ronggawarsita versions of the *Jayabaya* prophecy Déwaraja is generally rendered as Déwanata.

summary execution of that same son's father-in-law. The father-in-law had been a mountain hermit who himself had studied with Samsujèn. Jayabaya stabbed the hermit to death just as the hermit had presented him with a feast. The audacious hermit, Jayabaya teaches his son, earned the death sentence by the menu he served: a feast consisting of eight courses, seven dishes—plus one in the form of the serving girl. These eight dishes symbolized the eight eras of history yet to come. Serving the dishes to an already prescient king meant treason, an overstepping of the bounds of prophetic revelation. In a cryptic (second-level symbolic) explanation, Jayabaya interprets the symbology of the second of the eight dishes to his son:

> The single cup of *juwadah* porridge is the age of Andrapati Kala-wi[sésa] ["The Age of Power"]. Its kingship, I symbolize as "Sri Kala Rajapati-déwanata" [= déwaraja]. Its capital will be north of Mame-nang, and it will be called Majapahit. The produce of the earth will be called coin. It will last but eighty years till its destruction.[45]

This cryptic explanation then invites, or requires, further interpretation. C. F. Winter, the eminent Javanologist who supervised the production of the Major Babad and worked with the Ronggarwarsitas, interpreted King Jayabaya's explanation of the "name" of kingship in Majapahit as follows: since *rajapati* is "foremost among kings" and *déwanata* is "divine king," Jayabaya means that the kings of Majapahit were accorded respect to such an extent that they were just like gods descended to earth.[46] Other interpretations would be possible: in ordinary discourse *rajapati* means "man-slaughter" or "murder."

Should the audience of *Babad Jaka Tingkir* have missed the allusion to the Jayabaya tradition inscribed in the choice of this proper name for Majapahit's kingship, the poet repeats the allusion a few stanzas further on. Indicating the change in era that marked Majapahit's fall to Demak, the poet writes:

> "Gone, Vanished without a trace are the Works of the World"
> [Saka 1400 = A.D. 1478]
> At that time the era was changed

45. Ronggawarsita, *Serat Pustakaraja Madya: Jayabaya*. MS. RP D-128; SMP MN 15, pp. 469 recto–469 verso.
46. C. F. Winter Sr., *Javaansche Zamenspraken* (Amsterdam: Muller, 1858), 2:257.

To the Age of Dark Oppression [Kalawisaya], the world
Of Beautiful Hearts [Adiyati][47]

In the Jayabaya tradition, the "Age of Dark Oppression," or the Kalawisaya, is the last one-hundred-year subperiod (solar 1301–1400 / lunar [=
Saka?] 1340–1442) of the Kaliyuga, the middle period of historical time
(solar 701–1400). According to the Jayabaya *pralambang*, the world of
"Beautiful Hearts," or Adiyati, pointing toward the Islamic saints (*wali*),
designates political authority in Demak.[48] By choosing these proper names
to designate time and kingship, the poet composes intertextual allusions
which, by association, situate this *Babad Jaka Tingkir* in the realm of
prophecy. It should be emphasized, however, that these allusions, though
definitive, remain obscure. Even in the nineteenth century, only literary
adepts would have recognized the allusions inscribed with these names.[49]

The poet who composed the Tingkir history sprinkled his or her writing with a number of clues, some more obscure than others, to construct
the text of the *babad* as a kind of literary puzzle. The textual puzzle is to
some extent an esoteric one, written, on certain of its levels, for an audience of some sophistication. To solve the puzzle, which means to "read
in a certain way" the text, is to recognize and work through (at least some
of) the clues. Such a reading involves a recognition of how the poetry
turns in part upon the subtle interplay between concealment and revelation, for which the word is *semu*.

On Semu *and Vanishing*

The word *semu*, in its many usages, indicates the merely glimpsed perceptible dimension of the concealed. *Semu* is a subtle sign which points to
something other than that which it is—but not necessarily to something
else. For example, one's words may "appear to be tinged with anger"
(*semu duka*). They are not angry words, but in (or behind) them one can

47. "[Dhangdhanggula] Sirna ilang pakartining bumi / duk semana sinalinan jaman /
Kalawisaya alamé / Ngadiyati puniku" (*BJT* I:19).
48. *Pranitiwakya tuwin Jangkanipun Prabu Jayabaya* (composed Surakarta, mid to late
19th century; inscribed Mangkunagaran, Surakarta, s.a.). MS. RP B 177; SMP MN
409B, pp. 1–3, 13–14, 28.
49. Just how obscure these references are is indicated by the "mistaken" inscription of
wisaya for *wisésa* in the late-nineteenth-century copy of the *Pustakaraja* text cited
above.

discern anger. A person may be said to "have *semu*" (*asemu*); that is, her countenance radiates a "subtle aura" (*semu*) which indicates hidden profundity—she is more than she seems. Persons of excellence, those who are "never lacking in subtlety" (*tan kuciwa ing semu*), can read from these glimpsed perceptible signs toward their "inside," toward an understanding of their (only partially) hidden truth. And these adepts are also versed in the art of production of these signs (*limpat ing rèh pasang semu*) for communication of and around the concealed (the said unsaid).

The ability to produce these signs that *at the same time* conceal and reveal meaning is a learned skill from a shared body of knowledge, or science. One's discourse is valued as sophisticated and refined precisely for the extent to which it (apparently) masks meaning. To speak well, therefore, is expressly *not* to say what one means. For it is only the fool or the ignorant who speaks or understands directly.[50] Subtle discourse makes sense by means of masks. *And* it is by the very nature of *semu* that what it conceals is never really hidden. Indeed, the reality of something *as* hidden is produced by means of its revelation in *semu*. That there is revelation implies concealment—and the concealment subsists under the aspect of the revelation. *Pasemon*, a nominal cognate of *semu*, can mean "parable, allegory" or "the hint of a symbol." That is, it is something which indicates something more than itself, something which invites a reading (interpretation) by consciousness participating in a common epistemological universe. A *pasemon* is a kind of epistemologically constructed "mask" which reveals insofar as it appears to conceal. *Pasemon* also means "the [human] face" or "facial expression." *Pasemon* is at the same time a mask and a clue presenting itself to be read—in a reading guided by a system of conventions which comprises the "science of *semu*." Writing with *semu* means spinning webs of meaning that mask sense in a manner that would draw readers into making, for themselves, the senses that the writer herself intends.

The author of *Babad Jaka Tingkir* was a master of *semu*. The narrative of

50. Or rather *imagines* that she or he speaks or understands directly. For, as a function of its system of language levels, all Javanese discourse points to something other than itself. That is, to speak *ngoko* ("low" Javanese) *means* not to speak *krama* ("high" Javanese) and vice versa. How this works in Javanese discourse is argued beautifully and at length by James Siegel in his book *Solo in the New Order* (Princeton: Princeton University Press, 1986), pp. 3–33 and passim.

this Tingkir history, this "interrupted tale," begins with a highly significant disappearance, a vanishing:

> Now to be related here
> Is an interrupted tale:
> With the Fall of Majapahit
> Was Brawijaya's vanishing
>
> Vanished from the mortal realm
> Surging up in lightning body
> He rose to the realm of Release
> Not by way of death
> True return consummate
> To the realm divinely pure
> In absolute perfection
> His Majesty Brawijaya
> Perfectly realized *Jatimurti* ["Reality Incarnate"][51]

It is not fortuitous that this history opens with the vanishing of one of its
leading characters. For, as we shall see, vanishing is to be a major theme of
the poem. Let us pause to reflect on this initial instance of vanishing in the
babad. This vanishing of Brawijaya is a vanishing that (in the tradition of
semu) indicates something which is other than itself, but without pointing to something else. Vanishing (the production of absence) is for Brawijaya the means by which he realizes full—indeed absolute—presence.

Called *Jatimurti* (Reality Incarnate), Brawijaya's vanishing is both absolutely real and perfectly corporeal: it is true return. The word *jatimurti* is a
compound comprised of two Sanskrit-derived words: *jati* and *murti*. *Jati*
denotes "truth, reality, original state of being, birth"; *murti* means "body,
incarnation, material form." Brawijaya perfectly realized *jatimurti*; he was
an adept at the material realization of the state of absolute divinity (*sampun putus patitis ing jatimurti*). The poet underwrites the materiality of
this realization by selecting the word *patitis* to designate the degree of the

---

51. [Dhangdhanggula] kuneng kang winuwus / ing carita kang cinegat / sabedhahé
nagari ing Majapahit / musnané Brawijaya // Lenyep sangking manusapadèki / apan
sumengka mangawak braja / minggah mring muksapadané / datan kalawan lampus /
paripurna waluya jati / ing jaman kasuciyan / kasampurnanipun / Sang aPrabu Brawijaya / sampun putus patitis ing jatimurti (*BJT* I:12–13).

king's perfect mastery; one of the dominant meanings of the root verbal form *titis* is "to incarnate." This sense of the essential materiality of Absolute Reality and of the potential realization of that Reality in man, a sense that reverberates through nineteenth-century Javanese Sufi *suluk*, lies at the heart of the mystical thought of this poem.[52]

Together with vanishing (and return), a thematic of the interplay between absence and presence is woven into the texture of this unique version of *Babad Jaka Tingkir*. In this regard, the most conspicuous absence (and hence presence) in this Tingkir history is the Jaka Tingkir for whom it was named. Written in the contexts of prophecy and *suluk*, and written from a vantage of exile, the paradox of this central absence works together with the poem's thematics of marginality to generate novel possibilities for the future of the Javanese past. The reading initiated in this chapter has only begun to tease out some of these possibilities. In the following chapters I shall explain in more detail how these future possibilities take shape in the episodic fragments from the margins of the Javanese past that *Babad Jaka Tingkir*'s author (composer and scribe) has bound into this work of prophetic history.

---

52. To more conservative Islamic theologians, including orthodox mystics, this strain of material nonduality, called *wujûdiyyah*, comprises heterodoxy. In seventeenth-century Aceh, the orthodox Moslem mystic Nûru'l-Dîn al-Rânîrî attacked what he considered the heterodox, pantheistic *wujûdiyyah* of Hamzah Fansurî (see Syed Muhammad Nguib al-Attas, *Rânîrî and the Wujûdiyyah of Seventeenth-Century Acheh* [Singapore: Malaysian Branch of the Royal Asiatic Society, 1966]). *Wujûdiyyah* mysticism was *not*, however, exclusive to the Sufism of the Malay world; the most sophisticated theoretician of *wujûdiyyah* thought was the eminent Spanish-born mystic Ibnul 'Arabî (1164–1240). For a thoughtful and detailed treatment of 'Arabî's *wujûdiyyah* mysticism, see A. E. Affifi, *The Mystical Philosophy of Muhyid Din-Ibnu Arabi* (Cambridge: Cambridge University Press, 1938). For more on the implications of the paradoxical materiality of the spiritual in the text of *Babad Jaka Tingkir*, see below, chapter 6.

CHAPTER 4

A QUESTION OF VISIBILITY:
WRITING HISTORY IN JAVA

✸

Writing history in nineteenth-century Java meant composing a past for the future. A masterful writer would compose such a history under the aspect of *semu*, artfully concealing that which he or she would reveal. The anonymous poet who composed *Babad Jaka Tingkir* by "interrupting" the *History of Java* reflected upon these conditions of writing as he or she wrote. The first two episodes of the Tingkir history concern two marginal and marginalized Javanese princes: Jaka Prabangkara and Jaka Karèwèd. Their stories, while constituting a lengthy digression from "the story at hand," are artfully constructed to highlight the problematic of visibility (textual representation) and invisibility (a kind of textual absence) in the historical writing of Java. But before turning to a reading of these particular episodes, let us first review the *babad* in its entirety in order better to understand its structure of fragmentation and its thematics of marginality and vanishing. This review will identify, and thereby highlight, the six episodic fragments featured in this unique historical text, while at the same time recalling the narrative frames that shape the history's potential meanings.

Review of the Babad: *Frames and Episodes*

Babad Jaka Tingkir, a text comprising some 6,913 lines of poetry, opens with an extended introductory section of 683 lines. Beginning with the poem's invocation, of which I spoke at length in the previous chapter, *Tingkir*'s "introduction" then opens into a narrative that treats the (absent, that is, anticipated) hero's grandparents, Handayaningrat and the First Born Queen, and his vanished great-grandfather Brawijaya V. Then, instead of continuing in the narrative mode of a dynastic chronicle—in this case, that of the house of Pengging—this "introduction" is followed by what I term "the first and second episodes": that is, a poetic lingering on the tales of Brawijaya's sons Jaka Prabangkara and Jaka Karèwèd. And linger the poet does, devoting 2,121 lines to the histories of these two obscure princes. The episodes that constitute these histories are conjoined within one frame and thus were written to be read in relation to each other.

The narrative style of the first two episodes, moving in the register of sometimes fantastic detail, contrasts significantly with the much more schematic narrative that came before them. At the same time, the surprising content of these initial episodes—surprising in that it does not concern the ancestors of royal Javanese of succeeding generations—reveals the "introduction" as something other than what it had seemed. What had appeared the introduction to a conventional dynastic chronicle is now revealed as a prefatory frame that will set off a very different kind of historical discourse. The frames and episodes work together dialectically to shape the reading of the text: the frames act to contextualize the episodes, while in turn the episodes inform the reading of the frames.

Before continuing our review of frames and episodes, let us consider the shadowy heroes of the first two episodes. Jaka Prabangkara and Jaka Karèwèd, obscure figures about whom the dominant traditions of history are nearly silent, are both "illegitimate"[1] and unacknowledged sons of

1. In royal Javanese usage, the concept of the legitimacy or illegitimacy of kingly offspring is a relative or, better, "gradated" one. The most "legitimate" and most highly ranked of royal children are those born of a queen. Although according to Islamic law the king could have as many as four queens, he would rarely take more than three for reasons that will become clear below. Since the eighteenth century, it has been the eldest son born of a queen who has been favored to succeed to the throne. The children born of a *priyantun-dalem* residing at court would be next in the order of legitimacy. The *priyantun-dalem* (often mistranslated "concubine") were secondary, sometimes legally married wives of the king. The king (often through the stand-in of his *keris*) would temporarily marry these royal mothers on the occasion of their confinement. After the child was born, the mother would likely be divorced in order that the marriage license might be passed on to another mother on the eve of her confinement. Divorce, however, did not mean abandonment, and as many as fifty-three *priyantun-dalem* at once could continue on in the Kraton as kingly wives (as in the case of Pakubuwana IX). The next order of children would be those born to *lelangen-dalem* (roughly "royal playthings") residing at court. Many of the *lelangen-dalem* were court dancers. Although these mothers were not necessarily legally married by the king, their children recognized by him, and they remained part of the royal household. The

Brawijaya V. The mothers of the two half-brothers are both women of the butcher-folk (*wong jagal*), a group whose menial and bloody profession relegated them to the lowest strata of society. Both mothers are abandoned by Brawijaya. Prabangkara is the issue of that last ruler of Majapahit's brief dalliance with a young widow who had been served up to the king for a tryst that took place outside the palace walls. Karèwèd's mother is a girl who had been brought into the palace expressly for the king's sexual pleasure. But it is finally *her* sexual rejection of the king that leads to her eventual banishment from court. Jaka Prabangkara and Jaka Karèwèd, the products of these unions between the sovereign and women from among the lowest of his subjects, are then of mixed blood. Marginal and marginalized princes, they are both hyper-royal and hyper-common.

The first episode presents, in some 1,390 lines of poetry, the story of Jaka Prabangkara, a commoner-prince born outside the palace walls. We know nothing of his childhood or of his humble mother's subsequent fate. We are told that the youth Prabangkara comes at some point to be received into royal service, to serve as a court painter to the royal father who would not recognize him. Noted at his father's palace for his superb art, Prabangkara falls into royal disfavor through his too explicit portraiture of the queen. The portrait in question is marked by the telltale ink drop which too perfectly matches the queen's intimately positioned mole. For this excess of visibility, the punishment is exile (vanishing). It is by the devious ploy of the cast-off kite that Brawijaya effects the youth's banishment to China. Eventually Prabangkara makes a name for himself in China as a representational artist and is taken into the Emperor's household. It is clear that Prabangkara himself is never to return to Java. There is, however, the promise of a deferred "return" in the form of his descendants, the overseas Chinese.

---

lowest ranking of royal children would be the *lembu peteng* ("dark cows") like Prabangkara and Krèwèd, who were born of women outside of court and were not officially recognized by the king.

It was the Dutch colonials who imposed upon the Javanese courts a Western European concern for legitimacy *and* primogeniture as they became intimately connected with the internal workings of the court over the course of the eighteenth century. Evidence in the *babad* suggests that prior to that time succession might be determined on the more rational "traditional" basis of the candidate's prowess. The successor to the throne would be selected from a pool of candidates from the royal family on the basis of his demonstrable talents and accomplishments.

Following directly upon episode one is episode two: the history of Jaka Karèwèd, told at some length in 731 lines. As I mentioned above, Karè-wèd, like his half-brother Prabangkara, is a character significantly absent from the dominant historical traditions. Another illegitimate son of Bra-wijaya V, from yet another woman of the butcher-folk, young Karèwèd's life is notable for its distance and distinction from life at the court. A child of the village, he is almost a caricature of the rustic. It is by means of magic invisibility (vanishing from sight) that Karèwèd comes to penetrate the palace of his father, a palace from which he had been excluded. And this illicit penetration throws the court into an uproar. Eventually ap-prehended by an act of trickery that forces visibility upon him, this one-time outlaw is finally taken up into his father's court. However, once Karèwèd is taken into court, he vanishes from the scene of recorded history. No more is heard of him.

After the Prabangkara-Karèwèd episodes comes a brief (173-line) nar-rative framing interlude that brings the reader's attention back to the house of Pengging. Jaka Tingkir's father (Prince Kebo Kenonga) is intro-duced and then centered genealogically in relation both to the royal house of Majapahit-Demak and to the reigning ecclesiastical elite (the *wali*) who brought Islam to Java.

The third episode follows this interlude with some 509 lines on the erection of the Demak Mosque. *Babad Jaka Tingkir's* treatment of this marvelous and renowned ecclesiastical construction would not have been unfamiliar to the nineteenth-century Javanese audience, for this account both parallels and embellishes upon the dominant *babad* tradition's his-tory of this well-documented fifteenth-century construction project.[2] *Ba-bad Jaka Tingkir*, however, expands upon the account of the dominant tradition by (1) adding a catalog of the persons (categories of persons and sometimes the localities they represent) who come from all corners of the realm to construct (in a hierarchical manner) the mosque and (2) high-lighting the difficulties the *wali* encountered in their efforts to align the mosque with Mecca.

Another longer 591-line framing interlude follows upon the Demak

2. Compare, for example, this account with that of the Balai Pustaka (Major) *Babad Tanah Jawi* recension, vol. 3, pp. 14–17, and that of an early-nineteenth-century Mang-kunagaran recension, *Serat Manikmaya dumugi Demak*, Mas Ng. Rongga Panam-bangan, ed. (compiled Surakarta, 1813; inscribed Surakarta, [ca. 1850]). MS. RP B 100; SMP MN 184 (canto 86).

Mosque episode. This interlude opens with the tale of Sunan Tembayat's withdrawal from temporal authority on Java's north coast and his consequent rise to spiritual ascendancy in the Javanese heartland. It continues with abbreviated notes pertaining to dynastic succession in Demak. Along with the expected royal genealogy, this snatch of dynastic chronicle includes notes on successions among the ecclesiastical elite (the *wali*). The interlude closes with a striking narrative section that describes the transformation of Jaka Tingkir's father (now named Ki Ageng Pengging) into a charismatic rural *kyai* (master of an Islamic teaching foundation, or *pesantrèn*). Ki Ageng Pengging marks himself in contradistinction to the Demak court in style, attitude, and behavior. This ex-prince, who now speaks the language of a rural *kyai*, disregards a summons to present himself at court. It is in this interlude too that Pengging's teacher is introduced.

The poem's fourth episode tells in 654 lines the story of the trial and execution of this teacher, the remarkable Sèh Siti Jenar. A Sufi master, Sèh Siti Jenar reigns as traditional Java's most renowned "heretic." Although his story is treated, sometimes briefly, in several recensions of the dominant *babad*, Siti Jenar is best remembered in oral traditions and in *suluk*. In these traditions he is remembered as a representative of the common folk (a lowly worm risen to glory)[3] who was martyred for his reckless spiritual populism. This section of the *babad*, which does indeed read like a *suluk*, culminates in the ecstatic affirmation of *ngèlmu rasa* (Knowledge of, and that *is*, Feeling, Meaning, Mystery) uttered by Siti Jenar at his trial. The account underlines the very palpable mystery of Siti Jenar's life-in-death as the saint vanishes willfully into Mystery (*gaib*) after his execution.

This dramatic episode is followed by a 332-line framing interlude that treats the escalating resistance of Ki Ageng Pengging (Siti Jenar's pupil!) to submit himself to the authority of Demak. In this narrative interlude, Ki Ageng Pengging refuses—in an exchange of letters—the Sultan's second summons to court.

The fifth episode, in some 566 lines, tells the story of Sèh Malang Sumirang and sings a portion of his famous *suluk*. The character of Malang Sumirang is well remembered in oral traditions as well as in the

3. Literally, a worm. In many traditons, Siti Jenar was the transformation of worm who became man after listening in on the secret mystical teachings of Sunan Bonang to his disciples.

textual world of *suluk*. His story is not, however, inscribed in many *babad* texts. *Babad Jaka Tingkir* portrays Malang Sumirang as a character of remarkable audacity and impudence. Considered mad, his "madness" shows itself in his total disregard for the (Islamic) law. Tried and found guilty of his crimes, Malang Sumirang is roasted alive on the pyre. But alive and unharmed he remains. Indeed, it is in the raging depths of the fire that would not kill him that he writes—with some assistance from his pet dog—his final testament, the renowed *Suluk Malang Sumirang*. Emerging unscathed from the conflagration, he finally vanishes willingly into internal exile—leaving behind his *pusaka* text. And it is in the midst of this episode that the poet steps back from the narrative to reflect upon the conditions and the fruits of knowledge in passages which can be read as a discourse on knowledge and power.

The final 1,284 lines of the poem remember the final days (the triumphs and resistance), death, and postmortem of Ki Ageng Pengging—heir of Majapahit, pupil of Siti Jenar, and father of Jaka Tingkir. It is this section of the poem that I term the "sixth episode." With the birth of a son of promised greatness (Jaka Tingkir, at last), Ki Ageng Pengging's resistance to the court of Demak escalates. He engages in a series of debates (*bantah*) pertaining both to matters of Islamic mysticism and to relations between "the state" and the religious community. Finally he is executed by Sunan Kudus, who acts on the authority of Demak's temporal and ecclesiastical elite. Ki Ageng Pengging's manner of death is extraordinary, and so is his executioner. The vanishing of Pengging into death looks forward to his reappearance in the form of his son, Jaka Tingkir. At poem's close (without closure), the reader/audience is left with that expectation.

Frames as Episodes and Episodes as Frames

To call this final section of the poem the "sixth episode" is problematic and deserves further discussion. As even this brief overview should make clear, the poet's remembrance of the life and death of Ki Ageng Pengging does not in fact subsist as a separate episode. Rather it is the Pengging story that serves as the textual thread which sews the seams that both bind and separate all the poem's episodes. In all, the poem devotes 2,587 lines (over a third of its 6,913 lines) to the story of Pengging and his immediate antecedents. More than half those lines constitute the narrative interludes

> *Frame: Introduction (i:1–iii:18)*
> Invocation (i:1–i:9): genealogy of futures
> Pengging 1 (i:9–iii:18): genealogy

Episode i: Jaka Prabangkara (iii:18–ix:14)
visibility
exile
representation

Episode ii: Jaka Karèwèd (ix:15–xii:41)
invisibility
subversion
marginality

> *Frame: Pengging 2 (xii:41–xiii:17)*
> genealogy: Pengging & Wali

Episode iii: Demak Mosque (xiii:18–xvi:2)
relations
alignments
monuments

> *Frame: Wali & Demak (xvi:2–xvii:6)*
> Bayat (xvi:2–xvi:18): resistance & transition
> Demak & Wali (xvi:18–xvii:6): genealogy
> Pengging 3 (xvii:6–xviii:15): resistance & transition

Episode iv: Siti Jenar (xviii:15–xxi:5)
populism
dissemination

> *Frame: Pengging 4 (xxi:5–xxii:24)*
> resistance

Episode v: Malang Sumirang (xxii:24–xxiv:22)
transgression
knowledge & power
representation

> *Episode vi/Frame: Pengging 5 (xxiv:23–xxxii:7)*
> resistance
> undecidability
> genealogy of futures

Figure 13. *Babad Jaka Tingkir*: A Schematic Overview.

that frame the other five episodes. The climax of the Pengging story ("episode six") with which the poem ends could, then, be read as a "frame" turned inside-out into an "episode." This inversion (that is, this transformation of frame into episode) invites the reader to reread the preceding already-read episodes—but now as a series of frames that serve to inform (by fragmenting) her reading of "the Pengging story." The relationships among the episodes and the frames, the text(s) and the binding(s) are dialectical and productive ones. For a visual image of the interplay among these episodes and frames, see figure 13.

The remainder of this chapter and the following two chapters proceed through close readings of the six episodes and their frames. These readings work to disclose how the poet (writing from the vantage of exile) composed these fragments of history as a wishful prophecy. The textual investigation moves largely at the level of detail, sometimes with seeming serendipity, but—together with *Tingkir*'s author—always in the interest of a script for the future.

Jaka Prabangkara: A Figure of Visibility Disappears

Jaka Prabangkara, hero of the first episode, is a royal Javanese exile who earns his fame, as we shall see, through writing. He earns that fame *not* in Java, but in the faraway land of China. It is his descendants who are destined, with prophetic hindsight, to enjoy the prosperity that his talents will ultimately bequeath. Those descendants are notably *not* the Javanese nobility of the nineteenth-century "present" of the history's writing, but the notoriously successful overseas Chinese. Let us now look more closely at Prabangkara's curious story. What kind of person is he? How does the poet portray him? Wherein lies his excellence, and what betrays his faults?

The poet introduces Jaka Prabangkara as the very image of future kingship or, at the very least, of potential greatness. And we recognize in him his mother's son.

> Now the telling turns
> To Brawijaya's child
> Born of a lower wife, a handsome son

With brilliant radiance beaming
Like the moon at its fullness
Straight of body
With golden face alluring
Tall with silken skin
Enchanting of aura subtle [*asemu*]
Named Jaka Prabangkara
He was adept at every work[4]

Poetic (and sociopolitical) conventions dictate that persons of greatness—
especially kings/queens and candidate-kings/queens—be suffused with
light.[5] Indeed, in the world of royal Java, kingship itself descends upon the

4. [Sinom] Kuneng malih winarna / putraning Brawijaya / priya sangking ampéyan
pekik kang warna // Ulading cahya sumunar / lir wulan purnama sidi / lurus pasarira-
nira / jenar pamulu respati / pideksa lus kang daging / aparek driya asemu / ran Jaka
Prabangkara / wasis ing sabarang kardi (*BJT* III:18–19).

5. The association of kingship and light has been amply treated by Javanological scholarship: see Anderson, "The Idea of Power in Javanese Culture," pp. 16–18, and Day,
"Meanings of Change," p. 146 ff. Less attention has been afforded the association of
queenship (especially qua mother of a king) and light. In Javanese historical traditions,
however, the association of fertile queen and the light of royalty has been consistently
and powerfully drawn. One is reminded of the well-known flaming genitals of Ken
Dedes (wife of Ken Arok, founder of the Singasari dynasty), and the lesser-known
flaming genitals of the Princess of Pajajaran (who, according to certain Yogyakarta
babad traditions, mothered the "dynasty" of Dutch colonial rulers); see J. L. A. Brandes,
ed., *Pararaton (Ken Arok) of het Boek der Koningen van Tumapel en van Majapahit*,
Verhandelingen van het Bataviaasch Genootschap van Kunsten en Wetenschappen,
vol. 62 (1920), pp. 13–14, 57–58, and B. J. O. Schrieke, *Indonesian Sociological Studies*
(The Hague: van Hoeve, 1957), 2:70–74. *Babad Jaka Tingkir* highlights the striking
lustrous aura passed down from Ratu Dwarawati (Tingkir's great-grandmother) to her
daughter (Tingkir's grandmother) (*BJT* I:26–27). Ratu Beruk was still a (low-born)
little girl when her future husband, Pakubuwana III (r. 1749–88), recognized her as
candidate queen and mother of a king (that is, Pakubuwana IV) by a radiance beaming
from her navel. For a history of Ratu Beruk's (Kangjeng Ratu Kancana) ascent from
village hut to queenship, see R. Mantri Guru Sasrasumarta, *Serat Babatipun Kangjeng
Ratu Kancana* (composed Surakarta, 1936; inscribed Surakarta, ca. 1936). MS. SP 118
Ka; SMP KS 66. Surakarta royalty still delight in telling the story of how in October
1865 at a party in the home of the Dutch Assistant Resident, the *wahyu* descended on
the head of R.A. Koestijah—marking her instantly as Pakubuwana IX's queen-to-be
and Pakubuwana X's mother-to-be. For a witty retelling of this story, see Pemberton,
On the Subject of "Java," p. 80.

worthy candidate in the form of a very palpable ball of light (*wahyu*, especially *wahyu nurbuwat*). Suffused with the light of *wahyu*, the king (or candidate-king) in turn effuses that light, in an aura of power, from his person. And, it is the extent of the ruler's effusion of light that ideologically defines the limits of his authority. The light which is royal *wahyu* is both the source and manifest reality of the king's worldly and otherworldly powers. To attain greatness, then, is to be a seat of light. As such, the person of greatness is both a highly visible figure and a figure of visibility.

"With brilliant radiance beaming / Like the moon at its fullness" (*ulading cahya sumunar / lir wulan purnama sidi*). The description which opens the Prabangkara tale immediately identifies the hero as a figure of light and hence as a figure of visibility and greatness. "Enchanting, of aura subtle" (*aparek driya asemu*). However, Prabangkara's visible light indicates something else as well, something which remained partially invisible. He is possessed of the subtle aura which is *semu*, an aura which signals that "in" him dwells an even greater unseen profundity. In the discussion that follows, we shall see how *semu*, signifying the intersection of visibility (the revealed) and invisibility (the concealed), is the site of a vital problematic in the Prabangkara tale—a problematic of writing.

What else do these lines tell us of the youth Prabangkara? They disclose that he is "adept at [any and] every work" (*wasis ing sabarang kardi*). Its connotations perhaps too menial, this is not a standard textual attribute or epithet of royal prowess in traditional Java. But then Jaka Prabangkara is no typical royal offspring. The epithet calls into consideration the youth's other parent: his low-born mother. The stanza immediately following upon the introduction of the handy youth of light tells of the circumstances of Prabangkara's birth:

> As the tale goes, this Jaka Prabangkara
>
> Was not owned as son by
> His Majesty of Majapahit
> It began when His Royal Highness
> Was out on pleasure tour . . .
> (*BJT* III:19–20).

The text goes on to tell how this child, unacknowledged by his royal father, was the product of an evening of unrestrained royal lust in the course of the king's incognito foray into the butcher's quarter.

What, then, is Prabangkara's work? Prabangkara is a representational artist. He is a painter and, as we shall see, by extension a writer. In his early career at the court of Majapahit, Prabangkara's gift is his remarkable ability to make hidden things, the mysterious creatures who ply the seas and creep the forests, perfectly visible through art. His reward for this plenitude of perfect visual representation is his father's (hidden) love (*BJT* III:24–26). However, Prabangkara evidently takes perfect representation too far when he turns his artistic attentions to the reality of his father's court. By the unlucky chance (perhaps) of the ink drop, Prabangkara too perfectly reveals a too perfect knowledge of his father's queen (*BJT* III:26–30). To know too much and to reveal it in transparent mimetic representation is a scandal, and the reward for this excess of illicit knowledge made visible by ink is exile. And in exile, Prabangkara emerges as an adept of another, more "politic" form of representation.

But first let us consider further the sense the telltale ink drop makes in the *babad*. With the incident of the ink drop, the poet gives an early clue to the "true identity" of Jaka Prabangkara—that is, as a writer. For the tale of this drop of ink alludes to, as it recalls, another tale, one that belongs to Javanese literary history. That tale concerns the genesis of a classic text, the *Kekawin Bhâratayuddha*. It is well known to Javanese that the classic *Bhâratayuddha*, composed in 1157 under the patronage of King Jayabhaya (in modern Javanese, Jayabaya) of Kadiri, was written in two parts by two different authors. Empu Sedhah wrote the first part of the poem; Empu Panuluh, the second.

Ronggawarsita's nineteenth-century *Pustakaraja* provides a history of this dual authorship, explaining that it was Sedhah's untimely death that forced Panuluh to finish the poem. The history continues with an account of how and why Sedhah died: as it turns out, the poet was executed by order of Jayabaya for a crime much like that of Prabangkara. When Sedhah was but half finished with his writing, King Jayabaya asked to see the manuscript. The king was delighted with what he read until he came to the passage describing the charms of King Salya's wife and queen. For to King Jayabaya, Empu Sedhah's too beautiful, too erotic, and too knowledgeable depiction of this legendary queen too perfectly matched the real and very private qualities of his own queen. This too explicit portrayal at the very least betrayed the poet's indiscretion, and at the worst marked him the perpetrator of a treacherous adultery with his patron's queen. The punishment for the crime was death.[6]

This tale seems to have had wide circulation in nineteenth-century Java.[7] The literate nineteenth-century reader of *Babad Jaka Tingkir* would surely have recognized in the ink drop incident an allusion to this history of ancient writing. With this recognition would begin a chain of associations, or equivalences, that would lead to an identification of Prabangkara as a writer and suggest the danger of writing as a profession. While conflating notions of representation in the visual and textual arts, the allusion would also underwrite the critique of representation as mimesis already implied by Prabangkara's blunder. The allusion, moving to evoke the production of meaning, would not, however, explicitly determine the sense of its potential readings. No unseemly blot of ink itself, the poet's history of this unfortunate scene of writing moves in a more subtle register. The potential meanings toward which the allusion gestures are less than explicit. Composed with *semu*, allusions work as (sometimes coy) invitations to presumably knowing interlocutors to make for themselves a certain kind of sense.

The writer of *Babad Jaka Tingkir*, a master of *semu*, well understood the dialogic play of allusion. *Tingkir's* writer could be described as one

> Who is accomplished in precision perfect
> Even unto the play of subtle sign [*pasang semon*]
> Whose art shows in allusion[8]

This description, however, is of Prabangkara and is drawn in his father's parting letter, a letter that also serves as an order of banishment. In fact, Brawijaya's letter praises Prabangkara for the very skill at which he had proven deficient. The unstated crime for which this letter banishes him is, after all, the impolitic revelation of a too intimate knowledge of the queen, a revelation drawn explicitly with an indiscreet pen. Indeed, Brawijaya's laudatory letter of banishment is a study of double-speak that, were it not

6. R.Ng. Ronggawarsita, *Pustakaraja Madya: Jayabaya* (composed Surakarta, mid-19th century; inscribed Surakarta, mid to late 19th century). MS. RP D 128; SMP MN 15, pp. 283a–285b.

7. See P. J. Zoetmulder, *Kalangwan* (The Hague: Nijhoff, 1974), p. 271.

8. [Mijil] Kang wus putus ing titi patitis / trus ing pasang semon / ri sasmita katon lukitané ... (*BJT* V:22).

drawn in such simple and false reversal, would itself be a writing of *semu*. For example, in the letter Brawijaya acknowledges Prabangkara as son only by repudiating and exiling him; in it he admits his hatred for Prabangkara only to claim that this hatred was contrived with the better interests of this his newly acknowledged son at heart. Rationalizing the suffering he inflicts upon his son, Brawijaya declares that it is only through exile and hardship that the boy will gain success (*BJT* V:20–42).

If Brawijaya's letter is not itself written with *semu*, it is most certainly inscribed with *semu* into the manuscript witness of *Babad Jaka Tingkir* that we are reading. The text of this letter banishing the painter youth for his over-explicit portraiture is, in this manuscript, itself interrupted by a series of portraits and by the "dream notation" of an exiled nineteenth-century king. At the very textual moment that Brawijaya's letter declares to his newly acknowledged and banished son that he is, through the trials of exile, to become a "Master of wealth and master of accomplishment," the narrative is broken by the interpolations described in Chapter 1. After the interruption, the verse concludes with a "secret": the true harvest of the fruits this mastery will produce, in exile by writing, was to be enjoyed by those who would come after the fruits' producer:

> Master of prosperity perfect
> Master of virtue and of consciousness clear; the secret is
> The harvest of the fruits provides
> All of his descendants
> With greatness in the time to come[9]

As Brawijaya's letter catalogs in writing the future benefits of exile, the manuscript scribe interrupts his or her writing allusively to remind the manuscript's readers not only of the material production of his or her own writing in exile, but also of *its* projected future efficacy.

The quality of allusiveness that Brawijaya's fateful and duplicitous letter ascribes to his son (who shines as a figure of excess visibility) was the essential quality Prabangkara lacked in order to fulfill his promise for courtly office. Elsewhere, in an allusive play of language, the poet reflects (implicitly *and* explicitly at the same time) upon the association of this

9. [Mijil] Ing artawan myang guna [three interpolated leaves] wan titih / kertawan kinaot / susilawan budiman wadiné / pangundhuh ing wowohan ngemèhi / saturasira / padha mulyèng pungkur (*BJT* V:38).

quality with ancient (and ideal) kingship. The passage I have in mind is the one that expresses "the heartfelt anguish of the king" immediately after Brawijaya cuts the cord to Prabangkara's kite (*BJT* V:1–11). In the original Javanese, this passage generates its deeply textured sense of royal distress quite sensuously through sound by techniques of exuberant alliteration and assonance.

> Mangu-mangu manguneng nekani
> kakenan tyas képon
> lir kapesan kapasuk puseké . . .

> Distraught and whelmed with woe
> Of troubled heart aggrieved
> As one hopelessly anguish-stabbed . . .
> (*BJT* V:1)

As the language sensuously sighs and rustles Brawijaya's personal pain, the discursive line, however, moves off in another direction, away from personal grief toward a curious epistemological paradox that concerns royal power. The narrative moves in progression through a series of related topics: from the particular personal regret of this king, through more general reflections on progeny and futures, to denunciations of impetuous behavior, finally to a remembrance of the virtues of the "ancient kings" with didactic reflections upon exemplary kingship. The expression of "the heartfelt anguish of the king" culminates in the highly alliterative paradox:

kahananing nata nguni-uni
uninga wangening
wawenang winangun

Wangunaning naya kang winuni
wenang nganon tinon

The way of the ancient kings
Was to know the limits of
Structured authority

A structure of rule/allusion [*naya*] that is hidden/expressed [*winuni*]
Has authority to see and be seen
(*BJT* V:7–8)

The paradox turns on polysemic plays among the meanings of two Kawi words. The Kawi *naya* designates "rule, governance, wisdom, prudence" *and* "allusion." *Winuni* means both *and* at the same time "to be hidden" and "to be voiced" or "expressed." The light of true authority, however visible, appears under the aspect of a kind of hiddenness; it is expressed and recognized among veils. Mastery of the art of *semu*, then, marked both good governance (kingship) and good representation (as in the writing of history).

Excluded from the court of Majapahit, Prabangkara makes his fortune in exile. It is in China that this marginalized royal son regains both his proximity to and his promise of authority. He comes into that position by means of his industry, by his alliance with the poor Chinese widow woman, and especially by the irresistible power of his art. The present discussion will be restricted to his art: the textual art that he perfects in exile. By the time he reaches China, Prabangkara has learned his lesson. Perhaps indeed a result of the trials his (newly found and lost) father has granted him, he has gained sophistication in the play of *semu*. Consider, for example, how upon his arrival in the scrub woods of the provincial Chinese hill country, Prabangkara introduces himself to the widow Kim Li-yong. In this seemingly half-deceptive speech to his future foster mother, Prabangkara actually identifies wherein his true fault had lain:

> Verily mother, not nearly subtle enough
> To serve at royal court
> When charged by my Lord
> To study writing, I proved inept[10]

It was this ineptitude, he goes on to confide, that had earned him the king's wrath. Prabangkara had been a writer, and had proven himself a poor one at the courtly game of representation, whose art is not merely to represent perfectly (or simply to deceive), but rather to create a subtle balance between disclosure and veiling, between revelation and secrecy.

In Java, Prabangkara started and ended his career as a court artist. At the Majapahit court, his excess of visibility, his propensity to a too transparent representation of reality, had proven both his gift and his downfall. An inadvertent ink drop too literally revealing a royal "secret" earned Prabangkara a one-way kite trip to China. In far-off China, separated

10. [Pucung] Kula biyung, tan montra-montra ing semu / angawulèng nata / duk tinuduh ing nerpati / sisinaon ing tulis pan dèrèng bisa (*BJT* VII:5).

from Java and the royal center that had expelled him, the youth would work his representational art to more advantage. There, he would traverse a different and more successful career trajectory than he had on Java. Different too would be the character of the art of his Chinese period.

Prabangkara, the excluded prince, proves himself a businessman in China, and his business is portraiture, a form of writing that is drawing. "Writing was the work of the handsome one / Pictures did he draw" (*BJT* VII:46). Starting out an independent provincial artisan, he works his way up to service at (and marriage into) the imperial court of China. It is on his own initiative that he sets up this artful literary enterprise, using as starting capital the remains of his Javanese kite and jewels. Prabangkara the painter/writer sells the artful portraits he crafts on the free market. And sell they do indeed. It is said of Prabangkara's Chinese patrons: "They struggled to outbid each other, regardless of the price" (*BJT* VII:48).

What, then, was so attractive about these Chinese period portraits? In Kinanthi verse it is sung:

> A master of drawing was he
> Perfect likenesses were
> His artful portraits
> Seemed as if they'd speak themselves
> Of air [*semu*] his drawings seemed as not
> Crafted of paper and ink
>
> For as the truth were they
> Of the subject crafted by art
> In ceaseless stream did come
> Emissaries of all the kings
> And envoys of the nobles all
> Of the courtiers and officers
>
> All commissioning portraits
> Artfully crafted and painted
> Which seemed as if they'd move themselves
> In perfect agreement with that desired
> Rich were the returns
> For Ki Jaka the Painter[11]

11. Yèn akarya gambar putus / lir wantah tuhuning warni / punang gambar wewangunan / yayah bisa angling pribadi / semuning gambar tan montra / cinitrèng

The attraction of the portraits was not so much from the quality of "likeness" as from their "truth": a form of life produced from the inter-relationship (and tension) between likeness and artifice. Standing in between and transcending these two "representative" qualities was that allusive air that is *semu*. Perfect as-if-alive likenesses, these "artfully crafted and painted" portraits seemed as if they could speak or move on their own. Life would emerge from a portrait's surface at the very moment that same surface apparently disappeared: "Of air his drawings seemed as not / Crafted of paper and ink." It was as if the surface of the drawing was concealed or removed from view so that the patron gazing at the portrait could forget that the "face" of the portrait was really only "paper and ink." That forgetting was, however, a function of that same surface (a *sur*-face) through which shimmered the portrait's *semu*.[12] And life-engendering *semu* is precisely that which is "crafted by art." Not an inadvertent ink drop awkwardly calling attention to itself, *semu* is an artful supplement added to a portrait (the *sur* of the "sur-face") which draws attention away from the portrait's mimetic function. The air shimmering as *semu* was produced by art to reveal the portraits as something other than mere likeness or imitation. It was that air, a mysterious artful supplement alluding to something both other and more than mimetic representation, that betrayed the portraits' life, that effected in re-presentation a metamorphizing (living) coincidence of image and referent, the portraits' truth. *Semu* in portraiture produces truth at the mysterious point at which the image turns its effects upon that which is imaged. The allure of art that shimmers with *semu* is thus irresistible.

This aesthetic of allusion (the aesthetic of *semu*) upon which the Prabangkara story turns seems a particularly Javanese one. The poet, however, projects a kind of universality for this Javanese aesthetic. For here it is the Chinese whom it enthralled. It is the Chinese patrons who were

---

kartas lan mangsi // Pan kadi saèstonipun / barang kang cinitrèng warni / élur aselur kang prapta / dutaning para nerpati / myang dutaning pra satriya / punggawa praméya mantri // Samya mameling wewangun / ing citra warna sinu[ng]ging / ingkang yayah bisa molah / tan salaya kang kinapti / akathah wewangsulira / marang Ki Jaka Panyungging (*BJT* VIII:6–8).

12. "Sur-face" conveys the sense of *semu* in that while remaining something on its own, it always calls to mind something else (or more) which lies underneath or behind it. I am grateful to Ben Anderson for this observation and for the figure of "sur-face" for *semu*.

compelled to buy the portraits, thus assuring both wealth and fame for Prabangkara. The Chinese could look at the portraits he crafted and see in them their "truth," something which was at the same time alike and different from that which they presumably represented. The difference (and the irresistible attraction) is in the portrait's *semu*, the allusive air drawn by a Javanese writer in artful supplement.

The Chinese, precisely because they are not Javanese, would be particularly susceptible to this Javanese aesthetic with its imagined universality of appeal or allure. Imagined by the Javanese poet to be likely lacking in *semu* of their own, they would stand defenseless before the allusive allure of Prabangkara's paintings as well as before that of his person.[13] The Chinese of "all the land" rise up to acclaim the radiant Javanese prince who had literally descended into their presence:

> For, to be sure, he was handsome
>
> His face was like the moon
> At its time of fullness
> *A master of language*, of courtly mien
> Charming, incomparably able
> Polite, serene, unaffected
> Fit to be the talk of the land
>
> .   .   .
>
> Exquisite were his looks
> None was the like of him
> All the youths of China
> Were worsted in appearance (emphasis added)[14]

Not all Chinese, however, were imagined to be lacking in *semu*. The Chinese Emperor, for example, could read from Prabangkara's body, mannerisms, and erudition in the "classics" of Old Javanese literature the signs that all too obviously betrayed the youth's (Javanese) royalty. Intro-

13. In many texts of nineteenth-century Javanese literature, "the Chinese" are portrayed stereotypically as coarse, miserly, and greedy sorts who are interested in nothing but material-monetary gain. See, for example, *Suluk Condra* (composed s.l., s.a.), in *Serat Wulang* (inscribed Surakarta, 1899). MS. Rp 104 carik; SMP Rp 106 B, part 3.
14. [Kinanthi] . . . dhasar apekik kang warni // Pamulu yayah sitangsu / sedhengé purnama sidi / limpat ing tembung nor raga / sedhep bangkité dhèwèki / jatmika anteng pesaja / pantes khaojating bumi / . . . . // Tuhu bagusé pinunjul / tan ana kang angèmperi / jajaka ing nagri Cina / sami kasoran ing warni (*BJT* VIII:2–3 & 5).

ducing himself to the Emperor, the discernibly regal Prabangkara disclaims nobility by means of an erudite literary allusion to the Old Javanese *Nitisastra*:

> "I alone, Your Highness
> Am stupidest of all
> Of manner unfit to be
> Courtier to a king
> Short on intellect, fatuous
> Ignorant of decorum
>
> "I, a real ignoramus
> A wretch spoiled from childhood on
> 'Needs must [*pugung*] taste the flavors six'
> A mere lad without discretion
> A dunce unfit to know
> The taste then of the six . . ."[15]

The *Nitisastra* verse cited reads: "he who does not know (*punggung*) how to speak beautifully is [like one] ignorant of the six flavors" (*Nîti-çâstra* I:2).[16] In this widely read didactic classic, then, knowledge of the six flavors is directly associated with mastery of "beautiful language." With an interesting twist (or slip) of the pen, in the *babad* citation the *cecak* (◡) —*ng* over the syllable (ᰍ) *pu* is dropped, changing *punggung* ("ignorant") into *pugung* ("obstinate," translated above "needs must"). Although likely only a scribal variant,[17] the effect of the verbal transformation is nonetheless striking. By means of this scriptural twist, Prabangkara, the exiled writer, confesses to an obstinate persistence at his profession (the manipulation of beautiful language as a courtly writer) despite his unfitness for it. After this disclaimer, the "dunce" goes on to display his linguistic-literary prowess in an explication of these very "six" in the "beautiful language" of Kawi: "*Amla sarkara*, by which is meant . . ." In a clichéd play of *semu*, Prabangkara thus protests ignorance to display knowledge.

15. [Kinanthi] Amung kawula pukulun / ingkang balilu pribadi / ing bawa tan montra-montra / wong suwitèng narapati / cekak bui tanpa daya / tan uningèng tata titi // Amba dahad kumprung pengung / pugung marasé sadrasa / laré tan wrin ing dudugi / jugul tan montra uninga / ing rasa kang nem prakawis (*BJT* VIII:23–24).
16. "ring wwang tan wruha ring subhasita mapunggung mangraseng sadrasa," R.Ng. Poerbatjaraka, ed., *Nîtiçâstra* (Bandung, 1933).
17. The hand that wrote this manuscript habitually drops the *cecak*.

The allusion works by projecting a universality upon Javanese literary culture: the Chinese Emperor is assumed naturally conversant with the Javanese classics. *Babad Jaka Tingkir*'s author allows this conceit more pointedly to position Prabangkara as a literary figure and "the Prabangkara story" as a comment on textual representation in Javanese (if not just in Java). Appropriate to his "true identity" as court writer, immediately following this literary allusion and explication Prabangkara continues his apology to the canny Chinese ruler:

> Not nearly subtle enough
> Knowing not the secret most essential
> For service to a king
> Thus did I ever incur the wrath[18]

By stating that he had not known "the secret" in the past when he worked for Brawijaya, Prabangkara means to imply his present cognizance and hence to allay the Emperor's fears of any future blunders. Prabangkara now understands the secret essential for any writer's survival at court: perfect representation is not transparent mimesis; instead, to re-present perfectly in writing means to produce "truth" through the shimmer of *semu*. There would be no more of the "telling it straight" that got him into so much trouble in Java.[19] Prabangkara's marvelous Chinese portraits were not to be stained by any inadvertent ink drops. And so:

---

18. [Kinanthi] Tan montra-montra ing semu / tan wrin ing wadi gatining / sumi-wakèng naradipa / milanggung manggih ruruntik . . . (*BJT* VIII:26).

19. At this juncture one cannot but wonder what the writings of another impolitic writer, who—not unlike Prabangkara—earned exile from a Javanese court, might have been. That other writer was the elder Ronggawarsita (father of the famous "seal of the *pujongga*" Ronggawarsita). The elder Ronggawarsita, who had held the high rank of Lurah Carik (head scribe) of the Kraton Surakarta's Kadipatèn, was reputedly an accomplished writer. C. F. Winter, this Ronggawarsita's former student—and the man who set him up for capture—attributed to him a recension of *Panji Semawung* (*Javaansche Zamenspraken*, 1:189). No manuscript witnesses of that work or any other work signed by him remains in the major Surakarta repositories. Nor were any of his writings ever published—unless, of course, anonymously or under another's name. Political suppression and exile may explain this notable absence. The elder Ronggawarsita was arrested in 1828 (a year before the dated composition of *Babad Jaka Tingkir*) for anti-Dutch intrigues. His captors considered him extremely dangerous and said of him that he surpassed all the rest of the natives in intelligence. At the time of his arrest,

High Prince Prabangkara
Was acclaimed throughout the land

Unsurpassed in valor
Excellent of intellect
Heroic and heedful
He was adept at every work
With the sweet nature of an *ulama*
His character, burning incense
Striking [*kacap*] his every word[20]

At the end of the Prabangkara story we are returned to his beginnings: "He was adept at every work," but now with a couple of significant twists. Textually anticipating the history that would succeed him, the classical Javanese prince in exile has somehow become a Moslem scholar, an *ulama*. And his language (a fruit of exile's trials) has now become significantly empowered. Writing the "truth," his every word is "striking": what the exile writes is (potentially) engraved (*kacap*) in reality. Writing in exile with *semu*, Prabangkara produces a kind of truth that is to be bequeathed to those would come after him. Though he was never to return to Java himself, his success would ultimately shine through his descendants, the foreign-Javanese children who would return "in days to come to feed upon / The fruits of Java's land" (*BJT* IV:23). The success of those children, the notoriously wealthy and conventionally marginalized overseas Chinese, is doubly inscribed by *both* exiles' pens (Prabangkara in China and our anonymous scribe in Ambon), prophetically, *as* Javanese.

"all his papers" (along with some "military drums" and a banner inscribed in Arabic script) were confiscated. See Nahuys to the Kommissaris Generaal, Sourakarta den 19 April 1828, missive no. 41 geheim LªM, Ministerie van Kolonien (MvK) no. 4133 in the Algemeen Rijksarchief, The Hague. "His papers" confiscated and his writings suppressed, we cannot know if among the elder Ronggawarsita's faults was a deficit of *semu*. The elder Ronggawarsita, silenced as a writer, was exiled to Batavia, where he died, never to return to Surakarta (see Anjar Any, *Radèn Ngabéhi Ronggowarsito: Apa yang Terjadi?* [Semarang: Aneka, 1980]).

20. [Asmarandana] Dyan Harya Prabangkara / wus kasub ing bumintara // Kadibyané amumpuni / limpat pasanging grahita / prawiranjrah wiwékané / winasis sabarang karya / ambek merdu ngulama / budiné menyan katunu / kacap sabarang pangucap (*BJT* IX:11–12).

Jaka Karèwèd: A Figure of Invisibility Brought to Light

If Prabangkara shines as a figure of visibility, his half-brother Karèwèd tends to invisibility. What Karèwèd's invisibility "represents," I shall suggest, is a certain kind of textual absence, or gap, in the dominant *babad* tradition. Not represented in the standard dynastic chronicles are the stories of the *wong cilik* ("the little women and men"), the stories of those men and women who made up the overwhelming majority of traditional Java's population, stories that would constitute the greater part of a truly comprehensive history of any realm. I shall argue that the Karèwèd of *Babad Jaka Tingkir*, although a son of Brawijaya, is portrayed emphatically as his mother's son. Despite the admixture of royal blood, he represents a child of the *wong cilik*, a rustic village lad. The telling of his history, then, points toward the registration of another story: the more comprehensive history that is yet to be told. For, while telling the Karèwèd story cannot recuperate the lost history of the underclass, it may imply what such a recuperation, were it possible, could mean.

Jaka Karèwèd's father is Brawijaya V, the prolific final king of Majapahit, whose offspring are said to have numbered some 111 souls. Karèwèd's mother is the spirited daughter of a lowly officer from the palace butcher corps. When the pregnant butcher girl rejects Brawijaya sexually, he is "consumed with wrath." Cast out of the palace prior to her son's birth, the butcher maid raises Karèwèd to know nothing of court life. Socialized into a peasant world, Jaka Karèwèd becomes a simple—albeit exceptional—herd-boy. The herd-boy (*laré angon*) is the quintessential figure of rural idyll in Javanese representational art (textual and visual). *Babad Jaka Tingkir* portrays the herd-boy Karèwèd as a character of pristine innocence and naiveté. He is, above all, "natural." His sheer immediacy is the precise inverse of the courtly *semu* which came to be cultivated by his half-brother Prabangkara.

If what is at stake in the Prabangkara story is the sometimes dangerous intersection of concealment and revelation in art, something very different is happening in the case of Jaka Karèwèd. There is nothing contrived about the invisibility of Karèwèd. His invisibility, as opposed to concealment, is not produced by art; rather it is the (super)natural effect of a very real and corporeal (natural) magic found-object. Always artless, the boy along with his maternal kin are consistently portrayed as near caricatures of immediateness and naturalness. Fixing this characterization, the poet even goes so far as to have the boy forget his newly acquired magic invisibility when crying to his mother to give his "empty belly" some rice (*BJT* X:11–15).

By means of that same dialogue of mother and son, the poet reveals to the audience/reader the extent of the remove from court of this royal offspring and his mother. The language spoken by the two is that of a peasant boy and his peasant mother, not that of a (low-born) royal concubine and her princely son. The mother calls out to her little boy, appropriately for a peasant mother, in the *ngoko* ("low" Javanese) of superior to inferior: "*tholé, tholé ana ngendi*" ("Boy! [Jaka!] Where are you?"). He answers her in the *krama* ("high" Javanese) appropriate for inferior's speech to superior: "*wonten ngriki kula ibu*" ("Here I am, Mama" [*BJT* X:14–15]). The language spoken by the two is rustic, and as the dialogue progresses it shows the appropriate admixture of language levels characteristic of much Javanese speech.[21] The tonality of their discourse is intimate and conforms to the constraints that would govern (poeticized) linguistic exchange between a peasant mother and her young peasant son in rural Central Java. Their language, however, violates the courtly rules of language use which the genealogical relationship between Karèwèd and his mother would seem to dictate.

Courtly rules of linguistic exchange were rules established by convention—convention that would sometimes be codified into formal regulations.[22] At court, as elsewhere in Java, language use was determined by status considerations. However, in the palace, the "normal" status relationship between mother and child was often inverted. The sons and daughters of a king's concubine would be of considerably higher status than their mother. Indeed, the status differential was so marked that these children would not even call these women *ibu* ("mother"). Only an official queen had the right to be referred to as *ibu* and addressed in *krama*. The children of a royal concubine would call the queen(s) *ibu*, while

21. For a discussion of language levels in Javanese, see J. Joseph Errington, *Structure and Style in Javanese: A Semiotic View of Linguistic Etiquette* (Philadelphia: University of Pennsylvania Press, 1988), and Ward Keeler, *Javanese Shadow Plays, Javanese Selves* (Princeton: Princeton University Press, 1987), pp. 25–50.
22. According to the current ruler of the Kraton Surakarta, in earlier days there were courtiers who served as language police whose duty it was to mete out punishments to any who might transgress these linguistic regulations (Personal communication, I.S.K.S. Pakubuwana XII).

calling their own mother *bibi* ("auntie," a term of address for female domestics) and addressing her in *ngoko*. She in turn would call her children *Gusti* ("Your Highness") and speak to them in *krama inggil* ("high-high" Javanese).

There is nothing in the linguistic exchanges of Jaka Karèwèd and his spirited mother that even approaches proper courtly form. Not only does the boy *not* speak down to his low-born mother, she consistently uses the royal *ingsun*, a personal pronoun reserved for kings alone, to refer to herself when talking to him. It is particularly striking that she persists with this usage even at court in the presence of the king (*BJT* XII:19–21). Indeed, with the highly emotional and unaffected exchanges between mother and son throughout the Karèwèd episode, the poet effectively displays the characters' unselfconscious *disregard* for royal rule. The unselfconscious aspect of this disregard (a function of immediacy) lends poignancy to these exchanges. It underlines to the audience/reader the divorce of the boy from his royal origins. At the same time, these linguistic exchanges, contrived by the poet as the very image of artless discourse, constitute an important element in the poet's depiction of a pure idealized rural peasantry in the figures of Karèwèd and his mother. Marked by (and valorized for) their artlessness, these characters (anything but masters of *semu*) are moved, like the poet's imagined peasantry, by the sheer immediacy of desire.

How then does the poet portray Karèwèd's desire? Karèwèd's behavior under the cloak of invisibility is motivated by natural and straightforward desires: hunger, thirst, and especially curiosity. He satisfies his hunger at the lavish tables of the elite—his thirst, at the royal liquor cabinet. What then of the herd-boy's curiosity? Vanished from sight himself, what Karèwèd most desires is a particular kind of sight. He wants to see behind the *kraton* walls. What the invisible herd-boy wants sight of, then, is precisely that which it is denied him to see by the law those walls apparently represent. Signifying his exclusion from court, the very presence of those walls awakens the boy's "natural" desire to see what lies behind them. The pathos of that desire is written into the modality of the poetry that recounts his adventures on the other side of the walls: for the child's initial penetration of the palace is sung in the melancholy meter of Megatruh. The pathos of the desire expressed in song stands in tension with the naughty tonality which colors the verbal description of Karèwèd's exploits inside the royal harem.

Figure 14. Wall of the Kraton Surakarta, viewed from the outside. Rising behind the wall is the Sangga Buwana meditation tower. Photograph by John Pemberton.

> And now Ki Jaka wished to see
> The sights inside the *kraton* walls
>
> Ki Jaka, making straight for it
> Through the Gate of Watchful Waiting came
> Not a soul accosting him
> Heading straight for the king's zenana
> The Inner Sanctum did he penetrate
>
> From the Hall of Fragrant Flowers to the Queen's boudoir, her bath
> In and about ranging everywhere
> All over the royal harem
> He did not miss a thing
> And after everything was eyed
>
> Ki Jaka then withdrew most tired
> And he was very hungry too[23]

23. [Megatruh] yata Ki Jakarsa uning / kontha sajroning kadhaton // Nulya laju Ki Jaka

Figure 15. Guarding a portal to the Kraton Surakarta. Courtesy of the Mang-kunagaran Palace.

Invisible, Karèwèd manages to slip past a series of heavily guarded portals to find himself inside the most private, most "inside" pavilions of Brawijaya's palace.[24] Finally Karèwèd comes to the queen's boudoir—and her bath. What the boy eyes is precisely that which (she who) is reserved for the sight of the king alone. Naturally, the wide-eyed innocent village boy is exhausted by the experience. Like his half-brother Prabang-kara's, Karèwèd's "crime" involves illicit access to the royal women. In the case of Karèwèd, however, what the crime lacks is any criminal intent.

---

ing lampahipun / prapta manjing Sri Manganti / tan ana wong ngaru-biru / wus laju mring kenyapuri / Prabayasa wus kalebon // Purwakanthi miwah jroning Purwalulut / sadaya wus dèn-ubengi / sajajahaning pura rum / tan ana kang dèn-liwati / sawusnya telas kang tinon // Nulya metu Ki Jaka sayah kalangkung / lawan sanget dènya ngelih (*BJT* X:29–32). See also notes to *BJT* X:30–31.

24. The area of the Majapahit palace freely ranged by Karèwèd is, in fact, the inner sanctum of the nineteenth-century Kraton Surakarta—the royal harem to which no post-pubescent males, aside from the king and a few designated senior princes, were normally allowed access. We are reminded that the descriptions of the Majapahit and Demak courts in this *babad* incessantly map and comment on the nineteenth-century Surakarta palace.

Figure 16. The Inner Sanctum of the Kraton Surakarta: Dalem Ageng Praba-suyasa.

This lack of intent underlies the pathos of the segment while at the same time pointing toward a curious subversion of a cultural-political order which would erect walls that separate commoner from court. I shall say more on this below.

The crimes perpetrated by the "marvelous invisible outlaw" are considered serious ones by the authorities at court. Indeed, the grand vizier reads the outlaw's deeds of daring as evidence of a possible plot to overthrow royal power (*BJT* XI:1–4). The outlaw's crime consists of the transgression of boundaries and unlawful intercourse with things reserved for the royal hand and palate (the king's *pusaka gamelan*, his women, his table, and his liquor). According to the logic of royal *pusaka*, that the outlaw could with impunity gain intimate contact with these reserved objects indicated his excessive (and hence potentially royal) power. The established authorities presume him either one who was bent on wrestling power for himself, or an agent of such a would-be usurper. When the outlaw is captured, Brawijaya, seeing that he is a mere boy, thus asks in a way that is meant to explain, reduce, and negate the boy's own action:

> "Who then sent you here
> In a devious cunning plot

To topple thus our realm
To subvert by a *darma* of deceit?"[25]

The audience of *Babad Jaka Tingkir*, however, might well have other questions concerning Karèwèd's criminal escapades than did the royal victims the *babad* depicts. The audience already knows two things that Brawijaya has yet to learn: the marvelous outlaw is only a simple village boy at play, as it were; and this village boy is Brawijaya's own son. Karè-wèd is *both* an idealized commoner acting on his own "natural" desires *and* a marginalized cast-off prince claiming his "natural" birthright.

There is a good dose of humor in the poet's treatment of the panicky uproar at court brought on by the boy's innocent crimes. For example, in an unmistakably parodic voice, the poet depicts the outlaw's enjoyment of the royal liquor as the ultimate act of transgression. It is, after all, the losses to his liquor cabinet which finally cast the king, painted here in rather pathetic colors, into the deepest depths of anguish (*BJT* XI:3).[26] Consider also the parodic humor which colors the scene of Karèwèd's final apprehension (*BJT* XI:11–19). Literally "drunk under the table" by his royal father, the young boy lies passed-out in a pool of his own vomit. The overkill exercised in this capture is remarkable as the poet describes how the mighty Brawijaya mobilizes the entire state apparatus to subdue a single unconscious (!) village boy. The drunken child is surrounded and bound hand and foot by the king's soldiers. Then in a parody of the standard heroic battle scene, the king's courtiers hurl their challenges as though addressing a matched opponent in single combat. But here it is rather in chorus that their brave words rise, words that are cast at and over the sleeping and hog-tied figure of a solitary child. The inappropri-

25. [Sinom] Sapa silih kang angutus / ing rèh sandi-upaya / arsanjor ing praja mami / nyempaluki ing darma karti-sampéka (*BJT* XI:22).
26. Brawijaya's anguish over losses to his private reserves of liquor echoes a nine-teenth-century Surakartan concern with the contents of the royal liquor cabinet. A journal for the years 1843–53, kept by a European (probably Indo-European) servant of Pakubuwana VII, includes a detailed inventory of the king's liquor cabinet that faithfully notes items of missing service along with his careful ledgers of alcohol consumption at court—how much, what kind, when, and for what occasion. See [Josep Krep = Joseph Kreeft], [*Karaton Surakarta: Journal 1843–1853 and notes pertaining to financial affairs, taxation, and land administration*] = serat Baleniklan: awit ongka 1771 dumugi ongka 1773 (composed and inscribed Surakarta, 1843–53). MS. SP uncataloged; SMP KS 81a, pp. 214–24.

Figure 17. The Handrawina banquet hall of the Kraton Surakarta.

ateness of the court's response to the "criminal" suggests a collapse of order—a more radical collapse than the one suspected by either Brawijaya or his clever grand vizier.

The order to which I refer is that order whose interest it is to preserve the image of an inviolable difference between court and countryside. It is an order that is premised on the impenetrability of *kraton* walls. Interestingly, it is Jaka Karèwèd's mother who gives voice to this order (an ideology) in the course of her piteous plaint over her captive son:

> "O my darling, how could you dare
> To penetrate the *kraton*?
> Where many are the courtiers, the chiefs
> Many, the notables of the realm
>
> "You have yet to know the vengeance of the realm
> For you are but a commoner
> A lowly wretched wretch
> A villager who has no rule [*ukara*] . . ."[27]

27. [Mas Kumambang] Èh pagému nyawa dadak wani-wani / ngambah ing jro pura /

The word *ukara*, translated here as "rule," also designates "order" and rarely "greed." It is perhaps most widely understood as a linguistic or grammatical term denoting "sense, sentence, or syntax." To say that one has no *ukara* means that his or her behavior or language is without structure and is hence meaningless or nonsensical.[28] By pronouncing her son—because he is a commoner—as without *ukara*, Karèwèd's mother repeats the mythic notion that there is but one true or proper *ukara*, and that that *ukara* is the rule or grammar of the court.[29] If it were the case that there were but one *ukara*, and that *ukara* were the sole reserve of those inside the palace walls, then meaningful communication between court and countryside would be impossible.[30] The wall separating the "big" and "little" traditions would be truly impregnable. Taken to its extreme, such a notion would imply that if one cannot speak, move, or "be" according to the rules or grammar of the court, one does not properly speak, move, or "be" at all. In effect, alternative orders of discourse would be both essentially unreal and incommensurable with the single true order authorized by *the* (exclusive) royal center. Common folk, "having no order" as the butcher-girl claims, would remain forever radically other—essentially invisible, and outside of valid discourse.

With its characteristic *semu, Babad Jaka Tingkir* has these ideological lines issue from the mouth of a village woman whose own life, *not* atypically, bridged (breached) the *kraton* walls. Karèwèd's mother was both a lowly butcher-girl *and* a royal concubine. The nineteenth-century writer who composed *Babad Jaka Tingkir* knew well that such a mixed status was

---

akèh punggawa pra mantri / kèh wong gedhé jro nagara // Sira durung weruh sikuning negari / sira pan wong sudra / papa hina kawlas-asih / wong désa tanpa ukara (*BJT* XII:25–26).

28. This usage of *ukara* recalls the opening verse of R.Ng. Ronggawarsita's renowned *Kalatidha*, where the poet laments the loss of royal order in late-nineteenth-century Surakarta: "Mangkya darajating praja / kawuryan wus sunya ruri / rurah pangrèhing ngukara . . ." See also Errington, "To Know Oneself the Troubled Times," esp. pp. 117–18.

29. This notion belongs to a scholarly tradition which was promoted and ultimately entrenched by nineteenth- and early-twentieth-century Dutch colonial philology. It was a tradition that proclaimed the language spoken in or about the Kraton Surakarta the sole exemplar of "standard" (that is, correct) Javanese.

30. In order to avoid misunderstandings of my argument, I should like to emphasize here that *ukara* is *not* meant to designate any specific "language level," such as an imagined "kraton variety of *krama*" in opposition to, say, "village *ngoko*."

Figure 18. Women of the court moving in procession through a portal in the Kraton Surakarta. Courtesy of the Mangkunagaran Palace.

not at all extraordinary for women of the royal zenana. Javanese kings "traditionally" took attractive and talented daughters of their courtiers—both high and low—as concubines. Indeed, it was not unheard-of for such relatively low-born concubines to be elevated to queenly status, especially in the pre-1830 period preceding the high colonial age.[31] In the palaces of central Java many of the royal women who mothered the next generation of aristocrats were of humble village origin. Members of their families, as well as a host of other royal servants, passed back and forth—some of them daily—between court and countryside through the walls which encircled the nineteenth-century Javanese *kraton*. Nevertheless, despite the obvious evidence to the contrary, by the mid-nineteenth century the fiction of impenetrable *kraton* walls had become emblematic of the insuperable gap that was imagined to separate royal from other orders. Center and margin were ideally, if not really, incommensurable.

31. Consider, for instance the case of Pakubuwana III's queen, Kangjeng Ratu Kancana (Beruk). See above, note 5. When, in the late nineteenth century, Pakubuwana IX decided to elevate his favorite low-born concubine to queenly status, he met with considerable opposition from conservative members of his own family; see [K.R.A. Sasradiningrat IV], *Dhirilaksita* (composed Surakarta, [late 19th century]; inscribed Surakarta by Joyosayono, 1954). MS. Rp 290; SMP RP 60, p. 77.

This fiction of impenetrability gained such credence doubtless because there was an element of truth to it. That truth, however, pertained perhaps more to those inside the walls than to the "outsiders." It was, ironically, the king himself who was perhaps least free to pass through the walls encircling his own *kraton*. By the 1820s, the king had become a near prisoner in his own palace, no longer free to traverse the countryside as had been the royal prerogative of old. Any royal excursion required a prior letter of permission from the office of the Dutch resident or, for longer trips, from higher colonial officials. A *babad* composed at the Surakarta court around 1831 poignantly writes of this changed circumstance of Javanese kingship. The scene is April 1829, toward the end of the Dipanegara War. Pakubuwana VI would plan a trip to visit the Dutch commander of troops in the field several days' march away. A senior prince's cautionary response to the king's desire is as follows:

"Begging your pardon, Highness
Indeed 'tis more than fit
In the bygone age
He who reigned as king
Every year did make the tour
Round the compass of the realm
Rallying all the land

"It was as though the king did move
His court, the *pusaka* borne along
For a full month long
The ladies of the court
Those fit were borne along
But nowadays, I say
Ever since
The Company came to Java
That king-maker will not allow
You to tour as in days of old

"And if allowed to tour within the realm
You may not sleep the night along the way
Thus to this very day
No precedent is there

Save by the will of the Company
By order of the Governor . . ."[32]

However, the movements of village court women—like Karèwèd's mother—would have been of little interest to the Dutch governors. For persons like her, the walls' impenetrability was a more permeable fiction. Note, for instance, the hyperbolic ease with which Karèwèd's mother (and her mother again) make their highly emotional and unceremonious entrance into the king's audience hall. Upon hearing of Karèwèd's probable arrest:

> The Widow hoisted up her skirts
>
> Along with her mother; off rushed the two
> Eyes brimming with tears
> The two of them scurried on apace
> Straightway to the King's audience
>
> Arriving in the presence, the Widow let out a shriek[33]

These women were both of the center and of the margin; their (imaginary) lives, as did those of countless historical others, communicated among multiple orders. Nonetheless, and not uncharacteristically, in the royal presence Karèwèd's mother restates a division of orders which apparently negates extraroyal order as a meaningful category. Her discourse thus seemingly reinforces the position of the dominant-royal order at the expense of other orders. However, upon closer examination, her utter-

---

32. [Dhangdhanggula] kula nuwun Sang Prabu / mapan langkung déning prayogi / nenggih alaming kina / kang jumeneng ratu / ing saben warsu pepara / mubeng tapel-watesipun ing nagari / kerig wong sanagara // Sampun kados nenggih ratu ngalih / keprabon lan wasiyat binakta / ngantos sawulan laminé / parèstri jro kedhatun / ingkang pantes binakta sami / nanging mangké tur kula / ing salaminipun / kumpni nèng tanah Jawa / kang ngamadeg aji tan karsa ngidèni / papara kadya kina // Linilan pepara jro nagari / boten kinarsaken nyipeng marga / mila delasan ing mangké / tan wonten luwangipun / anjawi yèn sangking Kupeni / terang ing gupernur (*Serat Babat Sangkala* [composed Surakarta, ca. 1831] in [*Klempakan Warni-warni*] [inscribed Surakarta, ca. 1831]. MS. SP 6 Ta; SMP KS 1C.2, coll. I:pp. 205–6).

33. [Mas Kumambang] Ni Rondha ningseti sinjang // Lan rénanya lumayu tiyang kekalih / sarwi rawat waspa / ririkatan wong kekalih / laju maring paséwakan // Praptèng ngarsa Ni Rondha karuna anjrit (*BJT* XII:16–18).

ances and also the behavior of her son suggest a radical subversion of that dominant order, a subversion much more dangerous than had been feared at the outset by Brawijaya and his grand vizier.

What had been feared and suspected by Brawijaya was a plot to topple his kingdom, a plot perpetrated by the focal center of another, rival royal order. That the "marvelous outlaw"—this boy who lay exposed in front of the king—was merely a simple village boy acting on his own had been unthinkable. It was assumed such a character, insofar as he would be categorically outside royal order, could never, even under the cloak of invisibility, gain access on his unauthorized own to areas and objects (the royal *pusaka* and liquor) that belonged to the king alone. This is to say that according to the logic of a single elite/royal order, independent transgression by one like Karèwèd is virtually impossible. Thus Brawijaya must assume another elite mastermind (a *dhalang*) behind this "representative" of the "stupid masses"—those who have no order.[34] The most threatening of cases would be, of course, that Karèwèd (a figure for "the people") acted on his own. That a village herd-boy, the quintessential image of the *wong cilik*, would dare to penetrate the seat of the only true order, to touch the sacred regalia of the king (not with the rebellious intent of a rival prince, but rather out of the immediacy of his "natural" curiosity), and suffer no untoward effects from their supernatural royal powers, implies a crumbling of the mighty *kraton* walls that would separate the elite from common folk. Such a feat proclaims the absence of the categorical difference that the walls stand to define. Karèwèd's true transgression constituted the most dangerous of subversions.

Let us now turn to Karèwèd's "confession" better to understand the special nature of that transgression. Explaining how he came to range the palace, the prisoner Karèwèd tells the king:

> "As for what I've done
> All that, Your Majesty
> Was by my own design
> No one told me what to do
> It was because I wished
> To prove, Your Royal Highness

---

34. For an interesting treatment of the notion of the political *dhalang* in the context of contemporary Indonesia, see John Pemberton, "Notes on the 1982 General Election in Solo," *Indonesia* 41 (1986):15–16.

The book [*pustaka*] I chanced upon
In the middle of the mighty wood
Its form a banyan tree sprouting from the earth"[35]

Not only did Karèwèd act on his own, but his actions were propelled by a peculiar form of magic writing. By means, perhaps, of a scribal "error," *pusaka* ("power object") is transformed into *pustaka* ("book, writing"). It was that "book" which made the boy invisible (absent) in a way that won his presence at court. For with that "book" Jaka Karèwèd (the commoner) ruptured the wall of distinction that would pretend to exclude him from the center. By this strategic "slip" of the pen, the scribe (or perhaps the poet) again reminds the reader/audience of the potential power of scriptural interruption to effect a novel history that would tell "the other side of the story." *Babad Jaka Tingkir* is a text inscribed to suggest what it could mean to write a rather different kind of history for Java's future.

Let us reflect further upon the nature of Karèwèd's "invisibility." As long as he remained "in his place," Karèwèd (the emblematic commoner) was sheer absence from the seat of government. Thus would he/they remain radically invisible from the scene of written history. As long as she or he remained the image of sheer absence, the commoner did not have to be thought of or considered by the court. We have spoken of how, by the middle of the nineteenth century, the physical presence of concentric walls encircling the *kraton* had come to signify the inviolability of the distinction between elite and other orders. The walls stood to keep the elite (especially the king) inside, and to cultivate the fiction that commoners (the *wong cilik*) remained categorically outside. Since the physical presence at court of these same commoners was unmistakable, however, the fiction of categorical difference could only be preserved through mechanisms of denial that would erase the *wong cilik* from what was considered "meaningful" discourse at court. Their voices were present—both inside and outside the court—but seldom registered in the dominant discourse. A system of discursive denial assured that their stories would be rarely told.

What a story like this tale of Jaka Karèwèd does is to deny the system of

35. [Sinom] Déné ta pratingkah amba / makaten punika Gusti / pan kayun amba priyongga / tan wonten kang mumuruki / sangking kawula apti / angyektosaken puku-lun / pustaka [*sic*] gèn amanggya / wonten tengah ing wanadri / warni wit ing waringin tuwuh in kisma (*BJT* XI:26).

denial. This system can limp along quite effectively as long as the "invisible" commoners "know their place" within (that is categorically *outside*) order. These commoners "know" and keep to their place by pretending ignorance of their own productive participation in the order that conceptually excludes them. Jaka Karèwèd's possession of the *pus*[*t*]*aka*, the magic heirloom that *was* a book, propelled him to contest the pretense that founded the system of denial. The invisible herd-boy would no longer keep his place in an order that would erase him. From an invisibility which was sheer absence, the boy moved through a denial of denial to a different kind of invisibility which forcibly affirmed the presence of those persons the elite had refused to see in their midst. Karèwèd, the herd-boy with *pus*[*t*]*aka* behind his ear, dared to lay bare the fiction of difference. He eyed the royal women, touched the royal regalia, ate the royal food, and drank the royal liquor—*not* in an attitude of servitude, invisible in the shadow of his royal masters as did the other commoners-at-court, but invisible in a way that affirmed his presence, acting to satisfy *his own* natural desires.

Brawijaya sensed the danger such public "insolence" constituted. Contrary to appearances, it was not a feeling of charity that induced Brawijaya to recognize his paternity of Karèwèd.

> His Majesty the King was touched by wonder deep
> His heart pierced by care
> Tears welling in his eyes
> Bethought himself, his heart aware
>
> Decreed the King to his Vizier
> "This our Jaka here
> Is verily my son
> Take him home with you"[36]

The tears in Brawijaya's eyes were not for Karèwèd but for himself. His acknowledgment of Karèwèd was a last-ditch effort to reverse the subversion effected by the child's innocent transgression. By taking Karèwèd to himself he meant to appropriate for himself the child's behavior. If Karèwèd is recognized as his son-the-prince, rather than a mere commoner

36. [Mas Kumambang] Yata wau mangungun Sri Narapati / karantan ing driya / kumembeng waspanirèki / karaos èngeting driya // Sang ngaPrabu dhawuh mring Rekyana Patih / iki ta si Jaka / pan sayekti suta mami / gawanen mring wismanira (*BJT* XII:32–33).

(that is, his mother's son), the boy's actions could still be subsumed under the logic of the (imagined sole and exclusive) order of the court. That is: everything that Karèwèd did *really* belonged to his father-the-king. Thus Brawijaya could, perhaps, attempt to domesticate the danger Karèwèd's actions posed to his kingly authority. Was the domestication successful?

Even if we join Brawijaya in granting (and thereby recognizing) Karèwèd's princely status, the story told of him in *Babad Jaka Tingkir* remains the story of a village boy who is also of the court. Karèwèd is emblematic of a host of persons who lived between and among court and village orders in traditional Java. The telling of his tale points toward their tales— tales that remain, for the most part, untold. Where the character Karèwèd differs most significantly from those other court village personalities who routinely traversed the nineteenth-century *kraton* walls is not in his royal blood, but in the registration of his voice/story in a royal *babad*. Texts of the more dominant *babad* tradition barely touch upon, let alone linger upon, the lives of such seemingly insignificant personalities. Indeed, the rules governing the composition of those *babad* were of an order, an *ukara*, that seemed to proscribe such an interest.

Babad Jaka Tingkir, however, is a *babad* of another order. Among other things, it is precisely the presentation of an alternative set of rules (another grammar) for history writing that the text of this *babad* effects. This alternative grammar shows itself not only in this *babad*'s telling of untold stories by means of its serial focus on figures at the margins, but also in the anecdotal style with which it treats these marginal characters, a style that breaks the dominance of linear court narrative. A number of important figures in the dominant *babad* tradition too begin at or pass through the margins, perhaps most notably the figure of Jaka Tingkir himself. However, in the more typical court chronicle, these one-time marginal figures are finally incorporated into (and in control of) the center. The narrative of the dominant *babad* records the incorporation in a rationalized linear "genealogical" dynastic order. The Jaka Tingkir of the dominant tradition may start out fraternizing with crocodiles, but he ends up Sultan of Pajang, bequeathing power to his "foster son" the founder of the Mataram dynasty. The marginal figures of *Babad Jaka Tingkir*, though they rise momentarily and anecdotally, remain on the margins—exiled, lost in comfortable obscurity, killed, vanished, or left to roam.

With this in mind, let us turn finally to consider the *almost* invisible position of Jaka Prabangkara and Jaka Karèwèd within the historical memory of nineteenth-century Java. Both characters belong to the documentary margins: although occasionally listed among Brawijaya V's prodigious progeny, there is virtually no mention of them in the narrative texts of the dominant *babad* tradition.[37] Nor are they remembered in the oral historical traditions that still circulate in Central Java.[38] Nevertheless, these two characters do possess an apparently haunting textual presence in the Javanese past.

We find these shadowy protagonists in C. F. Winter's 1848 publication, the *Javaansche Zamenspraken* (Javanese Conversations). They appear in the context of one among many contrived dialogues the Dutch Javanologist, "Mr. So-and-so" (Tuwan Anu) pursued with his highly literate native informants. In this dialogue, the informant Parakawi ("The-Poet") catalogs for his colonial patron the contents, provenance, and authorship of the "great works" of Javanese literature. "The Poet" ends one of his many lists noting that "the *suluk* all comprise allusions (*pralambang*) that concern

37. Royal genealogies that do list these two shadowy princes note Prabangkara's exile to China and name Karèwèd as the "Adipati of Borneo." See, for example, *Serat Sajarah Citrasoma* (compiled s.a., s.l.; inscribed Surakarta, [late 19th century]). MS. RP B 85; SMP MN 247, and *Serat Sajarah-dalem Sampéyan-dalem I.S.K.S. Pakubuwana kaping X: sajarah ingkang saking pangiwa* (compiled Surakarta, [early 20th century]; inscribed Surakarta, early 20th century). MS. SP uncataloged; SMP KS 10E.

A variant of the Jaka Prabangkara tale is found in a manuscript that was inscribed (composed?) by or for B.R.T Suryadi (son-in-law and courtier of Hamengkubuwana VII, ruler of the Kraton Yogyakarta [1877–1921]) in 1906. This truly remarkable variant also draws Jaka Prabangkara's connection to writing. In this telling, which includes the story of the ink-stained portrait of the queen, it is two (nonroyal) youths (Prabakara and Purbèngkara) that Brawijaya sets to flight in the kite. The god Ywang Penyarikan (Citragotra), scribe (*carik*) of the gods, takes mercy on the hapless youths and draws their kite to heaven. He knows the youths are sinless, because it is he who inscribes the sacred tablet of God (Lokil Makpul, Ar. Lauhu'l Mahfûz). Peering in at the gates of heaven, the youths catch sight of two things: one in the form of a vessel (?) (*kentheng*), the other in the form of a carriage. The name of the first object is Sastra ("writing") Siring ("crooked, inclined; limit") Déwa ("god[s]") Metu ("emerge, come forth"). Finally Ywang Penyarikan expels the youths from heaven. Prabakara lands in Spain; Purbèngkara in China. Both lose their humanity to become rulers of spirit realms (*Babad Demak* I, ed. Slamet Riyadi and Suwadji [Jakarta: Departemen Pendidikan dan Kebudayaan, Proyek Penerbitan Buku Sastra Indonesia dan Daerah, 1981], pp. 161–67).

38. Variants of the Prabangkara story do, however, remain in oral circulation in East Java (R.P. Suryanto Sastraatmodjo, personal communication [November 1983]).

ngèlmu (Knowledge)."[39] It is at this precise moment that "Mr. So-and-so" recalls the titles of two half-forgotten texts: "I rather remember some time ago hearing of a couple of texts: one of them was called *Prabangkara*—the other, *Krèwèd*. Do they, in fact, exist?"[40] "The Poet" answers that indeed they do (or did), that they treat Majapahit history, and that they were composed by Carik Braja, the seventeenth-century *pujongga* to whom "The Poet" also attributes a number of mainstream *babad*. "The Poet" then continues his catalog, mentioning next the prophetic *Jayabaya* texts which provide "allusions [*pralambang*] that characterize Javanese realms through time."[41] In this textbook of Javanese language, literature, and culture that Winter composed in consultation with his literary colleague-informants from the Surakarta Palace, the titles *Prabangkara* and *Karèwèd* are recalled as texts already half-forgotten. And they are recalled, and thus textually situated, in between two very important genres of literary *allusion: suluk* and Jayabaya prophecies.[42]

In the textual work of our most allusive *babad*, the stories of these half-forgotten princes are composed in a manner which raises issues of representation and writing while at the same time highlighting the princes' marginal and marginalized (mixed blood) status. The histories of these youths, Javanese princes who are also and emphatically *wong cilik*, point suggestively to the nature of writing in Java. The story of Prabangkara is a cautionary tale on the danger and power of representation in writing. But it is also, and at the same time, a guide to how one should write (and rule) allusively with *semu*. Prabangkara's history is also a story of exile and of the possibility of success gained in exile by writing—and of the potential meanings of that success for the future. The Krèwèd tale reveals the imaginary status of the lines, or walls, erected to separate court from countryside, center from periphery, noble from commoner. The writing of the story of Krèwèd, who by means of a "book" penetrated the walls of the *kraton* that would exclude him, points toward the recognition and

39. "sawernining serat suluk punika sami pralambang ngèlmi" (C. F. Winter, *Javaansche Zamenspraken*, 1:192).
40. "Kula rumiyin mèngeti namaning serat kekalih, ènget kula setunggil nama Prabangkara, kalih Jaka Krèwèd, punika punapa yektos wonten?" (ibid., p. 192).
41. Ibid.
42. One cannot but wonder whether the Ambonese exile who inscribed *Babad Jaka Tingkir* into *His Majesty the Sixth's Correspondence* had read the 1848 *Javaansche Zamenspraken* as well as the 1845 *Javaansche Brievenboek*.

documentation of those of the margins who were always already "invisibly" present in the center itself. While questioning the centeredness of centers, the story of invisible Krèwèd's magic book bows in the direction of a history of the underclasses, a history that has yet to be written. The two episodes together, considered from the vantage of the nineteenth-century exile who inscribed them on Ambon, suggest to the future generations for whom they were written a new historiographic project—one that would turn allusively both to the increasingly visible world outside Java and to the invisible world within.

CHAPTER 5

THE DEMAK MOSQUE:
A CONSTRUCTION OF
AUTHORITY

❁

Tensions and struggles between centralizing authorities and more disseminate local powers were forces that worked to shape the historical
realities of Java. The author of *Babad Jaka Tingkir* explores this historical
dynamic, notably in the treatment of a monumental construction project
that took place in Demak at the close of the fifteenth century. An account
of the building of the Grand Mosque of Demak constitutes the poem's
third episode. With this episode, together with the framing interludes
that bind its telling, the *babad*'s author produces a critique of monumentalization as such, while at the same time introducing the power of Islam
on Java.

A Genealogy of Jaka Tingkir: Islam
Comes to Java

The Demak Mosque episode is preceded by a narrative interlude that
opens with an explicit reminder to the reader that what she has been
reading is an interrupted history. Revealing the delightfully fantastic adventures of Prabangkara and Krèwèd as a lengthy digression, the *babad*
abruptly returns to "the story at hand":

> Falling silent on Prince Jaka who had come into his own
> Let now be told in turn
> The tale interrupted by poetry [the poet]
> Of Pajang-Pengging sweet[1]

1. [Mas Kumambang] gantya kawuwusa / ingkang pinunggel ing kawi / ing Pajang
Pengging sarkara (*BJT* XII:41).

And with this narrative turn to a history of Pajang-Pengging and an introduction to our absent hero's father, Kebo Kenonga, and his uncle, Kebo Kanigara, we are returned to a genealogy of Jaka Tingkir. Then, revisiting the earlier textual moment of Brawijaya's vanishing: "with the Fall of Majapahit / Was Brawijaya's vanishing" (*BJT* XIII:5, literally repeating *BJT* I:12), we are back to the future that textually preceded the digressionary flashbacks we have been reading. The text proceeds to situate the two Pengging boys at the center of the new world of Islam in Java. These two grandsons of Majapahit's final king eventually become pupils at the Moslem ashram (as it is termed) of Sunan Bonang, the supreme *wali* of the time. Falling silent on the boys, whom our author leaves presumably immersed in their Quranic studies, the narrative then turns to the emerging world of Islam that the *wali* have introduced to Java. And that new world is initially articulated, through translation, as a transformation of professional categories. The old Sanskritic Buda religious orders have been exchanged for Arabic-titled holy men:

> Now at that time in Java's land
> All had become Moslem
> There was none who did resist
> All the mountain hermits [*ajar*]
> The ascetics [*wewasi*] and acolytes [*guguntung*],
>   the devotees [*manguyu*] and disciples [*cantrik*]
> Many converted to the faith
>
> And the royal Buddhist and Saivite monks [*sogata séwa*],
>   the Hindu priests [*resi-resi*]
> Were exchanged for *fuqaha* lawyers
> Great and mighty pundits
> Excellent learned *ulama*
> Mystic *zahid* and *mungahid*
> *Mufti* and *sulakha*
> Great and mighty *khukama*[2]

2. [Dhangdhanggula] duk semona ing tanah Jawi / pan wus Èslam sadaya / tan wonten barenjul / sagung ingkang para ajar / myang wewasi, guguntung maguyud (*sic*) cantrik / wus kathah nandhang iman // Myang sogata séwa resi-resi / wus liniron, kang para pukaha / pra pandhita gedhé-gedhé / pra ngulama linuhung / para sahid para mungahid / mupti lawan sulakha / khukama gung-agung (*BJT* XIII:19–20).

Next, by ranking the converters in a hierarchy of axial saints (or *wali kutub*) and listing a number of the most important converts (*BJT* XIII:21–28), the *babad* discloses the restructuring of authority that these saints are effecting as they establish a post-Majapahit Islamic state in Java. To concretize that structure of authority, the *wali* decide to build a Grand Mosque. As we shall see, that mosque comes to stand for, and thus becomes, the center of authority for the new state. This construction of order is not, however, without forces that would resist it.

The Demak Mosque: An Enduring Monument

The "figure" of the Demak Mosque, "hero" of the third episode, forms the exception to the rule of permanent marginalization that shapes *Babad Jaka Tingkir*. Not subject in the same way to the marginality experienced by the *babad*'s other heroes, the Demak Mosque qua *pusaka* of the realm is clearly and intentionally of the center:

> The desire of all the *wali*
> The eight who made the relic [*tilas*]
> A little something rather grand
> Was to create a new mosque
> A sacred site of power for the kingdom of Demak
> A *pusaka* for all the kings
> Of all the Land of Java[3]

By constructing the Demak Mosque to be a *pusaka*, the *wali* meant to embody in it their enduring legacy for kingship in Java. They built it (reputedly in A.J. 1420/A.D. 1498) to be a kind of "relic" or "trace" (*tilas*), a monument that would stand perpetually as a concrete material site both for pilgrimage and of supernatural power. It was to be the *bituwah* (sacred site of power) of the realm of Java and, at the same time, a *pusaka* for the rulers of that realm. The *wali*'s project was to produce "a little something" to stand for, and to stand as basis for, Moslem kingship in Java.

Evidently the *wali*'s project met with some success. *Babad* traditions

3. [Asmarandana] Karsaning kang para wali / wowolu kang karya tilas / sakedhik kang radi gedhé / angyasani masjid anyar / bituwah nagri Demak / pusakaning para ratu / nenggih ing satanah Jawa (*BJT* XIV:3).

("Major" and otherwise) confirm that long after the ascendancy of Demak had passed, its Grand Mosque continued to command a status as one of the major *pusaka* of the "Land of Java" and its successive rulers. By the beginning of the eighteenth century, the *pusaka* mosque of Java had stood firm for over two centuries while the capital of the realm had passed through four more or less turbulent moves: from Demak to Pajang, Pajang to Mataram (Kerta), Kerta to Plérèd, and finally Plérèd to Kartasura. The "Major *Babad*" tells the story of the Mosque's endurance as a source of royal power in the history of a fugitive king's surrender to Dutch forces in 1708. This king, Mangkurat III (r. 1703–8), had been on the run since 1705 when his Dutch-supported uncle (Pakubuwana I [r. 1704–19]) had taken his *kraton* by force. After Mangkurat III's surrender and subsequent exile to Ceylon, word came to the then-reigning Pakubuwana I that his exiled nephew had taken with him a number of Mataram's most important *pusaka*. Although deploring the loss, Pakubuwana I is reported to have said:

> "Even were all the *pusaka* of Java
> Carried off to Jakarta [and thence to Ceylon]
>
> Yea, all those in form of *keris* and spear
> I'd be not troubled in the least
> As long as there remains
> The Grave of Kadilangu [that is, the grave of Sunan Kalijaga]
> And the Demak Mosque, O Minister
> Mark this well
> Yea, these two are
> *Pusaka* of the Land of Java
> Whose greatness is equaled by none"[4]

The Demak Mosque retained its significance for the realm and its rulers up to and through the nineteenth century of *Babad Jaka Tingkir's* writing. When by 1842 the *pusaka* Mosque had fallen into grievous disrepair, it was Governor General Merkus (by then ruler of "all the Land of Java")

---

4. [Dhangdhanggula] nadyan kabèh pusaka ing tanah Jawi / ginawa mring Jakarta // Iya ingkang rupa tumbak keris / apan ora dadi galih ingwang / nanging sok maksih ing mangké / setana Ngadilangu / lawan masjid Demak apatih / èh iya wruhanira / kalih prakarèku / pusaka ing tanah Jawa / ingkang ageng datan ana malih-malih (*Babad Tanah Jawi* [Batavia, 1939–41], 18:27–28).

Figure 19. The Demak Mosque: "a *pusaka* for all the kings, of all the Land of Java." Photograph by Adhi Moersid.

who commanded the kings of Surakarta and Yogyakarta to see to its repairs.[5] A history composed at the Surakarta court, *Serat Nalika Bangun Masjid ing Demak* ("When the Demak Mosque was [Re]Built"), provides a firsthand description of that restoration project.[6] Opening with a note on Pakubuwana VII's (r. 1830–58) intense spiritual (that is, quintessentially royal) response to the Grand Mosque's precarious condition, the history goes on to relate royal Java's more material response to the Dutch governor general's initiative. After a grueling night in the meditation chamber, Pakubuwana VII summons two trusted courtiers whom he orders:

> "You, I order to Demak
> To attend to the disassembly of
> The *pusaka* Grand Mosque
> For it is to be rebuilt

5. *Serat Babad Sengkala: Kawit Pulo Jawi dipuniseni tiyang nalika taun ongka 1 dumugi taun 1854* (MS. SP 220 Ca-A; SMP 11KS 1A), p. 175.
6. *Serat Nalika Bangun Masjid ing Demak* (composed Surakarta, s.a.; inscribed Surakarta, 1885–86). MS. SP 203 Ra; SMP KS 81B.

Grandpa General, who is in charge
     [and/or: who had the idea in the first place]
Asks for our blessings
Go ye to Semarang
And I grant for the Mosque's [restoration] expense
Three thousand rupiah"[7]

The *babad* goes on to detail—sometimes with high drama—the adventures and misadventures of the restoration crew sent from Surakarta.

Now, almost five hundred years after its erection by the *wali*, the Grand Mosque of Demak still remains a force in Javanese governance. The Mosque's significance is not lost on the current New Order rulers. The most recent restoration of Demak's Grand Mosque was completed in March 1987. After opening the official ceremony commemorating the restoration with a ritual stroke on the Mosque's call-to-prayer drum (*bedhuk*), President Soeharto assured the assemblage that the restoration of the Mosque was neither a waste of money nor a luxury, but integral to the nation's development—in the largest sense of the word.[8] Indeed the president saw the restoration as part of an effort to build up the nation's "spiritual capital" (*modal rohani*) into a source of working capital that would powerfully propel all aspects of national development.[9]

Let us now turn to a reading of *Babad Jaka Tingkir*'s history of the construction of the Grand Mosque of Demak, this architectural *pusaka* that has for so long commanded such importance for rulers in Java. The text discloses that the express desire of the *wali* was to construct with it a relic whose efficacy would subsist under, and somehow be contained within, its material structure. The Grand Mosque of Demak was to be a monument: a permanent trace and a trace of permanence. And a monument it remains today. What, then, is it a monument to? How did it

7. [Dhangdhanggula] sira padha sun tuding mring Demak / anjenengi pangrurahé / pusaka masjid agung / apan arsa winangun malih / kaki jéndral kang murba / anjaluk pangèstu / sira jujuga Semarang / lawan ingsun paparing ongkosing masjid / cacah tri éwu rupyah (ibid., p 3).

8. The word *development* (*pembangunan*), denoting modern economic development, is *the* buzzword for New Order Indonesia. President Soeharto has taken the title "Bapak Pembangunan" (Father of Development). For an incisive study of "development" in late-twentieth-century Indonesia, see Ariel Heryanto, "The 'Development' of Development," *Indonesia* 46 (1988):1–24.

9. *Kompas*, 22 March 1987.

become monumental? And what, again in the terms of this *babad* of the margins, might it mean to construct such a monument?

On the Construction of a Monument

That the Grand Mosque of Demak is a monument to Islam in Java almost goes without saying. The architects of the Mosque were the very saints who brought Islam to Java, the legendary *wali* who are traditionally credited with the conversion of Java from the "Buda" faith[10] of the heathens to the True Faith as revealed to, and by, the Prophet Mohammed. Although *Babad Jaka Tingkir*, interestingly, does not speak directly of the *wali*'s proselytizing activities, it nonetheless shares in this tradition. For in our *babad* the construction of the Mosque itself stands for the process of conversion, and the architectural structure of the Mosque—as designed by the *wali* and detailed by this *babad* alone[11]—stands for the sociopolitical structure of newly converted Javano-Islamic society. In this regard we must remember that the Mosque's saintly architects are as well known for their temporal role in the formation of the first Islamic polity on Java as they are for their spiritual role in the propagation of the faith. These roles, of course, are not unrelated. *Babad Jaka Tingkir* twice tells us that the state that the *wali* established was one of a Javanese "caliphate," which meant (at least in theory) the instatement of Javanese kingship as the

10. When the term *Buda* is used to refer to religion or religious practice in Java, it does not denote specifically Buddhist belief or practice. Rather *Buda* indicates a multifarious pre-Islamic (or non-Islamic) complex of beliefs found in Java. This complex consists of animism, Hinduism, and Buddhism, as well as variously permutated blends of the three. Buda groups persist in the Badui highlands of West Java and the Ténggèr region of East Java. For an extended treatment of the Tengger people, see Robert W. Hefner, *Hindu Javanese: Tengger Tradition and Islam* (Princeton: Princeton University Press, 1985).

11. I have compared *Babad Jaka Tingkir*'s history of the construction of the Demak Mosque with that of several other *babad* and have consistently found in the 509-line *BJT* version a higher level of detail: in the architectural description, the named cast of productive characters, and in the recounted constructive action. Cf. *Babad Tanah Jawi* (Batavia, 1939–41), 3:14–17 (120 lines); *Serat Manikmaya dumugi Demak*, ed. Mas Rongga Panambangan (MS. RP B100; SMP MN 184), canto 86 (154 lines); *Babad Segaluh* (composed s.l., s.a. and 1887; inscribed [Yogyakarta?, 1904?]. MS. RP B24b; SMP MN 268, pp. 195–202 (256 lines); and *Babad Demak 1*, ed. Slamet Riyadi and Suwaji, pp. 213–14 and 221–24 (277 lines).

supreme temporal representative of God's dominion (see *BJT* I:22–24 and XIII:18–19). It was both the shape and the permanence of the sociopoliti-cal structure of this Javanese caliphate that the *wali* meant to build into the material structure of the Mosque. The Mosque was constructed to become a living *pusaka* that would serve for all time as a monument to, and of, a certain form of Islamic authority in Java.

Let us now consider in more detail *Babad Jaka Tingkir's* depiction of this construction of authority. The monument composes a seemingly perfect hierarchical structure, a wishful structure that would mirror the ideal sociopolitical configuration of the realm. The wishfulness expresses the desire of its architects, a desire that they project into the future in the material-spiritual form of the *pusaka*. The architects of the structure are the eight axial saints (*wali kutub*) of Islam in Java. It is they who assume and entertain the authority both to lay the plans and to mete out the tasks to be performed by all parties involved in the structure's production.

How, then, is the structure pieced together? As is the normal procedure in Javanese house building, the architects draw up plans and fix the mea-surements for the prefabrication of the structure's component parts (see figure 12); they also decide who shall work each component and deter-mine the date for later assembly and erection. The share that the eight saintly architects assign themselves (plus the ninth of their company whom they have installed as caliph) is the fabrication of the four master pillars (*saka guru*) (*BJT* XIV:12). Usually considered the most important structural components of such an edifice, the four *saka guru* constitute the master supports upon which the structure rests. To the auxiliary *wali* are assigned the auxiliary pillars (*saka pangendhit*). The rank and file of the spiritual elite (i.e., the *pradikan, ulama,* etc.) are to work the peripheral pillars (*saka rawa*). To the temporal authorities (the provincial lords, royal family, and nobility) are assigned the support-, tie-, hip-, and plate-beams. The provincial lords (the *adipati,* or princes-regent), whom the *babad* carefully lists, are to provide the primary beams, with members of the royal family and the nobility supplying the secondary beams along with the sheathing and "great roof boards" (*BJT* XIV:13–21). Structur-ally, the various beams both tie the pillars to one another and act as supports for the roof whose shape they frame; the great roof boards form the surface upon which the mass of roofing and shingles rests. The court-iers and military elite are to work the rafters and the fencing (*BJT* XIV:21–22). The rafters reinforce and define the roof-base, whereas the fencing defines the structure's boundaries. Finally, the roofing and the shingles are assigned to no single party; instead they are to be provided by general contribution (*sami urunan kéwala*), apparently by the public at large (*BJT* XIV:22). Ostensibly providing a superficial surface covering for the edifice, the roofing actually plays a rather more critical structural role. Why this is so shall become apparent below.

Translated into the sociopolitical index,[12] the architectural plans for the Mosque ordered by the eight *wali kutub* appear to lay out a schematized hierarchy of authority with the pinnacle (or, more precisely, the foundation) of that hierarchy secured for that eight *wali* who designed it and their anointed ninth (the caliph). Next in the hierarchy come the auxiliary rural *wali* and the lower "ecclesiastics" supporting the structure's periphery. The more obviously temporal elite, the provincial lords first and then the princes of the blood, tie the sociopolitical structure together. Connecting the main supports one to another, and resting upon them and their ultimate authority, the nobles also comprise a ground that supports, and a framework that shapes, those who follow in the hierarchy. The *babad* lists the provincial lords by place name. This listing, which textually precedes the construction, serves to map the territorial extent of the realm (see *BJT* XIII:26–28). Next in the hierarchy come the bureaucrats and military elite. According to this political blueprint, the reinforcement of the state structure and the guarding of its boundaries are the responsibility of the bureaucracy and the military. "The people" come last, in a multitude of undifferentiated "everyones"; they seemingly "just chip in" to cover over the structure and to provide its mass.

It appears that our *babad* has documented a tidy hierarchy indeed. A closer reading of this history of the Grand Mosque's construction, however, reveals a double subversion of the neat hierarchy that appears built into its structure. The more obvious subversion, and the one that our *babad* shares with both the dominant *babad* and the folk traditions of Java, is the one produced by the miracle of the wood-chip master pillar. For what could be more contestatory of the rigidity of the hierarchy than the fact that its grounding authority is nothing more, or less, than a fabrication from fragments and residues? *Babad Jaka Tingkir* relates the miracle as follows. As the day approaches for the raising of the Mosque, the

12. To call the Mosque a "metaphor" for the realm would be too weak—it would deny the real material efficacy of the monument for the realm, its rulers, and its ruled. Rather, I prefer the image of "translation" across related realities.

fourth master pillar, the assigned share of Sunan Kalijaga (sixth-ranked of the *wali kutub*), is still nowhere to be seen. Having been distracted by more "spiritual" pursuits, the maverick Kalijaga (a.k.a. Sèh Malaya)[13] has neglected his share of the work. Sunan Bonang, the supreme *kutub*, summons Kalijaga and chastens him. The wayward *wali* then withdraws to the work site, where he gathers fragments from the residues of everyone else's production, fragments that he then arranges in the form of a pillar. Then, spiritual activist that he is, Kalijaga—in a most material, and yet still spiritual, feat—wills the fragments one. And the miracle of the wood-chip pillar is done (*BJT* XIV:25–XV:4). That wood-chip pillar still stands today, nearly five centuries after the miracle of its residual production, and it stands today as the most sacred (that is, the most powerful) site of the newly refurbished *pusaka* Mosque of Demak.[14] The most sacred support, the ground, as it were, of the monument (the realm, authority) is a marvelous composite of residues.

Something should be said here of Sunan Kalijaga (a.k.a. Sèh Malaya), this most renowned of the *wali*. Sunan Kalijaga, the saint of Kadilangu, enjoys a privileged position in Javanese history. Indeed, among Central Javanese, Sunan Kalijaga is far and away the most famous and most beloved of the nine *wali*. The contours of his biography are known to Javanese subjects from all strata of society. Born of a Majapahit noble, the young Kalijaga was a boy gone wrong. The profligate youth was a gambler who went on to become a notorious highwayman. But when the young robber happened to prey upon the passing Sunan Bonang (in *BJT*: first-ranking of the *wali kutub*), his life's course changed radically. For finally the young criminal had more than met his match. Inspired by the magical powers of Sunan Bonang, Kalijaga left his life of crime. The youth then became Bonang's star pupil. After many trials (notably his

13. It is not by chance or merely to fulfill metrical requirements that Sunan Kalijaga tends to be called by his alias Sèh Malaya in this section of the *babad*. Sèh Malaya is the name the saint is known by in the *Suluk Sèh Malaya*, which is none other than an Arabicized version of the *Suluk Déwaruci*. In this more obviously Islamic version of the "classic" poem, Kalijaga as Sèh Malaya takes the Bima role to Nabi Kilir's Déwaruci.

14. The suggestion in the course of the 1842 restoration that the by-then rotten wood-chip pillar (*saka tatal*) should be replaced was rejected out of hand, for to replace that *saka* would mean to annihilate the Mosque's *pusaka*-ship. Instead the *saka* was reinforced with metal bands (*Serat Nalika Bangun Masjid ing Demak*, pp. 37–39). In the 1987 restoration the rotting *saka* was treated with chemicals and provided with further tin reinforcement (*Kompas*, 21 March 1987).

years-long "watch" [*jaga*] over a "river" [*kali*]), Kalijaga was finally initiated into the *wali*-ship.

Kalijaga is remembered for his humanity: that is, his quintessential "Javaneseness." He is also remembered as a devout Moslem, and as the most effective among the nine *wali* as proselytizer of Islam in Java. He has become emblematic of so-called Javanese Islam.[15] Kalijaga is also revered as an artist. He is remembered as the one who introduced *wayang kulit* (shadow puppetry) to Java. Attributed to him also is the authorship of several *macapat* verse forms. He is perhaps best remembered, however, for two (related) things: that miraculous wood-chip pillar and his special relationship to the kings of Pajang and Mataram. Stories (that is, histories) abound that underline the importance of these serial personal relationships for kingship in Central Java: from his meeting with young Jaka Tingkir in the fields of the boy's foster mother to his nineteenth-century (ghostly) rendezvous with Pakubuwana IX in the Solo River.[16] Indeed it was only with Kalijaga's support (along with that of Kangjeng Ratu Kidul, the Spirit Queen of the South Sea) that the genealogical line of the Mataram dynasty gained and then retained its ascendancy.[17] That Kali-

15. See Clifford Geertz, *Islam Observed* (Chicago: University of Chicago Press, 1973), pp. 25–29 and passim.

16. On his meeting with Jaka Tingkir, see above, chapter 3, p. 248. Pakubuwana IX (r. 1861–93) was apparently the last Mataram king to be actively and personally involved with Sunan Kalijaga. The relationship began when the king-to-be was still a child. The young Pakubuwana IX (son of the exiled Pakubuwana VI) was said to have suffered greatly under the authority of Pakubuwana VII (the usurper who had taken his father's throne). The unhappy child would steal away from the palace to meditate in the Solo River. It is there that he is said to have met with this most renowned of the *wali*. Kalijaga gave the ascetic young prince a *pusaka keris* and advised him of his future kingship. Many years later, following his coronation at Susuhunan, Pakubuwana IX constructed his beloved Langenharja retreat near the spot where he had met with the *wali* (Personal communication, G.R.A. Koes Moertiyah [Putri-dalem I.S.K.S. Pakubuwana XII], 1982).

In more recent times, President Sukarno, first president of the Republic of Indonesia, is alleged to have claimed genealogical descent from Kalijaga in a speech he delivered in Demak in 1958 (Solichin Salam, *Sekitar Wali Sanga* [Kudus: Penerbit Menara, 1974], p. 46).

17. Unique among stories I have heard concerning Sunan Kalijaga's relationship to the Mataram dynasts is a tale found in a *babad* composed (or copied?) by one Bagus Danang at the Kraton Yogyakarta in 1937. This singular tale treats the transmission of the *wahyu* of kingship to the Mataram dynasty. The tale is set in the Pajang period (mid to

jaga would have played the key role both in the fabrication and in the final placement of the Mosque that was to serve as *"pusaka* for all the kings / Of all the Land of Java"* is certainly consistent with his more obviously political role in the history of Central Javanese kingship.

Before turning to a consideration of the remarkably recalcitrant Mosque's placement at Kalijaga's hands, let us take another and final look at the structure's architectonics. Structures produced according to traditional architectural rules in Java are called *pendhapa* (roughly: "pavilion"). There are many kinds of *pendhapa*, and the various types are classed by roof forms. It is the roof form, not the configuration of its pillars, that defines (literally names) any structure. The Demak Mosque, for example, with its three-tiered pyramidal (*tajug*) roof is a *tajug lambangsari pendhapa* (figure 12).[18] The roofs of *pendhapa* are often large, sometimes massive; and yet they seem to be held up by a modicum of pillars. A mere thirty-six pillars, for instance, hold up the great three-tiered roof of the Demak Mosque, a structure that measures some 961 square meters. The four master pillars are commonly considered the structural key to the *pendhapa*; however, as we shall see, their structural "mastery" is, in fact, somewhat compromised.

In the early years of this century the truly remarkable physics of the *pendhapa* structure drew the attention of the Dutch architect Ir. H. Maclaine Pont. In a series of articles in which he traced the history of the

---

late 16th century). Kalijaga is wandering the southern coast of Java. The *babad* notes that since becoming a *wali* (i.e., pure) Kalijaga had never again moved his bowels— about one hundred years had passed since his last movement. Now, punished by God for the sin of pride, he was taken by the greatest urgency and rushed to the river. With heroic effort (the image given is one of childbirth) he finally "delivered" the feces. The feces, emitting the loveliest of fragrances and the brightest of radiances, started off upstream. It just so happened that Ki Ageng Pamanahan (i.e., Ki Ageng Mataram) was heading down the bank of that same river to perform ritual ablutions for his dawn *salât*. Spying the radiant object pushing against the current, he plunged into the river and grabbed it. Kalijaga then arrived to explain that with this object Pamanahan had won a great boon. The *wali* instructed Pamanahan to keep the feces as *pusaka* for his line's (future) kingship, and his descendants would rule in unbroken succession. This *pusaka*'s name was (is?) Kyai Ungkel. See *Babad Demak 2*, ed. Gina and Dirgo Sabariyanto (Jakarta: Departemen Pendidikan dan Kebudayaan, Proyek Penerbitan Buku Sastra Indonesia dan Daerah, 1981), pp. 183–86.

18. The *tajug* variety of *pendhapa*, of which the Demak Mosque is perhaps the prototype, is customarily associated with Islamic religious structures in Java.

Figure 20. Roof of the Demak Mosque. Photograph by A. Fanani.

pendhapa form, Maclaine Pont also explored its structural physics. In the course of an intricate technical argument, the Dutch architect demonstrated that it is far too simplistic to view the *pendhapa*'s structure merely as pillars-supporting-roof—that is, as it appears. For, on the contrary and at the same time, it is the very weight of the roof which produces the countertension against the pillars requisite for the integrity of the structure. The pillars depend as much on the roof for their stability as the roof depends upon them for its support.[19]

We can never know if the author of *Babad Jaka Tingkir* was aware of this fact of structural physics—whether or not he or she consulted with master builders to compose this passage that treats in such careful detail this monumental construction project. What we do know is that other *babad* do not even approach this level of detail in their accounts of the Mosque's construction.[20] *Tingkir*'s composer lingers on architectural detail, exhibits a notable concern with the sequence of the assembly, and underlines the hierarchical cast of the structure with a careful catalog of the subjects involved in its construction. This very care suggests that the poet may

19. Henri Maclaine Pont, "Javaansche Architectuur (Bouwkunst)," *Djåwå* 3 (1923): 112–27 and 159–79; 4 (1924):44–73.
20. See above, note 11.

well have been conversant with traditional architectural theory and may thus have understood the physical rationale for the *pendhapa*'s standing. The poet's painstaking provision of architectural detail and careful cataloging thus betray the second (and this time unique) subversive gesture written into this history of a monumental construction. Last mentioned in the catalog of constructive subjects who built the Mosque is the indeterminate "everyone" whose share is the roof whose mass, it turns out, determines the structure's integrity. With his or her characteristic *semu*, the poet thus indicates that the contestation of hierarchy, or order, is built right into that order. The poet, perhaps bearing in mind the egalitarianism of Islam, very subtly reminds the careful reader that the central authorities subsist only under the weight of "the people." Diminish or damage "the masses" and the rulers will decline, perhaps fall.

Setting the Kéblat: *A Relational Alignment and Localization of Authority*

Let us now direct our attention to that portion of the text which treats the problematic of the Mosque's placement (*BJT* XV:15–36). Curiously, it is only after the monumental structure is complete and fully raised that the *wali* concern themselves with this most vital issue of its placement.[21] By placement is meant the settling of the Mosque's "direction," its *kéblat* (from the Arabic *qiblah*) or "facing" (*adhep*) pointing in the most direct line to the Ka'bah of Mecca. The Ka'bah is the sacred cubelike building in the center of the Meccan mosque Masjidu'l-Haram that contains the holy Hajaru'l-Aswad, or "black stone." It is around this cube that all Moslems circumambulate when performing the *hajj* and toward this cube that all Moslems must face when performing their ritual prayers, or *salât*.[22] *Salât*

21. *BJT* shares this peculiarity with the "Major *Babad*" as well as the 1906 *Babad Demak* 1. The other *babad* consulted (*Babad Segaluh* and Rongga Panambangan's *Serat Manikmaya*; see note 11, above) have a slightly more rational sequence with the fixing of the *kéblat* after the erection of the central section of the Mosque (*saka guru* + beams and *mustaka* [crown]) but before the erection of the two subordinate sections or the installation of the roofing.

22. The word *salât* designates Islamic ritual prayer, or more precisely devotional *performance*. *Salât* is not prayer in the sense of a personal conversation with God; for that practice the Islamic term is *do'a*. Rather *salât* is a highly regimented devotional practice that must be performed according to carefully designated (legislated) rules. It is requisite of all Moslems to perform the *salât* five times every day, in the five specified time

performed in any other direction is invalid and hence ritually inefficacious. Thus all mosques everywhere must be oriented, that is, directed, precisely toward this single Meccan site. Every mosque is provided with a niche (*mihrab*) which indicates the true *qiblah/kéblat* to the faithful. In Java, the *kéblat* is to the west or sometimes west-northwest. The faithful in Java face west; their mosques open onto the east.

Kéblat and *adhep*, the Javanese words that concern proper Meccan orientation, are both semantically rich and ideologically charged. The verbal form *ngéblat* (*ng* + *kéblat*) means both "to face Mecca" and "to obey."[23] The Javanese word *adhep* (facing) also means "belief" or "obedience," and "the one [the authority] to which or whom one renders obedience and/or belief."[24] The polysemic potentials of these words are played to the full in the text of *Babad Jaka Tingkir*. For what is at stake in this section of the *babad* is the definition of a structure of belief for Javanese Moslems and the determination of the proper relationship between that structure of belief and the authority of universal Islam.

Babad Jaka Tingkir tells us that the Grand Mosque of Demak, the structure produced (literally patched together) by the *wali*, was not easily brought into alignment with the Ka'bah—the material-spiritual center of universal Islam. The Javanese structure, this completed edifice which was the monument to Islam in Java, to the conversion, and to the authority of the *wali*, just would not *ngéblat*. I would suggest that this deferral of the settlement of the *kéblat*, as written into the text of Javanese historical consciousness (perhaps especially into the text of *Babad Jaka Tingkir*), should be read as a detour sign meant to highlight the historicity of the conversion in Java. That the Mosque would not immediately *ngéblat* (obey) indicates the process of negotiation that surely marked the historical conversion, a process that would have been determined in part by how the new Javanese Moslems negotiated their understanding of obedience, or submission. What submission means is critical for a Moslem people; *islâm* is, after all, the Arabic word for *submission*. And among Moslems ("those who have submitted"), that submission is ultimately

---

periods. For an incisive description of the performance of *salât* in an Acehnese context, see James T. Siegel, *The Rope of God* (Berkeley: University of California Press, 1969), esp. pp. 109–15.

23. GR 1:553.

24. GR 1:141.

man's submission to God, rather than to any temporal authority. Were the Grand Mosque of Demak, this original site of Islam in Java, to have *ngéblat*-ed without any question or debate would have meant the passive and perhaps blind submission of the Javanese structure of Islam to the remote, and likely poorly understood, authority (*adhep*) of Islam's Meccan center. Ideally among Moslems, the submission to God that defines Islam is not passive and resigned, but active and informed. The resistance of this Mosque that embodied the society of the new Javanese Moslems who constructed it signifies that society's work both to define its *Islâm* and to establish itself, from its position on the margins of the Islamic world, as a center of authority. The *wali*, who ground that structure of nascent authority, debate among themselves the *kéblat* thus to negotiate a valid understanding of the Prophet's message that would properly inform the submission, the *Islâm*, of those whom they are converting.

The tale of the Demak Mosque's disputed *kéblat* as it unfolds in *Babad Jaka Tingkir* is a telling consonant with *and* amplified from the more mainstream *babad* texts. It is a tale that invites, as it recounts, a consideration of the meanings of submission (*islâm*) and of authority that arose in debate among the early Moslems of Java. What, then, is the nature of the debate? The *wali's* protracted dispute concerns a matter of vision (*pamawas*): the various *wali* have differing visions that would differentially define their local Islam's relationship to the universal center. The being of the center (Mecca/the original site of universal Islam) qua center is not ostensibly questioned. Rather, the interminable argument grows from the divergence among the *wali's* visions of that center as well as their visions of the relationship that should obtain between that center and their newly constructed *pusaka* Mosque—center of Islam in Java. This argument, which problematizes the nature (the substance) of Islamic authority in Java, is finally settled by the miraculous manipulation of Sunan Kalijaga, a manipulation of *both* the Meccan Ka'bah and the Demak Mosque.

The telling of this remarkable event in our *babad*, though not inconsistent with those of the more dominant traditions, does nonetheless distinguish itself from them. Notably, the *wali's* argument over the *kéblat* commands considerably more attention in *Babad Jaka Tingkir* than in these other *babad*.[25] This issue no doubt merits such extensive treatment

25. *BJT* devotes 108 lines to this matter as compared to the "Major *Babad's*" 49, *Serat Manikmaya's* 43, *Babad Demak* 1's 26, and *Babad Segaluh's* 24 lines.

in our *babad* in part because of its structural importance to the text's thematic development. In the course of (and because of) this more extended treatment, the "figure" of the *pusaka* Mosque itself seems to come forward almost "personally" to resist actively the complacence of a too easy submission to central authority. The poem has laid a textual ground out of which the reader/audience expects personality to emerge. The lingering upon this scene of resistance recalls other scenes of resistance and transgression, notably the tales of Prabangkara and Karèwèd; with the *babad*'s anecdotal structure of fragments, its tales of heroes on the margins, this lingering calls forth the Mosque as hero—or perhaps heroine—of the third episode. The Mosque lying on the margins of the Islamic world would negotiate the terms of its submission to a center. As the *wali* debate the *kéblat*, they nudge and—as it were—try to caress the feminized Mosque into alignment, but the Mosque will not come to rest. Like a coy woman prodded by an eager lover, the heroine resists bending to the other's desire:

> But all the *wali* eight
> Of vision still did clash
> The mosque nudged[26] to right and left
> Swinging to and fro from north to south
> Still never came to rest[27]

In response to "her" resistance, the *wali* miraculously condense the world in order to bring Mecca, the focus of universal Islam, "home" to Java:

> In a flash accomplished was
> The sovereign *wali*'s miracle
>
> Condensed the world was tiny
> And Mecca shone close by
> Allah's Ka'bah was nigh, manifest before them

26. The word translated here as "nudged" is *jinawilan* (from *jawil*), which is used to specify the communicative (message-sending) prodding or touching of another person—often to convey amorous intent.

27. [Gambuh] Nanging pra wali wolu / maksih pradongdi pamawasipun / punang masjid jinawilan nganan ngèri / ménga-méngo ngalo ngidul / sedanguné dèrèng manggon (*BJT* XV:28).

To estimate its distance
But three miles off it loomed[28]

Sunan Kalijaga completes the localization.[29] When, by his miraculous manipulation, the Mosque does finally bend into agreement with Mecca's Ka'bah, the Ka'bah at the same time is bent into agreement with the Mosque of Demak. Kalijaga's gesture, which borders on sacrilege, is a radical one:

Allah's Ka'bah did his right hand grasp
His left hand having taken hold
Of the uppermost peak of the mosque

Both of them he pulled
Stretched out and brought to meet
The Ka'bah's roof and the peak of the mosque
Realized as one being were
Perfectly straight strictly on mark[30]

By means of this double gesture, the two are realized, or proven (*dèn-nyatakaken*) as one being or substance. That reality of one-which-is-two, effecting the *kéblat*'s settlement, is established by a relational alignment between the Demak and Meccan structures in which the Meccan structure (though clearly senior) does not entertain absolute dominance. The agreement, manipulated by the maverick Kalijaga, results in the establishment of the Demak Mosque as a center—*a* center in a world of Islam that recognizes no single absolute temporal authority. This double gesture, which opens to a dissemination of centers, works by contesting the very "marginality" of the marginal.

---

28. [Gambuh] sami sakedhap wus kabul / kharamating wali katong // Ringkes buwana ciyut / ing Mekah pan wus celak kadulu / Khakbattullah parek katingal ing ngarsi / winatawis tebihipun / amung tigang ngemèl tinon (*BJT* XV:29–30).

29. I am indebted to Oliver Wolters for the term and concept *localization*. For a stimulating discussion of various "localizations" of foreign materials into various Southeast Asian contexts, see his *History, Culture, and Region in Southeast Asian Perspectives* (Singapore: Institute of Southeast Asian Studies, 1982), pp. 52–94.

30. [Gambuh] asta kanan anyandhak Khakbattulahi / asta kèri n[y]andhak sampun / sirah gada masjid kono // Tinarik kalihipun / sami mulur gya ingaben gathuk / payok Kakbat lawan sira gada masjid / dèn-nyatakaken sawujud / cèples kenceng datan mènggok (*BJT* XV:33–34).

It is this gesture that finally ordains the Grand Mosque of Demak as a true monument, that effects the monumentalization of the structure that the *wali* had designed to be *pusaka*. Contesting the binary opposition of margin/center, Kalijaga's hands manipulate a relationship that effectively localizes universal Islam in Java. This localization (the realization of one-which-is-two: not just one and not merely two) is the source of the Mosque's authority as a center (a center of authority). And it is the nature of centers of authority to move toward codification of their authority. Although born of a singularly radical gesture, we shall see how the monument, once ordained, begins to congeal toward a more rigid structure. The monumental, qua monumental, is precisely that which would resist change as it stands for perpetuity. How *Babad Jaka Tingkir* treats this move toward the codification of authority—and the countercurrents that contest it—will be addressed in the following sections.

Breaking the Frames: Countermoves

In *Babad Jaka Tingkir*, the *pusaka* Mosque of Demak comes to stand for, and as, the seat of authority for all Java. That standing is not, however, to remain unchallenged. Having approximated (with significant amplification) the more dominant *babad* in its account of this construction project, at the very textual moment the *pusaka* is (finally) in place, our *babad*'s telling turns from the dominant tradition to follow again its own, alternative trajectory.[31] Directly after the "Demak Mosque Episode," in a section I have deemed an interlude, *Babad Jaka Tingkir* moves away from this new establishment of authority to highlight those who would resist the *wali*'s order (*BJT* XVI:2–XVIII:15).

This counter-framing interlude turns on the adventures of two relatively well known historical characters: Sunan Bayat (the former prince-regent of Pandhanarang, or Semarang) and Ki Ageng Pengging (né Radèn Kebo Kenonga). The histories of these characters are recounted in the

31. In the other *babad* consulted, following the settling of the *kéblat*, the narrative continues with the miraculous appearance of the magic vest Kyai Antakusuma hanging from the rafters of the Mosque. The narrative of the "Major" Bale Pustaka *babad* and the *Babad Segaluh* then continue with accounts of the *wali*'s production of several *pusaka keris*. *Babad Demak* 1 and Rongga Panambangan's *Manikmaya* continue with an account of the battle in which the forces of Demak finally defeat Majapahit. See note 11.

form of two mini-episodes—but episodes that resist closure. The Bayat tale provides a crack in time that invites the reader to glance ahead in history, while the Pengging tale, by again reminding the audience that the poem is really a history of Pengging's son, Jaka Tingkir, faces both forward and backward, textually and otherwise.

The reminders and openings provided by this frame again direct the reader's attention to the future that this *pusaka* text would project: that is, its proper context. Presumably by this turn in the text the reader would have devised an informed strategy of reading. Having learned to apprehend the textual junctures I call "interludes" as something more than mere frames, she would have come to discern in them the seams of this prophetic history. Seams are at the same time sites of scission and of suture. The seams of the text, while marking the disjunctions that frame the fragments, are also the sites where the threads that bind the fragments are sewn to form the fabric of contestation that is *Babad Jaka Tingkir*. Let us now turn to these mini-episodes, these textual bindings, and to the issues that they raise.

Sunan Bayat: A Withdrawal into Power

No sooner is the *pusaka* Mosque of all Java raised than an important provincial lord, the Prince-regent of Semarang, demonstrates his resistance to the newly established central authority of Demak. It is not, however, to the centralization or hierarchization of authority as such that Prince Pandhanarang objects, but to his position in that hierarchy. For with the new architectonic political structure founded on the new supreme religious authority of the *wali*, the older seemingly secular elite now find themselves seated (literally) lower in the hierarchy than even the lesser of the officially sanctioned ecclesiastics (*BJT* XVI:8–9).[32] The

32. The protocol of seating (where and upon what one is seated) is of critical importance in the political and social affairs of Java. Indicative of just how politically important the issue of seating is among Javanese is the fact that seating arrangements (and intrigues surrounding those arrangements) are significant focuses of attention in traditional history writing, including the writing of *Babad Jaka Tingkir*. An extreme example of this focus would be a Kraton Surakarta manuscript dating from the later years of Pakubuwana X's reign: the manuscript consists entirely of seating diagrams for Kraton receptions in the years 1936 to 1938 (*Buku Péngetan palenggahan-dalem saha para*

humiliated Pandhanarang protests the new seating arrangements by resisting his obligation to pay fealty (and likely taxes) to the Demak caliphate: he refuses to come to court (*BJT* XVI:10). And, in the world of the
traditional Javanese polity, such a refusal is an act of open revolt, perhaps
a preface to armed rebellion.[33]

Sunan Kalijaga, seemingly always ready in a pinch, again steps forward
to overcome the crisis. He does so not by putting down the revolt, but
rather by fulfilling the rebel's desire for position. For by opening to him
the esoteric teachings of the *wali*-ship, Kalijaga takes the defiant prince-
regent (and his little brother) up the ladder of the newly restructured
hierarchy. Mastering Kalijaga's teachings, teachings that deliver the tran-
scendent material reality that is *Jatimurti* (Reality Incarnate),[34] the two
nascent rebels do indeed attain the status of candidate *wali* (*BJT* XVI:12).
Then abandoning their opposition to the center as they put themselves at
some remove from it, the candidate *wali* take for the hills of southern
Central Java, seemingly withdrawing from the world to devote themselves to spiritual practices (*BJT* XVI:16–17). For the former dissidents,
however, this move signifies an enhancement of worldly (as well as of
otherworldly) power, a power they will now enjoy from their position on
the margins of the realm. Although they leave their wealth and the royal
center behind, the brothers still win a net gain in the temporal sphere by
means of their ascent up the new sociopolitical hierarchy. Through spiritual enlightenment and ascetic "withdrawal" they gain both in prestige
and in power. Settling on Mt. Tembayat, Pandhanarang (now a *wali*) takes
the name Sunan Bayat. His brother, now called Panembahan Kajoran,
settles nearby. There, remote from the central authorities, the brothers
preside over their rural domains. And should they again visit Demak,
"these so exalted / To have attained the rank of *wali*" would surely find
themselves shown to better seats (*BJT* XVI:18). Having found their chosen
position in the hierarchy and authority over their appointed provincial
domains, the brothers would, it seems, have no further argument with the
center.

Tamu-tamu wiwit 16 Agustus 1936 [compiled and inscribed Surakarta, 1936–38]. MS.
SP 181 Na-A; SMP KS 166).

33. See, for example, Ki Ageng Tingkir's admonition to Ki Ageng Pengging, in which
he reminds his "younger brother" of this political reality (*BJT* XXVI:8–9).

34. On *Jatimurti*, see above, Chapter 3, p. 277.

The telling of the Bayat tale in this *babad* is notable. Sunan Bayat is a well-remembered figure in Java. Written as well as oral histories of his enlightenment and momentous move from Semarang to Bayat abound. The nineteenth-century audience would have been familiar with the outlines of this character's history and the history of the (then past) future that followed after him. That audience would, then, have been struck by the Bayat tale they heard in *Babad Jaka Tingkir*, for its version is apparently unique. This *babad* alone frankly addresses the issue of position (prestige and power) as the factor that directed Pandhanarang/Bayat on the way to spiritual enlightenment. More commonly it is an issue of wealth that is given credit for wakening the notoriously greedy prince of Semarang to the spiritual life. In the more mainstream tradition, the conversion comes when Kalijaga shocks Pandhanarang into a recognition of the triviality of his style of monetary acquisition. Kalijaga, disguised as a poor grass-cutter, is scorned by the prince-regent until the greedy noble starts finding nuggets of gold in the grass he had bought for pennies from the peasant. And when the clumps of dirt the peasant is casually hoeing up start turning to gold in front of the renowned miser, Pandhanarang knows he is utterly defeated. It is the sight of all that dirt turned to gold that wakens the wealthy noble to his error.[35] And so Pandhanarang falls down to submit himself as a disciple to the mysterious grass-cutter. The peasant reveals himself as Kalijaga and calls upon the prince to repent his avaricious ways. Divesting himself of all his possessions, Pandhanarang then turns to spiritual pursuits under the guidance of his new master. Before long, the ex-noble is on the adventurous road to Bayat with his yet to be enlightened miserly wife.[36]

Both versions of the Bayat tale deal with the convergence of temporal and spiritual interests, a convergence that characterizes so much of mystical practice in Java. The form of that convergence of interests, however, is

---

35. Interestingly it is not a demonstration of "dust to dust" that wakens Pandhanarang to the pursuit of the spiritual life. It is not gold reduced to dirt, but dirt to gold, that Kalijaga's miracle effects. What Kalijaga demonstrates is not the futility of wealth, but that there are more effective "spiritual" means for the acquisition and production of wealth.

36. On the more mainstream Bayat tale, see D. A. Rinkes, "De Heiligen van Java IV: Ki Pandhan arang te Tembayat," *TBG* 53 (1911):435–531. And on the contemporary significance of Bayat's connection with wealth in late-twentieth-century Indonesia, see Pemberton, *On the Subject of "Java,"* pp. 279–85.

developed along rather different lines in the two versions. The *Babad Jaka Tingkir* version adds the dimension of frank political ambition, while eliminating the traditional focus on wealth. It is remarkable precisely because it is *not* the tale the audience would have expected to hear. Instead of the expected shovelfuls of gold, the focus is on position in a sociopolitical hierarchy. The effect of the divergence from the more usual narrative is, then, to direct the attention of the audience away from the conventionally venal visions of gold to the potentially political meanings of Kalijaga's *jatimurti* teachings and Bayat's *subsequent* spiritual activism. By subtly writing against the grain of conventional history, this poet-historian strategically gestures toward a politically charged form of spiritual-temporal convergence—one that is somehow marked for the future by the paradoxical reality of *jatimurti*.

But there is still more to our *babad*'s foundational history of the holy Bayat complex. We noted above that the poet composed this history in a way that seems to portray Bayat's founder (this ex-prince and would-be rebel) as a provincial discontent whose resistance is reduced by drawing him up into the very order whose configuration he had protested. Sunan Bayat né Prince Pandhanarang would then, it seems, have been co-opted: for empty prestige, the authorities were able to lure him into a withdrawal that was silence-on-the-mountaintop. After all, no more is heard of him in the text of this *babad*. In Java, however, prestige was not and is not an empty category. And in Java a focus on spiritual pursuits does not necessarily, or ideally, mean a retreat from more worldly activism. The subsequent history of the rural religious complex of Tembayat-Kajoran, of whose founding *Babad Jaka Tingkir* writes, brings these truths home.

Historically, the Bayat complex was marked by a *persistent* conjunction of religious-spiritual practice and political activism that was often in opposition to royal centers. The power of this rural religious complex belonged to the localized and decentralized register of a margin that, in the name of Islam, persistently worked to elude the control of central royal authority. Historically, the spiritually powerful house and domain of Tembayat-Kajoran did anything but withdraw into silence. Rather, from the late sixteenth century up through the early nineteenth century, the spiritually active Tembayat-Kajoran complex was a focus of political opposition that veritably plagued the successive dominant centers of authority in Java.

A story from the life of Jaka Tingkir, our absent hero, marks the first instance I know of Bayat's subsequent oppositional positionality. According to the version of his history presented by the "Major *Babad*," it was Bayat's symbolic rejection of Jaka Tingkir, or Sultan Pajang, that conclusively signaled the end of both the sultan's reign and his life. When, after a defeat by the supernatural forces commanded by his rebellious foster son, the failing Sultan Pajang attempted a pilgrimage to the sacred tomb of Bayat, the door was magically locked against him. Returning home to Pajang from this failed pilgrimage, the Sultan fell from his elephant, sustaining injuries from which he was never to recover.[37] The opposition was not always "merely" symbolic or figurative, however. In the 1630s the Bayat-Kajoran complex again formed a more palpable center of resistance, rising in opposition to Sultan Agung, the grandson of Sultan Pajang's rebellious foster son. Again in the 1670s, the holy Bayat-Kajoran complex played a major role in the Trunajaya rebellion, a rebellion that effected the fall of Mataram's capital.[38] The reinstatement of the Mataram house (thanks to the intervention of Dutch colonial troops) and the sack of the holy complex did not mean an end to its self-consciously Islamic oppositional stance. At the time of the Dipanagara rebellion (1825–30), the Bayat-Kajoran complex again rose as a center of opposition to the colonial-royal rulers of Central Java. Indeed, in the widely circulated nineteenth-century historical allusion, *Lambang Praja* (Realms Symbolized), the Dipanagara War is figured: "the Time of Wrath, its *semu*: Semarang and Tembayat." In the allusion "Semarang" and "Tembayat" signify "the Dutch colonial forces" and "Javanese/Islamic rebels" respectively.[39] In this regard, we should remember that *Babad Jaka Tingkir* was possibly composed in 1829, toward the end of that rebellion, and that the sole surviving manuscript of it was certainly inscribed in an exile that resulted from that same rebellion.

The nineteenth-century audience of *Babad Jaka Tingkir* would have been well aware of Bayat's actual (and figurative) history of opposition to successive centers of royal and colonial authority. The poet, though silent on this future of the past that he or she writes, works through this shared historical awareness prophetically to craft a novel Bayat tale that subtly suggests a form of spiritually empowered political resistance whose home

37. *Babad Tanah Jawi* (Batavia, 1939–41), 4:68–70.
38. For an extended treatment of (Bayat) Kajoran as a center of opposition, see H. J. de Graaf, "Het Kajoran-vraagstuk," *Djåwå* 20 (1940):273–328.
39. C. F. Winter, *Javaansche Zamenspraken*, 2:255.

is on the margins. The poet thus weaves another thread into the empowered fabric of contestation for the future that *Babad Jaka Tingkir* apparently would compose.

Ki Ageng Pengging: A "Prince" of the People

Ki Ageng Pengging is the next to come forward in the text, and he comes with his own political ambitions and rather different strategy to power. We had previously met this character as Prince Kebo Kenonga, son of King Handayaningrat of Pajang-Pengging and grandson of the last Brawijaya. With the fall of Majapahit, he had gone with his elder brother to study at the hermitage of Bonang. Under the tutelage of Sunan Bonang (the then premier *wali kutub*), the Prince and his brother had learned the precepts of Islam and its law (*sharî'a*) (*BJT* XIII:1–10). Though the text then fell silent on the Prince of Pengging, the reader would have been expecting the return of this character, father of the *babad*'s namesake Jaka Tingkir.

How, then, does Kebo Kenonga resurface in the poem? Immediately preceding his textual return is a note on successions among the authorities in Demak. The *babad* records without elaboration the accession of Prince Trenggana, Kebo Kenonga's (junior) cousin, as the third sultan of Demak in A.J. 1432 (A.D. 1510). Second son of Demak's original sultan, Trenggana succeeds to the *kraton* of his short-lived brother who had but two years earlier succeeded their father (*BJT* XVI:23–24). The poet then notes the passing of two of the *wali kutub*. It is the report of the death in A.J. 1445 (A.D. 1523) of the Pengging brothers' teacher, Sunan Bonang, followed by that of their uncle, the Prince-regent of Madura, that apparently occasions Kebo Kenonga's return to the text (*BJT* XVII:4). When he does reappear it is as co-ruler, with his brother, of the ancestral domain of their father in Pengging.

Reminiscent of the story of the Prince-regent of Semarang, these Pengging princes are dissatisfied with their positions as provincial lords. For these brothers—whose lack of any involvement with the construction of the *pusaka* Mosque is notable—the problem is not with seating protocol, however. These most senior of Brawijaya's grandsons would not have lacked prestige at the court of their junior kinsman. Their ambitions evidently do not revolve around a desire to scale the hierarchy of authority established in Demak. They have something else in mind. The Princes of Pengging, having been led by their grandfather to expect something other than provincial vassalage, are averse to recognizing the parvenu authority of their Demak cousin and his officially sainted associates.

> The mighty nobles two, troubled in their hearts
> Refused to show themselves at the capital Demak
> So deeply shamed were they
> Within their hearts these nobles
> Did harbor deep resolve
> No summons would they answer
> Tormented by the fond hopes of old
> That with tender words their grandfather had raised
> Thus 'twas better they refuse
> To witness the celebration [of the new authority]
>
> Celebrating in their hearts, the mighty nobles two
> In Pengging their own realm, apart
> Considered then what they would do[40]

What they have been raised to expect and still desire is a celebration (a kind of ordination) of their own authority independent from Demak's rule. These brothers do not look to Demak or its newly constructed Mosque as a source for the authority they hope to celebrate. Nor are they satisfied with their provincial principality, at least not in the form that they have inherited it.

Ambition for something more disenchants both brothers from their fatuous petty royalty. But in their disenchantment the brothers turn in different directions. They differ both in their strategies of how to bring that "celebration" about and in the kinds of authority they desire. Kebo Kanigara, the elder brother, taking on the appearance of a pre-Islamic anchorite, withdraws with only his wife and children into silence-on-the-mountaintop. There he forgets (supé) his royalty and his principality (BJT XVII:8–10)—and is forgotten in inscribed history. Kebo Kenonga, the younger brother, remains at the seat of the old principality, but he works to transform that principality into a very different kind of domain. And

40. [Dhangdhanggula] Wong agung kalih kéwran ing galih / datan purun sumiwèng ing Demak / kalangkung sanget wirangé / ing batiné wong agung / kaletheké sajroning ati / cawengah ing pangundang kudanganing dangu / kinudang déné kang éyang / ya milané milalu amiwal kapti / sumaks[y]èng pamiwaha // Miwaha ring tyas wong agung kalih / anèng Pengging nagriné priyongga / kagagas-gagas karsané (BJT XVII:7–8).

his authority over that reformed domain is also a new form of authority, an authority self-constructed upon a transformed foundation. What had been a petty rural principality he makes into a thriving *pesantrèn*. Actively ridding himself of his aristocratic baggage (*dèn-ilang kencaraning priyayi*), the former prince becomes the *kyai* (master/patriarch) of an important rural center of Islam. The princely Kebo Kenonga vanishes to reappear as the devout and learned Kyai Ageng Pengging. No longer presiding as a noble over his subjects, he is transformed into a master of his disciples. He is *kyai* of the Pengging *pesantrèn*, a notably humble master who refuses deference and joins his followers laboring in the fields. And yet he commands the allegiance of some three thousand men, including seven hundred "inner disciples" (*BJT* XVII:10–13).

The *pesantrèn* (place of the *santri*, "student of Islam") is and has been a crucial institution in Javanese Islam and in rural Javanese political organization.[41] In the eighteenth and nineteenth centuries, these Islamic religious schools were residential communities that, often rural, were under the absolute mastery of a *kyai*. These religious-educational communities were usually economically independent and often made up *pradikan* ("freeholds") founded upon tax-free and compulsory service-free lands donated by the royal courts.[42] The *pesantrèn* were financed by mate-

41. For a comprehensive introduction to the *pesantrèn*, see Zamakhsyari Dhofier, *Tradisi Pesantren* (Jakarta: LP3ES, 1982). Though the institution of the *pesantrèn* is clearly centuries old, little is known of its early development. The renowned *Serat Centhini*, however, provides numerous vignettes of *santri* life (both social and academic) in the seventeenth-century rural *pesantrèn* of Central and East Java—as imagined by literati in the early-nineteenth-century Kraton Surakarta. See Sumahatmaka's convenient synopsis of the poem (*Ringkasan Centini* [*Suluk Tambangraras*] [Jakarta: Balai Pustaka, 1981]), the early twentieth-century partial Balai Pustaka transliteration (*Serat Tjentini*, 8 vols. [Batavia, 1912–15], the recent transliteration by Karkono K. Partokusumo (*Serat Centhini: Suluk Tambangraras*, 10 vols. [Yogyakarta, 1985–90]), or any of the many extant recensions in manuscript (see, for example, Behrend's review of the *Centhini* corpus in "The Serat Jatiswara," pp. 79–90). Soebardi has produced a valuable study that details the orthodox elements of *pesantrèn* Islam as depicted in the *Centhini*. This important work is written against the mainstream philological tradition which has tended to downplay the vital Islamic components of the poem in favor of its "encyclopaedic Javanism" (S. Soebardi, "Santri Religious Elements as Reflected in the Book of Tjentini," *BKI* 127 [1971]:331–49). *Suluk* literature, much of which was likely composed in the *pesantrèn*, is another as yet largely untapped source for improving our understanding of practice and theory in the premodern *pesantrèn*.

42. In the case of the *pradikan*, the *kyai* was not only the master of his pupils but also

rial contributions from the local population to their support (*zakat* and *sedhekah*), earnings from the foundation's (rice) lands (*wakaf*), and labor (sometimes obligatory) again contributed by the populace. Sometimes the labor of the pupils (the *santri*), both in the foundation's fields and within the institutional household, was an important factor in the *pesantrèn* economy. The land holdings of the *pesantrèn* were sometimes extensive, and the *kyai* were often wealthy men. Many *kyai*, especially in the later nineteenth century, performed the *hajj* to Mecca.

At the *pesantrèn* schools, the *santri* were taught by the *kyai* and his advanced pupils to read the Qur'ân. These Quranic lessons involved instruction both in vocal techniques and in Arabic language. The pupils were also instructed in the precepts of the sacred *sharî'a* law. Quranic interpretation as well as Islamic philosophy often comprised essential elements of the curriculum for the more advanced pupils. *Ngèlmu tasawwuf* (esoteric Sufi sciences), both practical and theoretical, pervaded premodern Islamic education in Java (as well as in most other areas of the Islamic world). Indeed, the premodern Javanese *pesantrèn* often served as a Sufi brotherhood (*tarékat*); the *kyai*, as a Sufi *syaikh*.[43] Javanese literature, writing in Malay, practical arts (including trade skills and magic practices), and fine arts were also taught at many *pesantrèn*. The *santri* consisted mostly of young men (although young women too occasionally numbered among the pupils). Most of the *santri* ranged in age from about ten to thirty. Although these youths came from all levels of society, when at the *pesantrèn* they lived a relatively egalitarian fraternal life. The *pesantrèn* tradition was not a monastic one. Upon completion of his education, it was only a rare *santri* who went on to become a professional "cleric" (for example, a *kyai*); most moved on to their chosen roles in the ordinary world of social commerce. These young men often traveled hundreds of miles from *pesantrèn* to *pesantrèn*, where they would study serially under a number of *kyai*, each with his own "specialty."

The *kyai* was the master of his *pesantrèn*, a master whose authority was founded not upon state sanction but upon his own knowledge of Islam, his personal charisma, and often upon his genealogical position within Java-wide familial networks of *kyai*. Given the relatively autonomous basis for

---

the headman/political leader of the community (*désa*) in which the *pesantrèn* was located.

43. Dhofier, *Tradisi Pesantrèn*, p. 34.

his authority and the sway of that authority over both his pupils and the local community, the *kyai* could (and often did, especially during the Dipanagara Rebellion and again in the latter nineteenth century) become a focus of opposition to central state (and especially infidel-colonial) authority.[44] The Ki Ageng Pengging of our *babad* is depicted as one such focus of resistance, if not outright opposition.

The relationship of the *pesantrèn's kyai* to indigenous royal power was not, however, a necessarily adversarial one. This was especially the case up to the early nineteenth century, that is, before the courts became subsumed under infidel-colonial rule in the post-1830 high colonial age. In earlier times a more productive and complicated relationship had been possible between these centers of authority.[45] A number of *pesantrèn* were, as noted above, established by royal foundation. And although, in theory, the authority of the *pesantrèn's kyai* subsisted apart from the court, the court and courtiers in these earlier years were not divorced from the *pesantrèn*. In the late eighteenth and the early nineteenth century, for example, there were particularly strong ties between the famous *pesantrèn* of Tegalsari-Ponorogo and the Kraton Surakarta.[46] During that

44. For an in-depth study of the role of the *kyai* as a revolutionary figure in late-nineteenth-century Java, see Sartono Kartodirdjo, *The Peasants' Revolt of Banten in 1888* (The Hague: Nijhoff, 1966), pp. 172–74 and passim.

45. And yet the tension between royal (and neoroyal) authority and certain elements among the more obviously spiritual authorities (the *kyai* and *ulama*) has been a persistent issue in Javanese history from at least the early seventeenth century—up through the late twentieth century. See, for example, my discussion above of Bayat as a center of ongoing opposition to royal power. Another case would be the decades-long struggle between the Mataram kings and the spiritual lords of Giri in the seventeenth century. Ki Ageng Pengging would seem to be another obvious oppositional character were it not that he belongs to both worlds: royal and spiritual/Islamic. My point here is that such a purely adversarial relationship was and is not necessarily (or ideally) the case. The two authorities are not defined against one another in sheer binary opposition.

46. F. Fokkens writes that Pakubuwana II (r. 1726–49) established the Tegalsari *pesantrèn* in gratitude to Kyai Kasan Besari I for the succor the holy man had provided him in 1742 during the course of his flight from Kartasura (Fokkens, "De Priesterschool te Tegalsari," *Tijdschrift voor Taal-, Land-, en Volkenkunde* [*TBG*] 24 [1878]:318–36). In about 1800 the Penghulu of the Kraton Surakarta forced Kyai Kasan Besari I's son, Kyai Yahya, to resign as the second Kyai of the Tegalsari Pesantrèn in favor of his younger brother Kyai Kasan Besari II (1762–1862). Kyai Yahya had been charged with malfeasance (ibid., pp. 321–22).

From another vantage, the extent and the depth of the relationship between the

period a large number of candidate courtiers, including virtually all that palace's court *pujongga*, pursued courses of *pesantrèn* study at Tegalsari as part of normal training for royal service.[47] By the middle of the nineteenth century, under the new colonial configuration of power, these ties were greatly weakened, as were both the Kraton Surakarta and the Tegalsari *pesantrèn*. The later nineteenth century was to be marked by a wave of small-scale rebellions led by (what the Dutch colonials deemed) "fanatic" rural *kyai*, rebellions that were inspired by (among other things) the dream of a new relationship between the religious communities and royal power.[48] That new dreamed-of relationship would be ushered in under the rule of "The Just King" (*Ratu Adil*) and would mark the dawn-

----

rulers of the Kraton Surakarta and the Kyai of Tegalsari can be seen in the marriage of one of Pakubuwana IV's (widowed) nieces to Kyai Kasan Besari II circa 1805. The son of that union was to become the Bupati of Ponorogo, R.M.T. Cakranagara (R.Ng. Wirapratana and [Ki Padmasusastra], *Sejarah Ageng ing Karaton Surakarta* [compiled Surakarta, ca. 1900–1940; typed s.l., s.a.]. MS. RP B77; SMP MN 690, pp. 91–92, and *Kagungan-dalem Serat Babat Sengkala: Kawi Pulo Jawi dipun-isèni tiyang nalika taun ongka 1 dumugi taun 1854* [MS. SP 220 Ca-A; SMP KS 1A], p. 69).

47. See J. F. G. Brumond, *Het Volksonderwijs onder de Javanen* (Batavia: Van Haren Noman & Kolff, 1857), p. 28. The most renowned of these courtly Tegalsari *santri* was R.Ng. Ronggawarsita (1802–1873), who is widely acclaimed as the greatest (and last) of the "true" Javanese court poets. A biography of Ronggawarsita compiled in the 1930s recounts the adventures (and misadventures) of the young and unruly poet-to-be under the tutelage of a sometimes exasperated Kyai Imam [Kasan] Besari (Komite Ronggawarsitan, *Babad Cariyos Lelampahanipun Suwargi Radèn Ngabéhi Ronggawarsita*, 3 vols. [Surakarta: Marsch, 1931–33], 1:5–36 & 86–126. The same document claims that Ronggawarsita's grandfather, R.T. Sastranagara (Yasadipura II), had been a "brother under one teacher" (*tarékat* brother?) with the same Kyai Imam Besari (ibid., p. 5).

48. There is some evidence to suggest that Pakubuwana IX shared in that dream. Although the (strategically up-beat) yearly Resident's reports are silent on this matter, Resident Spaan (served 1884–90) apparently confided his misgivings to an English visitor he entertained in 1889. The visitor, one Arthur Earle, writes of Surakarta: "The city is dominated by a fortress almost opposite the Residency, and this would be quite sufficient to quell any disturbances likely to arise in a place rather given to discontent of the Dutch Protectorate, kept alive by the hatred existing in the Emperor's Kraton (or Palace confines) towards the Government, and the constant preaching of the Hadjis, either real or sham ones, who, knowing it will please the Emperor, do what they can to foment sedition. Mr. Spaan is, however, not a man to be trifled with, and the soldiers are ordered out on the slightest provocation, which has a most salutary effect" ("A Month in Java in 1889," p. 29).

ing of a New Age of Moslem kingship, free from infidel Dutch rule, which kingship would promise a utopia of peace, prosperity, and righteousness for all.[49]

Babad Jaka Tingkir, though it preceded the "Just King" discourse of the later nineteenth century, would not have been unintelligible to it. Nor, I might add, was the dream inscribed in this *Tingkir* history identical to the messianic expectations that dominated that discourse. *Babad Jaka Tingkir* conveys a rather different dream: one dreamt by a fading ex-king in exile and one that would suggest a different form for the new relationship and a different shape for the new age. But that story is still unfolding in our reading of the *babad*. Suffice it to note at this juncture that, aside from Ki Ageng Pengging's absence from the court, what troubles Demak's new sultan is the strange newness of his rural (royal) cousin's ways. "Changing the tune of their ways / Their manners were strangely new."[50] Ki Ageng Pengging, the cousin who enjoyed genealogical seniority to the Sultan, turns from the sole (royal) order of the center to sing a "different tune" (*asalin lagu*). That tune, sung in the mode of the *pesantrèn-tarékat*, means the registry and sanction of other orders, and hence potential grief for the Sultan's rule.

Ki Ageng Pengging is not singing that new tune in isolation. Rather, this patriarch of the Pengging *pesantrèn* has joined a brotherhood of *kyai* (a *tarékat*) under the mastery of the remarkable Sufi *shaikh* Sèh Siti Jenar. The brotherhood numbers some forty[51] men who head what appears an integrated network of *pesantrèn* across the expanse of rural Central Java. Like the Ki Ageng of Pengging, the other *kyai* are identified in the *babad* by the names of the localities of their *pesantrèn* (*BJT* XVII:20–23). Of the toponyms that I have been able to identify, most name places in rural Central Java in the environs of Semarang, Japara, Salatiga, Klaten, and Surakarta. Mapped out, these localities compose a web that skirts and nearly circles the Sultan's court-city of Demak. These *kyai* and their

---

49. For more on the *ratu adil* movements of the nineteenth century, see G. W. J. Drewes's *Drie Javaansche Goeroe's: Hun Leven, Onderricht en Messiasp000rediking* (Leiden: A Vros, 1925), and Sartono Kartodirdjo's *Protest Movements in Rural Java* (Kuala Lumpur: Oxford University Press, 1973), and his *Ratu Adil* (Jakarta: Sinar Harapan, 1984).

50. asalin lagu pratingkah / ing rèh anyar-anyarin (*BJT* XVIII:2).

51. The *babad* states forty as the number of disciples. Including Ki Ageng Pengging, however, forty-three to forty-six co-disciples under Sèh Siti Jenar are actually listed; see *BJT* XVII:20–23 and notes to same.

followers, forming what might prove an oppositional net around the new "kraton of all Java," would have posed a formidable threat to Demak's hegemony. The Sultan would have been well advised to be uneasy about the potential of this *kyai* network—especially under the leadership of one like Sèh Siti Jenar. For he was:

> . . . a marvelous *waliyullah*
> Of wondrous power renowned of knowledge [*ngèlmu*]
> A wandering adept of practices austere [*laku*]
> A nimble wit, there was no catching him
> > [and/or: he could not be quoted]
> Proud and never cringing
> The consummation of knowledge
> Knowledge of *rahsa-surasa*[52]

Having mastered the esoteric knowledge (*ngèlmu*) of *rahsa-surasa* ("meaning's meaning, meaning's mystery, meaning's secret, the mystery of meaning, meaning-feeling, tasting's tasting" and more), Siti Jenar was the wholly Perfect Man (*lanang sejati, insan khamil*). Wholly real, he was Absolute Reality incarnate (*Sunyata Jatimurti*). And his word was the true word: absolutely authentic, his language was both noniterable (*datan kena pinethik*) and wholly effective. What he said (or thought) *became.* And it was this material authenticity of language and of person that the master shared with his students:

> When assembled all complete were
> The brethren under one master
> In Siti Jenar all of them
> Did discourse upon *rasa* ["meaning/feeling"]
> Deliberating on the knowledge
> Of the Sufi way whose knowledge is *rahsa* ["Mystery"]
> Precisely was their discourse on the Perfect Man [*insan khamil*]
> The binding of Release [and/or: The site where Release is bound][53]

52. [Dhangdhanggula] . . . waliyullah dibya / sekti koncara ngilmuné / kalana ahli laku / kesit datan kena pinethik / ladak norancak-encak / pambontos ing ngilmu / kang ngilmu rahsa surasa (*BJT* XVII:14).

53. [Dhangdhanggula] anuju pepekan kabèh / kadangé tunggil guru / anèng Siti Jenar pra sami / agenu-genu rasa / mufakating ngilmu / tasawuf kang ngèlmu rahsa / sami rasèh khusus ingkang insan khamil / pamuketing kamuksan (*BJT* XVII:24).

What the words "The binding of Release [The site where Release is bound]" might mean will be approached in the following chapter in a more extended discussion of Siti Jenar's Sufi activism and his politics of dissemination. We shall see how this activism and politics condemned him to death—and how this same activism and politics ensured that he could never be killed. Paradoxically, it would be his destiny rather to vanish into a wholly disseminate full presence. For he was:

> The perfection of body manifest
> A manifestation that never dies
> Vanishing in the end
> For ever ineffable is
> Its telling voiced in speech
> [and/or: Hidden is its telling][54]

Continuing to speak of that about which nothing can be said, the following chapter will also compare and contrast Siti Jenar's story with that of another unquotable and unbeatable Sufi master—the writer Malang Sumirang. Finally the chapter will return to a consideration of Siti Jenar's star pupil, Ki Ageng Pengging. The quiet defiance of this martyred father of Jaka Tingkir will be considered in relation to the stories of these other two vanished Sufi masters—and in relation to the generation of his future sons and daughters.

54. Paripurnaning ngongga muryani / wuryaning k[a]ng, tan kenaning pejah / lenyep ing kawekasané / pan tan kena winuwus / kauwusanira winuni (*BJT* XVII:16). As in *BJT* V:8, *winuni* means both, and at the same time, "to be hidden" and "to be voiced" or "expressed."

CHAPTER 6
THREE JAVANESE GURUS:
ON THE GENERATION OF
MARGINAL POWERS

❋

In 1925 the Dutch Javanologist G. W. J. Drewes published his *Drie Ja-vaansche Goeroe's* ("Three Javanese Gurus"), a study of three historical Moslem teachers whose lives and teachings earned them exile from nine-teenth-century Java. Sketching these men's biographies and analyzing some of the texts that the authorities seized from them at the time of their arrests, Drewes works to reinterpret what had seemed their potentially revolutionary messages. Absolving these teachers of the more sinister aspects of their treachery, Drewes's study works to drain Islamic meaning from their teachings by exposing their message as a (tired) traditional repetition of a Sanskritic messianism that he traces back to Old Java via Balinese manuscripts.[1]

The final section of *Babad Jaka Tingkir*, a nineteenth-century Javanese text that comes to us by the hand of a royal exile, inscribes the stories of three Sufi masters whose teachings emerge from the margins. My analy-sis is not interested in the possibly Hindu genealogy of their radical Moslem Sufism. Nor am I interested in quenching the revolutionary potentials of their messages. Rather I shall investigate how all three of these gurus—Sèh Siti Jenar, Sèh Malang Sumirang, and Ki Ageng Peng-ging—are depicted in this *babad*, as being, in some way or another, mar-ginal figures involved in forms of activity that threaten "the state." In the course of my investigation, I shall explore the manners in which these three masters of Islamic mysticism variously define the relationship be-tween spiritual and political interests. The various definitions will be read from practical actions performed both by and upon them as well as from

---

1. G. W. J. Drewes, *Drie Javaansche Goeroe's: Hun Leven, Onderricht en Messiasprediking* (Leiden: A. Vros, 1925).

their ideological statements. All three masters vanish: they are eliminated, without any among them suffering total defeat. I shall discuss the
significance of the three vanishings, each of which is quite different from
the other two.

Sèh Siti Jenar: A Figure of Dissemination

Sèh Siti Jenar is the best known of the three masters, retaining his renown
as Java's premier heretic-saint even today. Versions of his tale, both written and oral, abound.[2] He is a character who stands for dissemination, and
the dissemination for which he stands is of esoteric knowledge from the
exclusive cognizance of the political-spiritual elite into popular culture. It
was on account of this dissemination that the *wali* felt they had to eliminate Siti Jenar. They saw in him a clear and present political danger; for as
a figure of dissemination and populism he stood against the centralization
and unification of authority as such. In this regard it is notable that Siti
Jenar is remembered historically as the spiritual antecedent and progeni-
tor of subversives. In 1920s Central Java, his teachings were associated
with a radical rural wing (Sarékat Abangan) of the early Indonesian Communist Party.[3] And in the early 1980s certain commercial audio tape
recordings of his story were still considered dangerous enough to be
banned.

In popular consciousness, Siti Jenar is remembered as the patron of the
"little man" (*wong cilik*). The contours of his well-known biography underline his organic association with the lowest strata of society. In the

2. See, for example: D. A. Rinkes, "De Heiligen van Java II: Seh Siti Djenar voor de
Inquisitie," *Tijdschrift voor Indische Taal-, Land- en Volkenkunde* (*TBG*) 53 (1911):17–56,
and "De Heiligen van Java VI: Het graf te Pamlatèn en de Hollandsche Heerschappij,"
TBG 55 (1913):1–200; *Serat Centhini* (*Suluk Tambangraras*) = *Serat Cabolang* (canto
38), ed. Kamajaya, 1:130–33; *Babad Segaluh* (MS. RP B24b; SMP MN 268), p. 194 ff.;
Babad Demak (MS. RP B 31; SMP MN 193), pp. 12–16; *Walisana*, ed. R. Tanojo,
p. 121 ff.; R. Panji Natarata, *Serat Siti Jenar* (Yogyakarta: Kulawarga Bratakesawa,
1958); *Suluk Seh Siti Jenar*, ed. Sutarti (Jakarta: Departemen Pendidikan dan Kebudayaan, Proyek Penerbitan Buku Sastra Indonesia dan Daerah, 1981); Ki Sutrisno,
dhalang Kentrungan (asal Blora), "Lakon Siti Jenar" (performed at Gajahan, Surakarta,
11–12 November 1983).

3. Bratakesawa, *Falsafah Siti Djenar* (Surabaya: Djojobojo, [1954]), esp. pp. 7–12. For
more on the Sarékat Abangan, see Takashi Shiraishi, *An Age in Motion: Popular Radicalism in Java, 1912–1926* (Ithaca: Cornell University Press, 1990), pp. 197–203.

most widespread version of his tale, Siti Jenar is said to have been a lowly worm who was miraculously transformed into man.[4] The transformation resulted from the worm's accidental reception of the esoteric knowledge of Ultimate Reality. Once become man, the erstwhile worm then dared reveal that Knowledge to the masses. Presumably the transformation that the reception of such knowledge might effect on these other "worms" was a source of worry to the spiritual-political elite at the new capital of Demak. This worry is intensified in the *Babad Jaka Tingkir* version by Siti Jenar's association with the forty *kyai*, most especially with the troublesome Ki Ageng Pengging.

In addition to his sin of "baring the Secret" to the unworthy masses, Siti Jenar is also faulted for his disregard of the *sharî'a*, the sacred law of Islam. Many tellings of his tale also accuse him of the heresy of pantheism. For these sins, the most paramount and universally reported of which is the sin of Knowledge's dissemination, the saint was tried and sentenced to death. There are many different versions of the story of his "trial" and execution. Each of these versions needs to be understood against the background of the collective folk memory of his tale as well as that of the other versions. Particularly significant are the variant treatments of the final disposition of the saint's corpse; they range from one extreme of the transformation of the corpse into the stinking carcass of a dog to the other extreme (i.e., the *Jaka Tingkir* variant) of the saint's apotheosis and ascension to heaven. How the spectacular manner of Siti Jenar's final vanishing in *Babad Jaka Tingkir* underscores his identity as a figure of dissemination will be discussed below. But first his teachings and his "death."

Siti Jenar's Teachings: Naming a Saint

Babad Jaka Tingkir provides no in-depth analysis of Siti Jenar's teachings, that Knowledge whose dissemination so troubled the established authorities. The fullest exposition of his doctrine is found in the defense he offers his judges at the time of his trial (*BJT* XIX:8–23). That defense, which is in no way an attempt to elude the death sentence, takes the form

4. See, for example, *Babad Segaluh* (SMP MN 268), p. 194; R. Panji Natarata, *Serat Siti Jenar*, p. 11; *Suluk Sèh Siti Jenar*, ed. Sutarti, p. 7; Pak Trisno, performance, November 1983.

of a lyric expression of mystic union's Reality under the aspect of radical Oneness. The expression is couched in the idiom of *rasa* ("feeling, taste, meaning, essence, secret"). I shall have more to say on this lyric passage below.

Siti Jenar is first introduced into the *babad* as Ki Ageng Pengging's unnamed and marvelous teacher (*BJT* XVII:14). The famous name of this teacher is then withheld for some thirty-eight lines of praise for his mystic excellence. This deferral of identification acts (or pretends)[5] to arouse audience curiosity about the identity of the marvelous teacher who had come to Pengging. These evocative lines sing of this teacher that he was, among many other things, "The consummation of Knowledge [*ngèlmu*]" and "The perfection of body manifest." When he is finally named, he is hyperbolically named five times over: Prince Siti Jenar, Susuhunan Lemahbang, Ki Sèh Wali Lanang Sajati, Lord Jati-Minulya, and Sèh Sunyata Jatimurti (*BJT* XVII:17). The first two of these names are the common appellations of the saint and are known throughout the literature.[6] The last three names, however, are apparently unique to this text. Rather different from the (Western) proper name, these three names function as labels that identify the general curves of the saint's teachings, what might be called his ideology. They preface the poet's more direct identification of his teachings as a discourse on the Perfect Man (*Insan Kamil*), that is, "the binding of Release" (*BJT* XVII:24).

What, then, do these three names teach us? Each of the names, as a label or badge, is meant to be read for its semantic value, its indication of the master's teachings. The first of these names, Ki Sèh Wali Lanang Sajati or "Sir Shaikh Wali Perfect Man/Male," translates into Javanese

5. The more literate among the audience/readers would have known without being told that Siti Jenar was Ki Ageng Pengging's teacher.
6. The names Siti Jenar (*krama*: "Golden Earth") and Lemahbang (*ngoko*: "Red Earth") are also common toponyms that appear repeatedly across the Javanese landscape. The fact that persons' names, especially the names of religious and political leaders, were often taken from their locales (the Kyai or Sèh or Prince of X) has led to endless speculation concerning Siti Jenar's true seat of residence. *Babad Jaka Tingkir*'s author joins the speculation by placing the saint in a village of Siti Jenar/Lemahbang located somewhere to the north of Tingkir (*BJT* XVII:25). The poet probably had in mind the old village of Lemahbang on the Semarang-Surakarta road just south of Ungaran. Other *babad* locate Siti Jenar elsewhere, often placing his residence in the locale whereat the *babad* was composed.

the important Arabic-Sufi term *insan kamil*. In classical Sufi traditions (especially the writings of Ibn al-'Arabi and Abdul Karim al-Jili),[7] the Perfect Man is the Beginning and End of Creation, the realization of "Himself" to which the Sufi aspires. Echoes and variants of the classical conception of the Perfect Man pervade Sufi writings throughout the premodern Indonesian archipelago.[8] That *Babad Jaka Tingkir*'s Siti Jenar is called specifically *Lanang* Sajati ("Perfect *Male*" as opposed to a more neutral "Perfect Man") suggests that his teachings may be colored by the sexualized imagery that characterizes certain strains of Javano-Sufi thought.[9]

Again, Siti Jenar is called Lord Jati Minulya, a Sanskritic name that eludes easy translation. The name can be read discursively to mean "he whose essential reality has been returned to its prior more perfect state." The sense, then, is that the master who attains Perfection (the Perfect Man), rather than having attained a totally new state of being, has instead returned to, or better, realized a prior one. This priority is a logical or

7. See A. E. Affifi, *The Mystical Philosophy of Muhyid Din-Ibnu Arabi* (Cambridge: Cambridge University Press, 1938), esp. p. 77 ff., and Reynold A. Nicholson, *Studies in Islamic Mysticism* (Cambridge: Cambridge University Press, 1921), chap. 2.

8. See, for example, the works of Hamzah Fansurî in al-Attas's *The Mysticism of Hamzah Fansuri* (Kuala Lumpur: University of Malaya Press, 1970), 'Abdul-Ra'uf of Singkel's *Dakaik al-Huruf*, ed. and trans. A. H. Johns, *Journal of the Royal Asiatic Society* (1955), pp. 55–73, 135–58, and *The Gift Addressed to the Spirit of the Prophet*, ed. and trans. A. H. Johns (Canberra: Australian National University Press, 1965). See also Syed Naguib al-Attas, *Some Aspects of Sûfism as Understood and Practised among the Malays* (Singapore: Malaysian Sociological Research Institute, 1963), and Harun Hadiwijono, *Man in the Present Javanese Mysticism* (Baarn: Bosch and Keuning, 1967). The theme of man as microcosm, whether or not explicitly called *insan kamil*, is pervasive in the *suluk* literature of eighteenth- and nineteenth-century Java: see P. J. Zoetmulder, *Pantheisme en Monisme in de Javaansche Soeloek-Litteratuur* (Nijmegen: Berkhout, 1935).

9. An extreme example of this imagery is to be found in the *Suluk Gatholoco*, whose hero, the Sufi master Gatholoco ("rubbed prick"), is an opium-smoking ambulatory penis. The outrageous Gatholoco meets his match in Princess Perjiwati ("vagina"), and he falls limp after doing battle with her deep within a cave. See Philippus van Akkeren, *Een gedrocht en toch de volmaakte mens, De Javaanse Suluk Gatoloco, uitgeven, vertaald en toegelicht* (The Hague: Excelsior, 1951), and "The *Suluk Gatoloco*, Parts One & Two," trans. and ed. Benedict Anderson, *Indonesia* 32–33 (October 1981 and April 1982):109–50 and 31–88. See also note 24 below.

ontological, rather than a temporal, one. Hence, with the realization of that prior state, both nothing and everything is transformed. For the Perfect Man, Lord Jati Minulya, is (his "own") Reality Recuperate.

Finally, Siti Jenar is called Sèh Sunyata Jatimurti. Again challenging the translator while eluding ordinary meaning, the Arabic-prefaced Sanskritic name constitutes an oxymoron. The word *sunyata* denotes "the Absolute, Undifferentiated Void." The compound word *jatimurti* means "born or realized in [material] form." The name, then, indicates something like, "The Absolute Void Incarnate." Embodied Perfection, his person (body and soul) has been realized as the site on or in which Release is bound, "the binding of Release" (*pamuketing kamuksan*). His knowledge, a knowledge that he shares with others, masters the mechanism of this "binding." The name Sunyata Jatimurti and the concept of the "binding of Release" reaffirm the ideal of material (this-worldly) Perfection that—so important in much Javanese mystic thought—lies at the heart of *Babad Jaka Tingkir*.[10] The Siti Jenar who is Sèh Sunyata Jatimurti is not a world-renouncing ascetic retired to the silence of the mountaintop; he is on the move spreading his message of spiritual empowerment through networks of rural *kyai* dotted over the Javanese countryside.

The State Reconfirmed and Threatened

Having named Siti Jenar, and having thereby indicated his ideology, the poet once again frames that introduction with a return of Ki Ageng Pengging to center stage. The poet tells of the anxiety suffered in Demak owing to the Pengging lord's absence from the Sultan's court. The Sultan issues his first summons to the Kyai and receives his first rejection. That frame is closed by the opening of another scene: one that portrays the Garebeg Mulud festivities at the Demak court. This scene will lead into the trial and execution of Siti Jenar.

10. See, for example, Zoetmulder, *Kalangwan*, pp. 347–48 and passim. This form of realized material Perfection is claimed for a number of the *babad*'s heroes. Brawijaya V is said to have attained the state of *jatimurti* at the moment of his Release (*BJT* I:13). It is the knowledge of *jatimurti* that Sunan Kalijaga imparts to Adipati Pandhanarang (Sunan Bayat) and his younger brother (Panembahan Kajoran) (*BJT* XVI:12). Malang Sumirang was said to have realized this state of "spirit-body" (*BJT* XXIII:5 and XXIV: 16).

Celebrated in the third month of the Islamic calendar, the Garebeg Mulud commemorates the birth (*maulud*) of the Prophet Mohammad.[11] In the premodern royal polities of Java, the celebration was marked by the obligatory attendance at court of all the provincial nobility and all the kingdom's officialdom. Indeed, it was at this celebration that the unity of the kingdom was determined and reaffirmed precisely by the deferential attendance of the provincial elite alongside the elite of the capital. The Garebeg was also, and importantly, the occasion upon which taxes owed to the royal center were collected from the provinces.[12]

The success of the Garebeg at Demak in affirming the integrity of the still new realm is underlined in *Babad Jaka Tingkir* by the obedient and enthusiastic presence of the entire realm's officialdom and the orderly hierarchical attendance of these subjects in carefully tiered rows of seats (*BJT* XVIII:15–26). (Having newly reminded the reader of Ki Ageng Pengging's recalcitrance, the narrative "ignores" his absence from the celebration.) By picturing the Garebeg a success, the *babad* indicates, among other things, the success of the *wali*'s project to consolidate authority, the same project that had inspired the construction of the Demak Mosque. The new authority of the *wali*, who enjoy both spiritual and political ascendancy in Demak, is apparently holding firm.

With their power thus secured, the authorities (the *wali* and the senior *ulama*) assemble privately at the close of the Garebeg celebration, to discuss means by which they might more strictly enforce the tenets of Islamic law throughout the realm (*BJT* XVIII:27–28). A stricter enforcement of a more carefully codified code would mean, among other things,

11. For a description of the ceremony at the nineteenth-century Yogyakarta court, see J. Groneman, *De Garebegs te Ngayogyakarta* (The Hague: Nijhoff, 1895). See also John Pemberton's discussion and description of the Garebeg Mulud ceremonies in the Surakarta courts of Pakubuwana VII and Pakubuwana XI in *On the Subject of "Java,"* pp. 96–99.

12. In his illuminating commentary to the Old Javanese *Nâgarakrtâgama*, Th. Pigeaud traces the antecedents of this ceremony to the ritual politics of the kingdom of Majapahit (*Java in the Fourteenth Century*, 5 vols. [The Hague: Nijhoff, 1962]), vol. 4, chap. 14. Vincent Houben explains the significance of the Dutch colonial decision to retain the provision of the obligatory attendance of the provincial nobles to the Kraton Surakarta's Garebeg ceremonies even after the colonial government had wrested those provincial territories from Surakarta in the post–Dipangegara War contracts of 1830 ("Afstand van Gebied met Behoud van Aanzien").

an enhancement of the *wali's* authority and hence a confirmation of the royal polity. Conversely, transgression of the law would spell danger not only to Islam in Java, but also to the security of the realm. Having but recently been established *a* center of authority by a radical gesture involving the relational alignment of centers of authority within the Islamic world, Demak now turns to consolidate its power as a royal Moslem center. And so the *wali* convene their synod.[13]

Threatening the authority of the *wali*, and thus of the realm, are the actions and person of Siti Jenar (*BJT* XVIII:28–XIX:4). The paramount offense for which his senior colleagues indict him is his rash disclosure to the masses of the "Secret," the knowledge that is *sunyata jatimurti*, "the binding of Release." The second offense with which Siti Jenar is charged, transgression of the *sharî'a*, or the sacred law of Islam, is related to and extended by the first. He is faulted for revealing the Secret to the many "with nary a veil" (including and especially the veil of *sharî'a*).[14] His personal disregard of the law, in the context of his populist teachings, invites a more generalized breakdown of order. Sèh Sunyata Jatimurti's anti-authoritarian teachings and behavior effectively foster a radically populist, and potentially heterodox, mysticism that could and would actively undermine the more hierarchical and orthodox order that the *wali* are in the process of constructing. His teachings threaten both the law itself and the sole authority of the senior *wali* to determine and adjudicate that law on Java, that is, their authority to wield order as they define and construct it. Evidence of this threat is doubly inscribed in the text in the refusal of Siti Jenar's student Ki Ageng Pengging to submit himself to the court: a refusal proven both by Pengging's disregard of the Sultan's summons and by his (textually ignored) absence from the Garebeg ceremonies.

13. There are a number of texts which treat the "synod" or *musyawaratan* ("discussions") of the *wali*. These texts, often belonging to the genre of *suluk*, usually contain discussions among the *wali* upon matters pertaining to Sufi practice and theory. The "trial" of Siti Jenar is often imbedded in the context of these discussions. See Pigeaud, *Literature of Java*, 1:83–84.

14. Historically, mystical practice that rejects the sacred law has been condemned as heterodoxy if not heresy throughout the Islamic world, including the Islamic world of Java. Perhaps the most balanced and concise treatment of this issue in Javanese Islam is Soebardi's enlightening "Santri-Religious Elements as Reflected in the Book of Tjentini" *BKI* 127, no. 3 (1971):331–49.

The survival of the *wali*'s authority, that is, the survival of the Sultanate as Islam's center on Java, thus requires the elimination of Siti Jenar. The *wali* synod, then, has no choice but to execute the worm who had become a saint. This much is common to all versions of the Siti Jenar tale. There is considerable variation, however, in how the story of the saint's elimination is developed from version to version. The *Babad Jaka Tingkir* version appears alone in its depiction of Siti Jenar's vanishing as marking for him a perfect victory over the *wali*.

In the *Jaka Tingkir* version, for example, it is notable that Siti Jenar's "trial" constitutes no real contest. Unlike other versions, in which the trial is the scene of a *musyawarah* (or discussion) on matters concerning Ultimate Reality and on the "proper" relationship between God and man—a discussion that takes place among the accused and his accusers—in this version Siti Jenar's voice is the sole voice. His defense, the tonality of which is anything but defensive, is itself an exultant affirmation of his being the Perfect Man: the divine embodiment of that "relationship." The senior *wali* have no answer to his ecstatic defense. They remain silent aside from pedestrian pronouncements of accusations and verdicts.

Siti Jenar's defense turns on the semantic multivalence of the Sanskrit-derived Javanese word *rasa* (conflated with the again Sanskrit-derived *rahsa*, or *rahsya*) and its cognates. Perhaps the most dominant meaning of *rasa* is "feeling," a notion which in English already indicates the slippery phenomenological space in which the "outside" touches or impinges upon the "inside." Also denoted by *rasa* are notions akin to "emotion" and to "taste" and "touch." The word *rasa* also means "sense" in all senses of that polysemic English word. *Rasa* points toward "meaning," and also toward "speech," "voice," and "gossip." *Rasa*, especially but not exclusively in its form of *rahsa*, indicates "essence," as well as "mystery" and "secret."[15] Sung in the passionate, martial melody of Durma, Siti Jenar's ecstatic defense rides a current of language that culminates in a stream of *rasa* discourse that plays out the remarkable semantic fluidity of the word:

15. Paul Stange has written a thoughtful essay which explores the "meaning" of *rasa* in the context of contemporary Sumarah (a modern Javanese "mystical" [*kebatinan*] group) discourse, in "The Logic of Rasa in Java," *Indonesia* 38 (October 1984):113–34. See also Clifford Geertz's sensitive discussion of *rasa* in his seminal *The Religion of Java* (Chicago: University of Chicago Press, 1960), pp. 238–40.

"For he who has grasped the ultimate of *rasa*
Rasa that is Reality
The reality of *rasa*
Is surely not *rerasan* ["discourse"] voiced in speech
Nor the six *rasa* flavors
Nor again the *rasa*
Which is *rasa*-ed ["tasted"] by the lips

"Nor the *rasa* which is *rasa*-ed ["felt"] by the heart
Nor *rasa* fabricated
Nor again the *rasa*
Which is *rasa*-ed ["sensed"] by the body
Nor *rasa* which is *rasan*-ed ["spoken"] by the voice
Nor again the *rasa*
Of pleasure and afflicting pain

"The Reality of *Rasa* which authors *rasa*
Rasa Real mastering
Rahsa surasa
Rasa which is *rasa*'s navel
The king of *rahsa* all
Rasa exalted
Is *Jatimurti* recuperate"[16]

This passage, which is resonant with similar passages in other Javano-Sufi texts, points toward the ineffable and (im)possible interface of inside-and-outside, spirit-and-matter, divine-and-profane, Being-and-Nonbeing which is the Reality of *Rasa* or *Rasa* Real (*Rasa Sajati*). To grasp this meaning means to bind Release—which is to be the Perfect Man, or Jatimurti recuperate.

Also, and this is quite orthodox, to realize oneself as the Perfect Man is at the same time to cease to be (as such):

16. [Durma] Ujer sampun anyepeng pupusing rasa / rasa ingkang sajati / sajatining rasa / apan dudu rerasan / dédé rasa nem prakawis / lan dédé rasa / ingkang karasèng lathi // Dédé rasa ingkang karasa ing driya / dédé rasa kinardi / lawan dédé rasa / ingkang karasèng badan / dédé rasa dèn-rasani / lan dédé rasa / mukti myang suker sakit // Sajatining rasa kang amengku rasa / rasa jati mumpuni / ing rahsa surasa / rasa pusering rasa / ratuning rahsa sakalir / rasa minulya waluya jatimurti (*BJT* XIX:21–23).

"Encompassed by the Lord
Vanish does the creature
Dissolved, extinguished, and destroyed
Replaced by the Being of the Lord
His life is
Then the Life of the Lord

"*Lahir* and *batin*, his then is the Absolute's being
The one worshipped is the Lord
The Lord it is Who worships . . ."[17]

For, in reality, God is the sole Author of this realization; for the vanished (!) creature there is but "acceptance":

". . . for the receiver
There is but acceptance [*panarima*]
Eternal evermore
Beyond the limits of life
His life is beyond
The compass of the mind

"For he who has grasped the ultimate of *rasa* . . ."[18]

How then are we to understand this "acceptance"? The quality of *panarima* to which Siti Jenar refers is not—and this cannot be overemphasized—fatalistic. To "accept" (*nrima*) does not release the one who has "returned," the one who has "bound release," from the moral obligation to act. What it means is that in his or her actions such a Perfect Man realizes that it is not he or she as such who acts. For he or she is *Jatimurti* (God, in flesh, working on earth). The senior *wali*'s only answer to Siti Jenar's eloquent defense is to provide for it the label of heresy (Jabariyah) and to pronounce the sentence of death (*BJT* XIX:24–26).

The execution itself is depicted as a fiasco for the *wali*. They stage the saint's beheading as a spectacle for the ordered ranks of the entire realm, almost as though with it they hope to replay the reconfirmation of state

17. [Durma] . . . kalimputan in Gusti / ilang kawulanya / suh luyud sirna gepang / kagentèn ananing Gusti // Lahir batin pan wus kahananing Suksma / ingkang sinembah Gusti / Gusti kang anembah (*BJT* XIX:14–15).
18. [Durma] . . . kang nampani / amung panarima / ingkang langgeng nityasa / datanpa inganing ngurip / uripnya datan / kena cinakrèng budi // Ujer sampun anyepeng pupusing rasa . . . (*BJT* XIX:20–21).

authority defined by the Garebeg celebration. However, what becomes clear in full view of the realm is that the *wali* simply cannot kill Siti Jenar. First comes the miracle of the four-colored blood (a cliché of Javanese mystic discourse) and the lame attempts of the witnesses to rationalize it (*BJT* XX:1–7). Next follows the testament of the blood, a motif which, shared by a number of Siti Jenar variants, echoes the martyrdom of the most famous of all Sufi martyrs, al-Hallaj (*BJT* XX:8–11).[19] That common motif is then followed by another miracle, one apparently unique to this version. Siti Jenar's laughing and talking head fuses itself to its body in a passage that is couched to announce that union as a concrete expression of the mystery of the Perfect Man's union (body and soul) with God.

> With that the Honored Dead
> His head, that is
>
> Roared with laughter, while speaking oh so sweet:
> "Blood of my body all
> Return ye now in haste
> Lest ye be left behind
> And enter not into
> There your paradise"
>
> The blood then did return
> All of it, as if inhaled
> Vanished without a trace
> Then the head did circle
> Around its body
> Three times round
>
> Speaking all the while: "My fellows all
> None of you believed in me
> Your skepticism most extreme
> You took it as ridiculous
> Union with the Lord
> Fused in Being One"

19. It is told that at the almost unbelievably sadistic execution of al-Hallâj in Baghdad, A.D. 922, eighty-four drops of the martyr's spilled blood wrote the Divine Name "Al-lâh" on the ground. See Louis Massignon, *The Passion of al-Hallâj* (Princeton: Princeton University Press, 1982), pp. 553–54 and 616–19.

Thereat the head fixed on again
Perfectly in place[20]

Finally, by an act of his own will, Siti Jenar (body and soul) ascends to heaven in a flash of brilliant, fragrant light. Having attained the Perfection of spirit-body (*badan suksma*), Sunyata Jatimurti takes leave of the world and vanishes into Mystery (*BJT* XX:26–28). In contrast to most other versions of his tale, he leaves no body behind to be buried by the senior *wali*. The authorities at Demak are left behind wide-eyed with wonder and plunged in deep regret. Nevertheless, Siti Jenar's victory over the central authorities could appear a less than unequivocal one. For even though his vanishing was not effected by the agency of the center, that vanishing still serves the center's interests. The threat that dissemination (Siti Jenar) had posed to central authority has been, it seems, eliminated. Siti Jenar's apotheosis itself could be read as a domestication of his power.

The domestication of power that the retreat into Mystery might signify, however, is not realized in *Jaka Tingkir*'s Siti Jenar. Because Siti Jenar leaves behind no body, the senior *wali* are denied the normal means of appropriating his power to themselves, that is, the burial, care, and propitiation of his corpse. A properly constructed grave filled with Siti Jenar's mortal remains could have acted as a locus in which the dead saint's powers could have been concentrated and would have been accessed by pilgrims to the grave. In other words, the grave could have become, like the Great Mosque of Demak, another monument to and for the authority of Islam in Java under the leadership of the *wali*. Indeed, a number of versions of the Siti Jenar tale conflate Siti Jenar's grave with the Mosque itself, stating that the *wali* secretly buried the saint's corpse under the pulpit of the Mosque.[21]

The *Babad Jaka Tingkir* version of the Siti Jenar story goes on to relate a

---

20. [Mijil] . . . / yata sang alalis / utamangganipun // Sru gumujeng sarwi angling aris / kabèh getih ingong / padha sira baliya dèn-agé / manawa ta sira mengko kari / dadi nora manjing ing swarganirèku // Punang getih nulya sami bali / kabèh lir sinerot / sirna datan ana lelabeté / nulya utamongga angubengi / mring gagembungnèki / mider kaping telu // Sarwi muwus kabèh konca mami / tan angandel mring ngong / banget temen ing pamaidoné / ingkang ora-orané dèn-siri / panunggaling Gusti / pamoring sawujud // Nulya murda tèplok wangsul malih / cèples sampun manggon (*BJT* XX:13–17).

21. See, for example, the "Babad Tanah Jawa Poerwardja" version in Rinkes, "De Heiligen van Java VI," *TBG* 55 (1913):171–72.

final and desperate attempt of the *wali* to gain control over Siti Jenar's power despite that absence of a corpse. In a telling that is unique among versions I have consulted, the *wali* elect to erect a multiplicity of grave-stones to mark every place whereupon Siti Jenar had taught or meditated.

> No more said of him who was now Mystery
> Now it is related:
> Lord Sunan Drajat did command
> On all the sites used of old
> By Sèh Jatimurti
> Whereat he'd meditated
>
> And all the sites whereon he'd taught
> It was charged on all
> To mark them with tombstones
> Like graves the monuments
> Lest these sites bring curses on
> > [and/or (Engraved): "Don't bring curses on . . ."]
> Foolish unripe men [22]

The intent is for these stone markers to act as physical plugs that will hold in, and down, the traces of power left behind by the saint. The fear is that unless secured under these (engraved?) monuments, Siti Jenar's still un-tamed power may, by contagion, infect the masses—the "foolish unripe men." Further, by constructing these monuments, like graves, the *wali* hope to gain for themselves some institutional control over and access to the vanished saint's powers.

In the context of this *Babad Jaka Tingkir*, these desperate attempts to pin down Siti Jenar are, of course, doomed to failure. You will recall that in the case of the Demak Mosque, the marginal was marginalized to become its opposite, a center—something one can "get a hold of." Siti Jenar, the Perfect Man who was Sunyata Jatimurti, however, goes beyond simple reversal. Having himself "bound Release," he was, existentially, some-thing one can never "get hold of." "There was [and would be] no catching him" (*kesit datan kena pinethik* [*BJT* XVII:14]) anywhere, for he is always

---

22. [Mijil] Kuneng wau ingkang sampun aib / yata winiraos / Jeng Susunan Darajat dhawuhé / sagung panggonan tilasanèki / Sang Sèh Jatimurti / dènyanggung nane-kung // Tuwin tilas pamulanganèki / sadaya pan kinon / anengeri kijing maéjané / kadi kubur panyekarirèki / aja milalati / mring wong mudha punggung (*BJT* XX:31–32).

already both everywhere and nowhere at all. Having left no body behind, he remains instead:

> The perfection of body manifest
> A manifestation that never dies
> Vanishing in the end
> For ever ineffable is
> Its telling voiced in speech
>   [and/or: Hidden is its telling]
> There are no magic formulae
> Everything encompassed[23]

Vanishing thus, he denies the focus of any grave, including (and especially) the multiple graves erected by his executioners. He will not, and simply cannot, be appropriated. The Perfect Man who is the "binding of Release" is Himself boundless. He remains a power that owes nothing to anybody; he cannot be bribed and thereby controlled. His power remains on the loose, untamed, and disseminate. His is an absence that means presence. Though vanished from the world, he remains present (materially manifest) in it—and he has "work to do" (*BJT* XX:28). Something about the nature of that work may be glimpsed in the pious and other *works* of his pupil Ki Ageng Pengging depicted in the framing interval that follows on Siti Jenar's disappearance. That interval, which I will discuss in some detail below, lingers on the reciprocity of absence and presence, on the interplay between spiritual and material pursuits.

Sèh Malang Sumirang: A Figure of Anti-order

Malang Sumirang, whose name means "indecent, unseemly, anarchic," is a veritable icon of anti-order in Javanese writings, including the writing of *Babad Jaka Tingkir*. Like Siti Jenar, it is said of him that "There was no catching his nimble wit" (*datan kena pinethik kesité* [*BJT* XXII:27]). He too was not something or someone to be "got hold of." The word translated "catch" in the poet's depictions of both these saints is *pethik*, which means "to pluck" and especially "to cite" or "quote." The choice of the

23. [Dhangdhanggula] Paripurnaning ngongga muryani / wuryaningk[ang], tan kenaning pejah / lenyep ing kawekasané / pan tan kena winuwus / kauwusanira winuni / tan ana japa montra / kabèh wus kawengku (*BJT* XVII:16).

word *pethik* points toward language and implies that there is something in the words of these saints that cannot and will not be subjected to singular, univocal authority. Their words, like their selves, cannot be appropriated or controlled by another. And the "indecent, unseemly, anarchic" Malang Sumirang is best remembered as a master of words: he was a writer.

According to *Babad Jaka Tingkir*, Malang Sumirang's way is the "way of [Divine] madness." That madness originally shows itself in his inactivity, his passive disregard of the law (*BJT* XXII:31–33). But that passive disregard then turns to active defiance: his transgressions constitute frontal attacks on the sanctity of the *sharî'a*. Rather than (as Siti Jenar did) merely shunning *salât* in the mosque, Malang Sumirang is on the offensive, entering the mosque that he may defile it (*BJT* XXIII:2–3). Into the mosque he brings his pet dog, an animal so abominable to Islam that a Moslem touched by dog saliva must bathe seven times over to restore his or her ritual purity. A champion of sacrilege, Malang Sumirang might be called a "religious terrorist."[24]

It is for his outrageous offenses against the sacred law—and at the same time against the religious sensibilities of the pious—that Malang Sumirang is sentenced by the *wali* to death by fire. He is also accused (almost peripherally) of a theological heterodoxy reminiscent of Siti Jenar's "sin": his open claims to "spirit-body" and "Divine Existence" (*BJT* XXIII:5–7). But unlike Siti Jenar, Malang Sumirang offers no "defense" at his "trial"; his is to be a written testimony, and it will come later. The sentence is executed before the entire realm in yet another replay of a Garebeg-like spectacle. Like Siti Jenar before him, Malang Sumirang goes cheerfully to what was meant to be his death. And his execution, again like Siti Jenar's, marks another dismal failure for the *wali*. For Malang Sumirang it provides an opportunity to write.

24. Another interesting icon of anti-order in Javanese literary traditions is a character named Ki Lebé Lonthang. This figure also defies the law, but his style differs from that of Malang Sumirang. *Suluk Lonthang* describes graphically (and with great humor) the naked Lebé Lonthang's ejaculatory sexual forays against the market women, his (skirted) incursion into the mosque, and finally his intercourse in the middle of the road with his almost equally outrageous aging wife. See *Suluk Lonthang* in *Suluk Acih* (composed s.l., s.a.; inscribed Surakarta, 1867). MS. SP 15 Ca; SMP KS 502, pp. 77–80, and my discussion of this text in "Sex Wars: Writing Gender Relations in Nineteenth-Century Java," in *Fantacizing the Feminine in Indonesia*, ed. Laurie Sears (Durham: Duke University Press, forthcoming).

Writing of Malang Sumirang Writing

This telling of Malang Sumirang's story turns on, as it returns to, the theme of writing and the power of script. The scene of execution is transformed into a scene of writing. In a well-known tale, the poet describes how, attended by his dog, Malang Sumirang writes his testament in the midst of the fire. That testament is, of course, the famous *Suluk Malang Sumirang*. Although this tale of the writing in the fire is indeed widely known, and the *suluk* itself is among the most famous of *suluk*, this *babad*'s rendering of the tale and recitation of the *suluk* remain distinctive—and suggestive.

The poet's depiction of Malang Sumirang's act of writing in the fire is itself written in a manner that draws attention both to the process and to the product of that writing (see *BJT* XXIII:21–XXIV:3). Interestingly, it does so by composing the greater portion of this depiction in a manner that deflects attention away from a literal image of the saint writing. And because much of this passage on writing is written in direct authorial voice (*BJT* XXIII:23–29), the poetry reads as if the author has turned from the narrative in order to address the reader/audience in a voice that extends perpendicularly outward from the written page. This is the only extended passage in the entire poem so pointedly directed at the reader. The author's voice in the passage is a didactic one. And in it the author teaches the audience what it means to write, and to read, a text like that which Malang Sumirang is in the process of writing. At this point in the narrative, the poet stands back from the story to outline the conditions and the fruits of knowledge. And while admonishing the reader on these conditions (that which makes True writing—and reading—possible), the poet is at the same time creating a narrative space in which Malang Sumirang may write.

The passage affirms the Reality of Malang Sumirang as "The Consummation of Reality / The *rahsa* of Knowledge Ultimate" (*BJT* XXIII:22). And with this affirmation the poet thus confirms the Truth of what the saint is in the process of writing. The *babad*'s author goes on to caution the reader/audience on the dangers and difficulties of the pursuit of knowledge, that is, the danger of reading texts such as the one that Malang Sumirang writes. The author warns: "Most horrible the danger / A single slip spells ruin." The danger is presumably of falling into true heresy, and hence damnation. There is no such danger, however, "for him who knows." The true knower, having "already ascended to salvation" (*BJT* XXIII:24), knows how to read. According to the poet, the attainment of true knowledge requires ascetic practice as its precondition. Furthermore, that knowledge is to be embraced under the direction of a guru. However, the poet then cautions the pupil to dogged persistence and care in his or her quest for knowledge from the guru, lest he or she be so deceived as to take ordinary truth as True. In effect, the caution reminds the reader of the possibility that any guru's teaching may be contrived of deliberate "untruth" (*BJT* XXIII:25–29). The implication is that the final determination of Truth requires the pupil's "personal" attainment of the perfection that is *Jatimurti* ("The Consummation of Reality / The *rahsa* of Knowledge Ultimate").

Turning from the direct authorial didactic voice to a kind descriptive narrative voice which still does not return the reader to the action of the story, the passage ends with a comparison of Malang Sumirang's burning on the *alun-alun* of Demak to the trial by fire of the Prophet Ibrahim in the furnace of Babel (*BJT* XXIV:1–3). This metaphorical descriptive interlude brings Malang Sumirang's person and his act of writing into direct relationship with the sacred history of Islam, with sacred writ. This again emphatically underlines the stature of the mad/indecent saint's person and hence of his writing. At the same time, the metaphor prolongs the sense of narrative intermission that began with the poet's direct address to the audience. The audience is suspended in a narrative space of writing drawing attention to itself as writing. And this space is in some way the audience's "own" space. When Malang Sumirang finishes the writing of his testament and emerges unscathed from the fire, the *babad*'s poet returns the audience from the "meanwhile" of the didactic and metaphorical passage to the action of the story being played out on the *alun-alun* of Demak.

> Now again the telling turns:
> *By then* Sèh Malang Sumirang
> Had finished his writing [emphasis added][25]

The reader, having been suspended in the meanwhile of his or her own historical time to attend to the author's voice *while Malang Sumirang*

25. [Dhangdhanggula] Kuneng ingkang kawuwusa malih / Ki Sèh Malang Sumirang semana / sampurna ing panulisé (*BJT* XXIV:4).

wrote his suluk, is at this textual moment returned to the time and space of the narrative, to the unfolding story. This textual moment is crafted in a way that suggests an awareness of the interplay and coincidence among the diverse times and spaces that compose the *babad*'s writing. For it constitutes a moment of juncture among at least three apparently disjunct times and spaces: the historical time/space of which the poem writes, the narrative time/space of the poem's writing, and the potential phenomenological times/spaces of its reading. One of the effects of the moment is to draw audience attention to the process of writing—and hence to the status as writing of the *babad* being read or heard. By actively interrupting and intercepting the narrative, the passage also intensifies the effect of the episodic nature of the telling of the past that characterizes *Babad Jaka Tingkir.*

The Vanishing of Malang Sumirang: Reading and Not-reading His Suluk

Malang Sumirang's writing, which has already been confirmed as the Truth by the extraordinary circumstances of its production, is carried from the fire by the mad saint's dog (presumably in his drooling mouth). This writing, which is, of course, the renowned *Suluk Malang Sumirang,* is said to be a "framework (*penggalang*) for the self/body (*sarira*)" and "a stepping-stone to the Knowledge of / The *rasa* that authors *rasa*" (*BJT* XXIV:4 & 9). It is thus meant as a stage upon which (or from which) the reader can proceed in a movement of self-construction of his or her tomorrows. Specifically it is a piece of writing, the reading of which may lead toward the "binding of *rahsa,*" the realization of one's person (body and soul) as the Perfect Man. It is a piece of writing, like the *Babad Jaka Tingkir* into which it is inscribed, whose effectiveness is projected into the future. It is a trace (*tilas*) left behind by Malang Sumirang as his testament or legacy (*wasiyat*) for those who would come after him.

The nature of the testament's future effectiveness, and in whose interest that effectiveness would serve, are, however, problematicized in the *babad*'s writing of its publication. It is said of the *suluk* that it was received by Demak's Sultan "to be a relic in future times" (*mongka tilas ing wuri-wuri* [*BJT* XXIV:9]). For while *tilas* means "trace," it also means "relic" and "monument." This reception of the *suluk* into royal hands as a future relic suggests the possibility of a more constrained potentiality for it than might be imagined for "a stepping-stone to the Knowledge of / The *rasa* that authors *rasa*." Is *Suluk Malang Sumirang* to become (like the Grand Mosque of Demak, and unlike the "dead" Siti Jenar) a monument, which having been delivered into the hands of the Sultan, is to stand for and as a basis of central authority?

There are other elements in this *babad*'s telling of the Malang Sumirang story that seem to point in the direction of the monumentalization of the trace, to the domestication of Malang Sumirang's wild words by the state. Witness, for example, Malang Sumirang's seemingly docile retreat to internal exile in the forest at the close of the episode. He is exiled in the name and in the interest of the law (*shari'a*) and for the security of the realm (*BJT* XXIV:17–18). The security and stability of the Sultanate, founded as it is on order by law, requires the exclusion of this figure of anti-order. Sunan Kudus, spokesman for the conservative wing of the *wali* and Malang Sumirang's nephew, declares *after* the saint's miraculous escape from the fire:

> "Uncle, be resigned
> That better you go off far away
> Lest you bring about
> Confusion by subversion
> Loosening the knot
> Pulling down the palisades, breaking through the ranks
> Bringing low the flag . . ."[26]

Not only is his exile meant to expel danger from the realm, the *wali*'s intent is, by means of exile, to domesticate the saint's potentially dangerous powers in order that these powers may then be tapped by and for the realm. It is the express will of the *wali* that the exiled saint's hermitage be a "talisman of the realm" (*jimating praja*) (*BJT* XXIV:20). Although Malang Sumirang refuses the *wali*'s offer of a luxurious hermitage ("I wouldn't fancy something fine"), he does indeed agree "with great pleasure" to go off to the spectral forest (*BJT* XXIV:21). To the great joy of the central authorities, he retreats, seemingly to the silence of mountain and

26. [Dhangdhanggula] paman dipun-amuhung / meheng tebih sangking nagari / sampun ngantos akarya / kéron wowor-sambu / angendoni bubundhelan / ngarangaken pager ngelikabken baris / dhoyongaken bandéra (*BJT* XXIV:19).

forest.[27] Malang Sumirang vanishes into permanent and willing marginality.

But is the domestication of Malang Sumirang an unmitigated success for the authorities? Does his vanishing indeed eliminate him as a force with which to be reckoned? Was the *Suluk Malang Sumirang* he left behind to become a monument to authority? Hardly. Although his testament was received by the hand of the Sultan, it was not to be the Sultan's to master. This "relic for future times" remained Malang Sumirang's mad trace, a trace that was neither to be erased nor to be appropriated. Paradoxically, the irrepressible quality of the *suluk* is underlined in this *babad* by the narrative suppression of its reading.

Babad Jaka Tingkir provides but a partial reading of *Suluk Malang Sumirang*. That abbreviated reading is a public one and one performed by royal command. It is performed in song at audience by "the soldier whose office it was to read" (*BJT* XXIV:10). The reading of the *suluk*, which usually consists of some twenty or so stanzas of Dhangdhanggula meter, is cut off after a mere three stanzas—two of which are prefatory to the "*suluk* proper." And that abrupt cutting off is not by royal command, nor by the will of the singing soldier, but again (in another moment of narrative suspension) by the active and direct intervention of the *babad*'s author:

> Thus [or, Enough of this], the revealing of the secret
> Words writing the concealed
> The warning [and/or: "remembrance"] of the Watchful One
>   [Sang Manginté]
> To reason I will not refer
> This lesson of total knowledge
> I'll cut it off, I'll not unfold
> The unfolding of the sweet fragrance
> For I but follow the tale
> Done was the reading of the writing that is
> *Suluk Malang Sumirang*[28]

27. This retreat repeats a motif of the exclusion of (religious) disorder from the center of the realm found in other texts (notably the *Serat Cabolèk*). For a discussion of this motif see Anthony Day, "Islam and Literature in South-East Asia," in *Islam in South-East Asia*, ed. M. B. Hooker (Leiden: Brill, 1983), pp. 144–48.

28. [Dhangdhanggula] Nahan ta rèh wuryaning arempit / sipta-ripta rikang pipi-

Why cut off the reading? Why should the poet suppress Malang Sumi-rang's writing in the body of his or her own writing? And what has this suppression or censorship to do with "the Watchful One"? To whom or what does "Sang Manginté" refer? Although I have no definitive answers to these questions, I wish to suggest several possible rationales for this poetic choice. These rationales, though conflicting, need not be mutually exclusive.

Suluk Malang Sumirang is by no means a rare text. Given the large number and extensive dispersion of its manuscript witnesses, it may safely be claimed that this *suluk* was widely circulated and read in nine-teenth-century Java. "The secret," these "Words writing the concealed," were already very much in the public domain. Not inscribing them in full into the text of *Babad Jaka Tingkir* conceals or protects very little if any-thing at all. The literate reader/audience would already know and likely remember at least the outlines of this *suluk*'s teachings. Why then not repeat these words in the *babad*'s writing?

Let us begin with a consideration of what the censored *suluk* is about. What is the sense of the silenced "Words writing the concealed?" Al-though I have seen several versions of this famous *suluk*, all the versions I have consulted seem to share a common "message." Writing of mystic unity through the metaphors of the Old Javanese hero Prince Panji in disguise as a *dhalang*, and of the essential identity of the Hindu god Wisnu with the Mahabharata king Kresna, the *suluk* expresses an ideol-ogy of radical monism. The *suluk* usually includes several stanzas couch-ing that ideology in the idiom of *rasa*.[29] It then claims this ideology as the expression of the Truth of Islam. The true Moslem is only he who has Truly embraced the discourse of the infidels. The false Moslem (the true "infidel") is the pious fool who is preoccupied with the law (*sharî'a*). The

---

ngitan / pamèngeting Sang Manginté / ing nalar tan sun ulur / nalirahing ngèlmu sakalir / sun pu[ng]gel tan sun gelar / gelaring raras rum / mung ingsun amburu kondha / wusnya telas pamacané ponang tulis / Suluk Malang Sumirang (*BJT* XXIV: 14).

29. Indeed, the *rasa* passage from Siti Jenar's defense cited above is almost surely derived from a *Suluk Malang Sumirang* text. Compare *BJT* XIX:21–23 with comparable verses in the following *Malang Sumirang* redactions: verse 17 in G. W. J. Drewes, "Het Document uit den Brandstapel," *Jåwå* 7 (1927):108, and canto 11, verse 21 in Yasa-dipura I's *The Book of Cabolèk*, ed. Soebardi, p. 151.

suluk is always prefaced and usually concluded with disclaimers dismissing Malang Sumirang and/or his teachings as mad. The message, then, is one of anti-order and lawlessness (heresy), but a message that is conflicted by disclaimers. It is a complicated message. Impressionistic and rather "wild," the *suluk* is hardly a "lesson [or theory, *nalirah*] of total knowledge [*ngèlmu*]."

By cutting off the reading of a text with which the reader would already have been familiar, perhaps the poet is deferring to constraints of writing under the aspect of *semu*. The not-saying of the already-known Secret is a way of indicating its meaning under the aspect of concealment. The censorship "reveals" the saint's meaning without pretending to repeat his language. By not repeating the mad saint's words in the narrative, the poet underlines their originality, that is, their power. The silence thus acknowledges those words for what they are: frameworks (*penggalang*) for action, for "Self-Realization"—rather than iterable verbal monuments. The poet's cutting the *suluk* off can, then, be read as a bow in the direction of the efficacy of its words, to their resistance to the domestication of ordinary repetition in quotation (*datan kena pinethik*). Furthermore, by denying their quotation at this point in the narrative, that is, in a textual scene performed before the Demak authorities, the poet thereby preserves them from appropriation to and by central authority. Thus denying royal mastery of the "relic," the poet's suppression of reading leaves Malang Sumirang's wild "trace" open for more disseminate effect.

There remain other possible rationales for this self-censorship. Perhaps with this acknowledged silencing of *Suluk Malang Sumirang*, the poet is gesturing toward a more obviously "down-to-earth" motivation for his or her writing (history) under the aspect of *semu*.

> Thus, the [or, Enough of this] revealing of the secret
> Words writing the concealed
> The warning [remembrance] of the Watchful One [Sang Manginté]

The cutting off of the *suluk*'s reading is somehow related to a "warning," or a "remembrance" (*pamènget*) of the "Watchful One." But then who or what is this "Watchful One?" or "Sang Manginté?" Does the name refer to Malang Sumirang, or to someone or something else? I considered and then rejected a translation of "the All-Seeing" for Sang Manginté, thinking it perhaps a variant of the more common divine appellation, "Sang

Manon." Like the root *ton*, the Kawi *inté* does mean "to see," but *inté* means "to see" in a very special way—that is, "to peer at" or "to keep careful watch on." The reference is to surveillance, and draws attention to a reality that haunted nineteenth-century Javanese writing, perhaps especially court writing.

The nineteenth-century Surakarta court was awash with spies in the service of the Dutch colonial government. Notably, both the Sunan and his court were under constant surveillance by the forty European "honor guards" whom the Resident garrisoned inside the Kraton.[30] Court literati would certainly not have been among the least suspected of treason to colonial authority. Their activities and their writings were carefully monitored. Two of those writers, including the chief of the palace scribes (the elder Ronggawarsita) and his brother "the Haji" (almost certainly Ronggasasmita, whose call to reading unread texts opens this book), were accused of subversion and exiled in 1828, a year before *Babad Jaka Tingkir* is dated.[31] The reward for knowing too much and revealing it too transparently in writing was exile. I discussed in chapter 4 how the *babad* inscribes this lesson into the tale of the writer/painter Jaka Prabangkara, whose ink-stained portrait of the queen earned him a one-way kite trip to China. And now the poet's strategic censorship of the already-known words of Malang Sumirang's *suluk* serves as a device that (covertly) reminds the audience of the watchful eyes that ever constrain this *babad*'s writing. This remembrance or warning (*pamènget*) thus reminds the reader (again) to attend to the unwritten words, the implicate meanings, of the text.

But there is yet another plausible rationale for the censorship of *Suluk Malang Sumirang* in the context of this unique version of *Babad Jaka Tingkir.* Perhaps the poet censors the reading of the *suluk* to censure it. Perhaps he or she is in disagreement with the substance of Malang Sumi-

30. In his "General Report" of 1832, Resident MacGillavrij writes, "The Kaiser lives in the Dalm or Kraton, the palace of his forefathers, where there is with him at all times one of the honor-guards provided him by the Government, which honor-guard is comprised entirely of Europeans; this guard of forty cavalry men is garrisoned inside the Kraton and serves there a double end, namely: to watch over the Sultan and at the same time to keep a waking eye on everything that goes on there" (Algemeen Verslag Residentie Soerakarta, 1832. Solo Bundel 2/2, Arsip Nasional Republik Indonesia).
31. See above, Introduction, note 2, and p. 45; and Chapter 4, note 19.

rang's irrepressible mad trace, despite his or her sympathies with the person and pluck of the outrageous and unbeatable saint. Hence, the poet intercepts the narrative in order to exclude from his or her text the form of madness inscribed in the *suluk*.

The cutting off of the *suluk* is executed in direct authorial voice. That voice echoes back to its earlier and more lengthy intrusion that composes the didactic passage discussed above. You will recall that this earlier intrusion of the author into—and out from—the text had provided an interval of narrative suspension within which (like the fire) Malang Sumirang had written his *suluk*. At the same time the author had inserted his or her own brief lesson (remembrance and warning) into that interval. Now that direct authorial voice returns again to silence the reading of Malang Sumirang's writing from the fire. By thus silencing Malang Sumirang's voice, the poet replaces it with his or her own voice, the same voice that had shared the interval within which Malang Sumirang had written his *suluk*. The interception of the reading of the *suluk* marks the return of the poet's didactic voice as a displacement of the burning words of the saint.

Why, then, would the author of our *babad* wish thus to displace Malang Sumirang's words? You will recall that the dominant message of that singular, overtly didactic passage is that we (the readers/audience to whom the author speaks at that moment) should, through disciplined practice— and with utmost care and practiced skepticism—follow a teacher in pursuit of Self-Realization of the Truth. The dominant message of *Suluk Malang Sumirang* seems, on the other hand, to be one of "salvation" by way of radical anti-order and of exuberant heresy. Rather than suggesting the construction of an alternative order or orders, the mad *suluk* seems to deny all order in favor of an anarchy which is "the way of madness." That way can lead to a kind of marginalization that turns away from the world. The poem describes Malang Sumirang's madness:

> Lost in visions of rapt fancy
> He sat with absent gaze
> In thrall of excess ecstasy
> Heeding neither body nor soul
> Idling at home he sat
> In empty vacant musing

> Having forsaken all activity
> Nothing did he do[32]

The message of *Babad Jaka Tingkir*, on the contrary, is an activist one.

Ki Ageng Pengging: A Figure of Undecidability

Ki Ageng Pengging, as the father of the *babad*'s namesake Jaka Tingkir, is the figure in relation to whom the tales of this fragmented history's other heroes of the margins must be read. It is his story that frames and hence "contextualizes" the stories of the other five heroes: Jaka Prabangkara, Jaka Karèwèd, the Demak Mosque, Sèh Siti Jenar, and Sèh Malang Sumi-rang. Conversely, the stories of these other five heroes, these fragmented tellings of marginal pasts, inform the reading of the Ki Ageng Pengging story. Because of the progression of issues which these stories explore, we are able to recognize in the Ki Ageng Pengging story the still-suspended culmination of the *babad*'s potential meaning. Ki Ageng Pengging, as a figure of undecidability, stands beyond the category of choice between alternatives such as outside and inside, material/political power versus spiritual power. And, as the father of the orphaned baby Jaka Tingkir, he stands on the cusp of the future. The readers know that the baby Tingkir (Karèbèt), whose tale our *Babad Jaka Tingkir* will not tell, was to found the first Islamic kingdom of inland Central Java. The tale of the absent name-sake's father, then, breathes the anticipation of new beginnings.

As a figure of undecidability, Ki Ageng Pengging rejects relegation to the sidelines. He is a marginal figure who defies marginalization. He re-fuses the option that Malang Sumirang had accepted. He will not choose a spiritual life at the edges of society in contradistinction to "material" political authority at the center. Such a choice is simply not relevant to him. Nor does the choice between esoteric spiritual pursuits and the *sharî'a* law of Islam make sense to him. Beyond the binary categories of "either/or," his way is rather "both/and." In his final meeting with Sunan Kudus, Ki Ageng Pengging is challenged to choose for the last time. The

---

32. [Mijil] Linglang-linglung lenglenging panglingling / cengeng sapatemon / kan-dhem karem sangking sru nikmaté / jiwa raga wus datan katolih / kèndel anèng panti / lalu lengur-lengur // Sampun méngo sagunging pakarti / tan ana linakon (*BJT* XXII: 32–33).

choice that the central authorities demand of him is between the outside and the inside (that is, political power versus spiritual power *and* "external" Moslem practice versus "internal" Sufi consciousness), the above and below (ruling versus being ruled), being and nonbeing, and so on. The Kyai answers:

> "Were I to choose the inside I'd err
> To choose the outside I'm lost
> Wavering then in faith
> Were I to choose the above
> 'Twould be searching for an echo
> Were I to choose the front
> Truly I'd be most damnably lost
> Lost by seven schools of thought
> Below, above, left, and right are mine
> Nothing is mine"[33]

This refusal of Ki Ageng Pengging's to choose convicts him as an enemy of the state, and thereby signs his death warrant. And his interlocutor directly does execute the sentence. But it is only by Pengging's own will that the cut which Sunan Kudus makes to his elbow proves fatal; even with his death, the lord of Pengging has it both ways.

This quality of Ki Ageng Pengging's ambiguity, or ultimate undecidability, is first highlighted in the framing interlude that defines, as it divides one from another, the Siti Jenar and Malang Sumirang episodes (*BJT* XXI:5–XXII:24). In this interval a worried Sultan of Demak, whose futile attempts to plug the powers of the newly vanished Siti Jenar have just been related, sends a second summons to Ki Ageng Pengging ordering his presence at court. Pengging refuses the summons. Both the summons and the refusal are delivered in writing, as letters. The royal messengers, whose mission it is to convey those letters, at the same time function as the Sultan's intelligence officers. After himself reading Pengging's eloquent and evasive reply, Demak's Sultan asks the messengers for their reading of the true situation in Pengging. The messengers' spokesman answers:

33. [Dhangdhanggula] Yèn miliya jero mapan sisip / yèn miliya ing jaba pan sasar / semang-semang pangidhepé / yèn miliya ing luhur / pan kemandhang dipun-ulati / lamun miliya ngarsa / yekti sasar susur / sasaré pitung medhahab / ngisor dhuwur kiwa tengen duwèk mami / orané duwèk ingwang (*BJT* XXIX:15).

"The manner of your brother in Pengging
A secret does conceal
His manner's both *ramé* and *sepi*"[34]

The words *ramé* and *sepi* elude translation into English. Each of the two words comprises a semantic constellation, and each of these constellations stands in (binary) opposition to the other. The word *ramé* comprises a constellation of meanings connoting *presence*: noise, bustle, fullness, activity. The constellation around the word *sepi*, conversely, connotes *absence*: silence, solitude, emptiness, inactivity. By normal definition it does not make sense for something to be both *ramé* and *sepi* at the same time; but Ki Ageng Pengging is not subject to "normal definition." The messenger goes on to clarify how the manner and person of the Kyai of Pengging can be read as both *sepi* and *ramé*.

Pengging's Kyai is said to be *sepi* insofar as he has turned from the ways of nobility (*BJT* XXII:14–16). Embracing the "tune" (*lagu*) of a poor *santri*, he has abandoned "the practices of prestige" (*rèh kang mawi singgih*), those styles of practice—and especially language—that define, as they express, vertically graded status differentiations among persons. Since Javanese social and verbal discourse is founded upon, and subsists through, status differentiation, to abandon these "practices of prestige" means to ignore and hence subvert the received sociopolitical structure— to speak a "new language" that denies the essential superiority of one category of human beings (the nobility) over the rest. This subversion of the received order, the singing of a *santri* song, is the result of taking seriously the egalitarian precepts of Islam.[35] I shall have more to say on this social and linguistic subversion in a moment. Ki Ageng Pengging can

34. [Mijil] Rakitipun rakanta ing Pengging / asimpen wawados / ing pratingkah asepi aramé (*BJT* XXII:14).

35. For an interesting discussion of the differences between the *santri* "tune" and the more "normal" Javanese behavioral and verbal "song" in early-twentieth-century Java, see [R.Ng. Purbadipura], *Srikarongron*, 3 vols., ed. Moelyono Sastronaryatmo (Jakarta: Departemen Pendidikan dan Kebudayaan Proyek Penerbitan Buku Sastra Indonesia dan Daerah, 1981), 2:122–26. In this passage of the 1913-composed *Srikarongron*, a group of lower-level court servants discuss among themselves the king's (Pakubuwana X) recent attendance at the mosque of Ngèksipurna, Pengging. They contrast the social leveling in the Islamic context of the Friday prayers (pundi-pundi ya ing masjid / sami mawon boten wonten ingkang béda) with the status differentiations that characterize all other gatherings ("Bangsa luhur bangsa andhap boten campur / mawi pilah-pilah").

also be called *sepi* insofar as he often withdraws into solitude for quiet contemplation (*BJT* XXII:17). It is not his style, however, to remain wrapped
in the silence of the hermitage.

The person and ways of Ki Ageng Pengging are also *ramé*. The Sultan's
messenger cum intelligence officer goes on to describe as *ramé* in Pengging the ardent zeal of the Kyai and his *santri* as orthodox Moslems. That
zeal is evidenced by their actions: their strict adherence to the Prophet's
sharî'a, their faithful performance of ritual obligations (*salât*), and their
construction of a new and impressive mosque (*BJT* XXII:18–19). Also
mentioned are the Kyai's farming activities and how those activities would
give the impression that the Kyai were an ordinary peasant were it not the
case that he is clearly something other. An ambiguous character (a character of *semu*), the Kyai of Pengging acts like a farmer but lives in the
(powerful/*pusaka*) royal complex of his forefathers (*BJT* XXII:20–21).
Having turned from the ways of nobility, he nonetheless remains a prince.
But as a laboring *kyai*, what an extraordinary prince! Neither laboring in
the fields along side commoners nor piously adhering to the *sharî'a* is
behavior appropriate to the received image of what it meant to be royal in
traditional Java. But Ki Ageng Pengging, the potato farmer (*BJT* XVII:13),
is no ordinary royal figure.

Nor is he unique. Another royal figure who, through the letters he left
behind, we may associate with farm labor and Islamic piety is the exiled
Pakubuwana VI. In a verse letter sent from Ambon to his younger brother
in Surakarta, the ex-king wrote on 4 June 1848 (almost to the day one year
before his death):

> I am unfit for life in the capital
> Fit for life in the forest
> Growing corn and soybeans
> Peas, peanuts, and beans
> Chillies and sweet potatoes
> Is all I am good for
> Want of feeling, a hapless man
>
> You sent me a batik head-cloth
> And a batik shirt, Brother
> Yea, many are my thanks
> But 'tis not fit I wear them
> For me 'tis fit to wear

Skirts of black and black head-cloths
Yea, Ponorogo cottons[36]

Finished is this writing
Written in a rude hut in the fields[37]

Pakubuwana VI signed the letter: H.R.H. Sushunan Sayiddi Maolana Mokhamat Salim. In another verse letter dated the same day and addressed to one of his queens, the exiled king urges his wife to adhere to the *sharî'a* and to pursue sacred knowledge (*ngèlmu*). The pious ex-king would, he says, teach her himself—should God grant his return to Java; but now he looks forward only to death. The letter to the queen closes with several lines of Arabic quotation. These personal and highly emotional letters of Pakubuwana VI are preserved in the compilation whose final entry is the *Babad Jaka Tingkir* that we are reading.[38]

Babad Jaka Tingkir's Ki Ageng Pengging is the *kyai* of a *pesantrèn* who is also, and "underneath," a prince. But he is a prince who refuses the ways, the dress, and the language of the court.[39] And as a prince who is "really" a rural *kyai* with a large and zealous following, Pengging's defiance of court order is particularly troublesome to the central authorities. In my reading of the Jaka Karèwèd episode, I spoke of how the recognition of a presumed unitary grammar (*ukara*) of the court (those ways, that dress, and especially that language) as the sole correct or valid grammar

36. Skirts and especially head-cloths of blue-black (*wulung*) cotton from Ponorogo are emblematic of the dress of itinerant *santri*, and especially of *kyai* and *dhukun* (healers, sorcerers).
37. [Asmarandana] Tan patut anèng negari / mung patuté anèng wona / nandur jagung lan kadhelé / kecipir kacang lan kara / lombok lawan ketéla / gunaku amung puniku / tanpa ngrasa wong cilaka // Sira kirim iket bathik / lawan jarit bathik dhimas / ya banget panrimaning ngong / nanging tan patut sun goa / ingsun patut anggoa / jarit wulung iket wulung / iya lawon Panagara // Titi tamat ingkang tulis / tinulis nèng gubug sawah (*His Majesty the VI's Correspondence*, p. 72verso).
38. *His Majesty the VI's Correspondence*, pp. 72verso & 75recto–75verso; see Appendix I, Items 58 and 60.
39. This despite his fluency in, and occasional utilization of, that language. Witness, for example, the effectiveness of his eloquent and evasive letter to the Sultan in answer to the second summons. Although the Sultan recognizes that letter as harboring other hidden meanings (*ing jro simpen semu*) which spell trouble for the realm, its charming (court) language nonetheless effectively assuages the Sultan for the time being (*BJT* XXII:22–23).

was implicated in the construction of the fiction of the impenetrable *kraton* walls.[40] By actively rejecting that grammar, a grammar that he commands both by birth and by education, Ki Ageng Pengging joins in denying the walls' reality, and in exposing to the multitude their essential irrelevance, their permeability. And since the walls defining the center from the periphery are ephemeral fictions whose subsistence depends upon the populace's recognition of them as real (that is, as by nature impenetrable), Ki Ageng's rejection of court grammar constitutes an act of defiance that breaches the citadel. His defiance points to the cracks that are already present in the very structure of the walls, while at the same time gesturing toward another structure. His is an act of linguistic and social subversion that turns from the Sultanate as center to nod in the direction of a more populist Moslem egalitarianism under the *sharî'a*. His style, that is, his "tune," by rejecting the grammar of solitary, centralized royal authority, stands instead for a decentering of sociopolitical power within the context of Moslem brother/sister-hood.

As the *kyai* of a *pesantrèn* and a prince who has taken on *santri* ways, dress, and language, Ki Ageng Pengging is a formidable power—spiritually and politically. And his is, by choice, the power of a populist rural *kyai*. Hence, his is a power that recognizes other powers; the *kyai* is part of a constellation of powers: a brotherhood of *kyai* across the Javanese countryside and a brotherhood of pious Moslems across the Islamic world. The message of a populist *kyai* like Ki Ageng Pengging is that the faithful should recognize as ultimate authority—not any king, but—only Allah.

> [Asked Ki Ageng Tingkir]:
> "Are you not, Brother
> Subject to the King?
> The earth on which you move
> Yea, everything in Java
> Is all the property of him who reigns as king"
>
> Softly spoke [Ki Ageng Pengging]:
> "It is Allah who owns the earth"[41]

40. See above, chapter 4, pp. 307–12.
41. [Sinom] "Apa ta sira yayi / nora kabawah ing ratu / lemah kang sira ambah / saisiné tanah Jawi / pan sadaya, duwèké kang dadi nata // Kang rayi alon turira / Allah kang adarbé bumi (*BJT* XXVI:3–4).

Ki Ageng Pengging: Father of a King

And yet Ki Ageng Pengging's burning ambition seems to be the conventional royal one: to procreate a king. Following directly upon the vanishing of Malang Sumirang into the spectral forest, the *babad* turns to the scene of Ki Ageng Pengging's meditation. This turn in the narrative opens the final and culminating episode of the *babad*, the Ki Ageng Pengging episode that effects the inversion of frame and framed, figure and ground of the text. The Kyai, following a regime of intense ascetic practice, meditates for a son "Who'd be meet in future days / To finish out the tale" (*ingkang pantes ing bésuk / anutugna lalakonnèki* [BJT XXIV:25]). A divine voice answers his prayers, promising a son who will be king and master all Java. It is at this point that Pengging's hitherto relatively hidden resistance goes public. Shortly after his wife gives birth to this promised son (the future Jaka Tingkir), emissaries come from Demak with the Sultan's third summons to court. To this summons, Ki Ageng Pengging offers no more evasive and eloquent replies:

> "I, having been summoned
> By His Majesty the King
> Needs must beg pardon
> For I shall not go"
> Softly did the envoy speak:
> "Pray what reason for this?"
> Ki Ageng did softly speak:
>
> "I have no more reasons
> Just tell His Majesty
> That such is my reply"[42]

Nothing could be more conventional. The father of the would-be future king goes into open rebellion against the older center of authority in preparation for his son's coming establishment of a new royal center. It is a conventional vision that sees the exchange of one center for another,

---

42. [Asmarandana] Kawula dipun-timbali / marang Kangjeng Sri Naréndra / ing mangké nuwun dukané / kawula boya lumampah / gandhèk alon delingnya / punapa ta sababipun / Kiyageng alon delingnya // Tan wonten sababé malih / matura mring Sri Naréndra / yèn mengkono aturing ngong (BJT XXV:19–20).

rather than a transformation of the logic of the center. For of his son the voice had promised the Kyai:

> 'Tis he in the future whom God has ordained
> To be the staff of the multitude
> That means to be the king
> Who masters all Java[43]

Writing in Tension with the Tradition

But the Jaka Tingkir of whom our *babad* does not quite write figures, in anticipation, a different kind of kingship (of authority) than that usually inscribed in the dominant tradition. He, or perhaps *they,* figure an authority founded not upon mastery and subjugation but upon the recognized interpenetration of multiple orders. In his final meeting with Sunan Kudus, the Kyai of Pengging refuses again to honor the king's summons to court, repeating—with a difference—a traditional political, and also mystical, cliché:[44]

> "I do not serve as subject
> Am subject to no king
> Lord and subject are all the same
> The being of the subject has its source in the lord
> That of the lord in the subject"[45]

The scarlet thread which the Ki Ageng Pengging tale weaves through the *babad* is the refusal to accept as absolute the categories of lordship and subjugation. This thread is evident everywhere: in the framing interludes that develop the image of Ki Ageng Pengging as a populist potato-farming *kyai;* in the episodes that the intervals frame; and in the Kyai's final resistance and his resultant vanishing. Interestingly, with the telling of Ki Ageng Pengging's final stand and elimination (this final "episode"), comes the *qualified* dovetailing of *Babad Jaka Tingkir's* rendering of the past with

43. [Dhangdhanggula] iku bésuk pinasthi ing Suksma / dadya paugeraning wong ka-bèh / tegesé dadi ratu / tanah Jawa kang aduwèni (*BJT* XXIV:28).
44. Soemarsaid Moertono provides an extended introduction to the meaning of the *kawula-gusti* concept in the sociopolitical discourse of premodern Java, in his *State and Statecraft in Old Java,* pp. 14–26.
45. [Dhangdhanggula] manira tan ngawula / tan kabawah ratu / iya gusti ya kawula / kahanané kawula pan sangking gusti / gusti sangking kawula (*BJT* XXIX:12).

that of a corpus of texts from the dominant *babad* tradition. The ways in which these tellings both converge and diverge play out a tension between our *babad* and the dominant *babad* tradition. A reading of this tension demonstrates the difference between the dominant tradition's conventional vision of past futures and *Babad Jaka Tingkir*'s quite new, if not revolutionary, vision of futures born from pasts.

The corpus of texts with which lengthy passages of this final section of *Babad Jaka Tingkir* concur is a variant of the dominant *babad* tradition that I call the Galuh variant.[46] The dominant *babad* tradition, sometimes simply called *Babad Tanah Jawi*, comprises a constellation of variant textual corpora.[47] Among these corpora two variants prevail: that which was to earn the title "*The* Major Babad Tanah Jawi" and the "Galuh variant." Manuscript as well as published witnesses of the Galuh variant of the dominant *babad* tradition are many. The following analysis is based upon examination of, and comparison among, six of these manuscript witnesses.[48]

Babad Jaka Tingkir's cantos XXVI and XXVII are nearly identical to passages found in all the Galuh witnesses. There can be no doubt that

46. A comparison of opening lines of cantos indicates that this "Galuh variant" corresponds to the corpus of texts designated "Group II" by the Indonesian historian Hoesein Djajadiningrat in his 1913 *Critische Beschouwing van de Sadjarah Banten;* see Hoesein Djajadiningrat, *Tinjauan Kritis tentang Sajarah Banten* (Jakarta: Djambatan, 1983), esp. pp. 251 ff.

47. For more on the "dominant babad tradition," see above, chapter 3, pp. 265–68.

48. Those manuscript witnesses are: (1) canto 39 ff. of SMP KS 21 (*Serat Babad Pajajaran: Nyariyosaken Prabu Mundhingsari ngantos dumugi kawontenanipun lelampahan ing nagari Pajang* [composed Surakarta, s.a. and (1895)] [inscribed Surakarta, 1895]. MS. SP 190 Na). (2) canto 21 ff. of SMP KS 24A (*Serat Babad Pajajaran dumugi Pajang* [composed s.l., s.a.] [inscribed Surakarta, 19th century]. MS. SP uncataloged). (3) canto 92 ff. of SMP MN 184 (M.Ng. Rongga Panambangan, ed., *Serat Manikmaya dumugi Demak* [composed Mangkunagaran, Surakarta, 1813] [inscribed Surakarta, mid 19th century]. MS. RP B100). (4) canto 7 ff. of SMP MN 193 (*Serat Babad Demak* [composed s.l., s.a.] [inscribed Surakarta (early) 19th century]. MS. RP B31). (5) canto 22 ff. of SMP MN 196 (*Serat Babad Tanah Jawi: Sri Majapahit pungkasan dumugi Demak pungkasan* [composed s.l., s.a.] [inscribed Surakarta, 1871]. MS. RP B15a). (6) cantos 86 ff. of SMP MN 268 (*Babad Segaluh* [composed s.l., s.a. and 1887] [inscribed (Yogyakarta?, 1904?)]. MS. RP B24b).

Also consulted were cantos 58–59 of the published *Babad Demak I,* an out-of-the-mainstream *babad* which elsewhere diverges significantly from "the Galuh variant" (ed. Slamet Riyadi and Suwadji [Jakarta: Departemen Pendidikan dan Kebudayaan, Proyek Penerbitan Buku Sastra Indonesia dan Daerah, 1981]).

these two cantos, in "steady" Sinom and "plaintive" Asmarandana verse, compose extended quotation, carefully selected and edited, from one or more texts of the Galuh variant. Canto XXVI, in Sinom, treats Ki Ageng Tingkir's counsel to Ki Ageng Pengging, the birth of Jaka Tingkir, and the Demak Sultan's commission of Ki Gedhé Wanapala to put the choice to Pengging's lord. The very short canto XXVII, in Asmarandana, tells of Ki Ageng Pengging's refusal to choose. Canto XXVIII, in Pangkur, treats Sunan Kudus's journey to Pengging; portions of this canto are poetically transposed from passages composed in Asmarandana and Megatruh meters in the Galuh variant. Again among the verses of canto XXIX that treat Ki Ageng Pengging's death in Dhangdhanggula, some are nearly identical to their Galuh variant prototypes. But then following this quali- fied textual convergence around the death of Pengging's lord, *Babad Jaka Tingkir* again veers off on its own singular trajectory away from the narrative lines traced by these witnesses of the more dominant *babad* tradition. I will return to this point below.

To what effect, then, does the author of our alternative *babad* reinscribe these extended fragments from the more dominant tradition? A close reading of these passages suggests that the author repeats the works of that tradition in order thereby to contest and transform them. And the author produces this effect through a citational practice that turns on selective quotation, amplification, and elision.

Consider, for example, the passage in which Ki Gedhé Wanapala de- livers to Ki Ageng Pengging the Sultan's *bantah* that puts the choice to the recalcitrant *kyai*. In both the *Babad Jaka Tingkir* and the Galuh proto- types, when Wanapala demands that Pengging choose between "Being exceeding being" (*ana luwih sangking ana,* indicating "material/political power") and "absence of exceeding absence" (*kang suwung liwat suwungé,* indicating "spiritual salvation"), the Kyai answers: "I will not choose / For all of it I do desire" (*BJT* XXVII:8). But at this moment of refusal, which is at the same time an affirmation of multivalent desire, the composer of *Babad Jaka Tingkir* turns away from the Galuh prototype before him or her, thereby to interrupt (and contest) the meaning of the more dominant text. For while the more dominant *babad* continues with Pengging's rea- soned rationale for the refusal, our *babad* veers off to underline the dan- gerous ambiguity of the Kyai's answer. Compare the two sets of two verses in Asmarandana:

Babad Jaka Tingkir

"I will not choose
For all of it do I desire
Were I to choose
But one, 'twould be wrong
Brother, may this my answer
Be conveyed to His Majesty
No desire have I"

Ki Wanapala replied:
"That answer of yours, Lord
Has no end to it
Intrigue is your answer
To the Lord our King
Futile was my coming here
By order of Demak's king"[49]

A witness of the Galuh variant

"I will not choose
For all of it I do desire
Were I to choose but absence
Then absence of (royal) title there'd be
Would that not neglect
My descendants who come after me?
Were I to choose being

"How long then is the life of man?
How long the taste of power?
For there is no precedent
For a man to live a thousand years
Save the Prophet Adam

49. Kawula boten amilih / sadayané mapan arsa / yèn miliya awak ingong / sawiji pan siya-siya / adhi atur kawula / mugi katura Sang Prabu / kawula tan darbé karsa // Ki Wanalapa nauri / puniku atur panduka / tan ana wawekasané / sekuthu atur panduka / dhateng Sri Naranata / tanpa gawé lampahingsun / dèn-utus natèng ing Demak (*BJT* XXVII:8–9).

Who lived one thousand years
Other than him there's none . . ."[50]

The witnesses of the dominant tradition continue on in this explanatory vein for another eight or so verses. *Babad Jaka Tingkir*, however, having determined "intrigue" as the answer of the Kyai, cuts the *bantah* off short with Ki Ageng Pengging's last word:

"All of it do I desire
'Twould be wrong for me to choose
There is no end to it
When one does pick and choose"[51]

While the text of the dominant tradition rather prosaically considers royal titles and normal life expectancies, it looks forward literally to Ki Ageng Pengging's progeny. In the *Babad Jaka Tingkir* adaptation of that tradition, the meaning of the Kyai's refusal to choose is left open-ended. The refusal has, as the wise Wanapala noted, "no end to it." And its endlessness is of a different order from the prosaic endlessness of choosing between alternatives. Because of this open-endedness, Ki Ageng Pengging's refusal to choose in our *babad* is epistemologically more radical than the refusal written into the dominant tradition. For in *Babad Jaka Tingkir*, Ki Ageng Pengging's refusal is no cautious denial of risks, but a bold affirmation of power with the implicit promise of power's future dissemination.

The poet uses selective quotation, adaptation, elision, and amplification to elicit similar effects in the (derivative *and* creative) passages surrounding Ki Ageng Pengging's death at Kudus's hands. The tales of Sunan Kudus's journey is much the same in both versions, but only in *Babad Jaka Tingkir* is Kudus in *santri* disguise with the tongue-in-cheek assumed name of Ahmad Sapa-nyana (Ahmad "Who'd-ever-guess?"). Upon the unlikely Ahmad's arrival in Pengging, our *babad* again amplifies on the

50. Kawula datan amilih / sadayané apan arsa / yèn milihya suwung baé / pan suwung amengku gelar / punapa siya-siya / mring anak putu ing pungkur / yèn miliya ingkang ana // Pinten panjangé wong urip / pira rasané wibawa / pan dèréng wonten adaté / wong kang ngumur séwu warsa / liyané Nabi Adam / ingkang umur séwu taun / liyané iku tan ana (*Serat Babad Tanah Jawi: Sri Majapahit pungkasan dumugi Demak pungkasan* [MS. RP B15a; SMP MN 196], pp. 169–70).

51. [Asmarandana] sadayané kula arsa / sirik yèn amiliya / tanpa wekasing tumuwuh / yèn milih tuwin ngungkurna (*BJT* XXVII:11).

more dominant tradition with a more pointed politicization of the encounter. For it is at this point in *Babad Jaka Tingkir* that Ki Ageng Pengging, in defiance of yet another summons, definitively affirms the interpenetrability of lordship and subjugation in the "Lord and subject are all the same" passage quoted above (*BJT* XXIX:12).

Prefacing the Kyai's death, both the Galuh variant and our *babad* share the enigmatic refusal to choose that I quoted toward the beginning of this discussion of Pengging's Kyai:

> "Were I to choose the inside I'd err
> To choose the outside I'm lost
> Wavering then in faith
> Were I to choose the above
> 'Twould be searching for an echo
> Were I to choose the front
> Truly I'd be most damnably lost
> Lost by seven schools of thought
> Below, above, left, and right are mine
> Nothing is mine"
> (*BJT* XXIX:15)

In *Babad Jaka Tingkir*, Ki Ageng Pengging's death follows almost directly upon this declaration. There are, however, in the witnesses of the Galuh variant several verses separating the declaration from the execution. Adapting his or her poem from a Galuh variant, our *babad*'s poet excises one of these verses to place it elsewhere (i.e., *BJT* XXIX:13); other verses are simply eliminated, as had been the explanatory verses following upon the Kyai's earlier refusal voiced to Wanapala. Notably elided from our *babad* is Ki Ageng Pengging's rationale for this final refusal to choose, which, in the dominant text, he provides by explaining himself as: indeed a *santri*, indeed about to set up a kingdom, and indeed in truth Allah.[52] In the dominant tradition the Kyai's refusal is explained and hence offered up for domestication; by providing no rationale for Jaka Tingkir's father's resolve, our *babad* leaves all possibilities open.

---

52. ". . . sira iki andalih wong ngapa mami / pan ingsun tan suminggah // Lamun sira andaliya santri / iya santri yektiné waking wang / terkanen reraton mangké / nyata wijiling ratu / yèn nerkoa Allah sirèki / lah iya nyata Allah . . ." (*Babad Tanah Jawi: Sri Majapahit pungkasan dumugi Demak pungkasan* [MS. RP B15a; MN 196], pp. 181–82).

Ki Ageng Pengging: Opening to the Future

Following the death of Ki Ageng Pengging, *Babad Jaka Tingkir*'s telling of the past curves off from the Galuh variant in a vector that once again suggests resistance to closure. The death itself, in contrast to the would-be deaths of the other Sufi masters, is relatively normal. I say relatively normal, for the nick of Kudus's knife killed our absent hero's father only because the Kyai willed his own death. And Pengging did call out his parting "Peace" not at death, but *after* dying (*BJT* XXIX:16–17). His body is honored with a normal funeral and burial. His survivors attempt to avenge his death in battle with the "treacherous *santri*"; the vengeance is frustrated by Kudus's "magic" power. These textual elements are shared, though in different sequences and tellings, among our *babad* and the Galuh witnesses. At this point in the narrative there is, however, a crucial difference that distinguishes *Babad Jaka Tingkir* from the more conventional texts. In the Galuh witnesses, following relatively closely upon the telling of the father's death, comes the telling of the son's (Jaka Tingkir) rise to power, the beginnings of his move toward kingship in Pajang. *Babad Jaka Tingkir*, in contrast, lingers on the Kyai's funeral, the bereavement of his survivors, and Sunan Kudus's desultory journey back to court. Of the youth Jaka Tingkir, nothing is said.

When Prince Kudus finally arrives at court he is, in his brilliant success, likened to the white monkey emissary of the legendary King Rama. He comes to report the success of his mission to Pengging, his subjugation of the Kyai. That report is cut off abruptly—as is the *babad*—by a pen that ceased its writing:

> "But most averse [was Ki Ageng]
> To come before Your Majesty
> Not feeling himself subject
> By pretext he pressed his claims
> Refusing to pick and choose
> For all of it did he compass"[53]

Had the manuscript not broken off at this point, the writer would have had to have continued with Prince Kudus's rationale or rationalization for

53. [Sinom] Ananging sanget lenggona / sumiwèng nerpati / tan rumaos yèn kabawah / akiyas kedah ngengkoki / tan arsa nampik milih / sedayané pan winengku (*BJT* XXXII:7).

the execution. Rather, the writer leaves the martyred Kyai in his glory: "Refusing to pick and choose / For all of it did he compass."

And with the closure that completed report would have provided, soon if not next would have come the story of the boy, youth, man, and Sultan Jaka Tingkir for whom the *babad* is named. Had that story come, it would have proven difficult, if not impossible, to write it in a way that did not march through tales of marauding crocodiles and mad bulls in a trajectory toward the new inland kingdom of Pajang as a replacement of Demak—as center, as master of all Java. And that replacement, by implication, would have pointed to the one that followed close upon it: the replacement of Pajang by Mataram. Had the writing continued, the *babad* would, it seems, have been subsumed under the dominant tradition.

The writer of this *Babad Jaka Tingkir* (its composer and/or its scribe) apparently would not let this happen. We have spoken of how this *babad* was written against the grain of the dominant tradition, how it was written to interrupt the conventional narrative of the past. And I would argue that it is precisely for these reasons that this *Babad Jaka Tingkir* must break off when it does. In a manner similar to the cutting off of *Suluk Malang Sumirang*'s reading, the writer cuts off the text of the *babad* just as it is about to merge into the received text of conventional History. The hand of the royal Javanese exile who inscribed the manuscript in far-off Ambon lays down his or her pen to contest, in silence, that received text. For *Babad Jaka Tingkir* is the writing of another past for another future "Jaka Tingkir." The Jaka Tingkir it has in mind is not, I suggest, the founder of the Sultanate of Pajang. For this poem works to envision a radically different structure of authority for the future, one that would emerge out of a novel historical trajectory—an alternative trajectory that was not to be realized through the serial axial kings and royal centers whose rule had, by the middle of the nineteenth century, culminated in a moras of colonial domination. The poem cannot dictate that alternative future, but it can offer itself as a kind of (inscribed) framework or scaffolding (*galang*) upon which such a future might be constructed. *Babad Jaka Tingkir* proclaims itself *pusaka*, an object of magic potency that would work to effect, with its readers, the kind of future it envisions. And the real hero of the *babad* is, of course, Jaka Tingkir: the imagined sons (and daughters) of the future (those future readers) who have still "to finish out the tale."

CONCLUSION: HISTORY
AND PROPHECY

❉

In a personal memoir that chronicles his imprisonment and exile in post-colonial Indonesia, the renowned Javanese Indonesian writer Pramoedya Ananta Toer recalls the following exchange with a Jakartan journalist:

> "We have heard that you are now writing historical novels. Why not write about the present?"

> "First of all to avoid unnecessary risks. Secondly, in order to get a better understanding, and to invite a better understanding, of the present and the future."[1]

The interview with Pramoedya, arguably modern Indonesia's greatest writer, took place in December 1977 on the prison island of Buru, a remote eastern Indonesian island located just to the north and west of the island of Ambon where Pakubuwana VI spent his nineteenth-century, colonial exile. At the time of the interview Pramoedya had been a prisoner of Soeharto's New Order government for a little over twelve years, having been arrested along with hundreds of thousands of other left-wing activists in the wake of the abortive coup of 1 October 1965 that, blamed on the Indonesian Communist Party, had preceded Soeharto's rise to power.[2] This interview was occasioned by the first release of political

---

1. "Kami dengar Bung sekarang menulis roman-roman sejarah. Mengapa bukan tentang masa kini?"
"Pertama-pertama untuk menghindari risiko yang tidak perlu. Kedua untuk dapat memahami dan mengajak memahami masa kini dan masa depan lebih baik" (Pramoedya Ananta Toer, *Nyanyi Tunggal Seorang Bisu: Catatan Pribadi Pramoedya Ananta Toer dari tahanan Pulau Buru* [Wika Karya: Kuala Lumpur: 1988], typescript p. 228).
2. Pramoedya had been a central figure in LEKRA (Lembaga Kebudayaan Rakyat), a left-wing cultural organization associated with the Indonesian Communist Party. In the

prisoners from the roughly ten thousand who were incarcerated on Buru. Pramoedya had been led to expect that he would be among this first group of detainees to be released and repatriated to Java. Instead, he was to endure two more years of exile. Over the course of his fourteen-year imprisonment, Pramoedya composed orally, and then wrote, a number of historical novels.[3] He wrote these histories with the characteristically Javanese intention of touching his readers' presents and futures through commemorations of their pasts in writing. Pramoedya's writing repeats, with a difference, a historiographical vision remarkably similar to the one that prophetically informed the writing of *Babad Jaka Tingkir*.

It is with this kind of practical, self-consciously future-oriented histori-cal writing that this book has been interested. And that interest itself is oriented toward a future in which investigations of colonial pasts would move away from the more conventional interests of history as a disci-pline: that is, a disciplinary interest in colonized subjects and their Euro-pean colonizers as objects for studies and reconstructions of pasts within the framework of European notions of history. I envision a kind of history writing that would concern itself seriously with "Third World" subjects' reconstructions of their own pasts, historical studies that would investi-gate those reconstructions within the traditions, that is, the historical conditions, in and through which these subjects produced them. I cer-tainly do not mean, however, to suggest that I envision this historio-

---

aftermath of the coup of 1 October 1965, the forces of General Soeharto's emergent government led a purge of Communists and left-wing activists that left one-half to one million dead and hundreds of thousands imprisoned. For an account of Pramoedya's arrest, see Hamish McDonald, *Suharto's Indonesia* (Melbourne: Fontana, 1980), pp. 220–24. On the coup and its aftermath, see Harold Crouch, *The Army and Politics in Indonesia* (Ithaca: Cornell University Press, 1988), chaps. 4–5.

3. Not permitted writing utensils from the time of his capture in 1965 until 1973, Pramoedya first composed the novels orally as stories that he shared nightly with his fellow prisoners after their long days of labor in the hostile and infertile fields of Buru. Among these novels is a tetralogy, published and subsequently banned following Pra-moedya's release, that rereads the awakening of Indonesian nationalism at the turn of the twentieth century (*Bumi Manusia* [Hasta Mitra: Jakarta, 1980], *Anak Semua Bangsa* [Hasta Mitra: Jakarta, 1980], *Jejak Langkah* [Hasta Mitra: Jakarta, 1985], and *Rumah Kaca* [Hasta Mitra: Jakarta, 1988]). In 1973–74, Pramoedya also wrote "Arus Balik," a tale treating Java's history in the mid-sixteenth century (see *Nyanyi Tunggal*, pp. 111–23). That novel has yet to be published. He is also rumored to have written a history of Siti Jenar during his incarceration and exile.

graphical project as a quest for an authentic, essential indigenous perception of the past that would stand in sheer binary opposition to "Western history." Indeed, the fantasy that there could be such a thing as an authentic "Third World" sensibility arises in the same fabulous moment that would found an autonomous and universal "First World" logic. As Gyan Prakash has noted, the task of an enabling post-Orientalist historiography is not to substitute the "real" Orient for the "myth" of the Orientalists, but to trace "Third World" identities as relational, as shifting positions in history rather than as timeless essences.[4]

Shifting "Third World" perceptions and positions emerge in history in relation to, among other things, also shifting imperial "First World" sensibilities. In the case of Javanese historical writing, for example, those writings that are now considered traditional were themselves generated and regenerated under the changing conditions of Dutch colonialism. What I am suggesting is not, then, a historiographical approach that would revel in the presumed sheer difference of "Third World" histories, but an approach that would take seriously, as the subject of its research, "Third World" subjects' own textual explorations of their own pasts— thereby, perhaps, to interrupt and decenter the fabulous project of universalizing history itself.[5] I wish to suggest that by actually reading the

4. Gyan Prakash, "Writing Post-Orientalist Histories of the Third World: Indian Historiography Is Good to Think," in *Colonialism and Culture*, ed. Nicholas Dirks (Ann Arbor: University of Michigan Press, 1992), pp. 353–88.

5. I am certainly not alone in recognizing the significance of this subject for an understanding of Southeast Asian history. Among works of scholarship that explore the meanings inscribed in Southeast Asians' writings of their own pasts are: O. W. Wolters's *The Fall of Srivijaya in Malay History* (Ithaca: Cornell University Press, 1970), and *Two Essays on Dai-Viet in the Fourteenth Century* (New Haven: Yale Southeast Asia Studies, 1988); John Pemberton's *On the Subject of "Java"*; James Siegel's *Shadow and Sound: The Historical Thought of a Sumatran Kingdom* (Chicago: University of Chicago Press, 1979); M. C. Ricklefs' "The New Age in Javanese Literature: Serat Surja Radja, Babad Kraton, and the Literary Renaissance," in *Jogjakarta under Sultan Mangkubumi, 1749–1792: A History of the Division of Java* (London: Oxford University Press, 1974), pp. 176–226; Anthony Day's "Meanings of Change"; Jane Drakard's *A Malay Frontier: Unity and Duality in a Sumatran Kingdom* (Ithaca: Cornell University Southeast Asia Program, 1990); and C. C. Berg's "The Javanese Picture of the Past," in *An Introduction to Indonesian Historiography*, ed. Soedjatmoko et al. (Ithaca: Cornell University Press, 1965), pp. 87–117. See also Anthony Reid and David Marr's edited volume on indigenous Southeast Asian historiography, *Perceptions of the Past in Southeast Asia* (Singapore: Heinemann, 1979).

wealth of historiographical inscription that "Third World" subjects have left behind we might enter into a dialogue with these writers through which we could better understand the scenarios that they themselves envisioned not just of colonial pasts, but also for postcolonial presents and futures. This book is intended as one such reading.

With this book, an extended reading of a historical prophecy produced for the future by a nineteenth-century Javanese exile, I have attempted to evoke a sense of what it might have meant—and what it could still mean—to write and to read history in Java. I have worked to evoke that sense dialogically in the course of a lingering journey through the systems of signification inscribed in a particular historical text, a journey that moves, in part, through a consideration of that text's own historicity. The journey began with an introduction to the possibilities of reading in Java, proceeded through a consideration of the historical production of this particular history and then through the detailed by-ways that marked its translation, to end with an extended analysis of that translated text. In dialogue with this singular witness of the Javanese past, I have considered how this writing of history *makes* sense in the context of the nineteenth-century Javanese realities in and through which it was written—and, implicitly, in the late-twentieth-century postcolonial context in and through which I have read it. I have argued that the Javanese poet who composed this history produced its sense by writing against the grain of the more domi-

---

In his study of the modern Javanese chronicle tradition, M. C. Ricklefs provides the complete text and carefully annotated translation of a rare eighteenth-century *babad* (*Modern Javanese Historical Tradition: A Study of an Original Kartasura Chronicle and Related Materials* (London: Oxford University Press, 1978). Peter Carey has provided the field with two magnificently annotated works of Javanese historical writing in the form of contemporary accounts of nineteenth-century historical events: *Babad Dipanagara: An Account of the Outbreak of the Java War* (Kuala Lumpur: The Malaysian Branch of the Royal Asiatic Society, 1981), and *The British in Java, 1811–1816: A Javanese Account* (New York: Oxford University Press, 1992).

Also of interest is Mary Steedly's recent *Hanging without a Rope: Narrative Experience in Colonial and Postcolonial Karoland* (Princeton: Princeton University Press, 1993), an engaging study of narrative traditions among Karo subjects in East Sumatra. Vincente Rafael's *Contracting Colonialism: Translation and Christian Conversion in Tagalog Society Under Early Spanish Rule* (Durham: Duke University Press, 1993) is an incisive analysis of writing and translation among Tagalog subjects under colonial conditions. And Alton Becker's edited volume, *Writing on the Tongue* (Ann Arbor: University of Michigan Center for South and Southeast Asian Studies, 1989), works through readings of a number of Indonesian texts.

nant tradition of Javanese history. And I have suggested that the deeply textured meanings inscribed in this history emerge, in part, through self-consciously textualized plays that epistemologically question seemingly opposing realities: inside and outside, matter and spirit, center and periphery, ruler and ruled, text and context. *Babad Jaka Tingkir* is a historical text that was composed expressly to transcend the seeming boundaries of its own textuality—a text constructed to be a stage or framework (a context) for historical change in a world beyond (if not absolutely outside) the text. *Babad Jaka Tingkir* is, then, as real as any history might be: it is both a historical text that recounts the imagined past of a real Javanese world (that is, a world that was real to its Javanese author) and a historical event whose writing *in* history would construct a novel context for real Javanese futures. It is a *pusaka* whose effectiveness is projected onto coming generations. And it is a prophecy.

"This Writing of History"

The phrase "this writing of history" translates the Javanese word *mèngeti*, a word that occurs only once in *Babad Jaka Tingkir*—that is, in the initial line of the poem's second stanza: "It was Sunday when this writing of history began" (*Ing ri Akhad duk wiwit mèngeti* [BJT I:2]). Translated thus, the word *mèngeti* is understood to mean the production in writing of a certain form of historical consciousness. But what form of historical consciousness might it indicate? *Mèngeti* (from the root *ènget*, "memory; consciousness; awareness"), is a word that enjoys a remarkable semantic range.[6] Let us, then, turn to a consideration of the range of this *mèngeti* that opens *Babad Jaka Tingkir* as a strategic beginning to the conclusion of this book—thus to bring to a provisional end this exploration into the potential meanings that "this writing of history" would stage for a Javanese past and its futures.

Read in the context of the cited line, the dominant (though not the only) meaning of *mèngeti* seems to be "to record something; to write something down in order that it be remembered." This meaning is akin to the ordinary documentary notion of the historical record as a repository of what we consider to be "facts" about the past. In the context of Javanese writings about the past, this sense of *mèngeti* brings to mind the conven-

6. See GR 1:129–30 for an extended gloss of *mèngeti* and its cognates.

tion of prefacing entries in some chronologically arranged prose court chronicles with the word *pènget* (an intermediary form between *ènget* and *mèngeti* that means "note!" or "remember!").[7] The imperative note reminds readers that events are documented *in order that* they be remembered. What is interesting here is the element of desire implied by the practice of documentation: a desire for remembrance that is projected into the future.

This first documentary meaning anticipates a second meaning of *mèngeti*, which is "to commemorate, to celebrate a memory." To be commemorated, something has already to be a memory, to have been remembered. The celebrations, then, is a consummation of the desire that initiated the documentary record. A commemoration always looks back to that which has been, that is, to a remembered past, but in terms of a present celebration. The celebration actualizes that past-as-memory in the present of its commemoration. One species of commemoration would be the necessarily interpretive activity of writing *any* narrative history. The historian, traditional Javanese or not, cannot do otherwise than construct her narrative (a commemoration/a celebration in language) of any past in the historical moment of her becoming present.

In traditional Java, however, the relationship between the moment of desire (the impulse to record the past) and its consummation (the commemoration of the past-as-memory) is presumed neither coincidental nor accidental; that relationship is, instead, activated by another power of the "writing of history." *Mèngeti* also means "to predict" or, better, "to prophesy." The "writing of history" is not just the writing down of history (the record), nor is it simply narrative interpretation of the past (the commemoration). In its most active sense, the "writing of history" in Java prophesies its own future in ways that work to bring that future about—a writing of history can be a making of history. It is a prescient present's writing about a past which opens to a desired future.[8]

Historical texts in traditional Java treat events in time by writing those

7. See, for example, *Serat Babad Sengkala: Kawit Pulo Jawi dipunisèni tiyang nalika taun ongka 1 dumugi taun 1854* (compiled and inscribed Surakarta 1830–38 and 1845–47; MS. SP 220 Ca-A; SMP-KS 1A); and *Serat Babat Sangkala* (inscribed Surakarta, ca. 1924; MS. SP 6 Ta; SMP KS 1C.7).

8. *Mèngeti* also means "to give a sign of warning," or "to forewarn, admonish" (GR 1:130). To recognize the warning or admonition may be one way to understand how a text works, or would work, as a context for historical change.

events in poetry. That writing releases the event from the presumed past of its occurrence into the linguistic, literary, and sociopolitical-cultural structures of its contemporary inscription, its present commemoration in writing, and its future orientation as prophecy. The writing releases the event forward in time into the heterogeneous universe of Javanese (con)-textuality, a world of *semu*, to be read and realized. This release of the event produces a notion of history quite different from that in the dominant discourses of the post-Enlightenment West. The foundational projects of history engendered by the post-Enlightenment reign of reason have conventionally strived for the scientific recovery or recuperation of the past (what really happened) in transparent, representational language. These projects unselfconsciously imagine an authentic originary fit between language and its referent in which the reality of the event may be recovered under the transparent sign that the well-informed historian supplies. In traditional Javanese historical writing, however, the relations among the past event, the historian, and the language through which the historian writes the past are appreciated as more ambiguous.[9] Rather than attempt to recover a "really real" event in transparent language, these Javanese texts offer glimpses of events, of the past, among veils of *semu*. For the Javanese poet-historian, the event does not occupy a privileged extralinguistic position as a "really real" outside the writing of the poem. And yet this is not to suggest that the event is a mere fictitious construction of the poet. The past event is real to the poet and her audience (there is/was, in fact, a "there" out there), but its reality is neither absolute nor divorced from the linguistic reality of its writing in the poem. The past event that the poet writes is finally realized, historically, by being read and reregistered, prophetically, in the presents and futures of its readers. The inscribed past of the poetry becomes present and future when the audience dares to glimpse the veils in order, perhaps, to see and move beyond them.

If much historical writing in traditional Java is implicitly prophetic, *Babad Jaka Tingkir* is emphatically and explicitly so. Proclaiming itself a candidate *pusaka*, while associating itself with the shadowy and powerful worlds of *suluk* and Jayabaya prophecies, this history, with its episodic structure and focus on the margins, differs from the more mainstream

---

9. This is, of course, also the case for some of the more innovative recent theorists of history. Consider, for example, the writings of Michel Foucault, Michel deCerteau, Haydon White, and Joan Scott.

historical texts. Presenting itself as an inscribed stage or scaffolding (*pang-galang*) upon which a drama is yet to be played out, it writes a novel history of the past of a *still* to emerge future "Jaka Tingkir." It writes that history in order to effect this alternative Jaka Tingkir's emergence—in order that he, or they, may "finish out the tale" upon the stage that it has inscribed. That stage, or context for alternative futures, is constructed out of the interruption and fragmentation of the more mainstream tradition of historical discourse in Java. *Babad Jaka Tingkir* distinguishes itself from other texts of such a tradition both by the kind of future to which its history opens and by the mechanisms with which it inscribes that opening.

What Manner of Prophecy?

How then does this particular historical text, this *Babad Jaka Tingkir*, work toward the future? And what can this work tell us of the (past) present of its writing—its historicity? And how is one to read from the text, the nature of its (past) present inscription and the shape of its desired future? To begin to answer these questions, let us reflect yet again on the most active sense of the "writing of history" in the opening stanzas of the poem. From these stanzas we know that it is interruptions in "Java's story"—that is, the dominant tradition of history in Java—that are to be rendered in writing, to become worthy of remembrance. We also know that these interruptions are presumably in some way about Jaka Tingkir, and that they are related to the worlds of *suluk* and prophecy.

The first interruption in "Java's story" to be documented and commemorated by the poem is, however, no exploit of Jaka Tingkir or of his antecedents, but the poet's own act of writing. "It was Sunday when this writing of history began . . ." (*BJT* I:2). Immediately following this line comes the unusually emphatic (and problematic) dating of the beginning of the poem's writing that was discussed in chapter 1. In that discussion it became apparent that we might never be able to determine whether the poem was "really" composed in August 1829, or whether it was perhaps some twenty years younger. For the seeming hyperbolic precision in commemorative chronology yielded, instead of a definitive date of composition, chronological confusion.

This indeterminability itself points to other significant aspects of the text's writing. The sole surviving manuscript witness of the poem composes the conclusion to a volume of Kraton Surakarta archival documents (treaties and correspondence dating from 1812 to 1848), a volume titled "Copies of the Miscellaneous Correspondence of His Majesty the Sixth." We discovered that major portions of this unique volume of royal Javanese correspondence were, in fact, copied out of a Dutch textbook for colonial civil servants published in the Netherlands in 1845. Finally, because of the intrusion of "His Majesty's dream" of the "west monsoon" into the text of the poem, we came to recognize that its inscription was executed by a Javanese exile around 1849 on Ambon—where Pakubuwana VI had been imprisoned since 1830.

Given *Babad Jaka Tingkir's* thematics of marginality and its tales of vanishing heroes, is it not plausible to read this historical prophecy as an allusion to the hapless career and exile of Pakubuwana VI? The (displaced) writer who compiled *His Majesty the Sixth's Correspondence* on Ambon in 1849 surely read it thus; hence his or her decision to include this history of "medieval" Central Java in an archival volume that somehow belonged to that exiled nineteenth-century Javanese king. If the August 1829 date of composition is authentic, we might, then, have here a startling and disturbing example of the literal prophecy of that Surakarta ruler's future (June 1830) expulsion. Or could, perhaps, the "original" 1829 author have gotten wind of an exile already well in the works? By August 1829 the still secret colonial plans to depose the troublesome Pakubuwana VI and replace him with his "more agreeable" uncle Purbaya were already well under way.[10]

The 1829 composition of this history of vanishing heroes in the distant past as an allusion to more contemporary exiles could, however, have had nothing (at that point in time) to do with the particular, prophetic history of the young Pakubuwana. For the unfortunate Pakubuwana VI was by no means the only character to suffer exile in that turbulent time of rebellion and warfare. In the period anticipating the August 1829 date of composition there were a number of other captures and exiles that would have been highly significant in the literary and political worlds of Surakarta.

10. The government had even gone so far as to sketch out details of the scenario of the young Sunan's arrest and speedy transport to Ambon. See Nahuys aan den Minister van Staat, Sourakarta, den 28 November 1828, L.H.H. (Geheim); Missive van den Komissaris Generaal, den 17 Maart 1829, L^{a}P (Geheim); notes and report of Bousquet on the letter of 17 March 1829, Batavia den 28 Maart 1829, L^{a}H (Geheim) and especially L^{a}Q (Geheim); all in Solo Bundel 127 in the Arsip Nasional Republik Indonesia.

Mas Ronggawarsita, chief of the palace scribes and father of the seal of the *pujongga*, was sent into exile along with his brother the Haji (Ronggasasmita?) in May 1828.[11] Then in November 1828, Kyai Maja (Dipanagara's famous advisor and associate) was captured and sent off to exile in Menado.[12] After the *babad*'s putative 1829 composition, but before Pakubuwana VI's June 1830 exile, Prince Dipanagara himself was captured and shipped off to exile in March 1830. And yet we must not forget that, whatever or whoever may be the "real" reference of the "original" allusion, *in the form in which it now survives*, the prophecy *belongs* to the history of Pakubuwana VI. For thus was it recognized and hence determined in Ambon by the anonymous writer who inscribed it as the conclusion of *His Majesty the Sixth's Correspondence*.

Could, then, the curious inaccuracies of dating indicate a willful antedating of the poem? The anonymous compiler of *His Majesty the Sixth's Correspondence* could have been a poet who composed, as well as copied, texts. The *babad* could have been composed in late-1840s Ambon by that anonymous poet—with the pretense of having been written in 1829 Surakarta. If such were the case, the poet would have been writing prophecy both backwards and forwards at the same time. The poem would, then, have been the allusive historical prophecy of the expulsion of an already exiled Javanese king—and his futures. The possibility of willful antedating is pregnant with other significance as well. For an 1840s Javanese exile on Ambon to situate his or her writing in 1829 Surakarta would have been to return the inscription of an intended future back to a time, perhaps the last time, when traditional Javanese power had enjoyed a real possibility of moving in a world that had not yet been fixed as "tradition."

Let us, for the moment, thus suppose that *Babad Jaka Tingkir* was composed on Ambon around 1849. Who was the Javanese exile who wrote it? Inscribed in this volume of *His Majesty the Sixth's Correspondence* along with *Babad Jaka Tingkir* are four short *macapat* texts that were definitely composed in Ambon; these four texts are letters that were

---

11. *Babad Sengkala kang kaurut saking Kagungan-dalem serat Babad* (compiled and inscribed Surakarta 1830–38 and 1845–47). MS. SP 6 Ta; SMP KS 1C, II:127.

12. Ibid., pp. 89–90. Kyai Maja's *pesantrèn* (*pradikan*) was located just north of the village of Delanggu (not far from Pengging). He was, along with Dipanagara and Sentot, among the fiercest opponents faced by the Dutch in the course of the war. See Peter Carey's introduction of Kyai Maja in his annotations to *Babad Dipanagara: An Account of the Outbreak of the Java War (1825–1830)*, pp. 261–62.

written home from exile in 1848. Three of those letters were authored by Pakubuwana VI; the fourth, by his daughter R. Ayu Timur.[13] If *Babad Jaka Tingkir* was composed in late 1840s Ambon, it is not far-fetched, then, to suppose one of these two characters (or perhaps their ghostwriter) as its author. We know of *Babad Jaka Tingkir*'s composer that he or she possessed an intimate knowledge of the interior geography of the nineteenth-century Kraton Surakarta and considerable familiarity with the works and conventions of Javanese writing (especially of historical and *suluk* genres). Pakubuwana VI, at the time of his reign the *only* man with free access to the entire Surakarta palace, was described by his Dutch overlords in 1829 as well versed in Javanese historical traditions and as a "smart" writer.

It was by the interpolations that interrupt the text of *Babad Jaka Tingkir* that I was able to date its *inscription* to around 1849 and to place that writing in the Ambon of a royal Javanese exile. The last of those interpolations was the (prophetic/documentary) commemoration (*pémut*, a synonym of *pènget*) of a dream that "His Majesty" dreamt in 1849 at the time of the "west monsoon." This commemorative note, apparently haunted by the royal figure whose vision it marks, is silent on the dream's contents. Does not this very silence suggest that "His Majesty's dream" was nothing other than the same prophetic Tingkir history that its commemoration interrupts? Should we, then, suppose "this writing of history," this *Babad Jaka Tingkir*, the nostalgic dream of a failing young king in exile—the prophetic vision of a young king who had already grown old and was soon to die?

In the absence of any other manuscript witnesses, we may never "really" know when, where, by whom, and in allusion to whom or what the *babad* was originally composed. These questions remain undecidable, with an undecidability that echoes the undecidability underlying the teachings of the three Javanese gurus of whom the *babad* writes: Siti Jenar, Malang Sumirang, and, especially, Ki Ageng Pengging. Far from making the prophecy suspect, however, this ultimate undecidability actually acts to intensify the prophetic effects of "this writing of history." For between 1829 Surakarta and 1849 Ambon there yawns a gap that is defined by exile. The poem emerges, dreamlike, from that gap to point away from nostalgia for lost power toward something that had never been

13. *His Majesty the VI's Correspondence,* item nos. 58, 59, 60, and 62.

known. Although *Babad Jaka Tingkir* in some way belongs to the history of Pakubuwana VI, it moves beyond him toward something else. This *babad* does not merely prophesy defeated power in exile (Pakubuwana VI off in Ambon) or the return of quasi old-style power out of exile (the eventual succession of Pakubuwana IX to his exiled father's throne). "His Majesty's dream" is not merely a nostalgic dynastic fantasy, for what it envisions is the rise of a new form of power. This *Babad Jaka Tingkir* does not set the stage for "Jaka Tingkir, the Sultan of Pajang," that is, for the deadly continuity of dynastic power in Central Java. Rather, the stage is set for a novel figure—a "Jaka Tingkir" whose image foreshadows a more disseminate form of power for the Javanese future.

What Manner of Future?

The potential futures that *Babad Jaka Tingkir* presages for Java may be discerned, along with remembered past events, among the veils of *semu* through which are written the episodes and frames that compose this prophetic history. To begin with Prabangkara the Painter. I spoke of how the Prabangkara episode self-consciously raises the issues of writing and *semu*; it also entertains options for the future. Notably, this episode looks outside Java for the Javanese future. Prabangkara's own future was situated in China—thousands of miles from the royal center that had forcibly expelled him. There, he would gain success in exile, by writing. But in this exile was the promise of a deferred return. The exiled Javanese prince's success would return in another form: his descendants (the overseas Chinese) would go home to their Javanese origin "to feed off the fruits of the land." A number of things are happening here. In addition to redefining *as Javanese* the past of the nineteenth-century present success of the overseas Chinese, the episode anticipates an international, supra-Javanese arena where Javanese future successes must be won. It looks forward to a world that is not centered (ultimately) at a single point behind the constricting walls of the Javanese *kraton*.

There is also an obvious identification of Prabangkara's story with the history of Pakubuwana VI and his future. The writer (scribe and/or poet) of *His Majesty the Sixth's Correspondence* certainly recognized and registered this equivalence in his or her writing on Ambon around 1849. Rethinking the episode in terms of this exiled king's history gives new meaning both to this inscription of Prabangkara's Chinese adventures and to Pakubuwana VI's Ambonese imprisonment.[14] The writing of a tale characterizing success gained in exile by writing takes on new significance in the context of the volume in which it finds itself: this curious compilation of an exiled king's "correspondence." That compilation was itself constructed out of inscribed fragments of the Javanese past, many of which had come to Ambon via a Dutch publishing house. In Ambon those fragments, including *Babad Jaka Tingkir*, were reinscribed for their ultimate return to Java, that they might be read.

The writing of the Karèwèd tale envisions other future possibilities. Rather than looking outside to the supra-Javanese sphere, this story acts to displace the centeredness of the imagined royal Javanese center itself by allowing the margins in. It does so by revealing that the margins are already present at the very heart of that center. The telling exposes the imagined outside as very much inside; and the inside as a fiction dependent upon the pretended invisibility of the same outsiders who inhabit it. For the supposed outsiders (the servants at court and especially the women) were none other than the forces that silently reproduce that inside itself. This telling of the Karèwèd story registers that invisible presence by means of a marginal prince's magic book. The registration of this reality in 1829 (or in 1849 *as if* 1829), with its consequent displacement of the fantasy of a categorically exclusive center, looks beyond the structure of "Java" that was about to be born in the post-1830 high colonial age. It looks forward to a future society that would dare to lay bare the fiction of categorical difference, a fiction which, ever more clearly delineated, has worked, historically, to buttress structures of domination in Java.

The Demak Mosque episode, which ostensibly treats the construction of a new center of authority, also discloses a double displacement built into that very construction. Building upon and enhancing the telling of this tale in the more dominant tradition of history writing, *Babad Jaka Tingkir*'s account of the construction highlights the way in which this founding figure of central authority rests on residues and fragments, and stands under the weight of the people. Again, it is a telling that prefigures a future structure of authority that would recognize the (already present)

14. We are reminded, for example, of the exiled king's marriage in Ambon to the Chinese Nonah Kuwi. In his analysis of the nineteenth-century poem *Serat Bangun Tapa = Babad Nonah Kuwi*, Day suggests that the poem writes of that marriage in Ambon as engendering kingship in Surakarta ("Meanings of Change," pp. 146–62).

place of those elements of society that the dominant ideology would ignore. This episode also and at the same time looks outside Java, toward Mecca and the supra-Javanese world of Islam. It envisions a future which is negotiated between forces inside and outside Java. It sees Java and Javanese Islam as not only recognizing the center of international Islam in Mecca, but also as recognized by that center as a significant force in the Islamic world. This episode introduces a logic of "both/and" in contradistinction to—and transcending—an "either/or" binary structure of experience. And it identifies that logic with radical Sufi Islamic forces in Java.

The telling of the Siti Jenar tale anticipates the dissemination of knowledge that is power among the masses. Siti Jenar, the worm in us all, is in popular Javanese consciousness the figure of "the everyman." He is also the figure of heresy and of resistance. Vanishing into Mystery, he is the (disappeared) embodiment of a "both/and" logic. Siti Jenar, simultaneously realizing the material perfection of person and the material authenticity of language, speaks in a contestatory voice that is both noniterable and wholly effective. Because his perfection is always already fully present in the world into which it, or he, has (again, always already) vanished, this worm's truth cannot be quoted; and yet his perfection will be repeatedly realized in history through the works of his followers. The telling of the authorities' failed attempt to pin him down with the multiple gravestones, a telling that is unique to *Babad Jaka Tingkir*, underlines the irrepressibility and the imminent possibility of the worm's return—anywhere and everywhere.

The Malang Sumirang episode looks out toward the margins of society in the direction of those unruly forces that were, and are, never to be incorporated into the center. Malang Sumirang, the mad Sufi saint, is a figure of anti-order. Central authority simply has no sway over such characters. Like Jaka Prabangkara and Jaka Karèwèd, Malang Sumirang is associated with writing. And this telling, like other tellings of his story, relates how the mad saint leaves his famous *suluk* behind. In *Babad Jaka Tingkir*, however, the reading of that *suluk* (in the presence of the authorities) is expressly suppressed. I have argued that this suppression of reading is, among other things, the poet's caution against the appropriation and monumentalization of the wild traces on the margins in the interests of the center. A figure of resistance who lives a logic of "neither/nor," Malang Sumirang vanishes to the hills, leaving behind him writing that is meant as a stage (*panggalang*) for the construction of selves. The telling of the Malang Sumirang story envisions a future with individual options, including the option of madness.

Babad Jaka Tingkir's telling of the Ki Ageng Pengging story looks most emphatically to the future. It looks especially to a certain form of political Islam as a force in the Javanese future. Ki Ageng Pengging is a Moslem spiritual leader; he is a devout *santri kyai,* the popular and populist master of a rural *pesantrèn.* He is also a formidable traditional political force: he is the son, grandson, and father of Javanese kings. A figure of undecidability who lives (and dies) the "both/and" logic that his teacher Siti Jenar embodied, Ki Ageng Pengging leaves behind followers and a son. That son, Jaka Tingkir, is a figure for the one, or ones, "Who'd be meet in future days / To finish out the tale" (*BJT* XXIV:25). And that tale still awaiting its finish is this *Babad Jaka Tingkir,* a text inscribed to be a *pusaka*—a living context that would still move its readers to produce the script of their own futures.

Writing history—not just in Java—is a practice through which historically determined and desiring subjects compose narratives of selectively remembered pasts in order to produce documents for the future. With this book I have read a particular writing of Javanese history, one that composes the prophetic dream of a royal exile. And through my reading of this traditional Javanese writing of the past as an inscription for the future, I have meant, in part, to suggest how its writing anticipates both the decidedly contemporary postfoundational sensibilities that have come, in the late twentieth century, to inform some of the more innovative shifts in recent historiographical inquiry *and* the potential futures that contemporary Javanese Indonesians might still produce out of their traditional pasts. I would hope that this book, my writing of history, might thus suggest to readers on various sides of (as well as astride) what some would call the postcolonial divide the potential utility of actively reading traditional "Third World" histories—not as iconic exemplars of timeless traditions but as historically generated and generative fields of discourse, sites of significance where we may engage the sometimes forgotten subjects who wrote them in a dialogue through which, perhaps, something quite surprising, even revolutionary, might emerge.

APPENDIX I

DESCRIPTIVE TABLE OF CONTENTS
FOR *KUPIYA IBER WARNI-WARNI*
SAMPÉYAN-DALEM KAPING VI[1]

1. Treaty: I.S.K.S. Pakubuwana [henceforth PB] IV with the British Colonial Government (Surakarta, 4 August 1812). [*Javaansch Brievenboek*[2] {henceforth JB} #1]

2. Letter: PB IV to I.S.K.S. Hamengkubuwana [henceforth HB] IV re *tingkeban* pregnancy ceremony for the latter's queen (Surakarta, 19 Ruwah Bé 1744 = 5 July 1817). [JB #2]

3. Letter: PB IV to HB IV re the former's gift to the latter on the occasion of his queen's *tingkeban* (Surakarta, 21 Ruwah Bé 1744 = 7 July 1817). [JB #3]

4. Letter: PB IV to HB IV re birth of a son to the latter (Surakarta, 28 Sawal Bé 1744 = 11 September 1817). [JB #4]

5. Letter: PB IV to HB IV re the former's gift to the latter on the occasion of the birth of his son (Surakarta, 3 Dulkangidah Bé 1744 = 15 September 1817). [JB #5]

6. Letter: PB IV to HB IV re the installation of K.G.P. Adipati Anom (Crown Prince) in Yogyakarta (Surakarta, 18 Besar Bé 1744 = 30 October 1817). [JB #6]

7. Letter: PB IV to HB IV re death of the Yogya prince, P. Dipasonta (Surakarta, 4 Mulud Jimawal 1746 = 31 December 1818). [JB #7]

8. Letter: K. Ratu Kencana (PB IV's queen) to P. Adipati Mangkudiningrat of Pamekasan re death of Prince Suradiningrat (Surakarta, 28 Sawal 1747 = 9 August 1820). [JB #9]

9. Letter: K.G.P. Adipati Anom (Crown Prince of Surakarta = PB V) to HB IV re death of PB IV (Surakarta, 23 Besar 1747 = 2 October 1820). [JB #11]

---

1. *Kupiya Iber Warni-warni Sampéyan-dalem kaping VI* [Copies of the Miscellaneous Correspondence of Pakubuwana VI] (composed Surakarta and Ambon, 1812–48; inscribed [Ambon], ca. 1849). MS. SP 214 Ca; SMP KS 78. I include concordances with the 1845 edition of the *Javaansch Brievenboek*.

2. T. Roorda, *Javaansche brieven, berigten, verslagen, verzoekschriften, proclamaties, publicaties, contracten, schuldbekentenissen, quitanties, processtukken, pachtbrieven en andere soortgelijke stukken; naar handschriften uitgegeven* (Amsterdam: Muller, 1845).

10. Letter: PB VI to Governor General van der Capellen on the former's accession to the throne (Surakarta, 23 Sura Dal 1751 = 29 September 1823). [JB #39]

11. Letter: PB VI to Resident of Surakarta Nahuys re the death of R. Ayu Angabéhi (Surakarta, 16 Rejep 1757 = 11 January 1830). [JB #156]

12. Letter: PB VI to Commissaris Merkus and Commissaris Nahuys requesting that his three queens be sent after him to Semarang (Salatiga, [9] June 1830). [JB #166]

13. Letter: PB VI to Commissaris Merkus and Commissaris Nahuys re the former's impending journey, under arrest, to Batavia. PB VI requests that his queens, concubines, and children be sent after him ("Boyong," 14 June 1830). [JB #167]

14. Letter: PB VI to HB V re the former's impending marriage to the daughter of Prince Ngabéhi (she was to become K. Ratu Mas) and his sister's marriage to the Mangkunagaran prince P. Riya (Surakarta, 12 Jumadilakir 1751 = 12 February 1824). [JB #43]

15. Letter: Thank-you note PB VI to HB V for wedding gifts upon his and his sister's marriages (Surakarta, 28 Jumadilakir 1751 = 28 February 1824). [JB #44]

16. Letter: PB VI to Governor General van der Capellen re PB VI's divorce from K. Ratu Mas (Surakarta, 24 Sapar 1752 = 18 October 1824). [JB #49]

17. Report: PB VI to Lieutenant Governor General Merkus de Kock; on the dispatchment of P.H. Kusumayuda to attack the insurgents in Manorèh, Banyumas District (Surakarta, 19 Siyam 1753 = 26 April 1826). [JB #59]

18. Report: K.P. Adipati Kusumayuda to Resident Nahuys; field report from Pagelèn (Winong, 19 Jumadilawal 1755 = 8 December 1827). [JB #74]

19. Letter: PB VI to Commissaris General Du Bus deGisignies; farewell letter to the departing Commissaris General in anticipation of the inauguration of Governor General van der Bosch (Surakarta, 4 Ruwah 1757 = 29 January 1830). [JB #157]

20. Letter: Rongga Prawirasentika to Resident Nahuys; reports an attack upon the former which took place the previous month in Tunggul Madiyun, in essence an intelligence report identifying the *wong kécu* (bandits, rebels) (Tunggul, 3 Sura 1756 = 17 Juli 1828).[3] [JB #115]

21. Letter: PB V to HB V upon the latter's accession to the throne (Surakarta, 12 Rabingulakir 1750 = 26 December 1822). [JB #35]

22. Letter (demobilization orders): Lieutenant Governor General Merkus de Kock to K. Panembahan Buminata; re necessity to cut government expenses by returning troops to their home bases as soon as possible in light of the capture of Dipanegara (Magelang, 8 April 1830). [JB #161]

23. Letter: Lieutenant Governor General Merkus de Kock to PB VI; farewell letter promising to remember the Sunan always and informing him of the formation of the "Principalities Commission" (Magelang, 15 May 1830). [JB #163]

3. Not Kraton correspondence.

24. Letter: K. Panembahan Buminata to K.G.P. Mangkubumi in Ambon; reporting the death of PB V and the accession of PB VI. The letter tells of PB V's death-bed choice of PB VI as his successor. Also included is other family news (births, marriages, and deaths); apparently this is the first letter (= news) Mangkubumi would have received since his exile in 1816 (Surakarta, 23 Sapar 1751 = 29 October 1823). [JB #40]

25. Letter: K. Ratu Agung (PB V's mother) to P. Adipati Mangkudiningrat Pamekasan; re a "borrowing" of family members—the children have arrived safely in Surakarta. The queen reports on a [cholera] epidemic in Surakarta (Surakarta, 30 Dulkangidah 1748 = 29 August 1821). [JB #18]

26. Letter: PB VI to HB V; condolence letter on the death of the Sultan's great-grandmother, K. Ratu Kilen (Surakarta, 29 Besar 1751 = 24 August 1824). [JB #48]

27. Letter (directive): Resident Magillavrij to R. Adipati Sasradiningrat; re the need for strict enforcement of the wartime ban on sale of gunpowder and bullets (Surakarta, 18 January 1826). [JB #55]

28. Letter: Resident Magillavrij to PB VI; re the Resident's decision to send K. Panembahan Buminata, P. Adipati Arya Mangkunagara [henceforth MN], and R. Adipati Sasradiningrat to Klaten to meet with representatives of the Sultan of Yogyakarta. To be discussed is the surrender of Yogyakarta lands currently held by Surakarta nobility and courtiers (Surakarta, 18 January 1826). [JB #56]

29. Letter: PB VI to Commissaris General Du Bus deGisignies; letter of welcome to the new Commissaris General (12 Rejep 1753 = 19 February 1826). [JB #57]

30. Letter: P. Cakradiningrat (Bupati of Kediri) to Lieutenant Governor General Merkus de Kock; with a gift of two keris, the Bupati seals his military alliance with the Dutch commander (Kediri, 3 Rejep 1755 = 20 January 1828).[4] [JB #80]

31. Letter: G.P. Adipati Hangabéhi to J. F. C. Gericke; in answer to questions from Gericke, the then director of the Surakarta Institute of Javanese Language, Prince Hangabéhi explains some points of Kraton Surakarta language use. Transcribed by this royal informant is the standard dialogue between the Sunan and Grand Vizier in the context of a royal tiger fight. ("Bring out the tigers—Who killed them?— . . . What season is it?—What are my villagers doing?—In what condition, the river? . . .") ([Surakarta], 12 Sapar 1762 = 19 June 1834).[5] [JB #186]

32. Letter: Lieutenant Governor General Merkus de Kock to MN II; letter of commendation for the valor of the MN's troops in killing the rebel, Tumenggung Jayamenggala in the village of Gégér (Magelang, 23 Juli 1829).[6] [JB #143]

33. Letter: PB VII to Resident Maijor; re the return of crown lands (siti pangrembé) from the Kapatiyan to PB VII (3 Sura 1764 = 19 April 1836). [JB #191]

4. Not Kraton correspondence.
5. Not internal Kraton correspondence. Pangéran Hangabéhi resided outside the palace walls.
6. Not Kraton correspondence.

34. Letter: R. Adipati Sasradiningrat to Resident Maijor; re the return of crown lands) (3 Besar 1763 = 21 March 1836). [JB #190]

35. Letter: R. Tumenggung Purwadiningrat to C. F. Winter; re the firing of a recalcitrant *demang* of Prince Kusumayuda's (13 Jumadilakir 1770 = 21 July 1842).[7] [JB #219]

36. Proclamation: Lieutenant Governor General Merkus de Kock; re the capture and exile of Dipanagara. Noted is the Dutch refusal of the Prince's demand to be recognized as the leader of Islam in Java [March 1830]. [JB #160]

37. Letter: Ngabéhi Kartapraja, Panéwu Gunung to G.K. Panembahan Buminata; this Wedana Gunung Sentana Kasepuhan Surakarta complains that Surakarta princes are still trying to administer their own villages ([Surakarta], circa 1832). [JB #178]

38. Royal Charter (*Serat Nawala-dalem*) of PB [V?] assigning an apanage to Ngabéhi Wongsadiwirya (Surakarta, no date [1822?]). [JB #29]

39. Letter: P. Hadinagara to Resident Nahuys; re lease of land in Nglaban. This document demonstrates the web of indebtedness between Kraton nobility and Dutch lessees (Surakarta, 23 Sapar 1755 = 15 September 1827).[8] [JB #72]

40. Letter: PB VI to K.P.H. Mangkubumi in Ambon; re the marriages of the king and his elder sister. The letter to the exiled elder Kraton prince includes other family news as well (Surakarta, 24 Rejep 1751 = 24 March 1824). [JB #45]

41. Report: MN II to Resident Nahuys. MN II reports to the Resident on circumstances surrounding the death of PB IV. Of note is his account of PB IV's wish that MN's son be married to the daughter of the Crown Prince (PB V)—hence the wedding of PB VI's elder sister to a MN prince in 1824 noted above (see item nos. 14, 15, and 40) (Surakarta, circa October 1820). [JB #12]

42. Contract: Treaty of Accession PB V (Surakarta, 1 Sura 1748 = 10 October 1820). [JB #13]

43. Proclamation: Accession of PB V to the throne (Surakarta, 13 October 1820). [JB #14]

44. Oath of Office: PB V; this oath acknowledges the conditionality of the Sunan's rule (Surakarta, 31 October 1820). [JB #15]

45. Letter: PB V to R.M.H. Kusumaningrat in Juwana; PB V gives a wedding present of 500 *ringgit* for the marriage of H. Candradiningrat to the daughter of Tumenggung Blora (1 Sura 1750 = 17 September 1822). [JB #33]

46. Letter: K.P. Hangabéhi to R.M.H. Kusumaningrat; sends items of clothing as his wedding gift (Surakarta, 6 Besar 1749 = 24 August 1822). [JB #32]

47. Letter: K.P.H. Buminata to HB V; thank-you note to Yogyakarta for sending funeral

7. Not Kraton correspondence.
8. Not internal Kraton correspondence.

money upon the death of PB V (Surakarta, 9 Mukharam 1751 = 15 September 1823). [*JB* #37]

[Following are letters not found in the *Javaansch Brievenboek*]

48. Letter: Resident Nahuys to PB VI (Surakarta, 11 June 1830).

Having been arrested, PB VI has been taken off to Semarang.[9] Responding to PB VI's request that his three queens be sent to follow him (see item #12 above), the Resident writes that he has met and discussed the matter with the three queens. The Resident reports that of the three, only Ratu Anèm has agreed to follow her husband; the others (Ratu Mas and Ratu Maduretna) would decide "tomorrow." As for himself, the Resident explains that he is too busy to come to Semarang.

49. Letter: PB VII to PB VI (Surakarta, 15 Jumadilawal 1758 = 1 November 1830).

A letter of farewell, the letter concerns PB VI's imminent exile to Ambon. Answering a letter from PB VI, sent from Batavia on 2 July 1830,[10] PB VII reviews and responds to orders contained in that letter. PB VI's directives had pertained to the queens and concubines who did not follow him into exile and to the naming of the baby carried in the womb of Ratu Mas (that is, R.M. Deksina, the future PB IX). PB VII reports that no one in the Kraton has agreed to follow PB VI into exile. Although he would have been allowed a hundred servants, only five could be provided. PB VII refuses the request to send along Ratu Anèm's *keris*.

50. Letter: PB VII to PB VI in Makasar (again: Surakarta, 15 Jumadilawal 1758 = 1 November 1830).

Answering PB VI's letter sent from Makasar dated 7 Rabinguawal 1758 (26 August 1830), PB VII repeats the contents of that letter: PB VI has requested that several family members be sent after him into exile (notably his daughters Menthik and Sriti); he has also requested that specified items of clothing and jewelry, as well as his diaries (*serat dinten, buk kalih*) be sent on to him. PB VII refuses all these requests, suggesting that it would be more appropriate that such requests be directed to the Governor General in Batavia.

9. Pakubuwana VI left the Kraton in disguise on 6 June accompanied by only a few trusted courtiers. He traveled with them to the royal tombs of Imagiri and then on to the southern coastal beach of Parangtritis. There he was to meet with his spiritual consort, the Queen of the South Sea (Kangjeng Ratu Kidul). The king was arrested by colonial officials at Parangtritis on 8 June and charged with the crime of having left his *kraton* without their permission. He was taken by his captors to Semarang via Kalitan and Salatiga (*Babad Sangkala: Kawit Pulo Jawi dipunisèni tiyang nalika taun ongka 1 dumugi taun 1854* [composed Surakarta, s.a.; inscribed Surakarta, 1924]. MS. Sp 220 Ca-A; SMP KS 1a, pp. 163–66).

10. The official resolution to exile the incarcerated king was made on 3 July 1830 (V. J. H. Houben, "Afstand van Gebied met Behoud van Aanzien," [M.A. thesis, Leiden University, 1982], p. 9.

51. Letter: K.P.H. Suryabrata to his elder brother, PB VI (Surakarta, no date).

Responds to a letter received from PB VI which concerned the verdict of exile to Ambon. The copy, which is incomplete, includes family news, notably of births in the family on 28 Besar 1757 (20 June 1830) and 25 Rabingulawal [1758] (13 September 1830). Copy breaks off abruptly, midline. This letter likely accompanied the posting of one of the above letters from PB VII.

52. Letter: K. Panembahan Buminata to PB VI (Surakarta, 6 Sura Jé 1758 = 29 June 1830).

Reviews and answers (quite shortly) a letter from PB VI in which the incarcerated king had inquired as to why his two remaining queens have yet to join him. The king had gone so far as to ask whether or not the queens still loved him. Buminata responds that the two remaining queens absolutely refuse to follow the prisoner-king into exile.

53. Letter: K.P. Panji Priyabada to PB VI (Surakarta, 8 Sura Jé 1758 = 1 July 1830).

This letter from PB VI's young uncle reviews and responds to a number of requests made by the incarcerated king. The letter informs PB VI: (1) (again?) that his young daughter, R. Ajeng Sriti, will not be allowed to follow him into exile; (2) that the two *pusaka keris* which PB VI was forced to leave behind in Semarang have returned safely home to the Kraton along with the Ratu Anèm's jewelry; and (3) that his request that that jewelry be sent after him has been refused. Reviewed and affirmed are: (1) PB VI's chosen names, and wishes, for the baby to be born of Ratu Mas (i.e., Deksina/PB IX) and (2) greetings from PB VI and Ratu Anèm to various royal family members, court servants, and Dutch colonials in Surakarta. Finally the letter reports on the coronation of PB VI's rival Prince Purbaya as PB VII on 22 Besar 1757 (14 June 1830).

54. Letter: K. Ratu Mas to PB VI in Ambon (Surakarta, 12 Dulkangidah 1775 = 21 October 1847).

This letter from PB VI's queen (the mother of PB IX) acknowledges receipt of PB VI's letter of 2 Rabinguawal Alip 1771 (2 April 1843) as well as of the presents he sent her in the years Jé (1774 = 1845) and Dal (1775 = 1846). She sends greetings and a present to her husband and requests of him that R. Ayu Timur, the one daughter who had followed him from Surakarta into Ambonese exile, be sent home to the Kraton and that he grant permission for Menthik and Mublak (his daughters still in Surakarta) to be married. The tone of the letter is formal and rather stiff.

55. Letter: K. Ratu Maduretna to PB VI in Ambon (Surakarta, 12 Dulkangidah 1775 = 21 October 1847)

This letter from PB VI's other remaining queen acknowledges receipt of his letter of 2 Rabinguawal Alip 1771 (2 April 1843). She thanks him profusely for the presents he has sent her and sends presents to him and his Ambon family. The tone of the letter is friendly and newsy.

56. Letter: K.G.P.H. Prabuwijaya (= the future PB IX) to his elder sister Gusti R. Ayu Timur in Ambon; composed in *macapat* verse (Surakarta, 12 Dulkangidah 1775 = 21 October 1847).

Sending her a gift and greetings, the young prince asks his elder half-sister for permission to precede her in marriage. He notes and complains of the difficulty of correspondence across the expanse of the sea. The letter's tone is rather brash.

57. Letter: K.P.H. Suryabrata to his elder brother PB VI in Ambon; composed in *macapat* verse (Surakarta, 1 Dulkangidah 1775 = 10 October 1847).

Suryabrata's letter acknowledges receipt of PB VI's letter of 2 Rabinguawal Alip 1771 (2 April 1843) as well as of presents the exiled king sent over the course of several years. Among the gifts sent were four of PB VI's teeth which had fallen out. The teeth were distributed among the exiled king's younger siblings. The letter acknowledges PB VI's will: that the exiled king is not yet ready for Ratu Mas "to raise/care for a daughter" (R. Ayu Timur? a wife for Prabuwijaya?). Suryabrata conveys family news, especially noting recent (1843–47) deaths in the family. Suryabrata explains obliquely why he has not written for so very long (five years!). He claims to be, or to have been, afraid (*rinta sakalangkung ngajrih*). He says that he is weeping as he writes. Suryabrata sends with his letter gifts of clothing (textiles) to his exiled brother. A current of pathos colors the letter.

58. Letter: PB VI to K.P.H. Suryabrata; composed in *macapat* verse (Ambon, 2 Rejeb Bé 1776 = 4 June 1848)

Referring to himself as "I.S.K.S. Sayiddi Maolana Mokahamat Salim," this letter of PB VI is an answer to Suryabrata's October 1847 letter (item #57 above). The tonality of the exiled king's writing is tragic. He claims to be weeping as he writes. Complaining that his life has been a failure, he feels he has little left for which to live. He claims no use for the fine clothing his brother has sent him from Surakarta, for he is but a poor farmer of dry-field crops who writes this letter (through his tears) in a rude hut in the middle of the fields.[11] PB VI passes on the pitiful news of other exiles (i.e., news of their younger brother Suryaningrat who had been exiled to Menado). Entrusting his children (especially Prabuwijaya) to Suryabrata, the forty-one-year-old exiled king says he feels very old—"like a sun about to set." He begs his brother not to laugh at his senile writing. PB VI expresses his wish that his son Prabuwijaya be wed to Sajirin (Suryabrata's daughter). The exiled and failing king expresses his enduring hope to return home to Java.

59. Letter: PB VI to his queen K. Ratu Maduretna; composed in *macapat* verse (Ambon, [1848])

In this tender love letter, the prisoner-king sends the queen his love and longing as well as several gifts. Among the gifts are a prayer mat for her *salât* and a sarong he has worn—for her to use as her pillow. He asks after one of the concubines he had left behind in the Kraton. The letter answers her letter above (item #55). The copy is not dated and seems incomplete.

11. The exiled Sunan's description of himself here is reminiscent of the description of Ki Ageng Pengging in *Babad Jaka Tingkir*. For a translation of a portion of the letter, see above, chap. 6, pp. 380–81.

60. Letter: PB VI to his queen K. Ratu Mas; composed in *macapat* verse (Ambon, 2 Rejep and 25 Ruwah 1776 = 4 June and 27 July 1848)

In this affectionate letter to the mother of his son (*ibuné si tholé yekti*), the exiled king expresses the depth of his despair (*baya wis tan nèng donyèki / wis tan krasan anèng donya / urip tiwas becik mati*). He directs her to care for their son, and to keep the Prophet's Sacred Law (*aja sira lali iku / lakuning saréngat nabi*). Emphasizing piety, he advises her to take a religious teacher. Although PB VI would prefer to provide her religious instruction himself, in his absence he suggests as guru, Prince Hadinegara (the father of his other queen, K. Ratu Maduretna). He reports that he has a "new" (that is, for the past six years) Madurese concubine. A postscript to the letter grants their son Prabuwijaya the new name: Harya Prabu Suryaputrawijaya. In a second postscript, the Sunan records the loss of (another) tooth.

61. Genealogy of Sarifi Ibrahim Madyakusuma; composed in *macapat* verse (see Appendix II).

Genealogy traces the descent of this personage back to Adam via the Prophet Mohammad and the first seven of the twelve Imams of orthodox Shi'ah Islam.

62. Letter: G.R. Ayu Timur to K.G.P.H. Prabuwijaya; composed in *macapat* verse (Ambon, 2 Rejep 1776 = 4 June 1848)

Answering her younger brother's letter of October 1847 (see item #56), Gusti Timur grants him permission to precede her in marriage. The princess declares her intention (and sacred duty) to remain with their father in exile. She gratefully acknowledges his fine gifts and sends him in return some simple presents. The letter is written with grace and some lyric beauty.

63. *Babad Jaka Tingkir*

An allusive 6,913 line historical poem dated 23 August 1829, offering glimpses of Java's past around the turn of the sixteenth century. (Translated and annotated, chapter 2.)

APPENDIX II
GENEALOGY OF SARIFI IBRAHIM
MADYAKUSUMA[1]

Kinanthi
[1] Bismilah sinuryèng tembung
kinanthi pandoming manis
salasilah kang pinurwa
turas ingkang johar jisim
tumulat mring johar awal
tumandya mring badan kammih

[2] 'Al-fakuru illallahu
Ghanniyul Kammid Sarifi
Ibrahim Madyakusuma
ibnu Kusèn bin 'Alluwi
Babut bangsane dyan arya
ibnu Sarip Ngabdullahi

[3] Ibnu Sarif Muksimmahu
ibnu Sarip Ngumar sigih
ipnu Sarip ingkang raka
Mukhsim ibnu Ngabdullahi
ibnu Sarif Abu Bakar
ibnu Sarif Kusèn malih

[4] Bin Sarif Amat winuwus
bin Sarif Ngabdul Rahmani
ibnu Sarif Ngubud lawan
ibnu Sarifulla Ngali
ibnu Sarif Mukhammadda
ibnu Sarif Ngali malih

[5] Ibnu Sari Ngalwi Bakbut
ibnu Sarif Mukhammaddi
ibnu Sarif Ngali lawan
ibnu Sarib Mukhammaddi[2]
ibnu Sariful Ngaliya
bin Ngalluwi Abu Kasim

[6] Sariful Muhkhammad bintu
ibnu Sarip Ngapdulahi
ibnu Sariful Kusèna
'al-Khalis ibnu Sarippi
Ahmad ibnu Ngali Bakkra
ibnu Sarif ul-Ngisak-i

[7] Ibnu Sarif Mukhammaddu
al-Jawaddi ibnu Sarif
ibnu Sarif Mukhammadda
ibnu Sarip Ngali Ngaril
ibnu Sarib Musal Kalam
ibnu Sarip Jahfar Sadik

[8] Ibnu Sarif Mukhammaddu
Bakir ibnu Sarip Ngali
Jenal Ngabidin wa ibna
Sarip Kusèn al-Bastani
ibnu 'Amir ul-Mukminna
Ngalli ibnu Abu Talip

1. Item 61 of *Kupiya Iber Warni-warni Sampéyan-dalem kaping VI*, pp. 75recto–verso.
2. Inscribed and then crossed out here: "ibnu sarib ng-l-l-w-n."

[9] Akkrammalahu waz-atu
wahuwa waja-ojahi
Fatimmah Johar Karimma
ibnu Jeng Rasullulahi
sallala ngali wassalam
ibnu Ngabdulah Jeng Nabi

[10] Ibnu Hasimmala'abun
ibnu Kusyin bin Kilabbin
ibnu Marat ibnu Kangab
bin Luwiyin ibnu Ghalib
ibnu Fihrim Malik 'Abna
Nalar ibnu Kinnannahhi

[11] Ibnu Khujèmmah wa ibnu
Mudbikah ibnu Ilyassi
ibnu Malar ibnu Najran
bin Mangak ibnu Ngadnanni
ibnu Adam Makum'abna
Fakhur'abna Yatrah ibni

[12] Yakrab ibnu Yasjab bintu
Sabit Jeng Nabi Ismangil
ibnu Ibrahim-lillulah
ibnu Fajar bin Tarahtkhi
ibnu Fakhur bin Saruhkha
ibnu Rangu ibnu Falih

[13] Ibnu Giyar ibnu Saluh
bin 'Arwahsad ibnu Salim
ibnu Nuh ibnu Malika
ibnu Prabu Mutusálkhi
ibnu 'Ajwah bin Idrissa
ibnu Barad bin Mahlayil

[14] Ibnu Kènnan wau-wau
ibnu Yannas Ibnu Esis
ngala-ihi wasalamma
wa huwa ibnu 'Adammi
ngala-ihi wasalamma
wa 'Adam fitratullahhi

The eleven meters used in *Babad Jaka Tingkir,* together with their respective rules of *guru gatra, guru wilangan,* and *guru lagu,* along with directives for *ukara* and indications of *watak* are as follows:

Dhangdhanggula (10 lines)

10	i				
10	a				
8	é				
7	u				
9	i			*lithe; flexible*	
7	a				
6	u				
8	a		8	a	
		or:	12	i	
12	i		7	a	
7	a				

Sinom (9 lines)

8	a
8	i
8	a
8	i
7	i	*even; steady*
8	u
7	a
8	i
12	a

Asmarandana (7 lines)

8	i
8	a
8	é/o

plaintive; evocative of sorrow or longing

8	a
7	a
8	u
8	a

Pangkur (7 lines)

8	a
11	i

8	u
7	a

intense, impassioned, and/or weighty

12	u

8	a
8	i

Durma (7 lines)

12	a
7	i

6	a
7	a

impassioned, angry, or violent

8	i

5	a
7	i

Mijil (6 lines)

10	i
6	o

10	é
10	i

evocative of longing: erotic or mournful

6	i
6	u

Kinanthi (6 lines)

8	u
8	i

8	a	*erotic and/or didactic*
8	i	

8	a
8	i

Gambuh (5 lines)

7	u
10	u

12	i	*vibrant and rather brash*

8	u
8	o

Megatruh (5 lines)

12	u

8	i

8	u	*melancholic: evocative of sorrow or regret*
8	i	

8	o

Maskumambang (4 lines)

12	i

5	a	
8	i	*melancholic; evocative of deep sorrow or mourning*

8	i

Pucung (4 lines)

12	u

6	a	*lackadaisical*
8	i	

12	a

APPENDIX IV
OPENING LINES OF CANTOS:
BABAD JAKA TINGKIR

	Tembang	Pada	Lines	Opening Lines of Canto
I	Dhangdhanggula	30	300	*Nihan déning ngulun manulad sri, ring sarkara mamrih mamardawa*
II	Asmarandana	32	224	*Mangkana Sri Narapati, Brawijaya Majalengka*
III	Sinom	31	279	*Ing dalu Sang Nata néndra, lagya erem-erem pitik*
IV	Dhangdhanggula	27	270	*Kyana Patih Gajahmada prapti, wus jinarwan sakarsaning nata*
V	Mijil	46	276	*Mangu-mangu manguneng nekani, kakenan tyas képon*
VI	Gambuh	44	220	*Kambuh ing driya wimbuh, kambah barubah kabubuh-bubuh*
VII	Pucung	49	196	*Lah ta biyung, kula pan dédé lelembut, dédé perayangan*
VIII	Kinanthi	35	210	*Mangkana pan kamisuwur, tepis iring kanan kèri*
IX	Asmarandana	35	245	*Ngandika Sri Narapati, yèn mengkono kulup sira*
X	Megatruh	36	180	*Nulya wau, Ki Jaka susumpingipun, pinèt sinèlèh ing siti*
XI	Sinom	27	243	*Para dipati satriya, sami tinumutan bukti*
XII	Maskumambang	41	164	*Sang ngaPrabu èsmu kaduwung ing galih, dènya budi ganas*
XIII	Dhangdhanggula	28	280	*Kawuwusa natèng Pajang Pengging, Naradipati Handayaningrat*

GLOSSARY OF SELECTED
TERMS AND TITLES

adiluhung: the beautiful sublime, a popular designation for high Javanese culture in modern Indonesia.

ahlul-iman: (Ar.) men of faith.

babad: (meaning "to clear the forest") a generic term designating the (usually poetic) written texts of traditional Javanese history.

bantah: argumentation (usually in a series of riddled questions); debate.

batin: (Ar.) inside, interior; concealed, reserved; immaterial, spiritual.

Buda: pre- or non-Islamic religious complex.

darma: (Skt.) a code of conduct.

fakir: (Ar.) a mendicant; a poor wandering Sufi, a dervish.

fuqaha: (pl. of the Ar. *faqîh*) experts in Islamic law.

Hadîth: (Ar.) "traditions," the collected body of tales detailing practices of the Prophet Mohammad and his early associates.

hakim: (Ar. *hakîm*) judge of Islamic law.

halus: refined.

ijmâʻ: (Ar.) consensus, an Islamic legal term for the agreement of the community of Moslem legal scholars as a basis for juridical decision.

Jabariyah: (Ar.) a variant of Islamic thought characterized by radical determinism that is often associated with Wujudiyyah mysticism and with heresy.

Jaka: an unmarried youth; common as the first part of a (young) man's name.

Jatimurti: (Skt.) a state, or form, of material-spiritual enlightenment, or perfection; Reality Incarnate; Body of Reality.

kéblat: (Ar. *qiblah*) the direction to which a Moslem must face when performing *salât*, that is, pointing in the most direct line to the Ka'bah of Mecca. The verbal form *ngéblat* means "to face Mecca," or "to obey."

khukama: (pl. of the Ar. *hakîm*) judges of Islamic law.

Ki: variant of Kyai ("Master" or "Sir").

Ki Ageng: variant of Kyai Ageng ("Great Master").

kobongan: a chamber located in the center of the inner room (*dalem*) of a traditional (aristocratic) Javanese house. This chamber within a chamber is often glassed in and hung with curtains, and it constitutes the most hallowed/powerful point in the house/ palace.

krama: high Javanese.

kraton: from the root *ratu* (king or queen), *k[a]raton* designates "the seat of a king," hence: palace, reign, kingdom.

Kyai: "Master" or "Sir." The title Kyai (or Ki) is the usual one for the master of a *pesantrèn.*

Kyai Ageng: "Great Master."

lahir: (Ar.) outside, exterior; expressed, revealed; material, phenomenal.

Lauhu 'l-Mahfûz: (Ar.) the preserved tablet. In the tradition of the Hadîth, it is on this tablet that the decrees of God for mankind are inscribed from eternity.

mufti: (Ar.) canon lawyer authorized to promulgate a *fatwâ* or formal legal opinion.

mukmin: (Ar.) the faithful.

mukmin khas: (Ar.) the elect of the faithful.

mungahid: (a variant of the Ar. *mujâhid*) one who fights in the way of God, in the cause of religion.

ngabid: (from the Ar. *'âbid*) devout worshippers.

ngèlmu: (from the Ar. *'ilm*) knowledge, especially sacred or esoteric knowledge.

ngoko: low Javanese.

Ni: "Mistress."

Nyai: variant of Ni.

Panembahan: an extremely high Javanese royal title, the word *panembahan* means literally: the one to whom the *sembah* (act of obeisance) is appropriate. In the Kraton Surakarta it has been, since the nineteenth century, exclusively granted to exceptional senior princes (brothers of reigning kings).

pesantrèn: (usually) rural establishment of Islamic education.

pradikan: religious men of "independent" status. These were men of religion to whom the king would grant tax-free lands (also called *pradikan*). The *pradikan* were exempt from regular royal service but were expected to watch over royal (or other special) grave sites and/or provide religious education.

priyayi: originally from *para yayi* ("the younger siblings" [of the king]), the word has come to designate the administrative and/or bureaucratic elite of the realm (kingdom, colonial and postcolonial state).

pujongga: (supernaturally endowed) court poet; prophet.

pundit: (Skt. *pandhita*) [Islamic] scholar, sage, teacher, holy man.

pusaka: a thing or activity (or a class of things or activities) that are endowed with supernatural powers; a talisman.

qiblah: (Ar.) the direction to which a Moslem must face when performing *salât. See also* kéblat.

qiyâs: (Ar.) an Islamic legal term indicating a process of coming to legal decisions for novel cases by way of analogy to traditional cases from the Qur'ân and Hadîth.

rahsa: (Skt.) Mystery, secret, essence.

ramé: an adjective connoting "presence": noisy, bustling, crowded, full of activity.

rasa: (Skt.) feeling; taste; flavor; emotion; sense; meaning; thought; speech; voice; gossip; mystery; essence.

Ratu: "Queen" (wife or daughter of a king); rarely: "King."

salâm: (Ar.) peace. "Peace!" Also short for the standard Islamic greeting: "assalam 'alaikum," which is answered " 'alaikum salam."

salât: (Ar.) the ritual worship performed by Moslems at five specified times every day.

salèh: (Ar.) "the devout" or "righteous."

sangkala: chronograms. Aphoristic phrases, the words of which when read backwards signify, by a logical system of conventions, different numerical values.

santri: often itinerant students of Islamic religion and theology.

Sèh: (Ar.) Sheikh.

semadi: (Skt.) the final/perfect stage of yogic meditation.

sembah: a gesture of high esteem/deference in which one brings the hands (palms together as though in prayer) before the face with thumbs touching the nose.

semu: the merely glimpsed perceptible (often visible) dimension of the concealed.

Sénapati: a military commander, a commanding general; sometimes used as a royal title.

sepi: an adjective connoting a constellation of senses around the notion of "absence": silent, empty, lonely.

sharî'a: (Ar.) the body of rules that govern every aspect of life for a devout Moslem; the canon law.

sulakha: (pl. of the Ar. *sâlik*) travelers along the mystic path.

suluk: (from the Ar. *sulûk* [traversing the Sufi way]), an important and extensive genre of Javanese writing comprising Islamic mystical songs, mostly composed in *macapat* verse.

Sunan: (also Susuhunan, Susunan, Sinuhun) "He who is Revered." Royal and/or ecclesiastical title. Since the eighteenth century the title has been the exclusive right of the supreme rulers of Mataram; since 1755, of the ruler of the Kraton Surakarta. Originally the title was restricted to the hierarchy of Islamic saints (*wali*).

Sunyata: (Skt.) the Absolute Void, or the (mystic) state of emptiness.

tahlilan: (from Ar. *tahlil*) the practice of repeating the formula "there is no god but God," denoting sessions of collective Islamic prayer, or more precisely, chanting (*zikir*).

tarékat: (Ar. *tarîqah*) Sufi brotherhood.

ukara: sense, sentence, syntax; grammar; order, rule; greed.

ulama: (pl. of the Ar. *'âlim*) Moslem religious scholar.

wahyu: (Ar. *wahy'*) a supernatural (divine) radiant light that descends on certain persons (prophets, kings, poetic sages), instilling them with supernatural powers.

wajir: (Ar.) minister.

wali and *waliyullah:* (Ar.) "friend(s) of God, saint(s)," denoting the group of (usually nine) lords to whom the Islamization of Java is attributed.

wali kutub: (Ar.) axial saint.

wayang: theatrical performance; puppet; dancer. The term usually pertains to shadow-puppet theater.

wong cilik: little [wo]man; commoner.

zahid: (Ar.) an ascetic.

zikir: (Ar. *dhikr*) a form of Islamic ritual practice, characterized by chanting.

BIBLIOGRAPHY

'Abdul-Ra'uf of Singkel. *Dakaik al-Huruf*. Edited and translated by A. H. Johns. *Journal of the Royal Asiatic Society* (1955): 55–73, 135–58.

Affifi, A. E. *The Mystical Philosophy of Muhyid Din-Ibnu Arabi*. Cambridge: Cambridge University Press, 1938.

Serat Ajisaka ngeJawi sapiturutipun = *Babad Tanah Jawi*. Composed s.l., s.a.; inscribed Surakarta, 1866. MS. RP B 4b; SMP MN 187.

van Akkeren, Philippus. *Een gedrocht en toch de volmaakte mens: De Javaanse Suluk Gatoloco, uitgeven, vertaald en toegelicht*. The Hague: Excelsior, 1951.

Serat Ambiya. Composed s.l., s.a.; inscribed Surakarta, 1862. MS. RP 1D; SMP MN 280.

Anderson, Benedict R. O'G. "The Idea of Power in Javanese Culture." In *Culture and Politics in Indonesia*, edited by Claire Holt. Ithaca: Cornell University Press, 1972.

———. *Language and Power: Exploring Political Cultures in Indonesia*. Ithaca: Cornell University Press, 1990.

———. "The Last Picture Show." In *Proceedings from the Conference on Modern Indonesian Literature*. Madison, Wisconsin, 1974.

———, ed. and trans. "The *Suluk Gatoloco*: Parts One and Two." *Indonesia* 32 (October 1981): 109–50; 33 (April 1982): 31–88.

———. "A Time of Darkness and a Time of Light: Transposition in Early Indonesian Nationalist Thought." In *Perceptions of the Past in Southeast Asia*, edited by Anthony Reid and David Marr. Singapore: Heinemann, 1979.

Anjar Any. *Radèn Ngabéhi Ronggowarsito: Apa yang Terjadi?* Semarang: Aneka, 1980.

———. *Rahasia Ramalan: Jayabaya Ranggawarsita dan Sabdapalon*. Semarang: Aneka, 1979.

Arps, Bernard. *Tembang in Two Traditions: Performance and Interpretation of Javanese Literature*. London: School of Oriental and African Studies, University of London, 1992.

Arungbinang, R.T. *Serat Sri Pustaka Madyapada*. 29 vols. Composed and inscribed Surakarta, 1914–18. MSS. SP 249 Ca, 250 Ca . . . ; SMP KS 148–58.

al-Attas, Syed Muhammad Naguib. *The Mysticism of Hamzah Fansuri*. Kuala Lumpur: University of Malaya Press, 1970.

———. *Rânîrî and the Wujûdiyyah of Seventeenth-Century Acheh*. Singapore: Malaysian Branch of the Royal Asiatic Society, 1966.

———. *Some Aspects of Sûfism as Understood and Practised among the Malays*. Singapore: Malaysian Sociological Research Institute, 1963.

Babad Demak I. Edited by Slamet Riyadi and Suwadji. Jakarta: Departemen Pendidikan dan Kebudayaan, Proyek Penerbitan Buku Sastra Indonesia dan Daerah, 1981.

Babad Demak II. Edited by Gina and Dirgo Sabariyanto. Jakarta: Departemen Pendidikan dan Kebudayaan, Proyek Penerbitan Buku Sastra Indonesia dan Daerah, 1981.

Serat Babad Demak dumugi Pajang. Composed s.l., s.a.; inscribed Surakarta, ca. 1859. MS. Rp D82 (uncataloged); SMP Rp 20A.

Serat Babad Demak (Sèh Malaya). Composed s.l., s.a.; inscribed Surakarta, [early] 19th century. MS. RP B 31; SMP MN 193.

Babad Jaka Tingkir. Composed Surakarta, 1829. In *Kupiya Iber Warni-warni Sampéyandalem kaping VI*, 79verso–152recto. Inscribed [Ambon], ca. 1849. MS. SP 214 Ca; SMP KS 78.

Babad Jaka Tingkir: Babad Pajang. Edited by Moelyono Sastronaryatmo. Jakarta: Departemen Pendidikan dan Kebudayaan, Proyek Penerbitan Buku Sastra Indonesia dan Daerah, 1981.

Babad Langenharja. 30 vols. Composed and inscribed Surakarta, 1871–77. MSS. SP 187 Ra, 390 Ha . . . ; SMP KS 87–99.

Babad Langenharja. 3 vols. Composed Surakarta, 1872–73; inscribed Surakarta, late 19th century. MSS. SP 180 Na and 219 Ca; SMP KS 100–101.

Serat Babad Pajajaran. Composed s.l., s.a.; inscribed [Surakarta, early 19th century]. MS. Rp 140; SMP Rp 13.

Serat Babad Pajajaran dumugi Mataram. Composed s.l., s.a.; inscribed Surakarta, 1893. MS. SP 200 Na; SMP KS 25.

Serat Babad Pajajaran dumugi Pajang. Composed s.l., s.a.; inscribed Surakarta, 19th century. MS. SP (uncataloged); SMP KS 24A.

Serat Babad Pajajaran dumugi Sédanipun Kiyahi Ageng Mataram. Composed s.l., s.a.; inscribed Surakarta, [ca. 1893–1939]. MS. SP 28 Ca; SMP KS 24.

Serat Babad Pajajaran: Kagungan-dalem Gusti Kangjeng Bandara Radèn Ayu Prabuwijaya. Composed Surakarta, 1896; inscribed Surakarta, 1912. MS. SP 200 Na; SMP KS 22.

Serat Babad Pajajaran: Nyariyosaken Prabu Mundhingsari ngantos dumugi kawontenanipun lelampahan ing nagari Pajang. Composed Surakarta, s.a. and [1895]; inscribed Surakarta, 1895. MS. SP 190 Na; SMP KS 21.

Babad Pémut ing Nagari Surakarta. 14 vols. Composed and inscribed Surakarta, 1888–94. MSS. SP 5 Ca, 30 Ca . . . ; SMP KS 111–22.

Serat Babad Sampéyan-dalem Ingkang Sinuhun Kangjeng Susuhunan Pakubuwana kaping VI: Sri Naluri. Composed Surakarta, 1906; inscribed Surakarta, ca. 1906. MS. SP 177 Ca; SMP KS 80.

Serat Babad Sangkala. Composed Surakarta, ca. 1831. In [*Klempakan Warni-warni*], pt. 1, pp. 5–287. Inscribed Surakarta, ca. 1831. MS. SP 6 Ta; SMP KS 1C.

Babad Segaluh. Composed s.l., s.a. and 1887; inscribed [Yogyakarta?, 1904?]. MS. RP B24b; SMP MN 268.

Serat Babad Sengkala: Kawit Pulo Jawi dipunisèni tiyang nalika taun ongka 1 dumugi taun 1854. Composed Surakarta, s.a.; inscribed Surakarta, 1924. MS. SP 220 Ca-A; SMP KS 1A.

Babad Sengkala kang kaurut saking kagungan-dalem serat Babad. Composed and inscribed Surakarta, ca. 1831, 1847. MS. SP 6 Ta; SMP KS 1C.7.

Babad Tanah Jawi. 18 vols. Inscribed Surakarta, 1836. Leiden Oriental Collection, Codex 1786.

Babad Tanah Jawi. 31 vols. Batavia: Balai Pustaka, 1939–41.

Babad Tanah Jawi. Composed Surakarta, 1788; inscribed Surakarta: for R.M. Gondakusuma [= Mangkunagara IV], 1836. MS. RP 25d; SMP MN 191.

Babad Tanah Jawi: Wiwit Hyang Guru puputra Hang Wisnu jumeneng nata, ngantos dumugi Radèn Bondhan putra Prabu Brawijaya ing Majapahit ngèngèr dhateng Ki Ageng Tarub. Composed Surakarta, 1788; inscribed Surakarta, 1869. MS. RP B25b; SMP MN 192.

Serat Babad Tanah Jawi: Wiwit Prabu Majapahit pungkasan dumugi Demak pungkasan. Composed s.l., s.a.; inscribed Surakarta, 1871. MS. RP B15a; SMP MN 196.

Babad Tanah Jawi: Wiwit Sanghyang Guru dumugi Sénapati jumeneng Nata ing Mantawis. Composed Surakarta, 1788; inscribed Surakarta, 1831. MS. RP B 25c; SMP MN 189.

Barthes, Roland. "The Theory of the Text." In *Untying the Text,* edited by Robert Young. Boston: Routledge and Keagan Paul, 1981.

Becker, Alton L. *Writing on the Tongue.* Ann Arbor: University of Michigan Center for South and Southeast Asian Studies, 1989.

Behrend, Timothy E. "The Serat Jatiswara: Structure and Change in a Javanese Poem, 1600–1930." Ph.D. dissertation, Australian National University, 1987.

Benjamin, Walter. "The Task of the Translator." In *Illuminations.* New York: Schocken Books, 1969.

Berg, C. C. "The Javanese Picture of the Past." In *An Introduction to Indonesian Historiography,* edited by Soedjatmoko et al. Ithaca: Cornell University Press, 1965.

Brandes, J. L. A., ed. *Pararaton (Ken Arok) of het Boek der Koningen van Tumapel en van Majapahit.* Verhandelingen van het Bataviaasch Genootschap van Kunsten en Wetenschappen, vol. 62 (1920).

Bratadiningrat, R.M.T., et al. *Karaton-dalem Surakarta Adiningrat Sasana Pustaka: Mèngeti kuwajiban Abdi-dalem Juru Suranata, Maésa Lawung, Donga-donga, Nglabuh, Pados Sekar Jayakusuma, saha Mriksa Kasagedan Juru Suranata.* Compiled and inscribed Surakarta, 1941 and 1945. MS. SP 547 Ka; SMP KS 189.

Bratakésawa, R. *Falsafah Siti Djenar.* Surabaya: Djojobojo, [1954].

———. *Katrangan Tjandrasangkala.* Jakarta: Balai Pustaka, 1952.

Brenner, Suzanne. "Competing Hierarchies: Javanese Merchants and the *Priyayi* Elite in Solo, Central Java." *Indonesia* 52 (October 1991): 55–83.

Brumond, J. F. G. *Het Volksonderwijs onder de Javanen.* Batavia: Van Haren Noman and Kolff, 1857.

Buku Péngetan palenggahan-dalem saha para Tamu-tamu wiwit 16 Agustus 1936. Compiled and inscribed Surakarta, 1936–38. MS. SP 181 Na-A; SMP KS 166.

Serat Cabolang = *Serat Centhini* (*Suluk Tambangraras*). 10 vols. Edited by H. Karkono K. Partokusumo. Yogyakarta: Yayasan Centhini, 1985–1990. See also Ronggasutrasna.

Carey, P. B. R. *Babad Dipanagara: An account of the Outbreak of the Java War, 1825–1830.* Kuala Lumpur: Malaysian Branch of the Royal Asiatic Society, 1981.

———. *The British in Java, 1811–1816: A Javanese Account.* New York: Oxford University Press, 1992.

———. "The Sepoy Conspiracy of 1815 in Java." *BKI* 133, nos. 2–3 (1977): 294–322.

Serat Centhini (*Suluk Tambangraras*) = *Serat Cabolang.* 10 vols. Edited by H. Karkono K. Partokusumo. Yogyakarta: Yayasan Centhini, 1985–1990. See also Ronggasutrasna et al.

de Certeau, Michel. *The Writing of History.* New York: Columbia University Press, 1988.

Cohen Stuart, A. B. *Bråtå-Joedå, Indisch Javaansch Heldendicht.* Verhandelingen van het Bataviaasch Genootschap van Kunsten en Wetenschappen, vols. 27–28 (Batavia, 1860).

Crawfurd, John. *History of the Indian Archipelago.* 3 vols. Edinburgh: A. Constable and Co., 1820.

Crone, Patricia, and Martin Hinds. *God's Caliph: Religious Authority in the First Centuries of Islam.* Cambridge: Cambridge University Press, 1986.

Crouch, Harold. *The Army and Politics in Indonesia.* Ithaca: Cornell University Press, 1988.

Day, J. Anthony. "*Babad Kandha, Babad Kraton,* and Modern Javanese Literature." *BKI* 134, no. 4 (1978).

———. "Islam and Literature in South-East Asia." In *Islam in South-East Asia,* edited by M. B. Hooker. Leiden: Brill, 1983.

———. "Meanings of Change in the Poetry of Nineteenth-Century Java." Ph.D. dissertation, Cornell University, 1981.

Dhofier, Zamakhsyari. *Tradisi Pesantren.* Jakarta: LP3ES, 1982.

Dirks, Nicholas. *The Hollow Crown: Ethnohistory of an Indian Kingdom.* 2d ed. Ann Arbor: University of Michigan Press, 1993.

Djajadiningrat, Hoesein. *Tinjauan Kritis Tentang Sajarah Banten.* Jakarta: Djambatan, 1983.

Djatikusumo, G.P.H. "Sedjarah Politik ingkang Sinuhun Kangjeng Susuhunan Pakubuwana VI." Surakarta: Panityo Kol-Dalem PB VI, 1971.

Drakard, Jane. *A Malay Frontier: Unity and Duality in a Sumatran Kingdom.* Ithaca: Cornell University Southeast Asia Program, 1990.

Drewes, G. W. J. *The Admonitions of Sèh Bari.* The Hague: Nijhoff, 1969.

———. "Het Document uit den Brandstapel." *Djåwå* 7 (1927): 97–109.

———. *Drie Javaansche Goeroe's: Hun Leven, Onderricht en Messiasprediking.* Leiden: A. Vros, 1925.

———. *An Early Javanese Code of Muslim Ethics.* The Hague: Nijhoff, 1978.

———. "Wat valt er te verstaan onder het Javaanse Woord *Suluk?*" *BKI* 148, no. 1 (1992): 22–30.

Earle, Arthur. "A Month in Java in 1889." (typescript).

Echols, John M., and Hassan Shadily. *An Indonesian-English Dictionary.* 3d ed. Edited by John U. Wolff and James T. Collins. Ithaca, N.Y.: Cornell University Press, 1989.

Errington, J. Joseph. *Structure and Style in Javanese: A Semiotic View of Linguistic Etiquette.* Philadelphia: University of Pennsylvania Press, 1988.

———. "To Know Oneself the Troubled Times: Ronggawarsita's Serat Kala Tidha." In *Writing on the Tongue,* edited by A. L. Becker. Ann Arbor: University of Michigan Center for South and Southeast Asian Studies, 1989.

Faqier 'Abd'l Haqq, ed. *Suluk Sèh Malaya.* Yogyakarta: Kulawarga Bratakesawa, 1959.

Fasseur, C. "The French Scare: Taco Roorda and the Origins of Javanese Studies in the Netherlands." In *Looking in Odd Mirrors: The Java Sea,* edited by V. J. H. Houben et al. Leiden: Vakgroep Talen en Culturen van Zuidoost-Azie en Oceanie Rijksuniversiteit te Leiden, 1992.

Florida, Nancy K. "The Badhaya Katawang: A Translation of the Song of Kangjeng Ratu Kidul." *Indonesia* 53 (April 1992): 20–32.

———. *Javanese Literature in Surakarta Manuscripts.* Vol. 1, *Introduction and Manuscripts of the Karaton Surakarta.* Ithaca: Cornell University Southeast Asia Program, 1993.

———. "Sex Wars: Writing Gender Relations in Nineteenth-Century Java." In *Fantacizing the Feminine in Indonesia,* edited by Laurie Sears. Durham: Duke University Press, forthcoming.

———. "Writing the Past, Inscribing the Future: Exile and Prophecy in an Historical Text of Nineteenth-Century Java." 2 vols. Ph.D. dissertation, Cornell University, 1990.

Fokkens, F. "De Priesterschool te Tegalsari." *Tijdschrift voor Taal-, Land-, en Volkenkunde* [*TBG*] 24 (1878): 318–36.

Gallop, Annabel Teh, and Bernard Arps. *Golden Letters: Writing Traditions of Indonesia.* London: British Library, 1991.

Serat Gambaripun para Gupernur Jendral ing tanah Jawa. Compiled and inscribed Surakarta, ca. 1926. MS. RP B116; SMP MN 270.

Geertz, Clifford. *Islam Observed.* Chicago: University of Chicago Press, 1973.

———. *The Religion of Java.* Chicago: University of Chicago Press, 1960.

Gericke, J. F. C., and T. Roorda. *Javaansch-Nederlandsch Handwoordenboek.* 2 vols. Amsterdam: Muller, 1901.

Gibb, H. A. R., and J. H. Kramers, eds. *Shorter Encyclopaedia of Islam.* Leiden: Brill, 1953.

The Gift Addressed to the Spirit of the Prophet. Edited and translated by A. H. Johns. Canberra: Australian National University Press, 1965.

Gombloh. *Sekar Mayang.* Surabaya: Indra Records Golden Hand Series, 1980?.

de Graaf, H. J. "Het Kajoran-vraagstuk." *Djåwå* 20 (1940): 273–328.

de Graaf, H. J., and Th. G. Th. Pigeaud. *De Eerste Moslimse Vorstendommen op Java.* The Hague: Nijhoff, 1974.

Groneman, J. *De Garebegs te Ngayogyakarta.* The Hague: Nijhoff, 1895.

Guillot, C. "Dluwang ou Papier Javanais." *Archipel* 26 (1984): 105–15.

Hadiwijono, Harun. *Man in the Present Javanese Mysticism.* Baarn: Bosch and Keuning, 1967.

Hamzuri. *Rumah Tradisionil Jawa.* Jakarta: Departemen Pendidikan dan Kebudayaan, Proyek Pengembangan Permuseuman D.K.I. Jakarta, s.a.

Hardiatmo, Sri. "Tata Ruang dan Tata Bangunan Keraton Surakarta." Sarjana thesis, Institut Teknologi Bandung, 1982.

Hardjowirogo, R. *Pathokaning Njekaraken.* Jakarta: Balai Pustaka, 1952.

Hatch, Martin F. "Lagu, Laras, Layang: Rethinking Melody in Javanese Music." Ph.D. dissertation, Cornell University, 1980.

Hefner, Robert W. *Hindu Javanese: Tengger Tradition and Islam.* Princeton: Princeton University Press, 1985.

Heryanto, Ariel. "The 'Development' of Development." *Indonesia* 46 (1988): 1–24.

His Majesty the VI's Correspondence. See *Kupiya Iber Warni-warni, Sampéyan-dalem kaping VI.*

Hodgson, Marshall G. S. *The Venture of Islam.* 3 vols. Chicago: University of Chicago Press, 1974.

Houben, V. J. H. "Afstand van Gebied met Behoud van Aanzien: Een onderzoek naar de koloniale verhouding op midden Java in 1830." M.A. thesis, Leiden University, 1976.

———. "Kraton en Kumpeni: Surakarta en Yogyakarta, 1830–1870." Ph.D. dissertation, Leiden University, 1987.

Hughs, Thomas P. *A Dictionary of Islam.* Clifton, N.J.: Reference Book Publishers, 1965.

Jayadiningrat I, R.M.H. *Serat Mas Ngantèn.* Composed Surakarta, 1819. In *Serat Wulang,* pt. 1, pp. 1–48. Inscribed Surakarta, 1899. MS. Rp 104 carik; SMP Rp 106B.

———. *Serat Mas Nganten.* In *Serat Wulang.* Jakarta: Departemen Pendidikan dan Kebudayaan, Proyek Penerbitan Buku Sastra Indonesia dan Daerah, 1981.

"Journal of an Excursion to the Native Provinces on Java in the year 1828, during the war with Dipo Negoro." *Journal of the Indian Archipelago and Eastern Asia* 7 (1853): 1–19, 138–57, 225–46, and 358–78; 8 (1854): 80–174.

Kagungan-dalem serat Babat Sengkala: Kawit Pulo Jawi dipunisèni tiyang nalika taun ongka 1 dumugi taun 1854. Composed Surakarta, s.a.; inscribed Surakarta, 1924. MS. SP 220 Ca-A; SMP KS 1A.

Kamajaya. See Karkono K. Partokusumo.

Karkono K. Partokusumo, H., ed. *Serat Centhini: Suluk Tambangraras.* 10 vols. Yogyakarta: Yayasan Centhini, 1985–1990.

———. *Zaman Edan: Pembahasan Serat Kalatidha Ranggawarsitan.* Yogyakartz: Proyek Javanologi, [1983].

Kartodirdjo, Sartono. See Sartono Kartodirdjo.

Kartomi, Margaret. *Matjapat Songs in Central and West Java.* Canberra: Australian National University Press, 1973.

Keeler, Ward. *Javanese Shadow Plays, Javanese Selves.* Princeton: Princeton University Press, 1987.

Kidung Rumeksa ing Wengi. Composed s.l., s.a. In *Serat Suluk: Jaman Karaton-dalem ing Surakarta*, pp. 18–30. Inscribed Surakarta, by Ng. Hawikrama, 1870. MS. SP 244 Na; SMP KS 481.1.

Kidung Rumeksa ing Wengi. In *Sèh Amongraga*, edited by Moelyono Sastronaryatmo. Jakarta: Departemen Pendidikan dan Kebudayaan, Proyek Penerbitan Buku Sastra Indonesia dan Daerah, 1981.

Kitab Suluk 41. Leiden Oriental Collection, Codex 7375.

de Kock, H. M. "Beschrijving van het karakter en de hoedanigheden van den Keizer de Prinsen en de Rijksbestierder van Soerakarta." 1829. Solo Bundel 166, Arsip Nasional Republik Indonesia.

Kolff, S. "Een Baanbreker voor't Javaansch." *Djåwå* 2 (1922): 75–82.

Komite Ronggawarsitan. *Babad Cariyos Lelampahanipun Suwargi Radèn Ngebéhi Ronggawarsita*. 3 vols. Surakarta: Marsch, 1931–33.

[Krep, Josep = Joseph Kreeft]. [*Karaton Surakarta: Journal 1843–1853 and notes pertaining to financial affairs, taxation, and land administration*] = *Serat Baleniklan: awit ongka 1771 dumugi ongka 1773*. Compiled and inscribed Surakarta, 1843–53. MS. SP (uncataloged): SMP KS 81a.

Kumar, Ann. *The Diary of a Javanese Muslim: Religion, Politics, and the Pesantrèn, 1883–1886*. Canberra: Australian National University, 1985.

———. "Javanese Court Society and Politics in the Late Eighteenth Century: The Record of a Lady Soldier." Part I: The Religious, Social, and Economic Life of the Court." *Indonesia* 29 (1980): 1–46.

———. "Javanese Court Society and Politics in the Late Eighteenth Century: The Record of a Lady Soldier." Part II: Political Developments: The Courts and the Company, 1784–1791." *Indonesia* 30 (1980): 67–111.

Kupiya Iber Warni-warni, Sampéyan-dalem kaping VI. Composed Surakarta and Ambon, 1812–48; inscribed [Ambon], ca. 1849. MS. SP 214 Ca; SMP KS 78.

McDonald, Hamish. *Suharto's Indonesia*. Melbourne: Fontana, 1980.

Maclaine Pont, Henri. "Javaansche Architectuur (Bouwkunst)." *Djåwå* 3 (1923): 112–27 and 159–79; 4 (1924): 44–73.

Maier, Hendrik M. J. *In the Center of Authority*. Ithaca: Cornell University Southeast Asia Program, 1988.

Majumdar, R. C., ed. *The History and Culture of the Indian People*. Vol. 6, *The Delhi Sultanate*. Bombay: Bharatiya Vidya Bhavan, 1960.

Mangkunagara IV, K.G.P.A.A. *Serat Wédhatama*. In *Serat-serat Anggitan-dalem K.G.P.A.A. Mangkunagara IV*. Vol. 3. Edited by Th. Pigeaud. Jakarta: Noordhoff-Kolff, 1953.

Mangkunagara VII, K.G.P.A.A. *On the Wayang Kulit (Purwa) and Its Symbolic and Mystical Elements*. Translated by Claire Holt. Ithaca: Cornell University Southeast Asia Program, 1957.

———. "Over de wajang-koelit (poerwa) in het algemeen en over de daarin voorkomende symbolische en mystieke elementen." *Djåwå* 13 (1933): 79–97.

Serat Manikmaya = Babad Tanah Jawi. 3 vols. Composed s.l., s.a.; inscribed Surakarta, [late 19th century]. MS. RP B 97a, B 99, B 97b; SMP MN 169–71.

Massignon, Louis. *The Passion of al-Hallâj*. Vol. 2. Princeton: Princeton University Press, 1982.

Meinsma, J. J., ed. *Poenika Serat Babad Tanah Djawi Wiwit saking Nabi Adam doemoegi ing taoen 1647*. Transliterated by W. L. Olthof. The Hague: Nijhoff, 1941.

Moertono, Soemarsaid. *State and Statecraft in Old Java: A Study of the Later Mataram Period, Sixteeenth to Nineteenth Century*. Ithaca: Modern Indonesia Project, Cornell University, 1968.

Nadjib, Emha Ainun. *Suluk Pesisiran*. Bandung: Mizan, 1989.

Nahuys van Burgst, Baron. *Herinneringen uit het Openbare en Bijzondere Leven*. Utrecht, 1852.

Serat Nalika Bangun Masjid ing Demak. Composed Surakarta, s.a.; inscribed Surakarta, 1885–86. MS. SP 203 Ra; SMP KS 81B.

Natarata, R. Panji. *Serat Siti Jenar*. Yogyakarta: Kulawarga Bratakesawa, 1958.

Serat Nawawi. Composed Surakarta, 1789; inscribed Surakarta, ca. 1832 or 1841. MS. SP 129 Na A; SMP KS 527.

Serat Nawawi. Composed Surakarta 1817/18; inscribed Surakarta 1817/18. MS. SP 218 Na; SMP KS 525.

Nicholson, Reynold A. *Studies in Islamic Mysticism*. Cambridge: Cambridge University Press, 1921.

Niranjana, Tejaswini. *Siting Translation: History, Post-Structuralism, and the Colonial Context*. Berkeley: University of California Press, 1992.

[Padmasusastra, Ki] and R.Ng. Wirapratama. *Serat Sajarah Ageng ing Karaton Surakarta*. Composed Surakarta, ca. 1900 and 1940; typed s.l., s.a. MS. RP B 77; SMP MN 690.

Padmosoesastra. *Serat Urapsari*. Batavia: Kolff, 1896.

Pakubuwana IX, I.S.K.S. *Serat Wira Iswara*. Edited by Hardjana HP. Jakarta: Departemen Pendidikan dan Kebudayaan, Proyek Penerbitan Buku Sastra Indonesia dan Daerah, 1979.

——. *Wulang Putra*. Composed Surakarta, 1876. In *Serat Wira Iswara*, edited by Hardjana HP. Jakarta: Departemen Pendidikan dan Kebudayaan, Proyek Penerbitan Buku Sastra Indonesia dan Daerah, 1979.

Pemberton, John. "Notes on the 1982 General Election in Solo," *Indonesia* 41 (1986): 1–22.

——. *On the Subject of "Java."* Ithaca: Cornell University Press, 1994.

Pigeaud, Theodore G. Th. *Java in the Fourteenth Century*. Vol. 4. The Hague: Nijhoff, 1962.

——. *Javaanse Volksvertoningen: Bijdrage tot de Beschrijving van Land en Volk*. The Hague: Martinus Nijhoff, 1938.

——. *Literature of Java*. 4 vols. The Hague: Nyhoff, 1967–80.

Poerbatjaraka, R.M.Ng. "De Geheime Leer van Soenan Bonang (Soeloek Woedjil)." *Djåwå* 8 (1938): 145–81.

——. *Kapustakan Djawi*. Jakarta: Djambatan, 1952.

——, ed. *Nîtiçâstra*. Bandung, 1933.

Poerwadarminta. *Baoesastra Djawa*. Groningen: Wolters, 1939.

Prakash, Gyan. "Writing Post-Orientalist Histories of the Third World: Indian Historiography Is Good to Think." In *Colonialism and Culture*, edited by Nicholas Dirks.
Ann Arbor: University of Michigan Press, 1992.

Pramoedya Ananta Toer. *Anak Semua Bangsa*. Hasta Mitra: Jakarta, 1980.

———. *Bumi Manusia*. Hasta Mitra: Jakarta, 1980.

———. *Jejak Langkah*. Hasta Mitra: Jakarta, 1985.

———. *Nyanyi Tunggal Seorang Bisu: Catatan Pribadi Pramoedya Ananta Toer dari tahanan Pulau Buru*. Wika Karya: Kuala Lumpur: 1988.

———. *Rumah Kaca*. Hasta Mitra: Jakarta, 1988.

Serat Pranitiwakya and Jangkonipun Prabu Jayabaya. Composed Surakarta, mid 19th
century; inscribed Surakarta, by R.M.Ng. Samahatmaka, 1925. MS. RP A-101;
SMP MN 409.

Serat Pranitiwakya tuwin Jangkanipun Prabu Jayabaya. Composed Surakarta, mid 19th
century; inscribed Surakarta, by R.M.Ng. Sumahatmaka, 1925. MS. RP A-101;
SMP MN 409.

*Pratélan Luluhur para Wali Pangajeng ing Tanah Jawi wiwit kapranata Sunan Ngampèl-
denta dumugi jaman Karaton ing Mataram Wekasan*. Compiled, Surakarta, s.a. In
Sajarah-dalem Parisawuli, part 3. Inscribed Surakarta, 1943. MS. SP (uncataloged);
SMP KS 10H.

*Pratélan Wontenipun Bongsa Éropah angambah Tanah Jawi, tuwin Pratélan Kawon-
tenanipun Karaton Tanah Jawi, anggènipun lajeng Mamitran saha damel Prajang-
jiyan akaliyan Tiyang Bongsa Éropah*. Compiled Surakarta, [late 19th century];
inscribed Surakarta, 1922. MS. SP 179 Na; SMP KS 5.

Prijohoetomo. *Nawaruci: Inleiding Middel-Javaansche Prozatekst, Vertaling Vergeleken
met de Bimasoetji in Oud-Javaansch Metrum*. Groningen: Wolters, 1934.

Purbacaraka. See Poerbatjaraka.

[Purbadipura, R. Ng.]. *Srikarongron*. 3 vols. Edited by Moelyono Sastronaryatmo and
Sudibjo Z. Hadisutjipto. Jakarta: Departemen Pendidikan dan Kebudayaan, Proyek Penerbitan Buku Sastra Indonesia dan Daerah, 1981.

Purwadarminta. See Poerwadarminta.

Quinn, George. "The Case of the Invisible Literature: Power, Scholarship, and Contemporary Javanese Writing." *Indonesia* 35 (1983): 1–36.

Rafael, Vicente L. *Contracting Colonialism: Translation and Christian Conversion in Tagalog Society under Early Spanish Rule*. Durham: Duke University Press, 1993 [orig.
1988].

Raffles, Sir Thomas Stamford. *The History of Java*. 2 vols. London: Black, Parbury and
Allen, 1817.

Ras, J. J. "The Babad Tanah Jawi and Its Reliability: Questions of Content, Structure,
and Function." In *Cultural Contact and Textual Interpretation*, edited by C. D.
Grijns and S. O. Robson. Dordrecht, The Netherlands: Foris Publications, 1986.

———. "The Genesis of the Babad Tanah Jawi." *BKI* 143, nos. 2–3 (1987): 343–56.

Reid, Anthony. *Southeast Asia in the Age of Commerce, 1450–1680*. Vol. 1, *The Land
below the Winds*. New Haven: Yale University Press, 1988.

Reid, Anthony, and David Marr, eds. *Perceptions of the Past in Southeast Asia*. Singapore: Heinemann, 1979.

Ricklefs, M. C. *A History of Modern Indonesia*. London: Macmillan, 1981.

———. *Jogjakarta under Sultan Mangkubumi, 1749–1792: A History of the Division of Java*. London: Oxford University Press, 1974.

———. *Modern Javanese Historical Tradition: A Study of an Original Kartasura Chronicle and Related Materials*. London: SOAS, University of London, 1978.

Rinkes, D. A. "De Heiligen van Java II: Seh Siti djenar voor de inquisitie." *TBG* 53 (1911): 17–56.

———. "De Heiligen van Java IV: Ki Pandhan arang te Tembayat." *TBG* 53 (1911): 435–581.

———. "De Heiligen van Java VI: Het graf te Pamlatèn en de Hollandsche heerschappij." *TBG* 55 (1913): 1–200.

Robson, Stuart. *The Wedhatama: An English Translation*. Leiden: Koninklijk Instituut voor Taal-, Land- en Volkenkunde [KITLV] Working Papers No. 4, 1990.

Rongga Panambangan, M.Ng., ed. *Serat Manikmaya dumugi Demak = Babad Tanah Jawi*. Composed Mangkunagaran, Surakarta, 1813; inscribed Surakarta, mid 19th century. MS. RP B100; SMP MN 184.

Ronggasasmita, Mas. *Suluk Acih*. Composed Aceh, 1815; inscribed Surakarta, 1867. MS. SP 15 Ca; SMP KS 502.

———. "Suluk Martabat Sanga." In *Suluk Acih*. Composed Aceh, 1815; inscribed Surakarta, 1867. MS. SP 15 Ca; SMP KS 502.

[Ronggasutrasna, Ki Ng.], *Serat Cabolang* [composed Surakarta, ca. 1815]. In *Serat Centhini: Suluk Tambangraras*, edited by H. Karkono K. Partokusumo. 10 vols. Yogyakarta: Yayasan Centhini, 1985–90.

[Ronggasutrasna, Mas, R.T. Sastranagara, and Kyai Haji Muhammad Ilhar]. *Serat Tjentini*. 8 vols. [Composed Surakarta, ca. 1815; inscribed Surakarta, 1847]. Edited by Wirawangsa. Batavia: Bataviaasch Genootschap van Kunsten en Wetenschappen, 1912–15.

Ronggawarsita, R.Ng. [= Kiyahi Sarataka]. *Serat Jayèngbaya*. Composed Surakarta, ca. 1830. In [*Klempakan*], pt. 5. Inscribed Surakarta, 1920. MS. SP 135 Na; SMP KS 415.

———. *Serat Pustakaraja Madya: Jayabaya*. Composed Surakarta, mid 19th century; inscribed Surakarta, mid to late 19th century. MS. RP D-128; SMP MN 15.

———. *Serat Salasilah, Urutipun Panjenengan Nata ing Tanah Jawi, awit Panjenengan Ratu Prabu Déwatacengkar, Medhangkamulan*. Composed Surakarta [mid 19th century]; inscribed Surakarta, 1878. MS. RP B 84; SMP MN 245.

Roorda, T. *Javaansche brieven, berigten, verslagen, verzoekschriften, proclamaties, publicaties, contracten, schuldbekentenissen, quitanties, processtukken, pachtbrieven en andere soortgelijke stukken; naar handschriften uitgegeven*. Amsterdam: Muller, 1845.

Said, Edward. *Orientalism*. London: Vintage, 1978.

———. *The World, the Text, and the Critic*. Cambridge: Harvard University Press, 1983.

Serat Sajarah Citrasoma. Compiled s.a., s.l.; inscribed Surakarta, [late 19th century]. MS. RP B 85; SMP MN 247.

Serat Sajarah-dalem Sampéyan-dalem I.S.K.S. Pakubuwana kaping X: Sajarah ingkang saking pangiwa. Compiled Surakarta, [early 20th century]; inscribed Surakarta, early 20th century. MS. SP (uncataloged); SMP KS 10E.

Sartono Kartodirdjo. *The Peasants' Revolt of Banten in 1888.* The Hague: Nijhoff, 1966.

———. *Protest Movements in Rural Java.* Kuala Lumpur: Oxford University Press, 1973.

———. *Ratu Adil.* Jakarta: Sinar Harapan, 1984.

[Sasradiningrat IV, K.R.A.]. *Dhirilaksita.* Composed Surakarta, [late 19th century]; inscribed Surakarta by Joyosayono, 1954. MS. Rp 290; SMP RP 60.

Sasrasumarta, R. Mantri Guru. *Serat Babatipun Kangjeng Ratu Kancana.* Composed Surakarta, 1936; inscribed Surakarta, ca. 1936. MS. SP 118 Ka; SMP KS 66.

Sasrasumarta, R., R. Sastrawaluya, and R.Ng. Yasapuraya. *Tus Pajang: Pèngetan Lalam-pahanipun Swargi Radèn Ngabéhi Yasadipura I, Abdi-dalem Kaliwon Pujongga, ing Surakarta Adiningrat.* Surakarta: Budi Utomo, 1939.

Schimmel, Annemarie. *And Muhammad Is His Messenger: The Veneration of the Prophet in Islamic Piety.* Chapel Hill: University of North Carolina Press, 1985.

Schrieke, B. J. O. *Indonesian Sociological Studies.* Vol. 2. The Hague: van Hoeve, 1957.

Serat. See title: Serat *Babad,* Serat *Nawawi,* etc.

Shakespeare's Sonnets. Edited by Stephen Booth. New Haven: Yale University Press, 1977.

Shalahuddin Chaery, Shodiq H. *Kamus Istilah Agama.* Jakarta: C. V. Sienttarama, 1983.

Shiraishi, Takashi. *An Age in Motion: Popular Radicalism in Java, 1912–1926.* Ithaca: Cornell University Press, 1990.

Siegel, James T. *The Rope of God.* Berkeley: University of California Press, 1969.

———. *Shadow and Sound: The Historical Thought of a Sumatran Kingdom.* Chicago: University of Chicago Press, 1979.

———. *Solo in the New Order.* Princeton: Princeton University Press, 1986.

Simuh. *Mistik Islam Kejawen Raden Ngabehi Ranggawarsita: Suatu Studi terhadap Serat Wirid Hidayat Jati.* Jakarta: University of Indonesia Press, 1988.

Soebardi, S. *The Book of Cabolèk.* The Hague: Nijhoff, 1975.

———. "Santri Religious Elements as Reflected in the Book of Tjentini." *BKI* 127 (1971): 331–49.

Solichim Salam. *Ja'Far Shadiq.* Kudus: Menara Kudus, 1986.

———. *Sekitar Wali Sanga.* Kudus: Penerbit Menara, 1974.

Stange, Paul. "The Logic of Rasa in Java." *Indonesia* 38 (1984): 113–34.

Steedly, Mary Margaret. *Hanging without a Rope: Narrative Experience in Colonial and Postcolonial Karoland.* Princeton: Princeton University Press, 1993.

Steenbrink, Karel. *Dutch Colonialism and Indonesian Islam: Contacts and Conflicts, 1596–1950.* Amsterdam: Rodopi, 1993.

Suluk Condra. Composed s.l., s.a. In *Serat Wulang,* pt. 3. Inscribed Surakarta, 1899. MS Rp 104 carik; SMP Rp 106 B.

Suluk Gatholoco. Composed East Java, ca. 1860–80; inscribed Kalinyamat, 1880. MS. RP A 34; SMP MN 357.

"The *Suluk Gatoloco*: Parts One and Two." Edited and translated by Benedict Anderson. *Indonesia* 32 (October 1981): 109–50; 33 (April 1982): 31–88.

Serat Suluk: Jaman Karaton-dalem ing Surakarta. Inscribed Surakarta: by Ng. Hawikrama, 1870. MS. SP 244-Na; SMP KS 481.

Suluk Lonthang. Composed s.l., s.a. In *Suluk Acih,* p. 77–80. Inscribed Surakarta, 1867. MS. SP 15 Ca; SMP KS 502.

Suluk Sèh Malaya. Edited by Faqier 'Abd'l Haqq. Yogyakarta: Kulawarga Bratakesawa, 1959.

Suluk Seh Siti Jenar. Edited by Sutarti. Jakarta: Departemen Pendidikan dan Kebudayaan, Proyek Penerbitan Buku Sastra Indonesia dan Daerah, 1981.

[*Suluk Warni-warni*]. Composed s.l., s.a.; inscribed Surakarta, 1820–21. MS. SP 109 Na; SMP KS 480.

Sumahatmaka, *Ringkasan Centini* (*Suluk Tambanglaras*). Jakarta: Balai Pustaka, 1981.

Suranto Atmosopatro and Martin Hatch. "*Serat Wédatama*: A Translation." *Indonesia* 14 (October 1972): 157–82.

Sutherland, Heather. *The Making of a Bureaucratic Elite.* Singapore: Heinemann Educational Books, 1979.

Sutrisno, Ki (dhalang Kentrungan, asal Blora). "Lakon Siti Jenar." Gajahan, Surakarta: 11–12 November 1983.

Suwondo, Bambang. *Ceritera Rakyat Daerah Istimewa Yogyakarta.* Jakarta, 1982.

Suyanto, Sunar Tri. *Pahlawan Kemerdekaan Nasional RI: Sinuhun Banguntapa.* Surakarta: Tiga Serangkai, 1984.

Serat Tajusalatin. Composed [Kartasura, 1726]; inscribed Surakarta, 1826. MS. SP 140 Ca; SMP KS 340.

Serat Tajusalatin. Composed [Kartasura, 1726]; inscribed Surakarta, s.a. MS. SP (uncataloged); SMP KS 341.

Tanojo, R., ed. *Walisana.* Surakarta: Sadubudi, 1955.

Tarakusuma, *Serat Paturan ingkang sasambetan bab caranipun K.G.P.A.A. Mangkunagara IV nganggit serat.* Surakarta, 10 April 1941. MS. RP Bundel 19; SMP MN 530A.

Teresa of Avila, Saint. *The Interior Castle.* Garden City, N.Y.: Image Books, 1961.

Trimingham, J. Spencer. *The Sufi Orders in Islam.* London: Oxford University Press, 1971.

Tsuchiya, Kenji. "Javanology and the Age of Ranggawarsita: An Introduction to Nineteenth-Century Javanese Culture." In *Reading Southeast Asia.* Ithaca: Cornell University Southeast Asia Program, 1990.

Uhlenbeck, E. M. *A Critical Survey of Studies on the Languages of Java and Madura.* The Hague: Nijhoff, 1964.

Veth, P. J. *Aardrijkskundig en Statistisch Woordenboek van Nederlandsch Indies.* 3 vols. Amsterdam: van Kampen, 1869.

Vickers, Adrian. *Bali: A Paradise Created.* Berkeley: Periplus, 1989.

Walisana. Edited by R. Tanojo. Surakarta: Sadubudi, 1955.

Serat Wawaton Angger Tatakrama tuwin Adangiyah ingkang sampun kalampahaken wonten ing Karaton Tanah Jawi dalah Ada-ada Udanagara. Compiled Surakarta, s.a.; inscribed Surakarta, [late 19th to early 20th centuries]. MS. RP H3; SMP MN 542a.

Serat Wawaton Tatakrama Kadhaton. Compiled Surakarta, [mid 19th century]; inscribed Surakarta, [late 19th century]. MS Rp 74 carik; SMP Rp 76.

Weatherbee, Donald E. "Raffles' Sources for Traditional Javanese Historiography and the Mackenzie Collections." *Indonesia* 26 (October 1978): 63–93.

Wehr, Hans. *A Dictionary of Modern Written Arabic*. 3d ed. Edited by J. M. Cowan. Ithaca, N.Y.: Spoken Language Services, 1976.

Wijnmalen, T. C. L. "Nota van Dr. J. F. C. Gericke omtrent de Oprichting van een Instituut voor de Inlandsche Talen en Litteratuur." *BKI* 21 (1874): 313–19.

Winter, C. F., Sr. *Javaansche Zamenspraken*. Vol. 1. 3d ed. Amsterdam: Johannes Muller, 1882 [orig. 1848].

———. *Javaansche Zamenspraken*. Vol. 2. Amsterdam: Johannes Muller, 1858.

——— [with R.Ng. Ronggawarsita]. *Kawi-Javaansch Woordenboek*. Batavia, 1880.

———. *Serat Sultan Ibrahim Kawi Miring*. Inscribed Surakarta, 1846. Leiden Oriental Collection, Codex 2141.

Winter, J. W. "Beknopte Beschrijving van Het Hof Soerakarta in 1824." *BKI* 54 (1902): 15–176.

Woelders, M. O. *Het Sultanaat Palembang, 1811–1825*. The Hague, 1975.

Wolters, O. W. *The Fall of Srivijaya in Malay History*. Ithaca: Cornell University Press, 1970.

———. *History, Culture, and Region in Southeast Asian Perspectives*. Singapore: Institute of Southeast Asian Studies, 1982.

———. *Two Essays on Dai-Viet in the Fourteenth Century*. New Haven: Yale Southeast Asia Studies, 1988.

Yasadipura I, R.Ng. *Serat Cabolèk*. Edited and translated by S. Soebardi. The Hague: Nijhoff, 1975.

———. *Serat Déwaruci*. Composed Surakarta, 1794. In [*Serat Déwaruci tuwin Raja Kapala*], pp. 1–67. Inscribed Surakarta, ca. early 19th century. MS. SP 271 Ra; SMP KS 485.

———. *Suluk Déwaruci*. Composed Surakarta, 1794 and early 19th century. In *Serat Suluk: Jaman Karaton-dalem ing Surakarta*, pp. 198–242. Inscribed Surakarta by Ng. Hawikrama, 1870. MS. SP 244 Na; SMP KS 481.

———. *Serat Rama: Tilaran-dalem Sampéyan-dalem I.S.K.S. Pakubuwana kaping VI*. Composed Surakarta, late 18th century. Inscribed Ambon, 1846. MS. SP 106 Ca; SMP KS 428.

Yasadipura II, R.Ng. *Bimasuci Sekar Ageng*. In Prijohoetomo. *Nawaruci: Inleiding Middel-Javaansche Prozatekst, Vertaling Vergeleken met de Bimasoetji in Oud-Javaansch Metrum*, pp. 148–190. Groningen: Wolters, 1934.

Zoetmulder, P. J. *Kalangwan*. The Hague: Nijhoff, 1974.

——— with the collaboration of S. O. Robson. *Old Javanese–English Dictionary*. 2 vols. The Hague: Nijhoff, 1982.

———. *Pantheisme en Monisme in de Javaansche Soeloek-Litterateur*. Nijmegen: J. J. Berkhout, 1935.

INDEX

Abdurrahman, Suhunan (17th-c. ruler of Palèmbang), 102n

Adiluhung (the beautiful sublime), 32–40, 51

Agung, Sultan (r. 1613–45), 342

Al-Hallaj (Sufi martyr), 363

Allusions, in *Babad Jaka Tingkir*, 257–65, 272–75, 290–99, 340–42, 403–4. See also *Semu*

Ambiya texts, 263

Ampéyan (royal wives). *See* Women of the palace: concubines and wives

Anderson, Benedict, 30n, 47n, 87n, 256n, 295n

Architecture, *pendhapa* structure, 159–62n, 200–201n, 326–27, 330–32

Arps, Bernard, 22n, 31n

Asceticism, translation of terms, 165–66n, 174n, 242n. See also Sufism

Audience: and Bayat tale in *Babad Jaka Tingkir*, 340–42; and opening of *Babad Jaka Tingkir*, 249–52, 255–59, 264; for oral readings of traditional literature, 11–17, 22, 40–44, 372. *See also* Reading

Authority, as theme of *Babad Jaka Tingkir*: and Bayat episode, 337–43; and Demak Mosque episode, 321–37, 404–5; and invocation, 263; and Jaka Karèwèd episode, 306–15, 404; and Malang Sumirang episode, 366–77, 405–6; and Pengging episode, 343–51, 377–91, 406; and Siti Jenar episode, 357–66, 405

Authorship: of *Babad Jaka Tingkir*, 70, 78–80, 400–403; of *Serat Wéddhatama*, 34n; and writing in traditional Java, 19–21. *See also* Pakubuwana VI

Babad (history, chronicle), readings of in court community, 12–13. *See also Babad Tanah Jawi;* Historiography; History

Babad Jaka Tingkir ("The History of Jaka Tingkir"): authorship of, 70, 78–80, 400–403; compilation of, 60–64, 78–79, 400–401; dating of, 66–70, 75–80, 399–402; *His Majesty the VI's Correspondence* and, 53, 57–80, 399–404; and historical tradition of Jaka Tingkir, 246–49; interpolations in, 70–78, 119n; intertextuality of, 6, 69, 250, 257–65, 272–75, 289–90, 297–99, 317, 340–42, 369, 372–74, 384–89; introduction to, 8–10; invocation of, 251–68; Javanese historiography and, 249–51, 265–71, 300, 313–18, 341–43, 384–91, 396–99; manuscript of, 57–80; narrative structure of, 268–71, 277–86, 315, 338, 370, 377; prophecy and, 6, 9–10, 50, 249–50, 271–75, 338, 342–43, 391, 399–406; prosodic-melodic semantics of, 81–84; provenance of, 69–70, 75–80, 400–402; punctuation of, 84–85; as *pusaka*, 4, 255–57, 272, 391, 406; review of text, 279–86; *semu* and, 275–78; translation of, 5–8, 85–87

Babad Langenharja, 12–14n, 49n

Babad Tanah Jawi ("The History of Java"), 179n, 247, 256n, 264–68, 282n, 342, 384–89; Galuh variant, 385–89; genealogy of "Major Babad," 265–68; language of, 267–68n; narrative structure of, 267–68, 315

Bantah kawruh (debates), 225n, 386–88

Barthes, Roland, 5

Bayat, Sunan (15th-c. saint), 160n, 283; episode of *Babad Jaka Tingkir,* 337–43. *See also* Tembayat

Becker, Alton, 253n, 395n

Behrend, Timothy, 11n, 265n, 266n

Benjamin, Walter, 6, 8, 85–86

Berg, C. C., 21n

Bhâratayuddha, Kekawin (Panuluh and Sedhah), 289–90. See also *Bratayuda*

Bimasuci, Serat (Yasadipura II), 258–59

Bintara. *See* Demak; Patah

Bonang, Sunan (15th–16th-c. *wali*), 95n, 151–56n, 167n, 173n, 233n, 320, 328, 343

Bondhan Kajawèn, R. (marginalized Majapahit prince; ancestor of Mataram dynasty), 104–5n, 270n

Book-binding, *gula-kelapa* motif in, 59

The Book of Cabolèk (Soebardi), 14n, 260n

Bratayuda, Serat (Yasadipura I), 28, 31n, 33

Brawijaya V (15th-c. king of Majapahit), 92n, 104n, 107n, 151n, 161n, 177n, 233n, 277–82, 290–92, 300, 304–7, 312–16, 320

Brievenboek (Roorda). See *Javaansche brieven, berigten, verslagen, verzoekschriften, etc.*

Buda (pre- or non-Islamic religious complex), 94n, 152n, 155n, 325n. *See also* Religion

Cabolang-Centhini, 15n, 20. See also *Centhini*

Cabolèk, Serat (Yasadipura I), 14n, 260n

Calendars: Javanese, Islamic, and monsoon, 66–69, 75–79, 90–91n, 183n, 224n. *See also* Dating

Canon, of "Traditional Javanese Literature," 25, 30–31n. *See also* Literature, Javanese: and colonialism; Philology

Cara (costume or behavior style), 175n, 181n

Carey, Peter, 395n

Censorship: and *semu* in *Badad Jaka Tingkir,* 374; of *Suluk Malang Sumirang,* 372–77; of traditional literature in contemporary Java, 44; of the works of elder Ronggawarsita, 298–99n

Centhini, Serat, 15n, 20, 31n, 273, 345n

Certeau, Michel de, 52n

Childbirth, Javanese practices, 15, 224n

Chinese: as Javanese, 281, 286, 299, 403; stereotypes of in nineteenth-century Javanese literature, 296

Chronicle tradition, Javanese. *See Babad Tanah Jawi;* Historiography, Javanese

Cohen, Stuart, A. B., 28–29, 33, 45

Colonialism: and European notions of history, 393; Javanese historical writing and, 394; and Javanese literature, 22–30. *See also* Netherlands; Postcolonialism

Communist Party, Indonesian, 353, 392

Conduct, code of, 116n, 145n

Correspondence: compilation of royal, 60–66; formulaic address in Javanese formal, 118n. See also *His Majesty the VI's Correspondence*

Cosmology, Javanese, 111n, 188n, 232n

Coup of 1 October 1965, and political prisoners, 392–93

Court poets, 1–3, 14, 15n, 21, 38–39, 348, 375

Damar, Harya (15th-c. ruler of Palèmbang), 101–2n, 156n, 229n

Darajat, Sunan (15th–16th-c. *wali*), 153n, 173n

Darma (code of conduct), 116n, 145n

Dating, of *Babad Jaka Tingkir,* 66–70, 75–80, 399–402. *See also* Calendar

Day, Anthony, 2n, 11n, 266n

Demak (15th–16th-c. kingdom), 94–96n, 178n, 248–49, 274–75, 325–51 passim, 357–83 passim

cellaneous Correspondence of His Majesty the Sixth"). See *His Majesty the VI's Correspondence*

Kyai (head of *pesantrèn*), 107n, 345–50

Lambang Praja, Serat ("Realms Symbolized"), 342. See also *Jangka Jayabaya*

Language, Javanese: analysis of opening stanza of *Babad Jaka Tingkir*, 252–54; of *Babad Tanah Jawi* texts, 267–68n; courtly rules of exchange, 301–2; hierarchy and, 203n, 379–82; *krama andap/krama inggil* as style of, 226n; power of, 21, 38, 114n, 210n, 350, 366–67, 374; Pengging, Ki Ageng, and authority in *Babad Jaka Tingkir*, 381–82; punctuation of, 84–85; and *semu*, 276; translation of *Babad Jaka Tingkir*, 86; and traditional Javanese historical writing, 398. *See also* Philology; Translation; *Ukara;* Writing

Lawiyan (ancient district), 218n

Lawu, Sunan (spirit king), 107n

Lembu Peteng: of Madura, 152–53n, 343; as term, 100n, 281n

Lepiyan (venerable laid-by works), 2n

Liquor: consumption of, 143n, 306

Literacy: in context of prerevolutionary Java, 11–17, 252n; in "traditional" Javanese script, 37n

Literature, Javanese: and colonialism, 22–30, 266–70; as an icon of tradition, 31–40; preservation of manuscripts in museums and libraries, 35n–36n; reading in modern Indonesia, 22, 31–44; reading in traditional Java, 10–17; and the "Surakarta Renaissance," 26–30, 69; writing of in traditional Java, 17–21, 259. See also *Macapat* texts; Suluk literature

Localization, alignment of Demak Mosque and concept of, 332–37

Macapat texts: linguistic style of, 19, 252–55; *pesantrèn* and, 14; prosodic-melodic semantics of, 81–84; readings of in contemporary Java, 40–42; read-ings of in prerevolutionary period, 11–17

Maclaine Pont, Ir. H., 330–31

Magic, and power objects, 137n, 139n, 195n. See also *Pusaka*

Mahribi, Maulana (15th-c. saint), 161n, 179n

Maier, Hendrik, 8n

Maja, Kyai (exiled 1828), 71, 401

Majagung, Sunan (15th-c. saint), 151–53n

Majapahit (14th–15th-c. East Javanese imperial kingdom), 92n, 272–74, 277, 286–93, 300–318 passim

Malang Sumirang, Sèh (16th-c. saint): 205n, 269, 283–84, 405–6; episode of *Babad Jaka Tingkir*, 366–77

Malaya, Sèh. *See* Kalijaga, Sunan

Manggala (opening stanzas), 252; of *Babad Jaka Tingkir*, 251–62

Mangkubumi, Prince (of Surakarta), 71–75

Mangkunagara IV (r. 1853–81), 15n, 34

Mangkunagara VII (r. 1916–44), 32–33

Mangkurat III (r. 1703–8), 322

Marriage, Javanese royal: and concept of legitimacy, 102–3n, 134–35n, 280–81n

Mas Ngantèn, Serat (Jayadiningrat), 48–49

Mataram, Harya. *See* Mangkubumi

Mataram, kingdom and dynasty of, 27, 247–49, 265–68, 322, 329–30n, 342

Mecca: Ka'bah and alignment of Demak Mosque, 332–37; Ka'bah and Islamic prayer, 165n

Meditation chambers, in Javanese palaces, 217n

Memory, and writing of history in Java, 396–97

Mèngeti (historical consciousness), 396–97

Mimesis, and representation in Javanese historical tradition, 290

Moelyono Sastronaryatmo, 53n

Moertono, Soemarsaid, 384n

Moluccas, precolonial relations with Java, 99n

Monument: construction of Demak Mosque as, 325–32, 337, 364; grave(s) of Siti Jenar as, 364–66; *Suluk Malang Sumirang* as, 370–72; "Traditional Javanese Literature" as, 22, 29, 31–40

Nahuys van Burgst, Baron (Resident of Surakarta 1820–22 and 1827–30), 45n, 62, 64
Nalika Bangun Masjid ing Demak, Serat ("When the Demak Mosque was [Re]Built"), 323–24
Names, Javanese personal and royal, 92n, 355n
Narrative: review of text of *Babad Jaka Tingkir*, 279–86; structure of *Babad Jaka Tingkir*, 268–71, 277–86, 315, 338, 370, 377; structure of *Babad Tanah Jawi*, 267–68, 315
Nawawi texts, 263
Neoclassicism, in Javanese literature, 30–31
Netherlands, colonial policies in Java: 1830 as watershed in Javanese history, 23–25, 44, 56; Kraton Surakarta and Garebeg ceremonies, 358n; Kraton Surakarta and resistance to, 55–57, 74–75, 348n, 375; restrictions on movement of royalty, 310; suppression of elder Ronggawarsita, 298–99n; traditional Java and cultural policies under, 10–11, 23–30. *See also* Colonialism
New Order government: *adiluhung* rhetoric of, 33; and aftermath of 1 October 1965 coup, 392–93. *See also* Soeharto, President
Ngampèldenta, Sunan (15th-c. *wali*), 151–56n, 161
Ngèlmu (esoteric knowledge; knowledge as power), 170n, 262, 350, 368–69, 381
Ngèngèr (relationship of subjects to ruler), 127n
Niranjana, Tejaswini, 7n, 85n
Nitisastra, Serat, 131n, 297
Nur Mukhammad, 92n
Nûru'l-Dîn al-Rânîrî, 278n

Oral tradition: and Jaka Tingkir, 247; Sèh Malang Sumirang in, 283–84; Sèh Siti Jenar in, 283. *See also Macapat* texts
Orientalism, 23n, 26n, 47n, 394

Pajang (16th-c. Central Javanese kingdom), 247–49, 342
Pakubuwana I (r. 1704–19), 322
Pakubuwana II (r. 1726–49), 27n, 347n
Pakubuwana III (r. 1749–88), 287n
Pakubuwana IV (r. 1788–1820), 31n
Pakubuwana VI (1807–1849; r. 1823–30): and authorship of *Babad Jaka Tingkir*, 80, 402–4; biography of, 53–59, 77–80, 107n, 291, 310, 380–81, 392, 400–404, 411n; correspondence from exile, 64–66, 380–81; ghost of, 75–78; use of Arabic name, 74
Pakubuwana VII (r. 1830–58), 56, 64, 71, 74–75, 323–24
Pakubuwana IX (r. 1861–93), 57, 61, 65, 191n, 280n, 287n, 309n, 329, 348n, 403
Pakubuwana XII (r. 1945–), 263n, 301n
Pamrih (desire), 42
Panarima (acceptance), 189–90n, 362
Pandhanarang. *See* Bayat, Sunan
Panembahan (title), 96n
Pangéran (title), 160n
Panggalang (stage, context, framework), 213n, 271–72, 370, 391, 399, 405
Parody, *Serat Jayèngbaya* as, 50; in *Babad Jaka Tingkir*, 306
Patah, Prince (Sénapati Jimbun, Panembahan Bintara; 15th-c. sultan of Demak), 97n, 105n, 133n, 156n, 229n
Pemberton, John, 10n, 33n, 287n, 312n, 358n, 394n
Pengging, Ki Ageng (15th–16th-c. princely Kyai of Pengging), 150–54n, 246, 269–70, 282–86, 320, 337, 357–59, 366, 406; episode in *Babad Jaka Tingkir*, 343–51, 377–91
Perfect man (*insan kamil*). *See* Sufism
Pesantrèn (rural Islamic educational institutions), 14–15, 25, 175n, 345–50
Philippines, precolonial relations with Java, 99n

Philology, nineteenth-century Dutch colonial on Java, 23–30, 308n. *See also* Javanology; Literature, Javanese: and colonialism

Pigeaud, Theodore, 24n, 26n, 27–28, 358n

Plèsèdan ("slippage"; linguistic feature), 253, 271

Poerbatjaraka, R. M. Ng., 26n

Poetry, structure of *Babad Jaka Tingkir*, 81–84, 87; linguistic features of, 252–54

Portraits, interpolations in *Babad Jaka Tingkir*, 70–78

Postcolonialism: politics of translation, 7; reading of "Third World" histories, 406; and writing of history in Java, 392

Power objects. *See* Magic; *Pusaka*

Prabangkara. *See* Jaka Prabangkara

Pradikan (those of independent status), 161–62n, 345

Prakash, Gyan, 394

Pramoedya Ananta Toer, 392–93

Priyantun-dalem (wives of king). *See* Women of the palace

Priyayi (traditional elite), 32

Prophecy: *Babad Jaka Tingkir* as, 6, 9–10, 50, 249–50, 271–75, 338, 342–43, 391, 399–406; *Jangka Jayabaya*, 273–75, 317; reading history as, 50–51; and structure of authority, 390–91; writing of history and, 21, 38, 299, 398–406

Prosody, of *Babad Jaka Tingkir*, 81–84, 87

Provinces, pre-modern Javanese, 98n

Pujongga (court poet), 21, 38–39

Punctuation, of *Babad Jaka Tingkir*, 84–85

Purbadipura, R. Ng., 379n

Purbaya, Pangéran. *See* Pakubuwana VII

Pusaka (talisman or power object): *Babad Jaka Tingkir* as, 4, 255–57, 272, 391, 406; Demak Mosque as, 321–22, 326, 330, 337; handling of, 35, 146n, 197n, 229–30n, 233n, 305; manuscripts as, 3, 35, 256, 313–14; use of term, 90n, 142n, 158n

Pustakaraja Purwa-Madya-Wasana (Ronggawarsita), 273, 289–90

Queen of the South Sea. *See* Ratu Kidul

Queens. *See* Women of the palace

Rafael, Vicente, 7n, 395n

Raffles, Sir Thomas Stamford, 23n, 61

Rama, Serat (Yasadipura I), 31n, 59n. See also *Rama: Tilaran-dalem Sampéyan-dalem*

Rama: Tilaran-dalem Sampéyan-dalem I.S.K.S. Pakubuwana kaping VI, Serat ("The Book of Rama: Legacy of H.R.H. Pakubuwana VI"), 59, 78, 131n

Ras, J. J., 256n, 267

Rasa, concept of, 176n, 190n, 350, 360–61, 370–73

Ratu Adil ("Just King"), 348–49

Ratu Beruk (Queen of Pakubuwana III), 287n

Ratu Kidul (Queen of the South Sea), 56, 107n, 146n, 249, 329

Reading: of *Babad Jaka Tingkir*, 3–5, 50–51, 286, 406; Barthes on, 5; Ronggasasmita on, 1–3; in traditional Java, 10–17; of traditional Javanese writing in contemporary Java, 22, 40–50. *See also* Audience

Reid, Anthony, 11n

Religion, pre- and non-Islamic complexes in Java, 94n, 155n, 325n. *See also* Islam; Spirituality

Representation: *Babad Jaka Tingkir* and historical tradition, 289–95, 298; and mimesis in *Babad Jaka Tingkir*, 255, 289–90; politics of, 293–99, 313–18, 374–75

Rianto, B. J., 40–44

Ricklefs, M. C., 24n, 395n

Ronggasasmita, Mas (exiled 1828?), 1–3, 22, 45n, 375, 401

Ronggawarsita II, R. Ng. (exiled 1828), 1n, 14n, 45, 298–99n, 375, 401

Ronggawarsita III, R. Ng. (1802–1873), 1n, 14–15n, 20–21, 28–29, 37–48, 273–75, 289–90, 308n, 348n

Roorda, T., 62–65

Said, Edward, 7n, 21n, 26n, 47n

Saints: Sufi hierarchy of, 95n, 96n, 156n–57n. *See also Wali*

Salât (Islamic devotional practice), 158n, 164–65n, 175–76n, 231–32n, 239n, 332–33

Samir (ceremonial sash), 146n

Sangkala (chronograms), 68–69, 90–91n

Santri (students of Islamic religion and theology), 158n, 240–41n, 345–46. See also *Pesantrèn*

Sastranagara, R. T. *See* Yasadipura II

Script, Javanese: contemporary literacy in traditional, 36–37; power of as theme of *Babad Jaka Tingkir*, 368–70. *See also* Writing

Séla, Ki Ageng (16th-c. ancestor of Mataram dynasty), 47, 104n, 178–80n, 247–48

Sembah (gesture of esteem/deference), 112n, 221n

Semu (glimpsed perceptible dimension of the concealed), 275–76; and allusions in *Babad Jaka Tingkir*, 288–99, 317, 374–75; author of *Babad Jaka Tingkir* and, 275–78, 374; and language, 276; and writing of history in Java, 279, 308, 374–75, 398

Sénapati, Panembahan (founder of Mataram kingdom, r. ca. 1576–1603), 249

Serat. See specific titles

Sharî'a (sacred law of Islam), 152n, 354, 358–59, 367, 373, 380–82

Siegel, James, 158n, 276n, 394n

Siti Jenar, Sèh (15th–16th-c. saint), 160n, 177n, 269, 283; episode in *Babad Jaka Tingkir*, 353–66, 405; Ki Ageng Pengging and, 349–51; vanishing of, 360–66

Soebardi, S., 345n, 359n

Soeharto, President: and restoration of Demak Mosque, 324; on traditional Javanese script, 36. *See also* New Order government

Songsong (ceremonial parasol), 45–46n

Spirit mediums, 195n

Spiritual activism, 340–43, 350–51, 357,

359, 362, 372–82. See also *Jatimurti; Pengging, Ki Ageng; Siti Jenar*

Spirituality, Javanese: materiality of traditional practices, 262, 278. *See also* Spiritual activism

Srikarongron (Purbadipura), 379n

State and authority: in *Babad Jaka Tingkir. See* Authority

Steedly, Mary, 395n

Sufism: concept of *insan kamil*, 177n, 180n, 350, 355–57, 360–66, 370; concept of *Jatimurti* and, 170n; hierarchy of saints, 95–96n; premodern Javanese *pesantrèn* and, 346; state of *ghaib*, 197n; *tarékat* (order), 2n, 205n, 239n, 346–49; *wujûdiyyah* as form of, 278n; *zikir* practice in, 154n, 184n, 204n. *See also* Islam; Siti Jenar; Suluk literature

Sukarno, President, 329n

Suluk Acih (Ronggasasmita), 1–3

Suluk Déwaruci (Yasadipura I), 14n, 31n, 211n, 257–62, 328n

Suluk Gatholoco, 49, 356n

Suluk literature: *Babad Jaka Tingkir* and, 259–62, 278, 316–17; *Bantah kawruh* exchanges in, 225n; as genre of Javanese literature, 212–13n, 259–60, 359n; at the Kraton Surakarta, 49, 264; linguistic style of, 254n, 264; *pesantrèn* and, 345n; theme of man as microcosm, 356n

Suluk Lonthang, 367n

Suluk Malang Sumirang, 14n, 214n, 236n, 368–77

Suluk Sèh Malaya, 163n, 261n, 328n

Sunan (title), 95n

Supraba (heavenly nymph), 99n

Suryadi, B. R. T., 316n

Tajusalatin texts, 263

Tarékat. See Sufism

Tasawwuf. See Sufism

Tegalsari-Ponorogo, *pesantrèn* of, 14n, 39, 347–48

Tembang (metrical form), 81–84. See also *Macapat* texts

Tembayat-Kajoran, religious complex of, 171n, 341–42
Teresa of Avila, Saint, 87n
Textuality: conventions of Javanese, 19–20; text and context in Javanese historiography, 10, 396, 398. See also *Panggalang;* Writing
"Third World": politics of translation of literature, 7; reading of traditional histories of, 406; writing of history and, 393–94
Timur, Gusti R. A. (daughter of Pakubuwana VI), 61, 65, 77, 80, 402
Tingkir. See *Babad Jaka Tingkir;* Jaka Tingkir
Toer, Pramoedya Ananta. *See* Pramoedya Ananta Toer
Tradition: colonial cultural policies and, 24–25; twentieth-century emergence of, 10–11, 32–33; use of term "traditional Java," 10–11
Translation, of *Babad Jaka Tingkir:* as form of composition, 20, 255, 258–59; Javanese punctuation and, 84–85; theoretical issues, 5–8, 85–87; and writing in Ki Ageng Pengging episode, 384–89
Trenggana (Sultan Demak), 172n, 248–49, 343
Trunajaya rebellion (1670s), 342
Twin Banyans (*wringin kembar*), 208n

Uhlenbeck, E. M., 29n
Ukara (rule, grammar, sentence), 83, 91n, 110n, 149n, 307–8, 315, 381–82
Ulama (religious scholar), 134n, 155n, 299

Villages, organizational grouping of Javanese, 122n, 129n

Wahyu (divine and manifest light), 39, 205n, 287–88; and Javanese queens, 287n

Wali (15th–16th-c. saints who conveyed Islam to Java), 320–43 passim, 357–67, 370–71. *See also* Saints
Walisana, Serat, 161
Walls. *See* Kraton Surakarta
Wanalapa, Ki Ageng (15th–16th-c. kyai), 178n, 219n
Wanapala, Ki Ageng (16th-c. advisor to Sultan Trenggana), 219n, 386–87
Wandhan people, 103n
Wayang (shadow puppet theater), 32, 131n, 206n, 224n, 228n
Wéddhatama, Serat ("The Noble Wisdom") (Mangkunagara IV), 31n, 34–35
Winter, C. F., Sr. (1799–1859) 15–17, 45, 62–63, 266, 268n, 274, 298n, 316–17
Wiryakusuma, R. M. Ng., 34n
Wisaya, alternative uses of term, 94n
Wiwaha (celebration), 116n
Wolters, Oliver, 87n, 336n, 394n
Women of the palace: concubines and wives, 102–3n, 135n, 280, 308–9; moving among orders, 308–12; retainers, 135n, 220n; queens, 280n, 287n, 309n
Writing: and exile, 71, 291, 299, 317, 404; of history in Java, 21, 38, 52, 392–99; power of, 21, 36–38, 295, 299, 313, 317–18, 368–75; and prophecy in *Babad Jaka Tingkir,* 399–406; reading as form of, 5; and *semu* in *Babad Jaka Tingkir,* 288–99, 374–75, 398; as theme of *Babad Jaka Tingkir,* 368–70; in traditional Java, 17–21. *See also* Language; Representation; *Semu*
Wujûd, definition of, 253
Wujûdiyyah, as form of Islamic mysticism, 278n
Wulang Rèh (Pakubuwana IV), 31n

Yasadipura I (1729–1803), 1n, 3, 14n, 27n, 28, 59, 257–60, 266
Yasadipura II (1756–1844), 1n, 45n, 258–59, 348n

Nancy Florida is Associate Professor of Indonesian Language and
Literature at the University of Michigan in Ann Arbor. She is the
author of *Javanese Literature in Surakarta Manuscripts*, Volume I,
Introduction and Manuscripts of the Karaton Surakarta.

A transliteration of the entire Javanese text of *Babad Jaka Tingkir*
(MS. SP 214 Ca; SMP KS 78) is available from Duke University Press.
Address all inquiries to Anthropology Editor, Duke University Press,
Box 90660, Durham NC 27708-0660.

Library of Congress Cataloging-in-Publication Data
Florida, Nancy K.
Writing the past, inscribing the future: history as prophecy in
colonial Java / Nancy K. Florida.
Includes a translation and critical analysis of Babad Jaka Tingkir.
Includes bibliographical references and index.
ISBN 0-8223-1605-6. — ISBN 0-8223-1622-6 (paper)
1. Java (Indonesia)—History.   I. Babad Jaka Tingkir. English. 1995.
II. Title.
DS646.27.F56   1995
959.8'2015—dc20   94-45845 CIP